Perspectives on Cognitive Task Analysis

Expertise: Research and Applications

Robert R. Hoffman, K. Anders Ericsson, Gary Klein, Michael McNeese,
Eduardo Salas, Sabine Sonnentag, Frank Durso, Emilie Roth,
Nancy J. Cooke, Dean K. Simonton, **Series Editors**

Hoc/Caccibue/Hollnagel (1995) – *Expertise and Technology: Issues in Cognition and Human-Computer Interaction*

Hoffman (2007) – *Expertise Out of Context*

Hoffman/Militello (2008) – *Perspectives on Cognitive Task Analysis*

Mieg (2001) – *The Social Psychology of Expertise Case Studies in Research, Professional Domains, and Expert Roles*

Montgomery/Lipshitz/Brehmer (2004) – *How Professionals Make Decisions*

Noice/Noice (1997) – *The Nature of Expertise in Professional Acting: A Cognitive View*

Salas/Klein (2001) – *Linking Expertise and Naturalistic Decision Making*

Schraagen/Chipman/Shalin (2000) – *Cognitive Task Analysis*

Zsambok/Klein (1997) – *Naturalistic Decision Making*

Perspectives on Cognitive Task Analysis

Historical Origins and Modern
Communities of Practice

ROBERT R. HOFFMAN

LAURA G. MILITELLO

 Psychology Press
Taylor & Francis Group
New York   Hove

Psychology Press
Taylor & Francis Group
270 Madison Avenue
New York, NY 10016

Psychology Press
Taylor & Francis Group
27 Church Road
Hove, East Sussex BN3 2FA

Printed in the United States of America on acid-free paper
10 9 8 7 6 5 4 3 2 1

International Standard Book Number-13: 978-0-8058-6140-2 (Hardcover)

Library of Congress Cataloging-in-Publication Data

Perspectives on cognitive task analysis : historical origins and modern communities of practice /
    edited by Robert R. Hoffman, Laura G. Militello.
       p. cm.
    Includes bibliographical references and index.
    ISBN 978-0-8058-6140-2
    1. Cognition. 2. Task analysis. I. Hoffman, Robert R. II. Militello, Laura G. (Laura Grace), 1965-

BF311.P395 2008
153.4--dc22   2008006825

Visit the Taylor & Francis Web site at
http://www.taylorandfrancis.com

and the Psychology Press Web site at
http://www.psypress.com

Contents

Robert R. Hoffman would like to dedicate
this book to Peter Hancock, an incredible mind and
magnificent wit. He has been a supporter and friend
for many years. He epitomizes the scientist who is also
historian, something to which we aspire in this book.

Laura G. Militello would like to dedicate this book to
her Mom and Dad, who taught her to be curious,
and to Gary Klein, who taught her to be a scientist.

Series Editor's Preface

Robert R. Hoffman, the Editor of the book series *Expertise: Research and Applications* asked me as a member of the Series Editorial Board to prepare this Preface to *Perspectives on Cognitive Task Analysis*. I appreciate the opportunity to comment on the Series as well as on this volume.

The Series has been an important resource for the field of Cognitive Science. It has served as a forum for ideas and for the development of frameworks such as Naturalistic Decision Making. It has provided researchers and practitioners with a vehicle for disseminating their findings about the nature of expertise. It has made a critical contribution to expertise studies, and we are grateful to Robert R. Hoffman for editing this series, to Lawrence Erlbaum Associates for founding and supporting it, and now to Taylor & Francis and CRC Press for continuing to support it.

To study domain practitioners and to understand the nature of expertise, we need a variety of methods. Experts are not always easy to corner. They are often impatient with standard testing paradigms and especially with artificial, context-free tasks. And they are not always able to explain what makes them so good. Many of their skills depend on tacit knowledge that can be difficult to articulate. That is one reason why Cognitive Task Analysis (CTA) methods have been developed—to lift the veil covering the nature of proficient performance. CTA methods can also be applied across the proficiency scale, of course, to understand how practitioners at all levels of experience and skill make decisions and size up situations. But one of the most pressing needs for CTA is to help us figure out how experts do their work and how they are different from journeymen. CTA is a valued tool in helping us appreciate expertise, perform research with experts, and help people achieve higher levels of expertise.

But the notion of using CTA methods emerged only in the late 1970s. Previously, in the United States, the behaviorist tradition had discouraged the investigation of mental events and particularly discouraged the use of any methods that seemed in any way like introspection. Only after scientists started constructing computer models of cognition did American researchers begin speculating about mental activities. And, of course, the efforts to build expert systems required techniques to ferret out the rules that experts might be using. At the same time, additional lines of inquiry were opening the way for CTA methods.

How did that happen? What were the different threads linking up to create the canon of CTA methods? This is the story masterfully told by Hoffman and Laura G. Militello. In addition, they have shown how the evolution of CTA has come to include Cognitive Field Research methods.

We are fortunate to have the history of task analysis and CTA recounted by Hoffman and Militello. Robert Hoffman is one of the pioneers of CTA. He was doing (what we now call) CTA research in the early 1980s. Even then he was identifying different CTA methods and experimentally comparing and evaluating them, and he continues to develop new CTA methods and to incorporate existing methods into his repertoire as a researcher. Thus, he is a developer, practitioner, and researcher with CTA; researcher of CTA; and popularizer of CTA methods. On top of all these activities is his strong grounding in the history of experimental psychology that allows him to put CTA into a perspective going back more than a century. Laura G. Militello also comes well prepared to the job of writing about perspectives on CTA. She has been doing CTA research for almost two decades, working in different fields and applications and also teaching courses on CTA at the University of Dayton. I should also mention that both Robert and Laura are good friends of mine and frequent collaborators with me in CTA research efforts.

This volume is not a guide to conducting CTA. That exists as the Crandall, Klein, and Hoffman (2006) book *Working Minds: A Practitioner's Guide to Cognitive Task Analysis*. This book is a companion to that guide, providing us with a conceptual history of task analysis and CTA. Any student of expertise, any practitioner of qualitative methods for developing cognitive skills, anyone who is serious about CTA and Cognitive Field Research, or human factors psychology in general, will benefit from reading and studying this book to appreciate the origins and transformations of methods for investigating complex cognition.

Gary Klein
Dayton, Ohio

Preface

The purpose of this book is to provide a context for understanding Cognitive Task Analysis (CTA) in terms of its historical roots and recent origins in the traditional disciplines and emerging communities of practice. In the chapters of this book, we show how CTA came to be what it is today. We show where the many CTA methods have come from and what they are intended to do. We also provide integration by showing the relations, dovetailings, common themes, and common purposes of the various disciplines that have contributed to our modern understanding of CTA. We especially focus on the convergence with regard to the design of information systems, including intelligent technologies.

This book is intended to be a companion to *Working Minds: A Practitioner's Guide to Cognitive Task Analysis* (Crandall, Klein, & Hoffman, 2006), which goes into detail about the actual conduct of CTA methods. This book can also be seen as having a companion—Neville Moray's *History and Scope of Human Factors* (2005), which reprints many of the classic writings that are cited and encapsulated in this *Perspectives* book, including works by John Annett, Frederick Gilbreth, Donald Norman, Jens Rasmussen, David Woods, the classic paper on "man-machine task analysis" by R. B. Miller, and others.

In addition to providing a summary at the end of each chapter, we included an advance organizer at the beginning of each chapter. These organizers take the form of "Concept Maps" that lay out the key ideas. As concept mapping spreads around the world in its various applications in research, education, and Web work (see Cañas et al., 2003; Cañas & Novak, 2006; Hoffman, Coffey, Novak, & Cañas, 2005; Hoffman & Lintern, 2006; Novak, 1998), we present here a somewhat novel use of Concept Maps—to serve, in effect, as executive summaries. Learn more about *CmapTools* (including the research background) and get a free download at http://www.ihmc.us. A detailed "how-to" discussion of the use of Concept Maps as a knowledge elicitation method for creating knowledge models is in Crandall, Klein, and Hoffman (2006, chap. 4).

Acknowledgments

David Woods (Ohio State University), Emilie Roth (Roth Cognitive Engineering, Inc.), and Phil Smith (Ohio State University) provided valuable commentary on the material on the Cognitive Systems Engineering perspective. David Woods also coauthored with Robert Hoffman some of the initial draft material that eventually formed parts of chapters 5 and 15. John Annett (University of Warwick, United Kingdom) and Rob Stammers (University of Aston, United Kingdom) provided material about the history of U.K. industrial psychology and ergonomics, and clarified our understanding of the history of Hierarchical Task Analysis. Jean-Michel Hoc and Jaques Leplat (University of Valenciennes, France), Peter von Drunen (Reijksuniversität Gröningen), and Donald van Tol (Archives of Dutch Psychology, Gröningen) provided many useful pointers concerning the history of European and Francophone industrial psychology, psychotechnics, and activity analysis. Karol Ross (Klein Associates) provided detailed comments on the material on Naturalistic Decision Making. Bill Clancey (Institute for Human and Machine Cognition [IHMC]) and Sydney Dekker (Lund University, Sweden) provided detailed comments on ethnographic ideas and methods. Harry Collins (Cardiff University) helped with examples in the Sociology of Scientific Knowledge. Neelam Nakair (Defense Science and Technology Organisation of Australia) and Missy Cummings (MIT) provided comments on material on Work Analysis. Anne Bisantz helped with details about a project in Cognitive Work Analysis (our "wrapped package" in chapter 15). Mica Endsley and Debbie Jones (SA Technologies, Inc.) provided information about Goal-Directed Task Analysis. Walter Warwick of Micro Analysis and Design offered some pointers on the topic of computational cognitive modeling. Geoff Norman (McMaster University) offered some pointers on the topic of medical expertise. Renee Chow (Human Systems Engineering Group, Defence R&D Canada) pointed out some interesting subtleties in the comparisons of methods such as Hierarchical Task Analysis and Goal-Directed Task Analysis. Paul Feltovich (IHMC) offered helpful comments for the chapter on Expertise Studies. Rob Wozniak (Bryn Mawr) availed both himself and his vast library to help confirm some historical factoids.

All of the suggestions from these individuals were extremely valuable in helping us "get things more right" and also in realizing how many significant gaps there are in our understanding of the continuity from industrial psychology from the 1800s to Cognitive Systems Engineering of the present. We dare say we may not have hit the mark in all respects. We hope that those ways in which our treatment might be limited, questionable, muddleheaded, or simply wrong will be revealed in time and will serve as a springboard for discussion.

Portions of the material in chapters 7 and 15 have been reprinted and adapted from *Human Factors* (Hoffman & Woods, 2000), with permission from the Human Factors and Ergonomics Society. (Copyright 2000 by the Human Factors and Ergonomics Society. All rights reserved.)

The authors would like to thank the two anonymous reviewers for their very helpful comments.

The authors would like to thank Drew Bowers of the University of Dayton for helping compose the References section and the Author Index, and Brooke Layton of the IHMC for helping prepare the Subject Index.

The first author would like to thank Taylor & Francis/CRC Press for continuing the support of the book series, "Expertise: Research and Applications" that began with Lawrence Erlbaum Associates. Paul Dukes, Cindy Carelli, Lee Transue, and Robert Sims have all been extremely supportive, helpful and tolerant as we reincarnated the Series and, in parallel, got this book into production. The authors are pleased that this book is the first in the Series to appear under the Taylor & Francis banner.

The authors would also like to thank Elise Weinger for preparing the cover art.

Support for both authors was made possible by participation in the Advanced Decision Architectures Collaborative Technology Alliance, sponsored by the U.S. Army Research Laboratory under Cooperative Agreement DAAD19-01-2-0009.

About the Authors

Robert R. Hoffman, Ph.D., is a Senior Research Scientist at the Institute for Human and Machine Cognition in Pensacola, Florida. He is a Fellow of the Association for Psychological Science, a Fulbright Scholar, and an Honorary Fellow of the Eccles Center for American Studies of the British Library. He received his B.A., M.A., and Ph.D. in experimental psychology at the University of Cincinnati, where he received McMicken Scholar, Psi Chi, and Delta Tau Kappa honors. After a postdoctoral associateship at the Center for Research on Human Learning at the University of Minnesota, Hoffman joined the faculty of the Institute for Advanced Psychological Studies at Adelphi University. Hoffman has been recognized internationally in disciplines including psychology, remote sensing, weather forecasting, and artificial intelligence; for his research on human factors in remote sensing, terrain analysis, and weather forecasting; for his work in the psychology of expertise and the methodology of knowledge elicitation; and for his work on the human factors issues in the design of workstation systems, interfaces, and knowledge-based systems. Hoffman is the editor for the Department on Human-Centered Computing in *IEEE Intelligent Systems* and is the editor for the book series *Expertise: Research and Applications*. His major current project involves an effort to define the principles and methodologies for human-centered computing and complex cognitive systems. He is also helping lead an effort to establish a National Alliance for Expertise Studies. His latest books are *Working Minds: A Practitioner's Handbook of Cognitive Task Analysis, Expertise Out of Context, Minding the Weather: How Expert Forecasters Think,* and *The Cambridge Handbook of Expertise and Expert Performance.*

Laura G. Militello is a Senior Research Psychologist in the Human Factors group at the University of Dayton Research Institute. Her most recent work explores collaboration, particularly in the context of command and control in both military and crisis management settings. Before joining the University of Dayton Research Institute, she worked for Klein Associates where she contributed to the development of a set of applied cognitive task analysis methods (ACTA) for use by practitioners, as well as the design of techniques to train others in conducting cognitive task analysis. She has extensive experience conducting cognitive task analysis across a broad range of domains including critical care nursing, air campaign planning, weapons directing, and consumer decision making. She has conducted more than 20 cognitive task analysis workshops for human factors professionals and students, and currently teaches a course on cognitive task analysis for graduate students in the Human Factors Psychology Program at the University of Dayton. She has authored numerous reports, articles, and book chapters on related topics including interview techniques, knowledge representation, and team decision making. In addition to her research focusing on methods, Militello has worked as a senior user interface designer, applying findings from cognitive task analysis to design. She has worked in the medical device industry as a member of multidisciplinary work teams made up of software designers, mechanical engineers, marketing representatives, and industrial engineers. She has experience conducting multinational usability testing for medical devices, refining interface elements of existing products to reduce error and improve customer satisfaction, as well as designing new, first-of-a-kind interface elements for future ultrasound platforms. She received her M.A. in Experimental Psychology and Human Factors from the University of Dayton in 1995.

Part 1

History

1

Introduction to Section 1
History

That Was Then

Those who came before us were more aware of the key issues and arguments than we might give them credit for. Indeed, many modern researchers have reinvented the wheel and given it new names, often believing their work is distinct or special. In fact, Fernberger (1937) acknowledged that sporadic amnesia is inevitable:

> Scientific ideas become public and common property in spite of anything one may do. ... Examples of particular processes and modes of explanation become current in a laboratory and one does not remember whether one thought of them himself or whether they should be attributed to some one of one's colleagues. (p. xi)

One goal of this book is to draw connections from past approaches to current methods, tracing the historical roots of modern Cognitive Task Analysis (CTA), tracing the pendulum swings, the divergences and convergences. We hope that for a next generation this will reduce the need to reinvent the wheel and encourage efforts to improve on the wheels we already have.

Although we are hesitant to overly constrain the notion of CTA, we think it is necessary to place some boundaries around which approaches will be examined. First off, we need to look at the meaning of the word *task*.

What Is a Task?

The English word *task* has rich linguistic origins in the ancient Indo-European branch of language. The base of the word family is /tag-/, meaning "to touch" in Latin. From this base came many words, including the Latin *taxare,* meaning "to reprimand or blame." Among the many English words that derived are *tangible, attain, contingency,* and dozens of others. In many of these words we can see concepts that we can relate to the notion of task as in the modern phrase "Cognitive Task Analysis." *Webster's New Collegiate Dictionary* (G. and C. Merriam Company, 1979) links the word *task*

3

to the Latin *tasca,* meaning a tax imposed by a feudal superior. From this comes the notion that

> a "task" is a directive, given by a superior, that something is to be done or accomplished within a specified time, usually something hard or unpleasant that has to be done.

Industrial psychologists, human factors psychologists, and ergonomicists have studied proficient human performance in a great variety of domains and contexts (see Alluisi, 1967; Anastasi, 1979; Sanders & McCormick, 1992)—everything from the design of screwdriver handles to the design of information processing systems. The term *task analysis,* coined by R. B. Miller in 1953, has referred to methods that have been used in industrial psychology and ergonomics (Annett, Duncan, Stammers, & Gray, 1971; Eastman Kodak Company, 1983; Kirwan & Ainsworth, 1992; Meister, 1985; Wexley & Yukl, 1984). Task analysis can involve describing jobs in terms of individual physical actions (e.g., button pushing) or describing acts in terms of their higher level or functional foundations (e.g., goals, domain concepts, etc.).

Task analytic methods have been around since before World War I, after which they built on Frederick Taylor's Time and Motion Study approach to job analysis that was popular in the early 1900s. Applied psychologists have been studying aptitudes as a basis for personnel selection and training since the late 1800s. Industrial engineers have been studying work systems and how to make them more efficient since the Industrial Revolution, if not before. Certainly, ethnographers had been studying how history and culture affect work life long before the term *CTA* was ever coined.

A great variety of task analysis methods have been created and named so as to denote applicability in particular domains (e.g., operational sequence diagramming for industrial process control), the uniquenesses of particular methodologies (e.g., structured interviewing, hierarchical analysis, process tracing), or the goals of the procedure (e.g., fault tree diagnosis). The goals of task analysis can include the specification of entire occupations and jobs, the analysis of specific event sequences that lead to faults or accidents in industrial process control, the specification of ergonomic constraints on equipment design, and the development of training and remediational programs. (Lists of task analysis methods can be found in Chapanis [1996]; Drury, Paramore, Van Cott, Grey, and Corlett [1987]; Fleishman [1975]; Kirwan and Ainsworth [1992]; Meister [1985]; Nemeth [2004]; Salvendy [1987]; Shepherd [2001]; and Viteles [1922]. Diaper and Stanton [2004] provided a fine handbook on task analysis that includes overviews as well as chapters focusing on individual methods and approaches.)

Some researchers today hold that the *task* is not the proper unit of analysis because technology is always changing the work (Carroll, 1995) and therefore boundable tasks will be fleeting. Detailed, stepwise descriptions of tasks will be brittle—true today, gone tomorrow. Some define *task* as just the goals of particular activities or activity sequences. In part, this reduction of *task* to *goal* reflects the fact that in many jobs, worker activities cannot be completely (or well) described in terms of rulelike prescriptions or stepwise directives. Why? Because context, dynamics, and cognition are the keys. CTA methods are most often used in the study of adaptive work in complex contexts. Most commonly, these contexts include many people (teams) and many machines (computers), all acting as a system within a cultural, social, and organizational setting. Such contexts are referred to as complex cognitive systems

(Hoffman & Woods, 2005), joint cognitive systems (e.g., Hollnagel & Woods, 2006), and sociotechnical systems (Clegg, 2000; Vicente, 1999). Generally, CTA has the goal of designing better training, better technologies, and better teams to support cognitive work and the achievement of proficiency. However, CTA also has the goal of enriching our basic understanding of human cognition, reasoning, and perceptual skill.

CTA is a suite of scientific methods *and* (as the saying sort of goes) it is an art. As the associationist philosopher Alexander Bain pointed out in his book *Education as Science* (1879), this is not an either-or.

> The scientific treatment of any art consists partly in applying the principles furnished by the several sciences involved, as chemical laws to agriculture; and partly in enforcing, throughout the discussion, the utmost precision and rigour in the statement, deduction and proof of the various maxims or rules that make up the art. (Alexander Bain, 1879, p. 1).

The conduct of CTA requires practice, skill, and finesse.

CTA as Reflecting an Emerging Need

The phrase "Cognitive Task Analysis" began appearing in print in the late 1970s, primarily to express a need: How can we analyze the cognitive components of work? How can we help novices think and perform more like experts? The term emerged in the writings of instructional designers, expertise researchers, systems engineers, cognitive psychologists, and others. A number of researchers perceived a need for task analytic methods that would "define clearly what it is that an expert in a subject matter domain has learned" (Glaser & Resnick, 1972; Resnick, 1976, p. 209). Since about 1979 when the CTA phrase began appearing in print and the mid- to late 1980s when the phrase began appearing in the literatures of human factors psychology and instructional design, the phrase has come to be widely used as a designation for a number of different research and data analysis methods that all attempt to tap into or describe the cognitive processes that underlie proficient performance and its development, to reveal the patterns of human reasoning, problem solving, decision making, and collaboration and the content knowledge of domain expertise and skill. This emerging need is reflected in salient topics such as interface design and usability testing (e.g., Redish & Wixon, 2003). This emerging need is also reflected clearly in the advent of new communities of practice. Examples are the "Naturalistic Decision Making" community of practice (see chapter 9), the "Cognitive Systems Engineering" community of practice (see chapter 7), and the formation of the "Cognitive Engineering and Decision Making" Technical Group within the Human Factors and Ergonomics Society.

Workplace Changes

Recent decades have witnessed a shift in the sorts of things that task analysis is used to study and explain, moving from a traditional focus on relatively simpler and sometimes routine physical tasks—such as the assembly of vacuum-tube-based radios—to more complex problem-solving tasks, especially those that are involved in human interactions with complex information processing systems. Cognition has become the paramount aspect of the tasks performed by knowledge workers using information technology. Task analysis has placed increased emphasis on the specification of the cognitive elements of technical skill, especially the knowledge and reasoning components (Bailey & Kay, 1987; Bainbridge, 1979; Rasmussen, 1986b; Woods & Hollnagel, 1987). The goal is to understand complex interactions of humans and machines (see Gordon, Gill, & Dingus, 1987; Madni, 1988; Means & Gott, 1988; Moray, Sanderson, & Vicente, 1992; Sarter & Woods, 1995). If that is the case, it is argued, then one must engage in some sort of *Cognitive* Task Analysis (see Glaser et al., 1985; Gordon & Gill, 1997; Lesgold et al., 1986). There has been increasing demand for tools (including CTA methods and software support tools) aimed at helping researchers explore cognition in depth, unpack the influence of environmental factors on cognitive processes, and apply this in-depth understanding of cognition in real-world contexts to the design of technologies, interfaces, and training.

Emerging Interest in Studying Diverse Domains for Diverse Applications

Studies using CTA methods have been conducted on a great variety of domains— aircraft piloting, air traffic control, military command and control, industrial process control, reasoning in medicine, and electronics troubleshooting, to name just a few (see Hall, Gott, & Pokorny, 1995; Helander & Nagamachi, 1992; Klein, Orasanu, Calderwood, & Zsambok, 1993). Projects have had a great variety of purposes. CTA methods have been important for research and applications in such areas as training and remediation, the design of automated decision aids, the design of interfaces and workstations, the elicitation of expert knowledge for intelligent systems, the preservation of corporate knowledge, and the identification and mitigation of error (for examples, see Hall, Gott, & Pokorny, 1995; Hoc, Cacciabue, & Hollnagel, 1995; Hoffman, 1991a; Howell & Cooke, 1989; Klein, 1992; Marti & Scrivani, 2003; Merkelbach & Schraagen, 1994; Rasmussen, Pejtersen, & Goodstein, 1994; Redish & Wixon, 2003; Roth, 1997a; Woods, 1993). In addition to applications, CTA-based research has led to new models of decision making (see Klein, 1993a) and has enriched the ethnographic descriptions of the social construction of scientific knowledge (e.g., Collins, 1985; Hutchins, 1995a; Suchman, 1987).

CTA and CFR

The emerging need also involved the notion that the study of work cannot be conducted in isolation from the full, rich context in which tasks are performed, hence the need for what has come to be called Cognitive Field Research (CFR) (Hoffman & Woods, 2000 see DeKeyser, 1992; Rasmussen, 1992). The CTA community of practice emphasizes the study of complex cognitive systems in context. Hence, in this book we discuss CFR as well as CTA.

One purpose of the CTA–CFR distinction is to emphasize the fact that the analysis of tasks in terms of cognitive variables and functions can sometimes be somewhat divorced from empirical observation of actual activity in a realistic or real setting. That is, some CTA research is situated in laboratory or laboratory-like settings, whereas CFR is conducted in the place of work. These boundaries are of course fuzzy (see chapter 16 and Hoffman & Deffenbacher, 1992). Thus, a CTA interview procedure might be conducted in a meeting room next to the operations floor of a weather forecasting facility. That room would be essentially no different from a small cubicle in an academic psychology laboratory. So is it a laboratory, a natural laboratory, or a field setting? It is certainly laboratory-like: It is small, quiet, and includes a table and some chairs and a pile of research materials (instructions, note pads, data collection forms, etc.). But what if the interviewee weather forecaster sees a need to go back to his office and get some materials, say, satellite images, to refer to in the interview? When he comes back into the interview room, is that now a field setting?

The distinction regarding the location of the research (laboratory or field) may be a distraction. It may be more informative to consider the contrast between the objectives of CTA and CFR to retain as much real-world context as possible (even if the research must be conducted away from the work) and the traditional objective in laboratory research to control as many contextual variables as possible to isolate and examine a component of cognition. CTA and CFR embrace such notions as "cognition in the wild" (Hutchins, 1995a) and "situated cognition" (Clancey, 1997) (see chapter 10), both of which focus on explaining and studying cognition from an anthropological point of view in the context of work, culture, and political constraints. In this light, the assumption distinguishing CTA from CFR is the analysis of tasks in terms of cognitive variables and functions based on observation of real activity in the "real world," regardless of whether the goal is to influence the shape of technology or further our understanding of the cognition of domain practitioners. (To ease the flow of the discussion, we use the single acronym CTA throughout the remainder this book to refer to both CTA and CFR, unless otherwise indicated.)

Perspectives on CTA

CTA in its present form is a relatively recent development. However, to many who read or hear about CTA for the first time, the core ideas seem somehow familiar. In fact, many of the elements of CTA have evolved over time in the context of different fields of study. Psychologists have been using self-report methods (variants of introspection), combined with ethnographic methods, for many years. The buzz phrases "Cognitive Task Analysis" and "Cognitive Field Research" seem to be both ironic and oxymoronic. To many psychologists, *cognitive* does not quite seem to go with *task*—it hearkens to the pendulum swing of behaviorism versus mentalism. To others, the phrases are critical in capturing the implicit claim that for most human activities, cognitions are not only relevant in the description of behavior but necessary to explain the behavior because they play a causal role. The notion of "field research" seems to be an oxymoron to the experimentalist who prefers factorialization and laboratory control to the uncertainties and complexities of the real world, arguing that it is difficult, if not impossible, to engage in rigorous hypothesis testing in any form of field research.

So goes a historical pendulum of ideas, reactions, and counterreactions—this forms a recurrent theme to this book. The irony is that things that were said about psychological research methods decades ago (e.g., Fernberger, 1937) can be said today now about CTA methods:

- CTA has existed in a variety of forms and has a variety of uses.
- The methodology of CTA, and indeed its very existence, is linked to historical trends in the philosophy, goals, and even disciplinary agendas of both applied and academic psychology.
- Like all methods, CTA has both strengths and weaknesses.

The power of CTA is in how the needs and historical trends have come together to be applied to the challenges of the information age: using qualitative and quantitative methods to study cognition and expertise in the context of work, to explore a work domain with the objective of uncovering cognitive complexity, and to apply this knowledge to the design of tools, technologies, and work systems.

The Focus and Organization of This Book

By the 1990s the term *CTA* was often used to describe methods or approaches to studying the cognitive components of work—attempts to meet the need articulated beginning in the 1970s. Not long thereafter, the conversation shifted to how to best define CTA, what is actually new or different about CTA, and how it relates to historical as well as modern ideas about and methods for the study of work. This book documents and expands that conversation. In the chapters of this book, we do not shy away from discussing the difficulties and challenges of CTA and CFR. However, we also hope to convey the positive and rewarding aspects of the research, especially in terms of its fruitful applications.

We trace various historical and modern perspectives, or "communities of practice," that have components common to CTA, highlighting their use in different historical contexts, research paradigms, and real-world challenges. We highlight the CTA component present in modern-day perspectives that continue to seek novel ways to uncover, study, and support human cognition in the context of work. The juxtaposition of the perspectives will allow the reader to understand which aspects of CTA are well articulated and which are still somewhat murky, what has worked well and under what circumstances, and what has been suggested but not yet demonstrated. We discuss underlying theory where links have been made to specific CTA approaches.

The "how-tos" of CTA are described in detail, along with boilerplate data collection forms and experimental protocols, in Crandall, Klein, and Hoffman's *Working Minds: A Practitioner's Guide to Cognitive Task Analysis* (2006). This book is intended to be a companion to that guide. Three chapters in Stanton, Salmon, Walker, Baber, and Jenkins's *Human Factors Methods* (2005) present brief but well-illustrated rundowns of a number of task Analysis and CTA methods that we refer to in this book.

Thus, in this book we do not go into much detail about particular CTA methods and procedures. We do, however, refer to representative studies, and so in the course of our presentation, we give the reader a feel for the particulars of a number of CTA methods. Our main aim is to capture the essence of each of a set of differing perspectives on CTA. We do not presume to dictate hard and fast rules about what constitutes CTA. The field of Complex Cognitive Systems (Hoffman & Woods, 2005; Hollnagel & Woods, 2006) is relatively new, and the community of practice is still searching for accepted rules regarding which methods are best for what types of research, strengths and weakness of alternative methods, reasons why CTA has met with successes, and reasons why it has met with failures. In this regard, we attempt in this book to maintain a clear distinction between methods versus methodology, the latter being a term that is often and mistakenly used to mean the former. Methodology is the study and analysis of methods, and this book qualifies as just that, even though our treatment is largely historiographic.

Section 1

These chapters set the stage with a look at the historical origins of CTA in earlier forms of task analysis. Chapter 2 relays the origins of the concept of CTA over recent decades. It bounds the concept of CTA, as distinct from task analysis. Chapter 3 is a 'way-back machine,' charting the evolution of CTA from task analysis of the late 1800s, with chapter 4 focusing on the expansion of task analytic methods in the decades of World War II and thereafter. Chapter 5 focuses on events and trends since about 1980 that led to the introduction of the CTA designation and the recently emerged communities of practice—the "perspectives"—that use CTA in research.

Section 2

The chapters in section 2 cover each of the perspectives in detail: Cognitive Systems Engineering, Expertise Studies, Naturalistic Decision Making, Cognitive Work Analysis, Sociology-Anthropology, and Human-Centered Computing. Like any pie slicing, ours involves some sticky bits.

Each of the perspectives we discuss has its own

- historical origins,
- particular way of looking at CTA,
- particular CTA methods that are preferred (and that we will exemplify),
- particular views about methodology (i.e., the analysis of methods),
- particular core and theoretical notions and assumptions, and
- particular (sometimes outlandish) claims that raise the hackles of practitioners in other perspectives.

The intent of our pie slicing is not to make square slices out of round pies but to be comprehensive and inclusive. At the same time, we have to make some sense of the interwoven threads just to get the discussion going. Books, after all, have to have chapters.

Section 3

In the final four "synthesis" chapters, we pull things together by highlighting the similarities and differences among the perspectives, the things they agree on and disagree about, and some of the outstanding issues for CTA methodology. The perspectives diverge in many ways and dovetail in many ways. From the chapters in this book, the reader should see the full landscape of CTA from its rich history to the most current topics and issues.

Before exploring the modern perspectives and current state of CTA, we thought it made sense to lay out the evolution of CTA from task analysis. This is the top of chapter 2.

Summary

In this book we strive to recognize the credit due those who came before us in exploring methods for studying cognitive work. It is common throughout scientific history for ideas and arguments to be rediscovered without an awareness of the relevant work that has gone before. This phenomenon is no less true for practitioners of CTA. One goal of this book is to draw connections from past approaches to current methods.

CTA, by definition, is focused on the concept of task or work, sometimes characterized as goals. Regardless of the framework within which CTA is conducted, it is considered a suite of scientific methods and an art. As with the scientific treatment of any art, the evolution of CTA is dependent on the continued effort to better articulate and make explicit the maxims or rules that make up the art. We use the term *CTA* (inclusive of Cognitive Field Research [CFR]) as an umbrella to *designate methods that are intended to support the achievement of an understanding of human cognition and collaboration in the context of adaptive work in complex sociotechnical contexts.* Most commonly, these contexts include many people (teams) and many machines (computers) engaging in some complex activity, and all acting as a system.

The term *CTA* first emerged in print as a means to express a need for methods to aid in analyzing the cognitive components of work. These early discussions in the 1970s and 1980s appeared in instructional design and human factors literatures as researchers sought methods to understand human reasoning, problem solving, decision making, and collaborating. This stated need was no doubt a reaction to the shift in work that occurred as more sophisticated machines took over many of the routine, predictable tasks, leaving increasingly cognitively complex tasks to the humans (i.e., supervisory control). The challenges associated with work have become less physical and more cognitive for many workers as information technology has become pervasive.

Although discussions of CTA sometimes focus on the use of field research as an important distinction from laboratory-based methods, this distinction can easily become muddled. At times it is simply not feasible to conduct CTA studies in the actual work context (i.e., researchers are not welcome in military command and control cells during real-world conflict). A more important distinction is the attempt with CTA and CFR methods to retain as much real-world context as possible, in contrast to traditional laboratory research, which seeks to control as many contextual variables as possible to isolate and examine individual variables.

Although *CTA* is a relatively new term and is often presented as if it is a revolutionary new way to study work, CTA builds on ideas that have appeared and developed throughout the history of applied psychology. In this volume we begin in section 1 by tracing the historical threads, highlighting what they have contributed to modern CTA. In section 2, we discuss modern perspectives and themes that continue to seek novel ways to uncover, study, and support human cognition in the context of work. In section 3, we synthesize the perspectives, articulating similarities and differences among them.

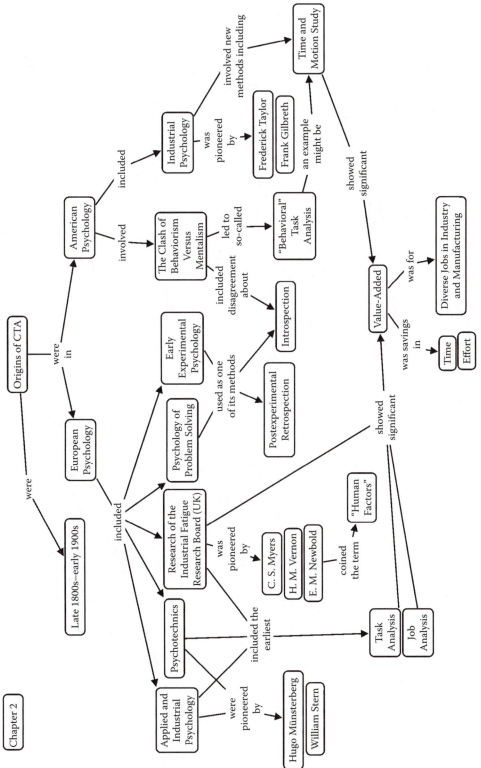

FIGURE 2.1 Chapter 2 Concept Map.

2

A History of Task Analysis

In recent years in psychology in America there has been a fashion to magnify "objective" techniques and to look askance at any technique which might be considered to have a subjective basis. It seems to me that the fashion is beginning to change and that some of the "subjective" techniques are again beginning to attain importance in current psychological methodology. Let me hasten to say that I have no quarrel with objective techniques nor with some of the magnificent results which have been obtained by them. The present paper is an attempt to reconcile some of the differences between the proponents of the two different points of view in the hope that psychologists will realize that all of us are working toward the same ends and that we are all working in the same scientific universe.

—Samuel W. Fernberger (1937, p. 207)

Hermann Ebbinghaus, pioneer in the psychology of learning and longtime editor of one of Germany's most prominent psychology journals, once said, "Psychology has a long past, but a short history." Roots of psychology can be traced to the most ancient of philosophies, but as an academic discipline, psychology dates to the latter part of the 1800s. A similar thing might be said of Cognitive Task Analysis (CTA), though on a different time scale. Its roots in task analysis can be traced back to the origins of industrial psychology, but CTA gained currency only some 20 years ago. This being said, there is a contrast one might draw: Task analysis was invented largely as a consequence of industrialization. It grew hand in hand with industrial psychology from within a single discipline—academic psychology. CTA was invented largely as a result of computerization, but it emerged in the 1980s in a number of disciplines ranging from instructional design to sociology.

Figure 2.2 provides a timeline highlighting several of the major influences leading to modern CTA. The need for methods for studying work and cognition is visible throughout history regardless of the political and scientific climate of the time—at times more openly acknowledged than others, but nonetheless present throughout.

Introspection

We begin with introspection for two reasons. One is that the method is often believed to have been the first empirical method of scientific (then mentalistic) psychology. The other reason is that among its variety of forms, versions can be found that are

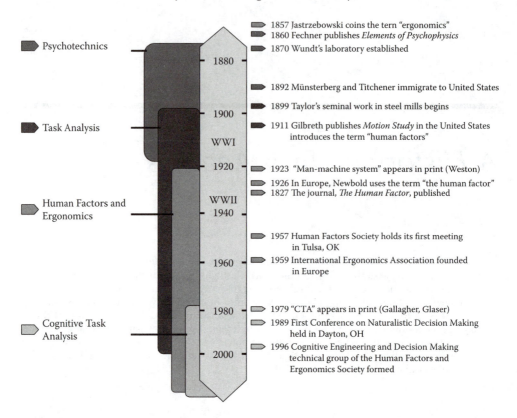

FIGURE 2.2 An evolution of method.

very like modern studies using the "new" methods of CTA. Even the very earliest researchers moved beyond classical introspection and employed methods that we today might term *process-tracing methods*, and used them in combination with performance measures.

Introspection evolved over many centuries out of discussions of methods of prayer and the nature of the human soul, by theologians such as Thomas Aquinas in his *Summa Theologica* (circa 1267/1945, especially the book, *The Mode and the Order of Understanding;* see Kenny, 1980). To some theologians, prayer was regarded not as talking to God but as thinking about oneself and one's perceptions, thoughts, beliefs, actions, and so on, all in relation to God. This could be readily recast as a method for scientific psychology by simply deleting the final phrase, resulting in a definition of introspection. French psychologist Théodule Ribot (1873, 1879) integrated the earlier philosophical and theological discussions and presented introspection in the context of the new science of psychology and its methodologies. Despite debate across the centuries concerning the validity of introspective reports, by influential figures such as Immanuel Kant, August Comte, John Stuart Mill, Franz Brentano, Carl Stumpf, and many others, by the mid-1800s psychology was defined not as a metaphysical science of the human soul but as the scientific study of mental phenomena. Ribot described introspection as "the psychical phenomena of the adult, civilized, white man" (Ribot, 1873, p. 17; see also pp. 81–89). It was generally believed that a main method, in addition to the physiological, psychophysical, and chronometric (reaction time) methods of the new psychologies (i.e., Donders, Fechner, Müller, Helmholtz, Weber), would be what was variously called "reflection," "interior observation," and "introspective observation" (see Dunlap, 1930, 1932; James, 1890, Vol. 1, p. 185; Ribot, 1873, pp. 16–22).

In the late 1800s, Wilhelm Wundt championed the establishment of psychology as a science, using new methods of psychophysics and also introspection and retrospection. Use of these methods spread to the United States as Wundt's student, Edward B. Titchener, took a position at Cornell, where he continued to promote and advance his particular introspection approach. A myth, perpetuated largely by introductory psychology texts (in English), is that introspection was used in Wundtian psychology as the sole method, but this could hardly be further from the truth. Most typically, introspective data were used to extend the explanation of data from either psychophysical or chronometric methods. And also most typically, the verbal report was retrospective rather than introspective (see Boring, 1953).

A variety of forms of introspection were used in psychological research in the late 19th and early 20th centuries, ranging from the prototypical introspective reports on the analysis of perceptions of simple stimuli into sensory elements, to the use of "phenomenological observation" in the Gestalt psychologists' studies of perceptual illusions (Wertheimer, 1912), to introspection for the analysis of the associative processes of schizophrenics (for reviews, see Bailey, 1932; Boring, 1913, 1953; Titchener, 1912) (for discussions of methodological issues, see Bakan, 1954; Benjafield, 1969; Gadlin & Ingle, 1975; Lieberman, 1979; Pepper, 1918; Radford, 1974).

It is interesting that protocols from Ruger's (1910) dissertation (under Wundt) on problem solving illustrate methods remarkably similar to those used much more recently in studying expert–novice differences (as in Bailey & Kay, 1987; Chi, Feltovich, & Glaser, 1981, for example). Ruger had adults learn to solve a mechanical puzzle called the "heart and bow," a familiar type of puzzle, this one having two intertwined wire constructions that had to be rotated and positioned just so to be untangled. On each of a series of trials, participants would attempt to solve the puzzle and then give a retrospective report.

Even more striking perhaps is the similarity of the modern CTA method of think-aloud problem solving to the method of introspection developed by Oswald Külpe and his students at Würzburg. They came to believe that classical introspection (i.e., reports on sensory attributes of simple stimuli used in psychophysical experiments) was inadequate for the study of the "higher mental processes." As a result, the Wurzburgers developed a technique they called "systematic post-experimental retrospection." In this interesting method, the participants would first engage in the complete task (e.g., constrained association reaction time, sentence comprehension reaction time, sentence recall, etc.) but then would be run through the experiment a second time, from start to finish, and retrospect about what they had thought or perceived during the initial run-through (see Boring, 1953; Mandler & Mandler, 1964, chap. 5). (Figure 2.3 is an adaptation of from Ruger's dissertation illustrates a version of this technique.) This technique bears remarkable resemblance to the cued retrospective interviews used in studying modern surgical teams, search and rescue teams, and firefighters (Mackenzie et al., 1995; Omodei, McLennan, Elliott, Wearing & Clancey, 2005; Xiao et al., 2005).

Trial 1: *I have no idea in the world how I did it. I remember moving the loop of the heart about the end of the bar, and the two pieces suddenly came apart. I think I can do it sooner next time, not because I know just how to do it, but I remember the parts of the puzzle which I brought together in the first success.*

The trial 1 attempt took 351 seconds to puzzle completion.

Trial 2: *Do not yet know what movements to make.*

Trial 2 took 256 seconds.

Trial 3: *Success was still largely by chance; did not anticipate except that I knew there was a certain part of the puzzle to work at. Hold the heart in the right hand and the bow in the left. Move the loop of the heart through the end of the bow. Can't describe the other movements; the rest is chance. Think I will get it next time.*

Trial 3 took 155 seconds, but on trial 4 the completion time dropped drastically—to only 27 seconds. For trial 4, the participant apparently offered no introspective report, but completion times continued to drop, down to 16 seconds on trial 10 at which point the participant reported:

Trial 10: *It is easier to run the loop of the heart under the end of the bar. Had done this before but just realized its importance.*

FIGURE 2.3 Transcript from Ruger's dissertation (1910) (as translated and summarized by Woodworth, 1938).

It is also important to note that participants in these studies were generally graduate students and professors who had experience with the tasks they were asked to perform. Although these studies did not focus on the concept of cognitive performance in the context of work, they were studying skilled performance, an important component of modern CTA.

In considering the history of introspection in science, we also must acknowledge that this method has fallen in and out of style several times throughout history. Not long after Titchener and others who studied under Wundt European scientists, the first generation of homegrown American psychologists reacted in one way or another to Wundt's use of introspection and retrospection (or Titchener's version of them, or various misrepresentations of what introspection was all about). Then, a next generation grew up under the influence of behaviorally oriented psychologists, especially John B. Watson, and behaviorally oriented methods in industrial psychology, such as the time and motion methods used by Frederick W. Taylor, Frank and Lilian Gilbreth, and the other so-called efficiency experts.

It was a mere decade or so after that when a second generation of American psychologists rediscovered the variety of the methods of introspection that had been developed and the variety of its uses (Fernberger, 1937). That generation also was discovering that what it had been led to believe about introspectionism did not quite tell the entire story. It was still clear in everyone's memory how Watson flamboyantly and thoroughly excoriated J. W. Baird (a Titchener Ph.D.) after Baird's embarrassing, if not merely boring, attempt to demonstrate Titchenerian introspection—at a meeting of the American Psychological Association, no less, with many of the country's major psychologists and their students in attendance (in 1914). But to Fernberger (1937), who was influenced by Titchener early in his career, that new generation seemed uninformed of the subtleties of the legitimate methodological issues and arguments that had been in the air concerning introspection and retrospection for decades, well before Watson was in the ascendance.

Although many cognitivists today are asked to justify the use of introspection-like and ethnographic interview methods, history shows that these methods are not new or in any way revolutionary. In fact, Fernberger made this point quite eloquently nearly 60 years ago in the quote at the beginning of this chapter.

Although introspection has been adapted and refined for use as a scientific method in psychology since the 1800s, adopting this approach for the study of work came later, as we will show. However, before we jump to the deliberate study of cognitive work via task analysis, we must consider the influence of the European "ergonomics" and "psychotechnics" movements in furthering our understanding of cognition and skill in applied settings.

Ergonomics

Research that we today would refer to as ergonomics, including the analysis of tasks, can be traced to the late 1800s, if not earlier. In Poland and Russia there was a movement similar to that of the German psychotechnicians. In fact, the Polish scholar Wojciech Jastrzebowski was the first to coin the term *ergonomics* from the Greek words *ergon* (work) and *nomos* (principle or law) in 1857. Jastrzebowski specifically included within his conceptualization of work "physical, aesthetic, rational, and moral work, that is Labour, Entertainment, Reasoning, and Dedication" (Jastrzebowski, 1857). Meister (1999) summarized research within this tradition through the early 1900s.

> The conceptual predecessors of Russian ergonomics include Mendeleev, who discussed in 1880 the general notion of adapting machines to man, and Arendt, who in 1888 discussed the adaptation concept with relation to the development of aeronautics. In 1915, Rudnev raised questions about the development of a standard cockpit for aircraft; in 1928, Rosenberg, using anthropometric data, determined the requirements of a cockpit layout. It is significant that, in discussing the development of Russian ergonomics, Lomov and Bertone (1969), from whose articles some of this material is taken and who unfortunately supplied no references in their article, also said nothing about the link between human factors and the two World Wars that were important in both Britain and the United States. These authors provide several early examples. ... Gellerstein and Ittin in 1924 with regard to redesign of the Russian type face to enhance the movements of the type setter; Berstein in 1929 with regard to the redesign of the tram drivers' workstation; and Platonov and Mikhailovskii in 1934 with regard to adjustable chairs for auto workers. In 1937, Zimkin and Aeple used a tachistoscope to study information reception form aviation instruments. (Meister, 1999, p. 161)

By the end of World War I, perhaps, but certainly in the lead-up to World War II, *ergonomics* had entered the English language. Floyd (1958) said that the term was a "post-war addition to the English language. It was used in 1950 by a group of workers, including engineers, to express in one word the application of ... psychological knowledge to the study of man and his working environment, a field of research which had become increasingly important during the 1939–45 war" (p. 75).

Psychotechnics

We have much for which to thank the psychotechnicians of the late 1800s and early 1900s. This was the other of two European groups that introduced the core idea that would come to be called applied psychology or industrial psychology. The core ideas, originating in Germany and then spreading throughout Europe and across the Atlantic to the United States, contributed significantly to our understanding of cognition. They developed instruments to measure aptitudes for personnel selection and training. The first simulators to train workers were developed and implemented during this era. The following is a brief history, highlighting aspects that have influenced modern CTA.

Psychotechnics in the early 1900s in Europe was aimed at measuring aptitude. Although the focus was clearly on cognitive skills such as perception and memory, the goal was to measure aptitudes to predict job performance. Skill was seen not in relation to a particular job but as a general quality a person possessed. A person was not necessarily apt at something in particular but had general aptitudes. The *skill bottleneck* was a term used to describe the prevailing belief that finding the people with the right aptitudes to do the job was a social and economic problem to be addressed (Sanderson, 2002).

Psychotechnicians studied the practices and methods, and the proficient workers, in diverse domains including the manufacture of ceramics and textiles, woodworking, radio repair, the sales and service industries, business management, the construction trades, and others. Research goals included vocational or aptitude testing, the optimization of productivity, the assessment of skill and proficiency, the creation of humane working conditions, and the issues of human–machine interaction. Domains of special concern in Germany in the years before and during WWI included piloting and gun operation (see Fitts, 1947; Maier, 1946, chap. 7; Poffenberger, 1942; Viteles, 1932, section 2).

Apparatuses were designed specifically to allow for careful examination of key elements. Widely used devices included the "Dubois ergograph" to study the effects of muscular fatigue on reaction time (repeated squeezing of a rubberized bulb, on cue, so as to lift a weight), and an assortment of reaction-time measuring devices, including a variation on Wundt's complication clock called the "estimating clock." (A comprehensive review of the psychotechnical research methods and results, and copious diagrams of psychotechnical apparatus, appears in Moede [1930, Vol. 1]; a thorough analysis of the history of German applied psychology appears in Geuter [1992].)

Perhaps the most influential accomplishment of the psychotechnics movement was the transition and adaptation of psychological methods from the academic laboratory to applied settings. The methods and theories that were employed in the earliest applied psychology stemmed directly from the classical laboratories (van Strien, 1998). In this psychotechnical research, jobs or tasks were analyzed in terms of basic psychological capabilities—the same elementary functions that had been researched

TABLE 2.1 Examples of Early Applied Psychological Research

- One of the most widely used tests of intelligence used in testing job candidates was the Ebbinghaus completion task (see Nestor, 1933).

- Otto Klemm, a Wundt Ph.D., conducted research at Leipzig on auditory localization and loudness judgments (dichotic presentation of clicks) (1918). Subsequently, Klemm applied his research to the task of antiaircraft gunners who had to target incoming airplanes using loudness and direction cues.

- In the years following their studies under Wundt and doctoral research at the educational psychology laboratory at Leipzig, in 1915–1917, Curt Piorkowski and Walther Moede investigated the problem of selecting men to serve as chauffeurs for the German army, and they built one of the very first simulator laboratories, to test candidates for jobs as railway motormen (see Gundlach, 1997; Moede, 1930, chap. 40; Nestor, 1933).

- Coinciding with events leading up to World War I, the first generation of applied psychologists in Europe, championed by Hugo Münsterberg (also a Wundt Ph.D.) and William Stern (a student of Hermann Ebbinghaus), had begun to conduct applied research that was motivated by the need for trained workers for new jobs as aviators, telegraphers, pilots, railway motormen, assembly line workers, delivery truck drivers, and so on (Dockeray & Isaacs, 1921; Viteles, 1932, chap. 5). The main focus was on personnel selection via psychometric testing and training.

in the academic laboratories. A rundown of these is presented in Table 2.1. Tests were then devised to assess an individual worker's ability to exercise those capabilities. Memory was tested, for example, by having the candidate remember the lengths of the lines in a simple diagram-like pattern. Spatial reasoning was tested by a variety of pattern completion tasks. Mechanical aptitude was tested by having the candidate indicate the directions in which the parts of a diagrammed machine would move when set in motion. Manual dexterity was tested in a variety of tasks in which, for example, the candidate would have to sort numbered disks into numbered compartments in a limited amount of time, or bend a piece of wire into a prescribed shape.

The psychotechnical methodology included a focus on cognitive factors and especially the assessment of individual differences in cognition. Along with such traits as tact, popularity, and attitude toward unionization, a number of traits or capabilities assessed by psychotechnicians that could be regarded as cognitive were general intelligence, knowledge, experience, memory, concentration, persistence, visual discrimination, auditory memory capacity, logical analysis, and others (see Gundlach, 1997; von Drunen, 1997; Wiendieck, 1997).

By 1914 there were over a dozen centers engaged in applied psychological research in Germany (Viteles, 1932, chap. 5). Major companies employed psychologists to conduct research on personnel selection and training, including Krupp, Zeiss, Siemens, and Allgemeine Electricitäts-Gesellschaft. The support from the German railroad authority included the creation of a traveling vocational testing research laboratory, housed in a special railroad coach (Couvé, 1925; Nestor, 1933). By the 1920s, institutes for the industrial application of psychology had been established in most of the major German cities (Geuter, 1992, chap. 2; Viteles, 1932, chap. 5).

From about the turn of the century up through WWI, applied psychological research was conducted in Czechoslovakia, France, Germany, the Netherlands, and Holland under the paradigm that Hugo Münsterberg christened "psychotechnics" (see Brozek & Hoskovec, 1997; Bültmann, 1928; Giese, 1927; Lahy, 1933; Laugier & Weinberg, 1936; Meyerheim, 1927; Moede, 1930; Münsterberg, 1912, 1913, 1914;

Stern, 1927/1961; see Viteles, 1932, chap. 5). (Walter Moede and Curt Piorkowski, whom we mentioned in Table 2.1, edited journals on industrial psychology and psychotechnics beginning in 1919.)

The rise of industrial psychology in Germany was paralleled to a great extent by research activities in the United States. The advent of the war-worthy airplane resulted in a flurry of psychological research in the United States as WWI approached. There also was a focus was on personnel selection and training. The various committees and boards on aviation psychology included such notable academics as (Major) John B. Watson, Edward L. Thurstone, (Major) Knight Dunlap, and Robert M. Yerkes. (Aviation psychology research on personnel selection and training was also conducted in Italy, France, and the United Kingdom; see Koonce [1984].)

The ideas of German industrial psychology were transported to the United States not only by Münsterberg (who championed the Applied Psychology Laboratory at Harvard University) but also by other former American students of Wundt. For instance, George M. Stratton, one of the first Americans to study under Wundt, conducted research at Leipzig on touch sensations (Stratton, 1896), but upon his return to America, he adapted the classical psychophysical methods to an applied problem, sponsored in part by the Pennsylvania Railroad Company—the problem of selecting colors for signal lamps that could be readily perceived under conditions of rapid movement at night (Stratton, 1909). Shortly thereafter, as WWI approached, Stratton would be but one of a number of prominent academic psychologists who would conduct research on the selection of aviators using tests, including simple and choice reaction-time tasks (e.g., Dunlap, 1919; Stratton, 1919; Thorndike, 1920; Yerkes, 1919; for a review, see Dockeray & Isaacs, 1921).

A key concept that grew out of this era was the notion of "mental work," which many today know only as the notion of mental workload. The concept appeared even before the turn of the century, for example, in the writings of William Stern in the 1890s (see Stern, 1927/1961) and R. S. Woodworth (1899) on motor skill and especially in Lindley's (1895) study of the motor movements accompanying mental work[1] and in the classic study of the acquisition of telegraphic skill by Bryan and Harter (Bryan, 1892; Bryan & Harter, 1897) (see also Swift's 1910 studies of telegraphers). Shortly thereafter, advances in the design and manufacture of typewriters (see Adler, 1973) led to a rapid widening of their use in business and also motivated the classic studies of the acquisition of typewriting skill (Book, 1908; Swift, 1904).

A concept of skill became entrenched in academic psychology: skill was regarded as well-adapted behavior involving central processes and organization (behavioral groupings, plateaus in performance, etc.) (see George, 1932; Lashley, 1930; McGeoch, 1931; Woodworth, 1903, 1938). What followed, up through the 1930s, was a great deal of research on mental effort (e.g., Bills, 1927, 1931; Freeman, 1931) and the speed–accuracy trade-off (e.g., Garrett, 1922; Hanson, 1922). The intense competition among the 100 or so typewriter manufacturers circa WWI was paralleled by a massive amount of research, including countless masters' theses, on the acquisition of typewriting skill (e.g., Bradford, 1915; Chapman, 1919; Hill, Rejall, & Thorndike, 1913; Hoke, 1922; Towne, 1922; Wells, 1916), the assessment of keyboard formats, and methods for teaching typewriting (for a review, see Dvorak, Merrick, Deals, & Ford, 1936). Much of this research, we might note, focused on the analysis of the performance of experts (see Book, 1924; Coover, 1923; Luton, 1926; Smith, 1922; Smith & Wiese, 1921). This research also shows that the concept of mental workload arose long before modern workload assessment methods such as the NASA Task Load Index (Hart & Staveland, 1988) and the Subjective Workload Assessment Tool (Vidulich, 1989) arrived on the scene.

Although the emphasis today has shifted more toward building better tools to support humans than toward fitting the human to the job, the methods used in these early applications of psychology have implications for modern CTA. The early psychotechnicians not only established the field of applied psychology but greatly advanced our understanding of cognition, the ways to study and assess aptitudes, and the ways to train specific cognitive skills.

The psychotechnics movements set the stage for the development of task analysis methods. As instruments for personnel selection and training became increasingly visible, work processes and tools naturally become an object of scrutiny in pursuit of further improving efficiency. Frederick Taylor is renowned for his highly effective methods for analyzing a task and identifying inefficiencies—and for successfully changing the way researchers thought about and studied work.

Task Analysis

The concept of task analysis is firmly rooted in Taylor's Time and Motion Study (TMS) (1911), which began by seeking ways to reduce muscle fatigue, increase efficiency, and improve safety for workers conducting physical tasks. Over time, however, those who were studying workers found that they could not ignore the cognitive aspects of work, and task analysis methods began to evolve to include more cognitive elements. This section provides a brief overview of the evolution of task analysis methods.

Studying Work: Time and Motion Study

Taylorism, or "scientific management," can be considered one of the earliest formalized method of task analysis. As such, it represents an important contribution to modern CTA. In particular, Taylor succeeded in shifting the focus from finding the humans with the right aptitudes to finding ways to study and improve the work environment to increase efficiency and reduce error. Taylorism was both a philosophy of scientific management espoused by Frederick W. Taylor (1911) and an associated method of TMS (See Figure 2.4). (Copley [1923] is a detailed biography of Taylor.) The method had roots in European psychotechnics, but it arose as a distinct methodology in the United States and then spread back to Europe (see Farmer, 1921).

Taylor started apprenticing at age 17, first at a machine shop and then at the Midvale Steel Company in Bethlehem, Pennsylvania. He worked first as laborer, then moved up the ranks to clerk, journeyman lathe operator, gang boss, and foreman of the machine shop, and eventually chief engineer (at age 31). In his role as manager, there were inevitable conflicts with workers, exacerbated by social class and attitudes: "One of the very first requirements for a man who is fit to handle pig iron is that he shall be so stupid and phlegmatic that he more nearly resembles in his mental make-up the ox rather than any other type" (Taylor quoted in Gies, 1991, p. 58). It was in that *Zeitgeist* that Taylor came to wonder exactly how management could measure "a day's work." Interestingly enough, Taylor began by studying not the dumb ox but the expert. A skilled machinist was pulled from the workforce and assigned the task of helping Taylor. The machinist conducted a variety of machining jobs while Taylor systematically changed the configuration of the tools and other artifacts in the work space. Taylor went on to examine proficient performance at numerous steel mill jobs, one job after another, across more than two decades at the Bethlehem Steel Company. He always began by identifying and then studying the proficient workers (the experts).

A majority of the hundreds of mill workers spent time slavishly shoveling ore and coal. Each worker owned his own shovel and differed from the other workers in the characteristic amounts lifted in each shovelful. In a study conducted in 1881, Taylor took two proficient shovelers and had them use shovels with various blade shapes and handle lengths, noting the time per load and the tonnage shoveled per day. The results showed that shoveling ore versus coal required different shovel shapes. This led to the establishment of a machine shop at the steel mill, for making various tools for different jobs.

Taylor's experience led him to constantly wonder what the best method was for doing each particular job, a question that would come to motivate all of the TMS research:

1. First, study how each of several highly skilled workers does the job.
2. Second, divide the job into elementary component activities.
3. Third, discard the useless actions.
4. Fourth, redesign the tools and the work space so as to maximize efficiency.

TMS was advanced significantly by Frank Gilbreth (a construction engineer and contractor) and his wife Lilian Gilbreth (a psychologist).

> I started learning the work of the construction engineer on July 12, 1885, as I had been promised that a thorough mastering of at least one trade, and a general practical experience with many trades, would be followed by rapid promotion to my particular line of engineering. I was, according, put to work between two specially selected, expert bricklayers, who were instructed to teach me the trade as rapidly as possible. They gladly agreed to do this. First one taught me, then the other, and, much to my surprise, they taught me entirely different methods. To make matters still more puzzling to me, I found that the methods that they taught me were not the methods that they themselves used. (Gilbreth quoted in Mogensen, 1932, p. 10)

Gilbreth's seminal studies in which he used a camera and a stopwatch to evaluate jobs, published in book form in 1911, demonstrated that many of the movements of bricklayers were totally unnecessary (e.g., piling bricks and placing mortar in such a way as to require the bricklayer to repeatedly bend over). When isolated and eliminated through redesign of the task environment (i.e., a new type of scaffolding), and after some training at the new sequence, fatigue was reduced, efficiency was increased, and accidents were avoided (Gilbreth & Gilbreth, 1919; Gilbreth & Gilbreth, 1917a).

It was not long before special photographic technology was developed to facilitate and extend TMS. "Chronocyclegraphy" involved placing a small lamp on each moving limb and adjusting the exposure in the camera to record a trace of limb motions over time on a single plate, the first "point light display" (see for instance

Lysinki's 1923 study of body movements while using different types of shovels to lift different weights). Gilbreth's stopwatch was made unnecessary when a motion picture camera was made that could record the passage of time on the film, at first as a series of regularly spaced dashes (see Gilbreth & Gilbreth, 1919, chap. 7) and later as a superimposed chronometer dial (see Barnes, 1937/1949; Mogensen, 1932).

In studying the procedures and practices of metal cutting, Taylor tackled the problem of degradation of the cutting tool due to temperature stress. Taylor systematically varied the temperature of the cutting tool, the metal that was being cut, and the speed of the cut, only to find that a red-hot cutting edge could slice through cold metal and have a lifetime greater than that of the standard (cold) cutting tool. This "fast steel" method was imported into French industry circa 1900 by the Sorbonne industrial chemist Henri Le Chatelier (Copley, 1923, Vol. 1, p. xxi). Le Chatelier had pioneered a scientific approach to the steel industry, inventing such things as pyrometers that could measure the temperature of molten metals in forges. He was, however, taken aback by many of the things that Taylor had accomplished, writing to Taylor, "I was somewhat ashamed to find the science of a practical man more developed than my own" (quoted in Copley, 1923, Vol. 1, p. 126). More than that, Taylor's research had revealed facts such as the utility of keeping a metal-cutting tool wet, facts that were "so easily verified that one is justified in being astonished that they are not known to everybody" (quoted in Copley, 1923, Vol. 1, p. 242). In subsequent correspondence, Le Chatelier said,

> Few discoveries in the arts [of metal cutting] have been the occasion of so many successive surprises as those of Mr. Taylor. At the time of the Exposition of 1900 in Paris, nobody quite believed at first in the prodigious result which was claimed by the Bethlehem works. ... The use of the high-speed Taylor-White steels spread rapidly in our manufacturing plants. (Le Chatelier quoted in Copley, 1923, Vol. 2, p. 116)

Taylor was "admired without reserve for the scientific method which controlled his whole work" (Le Chatelier, circa 1906, quoted in Copley, 1923, Vol. 2, p. 256). In fact, both Taylor and Gilbreth became notorious. A friend challenged Gilbreth to analyze a job during his visit to the 1910 Japanese–British Exposition; they then spied a girl who was rapidly pasting labels onto shoeboxes—about two seconds per box. Using a stopwatch and observing her do about 40 boxes, Gilbreth pronounced that half of her motions were completely unnecessary. Although irritated at first, she took his suggestions, and after a few tries at the new procedure, she was doing the task in less than a second per box.

Apart from such apocrypha, the real track record of TMS was quite impressive. Taylor's seminal work of 1898–1901 led to the elimination of hundreds of slavish shoveling jobs at steel mills and a halving of the cost of handling raw material. There were continuing advances in the design of typewriters, especially August Dvorak's creation of a new (today we would say "ergonomic") keyboard, with his successes attributed to the ideas and methods of Frank Gilbreth (see Dvorak et al., 1936).[2] New scaffolding methods in the construction trade led to a halving of the time taken to lay brick walls. The list of jobs affected goes on to include plasterers, cotton folders, office workers, and machinists, as well as crippled soldiers and other individuals with handicaps (see Barnes, 1937/1949; Gilbreth & Gilbreth, 1917b). Robert Kent, the editor of *Industrial Engineering,* saved the journal's secretaries considerable time by redesigning the task of preparing the journal's outgoing mail and correspondence (Kent, 1911). As the use of TMS spread, even more diverse success stories accumulated. Some examples are improvements in methods of the manufacture of machines, radio tubes, and radar coils; the sorting of day-old chicks; the peeling of tomatoes; and the assembly of the dropper tops for medicine bottles (see Mundel, 1947). For all manner of jobs, even fairly simple changes in the workplace and materials could result in up to a fourfold increase in productivity.[3]

Early in WWI, the governments of Germany, Holland, Russia, Italy, Spain, and Japan also realized the need for efficiency in industry and adopted the Taylor methods, especially in the steel industries (Copley, 1923, Vol. 1, p. xx). Right up through and even after WWII, TMS was part and parcel to industrial psychology. Evidence of the impact of Taylorism throughout the world is illustrated by the existence of organizations such as the "Taylor Society" and its presence in textbooks of the time, many of which had a significant lifetime (see Crane, 1938, chap. 3; Dietze, 1954; Gray, 1954, chap. 12; Griffith, 1934, chap. 30; Husband, 1934, chaps. 13–16; Maier, 1946, chap. 10; Poffenberger, 1942, chap. 20; Viteles, 1932, chaps. 22–24). Efficiency—as assessed through TMS—was the sole topic of dozens of books (see Barnes, 1937/1949; Maynard, Stegemerten, & Schwab, 1948; Mogensen, 1932; Mundel, 1947; Scott, 1921; Shaw, 1952).

In the United Kingdom, TMS was widely adopted. Maynard, Stegemerten, and Schwab (1948) discussed how one could design an efficient industrial production system with the aid of standardized data on reaction times and movement times. Perhaps the first important variation or extension of Taylor's task analysis was job analysis. Research conducted by the post–WWI British Industrial Fatigue Research Board (IFRB) extended TMS to job analysis. Job analysis was defined as the systematic examination of the components of occupations (including duties, working conditions, rewards, etc.) and their content and defining factors (see Moore, 1942, chap. 6). Job analysis included the classification of jobs into types on the basis of the required skills, hiring requirements, and types of tasks performed. Job analysis was not a single technique nor was it separate from TMS. Indeed, TMS (as defined by Taylor and the Gilbreths) was one of the main methods, if not *the* main method, for conducting a job analysis.

The second specific method used in IFRB job analysis was "job description," which consisted, essentially, of documentation analysis along with the use of questionnaires and interviews to define occupations (rather than the particular tasks involved in occupations). The third specific method used in job analysis was the "psychographic" (we would say psychometric) method (Viteles, 1932), which involved supplementing the description of occupations with a psychometric profile of the requisite worker abilities.

TMS has been described by some as a clear case of "behavioral task analysis" because of the focus on very fine-grained analysis of actions. Motions were coded for duration in hundredths of a second, using a variety of clever methods. For instance, Gilbreth photographed workers while they performed their tasks (e.g., seamstresses working at a sewing machine) in an enclosure in which the back and side walls and floor had been painted with a matrix of white lines, enabling the calculation of the three spatial dimensions of motion off of the film record. In another study (see Barnes,

1937/1949), the bolt-washer assembler wore a blouse that had a white matrix pattern, to provide a metrical background for the hand movements. Calculations were made of movement velocities, accelerations, and decelerations. Finally, the classified subtasks were laid out in "process charts" and "flow diagrams" in terms of actions such as "unload," "reach," and "grasp."

In 1912 Gilbreth coined the term *micromotion analysis* to refer to this approach (Gilbreth & Gilbreth, 1919, pp. 118–123). Perhaps the clearest and richest examples appear in Barnes (1937/1949). There one finds "simo charts" showing in thousands of a minute the amount of time spent (simultaneously) by the right and left arms, wrists, and hands in such tasks as the assembly of a linkage for a typewriter and the packaging of cheddar cheese. The numerous "time required" figures show such things as the time required to grasp washers of various thicknesses and the time required to position pins in beveled holes as a function of the pinhole clearance. Workers were given step-by-step instructions, accompanied by time-series photographs, explaining how to do such things as grasp a washer and position it on a bolt. Micro indeed.

In fact, to Gilbreth, the purpose of instruction was believed to be the instillation of motor habits or automaticities (see Gilbreth, 1911, pp. 37, 67–69). It was believed (almost literally, it seems) that the purpose of training was to educate muscles (see Griffith, 1934). Even so, components of modern CTA crept in, in three respects. First, the Taylorists studied people who were actually doing the work. It was quite clear to the Taylorists that they were indeed looking at jobs that required muscles more than wits. They studied the performer rather than the planner (Taylor, 1911), the laborer rather than the supervisor (Gilbreth, 1911, p. 72). The importance of studying the worker in the work context was realized. Second, and more important, even for such jobs there was a recognition that "first-class men" with the most skill should be highly respected and prized for their "natural power" to learn new methods quickly and to rapidly adapt to new circumstances without supervision (see Gilbreth, 1911, pp. 36–42). Those individuals were the ones targeted for the initial analyses of a job, hearkening to modern studies of expertise and proficiency training using the expert's performance as the gold standard. The concept of studying the skilled worker was established.

Third, and most important, cognitive factors were included in all of the categorization schemes of TMS analysis (at least as far as we can tell). When micromotion analysis was applied in the study of industrial operations (such as machining and machine tooling, etc.), a number of cognitive subtask elements simply *had* to be included in the analyses—mental operations such as "search" (manifested in eye movements), "select" (manifested in reaching movements), "inspect" (manifested in the machinist's use of his magnifying lens), and "plan" (shown when the machinist put his hand to his forehead and sat there, presumably, thinking) (Mogensen, 1932, pp. 87–91; Moore, 1942, chap. 11). Yes, the TMS researchers took photographs of people while they were sitting and thinking. Even as late as 1946 the analytical category of "inspect" was decomposed in terms that sound Wundtian in their mentalism—simple reaction time to inspect a visual stimulus takes about 225 milliseconds, choice adds on another 100 or so milliseconds, and so on (see Barnes, 1937/1949 chap. 13).

TMS researchers even analyzed their own job, where the consideration of reaction time went unmentioned, but cognitive functions seemed to be paramount:

> I believe then, as we review the requirements for a good methods man or motion analyst, as listed under Mental Quality, "open-mindedness," "freedom from prejudice or disposition to jump to conclusions," coupled with "an understanding of human nature" are the most important. I would also emphasize "ability to inspire and sustain the interest of others and secure active coopera- tion." I say this because I believe that the greatest need at present is for time-study engineers who can secure this cooperation which is so essential to success. (Mogensen, 1932, p. 19)[4]

In addition, and in hindsight remarkable, cognitive categories used in TMS include "adaptation to the machine," "adaptation to the materials," and "adaptation to tools" (see Fairchild, 1930). Here we see the hints of the emergent concept of the "man–machine system."

TMS firmly established the concept of studying work. The idea of observing the worker in context, so that leverage points for increased efficiency could be imple- mented (better tools, better processes, better training, better workstations, etc.), revolutionized the ways in which people thought about and conducted applied psy- chology. The study of cognitive elements of work—although largely limited to mea- suring time spent doing physical work—increased the visibility of cognition even in predominantly physical tasks. Furthermore, the systematic way in which TMS was conducted raised credibility among scientists as well as business leaders. This laid the foundation for the wider range of task analysis methods that would be developed.

Origin of the Concept of the Man–Machine System

In the pages of the research reports of the IFRB, one finds the first explicit notion of a man–machine system.[5] In his 1923 "personal contribution" to the annual report of the IFRB, H. C. Weston foresaw a need for a program of human factors research:

> The introduction and development of power-driven machines has effected an enormous savings of time and energy, not only by increasing the rapidity of production through substitution of mechanical power for human effort, but also by changing the character of the manipulations which remain to be performed by the operative. So great has this economy been, that it has brought with it a tendency to overlook the possibility that, while industrial machinery may be admirably adapted to the performance of its mechanical functions, it may be incompletely adapted to the needs of the human organism, upon whose efficient co-operation it depends for its productive use. (p. 71)

Weston went on to mention research detailing the discovery of serious design flaws in various machines, flaws that led to inefficiency and physical debilitation. For example, even commonly used lever shapes could result in serious physical debilita- tion if they were located in an improper position. Sometimes, attempts to correct one obvious problem led to another problem that went unrecognized by the design engi- neers. For example, the lightening of a roller in a laundry machine was not accompa- nied by a lightening of the load needed to depress the foot pedal controlling the roller, making the roller mechanism more difficult, not easier, to use.

> It is, therefore, most important that correct design should be secured in the first place. It is dif- ficult to see how this can be obtained to the fullest extent except as the result of definite research, undertaken with the object of determining such physiological and psychological facts as should be borne in mind when designing machines, the forms of mechanism and mechanical combina- tions which will conform to the needs of the operative. (Weston, 1923, p. 73)

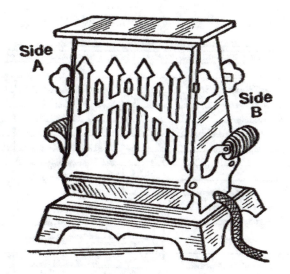

FIGURE 2.4 "An Electric Toaster." This figure accompanied a student exercise in creating a "man–machine" chart (see Table 2.2). Reproduced with permission from Barnes, R. M. (1937/1949). *Motion and time study* (3rd ed.) (p. 524). New York: John Wiley.

TABLE 2.2 Instructions Accompanying the Toaster Figure (see Figure 2.4)

The electric toaster shown in Fig. 310 is hand-operated, each side being operated independently of the other. A spring holds each side of the toaster shut, and each side must be held open in order to insert bread. In toasting three slices of bread in the above toaster, what method would you recommend to obtain the best equipment utilization—that is, the shortest overall time? Assume that the toaster is hot and ready to toast bread. The following are the elemental times necessary to perform the operations. Assume that both hands can perform their tasks with the same degree of efficiency.

Place slice of bread in either side	3 seconds
Toast either side of bread	30 seconds
Turn slice of bread	1 second
Remove toast	3 seconds

Make a man and machine chart of this operation.

One might say that therefore the basic concept of the man–machine system was present in industrial psychology as early as the 1930s. This is illustrated in the concluding line in the instructions accompanying a rather quaint figure in Barnes's (1937/1949) book *Motion and Time Study*, reproduced here in Figure 2.4. The instructions for this exercise are shown in Table 2.2.

An example of such a man–machine chart (also called a "simo" chart) is shown in Figure 2.5 (from Mundel, 1947). This chart is for the task of grinding a bearing for an aircraft engine. In such charts, the large open circles denoted operations, the small circles denoted movements, the open triangles denoted delays, and the filled triangles denoted the action of holding a part. (Other symbols, not needed in this case, were for such operations as inspect and count [see Shaw, 1952, chaps. 2, 3].) Such charts—thousands of jobs were analyzed this way between the 1920s and 1950s—depicted the operator's actions in interaction with the machine and materials being employed.

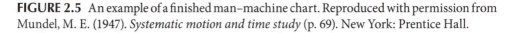

Original Man and Machine **OPERATION CHART**

Centerless grind aircraft engine bearing

LEFT HAND DESCRIPTION	SYMBOL	SYMBOL	RIGHT HAND DESCRIPTION
			Grinder
To material supply	○	○	*To feed control*
Pick up bearing	○	○	*Grasp control*
To grinder			
Place in grinder.			
			Start hydraulic feed
			During most of grind
			Finish grind
To finished bearing	○	○	*Back off*
Take bearing out	○		*To gage*
For gaging	▽	○	*Pick up gage*
			To bearing
		○	*Gage*
To finished parts box			*To bench with gage*
Place bearing in box	○	○	*Lay on bench*

Paste blank sheet 7¾" wide on here if additional length is required.

FIGURE 2.5 An example of a finished man–machine chart. Reproduced with permission from Mundel, M. E. (1947). *Systematic motion and time study* (p. 69). New York: Prentice Hall.

Intertwined Roots

We have described the three major historical roots of task analysis—psychotechnics, TMS, and job analysis in industrial psychology—as if these were somehow separate, when in fact they were not. We have discussed turns of events as if they were clearly punctuated by such things as national boundaries, the turn of the century, and the two world wars, when in fact there has been a fair continuity in the transmission of knowledge. In the works of Münsterberg and other European psychotechnicians, one finds copious references to the researches by Taylor, the Gilbreths, and other advocates of TMS (e.g., Frenz, 1920; Lahy, 1923; Münsterberg, 1912, 1913; Seubert, 1920; Tramm, 1921; see also Brozek & Hoskovec, 1997), and vice versa (see Barnes, 1937/1949).

One can find copious citations of the works of Münsterberg and the psychotechnicians in all of the industrial psychology books of that era published in the United Kingdom (see for instance Drever, 1921; Myers, 1925/1977, chaps. 2, 3; see also Shaw, 1952). One also finds copious citations of the work of Taylor and the Gilbreths. Indeed, the IFRB research relied on TMS methods (see Farmer, 1921; Farmer & Chambers, 1929). In the very essay in which H. C. Weston made a plea for a program of research on "machine design in relation to the operative," he also advocated the use of TMS:

Time and motion study, when it has been applied to mechano–manual operations, has enabled a better, or perhaps the best, method of work *with the existing machine*. (1923 p. 74)

Then he went on to advocate exactly the sort of experimental manipulations (i.e., changing the machine) that Taylor conducted three decades earlier:

… but the method which is really ideal for the worker is often unattainable without some alteration in the design and construction of the machine with which he has to co-operate. (p. 74)

In the works of numerous industrial psychologists after WWI, one finds references to the earlier researches of the psychotechnicians and the IFRB, as preserved and disseminated across the decades by the classic books of Burtt, (1929, 1957), Moede (1930), Münsterberg (1912, 1913, 1914), Myers (1925/1977), Poffenberger (1942), and Viteles (1932). For instances across the decades, see Anastasi, 1979; Dietze, 1954; Harrell, 1949; Maier, 1946; Ryan & Smith, 1954; Seymour, 1954.

Summary

Contrary to popular belief, research methods developed and extended in Wundt's lab in the late 1800s and early 1900s went beyond the exclusive use of introspection to include retrospective accounts of problem solving as well as examination of response speed and error rates. In fact, these methods could be characterized as early process-tracing techniques, methods that have been extended and adapted for use in modern CTA. Work emerging from Wundt's lab, in applied psychology, served as an important foundation for the study of cognition in context.

During this same time period, researchers in Poland and Russia spearheaded a related movement. It is this context that the term *ergonomics* was coined by Polish scholar Wojciech Jastrzebowski in 1857 and Russian researcher Mendeleev raised issues associated with adapting machines to man (Meister, 1999).

In 1991 Taylor formalized the study of work and changed the way the world thought about work with his TMS. It is interesting that Taylor was not a trained scientist but a laborer who moved his way up through the ranks to management within Midvale Steel Company in Bethlehem, Pennsylvania. His use of clearly defined methods and highly quantifiable metrics allowed for clear comparisons and cost–benefit calculations. TMS brought the study of work into the field, as observations and interviews were conducted firsthand in the context of work. Frank and Lilian Gilbreth, a construction engineer and psychologist, respectively, significantly advanced TMS, introducing specialized tools such as photographic equipment and motion pictures to facilitate the study of movements. TMS was widely adopted in the United Kingdom as well, showing up in the writing of the IFRB as a component of job analysis. TMS was widely influential both as an applied technique, increasing efficiency and the quality of work life for many manual labors, and as a research method, spawning a whole range of approaches to task analysis throughout the 20th century.

It is also worth noting that the concept of the man–machine system emerged during this time period. H. C. Weston explicitly discussed this notion in the 1923 annual report of the IFRB, calling for a program of human factors research. Industrial psychologists had begun thinking about and discussing the complexity of human and machine cooperation as early as the 1920s and 1930s.

Although the different research efforts described in this chapter occurred across somewhat disparate communities and vast geographic distances, cross-fertilization did occur. Examination of writings from this time reveals citations of work across countries and even continents. Although these various traditions are often described quite separately, they were in fact intertwined.

From the time Wundt's lab was established in 1870 to the appearance of Taylor's book *Principles of Scientific Management* in 1911 to H. C. Weston's IFRB report in 1923, many of the components of modern CTA emerged. Chapter 3 will take up where this chapter leaves off, continuing the evolution of methods through WWII to current Cognitive Task Analysis methods.

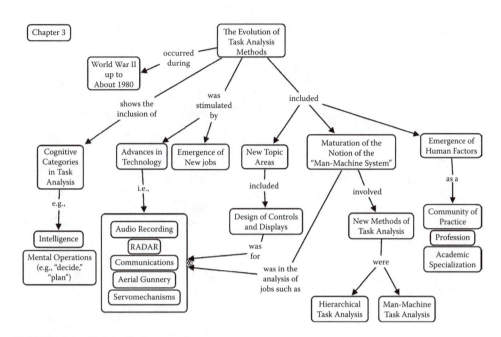

FIGURE 3.1 Chapter 3 Concept Map.

3

The Evolution of Task Analysis
Into Cognitive Task Analysis
From Time and Motion Studies
to Man–Machine Systems

As it had just twenty-four years earlier, world war would profoundly affect psychology. The Great War to End All Wars had transformed a tiny, obscure academic discipline into an ambitious, visible profession. World War II provided an even greater opportunity for psychologists to act together in pursuit of social good and their own professional interests.

—Thomas Leahy (1987, p. 354)

This chapter begins by highlighting the continued application of the Time and Motion Study (TMS) to the study of work in the years between the world wars and to the expanding palette of task analysis methods that evolved. This is followed by a discussion of applied psychology research organizations and the research issues they tackled in the political and social climate immediately prior to and during World War II. The subsequent sections describe four complex jobs that became critically important during WWII and the legacy concepts and methods that resulted. Although direct influence on modern Cognitive Task Analysis (CTA) may not be immediately visible, these studies certainly set the stage. Applied psychology and related disciplines were steadily progressing toward methods and theories to better understand work in complex settings. Cognitive elements were increasingly visible in discussions of human performance and how best to support it via both design and training. The final section of this chapter brings us to current organizations that support the dissemination of CTA methods and the study of complex systems.

Continuity Between the World Wars

The task analytic methods that were created in early industrial psychology, including TMS, were used right up through WWII (see Bonnardel, 1943; Clot, 1996). A clear example is a TMS study of the tasks of radar operators by M. E. Mundel (1948;

Anonymous, 1949; see also Bray, 1948, ch. 5). Mundel analyzed the hand movements of radar operators in the pencil-and-paper task of determining the track and speed of a target on an intercept plot. This plot is a circular map showing series of connected locations (the "tracks") of targets relative to some central position. From the location times and the tracks, one can compute target speed and predict next locations. (Mundel's simo chart for this task is reproduced in Chapanis [1959, p. 70].) Micromotion analysis resulted in a savings of about a third of the effort and time, simply by the creation of a specially calibrated ruler—navigators had been estimating speed by using a pencil (in one hand) and the thumb (of the other hand) as a ruler.

The continuity of WWI-era applied psychology with psychotechnics and TMS was even clearer in Germany. Walther Moede, a leader of the German psychotechnicans and author of a major text (1930), had been the first to use choice reaction-time methodology in tests for military personnel selection (i.e., automobile chauffers during WWI) (Moede, 1926). This approach of the psychotechnicians—adopting technology and methods from the early psychometrics laboratory (i.e., aptitude testing) and early experimental psychology laboratory (e.g., choice reaction-time, problem-solving tasks)—was maintained in the German's studies of military aviation (see Ansbacher, 1941 ; Geuter, 1992, 1997), especially piloting and gun operation (see Fitts, 1947).

German industrial psychology efforts during WWII were oriented mostly toward increasing the efficiency of the workforce, made acute by the increasing shortage of manpower. The backbone of the research was a type of TMS, despite the general unpopularity of psychotechnics and Taylorism, which were lumped together and widely regarded in Europe as being inhumane (see Fitts, 1946, p. 160). Nevertheless, during the years following the start of WWII (i.e., circa 1935), the Reich Committee for Work Study trained thousands of "time takers" who would go into various industries (i.e., Messerschmitt, I. G. Farben, and other major factories) to conduct efficiency analysis. In addition, German research emphasized the standardization of aptitude tests, the matching of aptitudes to jobs, and the establishment of special "selection camp" training program. The aptitude tests that were employed were referred to explicitly as "psychotechnical tests" (Ansbacher, 1944).

Continuity notwithstanding, WWII witnessed the development of new approaches and methods to solve new emerging problems.

An Expanded Palette of Task Analytic Methods

Up to WWII, task analytic methods, such as TMS and various forms of task reflection, were used in combination to study jobs and job performance (see Poffenberger, 1942), but during WWII, strategies and methods for task analysis really began to multiply Lists of task analysis methods can be found in Chapanis, 1996; Drury, Paramore, Van Cott, Grey, & Corlett, 1987; Fleishman, 1975; Meister, 1985; Nemeth, 2004; Salvendy, 1987; Shepherd, 2001; Viteles, 1922; Kirwan & Ainsworth, 1992, is a comprehensive review; Diaper & Stanton, 2004, is a fine handbook on task analysis that includes overviews and chapters focusing on individual methods and approaches. One driving factor behind this new palette of task analysis methods was the need to cope with the challenges and goals that emerged during WWII (see Chapanis, 1959;

Meister, 1999). For one thing, tasks shifted from those that required physical coordination and strength to those that required judgment and cognitive skill. In addition, applied psychology moved beyond personnel selection and training to include display design—a pursuit that requires contemplation of information, the ways it will be used, and the ways it will be presented. A third factor was the impact of cybernetics and ideas of servomechanisms and manual control theory. Even though psychologists initially approached these problems from the perspectives of industrial psychology and the academic psychology of learning and performance (Chapanis, personal communication, 1998), they began to stretch and adapt existing task analysis methods to accommodate the tasks and challenges they were studying.[1]

The Rise of Human Factors Psychology

As WWII approached, the emphasis in the United Kingdom and the United States shifted from concerns with productivity, accidents, and fatigue in the factory environment back to the military environment, especially soldiering, piloting, and navigating (see Christiansen, 1949). Organizations were formed and reformed to accommodate this shift.

In the United Kingdom, the Industrial Fatigue Research Board (IFRB) was reformed as the Industrial Health Research Board and pursued a broader mandate. In addition, the Applied Psychology Unit, under the aegis of the Medical Research Council (MRC), was formed in 1944 at Cambridge University to conduct psychological (we would say mostly cognitive) research. Personnel from the previous board (e.g., H. M. Vernon, Eric Farmer, and others) and psychologists and engineers from Cambridge University (e.g., Frederick C. Bartlett, Norman H. Mackworth, Kenneth J. W. Craik, and others) assisted the various military services with problems arising from WWII. Hywl Murrell, one of the founders of the Ergonomics Society, led the Naval Time and Motion Study Unit of the MRC, charged with studying the performance of sailors under adverse conditions. Also during the war, Churchill's advisors convinced him of the value of mathematical modeling. "At least as far as the UK was concerned, there were a variety of influences quite different from the US preoccupation with Behaviorism" (J. Annett, personal communication, 1998).

In the United States, the approach of WWII led to the establishment in 1940 of an Emergency Committee in Psychology (which included, among others, S. S. "Smitty" Stevens, Harry Helson, and James J. Gibson). Among its many activities, the Committee generated reviews of basic research on numerous issues relevant to WWII (e.g., fatigue, stress, propaganda; see Pratt, 1941), including the psychology of visual perception as it pertained to wartime needs (i.e., visual acuity and pilot selection; color perception and the detection of camouflage; the course of dark adaptation and the design of lighting for operations centers; the perception of space and motion via stereopsis for target acquisition by gunners, etc.) (Fernberger, 1941; Hunter, 1946).

It is safe to say that during WWII, the bulk of the efforts of the U.S. Applied Psychology Panel of the National Defense Research Council focused on personnel selection and training. (See, for instance, any of the notes on "Psychology and the War" edited by Donald G. Marquis in each of the issues of *The Psychological*

Bulletin that were published during the WWII years.) All branches of the military needed skilled radio telegraph operators, and training and performance measurement were priorities in the study of that job (Staff of the Personnel Research Section to the Adjutant General's Office, 1943). Thousands of jobs falling into nearly 100 "job families" were studied, with an eye toward the development of aptitude tests for selection and methods for training—aircraft assemblers, crankshaft servicers, electrical instrument servicers, electroplaters, hydrostatics servicers, milling machine operators, sandblasters, welders, and woodworkers. In all cases, the jobs had to be analyzed in terms of the required psychological capabilities, and the tests that were to be used for selection had to be validated in terms of posttraining performance, drop-out rates, and so on. The total wartime effort of the Army alone resulted in over 600 research reports just on the topic of aptitude testing for military jobs (Hunter, 1946).

Research on the psychology of aviation (i.e., pilot selection and training; see Yerkes, 1919) had been "abandoned almost immediately with the signing of the Armistice" (Viteles, 1945, p. 489), but the research program was picked up in about 1939 by the Civil Aeronautics Administration, which sponsored research by dozens of academic psychologists (Hunter, 1946). As WWII approached, research on aviation personnel selection and training was accelerated (Koonce, 1984; see, for instance, Harrell, 1945), and this time the research included the analysis of a variety of newer jobs in addition to piloting, such as bombardiering and navigating. Diverse aptitude tests were developed and employed: tests of alertness, visual-motor coordination, and so on; tests of background knowledge (i.e., tests of knowledge of how various machines work); and tests of "perceptual speed." In the report on this research, the basic idea for the "speed of response test" is attributed to R. A. Biegel's 1931 publication in the journal *Psychotechnik* (see Kurtz, 1944). However, the challenges of WWII required entirely new programs of research going beyond the ideas and methods of psychotechnics and involving the human factors of new systems such as radar (Fitts, 1946; Hunter, 1946; Poulton, 1964).

In addition, in both the United States and the United Kingdom, the research on the human factor came more and more to involve the problems of equipment design (Summers, 1996), as in the design of reticules for new gun sights (Hunter, 1946). The foundation stones for the framework in which problems were expressed had been set by Legros and Weston in 1926 when they noted in the preface to their IFRB report that many machines "require frequent manipulation of a release or control or some manual operation in which ... the work and machine form a single system" (p. iii) and, on page 8, "the combination of the machine and the operator requires to be considered as a unit no less than the combination of the machine and the work" (see also Weston, 1923). This framework was echoed by Kenneth Craik in the year of the founding of the Applied Psychology Unit: "[From] work of the type now in hand ... certain common principles have emerged ... that of suiting the job to the man, or suiting the man to the job ... and of improving the man's performance" (1944b, p. 476; see also Craik, 1947).

The palette of task analysis methods—rooted historically in TMS—had to be adapted to new challenges and goals during WWII (see Chapanis, 1959). Indeed, our current concept of the field of human factors psychology was shaped in the final years of WWII by research and theorizing that flourished in the 1940s and 1950s in the United Kingdom at the hands of Donald Broadbent (1957), W. E. Hick (1945,

1951, 1952), N. H. Mackworth (1950), and R. B. Miller (1953), among others, and in the United States by Alphonse Chapanis (1949), Paul Fitts (1954), and others who instituted the Psychology Branch of the U.S. Air Force Aero Medical Laboratory.

Aerial Gunnery

The analysis of the complex and difficult tasks of aerial gunners by the Applied Psychology Panel of the National Defense Research Council was mandated by the need to facilitate training. The Flying Fortress carried a great many gunners, and casualty rates were high for bomber crews. This led to the creation of the pedestal gunnery simulator, which provided simulated targets and feedback on hits and misses. The analysis of the tasks of aerial gunners also made clear the basic problem of task allocation among members of a team and not just allocation among the effectivities of the individual gunner (see Bray, 1948, chap. 6). Specifically, the creation of "computing machine gun sights" for the B-29 bomber changed the problem of allocating tasks to people (gunner, tracker, targeter) to the problem of allocating tasks to human versus machine. Although gunners and flight crew members still had to cooperate on many tasks, the individual gunner had several distinct and challenging tasks. The new computing sights also made salient the problems of display design: "The relation of the gunner to target and guns was indirect. … In many systems the target could not be seen directly. The representation of a target by a dial pointer or an oscilloscope blip did not necessarily look like the target" (Bray, 1948, p. 157).

A report from the Applied Psychology Panel on the research on the design of gun sights referred to a number of ways in which cognitive factors played a critical role: Ideally, the design of the gun sight computing system should not require the gunner to understand the computing system to operate the gun; the sight should "reduce as far as possible the need for the gunner to know deflection angles, to judge target direction, and to estimate target angles in order to reduce computer error" (Bray, 1948, p. 214). Bray quite clearly articulated the goal of using the computing system to reduce cognitive load on the human.

Paralleling the involvement of psychologists in the U.S. program on computing gun sights, the German military also recognized that new technologies mandated a program of psychological research to support equipment design (see Fitts, 1946, p. 159). It was in the United States, however, that the research had a significant culmination—the development of control theory and the general concept of the servomechanism (see Brown & Campbell, 1948; Wiener, 1948), both of which have greatly influenced modern CTA (Flach & Dominguez, 1995; Jagacinski & Flach, 2003).

Radio Coding Operations

When it was discovered that the thousands of men who had undergone training to be radio coders did not achieve the proficiency needed to handle tasks during actual military operations, the Applied Psychology Panel was tasked by both the Army and the Navy with improving methods for instructing radio coders. The panel's approach, including efforts by Harold Seashore, L. L. Thurstone, and the staff of the Psychological Corporation, was to analyze the task using phonographic recording technology, determine the rate at which operators could handle code, and then use the results in the design of proficiency tests (see Bray, 1948, chap. 5). A second approach taken by the panel was to develop new training methods, based largely on ideas from the psychology of learning such as the method of paired associates, the provision of immediate feedback, and the reliance on distributed practice.

Radio Detection and Ranging

Radar introduced a number of new and complex jobs to the military. One might think that the task of the "scope dope" was simple and boring—staring at a small circular screen to detect blips. But the operator's task was (and still is) actually very complex, involving not just target detection but also such tasks as determining bearing and altitude. In addition, radar operators needed to tune and calibrate the radar, a task that was critical, because error in radar readings due to detuning (e.g., from being in an overnight standby mode) and error due to the aging of the oscilloscope tube could be far greater than any portion of error due to the human factor (Chapanis, 1959, chap. 6). (Even identical radars could provide target bearings differing as much as 5 degrees.) Furthermore, there was a variety of types of radar, each designed for unique tasks—antiaircraft targeting, low altitude radar-controlled bombing, ground-controlled approach systems, submarine detection radar, and so on (Chapanis, 1951). To make matters even more complex, the design of radar systems and their control mechanisms and associated mechanical and computational aids evolved very rapidly, within the span of just a few years.

    Study of this rich domain and the complex tasks associated with it greatly increased our understanding of the cognitive challenges associated with work and led to a number of innovations in task analysis techniques. New concepts that emerged from this line of research included methods for analyzing vigilance tasks, the use of synthetic trainers, research on display and indicator design, and research on the acquisition and maintenance of what we today would refer to as mental models. Here are several of the challenges researchers faced in studying radar operators and the important innovations that resulted:

- The radar operator's task made salient the need to analyze "vigilance"—performance over prolonged periods of watch involving the detection of weak, ambiguous, and intermittent signals in a very fairly simple visual display.
- Task analysis (conducted by a team including prominent psychologists John Darley and Wendell Garner) of the radar operator job revealed that the critical aspect of performance was not a tool-use skill but a set of cognitive and visual perception skills. This led to an emphasis in personnel selection on such measures as visual acuity and convergence accuracy.
- Researchers also discovered that the standard 3-week training program could not possibly instill all the knowledge that operators needed (i.e., how the radar works, the hows and whys of target identification, the hows and whys of interference and jamming, plus all the ancillary procedures, such as for communications). The report emphasized the need to regard radar operation as a skill, entailing a great deal of practice at such tasks as target identification, for true proficiency to be achieved (see Bray, 1948, chap. 5; Lindsley, 1945).

- Although it was found that much of the dynamics of radar operator tasks could be captured in paper-and-pencil methods, synthetic trainers were also needed to facilitate training and retraining (using motion picture technology and mock oscilloscopes to simulate the actual radar systems).
- The development of radar technology also introduced the new visual display device, the oscilloscope, and new data types to display (i.e., bearing, range, etc.). This necessitated research on display and indicator design, some of which was contracted to the Psychology Laboratory at Johns Hopkins University (Chapanis, 1946, 1947, 1949; Gebhard, 1948).
- The Johns Hopkins studies used a high-fidelity simulation radar console. A main finding was a relation of time and accuracy, that they were inversely related—the longer the operator took to estimate a target range, the less the error in the range estimate.
- A subsequent study (Gebhard, 1948) investigating a new mechanically aided method of tracking targets confirmed that the radar operators were indeed able to rapidly generate a mental model (as we would say using modern parlance) of target track and speed after tracking only one or two sweeps of the beam.
- Ultimately stemming from the reports of the U.S. (Lindsley, 1945) and U.K. (Mackworth, 1950) radar projects was a great deal of basic and applied psychological research on signal detection and vigilance (attention and arousal for prolonged periods when under stress) (see, for instance, Nicely & Miller, 1957).
- The research on radar also confronted psychologists with some significant problems of measurement and statistical analysis in human and machine information processing. Early radar systems were limited in terms of their accuracy (i.e., in targeting for location, range, speed, altitude, course, etc.). This made it unclear what sort of standard to use in assessing radar operator performance, with the human operator being another source of error. In addition, the interaction of the operator with the radar was a third source of error, and these three sources, which could not be defined independently of one another, had to be disentangled somehow and apportioned into constant, variable, and cumulative error components (Chapanis, 1951).

Voice Communications

Spearheading a collaboration of psychologists and engineers was S. S. Stevens of the Harvard University Psycho-Acoustic Laboratory. The military was confronted by the problems of using the telephone (and radio) under circumstances involving the communication of complex information in noisy environments, under stress and time constraint. The goals of the psychological research focused less on personnel selection than on training and the engineering of systems that facilitate the transmission of speech by reducing the signal-to-noise ratio.[2] The systems engineering work included the development of a standardized test of message intelligibility, the development of standardized message formats to help avoid communication breakdowns, the establishment of speaker and amplifier loudness levels that would maximize audibility for various types of microphones (Bray, 1948, chap. 5), the establishment of facts concerning the effects on intelligibility of the way that a microphone is held (Hunter, 1946; Office of Scientific Research and Development, 1946), and the effects of various kinds of noise on intelligibility (e.g., the noise of airplane propellers; Office of Scientific Research and Development, 1946; see Chapanis, 1959, chap. 8). The human factor in voice communication led to the discovery that voice communication in noisy

FIGURE 3.2 A depiction of an early theory of the general communications system.

environments can be facilitated by clipping the longer wavelengths and amplifying the shorter ones—"tailoring the speech and radio procedures to the requirements of the human ear" (Anonymous cited in Hunter, 1946, p. 487).

This research addressed all of the major aspects of the communication system, as shown in Figure 3.2.

In the ensuing decades, these components would form a core metaphor of the information theory and the information processing approach for research on such topics as speech compression, the measurement of redundancy in spoken and printed language, Markov models of sentence structure, the problem of phonemic segmentation, the analysis of speech waveforms, and so on (see Jacobson, Fant, & Halle, 1952; McMillan, 1953; Miller, 1953; Miller, Heise, & Lichten, 1951; Pollack, 1952; Shannon, 1951; Shannon & Weaver, 1949; Weaver, 1949).

The Culmination: Additional Methods of Task Analysis

Much of the wartime research involved new methods of task analysis that were variations on some traditional methods, even though the new jobs were not so strictly physical or repetitive (Chapanis, 1959, chap. 2). Perhaps the clearest case is the use of "activity sampling," which seems to be a variation on the theme of job analysis. In activity sampling, the observer notes the specific tasks in which the operator is engaged at predetermined points in time during a period of watch (i.e., every 5 or so seconds, in the case of aerial navigation). From these observations, estimates are made of the percentage of time allotted to the various tasks and the average amount of time spent in each of the various tasks. In the case of the research on new radar jobs (Christiansen, 1949, 1950), for instance, task activities included log work, sextant work, eating, astrocompass work, drift reading, and so on. What Christiansen's radar research showed was that the navigators spent most of their time doing paperwork (log work, chart work) and that the size of the air crew could be reduced by two (a significant savings) by eliminating needless data recording and by providing better plotting tools and charts (Chapanis, 1959, chap. 2). New methods of "man–machine task analysis" (Miller, 1953) also included:

- task allocation to design man–machine systems (see Fitts et al., 1951; Gagné, 1965; Kidd, 1965; Wulfleck & Zeitlin, 1965),
- the Critical Incident Technique of in situ interviewing and retrospection to determine the cause of accidents (see Fitts & Jones, 1947; Flanagan, 1954), and
- link analysis to chart the interactions and communications of team members (Chapanis, 1959).

The methods used during this time and the applications to which they were applied are sometimes referred to somewhat dismissively as "knobs and dials" era research.

Knobs and Dials

Diverse studies at the U.S. Air Force Psychology Branch used task analysis in the study of cockpit design, leading to the designation of this as the "knobs and dials" era in human factors psychology (Summers, 1996). It is easy to find clear instances, one of the best being Paul Fitts's chapter in Stevens's *Handbook of Experimental Psychology* (1951; see also Chapanis, 1959). One set of studies, for example (Chapanis, 1946, 1947), used displays of increasing levels of realism (going from a mock-up panel having counters and dials to a realistic mock-up of a variety of radar consoles) showing in every case that radar operators were better at reading target bearings from dials than from counters.

However, the "knobs and dials" designation is both misleading and unfair. The unfairness is made clear when one realizes how crucial the psychological research was in the design of such devices as the computing machine gun sight, involving answers to a variety of problems in stereoscopic vision and reticule design (Hunter, 1946), as well as the design of control knobs and indicators. The redesign of fire control equipment, including the establishment of the operating doctrine expressed in "operations manuals," saved the military months of time in comparison with previous procedures in the use of new weapons systems (Hunter, 1946, p. 484).

The "knobs and dials" designation is misleading because a great deal of research in the knobs and dials era involved alternative designs for entire display systems. For instance, Sinaiko and Buckley (1957) described an experiment in which naval officers rated tactical display systems, comparing a conventional display system to newer approaches, finding that even though a new display format resulted in improved performance (in the ability of a combat information center to keep track of multiple targets), tradition had significant momentum in terms of officers' preferences. This somewhat frustrating result will ring true with many modern applied psychologists who are involved in the design of new information processing display and workstation systems.

The "knobs and dials era" designation is also misleading because decades before WWII, a great deal of research had already laid out some basic facts on the optimum design for control knobs, levers, and handles, for such devices as turret lathes (see Barnes, 1937/1949).

New Perspectives

On the surface, the common theme of the American WWII work—on gunnery, communications, and radar—was its applied focus, having to do with aiding (equipment design) and quickening (through both equipment design and training). But at another level, the theme that came to unify both the research and the newer theories of communication and information was the view of the human as a controller, a component in a larger cybernetic system. Both in the United Kingdom (Craik, 1947; Hick, 1952) and in the United States (see Fitts, 1951), a focus (in addition to information theory) was the theory of servomechanisms (as in Brown & Campbell, 1948; Wiener, 1948). The servo system was conceived of as having components including comparator, amplifier, motor, and stabilizer. Such components were applied literally to analysis of pathways in the human nervous system (see McCulloch, 1949; Ruch, 1951) and were used to explain results from a great deal of research (both old and new) on the time and force patterns of simple motor responses in perceptual-motor tasks (aiming and tracking) and such phenomena as the speed–accuracy trade-off.

Servomechanism

The research on these topics that stemmed from the efforts of WWII was conducted largely in service of the design of controls (see Fitts, 1951), but the servo concepts were also applied conceptually, in a view of perception and decision making as controlling functions that operate by providing feedback that regulates the control of movements: "The behavior of a servo is governed, not by the input signal alone, but by the difference between the input and some function of the output" (Fitts, 1951, p. 1319), with "some function" implying central processes. (In other words, mental representations and judgments.) The next step would be to focus on those central processes, regarding them as involving a hierarchical organization of feedback loops, loops that are based on the processing of information and that are defined in terms of goals that are taken at more than one level of abstraction.

The servo concept of input signals, acted upon by central process to influence output, was a core component of theories in the emergent fields of cognitive psychology and artificial intelligence (as in Donald MacKay's discussion of automata, 1956a, and Miller, Galanter, and Pribram's *Plans and the Structure of Behavior,* 1960). This was the approach taken in the development of new methods of task analysis (see Annett & Kay, 1956). A clear instance is "Hierarchical Task Analysis" (Annett, 2000, 2004; Annett & Duncan, 1967; Walls, 2006), in which tasks are decomposed in terms of fundamental goals and the information processing requirements on cognitive activities (see chapter 9; for more examples; also see chapters 7–16 in Kirwan & Ainsworth, 1992).

It is also worth noting that this wartime work fostered the maturation of the concept of the man–machine system (as, for instance, in Craik, 1947). That notion had been around ever since the work of Weston and the IFRB in the 1920s, but it became salient in WWII-era research in the United States (Chapanis, 1951, p. 224; see also his foreword; Hunter, 1946). The concept of the man–machine system, along with the pursuit of optimal function allocation between humans and machines, characterized much of the research of this time.

Man–Machine System

The man–machine approach was pursued with vigor at the Aeromedical Laboratory (during the so-called knobs and dials era) and can be clearly seen in the titles of a great many of post-WWII psychological researches, such as Birmingham and Taylor's (1954) general description of the approach for an audience of engineers and Sinaiko and Buckley's summary report (1957) for the Navy. The notion of the man–machine system formed the core of post-WWII discussions of system development and achieved another level of refinement as the topic of the "man–computer" system and the psychology of programming became ever more salient (see Edwards, 1965a, b).

More to the present point, however, it is important to acknowledge that many studies in this era had cognition through and throughout their task analyses. We see deliberate, studied attempts to understand cognition in the context of work. Categories of subtasks or activities that were used in task analyses included, for example, "sensing," "identifying," "interpreting," and "problem solving." Studies by Crossman (1956) and Seymour (1954) in the United Kingdom relied on diagrams that not only charted hand movements but also had activities such as visual search and decision making as analytical categories. The prevailing approach at the time was to categorize cognitive functions so that they could be allocated to the appropriate member of the man–machine system (see Gagné, 1965). Although the concept of function allocation eventually came to be understood as an oversimplification, researchers today look to this era as a step in helping us understand that cognition is often shared among team members (as opposed to residing in a human or a machine), is generally difficult to place into discrete categories, and is highly changeable as processes, technologies, and environmental conditions vary over time.

Furthermore, many studies—of such things as aircrew communication and pilot reasoning—were conducted in the field setting. This work could easily be described as Cognitive Field Research.

A Bifurcation: Personnel Selection Versus Design of Controls and Displays

Unlike the case for the clear linkages between psychotechnics and the industrial psychology of the WWI era, a bifurcation occurred after WWII, with one path continuing the research on personnel selection and training and the other pursuing the special challenges facing knowledge workers.

The first path, issues in personnel selection and training (a focus of psychotechnics), remained of paramount importance throughout WWII (Harrell & Churchill, 1941; Hunter, 1946). The study of industrial and job-related accidents continued to be a main focus of applied psychology (see, for example, Burtt, 1957). Furthermore, the methods of job analysis that had been used to develop training programs maintained the approach of TMS, with an emphasis on the analysis of tasks at a microlevel and the elimination of unnecessary details or task elements through simplification and combination and through the redesign of the work space and tools (see War Manpower Commission Bureau of Training, 1945). Not only did the use of TMS in the analysis of industrial tasks continue unabated (see, for example Maynard, Stegemerten, & Schwab, 1948; Shaw, 1952) but micromotion study was used in the analysis of military jobs.

The second path of the bifurcation stemmed from the new program of information theory and measurement. This path focused on such topics as information coding methods and stimulus-response compatibility in the design of controls and displays. These works, representing both U.S. wartime efforts (e.g., McMillan et al., 1953; Quastler, 1955) and U.K. wartime efforts (e.g., Bartlett, 1947; Craik, 1944a; Jackson, 1953; Mitchell, 1948; Mitchell & Vince, 1951), included essentially no references to any of the topics, methods, and results from pre-WWII industrial psychology. Rather, they referred almost exclusively to the pioneering studies and the new ideas and applications of information theory and measurement, especially the influential technical reports (e.g., Andreas & Weiss, 1954; Hick, 1945; Shannon, 1948), the influential reviews (e.g., Weaver, 1949; and later, Cherry, 1955; Cronbach, 1953; MacKay, 1969), and the seminal publications (e.g., Hick, 1951, 1952; Hyman, 1953; MacKay, 1951, 1956a, 1956b; Shannon & Weaver, 1949; Wiener, 1948). In these works one finds few substantive references to the methods and results from research conducted before WWII.[3]

Cited more often were the new classics, such as Hick's (1952) pioneering studies of choice reaction time and the "rate of gain of information." Hick relied on a new framework—measuring the transmission of information in terms of binary digits (Shannon & Weaver, 1949) and new technology—the punched-tape reader—to control the illumination of arrays of lights in various combinations. Equipped with new theory and new apparatus, he tested hypotheses about choice and classification reaction time in a way that would have been impossible in Wundt's laboratory.

The "look" of the field of applied psychology was changing, and it was not only the new ideas in information measurement and the theory of servomechanisms. An important additional factor was that the wartime projects—on the design of new gun sights, new radar systems, the methods of voice communication, and so on—all involved teams of psychologists working in collaboration with teams of engineers (see Bray, 1948). For instance, one of the earliest of the wartime efforts, that on the selection and training of radio coders, led to the notion that skilled performance could be more easily achieved and maintained if the coding device automatically produced a record of what the operator had sent (i.e., immediate feedback) (Hunter, 1946). From the very start of WWII, psychologists helped engineers build things, in this case, the Morse Code Actuated Printer.

> The psychological contributions ... point to certain activities which should be continued by the Services. ... The study of the role of the human factor in the design and operation of all types of new equipment utilizing the *joint efforts of experimental psychologists and engineers* [italics added]. (Hunter, 1946, p. 492)

The applied psychology effort of the Psychology Branch of the U.S. Air Force Aero Medical Laboratory, established in 1946, was retitled the "Human Engineering Division" just a few years after WWII (Summers, 1996). The momentum for a human factors psychology was not to be lost: "The determination of whether or not there is a human factor problem involved [in the design of new equipment] should not be left to the offhand judgment of materiel men!" (Hunter, 1946, p. 492).

Following WWII, one would find that books on industrial psychology still discussed TMS and the work of the IFRB, not in chapters on efficiency but instead in chapters titled "human engineering" (see, for example, Harrell, 1949). Indeed, the new topic of human engineering became a book of its own, with the discussion of the older methods and results from industrial psychology now summarized in the chapters on methodology (see Chapanis, 1959, chap. 2). H. C. Weston's (1923) notion of the man–machine system had been embraced by the ergonomics and human factors communities. In his address to the Ergonomics Research Society in the United Kingdom in 1954, Sir Wilfred Le Gros Clark said, "A man and his machine may be regarded as the functional unit of industry, and the aim of ergonomics is the perfection of this unit so as to promote accuracy and speed of operation, and at the same time to ensure minimum fatigue and thereby maximum efficiency" (Clark, 1954).

Human Factors and Ergonomics as a Community of Researchers

The final piece needed to set the stage for CTA was a means for people who were studying work, cognition, and expertise, as well as those designing training, technology, and systems to communicate with each other. Early efforts to institutionalize applied psychology went through several incarnations. Psychotechnics began as a very small community. Many of the first practitioners came from Wundt's laboratory in Germany. His students became conduits of information and methodology, spreading them across continents. Shortly thereafter, Britain institutionalized applied psychology in 1918 with the IFRB, which published a number of widely disseminated reports. In the United States, the Emergency Committee on Psychology and the Panel of the National Defense Research Counsel both began efforts in the 1940s, serving to bring researchers together. It wasn't until the 1950s, though, that human factors and ergonomics researchers became organized as a community. The American Human Factors Society held its first meeting in Tulsa, Oklahoma, in 1957, and the International Ergonomics Association was founded in Europe in 1959. Figure 3.3 depicts a timeline of key research institutions and organizations devoted to the study of work from WWI to today. All of these organizations provided means for researchers to share their findings, methods, and tough problems with colleagues, pushing forward our understanding of cognition, work and expertise, as well as the many other broadly ranging topics addressed by human factors researchers and ergonomicists.

Task Analysis and Cognitive Task Analysis

A look at Nemeth's (2004) *Human Factors Methods for Design* shows that task analysis, as conceived and conducted by human factors psychologists, is rife with consideration of cognitive factors, including in its roster such methods as think-aloud problem solving and usability–usefulness analysis. A main takeaway from this chapter, and chapter 2, is that task analysis has *never* been void of cognition. Here are two striking examples of this.

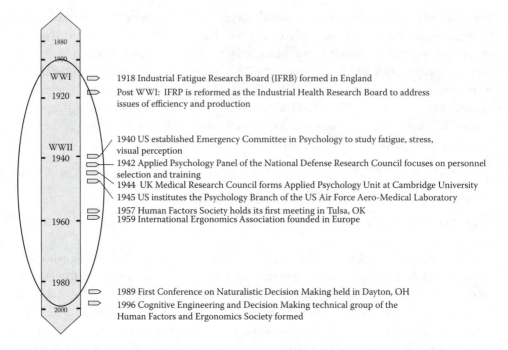

FIGURE 3.3 A timeline of key research institutions and organizations devoted to the study of work.

Example 1. In his classic wartime researches on vigilance at radar tasks, Norman Mackworth (1950) focused not just on observer performance but also on the physiological changes that take place (e.g., changes in body temperature). His approach was not just physiological but in fact Pavlovian—the performance decrement was explained in terms of conditioned inhibition and disinhibition. On close read, however, cognitive factors seem to have won the day:

> [The tests] gave some evidence which was crucial in deciding whether (1) experimental extinction, (2) secondary extinction, or (3) conditioned inhibition was responsible for the main downward trend in performance. It was deduced that were this deterioration due to experimental extinction, the decline could be prevented by the addition of the missing reinforcement ... knowledge of results did in fact prevent the falling-off in efficiency. (p. 89)

Mackworth went on to describe research (e.g., Hilgard, Campbell, & Sears, 1938) showing that conditioning in humans (the eye-blink response) was affected by the participants' knowledge of the stimulus relationships and the expectations that are entailed in the instructions.

Example 2. During WWII, German industrial psychologists developed special "thought analysis" tests to assess reasoning skill using "what-if" sorts of reasoning problems. The German government was made painfully aware by the Reich Committee for Work Study that the German workforce was dominated by individuals with "practical-manual" aptitude and that this had to be counterbalanced by identifying workers possessing "theoretical-intellectual" ability (Ansbacher, 1944). Likewise, American psychologists at the Psychological Laboratory of the War Department who interviewed prospects for officer training focused on the assessment of reasoning skill along with other factors such as command ability (Ansbacher, 1941; Fitts, 1946).

In the United States, the program of research on pilot aptitude testing by the Civil Aeronautics Administration integrated the research on both civilian and military aviation, concluding that a number of the available tests had limited usefulness (i.e., psychomotor tests, physical fitness tests, prior school performance) whereas others were more promising, especially those focusing on knowledge and experience (i.e., biographical data, the Aviation Classification Test, and a test of mechanical comprehension) (Viteles, 1945). Likewise, the study of aptitude testing and training of radio operators revealed that proficient performance was related more to knowledge of electronics and mathematics than to general intelligence or even prior radio experience (although college experience and motivation were factors of some importance as well) (Hadley, 1944).

Task analysis has always involved cognitive categories and phenomena as a part of what it means to decompose and understand tasks. Even the clearest case of what might be called "behavioral task analysis" embraced notions of cognition. What has happened is that as tasks have become more complex and more reliant on cognition than on physical labor, the cognitive work in complex sociotechnical contexts has become more salient and more important as a topic for scientific understanding.

The maturation of the concept of the man–machine analyzed as an interactive and sometimes highly "cognitive" system in the post-WWII years had its origins in research findings dating back to the early 1920s, if not even earlier. A myth seems to surround the notion that WWII-era task analysis was "behavioral." Between the two world wars, behaviorism was a dominant school of thought in American academia. We suspect that that the dominance of behaviorism in American academic psychology between the world wars, combined with the (apparent) knobs and dials emphasis of much of the WWII-era human factors psychology, contributed to the behavioral feel of early task analysis. However, careful examination reveals that the seeds of present-day CTA methods were increasingly visible as researchers sought to address the more cognitively complex tasks created by WWII weapons technology.

An encapsulation of historical findings related to cognition in the context of work is presented in Table 3.1. As this table shows, even in the years before WWI, when TMS was transforming the world of work, task analysis was not cognition free. Cognitive elements continued to appear after WWI despite the rising popularity of the white rat and behaviorism. Cognitive elements became even more visible during WWII, when emerging technologies increased the cognitive load on many war fighters. In this chapter we have made a case that, although it is only in recent years that the research community has made a deliberate shift in language and recognize the increasingly complex nature of work, there was *always* cognition in task analysis in some form. Modern forms of task analysis, cognitive and otherwise, trace their origins to basic ideas that have been on the table for decades (and in some cases, more than a century).

Examining the right column of Table 3.1, one can see the movement toward cognitive task analytic approaches from the early psychotechnicians looking for general aptitudes such as intelligence, to the Taylorists and industrial researchers of the early 20th century looking at how long different mental activities take in the context of a

TABLE 3.1 An Overview of the Historical Roots of Cognitive Task Analysis

Focus	Research Topics	Participants	Primary Units of Analysis	Cognitive Units of Analysis
Psychotechnics: 1880s–1930s				
Selection, Training	Railroading, Telegraphy, etc.	Workforce in general	Abilities (e.g., manual dexterity, memory capacity)	Intelligence, Knowledge, Memory, Reasoning, etc.
Time and Motion Study: 1890s–1930s				
Efficiency, Safety, Tool Design, Workplace Design	Industrial Jobs	Workforce in general, but studies began with the analysis of proficient workers	Physical movements	Mental operations such as "plan" and "inspect"
Industrial Research, United Kingdom: 1910s–1930s				
Efficiency, Safety, Work Environment	Industrial Jobs	Workforce in general	Physical movements, Mental activities	Attention, Speed of Judgment, Logical Reasoning, Planning
Human Factors: World War II era				
Selection, Training, Equipment Design	Communications, Radar, Gunnery	Recruits, trainees, and proficient individuals	Physical movements, Mental activities, Verbal reports, Retrospections	Comprehension Skill, Perceptual Skill, Knowledge

specific task, to WWII-era research that involved the study of perceptual skill in the context of a specific task. This movement toward studying cognition in the context of work, going beyond a list of cognitive aspects of work and how long each might take, was a slow and steady progression over the past century.

Historically, task analysis has been strongly associated with job analysis and job design (cf. Ryan & Smith, 1954, chap. 3; Shartle, 1950). Especially in the eras of manual labor, industrial psychologists and human factors psychologists thought of jobs as being composed of many tasks. Wei and Salvendy (2004) described the history of job analysis and showed how a result of recent trends, especially computerization, has been that job analysis in service of job design has become *Cognitive* Task Analysis.

> Traditional methods for task analysis break down jobs into discrete tasks composed of specific action sequences and identify prerequisite knowledge and skills for each task. Although these methods have been effective for designing jobs for simple procedural skills, they offer little insight for analysis of jobs involving complex cognitive skills. … The operators' tasks in highly automated systems contain more and more planning and decision components. The analysis of these components includes mental activities [used in] traditional techniques; however, only task-oriented behavior is analyzed, at the level of skill-based and rule-based action patterns … the design of a properly functioning job requires a different kind of knowledge to describe the cognitive or mental functions at the knowledge-based information processing level. (Wei & Salvendy, 2004, p. 275)

In their review and summary of CTA for job analysis and design, Wei and Salvendy (2004) presented a table listing dozens of methods of CTA (types of interviews, diagramming methods, ratings and scaling tasks, modeling methods, etc.), and their list corresponds with listings that Cognitive Systems Engineers have offered of CTA methods, in general and not just with reference to job design (cf. Bonaceto & Burns, 2007).

Without knowing this historical background, one might suppose that modern discussions of *Cognitive* Task Analysis represent something of a leap. It might be more accurate to depict modern CTA as a shift to accommodate the changing nature of work and an increased understanding of the impact of technologies on human cognition. As we show in the next chapter, modern notions of CTA represent a logical culmination of recent historical trends as well as the culmination of the broader history.

Summary

The use of TMS and other task analytic methods developed prior to WWII continued through the WWII era. However, new technologies, such as radar and computational devices, accelerated the evolution of the notion of the man–machine system. New methods of task analysis were developed, and new issues arose, involving such topics as display design and task allocation. New frameworks emerged for understanding cognition, including the notions of cybernetics and the information theory of communication. Human factors and ergonomics, as a profession and a community of practice, supplanted the earlier psychotechnics.

Human factors psychology was on the rise as WWII brought about the reformation of the IFRB as the Industrial Health Research Board. In addition, the Applied Psychology Unit was formed at Cambridge University in 1944. In the United States, an Emergency Committee on Psychology was established in 1940, and the Applied Psychology Panel of the National Defense Research Council focused its research on personnel selection and training for wartime tasks. During WWII, these organizations brought together top researchers who advanced and adapted existing methods in the context of the increasingly complex jobs military personnel were called on to perform. Aerial gunnery, radio coding operations, radio detection and ranging, and voice communications represent four wartime jobs that served as fertile ground for advancing human factors research and our understanding of human cognition in the context of work.

New perspectives resulting from this wartime research included servomechanisms as well as the maturation of the concept of the man–machine system. Post-WWI a bifurcation occurred in which one path continued to focus on personnel selection and training, whereas a second path tackled issues associated with information theory and measurement. As research on these and related issues continued, organizations dedicated to the advancement of human factors emerged in both North America and Europe in the form of the Human Factors Society in 1957 and the International Ergonomics Association in 1959.

In our presentation of this history, we have highlighted important links and historical roots. This presentation may be surprising to modern CTA researchers. Many current researchers would characterize CTA methods as a new perspective and would credit CTA with advancing the use of qualitative methods in applied psychology. In fact, the emergence of CTA methods has *felt* revolutionary—perhaps in the same way that self-report methods felt revolutionary in Fernberger's time. Historical analysis, however, suggests that modern CTA represents a shift to accommodate the changing nature of work rather than a major leap. The previous chapters detailed how components of modern CTA emerged across history. The next chapter will examine how these elements have come together in a new way and have been applied to new problems under the term *CTA*.

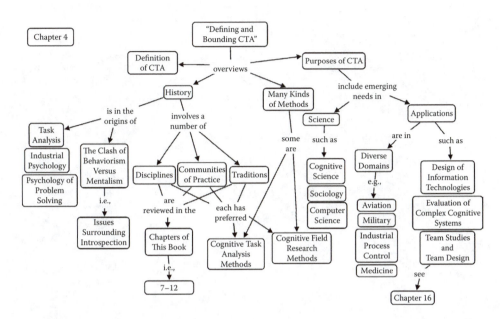

FIGURE 4.1 Chapter 4 Concept Map.

4

Defining and Bounding Cognitive Task Analysis

Central to a concern with instructional processes is the problem of task analysis; analytical description is required of what it is that is to be learned. What has a competent performer in a subject-matter domain learned that distinguishes him from a novice? What distinguishes a skilled reader from an unskilled one? ... Analyzing the content of instruction means studying tasks considerably more complex than those typically studied in the laboratory. It also requires techniques for the detailed analysis of performance in terms of the demands placed on cognitive processes and on knowledge and skills assumed to be in the learners' repertoire as acquired through instruction, development, or self-learning.

—Robert Glaser (1976b, p. 9)

Historical Origins of the Phrase "Cognitive Task Analysis"

At the University of Pittsburgh's Learning Research and Development Center (LRDC), Robert Glaser, Alan Lesgold, and others were using what they referred to as "rational task analysis" in the early 1970s, in the study of instructional problems. This designation was meant to refer to the fact that task analysis was thought to be mostly about skill and physical action, yet the flowcharts developed at the LRDC had cognitive components (A. M. Lesgold, personal communication, November 2001). In David Klahr's 1976 edited volume *Cognition and Instruction*, Robert Glaser, James Greeno, and Lauren Resnick referred to notions of task analysis in the context of instructional design, in a way that seemed to beg for the coining of the phrase "cognitive task analysis."

As far as we can tell, the earliest use of the phrase "Cognitive Task Analysis" in a published article was in a review by J. P. Gallagher (1979) on the theory and method of instructional design. He used the phrase twice, once in the abstract and once again as a section header. Gallagher reviewed some findings in cognitive psychology pertinent to instructional design, such as Ausubel's theory of "meaningful learning," which stresses the role of knowledge structures and processes of assimilation and accommodation (Ausubel, 1968), and Mayer's (1977) discussion of "schema assimilation." Gallagher summarized a number of studies using observational methods to reveal teacher's reasoning and strategies (e.g., Shavelson, 1972). Gallagher also summarized Robert Glaser's (1976b) ideas about the theory of instructional design and James Greeno's discussions of knowledge types (1973). All of these writings, and more besides, emphasized the importance of studying and analyzing the learner's knowledge structures:

> The analysis of complex instructional tasks in terms of formal process models constitutes perhaps the newest application of cognitive/information processing psychology to instruction. … The analysis of propositional content and emphasis on the storage of knowledge in human memory may be particularly helpful in indicating appropriate sequences for the presentation of material, as well as prescribing the use of advanced organizers to assist in the integration of instructional material with existing memory structures. (Gallagher, 1979, pp. 401, 403)

At an Office of Naval Research meeting in March 1978, James Greeno gave a presentation titled "Some Examples of Cognitive Task Analysis With Instructional Implications," which appeared in print 2 years later (Greeno, 1980). At the same time, Sherri Gott of the Air Force Research Laboratory made a case that the Air Force should support more research aimed at improving instruction, and the term "Cognitive Task Analysis" was heard at AFRL contractor meetings. At least by 1983, the notion of CTA was established in contracts to the LRDC from the U.S. Air Force and U.S. Navy. By the mid-1980s the term "Cognitive Task Analysis" was appearing in LRDC reports (cf. Bonar et al., 1985; Glaser, Lesgold, & Lajoie, 1985; Glaser et al., 1985;. Lesgold, 1985; Lesgold et al., 1986). Also we see in this community of practice an increasing interest in the study of expert–novice differences, in service of instructional design (cf. Chi, Glaser, & Rees, 1982; Feltovich, 1981; Means & Gott, 1988).

In the early 1980s, a young Ph.D. named David Woods was working with General Electric on human factors of the electric utilities, and plant workstation design in particular. He began a collaboration with Erik Hollnagel (see chapters 5, 7) when Woods visited the Institute for Atomic Energy of the Halden Reactor Project in the Netherlands. Starting in 1982, they began drafting the first paper titled "Cognitive Task Analysis." In their first draft, Hollnagel (1982) discussed the importance of a human–machine systems viewpoint and the limitations of traditional task analysis (citing the paradigm of "scientific management" in industrial psychology of the early 20th century; see chapter 2). Hollnagel stated,

> The functional analysis of the machine … is not sufficient for making a task analysis, since that requires that the human was completely under the control of the machine. This state of affairs seemed attractive for the task analyses made in the first decades of the century, in the so-called Scientific Management movement, and was to a certain extent also possible with simple industrial machines and processes. But it is neither attractive nor possible with the complex systems we now have which generally involve process control rather than manipulation. (Hollnagel, 1982, p. 3)

To reach the goal of good design for complex systems, Hollnagel, Woods, and their colleagues referred to CTA as involving "studies of worker activities," the discovery of "decision requirements," and the study of the expert's skills, rules, and knowledge (see Rasmussen, 1979, 1983, 1985; Woods, 1982a, 1982b). The phrase "Cognitive Task Analysis" was promulgated at the April 1982 Workshop on Cognitive Modeling of Nuclear Plant Control Room Operators, supported by the Nuclear Regulatory Commission, attended by cognitive scientists and human factors psychologists, including David Woods, Donald Norman, Thomas Sheridan, William Rouse, and Thomas Moran.

Some researchers developed other designations for CTA. For example, Dan Diaper and Peter Johnson (in the United Kingdom) referred to "task analysis for knowledge descriptions" (Diaper, 1989b). But in the early 1980s, the phrase "Cognitive Task Analysis" began to crowd out the competition, in a number of communities of practice. For instance, from 1982 to 1984, educational psychologist Joseph Scandura referred to "structural (cognitive) task analysis" in three papers on what he called "structural learning" (1982, 1984a, 1984b). He cited an unpublished paper by T. F. Merrell that is said to refer to CTA, but he also cited Lauren Resnik's chapter in the Klahr volume (Klahr, 1976), which we mentioned earlier. Scandura pointed to problems in defining learning and assessment solely in terms of "behavioral objectives," revealed by "traditional task analysis," and he yet described his methodology as having its anchor and origins in behavioral research of the 1960s. It is perhaps no surprise therefore that the real underpinning of his structural learning approach is basically a hunt for procedural rules and algorithms. In his method, one classifies problems (e.g., geometric puzzles, mathematical problems, etc.) into types and then writes general ("operationalized" or "behaviorally valid") rules for solving each kind of problem. One might wonder about the depth of cognitive analysis culminating in such rules as the following:

> Construct a picture of the problem as solved. Does the picture contain a point X that satisfied two locus conditions? If so, store the rule (a "high-level" rule in a geometrical example).

Or:

> Position slot for the quotient above the line and one slot to the right of the last digit in the initial dividend (a "low-level rule" in a mathematical example).

And one might wonder about the assertion that such rules *are* cognitive processes (Scandura, 1984a, p. 6). Although Scandura said, "People are assumed to have minds," he also asserted that his methods are "firmly rooted in behavior" (Scandura, 2006, p. 8). The only thing arguably cognitive about the methodology involves the analyst, not the learner:

> The analyst must be thoroughly familiar with the content ... the analyst must be able to verbalize or otherwise adequately represent his content and population knowledge ... the analyst must be able to identify the important features of the problems and the solution rules ... [there must be] expert and non-expert analyses of content. (1984a, pp. 8–9; 1984b, p. 173)

Be that as it may, our point is that the notion of CTA was emerging in a number of historically distinct, even divergent, paradigms and communities of practice.

In 1986, Jerker Rönnberg published a review of research on cognitive dysfunction in the *Scandinavian Journal of Psychology,* in which he discussed the use of laboratory methods for the study of memory, attention, and comprehension in the analysis of cognitive dysfunction. He mentioned CTA (in the paper's abstract) as a method necessary for understanding the relations of neuropathy and learning.

In 1987, when the field of knowledge engineering was in its infancy and was referred to as "expert systems," Phil Barnard and his colleagues at the Medical Research Council Applied Psychology Unit in Cambridge, England (Barnard, Wilson, & MacLean, 1987), discussed the inadequacies of task analysis for the creation of expert systems. They argued that CTA is needed to model the "users" of information processing systems. The models would rely on concepts from cognitive psychology to describe users' mental activity (knowledge, perceptions), supporting the creation of rule-based decision aids that make "performance predictions by reasoning about cognitive representations and their processing" (p. 21). Barnard et al. attempted to create a "general architecture for human information processing" that could be used as a tool kit to help others in the generation of procedural rules for expert systems. Reasoning rules, or heuristics, were revealed by experts' answers to questions (e.g., about keystroke operations and their order, hierarchical structure, etc.), and these would be used to specify a "task model" for the operations of the inference engine.

About this same time, the notion of intelligent tutoring systems was emerging (also called "machine-mediated learning"), and researchers with backgrounds in cognitive psychology and instructional design began working this area. Alan Lesgold (1986) discussed limitations of the computer-based teaching machines of the day (e.g., that the primary teaching strategy was to basically support the learner in redoing problems, failing to help the student in developing knowledge through a deep understanding of the reasons for failure). Barbara Means and Sheri Gott (1988) discussed the use of CTA for the development of better intelligent tutoring systems, and Lajoie and Lesgold (1989) published their report on the development of SHERLOCK, an intelligent tutor for avionics electronics troubleshooting, created through U.S. Air Force funding and based on CTA of expert knowledge.

In 1989, Richard Redding (University of Virginia) presented a review at the annual meeting of the Human Factors and Ergonomics Society, with the emphasis shifting (understandably, for that venue) from education to training. He cited developments at the LRDC (Lesgold et al., 1986), which influenced him considerably (R. E. Redding, personal communication, March 1998). His discussion focused on the new notions of CTA, contrasting it with "the traditional behavioral approach to task analysis," and pointed to a need for richer analysis and understanding of this new CTA methodology. "No formal procedures for cognitive-task analysis have yet been proscribed" (Redding, 1989, p. 1349). He referred to the matter of requiring an "indirect approach" (because cognition is not directly observable), the ways in which CTA procedures can be difficult and time consuming, the need to study domain experts, and the challenges in revealing learner's mental models. Some of the challenges that Redding pointed out (e.g., "cognitive analysis is often not considered cost effective for applied purposes," p. 1351) remain issues today.

What Is CTA?

CTA is commonly regarded as the determination of the cognitive skills, strategies and the knowledge required to perform tasks (Essens, Fallasen, McCann, Cannon-Bowers, & Dorfel, 1995; Gordon, 1994; Redding, 1989; Roth, Woods, & Pople, 1992).

CTA involves specific methods and guidance in probing cognitive processes, a feature that is believed to set CTA in contrast to task analysis (Klein, 1995). However, just as task analysis has rarely (if ever) been purely behavioral (as we showed in chapter 2), CTA is not purely cognitive. For instance, some CTA research relies on the analysis of individual keystrokes in human–computer interaction from which cognition is inferred (Card, Moran, & Newell, 1980a, 1980b, 1983; Gray, John, & Atwood, 1993).

Our definition of CTA is as follows: CTA is a methodology for the empirical study of workplaces and work patterns, resulting in: (a) descriptions of cognitive processes and phenomena accompanying goal-directed work, (b) explanations of work activity in terms of the cognitive phenomena and processes, and (c) application of the results to the betterment of work and the quality of working life by creating better work spaces, better supporting artifacts (i.e., technologies), and by creating work methods that enhance human satisfaction and pleasure, that amplify human intrinsic motivation, and that accelerate the achievement of proficiency.

A few notes are in order:

- We do not rely on a notion of "task" in our definition, for the obvious reason that this would tend to make the definition circular. More important, the wording of our definition is intended to divorce CTA from the traditional notion of task as a directive to engage in particular, prespecified, stepwise behavioral acts (see chapter 2).
- We do rely on the notion that cognitive work is goal directed. This too helps us avoid any assumption that "task" must be the single or preferred unit of analysis. As Jens Rasmussen has pointed out (see chapter 10), cognitive work involves making knowledge-driven, context-sensitive choices among activities, not the conduct of "tasks." That being said, most researchers, most of the time, refer to CTA as Cognitive *Task* Analysis. Hence, we do too. But throughout any discussion of CTA, one has to try to hold the historical baggage of the word *task* in limbo.
- By "cognitive" we do not mean to limit the "processes and phenomena" to ones that would be coin of the realm in mainstream cognitive psychology (or information processing psychology)—concepts such as learning, memory, perception, and the like. We definitely mean "cognitive" to include team communication, social-psychological, and socio-cultural processes and phenomena (e.g., collaboration, organizational constraints on cognitive work, etc.).
- Although we are tempted, we do not limit CTA to the study of cognitive work in "complex sociotechnical systems." Such a boundary might rule out many legitimate domains or venues of study, such as consumer behavior and marketing. This being said, CTA is often conducted within, and for the betterment of, complex socio-technical systems, and CTA often reveals the ways in which cognition adapts to complexity.
- The phrase "the betterment of work" captures such goals as making work more efficient and productive (often a primary goal of CTA), but we counterpoint this with assertions about the quality of work, that the work be "human centered" (see Table 12.1).

Today, CTA is regarded by research agencies worldwide as being not just an important component of research and development efforts for complex human–machine systems but a *necessary* component, because the work that is being analyzed is *cognitive* work.

Cost considerations also enter the picture in a significant way:

> There are few claims and very little research concerning the economic benefits of CTA ... many military training specialists suggest that CTA is the only strategy which has been found to work for training on, for example, the troubleshooting of complex technological systems. One of the most dramatic claims was advanced by Means and Gott (1988) who speculated that the equivalent of five years of job knowledge can be transmitted in 50 hours of training based on CTA. What Means and Gott do not explain is the cost and amount of effort required to conduct a task analysis that will result in the 50 hours of training. Informal estimates one hears from specialists in this area suggest that approximately 30–35 hours of CTA activities involving both a CTA specialist full-time and at least two part-time task experts are required to produce the knowledge content for one hour of training. However, if Means' and Gott's estimate is accurate, one year of experience for many on-the-job apprentices would cost much more than the CTA and training design time required for all trainees plus 10 hours of training time salary time required for each trainee. (Clark & Estes, 1996, pp. 410–411)

Clark and Estes cited a study in which there was an opportunity to compare traditional training with a new training package based on CTA. The course, for managers in a large European company, focused on legally mandated safety procedures. It took managers 2 days to take the traditional course and pass the exam, whereas the new course took 1 day and resulted in comparable performance levels on the part of the trainees. "The overall financial benefit from the CTA-based course was estimated to be equivalent to 2.5 years of the average manager's salary, every time a manager was required to take the course" (p. 411).

A great many applied projects using CTA have come to fruition, their success sometimes being attributed to the use of particular CTA methods. Researchers believe that CTA and CFR (Cognitive Field Research) yield valid information—that the data from CTA really do capture knowledge and reasoning and do so in such a way as to support such activities as training and technology design.

The Main Purpose of CTA and CFR

Research over the past decade that has involved examination of cognitive work in complex sociotechnical contexts has relied to a greater or lesser extent on methods that either were referred to as CTA or might legitimately be regarded as CTA or CFR. The study of cognitive systems in context is discovering how the cognition and behavior of practitioners are coadapted with two other sets of factors:

1. The purposes and constraints of the field of activity, and
2. The characteristics of the complex physical systems (usually, information processing systems) with which they interact.

The main reason for using methods of CTA is to address issues about how to study the interaction of complex tools and cognition in the field setting or workplace as well as the laboratory (Hoffman & Woods, 2000). Sociotechnical contexts involve emergent phenomena—ones that exist only at the intersection of people, technology, and work. Additional new phenomena emerge as technology and organizational change transform work activities. Studies of cognition at work do not see cognitive activity as being located or isolated in a single individual, but rather cognitive activity goes on distributed across multiple agents as a part of a stream of activity (Hutchins, 1990, 1995a; Klein, 1998). Individual cognitive work is embedded in larger, professional, organizational, institutional contexts, which constrain activity in many ways (e.g., rewards and punishments, not altogether consistent goals, limited resources, etc.) (Woods, Johannsen, Cook, & Sarter, 1994). Overall, cooperation and coordination are ubiquitous, because cognitive work is distributed over multiple human and machine agents. We expand on this idea in chapters 6 and 7.

Technology change transforms cognitive systems, creating new roles, changing what is standard and what is exceptional, changing the kinds of errors and paths to failure, and changing the ways people adapt to achieve their goals and cope with error (Woods & Dekker, 2000). For example, the shift to computer-based displays of data in a control center creates a large network of displays behind a narrow display keyhole. This narrowing can create a risk of people ("users") getting lost in the network of displays and menus, but because they can be aware of the danger, people can adapt by devising techniques and reshaping the artifacts to avoid navigation in the interface and the associated cognitive costs (Koopman & Hoffman, 2003; Watts-Perotti & Woods, 1999).

This process of transformation and adaptation creates a challenge of prediction:

- How will envisioned technological change shape cognition and collaboration?
- What are the new roles for people in the system?
- How will practitioners adapt artifacts, given mismatches to the actual demands and pressures they experience?

The process of studying cognition at work changes quite dramatically our psychological concepts about the boundaries of cognitive activity (e.g., Hutchins, 1995b). To what extent is cognition distributed in teams? To what extent is memory "embodied" in artifacts? The process of studying cognition at work changes quite dramatically our concepts about the goals of Cognitive Science. Rather than just seeking a broad, general theory of learning or cognition, one must examine failure as well as successes, expertise as well as error. What challenges practitioners? What makes situations hard? How do practitioners succeed despite the constraints under which they engage in cognitive work?

CTA can be intended to reveal knowledge about domain concepts and principles (whether these are known explicitly or implicitly by the expert); schemas for typical scenarios; problem types, data types, displays, tools, and so on; routine plans and goals; reasoning rules and heuristics; and memories about rare or tough cases, unusual situations, and critical incidents. CTA and CFR can be intended to reveal information about mental processes, including sense making, learning (perceptual learning, the progression from novice to expert, etc.), mental modeling (of situations or of the systems or processes that an operator controls or interacts with), strategies for adapting to unexpected circumstances, and circumstances leading to and contributing to error.

CTA Methods

The palette of CTA and CFR methods is quite rich. CTA methods can be placed into just a few categories (e.g., Hoffman, 1987b) or can be placed into many categories (Hoffman, Shadbolt, Burton, & Klein, 1995; Wei & Salvendy, 2004). Methods for modeling cognition can be included, as well as methods more like those used in the traditional psychology laboratory. So, depending on how one slices the pie, there are only a few basic methodological approaches, or dozens of methods, that are distinguishable in either subtle or gross ways (Bonaceto & Burns, 2007). Furthermore, methods can be (and often are) combined in various ways (Hoffman et al., 1995), and new methods can be concocted on the fly. Examples of all of these will be presented in the chapters of this book. (See also Crandall, Klein, & Hoffman, 2006.)

Methods that have been used in the examination of the cognition of experts can be grossly classified as being either a kind of interview, a kind of observation or analysis of performance, or a kind of "contrived" or more laboratory-like task.

Storytelling Methods

As we discussed in chapter 2, some CTA methods have roots in introspection. In modern times, the self-report methods used in CTA have been adapted and refined, emerging as a distinct category of methods termed "process tracing" (Mitchell & Sundstrom, 1997; Svenson, 1979; Todd & Benbasat, 1987; Waldron, 1985; Woods, 1993). To introspect is to think about, and verbally report on, one's perceptions, thoughts, beliefs, judgments, and so on (see Ribot, 1873). In Titchener's laboratory, the "Observer" would look at some sort of fairly simple stimulus, think about what is being perceived, the phenomenal experience of thoughts and "apperceptions." The Observer would provide a running account of the contents of consciousness. This would be a dissection according to a prescribed list of primary qualities and what were believed to be elementary units of thought and percept (e.g., "Then I had the clear impression of the color red"). In contrast, in a type of process tracing called "think-aloud problem solving" (e.g., Duncker, 1945), one reads some sort of real problem or is presented some sort of real puzzle and then verbalizes his or her thoughts *about the problem*. Mental acts are charted, so are task activities (i.e., reaction time and other performance measures) (see Bailey & Kay, 1987; Benjafield, 1969). But the verbal report is about the problem information the interviewee attends to and how he or she makes sense of that information, *not* about mental phenomena, percepts, and so on. This is the key distinction between *introspection* (on one hand) and *task reflection* (or *retrospection*) on the other hand. Many CTA methods involve participants in tasks in which they "think out loud" about the problems they are working or have worked in the past.

An example of a task reflection method is think-aloud problem solving, with the data subjected to an analysis technique called protocol analysis (Ericsson & Simon, 1993). Think-aloud problem solving combined with protocol analysis is a method that has been relied on heavily in psychological studies of expert–novice differences (e.g., Chi, Glaser, & Farr, 1988; Ericsson & Smith, 1991a; Feltovich, Spiro, & Coulson, 1989;

Foley & Hart, 1992; McKeithen, Reitman, Reuter, & Hirtle, 1981; see chapter 5). The researcher's goal is to infer from the protocol a description of the temporal sequence of mental events and especially the momentary contents of working memory (e.g., memory access, reasoning operations, etc.) and the cycle of perceiving, reasoning, and acting (as in Duncker, 1945; Neisser, 1976, 1993; Newell, 1985; Simon, 1979.

CTA can involve something like introspection, however. For instance, in one study of weather forecasters (Hoffman, Coffey, & Ford, 2000), models of expert reasoning were validated through work-patterns observation. If a forecaster had said that he began the forecasting procedure by inspecting satellite images to get the "big picture," that could be verified by observing that the forecaster does that when beginning a work shift. If the forecaster had also said that after inspecting other data and reaching an understanding of the larger-scale weather forces at work, he tries to build a "mental picture" of what is happening and what will happen more locally. The only thing in work activities that might reflect that is a pensive pause. At that point the researcher could intrude, asking, "What are you thinking?"

Interviews

CTA involves asking people questions. In one type of interview task, for example, experts are asked a series of preplanned probe questions and their functions (Burton, Shadbolt, Rugg, & Hedgecock, 1988; Wood & Ford, 1993). Questions can be intended to yield information about domain concepts and their interrelations (e.g., "Could you tell me about a typical case?" "Can you tell me about the last case you encountered?" "Can you given me an example of an X?" "Does X include Y?"), information about domain procedures and reasoning rules (e.g., "Why, how, or when do you do that?" "What do you do at each step in this procedure?" "What alternatives are there?" "What if it were not the case that X?"), or information about rare cases and special procedures (e.g., "Can you tell me about an unusual case?").

Laboratory-Like Tasks

An example of a constrained or laboratory-like task is when experts work with elicitors in creating a Concept Map (like the advance organizers for the chapters of this book), which can be a representation of the domain in terms of the relationships (graphical links) among domain elements (concept nodes) (Adelman, 1989; Crandall, Klein, & Hoffman, 2006, chap. 4; Gordon & Gill, 1997; Gordon, Schmierer, & Gill, 1993; Hoffman, Coffey, Carnot, & Novak, 2002; Hoffman, Coffey, Novak, & Cañas, 2005; Hoffman & Lintern, 2006; Kaempf, Thordsen, & Klein 1991; Novak, 1990, 1991, 1998; Shadbolt & Burton, 1990a, b). (Many examples can be viewed at http://www. ihmc.us.) Alternatively, the expert can be asked to construct a diagram that depicts operational procedures or that depicts what occurred in a particular case that is presented for analysis. Graphs can take the form of timelines that depict the unfolding of events, decision points, and so forth over the time course of a scenario. Individual graphs can use symbols, icons, arrows, and so on to depict situations at particular points on a timeline, and the graphs can be composed into a storyboard series that paints a picture of an event or case.

In addition to generating domain knowledge and descriptions of scenarios, diagrams can be used to scale proficiency; that is, identify differences in reasoning across the experience continuum (e.g., Cooke & McDonald, 1986). Graphical representations have proved themselves to be useful in interface design (Redish & Wixon, 2003; Sowa, 1984), an instance of the widely recognized utility of using graphical displays to convey information (Andre, Wickens, Moorman, & Boschelli, 1991; Bauer & Johnson-Laird, 1993; Gordon et al., 1993; Sanderson, Haskell, & Flach, 1992; Vekirl, 2002; Wickens, Merwin, & Lin, 1994). Conceptual graphing has also formed the basis of some "automated knowledge acquisition tools" that permit the transformation of diagrammed information directly into rules or other knowledge representation formats that can be implemented in decision aids or expert systems (see Berg-Cross & Price, 1989; Motta, Rajan, & Eisenstadt, 1989; Solvberg et al., 1988).

Strengths and Applications

As is true of all empirical methods, particular CTA methods have strengths and limitations. Wei and Salvendy (2004, Table 2) discussed four broad families of CTA methods, not terribly dissimilar from the classes of methods we laid out previously, and for each of 40 methods, they listed method strengths and weaknesses and some of the appropriate use contexts for each. The kinds of strengths and weaknesses that are indicated include time and effort required, reliance on researchers' observational skill, effectiveness at generating a broad domain overview, effectiveness at revealing details, knowledge and expertise required of the researchers, and other factors as well. A capsule view of this material is summarized in Table 4.1.

This sort of clustering of CTA methods into families, accompanied by this sort of evaluation of strengths, weakness, and appropriate uses, is common to many summary

TABLE 4.1 Appropriate Uses for Cognitive Task Analysis (CTA) Methods within Each of Wei and Salvendy's (2004) Major Families of CTA Methods

Family	Particular CTA Methods	Appropriate Uses
Observations and interviews	Many types of structured interviews are listed, such as the Critical Decision Method	Useful to define and circumscribe the domain. Useful for domains where specific task procedures are not well definedUseful for the analysis of tasks that are skill based
Process tracing methods	Verbal reports	Useful when it is easy to define representative tasks and scenariosUseful when it is important to evaluate task (or dual-task) performance. Useful for the analysis of tasks that are skill based or rule based
Conceptual techniques	Graphing tasks, ratings tasks	Useful when it is important to reveal domain knowledge. Useful for the analysis of tasks that are rule based or knowledge based
Formal models	ACT-R, GOMS modeling	Useful for modeling tasks that do not change much. Useful for the analysis of tasks that are rule based or knowledge based

Note: ACT-R = Adaptive Control of Thought-Rational; GOMS = Goals-Operations-Methods-Selection Rules.

reports on CTA (e.g., Cooke, 1994; Crandall, Klein, & Hoffman, 2006; Hoffman et al., 1995; Means & Gott, 1988).

Combinatorics

CTA tasks as they are often employed combine the methods and elements we have illustrated. For example, the Critical Decision Method is a type of interview, but it involves task retrospection. Most researchers and system developers have used combinations of particular methods (Gordon & Gill, 1997). For example, the think-aloud problem-solving task has been combined with a variety of other tasks, such as a judgment task in a study of expert highway engineers (Hammond, Hamm, Grassia, & Pearson, 1987), a categorization task analysis in a study of medical diagnosticians (Fox, Myers, Greaves, & Pegram, 1985), and a contrived "limited information" task in a study of expert aerial photo interpreters (Hoffman, 1987b). In the method called PARI (Precursor, Action, Result, Interpretation), which was developed to capture the cognitive and behavioral demands of troubleshooting complex systems (Hall, Gott, & Pokorny, 1995), experts work in pairs; they think aloud while solving test case problems; they are encouraged to draw pictures, timelines, or diagrams; and they also are presented with probe questions. Many combinations of particular tasks are possible, and we will illustrate those in many examples in the remaining chapters of this book.

Summary

Early discussions of CTA took place at the University of Pittsburgh's LRDC in the 1970s. Researchers such as Robert Glaser and Alan Lesgold were searching for new methods of task analysis for use in instructional design for cognitive tasks. At an Office of Naval Research meeting in March 1978, James Greeno gave a presentation using the term, also relating it to instructional implications. The earliest use of the term in writing that we have been able to find is in a review by J. P. Gallagher in 1979 on theory and method instructional design. A year later, Sherri Gott of the Air Force Research Laboratory made a case that the Air Force should support more research aimed at improving instruction, using the term "Cognitive Task Analysis." In 1982, Eric Hollnagel and David Woods drafted a paper titled "Cognitive Task Analysis" in their work on nuclear power plan design. In the United Kingdom, Dan Diaper and Peter Johnson referred to "task analysis for knowledge descriptions" in 1989. Jerker Ronnberg used the term "Cognitive Task Analysis" in the *Scandinavian Journal of Psychology* in a review paper on cognitive dysfunction in 1986. These examples and others suggest that the need for methods to better understand human cognition in the context of work was recognized independently across a range of settings throughout the 1970s and 1980s.

Now just 30 years later, CTA has come to be considered a necessary component of research and development efforts for complex human–machine systems. It is generally defined as the determination of cognitive skills and strategies and the knowledge required to perform tasks. In the past two decades, research that has involved examination of cognitive work has relied largely on CTA methods (although not always referred to by the term CTA). CTA researchers acknowledge the importance of discovering how the cognition and activities of practitioners are coadapted with the purpose and constraints of the work setting and the characteristics of the physical systems (usually information technology) with which they interact. This includes issues such as to what extent cognition is distributed in teams and to what extent memory is embodied in artifacts.

A rich set of CTA methods exists today, including retrospective interview techniques, real-time observations, think-aloud problem solving, and constrained tasks resulting in Concept Maps. Most researchers use combinations of methods, depending on the task to be studied and the resources available. The next chapter will discuss key communities of practice that have supported the application and refinement of these methods.

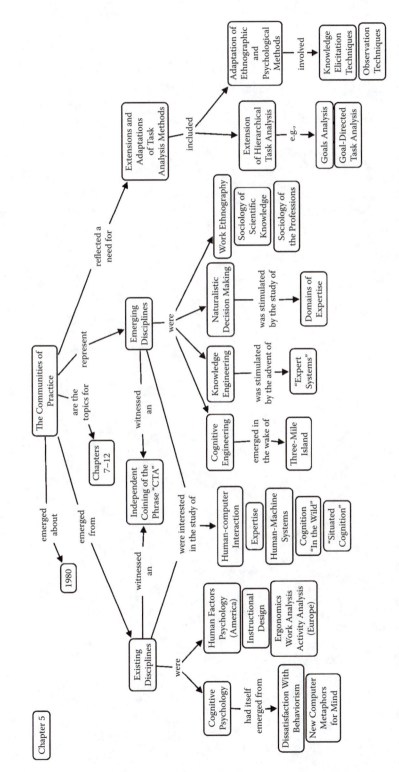

FIGURE 5.1 Chapter 5 Concept Map.

5

Emergence of the Communities of Practice

Robert R. Hoffman and Laura G. Militello,
with contributions by David D. Woods

The definition of a task implies that the human is necessary for the machine to function, hence for the total man–machine system to achieve its goal. The functional analysis of the machine is, however, not sufficient for making a task analysis since that would require that the human was completely under the control of, or subsumed by, the machine. This state of affairs seemed attractive for the task analyses made in the first decades of the century. But it is neither attractive nor possible with the complex systems we have now. ... This indicates that a task analysis must be made along two different dimensions. One is the engineering analysis of the functional requirements of the machine. Another is an analysis of the performance characteristics of the operator, i.e., a cognitive analysis of the basis for human performance. This is so obvious that no further arguments are needed.

—Erik Hollnagel (1982, p. 3)

Introduction

In chapters 2 and 3 we laid out what might be called the "ancient history" of Cognitive Task Analysis (CTA), showing that it has roots in the early scientific psychology and showing that task analysis was never purely behavioral and never in any sort of state of denial over the causal role of mental events. In this chapter, we trace the modern trends and developments that mark the specific origins of CTA and Cognitive Field Research (CFR). A variety of events, trends, and problems falling at the intersection of cognition, collaboration, technology, and work became salient circa 1980. Many people at many laboratories and organizations found it natural to speak of and carry out what they called "Cognitive Task Analysis," with multiple parallel and independent origins of the activity and coinages of the term, or related terms.

Eight communities of practice in the modern history of CTA emerged in the 1980s. Most of these originated in an existing or traditional academic discipline. Each was driven to some degree by needs—either training high-performance skills or aiding performance online given the potential for failure. Each community was driven to some extent by perceived limitations of traditional methods, such as traditional task analysis or early knowledge acquisition techniques. Each thread was driven to some extent by new opportunities to shape computer technology in supporting cognitive work and coordinated activity. The communities of practice were as follows:

1. Cognitive Psychology
2. Human Factors Psychology and Ergonomics
3. Cognitive Engineering
4. Instructional Design
5. Experimental Psychology
6. The Ethnography of Workplaces and Cognitive Anthropology
7. Naturalistic Decision Making
8. European Work Analysis and Ergonomics

We discuss these in this order, although they could be described in any order, because they emerged in parallel. They were, furthermore, not entirely independent, because there were cross-influences and cross-fertilizations, which we will point out as we go.

The Rise of Modern Cognitive Psychology

Prior to the dominance of behaviorism, primarily in the United States, psychology had always been mentalistic in orientation. Psychology also had a significant applied aspect in which the study of cognitive processes was salient (e.g., Münsterberg, 1914; Stratton, 1896, 1909). Then, beginning with the emergence of the pragmatic "behavioral attitude" in the years just after World War I (see Dunlap, 1932), and especially the writings of John Watson (1913), the paradigm of behaviorism rose to prominence and then dominance in American academic psychology. Conditioning methods for studying behavior were touted as being rigorous, objective, genuine science. Criticisms of the European mentalistic psychology and criticisms of the methods of introspection had a great influence. Behaviorism would hold sway for over half a century, despite arguments from within that the paradigm had important limitations (e.g., Lashley, 1951).

In 1951, the Carnegie Institute sponsored meetings of linguists, psychologists, and computer scientists (Carroll, 1953; Cofer, 1961; Osgood & Sebeok, 1954) that were seminal for the "psycholinguistic revolution." Linguist Noam Chomsky had a profound impact through his work on the formalisms and ideas of generative transformational grammar and his criticisms of the behaviorist approach to language (Chomsky, 1957, 1959). Notions from the WWII-era applied research also had a critical impact. Developments in sonar, audio recording, and signal processing technologies led to a research on speech perception (e.g., Liberman, Delattre, & Cooper, 1952). Information theory and signal detection theory (e.g., Shannon, 1948) led directly to a number of programs of research on perception, attention, and vigilance (see chapter 3). Also in the 1950s, steps were taken to found a field of "artificial intelligence" (von Neumann, 1958; Wiener, 1948), including the introduction of the notion of "programming languages" (Newell & Simon, 1956). Marvin Minsky (1961) laid out the central goals for the field, and through the 1960s, systems were created for solving geometrical puzzles, playing chess, and proving theorems in symbolic logic. The notions of cybernetics, control theory, and the general-purpose linear digital computer had a major impact on the rise of cognitive psychology. The computer metaphor for mind spawned flowchart models that postulated stages of mental operations and decision making (e.g., Atkinson & Shiffrin, 1968; Waugh & Norman, 1965).

Calls for a mentalistic revolution were made in the 1960s (Hebb, 1963), and the Center for Cognitive Science was established at Harvard (Miller, 1979, p. 11; see Baars, 1986) by George Miller and Jerome Bruner. Neisser's *Cognitive Psychology* (1967) was responsible for introducing an entire generation to the new field. New journals appeared, including *Cognition* (in 1972) and *Cognitive Psychology* (in 1976). Few graduate schools at the time had courses in cognitive psychology, and courses in learning spent as much time on rat research as on human research. But Miller, Bruner, Neisser, and others showed that it was scientifically respectable to study cognition and even necessary to a science of psychology broadly defined, as George Miller did, as the scientific study of behavior *and* mental life.

In the mid-1970s, a number of scientists called for a new interdiscipline to be called "Cognitive Science," integrating philosophy, artificial intelligence, and psychology and focusing on the study of the mind (Abelson et al., 1976). The Cognitive Science Society was founded and launched its namesake journal in 1977. The first international conference of the society was held in 1980, at which Herbert Simon declared that mainstream psychology had converged around the information processing framework.

This academic climate profoundly shaped the development of CTA methods in the 1980s, but much of the influence also came from applied disciplines and research efforts.

Advances in Human Factors Psychology and Ergonomics

Beginning in WWII, cybernetic and information processing systems mandated new approaches to the description and design of tasks for human–machine interaction. One important historical marker is R. B. Miller's (1953) "A Method for Man–Machine Task Analysis." Although in hindsight it can be faulted for characterizing the human solely in terms of "input–output functions," Miller's method opened up task analysis in the sense of understanding that the particulars of any analytic method would depend at least to some extent on the goals of the research project (see Drury, Paramore, Van Cott, Grey, & Corlett, 1987; McCormick, 1976). As it came to be applied to information system design and came to be adopted broadly in system development and procurement, task analysis came to be seen as a suite of methods, with many possible variations on the theme, rather than as any single method.

Well into the 1980s, task analysis, at least as it was conducted in North America, retained much of the action orientation that task analysis had from the beginning. Drury et al. (1987) gave the example of the task of a preassembly-line worker, which included activities such as "move pallet to the side of the conveyor" and "put bar code sticker on carton." On the other hand, cognition crept in. For the activity, "enter shipping information for invoice," the corresponding ergonomics issue was, "Is the data input dialog user-friendly?"

Although definitions of *task* stuck to the idea of sequential actions having clear-cut beginning and ending points (see Drury et al., 1987; Singleton, 1974), there was also a recognition that there are "branching tasks" where "task sequence is determined largely by the outcome of particular 'choice' tasks in the operation" (Drury et al., 1987, p. 374). Drury et al.'s inclusion of the word *choice* inside scare quotes can easily be interpreted as a legacy of behaviorism, but more important, the inclusion of branching tasks—conditional dependencies that mandate that task descriptions be hierarchical rather than linear—shows how work was changing and how the era of task analysis was leading to an era of CTA.

Contributing to the emergence of more powerful task analytic methods was recognition that methods are adapted to purposes and contexts. Much of the task analytic work in the decades between WWII and the introduction of computers took the form of analysis of tasks, as they were conducted using technologies that already existed. Human factors (in the United States) and ergonomics (in Europe) seemed intent on justifying themselves by contributing to redesign (for examples, see Singleton, 1974). Thus, a distinction was drawn between task description, task specification, and task analysis. Description involved understanding the system (i.e., machine, work space, technology). Specification involved laying out the requirements for the human (strength, reading skills, math skills, etc.). Analysis involved injecting human factors and ergonomics considerations (e.g., the foot rest is too high, the display is too far away) for possible redesign of the machine (work space, technology, etc.).

This effort at justification based on successful redesign, however, opened a window to the detailed analysis of skills, especially because skill was critical in such activities as choice and crucial in the conduct of tasks that involved dependencies (i.e., conditional branchings). Knowledge and perceptual-motor skills were coming to be understood as being critical, even in industrial contexts (Crossman, 1956; Seymour, 1968).

> Although nonmanual skills have always been part of supervisory and managerial jobs, in recent years there has been a rapid growth of shop-floor jobs that largely involve nonmanual skills, particularly in the process industries. Here, the skill is essentially a mental one, with operators being concerned with decision-making and the handling of information in circumstances that rarely occur in a predetermined order (Drury et al., 1987, p. 379)

Thus, in task analysis,

> For each task in the job, the knowledge and skill required are determined. To do this, the analyst must work with the operator to consider, for instance, what knowledge the operator requires to set up, operate, or inspect the work, how this will be obtained, and how and when it will be used. Sources of information, whether they be handbooks, written instructions, or memory, must be considered, as must be the limits of the operator's discretion with respect to these instructions. When considering skill content, the analyst must decide what the operator does and how he does it. … Thus the skilled performance is observed as closely as possible over several cycles, with each movement being recorded in detail. The analyst then gains additional information by questioning, attempting the task himself, or various other methods appropriate to the case under study (Drury et al., 1987, p. 378)

Although couched in terms of the analysis of "operators" conducting industrial tasks and engaged in "muscle movements" and "sensory checks," this description can be used to good effect in any discussion of modern CTA. Knowledge and reasoning stand between input and output.

Historically, the understanding that tasks in an age of new technologies involve conditional branchings, and require choice, skill, and knowledge, gave rise in the United Kingdom to the idea of Hierarchical Task Analysis (HTA), pioneered by Annett and Duncan (1967). HTA came to grips with complex tasks with a significant mental component. This was

> ... a radical departure from contemporary approaches. The cognitive revolution had yet to spread to applied psychology and ergonomics, where the behavioristic paradigm was still dominant, although it had been on the wane in experimental psychology through the 1960s. In applied psychology it was still considered unscientific to infer cognitive processes, and the focus remained principally on observed behavior. (Stanton, 2004, p. 578)

Although it can be argued that HTA involved bucking the behavioral establishment, European ergonomics and academic and applied psychology were less influenced by behaviorism to begin with. As Annett (2004) pointed out, HTA was initially and explicitly created to overcome some of the perceived limitations of the Time and Motion Study methods of Taylor and Gilbreth, at a time when the basic ideas of cybernetics and information theory were being extended from the analysis of relatively simple perceptual-motor tasks to the acquisition of higher level skills (e.g., Annett & Kay, 1956; Miller, Galanter, & Pribram, 1960) and from individual cybernetic devices to man–machine systems at a larger scale (e.g., Chapanis, 1951).

To illustrate HTA, we prepared a reasonably realistic example, from the domain of weather forecasting, presented in Figure 5.2. This diagram is only fractional, in the sense that it presents only a very few of the many nodes and branchings that would be involved in this activity.

Although seminal, the concept of HTA led immediately to a new problem: how to know when to stop an analysis. As tasks became more complex and involved more conditional dependencies, analysis could go into ever more detail. If the level of detail were to involve the individual "muscle movements" of the previous era of task analysis circa WWI (e.g., for lathe operation), then task analysis would be significantly distanced from the design of training for knowledge and skill-based tasks. There was thus the important question of what are the "essential" operations.

A solution involved a distinction between tasks and goals. Consider glassmaking as an example. The specific task of melting glass can be described in great detail of subtasks and activities. But the task, and its subtasks, can be involved in a number of differing goal-directed activities at both higher and lower levels of action and purpose. One can melt a blob of glass to shape it, but one can also melt a blob of glass to remove bubbles. A hierarchy showing the sequential and dependency of tasks and subtasks might not clearly show their rationale, that is, the goals and subgoals. A high-level goal is to "make the right glass," and this has a subgoal to "avoid small bubbles," which has a sub-subgoal to "control the hot spot," and so on.

In a seminal paper titled "An Improved Tabular Format for Task Analysis," Shepherd (1976) introduced the idea of describing tasks in terms of hierarchies of goals rather

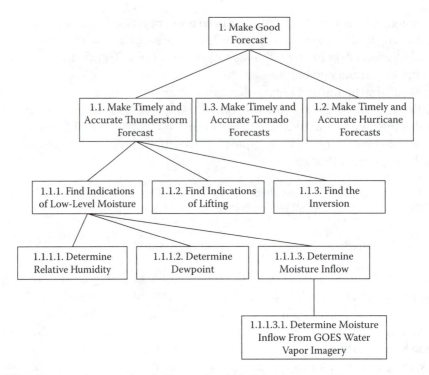

FIGURE 5.2 A simple example of a Hierarchical Task Analysis.

than in terms of hierarchies of subtasks. In most applications of HTA, tasks are labeled according to their goals and subgoals. In Bainbridge's (1979) "goal-directed program," the task analysis admits that the task sequence, and even the operations themselves, vary depending on the conditionalities (i.e., the data received, the decisions made) (Drury et al., 1987, p. 378). This in turn suggested an approach to the problem of the "essential" operations. If one were to describe the glassblower's job in terms of goals and subgoals and then apply that description in an analysis of glassblowing for, say, the goal of creating a goblet, then HTA allows analysis of subgoals to proceed to whatever level of detail is appropriate for achieving the goal. That is, the required level of detail can vary, as appropriate, for subgoals (Drury et al., 1987).

What distinguishes HTA from other (especially, the historically earlier) forms of task analysis is the (a) recognition that some tasks cannot be described as single sequences of activities but instead have contingencies or conditionalities, represented as branchings in a tree diagram; and (b) recognition that tasks can be analyzed not just in terms of sequences of actions but also in terms of goals or functions.

According to Shepherd (1976), the questions that HTA seeks to answer are as follows:

- What is the goal of the task?
- What information is required to conduct the task?
- What decisions are involved in conducting the task?
- What are the consequences of actions (including feedback)?
- What problems can occur?

This roster, like the previous quotation from Drury et al. (1987), can be used to good effect in any discussion of modern CTA. Indeed, it mirrors William Wong's (2004) roster in his discussion of the Critical Decision Method.

HTA is today said to be the most widely used method of task analysis in the United Kingdom (Annett, 2003, 2004). Stanton (2004) attributed its utility to its flexibility as a framework or a suite of methods for analyzing tasks (see also Shepherd, 2001). Annett (2000, 2004) provided a general discussion of how to analyze tasks in terms of goals and illustrated the process of "successive unpacking," which results in a nested hierarchy of subgoals. His presentation includes example goal hierarchy diagrams and shows how these can be used in design. Ormerod and Shepherd (2004; Ormerod, 2000) provided detailed guidance on the conduct of HTA, intended to gently lead the trepidant novice in the conduct of the procedure. This includes a task classification scheme and data collection templates.

Task analysis as it was understood in North American human factors psychology underwent a similar shift that expanded on the traditional forms. The change also came in recognition of the changing workplace and the impact of information technology. A clear example is Goal-Directed Task Analysis (GDTA) (Endsley, 1988, 1995a). GDTA is a type of structured interview that seeks to elicit from the domain practitioner details concerning the task goals and decision requirements. Just like HTA, GDTA charts describe tasks in terms of levels of goals and subgoals. In the interview procedure, goals and subgoals are described to a fine level of detail sufficient to support the creation of new information technologies. Also like HTA, GDTA represents an adaptation of task analytic methods to the fact that that work is not always sequential and linear. Not only do tasks involve conditional branchings but much practitioner reasoning involves a constant juggling back and forth between multiple goals and processing of information in a very non-linear fashion (Endsley, Bolte, & Jones, 2003).

The GDTA procedure involves the following: (a) an interview with one or more domain practitioners to first develop a high-level hierarchy of goals and major subgoals, (b) successive interviews in which the major subgoals are split out and hierarchies are made at finer levels of detail, and (c) an interview in which, for each subgoal at a fine level, the practitioner is asked about requirements for making decisions and maintaining an awareness of ongoing situations (e.g., the sorts of information needed).

As HTA was emerging in human factors psychology, another community of practice was converging on the same problem—designing information technologies to support work on complex human–machine contexts.

The Emergence of Cognitive Engineering

Cognitive Engineering emerged from the need to understand patterns and principles in human–computer interaction and support the design of human–computer interfaces. Research in this thread attempted to map mental mechanisms at a microcognitive scale onto specific tasks that centered on interaction with computers and computerized devices. This emerged following on Card, Moran, and Newell's (1983) work on the "keystroke model" and the later GOMS model (goals, operators, methods and selection rules). Such modeling hinges on notions of short-term memory capacity, the time taken for attention shifts, and so on. The work on cognitive architectures allowed researchers such as David Kieras and Peter Polson to develop cognitive simulations of the microstructure of the cognitive work required to accomplish particular fixed tasks (e.g., Kieras, 1988; Polson, 1987). Early successes predicted learning times for different human–computer interface designs. Later work examined how task demands could impose working memory bottlenecks that might lead to predictable errors. Microcognitive modeling along these lines remains an active area of research and applications.

But there is much more to this thread, specifically, the emergence of Cognitive *Systems* Engineering. The broader focus, beyond the one person–one machine interaction, is how the behavior of practitioners, such as controllers in nuclear power plants, is adapted to the constraints imposed by the domain, organizational goals and pressures, and characteristics of information technology (Hollnagel & Woods, 1983; Norman, 1993; Rasmussen & Lind, 1981). Cognitive Engineering emerged in response to accidents such as the Three Mile Island accident of 1979. This showed the need for academic cognitive psychologists and human factors engineers to broaden their horizons to study cognitive work and escape the "knobs and dials" legacy (however inappropriate that designation may have been) of the post-WWII human factors work. At the same time, advances in computer graphics and computer technology provided a basis for creating new support systems and interfaces for process control (Hollnagel et al., 1986). A new generation of cognitive psychologists confronted cognitive work in control centers and tried to extend concepts from psychology to deal with actual practitioners performing substantive tasks with many kinds of tools (Woods, 1982b, 1994b; Woods & Roth, 1988a, b; see also chapter 1).

The designation CTA as a method became commonplace in Three Mile Island follow-up meetings in the early 1980s. This community coined the label "Cognitive Task Analysis" in 1981–1982. Just as the research and research needs seemed to beg for the coining of the term "Cognitive Task Analysis":

> The words just seemed to be self-evident and "in the air" at that time. But at the 1982 meeting Jens Rasmussen and I mainly were forcing people to look at the domain operators' relationships as from a Gibsonian perspective. This is what I was doing in our control room redesign project at Westinghouse and as in the discussions we were having with Jens Rasmussen and others at Risø in Denmark. (D. D. Woods, personal communication, 2002)

CTA was used in the Nuclear Regulatory Commission technical report (Sheridan, Jenkins, & Kisner, 1982) and a follow-up publication by Erik Hollnagel and David Woods (1983). Research that followed the Three Mike Island accident orchestrated multiple analytical and empirical techniques to discover how practitioner strategies were adapted to artifacts, problem demands, and organizational pressures (Rasmussen, 1983, 1985, 1986a; Woods & Roth, 1988a). In addition, there was a desire to discover general patterns in the relation of cognition, collaboration, technology, and work demands to generalize from the unique details of specific technologies and domains. A complementarity came to the fore—the studies served practical local goals, and the field context became a laboratory to examine broader themes. The CTA process was more than the use of a single technique to examine cognitive and collaborative work. Research addressed themes that cut across phenomena and particular application domains, including anomaly response, automation surprises, and how to make intelligent systems team players (Rasmussen, Pejtersen, & Goodstein, 1994; Woods & Hollnagel, 2006).

Developments in Instructional Design

Concurrently, research regarding the nature of expertise and ways to promote its acquisition was producing new forms of training. This led to studies of the basis for expertise and the knowledge organization of people at different stages of acquiring expertise (e.g., Glaser et al., 1985; McKeithen, Reitman, Reuter, & Hirtle, 1981). This thread emerged initially from learning research (Glaser, 1976a, b), studies of the nature of expertise (Chi, Feltovich, & Glaser, 1981; Means & Gott, 1988), and the need for better methods for training people for high-performance jobs (Lesgold et al., 1992; Katz et al., 1998; 1993). Starting in the early 1970s, a group of researchers affiliated with the Learning Research and Development Center at the University of Pittsburgh and the Psychology Department at Carnegie Mellon University launched a number of research projects on issues of instructional design in both educational contexts (e.g., elementary-school-level mathematics word problems; college-level physics problems, etc.) and technical contexts in military applications (e.g., the problem solving by electronics technicians) (Glaser et al., 1985; Lesgold et al., 1986).

The research methods that were used evolved out of the decomposition of problem-solving behaviors in terms of "learning hierarchies" (Gagné, 1968), that is, sequences of learning tasks arranged according to difficulty and directional transfer. There was some debate about the extent to which what was perceived as a "behavioral" approach to task analysis could succeed without reference to cognitive structures (V. Shalin, personal communication, 1998), triggered in part by such papers as Gagné's 1974 article "Task Analysis—Its Relation to Content Analysis." Many of the task decompositions did seem largely behavioral or at least microscale, literal descriptions of individual mental actions. For example, Step IVa in a decomposition of the task of adding integers was "use the whole number 0 as the additive identity" (Gagné, Mayor, Garstens, & Paradise, 1962).

In the 1970s, Skinnerian behaviorism was still a force in academic psychology, and "knowledge" was frequently referred to as "verbal association" (see Dixon & Horton, 1968). However, methods referred to as behavioral task analysis, methods that had been used in curriculum design, began to seem incomplete and insufficient. Specifically, they did not capture domain knowledge. They also failed to capture mental processes and strategies, such as the ways that some learners seem able to effectively skip parts of hierarchical behavioral task sequences. Research on problem solving circa 1968–1975 (e.g., Loftus and Suppes's study of computer-aided instruction, 1972) pointed to a need to study underlying processes (of reading comprehension) and the knowledge structures involved in the mathematics domain.

Cognitive Science was on the ascent. A 1974 symposium on cognition and instruction (Klahr, 1976) included investigations that seem to us today to beg for someone to coin the phrase "Cognitive Task Analysis" (see chapters by Greeno, Gregg, Resnick, and Simon and Hayes), having titles such as "Task Analysis in Instructional Design" and "Methods and Models for Task Analysis in Instructional Design." The notion of CTA (if not the explicit term) was seen as a natural contrast with behavioral task analysis (Greeno, 1989). In that same span of a few years, the phrase "Cognitive Task Analysis" was used in a technical report (Greeno, 1978), which appeared in print in 1980 (Greeno, 1980), and also in an article by Gallagher (1979), making a similar plea for the incorporation of the analysis of cognitive tasks into the instructional system design process.

Interest in instructional design quickly became linked to a program of investigation into expertise. In parallel with the other threads described here, researchers in the field of Expertise Studies began to use the term "Cognitive Task Analysis" to refer to the process of identifying the knowledge and strategies that make up expertise for a particular domain and task (Glaser et al., 1985; Lesgold et al., 1986). Study samples shifted from naive, college-aged "subjects" who participated in laboratory tasks using artificial materials (in service of "control" and "manipulation" of variables) to highly skilled, domain-smart participants engaged in tasks that were more representative of the real world in which they practiced their craft (Chi, Feltovich, & Glaser, 1981; Chi, Glaser, & Farr, 1988). Investigators began to shift their attention from artificial and simple problems (e.g., statistical reasoning puzzles, syllogistic reasoning puzzles) to the exploration of human capabilities for making decisions, solving complex problems, and forming "mental models" (Gentner & Stevens, 1983; Klahr & Kotovsky, 1989).

Advances in Knowledge Engineering

The emergence of Expertise Studies in instructional design occurred in parallel with another development that led experimental and cognitive psychologists to conduct CTA. Computer simulation of thinking (e.g., Newell & Simon, 1972) seemed to require methods of protocol analysis, but another strong motivation to develop methods and a methodology was to capture the knowledge and reasoning of subject matter experts (Hoffman, 1986, 1987b).

During the era of expert systems, roughly the late 1970s through the late 1980s, literally hundreds of domains were the subject of system development efforts. In the development of expert systems, there must be some sort of "knowledge elicitation" procedure, as one component to the total process of knowledge acquisition (which also includes knowledge representation, instantiation, and prototyping) (Regoczei & Hirst, 1992; for reviews, see Cooke, 1992, 1994; Gordon & Gill, 1997; Hoffman, Shadbolt, Burton, & Klein, 1995; Olson & Biolsi, 1991). Knowledge elicitation procedures, as these are used in expert system development, would constitute an example of CTA (Hoffman & Lintern, 2006). Although the elicitation of knowledge about domain concepts and principles (the "knowledge base") can be regarded as somewhat distanced from the analysis of physical tasks, the elicitation of experts' reasoning (for the development of an "inference engine") forces one to examine experts' familiar or routine tasks.

A great deal of effort at knowledge acquisition is necessary for the development of expert systems, and thus hundreds of knowledge engineers found themselves immersed in the analysis of diverse domains of human expertise using methods that could be called CTA and CFR. Conversely, the questions about knowledge elicitation led experimental psychologists into Expertise Studies. Some explored the utility of adapting ethnographic interview and observation methods as a means of knowledge elicitation. Others adapted traditional experimental methods for use in eliciting information about cognitive processes.

Thus, the advent of expert systems was interwoven with a shift that occurred in basic research on instructional design and higher cognitive processes. Many researchers came to emphasize such notions as ecological validity and design representativeness (Hoffman & Deffenbacher, 1992; Hoffman & Palermo, 1991; McCabe & Balzano, 1986; Neisser, 1993). As in the field of instructional design, study samples shifted from "subjects" to highly skilled, domain-smart participants (Ericsson & Simon, 1993; Hoffman, 1992b; Shanteau, 1992). Likewise, investigators shifted attention from traditional laboratory topics and methods to the exploration of human capabilities for making decisions and solving complex problems (Anderson, 1983; Cohen, 1989; Gentner & Stevens, 1983; Neisser, 1982; Scribner, 1984; Simon, 1973a, b; Sternberg & Frensch, 1991). Expertise Studies has spanned a wide gamut of topics, some of which seem more relevant to academia (e.g., physics problem solving), but many that extend well beyond traditional experimental psychology (e.g., expertise in manufacturing engineering, medical diagnosis, taxicab driving, bird-watching, etc.). Cognitive psychology took something of a turn toward applications (see Barber, 1988), triggering considerable debate (e.g., Banaji & Crowder, 1989; Hoffman & Deffenbacher, 1993). Nevertheless, today the phrase "real world" seems to no longer require scare quotes (see Hollnagel, Hoc, & Cacciabue, 1995).

Developments in Ethnography and Sociology

Ethnographic study of the workplace emerged along with "cognitive anthropology" and an interest in understanding how work cultures are affected by technology change. This led to field observation of practitioners at work in their world, and ethnographies of work (e.g., Jordan & Henderson, 1995; Lynch, 1991), and studies of "situated cognition" (Clancey, 1997). Ed Hutchins's research, first at the Navy Personnel Research and Development Center and then at the University of California–San Diego, contributed to new concepts for human–computer interaction such as the idea of the direct manipulation interface (Hutchins, Hollan, & Norman, 1985) and to new ideas about the study of "cognition in the wild" (Hutchins, 1995a). Classic studies in this area include the following:

- Hutchins's (1995a) studies of navigation, in which he described the interplay of navigation tools and collaborative activity in maritime navigation,
- Hutchins's (1995b) study of flight crew teamwork,
- Orr's (1996) study of how photocopier repair technicians acquire knowledge and skill by sharing their "war stories" with one another, and
- Lave's (1988, 1997) studies of traditional methods used in crafts such as tailoring and the nature of math skills used in everyday life settings such as shopping and dieting.

Lucy Suchman's work (1987) is regarded as a landmark, highlighting an explosion of interest in ethnography of the workplace (e.g., Barley & Orr, 1997; Orr, 1985). Suchman asserted that many problems are solved "on-the-hoof" and utilize resources that are inherent in the problem context to support problem solving—in contrast to notions that problem-solving behaviors are structured by preformulated mental representations and procedures, such as plans (cf. Miller, Galanter, & Pribram, 1960). Situated cognition theorists advocate a view that such representations are "best viewed as a weak resource for what is primarily ad hoc activity" (Suchman, 1987, p. ix).

Related to cognitive anthropology is a field known as the "Sociology of Scientific Knowledge" (e.g., Barnes, 1974; Collins, 1993, 1997; Knorr-Cetina, 1981; Latour & Woolgar, 1979; Lynch, 1991, 1993; Lynch & Edgerton, 1988; Williams, Faulkner, & Fleck, 1998). Researchers within this approach proposed that the acquisition of scientific knowledge is as much a social accomplishment as a process of objective empiricism and thus argued that science is a largely "constructive" process that cannot be analyzed without consideration of the historical, cultural, and social context in which it occurs. Research in this area has involved detailed analyses of science as it is practiced, for example, the history of the development of new lasers and of gravity wave detectors, the role of consensus in decisions about what makes for proper practice, breakdowns in the attempt to transmit skill from one laboratory to another, and failures in science or in the attempt to apply new technology.

Methods of investigation used in ethnography and the Sociology of Scientific Knowledge vary widely but could be described as ethnographic in nature. Ethnography is the empirical–observational study of a particular group or society, and makes great use of fieldwork to study the behaviors and activities of humans in their environments (see Clancey, 2001; Dekker, Nyce, & Hoffman, 2003; Fetterman, 1998). In this approach, cognitive variables are regarded as part of a complex and dynamic mix, which includes social, cultural, and historical aspects of the work context. The objective is to gain a deeper appreciation of how skilled actions depend on the context that includes groups of individuals, the space they work in, and the tools they work with (Anderson, 1994; Clancey, 2001). These considerations might, or likely would, be missed during traditional process descriptions of "on-task" work that might concentrate on sources of work information such as written procedures, policy manuals, job descriptions, business process models, and work-flow models. Ethnographic investigation also considers broader social factors, such as the ways in which expertise might be socially determined, how expertise relates to power politics, the ways it may or may not give rise to successful technological innovation, the ways in which expertise may or may not relate to effective social policy making, and the implications of all this for such things as the management of technological change (see Fleck & Williams, 1996; Harper, 2000; Mieg, 2001) and the creation of new technologies (Ball & Ormerod, 2000; Dekker et al., 2003).

In the ethnographic approach, actual situations are taken as natural laboratories wherein investigators shape the conditions of observation through scenario design. A variety of methods can be used that allow the observation and recording of a given work domain by researchers. Researchers are likely to be involved in the domain for a considerable length of time, sometimes more than a year. For example, in her paper on the use of metaphors in the scientific laboratory, Knorr-Cetina (1995) drew on 5 years of ethnographic research conducted in physics and biology laboratories.

More specifically, the research methods used within this approach include directly observing and documenting behavior using note taking, detailed analysis of videotaped events of behavior, and formal and informal interviews with domain participants (for examples, see Ball & Ormerod, 2000; Clancey, 2001; Knorr-Cetina, 1981). The researcher may shadow, or actually work with, the people being studied. As Knorr-Cetina (1981) argued, a good understanding of a domain, and the operatives who work within it, is unlikely "to be gained from observation alone. We must also listen to the talk [by operatives] about what happens, the asides and the curses, the mutterings of exasperation, the questions they ask each other, the formal discussions and lunchtime chats" (p. 21). More traditional laboratory studies are also used, but natural, real-world situations are taken as the starting point for their creation. Laboratory studies are regarded as just *one* method of investigation among many, in contrast to the sole method of investigation in the Cognitive Sciences. Some traditional Cognitive Science methods such as protocol analysis are also employed. These techniques have been used by ethnographers to analyze the interplay of people within groups and with technology in the observed situations (Cross, Christiaans, & Dorst, 1996).

An example of work in this thread is the study by Bruno Latour and Steve Woolgar (1979). They spent 21 months observing endocrinologists in the laboratory. They made field notes throughout, and analyzed research papers produced out of work undertaken in the laboratory and documents relevant to the daily activities of the scientists. Formal interviews were conducted with members of the laboratory teams and with staff from other laboratories. The researchers also worked within the laboratory as technicians and, therefore, were able to learn about laboratory life from within the culture by participating in conversations among scientists and actually experiencing the nature of the work. Latour was given his own office space in a prominent area of the work domain and proposed that his physical proximity to the work being undertaken aided the research process. (See Knorr-Cetina [1981] for details of the application of similar methods in the domain of science.)

The Emergence of Naturalistic Decision Making

Attempts to apply theories and methods from the field of "Judgment and Decision Making" to complex, real-world settings led to new methods of conducting structured interviews for studying decision making and to new models to describe decision making in real-world settings (e.g., Klein, 1989a, b). Researchers who studied domains such as firefighting and clinical nursing began to note that observations from field studies of experts in action in complex settings were at odds with formal models of decision making that had come from research in the field of Judgment and Decision Making. Those models were analytical and normative. That is, they described how decision making *should* proceed if it is to be "good." The prototypical theory–method is utility analysis, in which all of the alternative decision paths are specified and each is evaluated in terms of costs, benefits, risks, and so on.

The inability of such models to account for, or even make meaningful contact with, results from the field studies prompted the Army Research Institute to sponsor a conference in Dayton, Ohio, in 1989. That conference helped define a new community of practice labeled "Naturalistic Decision Making" (Klein, Orasanu, Calderwood, & Zsambok, 1993). Standard methods were inadequate to investigate how people were actually making decisions. Instead, new methods for observing and interviewing were needed. Klein, Calderwood, and Clinton-Cirocco (1986) described the "Critical Decision Method" to identify and probe the challenging decisions during critical incidents. (See Klein, Calderwood, and MacGregor [1989] and Hoffman, Crandall, and Shadbolt [1998] for descriptions of the method and Klein [1998] for a discussion of its historical development.) Naturalistic Decision Making researchers quickly expanded their focus of interest beyond decision making to encompass a wider array of cognitive functions and processes, including problem detection, planning, and sensemaking (Klein et al., 2003).

Like the other threads, the Naturalistic Decision Making approach dovetailed with work emerging from other arenas, particularly the ethnography and work analysis threads. The analysis of proficient performance had to extend beyond the laboratory to investigate cognitive activity in the field setting. Human factors psychologists found that they needed to focus on decision making in situations marked by time pressure, high risk, ambiguous or missing information, and conflicting goals (Lipshitz, 1993; Orasanu & Connolly, 1993; Woods, 1993), which are the hallmarks of the Naturalistic Decision Making paradigm (see Klein et al., 1993).

Advances in Work Analysis

European academic psychologists, applied psychologists, and industrial (or ergonomics) psychologists had never been "captured" by behaviorism. For example, Adriaan de Groot (1945) used a form of task reflection to explore the strategies of chess masters. In Europe, psychology and applied or industrial psychology evolved more or less continuously (with interruptions caused by the world wars) from psychotechnics to post-WWII observation and interview techniques developed in response to the questions and issues that were being addressed. The paradigm of work analysis has its origins primarily in ergonomics in France, Belgium, and Denmark (see Christensen-Szalanski, 1993; De Keyser, 1992; De Keyser, Decortis, & Van Daele, 1988; Galegher, Kraut, & Egido, 1990; Schraagen, Chipman, & Shalin, 2000, chap. 1; Vicente, 1999).

Engineer Jens Rasmussen and his colleagues at the Risø National Laboratory in Denmark made some important inroads in the engineering aspects of safety in the nuclear power industry, but they found that accidents still happened (Rasmussen, 1981; Rasmussen & Lind, 1981). Hence, they began to conduct observations in the workplace and conduct interviews (e.g., analyses of prototypical problem scenarios). Studies of accidents in domains including aviation as well as nuclear safety showed that safety considerations could not be taken solely from a technical engineering standpoint (see Rasmussen & Rouse, 1981). Research was conducted on domains including electronics troubleshooting, and these investigations revealed additional aspects of human problem solving and strategic reasoning (Rasmussen, 1992).

This European work analysis tradition understood that the study of proficient behavior must extend beyond the laboratory to investigate behavioral and cognitive activity in the field setting (Christensen-Szalanski, 1993; De Keyser, 1992; Galegher, Kraut, & Egido, 1990; Rasmussen, 1992; Sarter & Woods, 1992; Woods, 1993). One of the reasons that the work of Rasmussen et al. is regarded as a landmark is because this notion was taken a step further: The analysis of work in complex sociotechnical systems cannot be conducted solely from a single perspective (see Rasmussen, Pejtersen, & Schmidt, 1990). A variety of perspectives and analytical procedures need to be brought to bear for the researcher to come to a rich understanding of human factors and engineering design issues:

- the larger organization and its values and goals (how roles are allocated to individuals; how the organization is managed and coordinated);
- the work domain (e.g., the analysis of problem spaces);
- the abstract or general functions that the organization, worker, worker–machine system conducts;
- the specific functions that the organization, worker, worker–machine system conducts;
- the cognitive capacities of the human worker (mental models, levels of expertise);
- the worker's activities expressed in domain terms; and
- the worker's activities expressed, for example, in terms of information processing models (i.e., decision trees).

The Risø work had a profound impact on the first generation of cognitive engineers. In discussing the threads we have pointed to other dovetailings and cross-influences. We can now turn to a discussion of the common ground of the threads.

Finding Common Ground

The communities of practice all occurred at the boundaries of traditional, or at least preexisting, areas. This afforded opportunities for sharing and learning. Individuals working in each of the threads or traditions found themselves learning from the findings coming from the other communities, and rediscovering things that had been long known by the others. There also has been cross-fertilization in terms of methods, as people created innovative methods brought them to bear on both old and new problems, and opportunistically learned about each other's work and the traditions from which they had come. Ideally, researchers who study cognitive systems in context, regardless of their specific community, paradigm, or discipline of origin, would come together to identify common core concepts and basic techniques, to delineate various meaningful avenues to reach common goals, and to advance the maturity of field research techniques.

Although we have discussed history in terms of separable communities, these communities are neither conceptually nor empirically distinct. For example, studies from the Cognitive Engineering CTA thread found the same patterns that had been found by ethnographers and expertise researchers (see Suchman, 1988; Woods et al., 1990). Applied cognitive psychology, which some regarded as a form of "Neo-functionalism," placed an emphasis on fieldwork, which had European roots that had already intertwined to some extent with ethnography. But cognitive science added experimental values, because simulators and rapid prototyping technology allowed investigators to control the problems that practitioners faced and allowed the study of new artifacts and the manipulation of interface features to help reveal strategies and work practices. The tradition of critical incident studies in human factors (Flanagan, 1954) was updated to a cognitive work context (e.g., Hoffman, 1987b; Hoffman et al., 1998; Klein, 1989b) to provide another complementary approach to understand what it means to practice in a field of activity.

This being said, historical differences have contributed to a fragmentation of approaches, labels, agendas, claims of priority, technical imperialism, and so on. This makes coherent assessment difficult for all, but it makes things especially confusing for those who are not steeped in any of the individual historical trends. So, what lies at the heart of these different communities? Each has represented an attempt to understand aspects of cognition in context:

- The fundamental reference point for all of these trends is the field or real-world setting.
- All of the communities describe, study, model, and design operational systems in terms of cognitive concepts.
- Each of the communities has been drawn to contextualized study, looking at how experts and teams of practitioners confront significant problems, aided by technological and other types of artifacts—the cognitive system triad (Hoffman, Coffey, et al., 2002).
- The communities share a general approach (and some share methods but give them different names) to capture and apply concepts about cognition in response to challenges created by the transformation of the workplace to place greater emphasis on cognitive and collaborative work.

As they emerged, all of the communities quickly had to confront the challenges in linking analysis to design. These challenges continue to dominate thinking about CTA (Woods & Hollnagel, 2006). How do studies of cognitive work help decide where to spend limited resources in order to have significant impact (because all development processes are resource limited)? How do studies of cognitive work support the innovation process (the studies are necessary but not sufficient as a spark for innovation)? How do the results that characterize cognitive and cooperative activities in the current field of practice inform or apply to the design process, because the introduction of new technology will transform the nature of practice? How does one predict and shape the process of transformation and adaptation that follows technological change? These are the sorts of questions that weave through the following chapters of this book and that we return to in the synthesis in section 3.

Summary

Eight communities of practice in the modern history of CTA emerged in the 1980s. Each was driven by needs arising in a changing world, perceived limitations of traditional methods, and opportunity afforded by new computer technology.

Cognitive psychology arose in the United States, in part, as a reaction against behaviorism. Noam Chomsky's work in linguistics; WWII-era applied research on speech perception, attention, and vigilance; as well as the new field of artificial intelligence in the 1950s set the stage for the mentalistic revolution of the 1960s. Miller, Bruner, Neisser, and others demonstrated that it was scientifically respectable to study cognition. In the 1970s, the Cognitive Science Society was formed, creating an interdiscipline integrating philosophy, artificial intelligence, and psychology. This academic climate profoundly shaped the development of CTA methods in the 1980s.

As previous chapters have detailed, *human factors and ergonomics* researchers were moving toward new approaches for describing and designing tasks for human–machine interaction throughout much of the 20th century. One of the earliest task analysis methods proposed for capturing cognition was HTA developed by Annett and Duncan (1967) in the United Kingdom. Key elements of this seminal work include recognition that some tasks cannot be described as linear sequences of action but instead have contingencies or conditionalities, and an emphasis on goals rather than on sequences of actions.

Cognitive Systems Engineering began with attempts to map mental mechanisms at a microcognitive scale onto specific tasks requiring human–computer interaction. However, this soon led to a broader focus on Cognitive Systems Engineering, which addressed multiple humans interacting with complex technology such as operators in a nuclear power plant control room. After the Three Mile Island accident of 1979, academic cognitive psychologists and human factors researchers sought to extend concepts from psychology to create safer power plants. This rich domain of study was fertile ground for the development of CTA methods, as well as the investigation of anomaly response, automation surprises, and how to make intelligent systems team players.

Instructional design also began to take on a new perspective as research on learning and the nature of expertise changed strategies used for training and education. Work at the University of Pittsburgh's Learning Research and Development Center starting in the 1970s explored instructional design in both education and technical contexts. The research raised questions about whether a behavioral approach to task analysis would be sufficient. Studies of expertise linked to instructional design shifted from using naive, college-aged subjects to highly skilled, domain-smart participants. The tasks of study transitioned from laboratory tasks using artificial materials to real-world tasks.

Within *Experimental Psychology* a need for CTA methods was recognized. As the development of expert systems came to the forefront in the 1970s and 1980s, the need for "knowledge elicitation" procedures to capture knowledge from subject matter experts arose. In this climate, hundreds of knowledge engineers found themselves using methods that could be called CTA and CFR. Questions about knowledge elicitation led some experimental psychologists into studies of expertise. Others explored the utility of adapting ethnographic methods as means of knowledge elicitation. Still others adapted traditional experimental methods for use in eliciting information about cognitive processes.

Within *ethnography* and *sociology* efforts to study the workplace spawned terms such as "cognitive anthropology," focusing on how work cultures are affected by technology change, and "situated cognition," integrating the complexities of the workplace into the study of cognition. The related field of Sociology of Scientific Knowledge posits that scientific knowledge is as much a social accomplishment as a process of objective empiricism. Research methods within these disciplines are ethnographic in nature, considering cognitive variables in the context of social, cultural, and historic aspects of work.

The field of *Naturalistic Decision Making* appeared on the scene as researchers realized the limitations of utility theory in decision-making research. Researchers studying domains such as firefighting and nursing noted that decision making in these settings was quite distinct from the prescribed formal models of decision making that had come from the field of Judgment and Decision Making. Naturalistic Decision Making focuses on studying decision making in situations characterized by time pressure, high risk, ambiguous or missing information, and conflicting goals.

European *work analysis* as advanced by Jens Rasmussen and his colleagues at the Risø Institute addressed the study of accidents in nuclear power plants, aviation, as well as electronics troubleshooting. Work analysis went beyond the study of cognitive activity in field settings to include the notion that analysis of work in complex sociotechnical systems cannot rely solely on a single perspective. Instead, a variety of perspectives and analytical procedures must be brought to bear.

Although cross-fertilization of communities has occurred, historical differences have contributed to a fragmentation of approaches, labels, agendas, claims of priority, technical imperialism, and so on. In spite of these differences, there is a shared goal of understanding cognition in the context of work.

Part 2

The "Perspectives"

6

Introduction to Section 2
The Perspectives

The chapters in section 2 go into detail concerning each of the "perspectives" (or communities of practice): Cognitive Systems Engineering, Expertise Studies, Naturalistic Decision Making, Work Analysis, Sociology/Ethnography, and Human-Centered Computing. In each case, we highlight the key ideas and the ways in which communities have distinguished themselves by reacting against other traditions and views. We provide descriptions and illustrations of the preferred methods of Cognitive Task Analysis (CTA) that are employed and the methodology or theory underlying the methods.

The field of human factors is discussed across chapters and is not represented by a chapter of its own. This deserves some explanation—where did we get these perspectives that we are talking about? Members of some communities of practice are not closely connected to other communities. For instance, until the recent emergence of the study of the sociology of expertise (e.g., Fleck & Williams, 1996; Mieg, 2001), sociologists who studied scientific practices and the sociology of technological innovation were generally not involved in dialog or collaboration with researchers in the area of Expertise Studies. Although some researchers in Expertise Studies are very active in the human factors community, a great many are not. Until recently, ethnographers who studied the modern workplace were largely not involved in dialog and collaboration with Cognitive Systems Engineers, and even saw the Cognitive Systems Engineering view as antithetical to theirs because of Cognitive Systems Engineering's roots in an information processing approach. Researchers in ethnography and in the Sociology of Scientific Knowledge would see little benefit in referring to their methods as CTA. Indeed, they might be a bit off-put at the notion, because their field is, in part, a reaction against information processing psychology, and from their perspective CTA has its main roots in mainstream cognitive psychology. Such contrasts define and shape the boundaries of the various perspectives, boundaries that emerged and persist despite historical and contemporary cross-influences.

This being said, many researchers do live in more than one community of practice. In some cases, they have no single home. For instance, many researchers who consider themselves members of the Naturalistic Decision Making community are also active in the Human Factors and Ergonomics Society. Many Cognitive Systems Engineers see their community as having evolved out of human factors psychology, and indeed see their community as being nearly synonymous with modern human factors—as contrasted with ergonomics. This is related to the reasons why the Human Factors Society renamed itself the Human Factors and Ergonomics Society, with U.S.-based ergonomics having more to do with physical work and anthropometry (e.g., the design of ergonomic chairs, workplace safety issues, etc.). At the same time, there are numerous features that make human factors stand out. One is the historical origins of task analysis in industrial psychology and its post-WWII extension by North American human factors psychology—which we detailed in section 1. Another is the fact that many of the perspectives define themselves, in part, in terms of what they see as the limitation of so-called traditional human factors.

All of these subtleties and complexities of trends and influences will be made clear in the chapters of section 2. Our "gravitational collapsing" of the field of human factors into the Cognitive Systems Engineering perspective emerged as we wrote the book. This being said, the field of human factors does receive special attention and consideration in many places in section 2 and throughout the book.

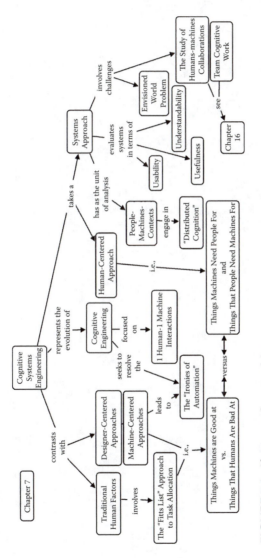

FIGURE 7.1 Chapter 7 Concept Map.

7

Cognitive Systems Engineering

Cognitive Engineering, a term invented to reflect the enterprise I find myself engaged in: neither Cognitive Psychology, nor Cognitive Science, nor Human Factors. It is a type of applied Cognitive Science, trying to apply what is known from science to the design and construction of machines. It is a surprising business. On the one hand, there actually is quite a lot known in Cognitive Science that can be applied. But on the other hand, our lack of knowledge is appalling. On the one hand, computers are ridiculously difficult to use. On the other hand, many devices are difficult to use—the problem is not restricted to computers, there are fundamental difficulties in understanding and using most complex devices. So the goal of Cognitive Engineering is to come to understand the issues, to show how to make better choices when they exist, and to show what the tradeoffs are when, as is the usually case, an improvement in one domain leads to deficits in another.

—Donald A. Norman (1988 p. 31)

Introduction

In the years following World War II, the linear digital computer was adopted as a model for human cognition, and circa 1965 "cognitive psychology" was proclaimed as a valid topic area. Beginning in the 1970s, psychologists could wear two hats—that of the computer scientist and that of the psychologist. "Cognitive engineers" conducted research on human–computer interaction and concerned themselves with such issues as interface design (Redish & Wixon, 2003). Also beginning in the 1970s, one of the pioneers of cognitive psychology who paved the way for the discipline of Cognitive Engineering, Donald Norman, began a series of conceptual and empirical investigations into the design of tools, ranging from household appliances to computers (Norman, 1988, 1990, 1993, 1998). In parallel, researchers in the nuclear power industry were investigating issues of cognitive complexity of power plant control rooms (Hollnagel & Woods, 1983; Rasmussen, 1981).

In this context, two related terms emerged. *Cognitive Engineering,* also known as "human–computer interaction," focused on the study of the "one person–one machine" dyad. This focus was a natural consequence of the introduction of the personal computer, the "workstation," and advances in graphical display and interface design (i.e., menu and mouse). At the same time, work in the nuclear power industry was described as *Cognitive Systems Engineering* (CSE), reflecting a focus on complex sociotechnical systems. These two terms have come to be used somewhat interchangeably, and the two lines of research have many connections. Nevertheless, in this chapter we refer to *Cognitive Systems Engineering*, because Cognitive Task Analysis (CTA) is more tightly linked to the broader systems view that is associated with CSE.

As we pointed out in chapter 1, the phrase "Cognitive Task Analysis" traces its origins, in part, to the field of CSE. To reach the goal of good design for complex systems, pathfinders Erik Hollnagel and David Woods (see Woods, 1982a, b) referred to "studies of worker activities," the discovery of "decision requirements," and the study of the expert's skills, rules, and knowledge. Neither Woods nor Hollnagel saw CTA as being separate from or a precursor to the process of design—design was, and is, regarded as part of cognitive analysis (Hollnagel's marginal notes to Woods, in Woods, 1982a). *Cognitive Systems Engineering* is an umbrella term used to describe a range of approaches, all of which rely on forms of CTA and CFR (Cognitive Field Research), and all of which are intended to lead to technologies (typically, software and workstation systems) that support cognitive work. For example, Cognitive Work Analysis (see chapter 8) would be a considered a CSE approach, as would Decision-Centered Design (see chapter 9) and Situation Awareness-Oriented Design (Endsley, Bolté, & Jones, 2003). New approaches such as Eggleston's (2003) "Work-Centered Design" continue to emerge. However, regardless of the designations and differing emphases, all rely on CTA in some manner to inform the analysis of work and the role of cognition in the work. CTA generally takes a form that Woods (1993; see also Todd & Benbasat, 1987; Waldron, 1985) referred to as "process tracing," taken to mean the analysis by observation of processes of work, involving primarily observations of work, the study of communication patterns, and various types of cognitive interviews.

This chapter focuses on aspects of CSE that have changed the way we think about design, many of which have been presented in the writings of Donald Norman, David D. Woods, and Erik Hollnagel. This chapter also focuses on issues of CTA and CFR methodology, and in particular the scientific status of CTA and CFR relative to laboratory experimentation.

Cognitive Systems Engineering and Human Factors

As we know from the history of science, emerging fields and communities of practice often define themselves, at least in part, in terms of what they are not, in terms of some existing or traditional field against which they are reacting. Sometimes this broaches on describing the traditional field in terms of "straw men," that is, a somewhat simplified or even misleading view of the traditional field. In the case of applied psychology, as we have seen in previous chapters, it is possible to react against "traditional" task analysis to justify CTA, when in fact task analysis was never void of cognition (see chapter 2). It is also possible to react against traditional human factors psychology by arguing that the topic of study (human–machine interaction) necessitates a systems approach. We see this in play in the recent history of CSE.

Both Donald Norman and David Woods found themselves reacting against what they took to be a "traditional" human factors viewpoint, characterized as an approach in which jobs can be broken down to particular tasks, each having well-defined and sequential subtasks that can be specified in terms of physical and cognitive actions and that result in the achievement of fixed and well-defined goals. Other scientists also noted a particular design philosophy to the human factors approach, which Phil Agre (1997) referred to as the "command-and-control" approach:

- Using task analysis, the designer creates what is believed to be an optimal plan, based on existing practices.
- To the greatest extent possible, the existing practices are replaced by computers that enforce plan.
- The human executes a set of fixed rules for the activities that cannot be automated.

Although this philosophy may have worked well for relatively simple tasks that could be well specified (i.e., during the "knobs and dials" era), it seemed to Phil Agre, Erik Hollnagel, David Woods, Jens Rasmussen, and others, that it does not work for the design of complex systems. Traditional task analysis may work for specific actions conducted by individuals who are performing particular, well-specified tasks with well-specified goals. For that very reason, however, the task protocols are brittle: Normatively designed devices, or protocols that prescribe one best way of doing things, are applicable only to the tasks that have been identified and the particular ways of conducting them that have been specified. Normatively designed devices are limited because of their inability to cope with context-conditioned variation. Workers encounter situations for which the device was not well designed, and as a result they cannot and sometimes should not follow the prescriptions. Hence, normative task analysis ends up not being very useful for the analysis of sociotechnical systems.

Another premise taken to typify traditional human factors was that machines are to be designed to compensate for the limitations of the human operator (Flach & Hoffman, 2003). This premise was couched in "Fitts's List." Paul Fitts, leading a panel of academic and U.S. Air Force human factors psychologists, described the human factors approach to machine design (Fitts et al., 1951) by beginning with the idea that some tasks are better performed by machines than by humans, because of human limitations. For instance, calculating is something machines can do better than humans, whereas only humans can perceive patterns and make decisions. Fitts's List is presented in Figure 7.2. The assumptions of this "task allocation" theory are that

1. Functions can be allocated without adjustment for contextual factors, and
2. Functions are allocated statically; that is, once a function is assigned to the human (or the machine), that function will always be conducted by the agent to which it assigned, independent of context and circumstances.

This view has been called MABA–MABA (Machines Are Better At–Men Are Better At) and also the "Machine-Centered view." Donald Norman's expression of the Machine-Centered view is presented in Table 7.1.

A number of scientists have reacted against this normative aspect of traditional human factors psychology, pointing out many weaknesses and issues.

HUMANS SURPASS MACHINES IN THE:

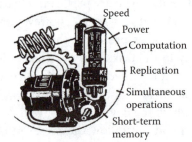

- Ability to detect small amounts of visual or acoustic energy
- Ability to perceive patterns of light or sound
- Ability to improvise and use flexible procedures
- Ability to store very large amounts of information for long periods and to recall relevant facts at the appropriate time
- Ability to reason inductively
- Ability to exercise judgment

MACHINES SURPASS HUMANS IN THE:

- Ability to respond quickly to control signals, and to apply great force smoothly and precisely
- Ability to perform repetitive, routine tasks
- Ability to store information briefly and then to erase it completely
- Ability to reason deductively, including computational ability
- Ability to handle highly complex operations, i.e., to do many different things at once.

FIGURE 7.2 Fitts's List. Reproduced with the permission of the National Academies Archives.

TABLE 7.1 The Machine-Centered View (after Norman, 1988, 1992, 1993, 1998)

People	Machines
Vague	Precise
Disorganized	Orderly
Distractible	Not distractible
Emotional	Not emotional
Illogical	Logical

Limitations of the Machine-Centered View

The Machine-Centered view assumes that machines are static, that is, their capabilities and functionalities are relatively fixed, when in fact they are always being improved. Furthermore, the more "intelligent" machines become, the more they can "starve cognition" in the sense of making it more difficult for the human to understand what the machines are doing and why. In this way, machines can make it less likely for people to develop their own knowledge and skills; people can become "de-skilled" (Bainbridge, 1981, 1983, 1989, 1992; Sheridan, 1997).

In one of his treatments of the topic, Donald Norman focused on the value judgments that are integral to the Machine-Centered view:

1. The capabilities of machines are valued more highly than the capabilities of humans.
2. Machines have certain needs, and the role of the human is to fulfill them.

> Machines need precise, accurate control and information. No matter that this is what people are bad at providing, if this is what machines need, this is what people must provide ... The industrialized, machine-centered view of the person includes such terms as imprecise, sloppy, distractible, emotional, and illogical. Each one is a negative attribution of people, especially compared with machines. Machines are precise, neat, orderly; they concentrate on their task, they are logical. See what a badly engineered piece of machinery we are? (Norman, 1993, p. 223)

The parts that could be automated were automated, and the leftovers were given to humans.

According to the Machine-Centered view, machines are said to be more reliable than humans. However, sociotechnical workplaces are characterized by unanticipated and surprise events, variability, and rapid change (Woods, 2002; Woods & Dekker, 2000; Woods & Shattuck, 2000). Humans are context sensitive and, therefore, are able to update their priorities and expectations in any given scenario on a moment-to-moment basis based on the changing context, whereas machines are literal minded and disconnected from the world and thus are context insensitive. As a consequence, in modern work environments, a machine might respond reliably, but to outdated contextual information, and thus humans would soon learn not to rely on the machine. Cognitive scientists have argued that the human is required to intervene to repair the shortcomings of machines in many scenarios and events that characterize the modern workplace.

Machines have become labeled as "brittle" devices because the external environment (such as tasks, goals, and problems) must always be fitted to the machine, a process that requires time and effort by the human. Brittle designs have profound negative consequences:

> [The] automation works best when conditions are normal. When conditions become difficult—say, there is a storm and an engine, a radio, an electrical generator fails—then the automation takes over when it is least needed, gives up when it is most needed. When the engine fails, often with no advance warning, people are suddenly thrust into the process, suddenly asked to figure out the current state of the system, what has gone wrong, and what should be done. (Norman, 1993, p. 225)

An even stronger argument against the Machine-Centered View of task analysis and task allocation is that it is literally impossible to design good technologies by following traditional notions and methods. For instance, leading human factors specialist Thomas Sheridan argued,

> There is a tendency to fall into the trap of analyzing the task as a series of steps for a human to look at particular existing displays and operate particular existing controls—the very displays and controls which constitute the present interface one seeks to improve upon or automate. The correct way to analyze the task is with each named step, to specify the information to be obtained and/or stored, the decisions to be made, and the actions to be taken, independent of the human or machine means to achieve those steps. (1997, p. 90)

Donald Norman (1988; see also Billings, 1997; Flanagan, Huang, Jones, & Kasif, 1997, pp. 65–67; Sarter, Woods, & Billings, 1997; Sheridan, 1997) identified a host of things that are wrong with technologies that are designed according to the Machine-Centered view.

Claim made about the new technology: Work will be enhanced. Experience shows that, in fact, work and roles are changed. Although some things may be made easier, new things will be hard. New types of clumsiness appear. People get bewildered. Computers can be hard to use and difficult to understand. "Automation can starve cognition if the human is not kept in sufficient communication with what the automation is doing or intending" (Sheridan, 1997, p. 89).

Claim made about the new technology: Worker resources will be freed up by off-loading work to the machines. Experience shows that what actually happens is that new kinds of cognitive work are created, and they often have to be conducted at the wrong times in terms of the worker's mental workload.

Claim made about the new technology: The machine will provide the kinds of feedback the worker needs. Experience shows that new and unanticipated types of feedback are needed to support people's new roles.

Claim made about the new technology: The machine will be more flexible than previous machines. Experience shows that there is an explosion of new features, options, and operating modes that create new demands, new kinds of errors, and new paths to failure.

Claim made about the new technology: The machine will reduce human error. New forms of error are created because of new kinds of coordination breakdowns.

Claim made about the new technology: Data overload will be mitigated. Experience shows that the computers do not help people cope with data overload and in many circumstances actually contribute to it. As software gets fancier and fancier (what Norman, 1988, called "creeping featurism"), it requires the user to know more and more.

Claim made about the new technology: Worker resources will be freed up by focusing the worker's attention on the right things and requiring the worker to possess less knowledge. Experience shows that the worker has more threads to track, making it harder to maintain awareness of all of the activities. New knowledge and skills are required.

Claim made about the new technology: The machine will be able to act autonomously. Experience shows that the machine does not operate as a team player. When acting on its own, it does things the human does not anticipate or understand.

Some of the reasons for the gaps between the promise of technology and the results of technological interventions lie in the nature of the complex sociotechnical workplace and its mismatch with the Machine-Centered view. This complexity is illustrated by studies performed by David Woods and his colleagues in such domains as nuclear power plant operation and operations at NASA's Mission Control (Patterson, Watts-Perotti, & Woods, 1999). Communication loops link workers, facilitating human-to-human coordination. For each link, different meanings are communicated and different things are coordinated, planned, and synchronized. Communication supports error correction and detection at the team and organization levels. Machines present data, but workers talk about events in ways that are sometimes abstracted from the data and signal the activities that have been spawned. Communications also involve conveying a stance or opinion about decisions. Puzzlement, subteam conflict, or disagreement gives cues about when someone needs to step in with resolutions. Cooperative advocacy debates spawn alternative hypotheses and alternative plans, more possibilities come to mind, and a deeper exploration of assumptions and consequences occurs. Workers in sociotechnical contexts cope with complexity not just through fancy machine mediators and complex highly specified procedures but also through coordination and continuing investments in sharing knowledge and expertise.

Some of the reasons for the gaps between the promise of new technology and the results of technological interventions lie in the nature of the process by which new technologies are created. Arguments on this topic involved a reaction not just against the Machine-Centered view but also against another acronym in the acronym soup.

Cognitive Systems Engineering Contrasted With Designer-Centered Design

"Designers have incomplete and inaccurate models of how workload is distributed over time and phase of task and of how practitioners manage workload to avoid bottlenecks in particular fields of activity" (Flanagan et al., 1997, p. 66). "All designers in some sense believe they are taking a 'human-centered' approach, but ... their own intuitions of 'what the user needs' somehow get in the way" (Roth, 1997b, p. 250). Woods and Patterson (2000) argued that there is a striking contrast between the effects that designers proposed before design implementation and the actual post-implementation effects. Similarly, Norman (1988, cited in Winograd & Woods, 1997) and others have commented that modern computer system designers appear to have formed a conspiracy against human memory after observing the effects of memory burdens imposed by modern computers. "Enter a workplace and we almost always find that users keep paper notes as a kind of external memory to keep track of apparently arbitrary things that a new computer system demands they remember to be able to interact with the system" (Flanagan et al., 1997, p. 66).

During the Gulf War, technology that was designed to circumvent challenges facing soldiers actually ended up creating new challenges:

> Much of the equipment ... was designed to ease the burden on the operator, reduce fatigue, and simplify the tasks involved in combat. ... Almost without exception, technology did not meet the goal of unencumbering the military personnel operating the equipment. ... As a result,

virtually every advance in ergonomics was exploited to ask military personnel to do more, do it faster and do it in more complex ways. ... One very real lesson of the Gulf War is that new tactics and technology simply result in altering the pattern of human stress to achieve a new intensity and tempo of combat. (Codesman & Wagner, 1996, p. 25)

It is during what Woods and Patterson (2000) called periods of "escalation" that the shortcomings of technology are revealed, and it is at these times when system failures are most catastrophic. For example, Cook and his colleagues (Cook & Woods, 1996; van Charante, Cook, Woods, Yue, & Howie, 1993) studied physicians in operating rooms who were working with a new interface displaying information about the medical status of patients. They observed that physicians needed to allocate more attentional resources to, and therefore recall knowledge about, the interface during critical periods of the operation, that is, during periods when cognitive resources were needed for patient care.

Another negative consequence of Designer-Centered Design involves the problem of data overload (Woods & Watts, 1997). Human ability to digest and interpret data has been exceeded by the quantity of data that can be produced by powerful new technologies, such as sensor systems. Technologists have designed systems that can deliver large quantities of data to the user easily and sometimes quickly. Examples include systems that allow switching among multiple displays that comprise a variety of documents and other data sources: It is easy and common for developers to create large collections of data and hide them behind a narrow keyhole (paraphrased from Woods & Watts, 1997, p. 619). However, navigating across the screens demands time and cognitive resources if the operator is to avoid getting lost or disoriented. This allocation of time and resources interferes with, and detracts from, the operator's actual work. As a consequence, less of the data is used than would be desirable. For example, Woods, Patterson, and Roth (1998) conducted a study of intelligence analysts searching for information using an information search software agent. They found that analysts did not take full advantage of the data sets, owing to the large amount of information available and the shortcomings of the search system. To elaborate, analysts did not characterize the database available to them, they narrowed in on a small set of documents, they appeared to read the first documents they opened more carefully than later ones, and they did not conduct new searches after initial ones.

Woods and Watts (1997) provided examples from studies of system control to demonstrate the effect of display disorientation. In a study of nuclear power plant control (Easter, 1991), a new control room design that was under development was found to have over 16,000 screen displays that could be navigated. Developers realized that this would cause users to be very inefficient when searching for the correct configuration of displays required for a particular task. Woods and Watts argued that in domains such as piloting, space flight control, hypertext searching, nuclear power plant control, and medical practice, these shortcomings have serious ramifications for performance: People spend their time adapting and developing strategies required to work around technological shortcomings rather than on leveraging the strengths of the technology.

Another inclination in Designer-Centered Design is to attempt to automate every-thing that can be automated (e.g., Sarter & Woods, 1992, 1995, 1997). Cognitive scientists have discovered various shortcomings with automated systems that have lead them to warn against trying to automate tasks wherever possible. Sarter and Woods (1992, 1994, 1995, 1997; see also Mosier, 1997) identified a class of automation-related problems that they labeled *automation surprises*. Automation surprises occur when users are surprised by actions taken (or not taken) by automated agents. Surprises are caused by miscommunication and misassessments due to the lack of feedback between the automation and users, which can lead to a gap between the user's under-standing (mental model) of what the automated systems are set up to do, what they are actually doing, and what they are going to do. Thus, automation surprises occur when machines act in a way that contradicts the expectations of their operatives. Surprises have been shown to be a significant cause of accidents (Sarter, Woods, & Billings, 1997; Woods & Sarter, 2000).

> The complexity created when automated systems are not human or practice-centered is best expressed by the questions the users posed when working with "clumsy" machine agents: "What is it doing now?," "What will do next?," "How did I get into this mode/state?," "Why did it do this?," "Why won't it do what I want?," "Stop interrupting me while I am busy!," "I know there is some way to get it to do what I want," "How do I stop this machine from doing this?" (Woods & Sarter, 2000, p. 329)

Woods and Roth (1988b) provided an example from the European Coal and Steel Com-munity (1976) of the negative consequences of the introduction of automated systems:

> The 1976 Hoogovens [steel plant] report details how supervisors of newly commissioned process control systems in steel plants had little ability to see the autonomous process in action, and the complexity of process activities obscured sources of problems and malfunctions. To supervisors it was often unclear what kind of intervention should take place, and when or whether they should intervene at all. Unsure of how their manual intervention would interfere with automatic anomaly compensation, supervisors frequently left anomalies to escalate. (p. 16)

Escalation, display disorientation, and automation surprises are created in part by the "substitution myth" that lies at the heart of Designer-Centered Design: the naive assumption that attempting to replace human manual work with an automated alternative will not cause additional changes in interactions between the processes involved in the work and the other ongoing processes in the work environment (Chow, Christoffersen, Woods, Watts-Perotti, & Patterson, 2000).

The negative consequences of Designer-Centered Design can be expressed as "ironies of automation."

The Ironies of Automation

> Despite steady technological advances operators are still required to intervene in the control of automated systems, for instance to cope with emergencies or to improve the productivity of a discrete manufacturing process. Expertise … on which the support system is based [should be] apparent from the way the system works. Automation and support systems should not be impenetrable black boxes. (Hollnagel, Hoc, & Cacciabue, 1995 p. 282)

In a study of the activities of nuclear power plant operators in simulated emergencies, Emilie Roth (1997a) demonstrated the limitations of detailed procedural guidance. For one thing, even in normal situations, "pre-planned procedures do not eliminate the need for operators to develop diagnostic and response strategies on their own" (p. 181). In both routine situations and abnormal ones, operators engage in knowledge-based reasoning in a search for causal understanding, the generation of expectations, and adaptation to changing circumstances. "While operators did need to know pre-planned procedures, that did not relieve them of the challenge of developing their own understanding. Not only did they need to understand events in the plan, but they also needed to know the assumptions and logic underlying the pre-planned procedures, the response plans that the procedures embodied, the rationale of the response plans" (p. 181). This seems ironic, because preplanned procedures are supposed to lessen the burdens of operators.

A number of ironies of automation have been eloquently described by Lisanne Bainbridge of University College London (Bainbridge, 1983). In the context of automation for process control, Bainbridge described a number of ironies, some of which refer to operator tasks and some to proposed solutions. Though expressed as cautionary tales for CSE back in 1983, they ring true today.

One consequence of automation is that the human is actually given a nearly impossible task. If a process can be specified and a computer can make complex decisions more quickly and effectively than a human, the operator must determine when the automation is working properly. "The monitor needs to know what the correct behavior of the process should be. ... Such knowledge requires special training or special displays ... [there may be] no way in which the human operator can check in real-time that the computer is following its rules correctly" (p. 776).

A second consequence is that skills deteriorate when they are not used. As we know from studies of vigilance, "an operator will not monitor the automatics effectively if they have been operating acceptably for a long period" (p. 776). The operator has less opportunity to explore and understand how the process is working. "An operator will only be able to generate successful new strategies for unusual situations if he has an adequate knowledge of the process ... the operator has in his head not raw data about the process state but the results of making predictions and decisions about the process which will be useful in future situations." This develops only through practice with feedback, and the monitoring role often precludes that.

A third consequence involves what happens when an automated process goes awry. "If the human is not involved in on-line control he will not have a detailed knowledge of the current state of the system. ... When manual take-over is needed there is likely to be something wrong with the process so that unusual actions will be needed to control it, and one can argue that the operator needs to be more rather than less skilled. ... By taking away the easy parts of his task, automation can make the more difficult parts of the human operator's task more difficult" (pp. 775, 777; see also Mosier, 1997). Monitoring is often predicated on the notion that the operator can call in specialized expertise in unusual situations. Here too is an irony: "The supervisor too will not be able to take over if he has not been reviewing his relevant knowledge or practicing a crucial skill" (p. 776).

In sum, the monitor has a job that is at once very boring and very responsible, "yet there is no opportunity to acquire or maintain the qualities required to handle the responsibility ... [when] the job is 'de-skilled' by being reduced to monitoring" (p. 776). Bainbridge cited studies showing that job satisfaction is higher and stress lower when workers are actively engaged in the control of processes that are complex yet highly controllable.

Potential solutions to these conundrums have themselves resulted in ironies of automation. One approach is to create alarms and specialized displays for use in certain kinds of unusual situations. Catastrophic problems can be easy to detect. However, the trends that show a path to failure are not always obvious; displays that are ideal for normal situations may disguise abnormal ones. Furthermore, the automated systems work constantly to correct deviations from the norm, and thus when an alarm sounds or a catastrophic break has occurred, the trend may be beyond the capacity of the human monitor to understand and act on quickly, compounded by the fact that the operator will be most practiced in using the displays that are for routine operations and routine monitoring activities. And if the human operator does not believe or agree with the computer, he may be unable to trace back what it was that the computer did.

Another approach is to create displays that are designed to match the operator's level of skill (perhaps based on Rasmussen's levels of skills versus rules versus knowledge; see chapter 8) or proficiency level (e.g., trainee versus journeyman versus expert). In theory, the computer could detect the level of skill or strategic style of the operator and adjust the display accordingly. Bainbridge argued that such capabilities of multiple displays might confuse rather than help:

> The changes between knowledge-based thinking and "reflex" reaction is not solely a function of practice, but also depends on the uncertainty of the environment, so that the same task elements may be done using different types of skill at different times. ... We do not know how confused operators would be by display changes which were not under their own control ... although operators evidently do think at different levels of complexity and abstraction at different times, it is not clear that they would be able to use, or choose, many different displays under time stress. (p. 778)

Another irony that stems from the creation of better interfaces links back to the issue of the degradation of knowledge:

> The more processing for meaning that some data has received, the more effectively it is remembered. This makes one wonder how much the operator will learn about the structure of the process if information about it is presented so successfully that he does not have to think about it to take it in. It certainly would be ironic if we find that the most compatible display is not the best display to give the operator after all! A highly compatible display [that] supports rapid reactions [may not support] acquisition of the knowledge and thinking skills needed in abnormal conditions. (p. 778)

There are also ironies that are resultant from training. "It is inadequate to expect the operator to react to unfamiliar events solely by consulting operating procedures. These cannot cover all the possibilities, so the operator is expected to monitor them and fill in the gaps. However, it is ironic to train operators in following instructions and then put them in the system to provide intelligence" (p. 777). High-fidelity simulations can help workers maintain skills and can provide opportunities to practice some nonroutine situations, but they cannot help in dealing with unknown faults and complex failures having multiple causes that cannot be anticipated (and hence cannot be simulated). A final irony is that "the most successful automated systems, with rare need for manual intervention ... may need the greatest investment in human operator training" (p. 777).

Thus, for a number of reasons it is necessary for the human to be able to understand and follow the operations of the automation. This is, of course, an irony that the automated system was created to help the human cope with the complexity of process being controlled but ends up forcing the human to understand the complexities of the automated system. This can make human performance worse in a number of ways. For instance, when the operator does not understand or trust the automation, he will attempt to make control decisions anyway, and so the additional task of having to monitor the automation adds to workload—ironic, because automation is intended to reduce workload.

Bainbridge cited instances in which automation does help, for instance, aircraft autopilots that work to free the pilot from online control and thus allow the pilot to think about the challenges or abnormalities.[1] In such cases, the human knows which process the computer is thinking about and (to some degree) what the computer is trying to accomplish. Good interfaces are ones in which key types of information are presented in dedicated displays (e.g., one display of process plant layout and another of process functionality). "Operators should not have to page between displays to obtain information about abnormal states in parts of the process other than the one they are currently thinking about, nor between displays giving information needed within a single decision process" (p. 778).

This brings us to the viewpoint that CSE has established to counter the Machine-Centered and Designer-Centered views.

The Human-Centered Viewpoint

Woods and Watts (1997) reviewed interface use across a variety of domains and found that users who were provided with interfaces with a flexibility to specify various features, displays, and user modes preferred to specify a simple and spatially dedicated representation of their work domain. The display was then left largely unchanged by users. This strategy contributed to efficiency: Users tailored the display so that it provided satisfactory service without consuming cognitive resources that were needed for their work. This finding concerning the mitigation of display disorientation hints at the value of what came to be called a "Human-Centered" approach, in contrast with both Designer-Centered Design and the Machine-Centered view.[2]

Norman (1993, 1998) also expressed a Human-Centered view, offering a different characterization of the five attributes given in Table 7.1. This different view is presented in Table 7.2. The focus here is on the things humans are good at, their natural abilities—things that are not referenced in the Machine-Centered view.

As Table 7.2 indicates, the Human-Centered view emphasizes human cognitive capabilities that machines cannot possess rather than human weaknesses for which

TABLE 7.2 Norman's Human-Centered View

People	Machines
Creative	Dumb
Flexible	Rigid
Attentive to change	Insensitive to change
Resourceful	Unimaginative
Decisions are flexible because they are based on qualitative as well as quantitative assessment, modified by the special circumstances and context.	Decisions are consistent but only because they are based solely on quantitative evaluation of numerically specified, context-free variables.

TABLE 7.3 An "Un-Fitts List" (adapted from Hoffman, Feltovich, et al., 2002)

Machines		People	
Are limited in that …	Need people to …	Are not limited in that …	But need machines to …
Sensitivity to context is low and is ontology limited	To keep them aligned to the context.	Sensitivity to context is high and is knowledge and attention driven.	To keep them informed of context.
Sensitivity to change is low and recognition of anomaly is ontology limited.	To keep them stable given the variability and change inherent in the world.	Sensitivity to change is high and is driven by the recognition of anomaly.	To align and repair their perceptions because they rely on mediated stimuli.
Adaptability to change is low and is ontology limited.	To repair their ontologies.	Adaptability to change is high and is goal driven.	Affect positive change following situation change.
They are not "aware" of the fact that their model of the world is itself in the world.	Keep the model aligned with the world.	They are aware of the fact that their model of the world is itself in the world.	To computationally instantiate their models of the world.

machines might compensate. Another way of expressing this is in terms of the Woods-Hoffman "un-Fitts List" (Hoffman, Hayes et al., 2002), presented in Table 7.3.

The Human-Centered view also involves a number of guiding principles that stem from its position that sociotechnical workplaces must be understood from a systems perspective.

Distributed Cognition

Traditional human factors designers have tended to regard cognition involved in workplaces as if it were relatively isolated as a single activity. However, cognition in collaborative work environments is often distributed:

> One can look at operational systems—the individual people, the organization both formal and informal, the high technology artifacts (display alarms, intelligent tutoring systems, computer-based visualization) and the low-technology artifacts (displays, alarms, procedures, paper notes, training programs) intended to support human practitioners … as a single cognitive system. (Woods, 1994b, p. 3).

This concept of distributed cognition is explored further in the chapter on sociological perspectives (chapter 7). Ed Hutchins and others have highlighted the importance of looking at cognition as an embedded activity rather than a process that takes place solely in the head of an individual (Hutchins, 1995a; Suchman, 1987).

Cognitive Systems Engineers have attempted to move the unit of analysis for design beyond that of the "one computer–one human" dyad:

> In building and studying technologies for human use, researchers and designers often see the problem in terms of two separate systems (the human and the computer) with aspects of inter-action between them. This focuses attention on the people and the technology in isolation, de-emphasizing the activity that brings them together. In human-centered design we try to make new technology sensitive to the constraints and pressures operating in the actual field of activity. (Woods & Sarter, 2000, p. 339)

Woods has asserted that an appropriate approach to the design of workplaces begins with an investigation of the intersection of the people who do the work, the technology used to do the work, and the environment in which the work is done. These three aspects of cognitive work in context have been called the cognitive systems triad (Winograd & Woods, 1997; Woods & Roth, 1988b), and it is the study of the interaction of the aspects of the triad that would yield better design results. In contrast, systems research and development has been focused on exploiting advances in technology. This focus has caused many issues to be overlooked (van Charante et al., 1993; Woods & Cook, 1991). As Norman (1993) recalled, system design in the past was succinctly described by the motto for the 1933 Chicago World's Fair: "Science finds, industry applies, man conforms." This approach still influences the design process of many modern work systems: Consider this example from air traffic control (ATC):

> Despite the intentions of those involved in ATC improvements, many developments remain fundamentally technology-centered. Developing the technology (automatic dependent surveil-lance, conflict probes, digital communications) remains the primary activity around which all else is organized. The focus is on pushing the technological frontier; on creating the technologi-cal system in order to influence human cognition of human activity. These efforts are likely to produce ideas … that are based on generous assumptions about human performance. Similarly, these efforts are likely to produce computerised support that is not cooperative from the human controller's perspective. Indeed, it can make the easy problems in a controller's life go away, but make the hard ones even harder. (Dekker & Woods, 1999a, p. 95)

Thus, Norman (1993, cited in Winograd & Woods, 1997) and Woods (1996) argued that better design results would be obtained if the process of design was rearranged as "People propose, science studies, technology conforms."

The Environment–Cognition Relationship

Also related to the systems stance, CSE emphasizes how the environment might influ-ence human cognition and activity, as evidenced by the environmental component of the cognitive systems triad. The notion that mental phenomena are the predominant influences on cognition is not really abandoned, but environmental phenomena are given equal consideration in terms of their influence on work. As the previous example about the context sensitivity of humans showed, cognition is an activity that is not always entirely private, isolated, and pensive but often inextricably related to the context in which it occurs, in that it is an integral part of ongoing activity and fundamentally social and interactive (see also chapter 11). Woods (1998a) commented that research has revealed that work systems comprise a variety of human and machine agents that are embedded in a larger group, profession, and organizational institutional context that both constrains and provides resources for their activities.

As a consequence, the manner in which a problem is represented in the environment (e.g., through interface design) affects the cognition required to undertake that problem in an either facilitating or impeding way. For example, the nature of artifacts, such as technological devices, shape the cognitive work required to solve that problem (Norman, 1993; Zhang & Norman, 1994). The same problem scenario presented in different environmental contexts leads to different cognitive work, different solution processes, and, in turn, different performance levels and outcomes (Woods, 1995; Woods & Sarter, 2000). Both the agent and the environment must be understood in terms of their relationship to each other; what Woods (1994b) called the agent–environment mutuality.

"Wrapped Packages"

According to Cognitive Systems Engineers, "traditional" task analysis is of limited value because it does not take a systems approach. It focuses on specific actions conducted by individuals who are performing particular, well-specified tasks with well-specified goals. It treats the machine as an artifact that can be designed independently of the needs and capabilities of the human operator. However, in complex sociotechnical contexts, the more or less visible activities are part of a larger process of collaboration and coordination, shaped by the artifacts and shaping how those artifacts function in the workplace and how they are adapted to the multiple goals and constraints of the organizational context and the work domain. These factors of complex artifacts, dynamic worlds, cognitive work, coordinated activity, and organizational dynamics do not present themselves to CTA researchers one at a time, pristine and isolated. Rather they come in association with each other, embodied in the particular, cloaked by some observer's vantage point. In other words, cognitive systems in context come in a "wrapped package" of interdependent and changing variables (Woods, 1993).

Richard Cook (2006) provided examples of the concept of a "wrapped package" in his work on medical safety. Cook's study was concerned with hospital intensive care units (ICUs) and showed how decision making and sources of error in the hospital workplace were determined not just by technical aspects of the domains (e.g., medical expertise) but by interactions among technical and organizational aspects that included resource availability, procedural rules, and team issues; hence, a wrapped package. In the hospital studied by Cook, workers had developed an argot for efficient communication purposes. One such example of this argot was the term *bumpable.* This term applied to a patient who was occupying a bed in an ICU but could be moved out of the unit if more critical patients needed to be admitted under emergency circumstances. However, being bumpable had additional connotations and implications for the various work areas within the domain that extended beyond this simple definition. An excerpt from Cook describes this:

> Practitioner argot is often regarded as simple shorthand for specific technical domain language. But the suggestion here is that argot performs a more complex function than simply standing in, one for one, for technical terms. The practitioner language provides useful aggregates of domain knowledge. … Being bumpable means having temporarily taken on a certain characteristic that has individual and larger group meanings. Medical stability, the threat of future clinical events, the ease with which these may be detected, the consequences of failing to detect them, all play into the assignment of this state. But being bumpable is more; it depends not only on inherent characteristics of the patient but on the states of the other patients, the needs of the other units, the other available resources. Being bumpable involves comparisons, contrasts, and expectations. It is not a static circumscribed technical term, like "coronary artery disease" or "diabetic ketoacidosis," but a fluid, dynamic, complex, time limited, assessment—characteristics that it shares with the domain. It subsumes a variety of local factors, local issues, local limits and local capabilities. Bumpable is not ephemeral or insubstantial; it has real meaning that is subject to negotiation between practitioners and throughout the organization. The argot is a powerful tool used to express the relationships between higher and lower abstraction levels, neither just technical nor just organizational but rather both. That practitioners develop and employ such argot indicates that their work is not divided between technical and organizational elements but about the interplay between these. (p. 33–34)

Cook investigated an incident in the ICU that resulted in a shortage of beds at a time when the need for them was most critical, despite the existence of a planning strategy that had been implemented in an attempt to prevent such a shortage. The cause of this shortage was purported to be "human error." A hospital porter, new to the job, had left a bed trolley in an incorrect location, resulting in incorrect conjectures about the availability of ICU beds. Cook reported that this error was the most "proximate" to the staff concerned and thus was the focus of their attention during an assignation of blame. However, as Cook observed, the cause was much more complex than originally proposed. It lay not only with the porter but also with work methods of the hospital. As Cook, Woods, and Miller (1998) stated, the label "human error" is often applied at the conclusion of an investigation, often so that blame can be meted out, but it should be used as an initiation of an investigation because more complex systemic causes of error that occur at an organizational level are nearly always revealed. In this excerpt, Cook (2006) was critical of how the cause of the error was sought:

> No thought [about the cause of the error] was given to the nature of ICU resource use or scheduling, the roles of various parties in resolving resource conflicts, the impact of operating a hospital at or near its theoretical capacity, the potential consequences of the extra activities required of the many people in the ICU and in the floor to cope with these circumstances, or the implications of the "hiding" of … [an] (unused) … bed. (p. 33)

Similarly, Cook et al. (1998), in a more general investigation of patient safety in hospitals, reported that the focus for error prevention should be broadened from its typical use in evaluating the performance of practitioners to evaluation at the organizational or system level. Reason (1990, 1997) referred to this as the contrast of analysis at the "sharp end" (individual worker) versus at the "blunt end" (organizational constraints).

Cook et al. proposed that multiple events that arise from, and are shaped by, systemic factors, and not individual ones, are often the real cause of safety lapses: "Accidents in complex systems only occur through the concatenation of multiple small factors or failures, each necessary but only jointly sufficient to produce the accident" (Woods & Cook, 1999, p. 143). (See Reason [1990, 1997] for additional discussion of "sharp end" versus "blunt end.") They also proposed that safety cannot be achieved without consideration of other aspects of the health care system, that is, technical, individual, organizational, regulatory, and economic aspects. Safety is complex and dynamic and not a stand-alone entity that can be manipulated or achieved in isolation from its layers of context. These examples from CTA applications in the study of health care show how work systems can be considered wrapped packages, that is, complex conglomerates of interrelated variables that need careful exploration and consideration during system design.

Roth, Malin, and Schreckenghost (1997) explored related themes via review of a series of real-world systems and provided guidance regarding the use of machine intelligence. They suggested that the most effective intelligent interfaces act as cognitive and cooperative tools either providing critique or taking on the role of a team player. They documented limitations of the so-called Greek Oracle approach to machine intelligence in which the machine solves problems and the human acts as a data gatherer and solution filter. Difficulties with this approach include lack of user acceptance, brittleness in the face of unanticipated variability, deskilling as humans have fewer opportunities to solve problems and build an experience base, and biasing the human decision process by narrowing the hypothesis set. More effective technology allows the human an active role in problem solving while machine intelligence processes and synthesizes information to reduce information overload. One successful paradigm is described as a critiquing system. The machine intelligence acts as a mentor or colleague offering advice in response to human-generated solutions (Guerlain & Smith, 1996). Another effective paradigm for machine intelligence uses cooperative teams as a metaphor. In this case, the human has a leadership role and intelligent agents act as subordinates to whom tasks may be delegated.

The ideas we have presented concerning the CSE perspective entail challenges for the design of complex cognitive systems.

Challenges for Design

Advancing our understanding of cognitive work is not the only purpose of using CTA to study cognitive systems in context. That understanding must be instrumental; that is, it must contribute to the process of designing not just new technologies and training methods but the complete cognitive systems of which they are to be a part (Hoc, Cacciabue, & Hollnagel, 1995; Hollnagel, Hoc, & Cacciabue, 1995; Hollnagel & Cacciabue, 1999). Ultimately, the purpose of studying complex cognitive systems is to inform design—to help in the search for what is promising or what would be useful in changing fields of practice (Woods, 1998a; Woods & Roesler, 2007). Thus, methods for studying cognitive work are means to stimulate innovation and not just ways to build up the pattern base (Woods, 2002).

In Designer-Centered Design, the designer's hypotheses get manifested as features of the artifacts. An argument from CSE is that in this process, the developers of technology commit a version of William James's psychologist's fallacy: The empirical investigation of the actual impact of new technology is swapped out for the designer's vision of the intended impact of the technology.

In the study of cognition in context, the usually separate roles of researchers and designers converge and become complementary when it is recognized that arti-facts embody hypotheses about how technology shapes cognition and collaboration (Carroll & Campbell, 1988; Woods, 1998a). As discussed earlier, this is because the artifacts shape the cognitive work required to solve problems (Woods, 1995; Woods & Sarter, 2000; Zhang & Norman, 1994). The researcher functions as a designer, because, if we truly understand cognitive systems, then, as a test of that understand-ing, we should be able to develop designs that enhance cognition and collaboration in operational settings (Woods, 1998a). The designers function as researchers, because the artifacts they develop embody hypotheses about what will be useful and about how the field of practice will be transformed by new artifacts.

CSE lays out a number of significant challenges for the design of complex cognitive systems, and all of these relate to methods and methodology for CTA.

The Envisioned World Problem

When people study cognitive systems in context, a significant challenge is the "envi-sioned world problem" (Dekker & Woods, 1999b; Hoffman & Woods, 2000; Smith et al., 1998). How do the results of a CTA characterizing the current domain inform or apply to the design process, because the introduction of new technology will trans-form the nature of practice (Flores, Graves, Hartfield, & Winograd, 1988; Hollnagel & Woods, 1983)? New technology introduces new error forms; new representations change the cognitive activities needed to accomplish tasks and enable the development of new strategies; new technology creates new tasks and roles for people at different levels of a work system. New technology is an experimental intervention into fields of ongoing activity (Flores et al., 1988; Woods, 1998a). Changing artifacts, and the process of organizational change it is a part of, can change what it means for someone to be an expert and the kinds of breakdowns that can occur. An example is efforts at designing new weather forecasting workstations even while the operational systems are undergoing modification, and local kludging (Hoffman, 1991a). This is a perennial challenge for military systems as the nature of warfare, the types of missions, and the technology available continuously change, yet the need for constant, safe, and effective performance is constant. Woods and Dekker (2000) likened this problem to trying to hit a moving target.

Woods et al. (1998) discussed an example of the unforeseen effects of system design. In older power plant control rooms, artifacts that displayed information were often hardwired so that each type of information was displayed at a spatially separate location (see also Woods & Watts, 1997). This was a problem for operators because the integration of the different types of data used to build up an overall mental model of system state required operatives to move physically (and cognitively) between each information location. It might seem to be beneficial to combine these information displays into one display unit, or at least into colocated display units, so as to facilitate data integration. However, Woods et al. (1998) argued that the older control room layout had some important properties that would have been lost by the integration of displays. For example, in the older control room, an operator who glanced up momentarily from his or her work to look at the rest of the control room could gain information about the locations of other operators and thus what types of information or problems were receiving attention, because the display units were spatially separated and dedicated to certain functions. In turn, the operator could make a rapid inference about the system state.

For example, operators clustering around a heat sensor panel would indicate that there was a heating problem occurring in the plant. As a consequence, the operators could "remain in touch with the big picture"—that is, any one operator could update his or her mental model even though he or she might be concentrating predominantly on detailed work at his or her own workstation. These advantages would have been lost during implementation of the new design, but this loss would have been difficult to envision beforehand. This difficulty would have been compounded if designers had adopted a traditional approach of focusing predominantly on the technological elements (integration of displays) rather than on the human elements (location of operatives) of system design.

Another facet of the envisioned world problem is what Woods and Dekker (2000; see also Woods, 2002) called "the law of stretched systems." This law is well illustrated by the Gulf War example (Codesman & Wagner, 1996) that we used in the Designer-Centered Design section. Operators are often aware of system vulnerabilities from their experience of working in the system, especially during times when it has been worked to its limits. Imagine that designers are brought in to identify these vulnerabilities and implement changes to overcome them. In turn, a new higher level of operation will be achieved. The law of stretched systems states that a new system will always become stretched so that it is once again worked to its limits:

> Every system is stretched to operate at its capacity; as soon as there is room for improvement, for example in the form of new technology, it will be exploited to achieve a new intensity and tempo of activity. Under pressure from performance and efficiency demands, advances are consumed to ask operational personnel to "do more, do it faster or do it in more complex ways." (Woods, 2002, p. 2; see NASA's Mars Climate Orbiter Mishap Investigation Board report, 2000, for an example)

The new system vulnerabilities will become exposed under such conditions but will not have been experienced, and thus not predicted, by the system operators (Woods, Johannsen, Cook, & Sarter, 1994; Woods & Patterson, 2000).

Coping with the envisioned world problem will require our CTA and CFR methods to predict the evolution of a dynamic process (Hoffman & Elm, 2006). How does one envision or predict the relation of technology, cognition, and collaboration in a work context that does not yet exist or is in a process of becoming? How can we predict the changing nature of expertise and new forms of failure as the workplace changes? Studies of complex cognitive systems usually occur as part of a process of organizational and technological change spurred by the promise of new capabilities, dread of some paths to failure, and continuing pressure for higher levels of performance and greater productivity (systems under "faster, better, cheaper" pressure). This means that CTA researchers, through observing and modeling practice, are participants in processes of change in those fields of practice.

Woods and Dekker (2000) highlighted four properties of design problems that constrain prediction. First, the *plurality property* describes the phenomenon that for each system design problem there exist multiple versions of how any novel design will affect the future field of practice. Second, the *underspecification property* describes the phenomenon that each proposed design will inevitably underspecify the details of the practice field; that is, only a partial representation of the field can be established prior to system implementation. Third, the *ungrounded property* describes the phenomenon that, during the design process, the proposed system can become easily disconnected from, and not grounded sufficiently in, the data used to form predictions of the effects of various designs. Fourth, the *overconfidence property* describes the phenomenon that designers can be overconfident in their assessment of the anticipated consequences of the design; their assessments of the anticipated consequences are often oversimplified because there is a tendency to see complex phenomena as more simple than they actually are (Feltovich, Hoffman, & Woods, 2004; Feltovich, Spiro, & Coulson, 1997).

All of these challenges revolve around the issue of how studies of cognitive work help one decide where to spend limited resources and yet have significant impact. In response to these challenges, Cognitive Systems Engineers have argued that success will ultimately come to those who can predict the consequences of change early in the design process so as to avoid unintended and negative design effects. Woods and Dekker (2000) proposed a process to facilitate such prediction. They recommended that research should be conducted to establish a corpus of data on how organizational and technological change affects cognitive and collaborative demands and activities and to identify where new forms of potential error are created. Over time, patterns of effects can be identified from such data, and, in turn, models of design effects can be created. These models could then be used to predict the consequences of change before designs are implemented.

Other methods have been suggested to help avoid unintended and negative design effects. Woods and Dekker (2000) proposed that prototype designs can be used to observe the potential impact of a fully developed system. Observations of practitioners' activities, in terms of how they respond and are required to adapt to the prototypes, can be used to inform modifications of the design for a next set of prototypes. This process can iterate between designing, testing, and modifying the prototype until a final design solution is found. Another suggested approach is the Future Incident Technique (Dekker, 2005; Dekker & Woods, 1999b) in which attempts are made to identify the potential for errors in proposed systems by using current knowledge about classic technology-related design errors and about extratechnology vulnerabilities in the field of practice.

Some of these potential problems might be dealt with through an approach suggested by Hoffman and Elm (2006). This involves "folding the exploration of the envisioned world into the procurement process" by situating the prototype in the workplace. As the prototype is refined by having the practitioners work with it, the practitioners would come to use the new technology more often to get their jobs done and come to use the legacy technologies less. Over this same time span there would be opportunities to observe (and refine) the envisioned world during epi-sodes of coping with rare, tough, and challenging cases, as well as episodes of dealing with routine cases. In addition, as the technology development activity reaches its culmination, one will have a ready-made cohort of individuals who are accustomed to (i.e., trained in) working in the new context.

How to Facilitate Cooperation Among Humans and Machines

Many modern workplaces are characterized by work systems that are cooperative, in that they comprise humans and machines working together toward a common goal. A substantial area of research by Cognitive Systems Engineers has been on the design of, and challenges to, effective human and machine cooperation in work settings (Klein, Woods, Bradshaw, Hoffman, & Feltovich, 2004). Woods and Patterson (2000) argued that one factor contributing to effective cooperation was the extent to which agents coordinate their efforts. Successful coordination helps people avoid problems such as automation surprises and the resultant accidents. This issue is discussed in the following excerpt by Chow et al. (2000):

> The bottom line is: if we are going to introduce automation to do a task previously performed by humans, we have to design the coordination capabilities as carefully as the ability to do the target task. "Intelligent" automation that has strong cognitive capabilities but weak coordina-tive abilities can threaten safety and productivity in the work environment as much as, if not more than "unintelligent" automation that is inadequate in its capability to perform its target task. (p. 41)

Cognitive Systems Engineers have suggested that the identification and specifi-cation of a "competence model" of human–machine coordination can be obtained through CTA studies of competent human–human coordination (e.g., Chow et al., 2000). For example, Patterson, Woods, Sarter, and Watts-Perotti (1998) argued that one factor affecting the ability of humans to coordinate their efforts successfully is the extent to which a representation of the problem situation is shared by individu-als. This representation has two parts: a shared representation of the current problem type (e.g., what type of problem is this?) and status (e.g., what solution attempts are being considered or implemented?), and a shared representation of the status of the other individuals (e.g., what aspects of the solution process are the other individuals working on and how are they progressing?) (see also Hutchins, 1990, 1995a). A shared representation enables the individual to anticipate the future actions of other opera-tives so that the individual can perform a task with the expectation that those efforts will coordinate with the efforts of the other operatives.

As discussed earlier, one drawback to work systems that include automated machine agents is that the human is often provided with limited information about the activ-ity and intent of those agents. As a consequence, this does not allow humans to build a shared representation about the status of the machine agents, exemplified by state-ments such as, "What is it doing now?" In turn, the coordination of efforts required for cooperative work is undermined. In human–human interaction the status of other humans is often signaled and easily observable. For example, in work on an assembly line, an employee can easily monitor the activities of other employees by looking around the line to see what tasks are being performed and which employees are performing them. The work system status can be inferred from this information (e.g., a group of mechanics gathered around a piece of machinery might mean that the machine has developed a fault). Another example of the availability of information about human activity is that humans in cooperative environments will tend to explain out loud their assessments of, and attempted solution pathways to, a given problem as they proceed through a solution process (Patterson & Woods, 2001). As a consequence, coordination is facilitated.

However, when agents are organized in a more covert operational form, as is typical in automated systems, the agents must be designed such that information about their status and intent is observable. Obradovich and Woods (1996) used an example from a home medical device designed for the control of preterm labor to illustrate how the lack of observability is unhelpful and frustrating for the user. The user was required to enter a sequence of commands to operate the device. However, the device had several different modes of operation and did not clearly display its current mode of operation. If the commands entered by the user were not appropriate to the mode (despite being appropriate to the mode the user believed the device was in), the user did not receive the display expected. Indeed, no information was displayed for up to 7 seconds, and then the machine switched back to the default display. No feedback was given concurrent with, or after, the user's actions about any incorrect actions taken, and thus the user was left wondering what she did wrong.

Woods and Sarter (2000) suggested that increases in the complexity and autonomy of machine agents require a proportional increase in feedback from those machines to their human coworkers about agent status. These authors also argued that current technologies that have been designed to provide feedback do so in the form of one-shot retrospective explanations of the operations the agent had been performing, such as an alarm indicated an error. Woods and Sarter argued that this "after the fact" information is of limited use to the operator. Thus, feedback must be in the form of indicators that display information about ongoing and future events, so that humans can build a shared representation of the system. Woods and Sarter recommended that these types of feedback should be presented in a pattern-based form so that operators might rapidly perceive important information and detect abnormalities. The consequence of the provision of feedback is facilitation of ongoing decision making, anticipation, and, in turn, the coordination of future events. Technologies that support anticipation have been shown to contribute to error prevention and overall safety (Woods, 2000). Furthermore, anticipation achieved through shared representations also achieves a reduction in the communication required to undertake tasks and, in turn, the associated costs of communication, because agents need to communicate less about upcoming tasks. Woods (2000) reported that short updates can replace lengthy explanations in agent–agent coordination.

Another quality of feedback that is important to coordination is timing. Patterson et al. (1999) studied a voice loop groupware device in NASA's Mission Control center and showed that humans seldom interrupt ongoing conversations or activity unless it is important. This is because humans are context sensitive and thus can identify when the demands on the intended recipient of their communication are too high for the message to be received successfully and subsequently attended to. By contrast, machines are not context sensitive and thus do not know how to time their communication properly. For example, Woods et al. (1994) reported that important contributions from intelligent machines can go ignored if delivered during periods of high demand, as myriad other messages and data flood human operatives.

Another factor that contributes to cooperation between humans and machines is directability. The extent to which automated agents can be directed during their operation is related directly to the level of cooperation a system can achieve (Billings, 1996). Humans can undertake some situations more competently than machines, and thus a device must allow for human intervention at any time. Cognitive Systems Engineers have asserted that the machine agent has been treated as the locus of expertise in many modern systems, which is said to be a legacy of normative human factors (Woods, 1994a, b). However, as discussed earlier, Cognitive Systems Engineers consider cognition in modern work systems to be distributed across multiple machine and human agents, and thus treating the machine as the locus of expertise tends to lead to designs wherein technological agents become poor "team players" (Woods, 1994b).

Rather than implementing an alternative design in which there is a dichotomous switch in responsibility between human and machine, Woods and Sarter (2000) recommended that designers explore ways in which responsibility can be allocated, and reallocated, dynamically and incrementally as needed. In such a work system, machine efforts could be directed flexibly toward areas of problem solving in which machines have strengths, such as raw computational power, and human efforts can be directed toward areas in which humans have strengths, such as innovation and creativity. For a cooperative work system to function most effectively, humans should be able to decide how much of the work they wish to control and not suffer the inflexibility of having such decisions made for them by machine agents.

Despite these considerations for coordination, the implementation of directable machine control and dynamic, adaptive task allocation will remain a challenge for technologists and Cognitive Systems Engineers (Dekker & Woods, 1999b; Sheridan, 1997). For example, if an automated agent is responsible for some element of problem solving and a human agent intervenes early in this solution process to take some control, the capabilities of the machine might not be leveraged fully, and, by relation, human resources and expertise, which are often in scarce supply, might be wasted. Alternatively, if a human agent decides to intervene late in the solution process, the human's shared representation of the problem solution must be updated (Johannesen, Cook, & Woods, 1994; Patterson & Woods, 2001). Updating the representation takes time and cognitive resources and thus impacts on system performance. Patterson et al. (1998) described such a problem in a human–human coordination scenario:

> In an envisioned new form of air traffic management, authority to control flight paths will be distributed mostly between pilots and company dispatchers. Air traffic controllers will monitor the aircraft and intervene only to preserve safety. ... Decker and Woods investigated how this ... creates a dilemma for the distant supervisor about whether and when to take back partial or complete control over what flight path some subset of aircraft will fly. If the supervisor intervenes early (when it is easy to understand the situation and act constructively), it will tend to be seen as over intervention. If the supervisor intervenes late, it will be very difficult to act constructively given the tempo of the situation and the workload involved in assessing and directing multiple aircraft. (p. 19)

Dekker and Woods (1999b) argued that a prerequisite to directability is good observability, a concept we mentioned previously. A machine agent that continuously provides information on the difficulty of a problem or the increase in effort required to keep relevant parameters on target helps the human make appropriate decisions about when to assume control. In a more futuristic scenario, the machine agent would be able to monitor ongoing events for problems that are identifiable as being better handled by human than machine and in turn would alert the human colleagues accordingly (Patterson & Woods, 2001).

We have focused this chapter on laying out the general approach and view held in CSE. Emilie Roth and her colleagues have provided some excellent reviews of CSE that delve into greater detail about design (Roth, Malin, & Schreckenghost, 1997; Roth, Patterson, & Mumaw, 2002). We would be remiss not to say something about the CTA methods of CSE, and this is the topic with which we close this chapter.

Cognitive Systems Engineering and Cognitive Task Analysis

Research and development efforts in CSE rely on a rich palette of CTA methods. This includes documentation analysis, numerous forms of structured interviews, workplace analyses, work patterns analysis, surveys, questionnaires, and the like. All of these show that there is considerable overlap with the CTA methods palettes of the other perspectives and communities of practice, including the sociological and ethnographic perspectives. CSE also relies on the more traditional types of task analysis (e.g., activity analysis) and also on various forms of process tracing, including think-aloud problem solving. CSE research often has a focus on understanding domain expertise, showing considerable overlap and convergence with Expertise Studies. CSE does stand out, in a sense, because it also relies on experiment-like methods, which is not surprising given its roots in experimental and applied experimental psychology. But in addition, it also relies heavily on simulations and formal computational modeling. Indeed, some reviews of CTA methods list various formal modeling procedures *as being* methods of CTA (e.g., Bonaceto & Burns, 2007; Stanton, Salmon, Walker, Baber, & Jenkins, 2005; Wei & Salvendy, 2004). This is not surprising given the roots of CSE in computer science reflecting the influence of the works of such scientists as Herbert Simon and Alan Newell.

A general goal of research is to create decision support systems, through a detailed understanding of cognitive processes in decision making (Smith & Geddes, 2003). Research examines the role of biases in decision making, the forms of human error, the nature of domain expertise, and many other factors that play into the design of information technology.

Much of the research has been shaped by a key finding from the work on "expert systems" of the 1980s. A great deal of effort went into creating models of expert knowledge and reasoning in literally hundreds of domains (Hoffman, 1992b). The creation of an expert system relied on some form of knowledge elicitation, a type of CTA, and led to what was called the "knowledge acquisition bottleneck," which in turn contributed to the advent of CTA (see chapter 8). Expert systems relied on a knowledge base of domain concepts and principles and also an "inference engine" that could take input from the human (e.g., case features) and apply methods of inference to generate classifications or other determinations. A key finding was that such systems were often "brittle," that is, insensitive to context and any factors not included in the knowledge or reasoning models. This finding contributed not only to the shift within computer science from "expert systems" to "intelligent systems" but, in CSE, promoted the investigation of other ways in which knowledge-based technologies might play a role in training support and decision support.

Smith and Geddes (2003) presented a number of case studies that richly illustrate alternative approaches to decision aiding, including a case in the design of a software tool to aid diagnostic decision making at blood banks, conducted by Stephanie Guerlain and her colleagues (Guerlain et al., 1999). In this study, the researchers used a combination of CTA and work domain analysis methods including workplace observations, documentation analysis, interviews, and process tracing methods to understand the process for making decisions about assigning blood for transfusions. The primary decision task for blood bank technicians is one of diagnosis, involving abductive inference over multiple variables, which occurs in two stages. Initially, blood type and Rh factors are identified. Then the technologist searches for evidence of antibodies and alloantibodies via a series of tests. Blood bank technologists relied on a computer data-entry system that used a color-coded matrix display to show the results of various antibody tests. The task for the technologist is to go from that depiction to a decision (e.g., blood type B, Rh positive). The process could not be automated because the full range of cases was too diverse, the possible combinatorics of the tests were too numerous, and decision making is susceptible to brittleness because of such things as incomplete data.

> The task of determining the alloantibodies present in a patient's blood is a difficult one for many technologists. A variety of causes of errors were observed, including slips, perceptual distortions, incorrect or incomplete knowledge. (Smith & Geddes, 2003, p. 665)

With the goal of reducing errors and supporting decision making, Guerlain and her colleagues designed a decision aid that relied on algorithms for inferencing and also a rule base not unlike those of traditional expert systems. This system, however, did not act like traditional expert systems, which often present answers without providing much in the way of explanations. Instead, it engaged the human user in a process of "critiquing" in which the computer acts as a critic rather than a problem solver, providing the technician with the following kind of feedback:

> Group B individuals have no A antigen on their red blood cells, so you would expect a reaction with anti-A but not anti-B. Also, group B individual will have anti-A in their serum but not anti-B, producing a reaction with the A-1 cells, but not the B cells. Therefore your answer is incorrect.

This approach to leveraging the computational capabilities of the computer kept the human fully engaged in the decision-making process and mitigated bias, because the computer would not offer a determination before the human had understood and integrated the data. In addition, the designers of this decision aid employed the use of metaknowledge so that the decision aid was designed to alert humans to tricky or unusual cases, encouraging the user to take additional care when warranted. To reduce brittleness, the designers developed the decision aid so that it aided the user in seeking converging evidence from a range of problem-solving strategies and data sources before reaching a diagnosis.

After prototype software was developed, it was evaluated in an experiment-like procedure in which error rates were compared for 37 technicians across seven hospitals when using, versus when not using, the critiquing tool. Errors were reduced significantly by the use of the critiquing tool, even for a case where the software was not fully enabled with all of its inferencing capabilities.

The general approach used here was not to create software that fully emulated the human decision maker but to create a "reasoning assistant" that works with the human.

The second example provided by Smith and Geddes (2003) was a study in the domain of aviation. A system called the "Pilot's Associate" was created to assist military aviators in maintaining situation awareness, planning, responding to emergency situations, and determining air combat tactics.

> The user interface to an associate system is surprising in its simplicity as a result of the information management process. When the associate is aiding the user, there are few overt outward signs of the behavior of the associate. Instead, the user finds that his situation, options, or potential outcomes are organized and displayed for him without the need to perform frequent interactions with the user interface. (Smith & Geddes, 2003, p. 668)

This is accomplished by having the Associate use plans as a way to evaluate actions and the current situation to determine the pilot's intent, monitor progress, detect possible errors, and determine useful forms of aiding. For example, the Associate can determine the pilot's workload based on a model of performance and can provide additional assistance as needed. The Pilot's Associate was costly to create, and it underwent extensive testing. Here we find another CTA method in the methods palette used in CSE: simulations. The Pilot's Associate was evaluated and refined over many years of testing in high-fidelity simulators using a great variety of piloting and air combat situations.

> The Pilot's Associate … had many significant issues of user trust and commitment to overcome. At the outset, pilots were extremely skeptical of automation as a direct result of their experiences with its brittleness in combat situations (Sewell, Geddes, & Rouse, 1987). … It was widely felt by pilots that no machine could produce anything other than weak or outright silly advice. The results of using the Pilot's Associate were very different, however. Whereas most pilots maintained an opinion of guarded trust, all pilots universally embraced the Associate. … Many of the test subject pilots acknowledged that, despite their years of operational experience in combat aircraft, they actually learned new and powerful strategies and tactics form their interactions with the Associate. (pp. 669–670)

A third example, from Smith, Geddes, and Beatty (in press), explores human interactions with unmanned aerial vehicles (UAVs) used for reconnaissance and surveillance, as well as for suppression of enemy air defenses. One commonly stated goal for UAVs is that a single operator will control four or more UAVs in a combat setting. In this context, research suggests that a decision aid must support situation awareness, planning and resource commitment, coordination and acting, and understanding and responding to irregularities (Elmore, Dunlap, & Campbell, 2001; Geddes & Lee, 1998).

A software tool designed to meet these challenges, AUCTIONEER, uses both a cognitive model of decision making and a market-based auctioning method (Atkinson, 2003, 2005). This tool was designed specifically to open the "black box" of automation, allowing and encouraging human involvement. The AUCTIONEER includes a distributed model of beliefs that combines information provided by each UAV and the human operators to create a concept graph depicting the current situation. Distributed planning in AUCTIONEER leverages market-based auctioning, allowing each member to initiate an auction for a task that must be completed. Any team member can bid on the task.

The AUCTIONEER tool was evaluated with both passive and active operator involvement. An initial study examined AUCTIONEER in a fully autonomous mode and found that the auction process was effective for allocating resources. More targets were attacked in a shorter time, fewer tasks were abandoned, and there were shorter average timelines to attack targets. The second study included a human operator with the ability to intervene in the auction process. Findings from this study indicate that human effectiveness was limited because they did not have direct insight into the auction process. The design intention to provide insight into the black box was not successfully implemented in this case. As a result, Atkinson and her colleagues developed guidance for improving AUCTIONEER, including the following:

- *Communication of beliefs.* The operator should be able to view the beliefs held by each member of the flight and act to modify those beliefs when required. This provides assurance that the members of the flight are acting with a common assessment of the situation and are exploring all available information.
- *Communications of intentions in the context of a bid.* If the only information available to the operator about an offered bid for a task is its total cost, the operator loses important information about the context of the bid. By allowing the operator to view the chain of intentions that led to the bid, as represented in the plan goal graph, the operator would be able to understand how the bid was composed and to be assured that the bid was proper.
- *Communication of direct commands.* Operator commands need to be recognized as distinct from task-auction request. This would allow the operator to act with assurance that his or her commanded action would be carried out by the aircraft and resource that was directed, rather than incurring an auction response of uncertain outcome. Any addition task reallocations that result for the operator's command may be automatically handled as auctions

The case study illustrates clearly the difficulty associated with designing effective decision aiding and the importance of iterative design. It provides important lessons learned about how to open the black box using explicit models of belief, goals, and intentions as a basis for communication between automated and human team members.

Another class of CTA methods used in CSE is the computational modeling of cognition. This has a number of purposes. One is to develop what are believed to be full-blown theories of cognition, with the computer model being regarded as a theory

(Newell, 1981, 1990; Simon, 1991; Simon, Langley, Bradshaw, & Zytkow, 1987). This area of work entails many philosophical and scientific issues, in discussions that fill libraries and go well beyond the scope of this book (for instance, see Warwick & Hutton, 2007). In a nutshell, if the computer can be made to behave in ways similar to how humans behave, then it might be taken as a veridical model. Thus, computational models predict such things as decision reaction time based on known facts of cognition, such as memory capacity, attentional limitations, and so on. Earlier we pointed to the view that computational cognitive modeling is a form of task analysis. Proponents of computational models as theories of cognition have theoretically inspired views on how to conduct a CTA, what kinds of knowledge can be elicited, how to represent it, and so forth. Computational cognitive models can certainly be used to embody the results of task analysis. One might regard computational models as testing grounds, not as CTA methods per se. CTA is all about methods for collecting data about (human) cognitive work. There is a fine line here, however, in that the process of collecting data can stretch to the collection of data that are the outputs of a model of the cognitive work and then stretch to the use of those data in a comparison to the human data for theory validation and refinement. Furthermore, other ways in which CTA data are collected and analyzed can result in "models" of a sort, although these may not *do* anything (e.g., Abstraction-Decomposition matrices, Goal-Directed Task Analysis diagrams, Concept Map knowledge models, etc.).

Once a computational cognitive model is created and validated, it can be used for a second purpose, which is to test hypotheses about cognitive work and the impact of technology, such as a new software tool. Modeling enables one to predict the actions of humans who are skilled at the given task being modeled, for example, the amount of time it will take a person to conduct a task, the error rates under high levels of mental workload, or the long learning times for poorly designed interfaces. It is sometimes said that these models fall at the "keystroke" level, meaning that the model is created on the basis of individual actions. One can note a similarity to the "man–machine" diagramming methods of early industrial psychology (see Figure 2.5), even though at the modeling level where the behavioral data are interpreted, cognitive concepts (e.g., human short-term memory capacity) are used to shape the architecture.

A great many schemes and approaches have been devised to conduct computational cognitive modeling (ACT-R, SOAR, EPIC, many others), and each basic approach has spawned a great many variants and spin-offs. These computational models are often described as being like programming languages, because they allow one to create a model of a task and then run it to produce a step-by-step trace of the cognitive operations that are involved in performing the task. Operations include sensory encoding of stimuli, encoding in memory, executing motor commands, and so on—the so-called atomic components of thought. Operations have associated with them a time parameter and an error parameter, allowing the model to predict performance times and error rates.

Most of the major models began as attempts to model the sorts of tasks that were common in the traditional psychology laboratory, such as the Tower of Hanoi problem, the task of memorizing a list of words, or the task of using a simple word processor. It was not many years, however, before the modeling efforts expanded their range considerably both in the scope of cognitive tasks (category learning, the Stroop task, causal learning, mathematical problem solving, etc.) and in the scope of real-world tasks (piloting, information search, programming, etc.).

Discussion of the details of any of these systems would take us well beyond the scope of this book, but there are a number of centers, institutes, and research groups and a great many conferences that discuss them. Excellent recently edited collections and reviews are Gluck and Pew (2005) and Newell (1990). For illustrative purposes, we provide a capsule description of two cognitive modeling frameworks: Anderson's (1983, 1987, 1991) Adaptive Control of Thought (ACT) modeling approach and the Goals-Operations-Methods-Selection Rules (GOMS) approach of Stuart Card, Alan Newell, and their colleagues (Card, Moran, & Newell, 1980a, 1980b; Kieras, 1988).

ACT is a family of models that all rely on a core architecture consisting of memory modules (declarative memory of facts) and procedural memory (of procedures that describe how things are done), buffers that contain information about the current state, and a pattern matcher, which searches the production rules for ones that match with the current problem state stored in the buffer. ACT is referred to as a "hybrid architecture" in that it operates at both the symbol level (i.e., in the representation of declarative knowledge) and the "subsymbolic" level, where mathematical equations, operating in parallel, work to select operators based on calculations of utility and determine the speed with which facts are retrieved from memory and stored in the buffer. Like other models and modeling approaches, ACT-R (Adaptive Control of Thought-Rational) generates estimates of task performance time and accuracy.

GOMS is a family of models that have a representation of knowledge (e.g., knowledge of goals) and of procedures (referred to as procedural rules, which are essentially "if–then" conditional statements). Methods are sets of operators that describe how one gets from some current state to some goal state (e.g., place cursor at beginning of text, push mouse button and hold, move cursor to end of selected text, push "delete" key). Methods are arranged in a form of hierarchical goal decomposition. Operators are acts (believed to be elementary) that cause a change in the problem state representation or the task environment. These can be motor acts (select from menu), perceptual acts (recognize x), or cognitive acts (decide z).

The general computational cognitive modeling approach has met with considerable success in identifying usability problems with new software tools and new interfaces, estimating the cost of training, evaluating alternative designs for new technologies, suggesting ways of improving on software to decrease task execution times, and forming the basic framework for training aids and intelligent tutoring systems that can predict the errors students are likely to make given the stage of their skill development.

A good example is Project Ernestine, named after comedienne Lily Tomlin's spoof of a rude telephone switchboard operator. NYNEX was considering the acquisition of a new workstation and work method for operators who handled international phone calls. The new work system held promise for saving the company millions of dollars per year, in part because data displays worked faster and the operator was required to make fewer keystrokes to enter data. Even a few seconds saved in handling individual calls could add up to millions of dollars in terms of total workforce productivity.

Wayne Gray, Bonnie John (a student of Alan Newell), and Mike Atwood (1993) used a version of GOMS to model the task of operators using both their current system and the proposed new system. To their surprise, the modeling results showed that work with the new system would not result in savings and in fact would make the processing of most calls take a fraction of a second longer. These modeling results were met with skepticism, but a subsequent field trial, comparing the old and the new systems, confirmed the result. Why did the new system not live up to its promise? It turned out that the savings in terms of eliminated keystrokes came at a time when the operator was multitasking (e.g., listening to the caller while simultaneously entering data). The "critical path length" in the task was not much affected. The new work system would end up costing the company on the order of $2.5 million a year because of the number of calls an operator could process in a given time, and so NYNEX decided not to adopt it.

Project Ernestine is widely regarded as one of the outstanding success stories of CSE. Along with a number of success stories, it is recounted in rich detail in Nancy Cooke and Frank Durso's *In the Aftermath of Tragedy* (2007), which we highly recommend as a primer in the value and role of both CSE and CTA.

There remain significant challenges to computational cognitive modeling raised by considerations including macrocognition (high-level cognitive processes are parallel and highly interacting; see chapter 8) and especially cognitive work in complex systems, where one must consider adaptation, opportunism, dynamicism, and the unexpected rather than routine, well-learned, separable, tasks. When a human who is working on a tough problem in context has to deviate from known task sequences to engage in problem solving, collaborative problem solving, or similar activities, the models become less applicable. Furthermore, the models are designed to generate estimates of task execution time and error rates, but as the diversity of CTA shows, there is more, far more, to cognitive work.

It is also noteworthy that the computational cognitive models do not support human-machine interaction using natural language, which is a critical feature of all cognitive work (Wayne Zachary, personal communication, May 2008). One can debate whether the computational models really capture much "knowledge" or "reasoning," and this brings us back to the point that this area of work is deeply involved in many philosophical issues. Nevertheless, the field as a whole is confident that the capability for computational cognitive modeling will be expanded in years to come.

Summary

Early cognitive systems engineers such as Donald Norman and David Woods reacted against what they took to be "traditional" human factors. This includes a reaction against the idea that jobs can be decomposed into well-defined and sequential tasks and subtasks that can be specified in terms of actions that result in the achievement of prespecified goals. Other notions against which Cognitive Systems Engineers reacted include the idea that automation should take over as many tasks as possible, leaving the human to complete tasks that cannot be automated, and the idea that machines are designed to compensate for the limitations of humans.

CSE has identified a number of problems with a "Machine-Centered" view of design. For example, rather than assuming that increasing automation is always a positive step, CSE points out that more intelligent machines can inhibit the ability of people to develop their own knowledge and skills. The notion that machines are more valued than people leads to brittle designs that fail when unexpected, nonroutine events occur. Furthermore, humans are left with little understanding of the events and actions that led to the failure, making it difficult if not impossible for them to know what has gone wrong and what should be done to correct the situation.

Experience has shown that a number of claims often made about the introduction of new technologies are often dubious. Rather than enhancing work, new technology often changes the nature of work and the roles required to accomplish it, resulting in clumsy technology and confused humans. Rather than off-loading work from humans to machines, new kinds of work are created, often emerging especially during high workload settings. Rather than providing the kinds of feedback the worker needs, new and unanticipated feedback needs emerge. Rather than being more flexible than previous work methods, the increasing number of features, options, and operating modes of the machines results in new demands, new errors, and new paths to failure. Rather than reducing human error, new technologies often create new forms of error associated with collaboration. Rather than mitigating data overload, information technology often contributes to it. Rather than focusing worker's attention and requiring a reduced amount of knowledge, new technology requires that people have more threads to track, making it hard to maintain awareness of all the activities. Rather than acting autonomously, the new technology does things that humans do not anticipate or understand, requiring the humans to compensate by developing new strategies for collaboration.

"Designer-Centered Design" refers to the tendency of designers to overestimate the depth and quality of their understanding of the actual work. Often the impact designers propose is not realized after implementation. In fact, technology intended to reduce memory demands and circumvent challenges often results in the need for humans to remember more and to complete tasks more quickly and in more complex ways. In spite of good intentions of designers, new technologies often result in increased data overload, display disorientation, and automation surprises. It is ironic that automation often results in nearly impossible tasks for humans, skill deterioration, reduced understanding of the current system state (particularly troublesome when something goes wrong), and limited human processing of data resulting in reduced memory.

The "Human-Centered" viewpoint is offered in contrast to the Machine-Centered view and Designer-Centered Design. This view emphasizes human cognitive capabilities that machines cannot possess rather than the human weaknesses for which machines might compensate. Associated with the Human-Centered viewpoint is the notion of "distributed cognition," the idea that a cognitive system is composed of humans, technology, and the environment. CSE posits that examining the interaction of the elements of this cognitive systems triad results in better design. A key concept within CSE is that "traditional" task analysis is of limited value because it does not take a systems approach. A systems approach implies that in complex sociotechnical systems, the visible activities are taking place in a larger process of collaboration and coordination shaped by artifacts and constraints of the domain. These factors of complex systems come not in discrete, individual components but as "wrapped packages," closely associated with each other and embodied in the particular.

CSE seeks to address a range of design challenges associated with complex socio-technical systems. This includes the envisioned world problem or how to design first-of-a-kind systems. Given that it is impossible to anticipate all the possible ways in which humans, technology, and the environment will interact, and that the world itself is constantly changing even as new systems are proposed, envisioning a new work system effectively is a significant challenge for designers. Developing strategies to minimize unintended consequences is a key component of CSE. A second design challenge is how to facilitate cooperation among humans and machines. Increased automation has created a range of new coordination challenges. Cognitive Systems Engineers have suggested that a "competence model" can be identified by studying proficient human–human coordination. For example, research suggests that a shared representation of the problem situation is a key factor in successful human–human coordination. These and other factors influencing human coordination may have important implications for human–machine coordination.

Examining CSE in terms of its uses of CTA, one finds reliance on a diverse set of methods of observation, process tracing, and so forth, which CSE shares with other communities of practice. One also finds success stories that validate many of the CSE ideas about how Machine-centered or Designer-centered technology can negatively impact work, and how Human-centered technologies can improve cognitive work. Examples include the Pilot's Associate intelligent system, and the use of a computational cognitive model to predict the negative impact of a hew work method on the task of telephone switchboard operators. Given its roots in cognitive science, it is no surprise that computational cognitive modeling is regarded by some as being a CTA method, and likewise no surprise that CSE links directly to theoretical and philosophical issues on cognitive science and artificial intelligence.

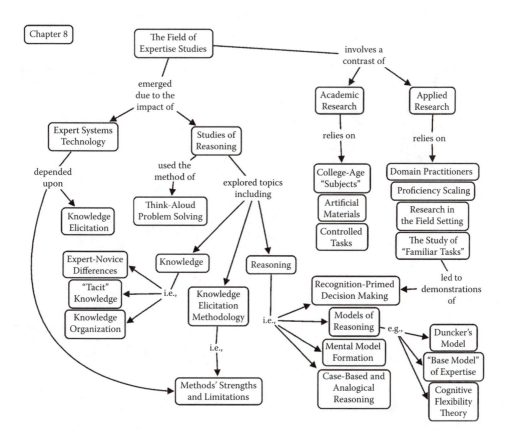

FIGURE 8.1 Chapter 8 Concept Map.

8

Expertise Studies

Amateurs work until they get it right; professionals work until they can't get it wrong.

—General Motors Corporation television commercial (August 2006)

Apprentices make the same mistake twice; experts make the same mistake once.

—Guillermo Alvarado (2006)

Introduction

In recent decades, the word *expert* has become salient in popular culture. It is even used to name a brand of pet food. As a Web search shows, the word is used in the names of a great many companies and countless software products for all manner of applications. One of the threads in the emergence of Cognitive Task Analysis (CTA) is Expertise Studies. In the study of expertise, and expert–novice differences, a great many methods have been used in research, and many of these can be considered to be CTA.

Since its emergence in the 1980s, the field of Expertise Studies has taken on considerable significance. If one includes in Expertise Studies the many earlier studies in the field of judgment and decision making that (in hindsight) involved experts, the literature that is encompassed is rather huge. In this chapter we could not possibly encapsulate that literature. A handbook by Ericsson, Charness, Feltovich, and Hoffman (2006) provides in-depth treatments of the history of the field, discussions of research methods, and chapters on selected domains of expertise, including chess, art, dance, sports, and medicine. Also in that volume, Jan Maarten Schraagen (2006) presents case studies in the use of task analysis methods.

After briefly reviewing the history of the field of Expertise Studies, we focus on topics that are at the core of the present book: the sorts of things that have been learned about expertise through the application of CTA methods and the selected issues concerning CTA methods and methodology that have arisen in the study of expertise.

History of This Community of Practice

Expertise Studies emerged in the 1980s, in part because of the development of "expert systems" in the field of artificial intelligence (see Buchanan, Davis, & Feigenbaum, 2006; Hoffman, 1992a). However, Expertise Studies has a rich history, historically speaking (see Amirault & Branson, 2006; Ericsson, 2006a; Feltovich, Prietula, & Ericsson, 2006). It is possible to look into the archives of psychology and find many writings and studies pre-1980 that could be embraced under the banner of Expertise Studies.

Even in the years before Wilhelm Wundt championed the founding of experimental psychology by divorcing it from philosophy departments and establishing graduate programs, reaction-time measures (of detection, recognition, and judgment processes) had stemmed, in part, from the problem of measuring individual differences in the perceptual judgments of professional astronomers (Boring, 1950). That work could be counted among the earliest formal experimental studies of experts and might also qualify as Cognitive Field Research.

Moving across the history of psychology, the study of reasoning using introspection (e.g., Thumb & Marbe, 1901) evolved into the think-aloud problem-solving task (TAPS). This was combined with the process now called "protocol analysis" in classic research on problem solving by Edouard Claparéde (1917) and Karl Duncker (1945). Today, TAPS is a main method used in the psychological exploration of expertise (and we will be discussing it at length in this chapter). Book's (1924) study of "world champion" typists and Bryan and Harter's (1897) study of telegraphers—both classics in experimental psychology—were oriented toward basic questions about motor skill acquisition (i.e., the occurrence of plateaus in learning curves of complex performance; Woodworth, 1938, chap. 7). But in hindsight these studies could be embraced under the banner of Expertise Studies, because expertise involves proficient skill as well as knowledge. Learning, transfer, and related phenomena are fundamental to the development of expertise, and therefore a great deal of learning research is potentially germane to the understanding of expertise.

In the areas of organizational behavior and decision making, researchers have put a great deal of effort into the study of individuals who could be called experts, in such diverse domains as accounting, auditing, management, livestock judging, finance, and so on (Fischhoff, 1989; Libby & Lewis, 1977; Shanteau, 1988). The archives of human factors psychology are laden with studies of performance in complex environments such as aircraft piloting, radar operation, and air traffic control. Many of these studies relied on highly experienced participants who had achieved high levels of proficiency or, we would say, were experts.

Studies on topics relating to expertise abound in the archives of psychometrics. Brown and Ghiselli (1953) used a battery of standard aptitude tests in an (unsuccessful) attempt to predict the proficiency of taxicab drivers. Jenkins (1953) employed questionnaires and standardized achievement and aptitude tests in a somewhat successful attempt to assess the aptitudes of weather forecasters, comparing the data to task analyses and forecasting skill scores. On the side of clear successes, Hammond (1966) laid out a program of research on nursing, involving field studies that disclosed the sorts of problems nurses encounter and laboratory studies using "test case" problems that disclosed nurses' patterns of clinical inference.

In general, within the broad history of experimental psychology, the study of expertise has tacitly been regarded as having value, because it touches on basic questions having to do with cognition, perception, and decision making, and applications involving skills training and the preservation of knowledge. Furthermore, the literature on expertise into which we might tap is not restricted to fields of psychology. For instance, a considerable literature in the philosophy, sociology, and psychology of science is germane to the study of expertise, because scientists are (presumably) experts and because science is (presumably) the epitome of rationality (cf. Dunbar, 1995, 1999, 2000; Dunbar & Fugelsang, 2005a, 2005b, 2006; Gorman & Carlson, 1990; Gorman, Tweney, Gooding, & Kincannon, 2005; Kulkanni & Simon, 1988; Miller, 1984).

The field of Expertise Studies emerged as a convergence of events and trends in computer science and psychology (Feltovich et al., 2006). As we explained in chapter 5, the development of expert systems helped bring attention to the phenomena and importance of expertise, and made the problems of knowledge elicitation salient. This brought some experimental psychologists into collaboration with computer scientists (e.g., Cooke, 1992; Foley & Hart, 1992; Ford & Adams-Webber, 1992; Gordon, 1992; McGraw, 1992; Prerau, Adler, & Gunderson, 1992). At about the same time, other psychologists had begun studying expertise in a number of domains, with the goal of advancing cognitive theory and contributing to instructional design.

Today, the field of Expertise Studies is flourishing and gaining in prominence in cognitive psychology:

> Our civilization has always recognized exceptional individuals, whose performance in sports, the arts, and science is vastly superior to that of the rest of the population. Speculations on the causes of these individuals' extraordinary abilities and performance are as old as the first records of their achievements. Early accounts commonly attribute these individuals' outstanding performance to divine intervention, such as the influence of the stars or organs of their bodies, or to special gifts (Murray, 1989). As science progressed, these explanations became less acceptable. (Ericsson, Krampe, & Tesch-Römer, 1993, p. 363)

Expertise as a topic now has its place in cognitive psychology textbooks and is a frequent focus in the experimental psychology literature (see Ericsson et al., 2006), by virtue of its implications for basic theories of learning, skill, and cognition. Cognitive scientists have studied complex problem solving in a great many domains, including science, public policy and administration, English composition, mathematics, jurisprudence, electronics, computer programming, medicine, aviation, and so on (e.g., Campbell, Brown, & DiBello, 1992; Simon, Langley, Bradshaw, & Zytkow, 1987; Sternberg & Frensch, 1991; van Someren et al. 1994).

Expert reasoning and knowledge have been two primary areas of research, and thus we emphasize these two topics in this chapter. However, it should be pointed out that other psychological considerations are critical, such as motivational factors. Some people decide to enter a profession because they "love" the domain, based often on previous experiences. As an individual progresses in skill and achievement, a love for the domain is something that will always remain open to change, for any of a variety of reasons. Likewise, motivation to improve can decrease or increase over time. And if anything distinguishes experts from nonexperts, it is the willingness and will to maintain a regimen of practice aimed at stretching their abilities. This has been shown clearly in Ericsson et al.'s (1993) analysis of advanced violinists and piano players at the Berlin Academy of Music, in which the musicians retrospected about their musical development and practice habits.

CTA or Not CTA?

From the standpoint of methodology, one might say that nearly all research in the area of Expertise Studies involves CTA, with the emphasis on *cognitive,* that is, research to reveal and explore phenomena of cognition. Many researchers would find such a wholesale adoption troublesome, however, when the emphasis is on *task.* Not all research on expertise focuses specifically on task analysis in the sense of breakdown of the day-to-day tasks that experts conduct. For example, many studies of medical expertise (e.g., radiology) rely on the analysis of eye movements (Carmody, Kundel, & Toto, 1984; Kundel & LaFolette, 1972; Kundel & Nodine, 1978; Kundel & Wright, 1969; Myles-Worsley, Johnston, & Simons, 1988). Studies have shown that within the first few seconds of viewing films, the expert radiologist can correctly identify abnormalities. "Training and experience result in a more effective use of global fixations and thus increase efficiency, perhaps because of a better prototype for the normal image" (Kundel & Nodine, 1978, p. 532). Although informative of perception and cognition, such studies seem fairly distanced from CTA, for example, knowledge elicitation forms of CTA.

On the other hand, research in Expertise Studies often does provide clear instances of CTA. Again using the study of medicine as an example, Alan Lesgold and his colleagues (Lesgold, Rubinson, Feltovich, Glaser, Klopfer, & Wang, 1988) analyzed TAPS protocols from oral diagnoses during which probe questions were presented to radiologists. The researchers also used a recall task in which radiologists viewed a film for only 2 seconds, then reported what they saw, and made a drawing of the key anatomical and diagnostic features they recalled. Included in the findings was a demonstration of some fundamental differences between senior radiologists and residents. The experts made more observations and more inferences. Such studies of medical reasoning have led to a richer understanding of expert reasoning strategies, and led to Cognitive Flexibility Theory, which we discuss in more detail later (Feltovich, Spiro, & Coulson, 1997; Spiro, Coulson, Feltovich, & Anderson, 1988). Research comparing reasoning across levels of proficiency (students, interns, residents) has also revealed the ways in which learners tend to create simplifying mental models of complex dynamic processes (the "reductive tendency") and, related to that, a roster of "knowledge shields" that they fall back on when motivated to preserve their simplifying concepts and assumptions (Feltovich, Coulson, & Spiro, 2001; Feltovich, Spiro, & Coulson, 1989).

There is, of course, a fuzzy boundary between CTA and not-CTA. We might compare two studies, one in which students (nonexperts) and professors (experts) are situated in an academic laboratory and are given textbooklike domain problems in a TAPS task. The results would tell us about expert reasoning versus nonexpert reasoning on problems that are of a somewhat familiar type. In another study, domain practitioners versus apprentices are asked to think aloud concerning how they usually conduct a case analysis, using archived case materials. The results would tell us about reasoning in their familiar task. One can ask the following:

- How similar is the experimental task to the expert's familiar task?
- Is the focus on cognition or on cognitive work?

We then try our best to divide studies accordingly into CTA versus laboratory experimentation categories, but it is always slippery and not necessarily even valuable.

An example study that seems to fall rather clearly on the experimental-laboratory side of the distinction engaged participants in a simple problem-solving task—the construction of a device using an erector set (Bailey & Kay, 1987). Problem-solving behavior was analyzed in terms of specific actions, such as the bolting of two parts together. Participants' utterances were categorized according to their reference, such as the goals of a particular action that was being planned or the evaluation of the outcome of a test of a component. On the basis of the goals, references, and intentions, the specific actions were grouped into meaningful episodes, and the episodes charted out, revealing an overall pattern of goal decomposition that had been used by the problem solver. Only with the aid of the think-aloud protocols could sense be made of the behavioral data, for example, why a subassembly might be taken apart following a realization that it would not fit right with another subassembly. Protocol data also permitted explanation of behaviors that reflected disorganized, out-of-sequence reasoning.

Is this *cognitive* analysis? Yes. Is it analysis of cognition at a *task*? Yes. But is it CTA as this term is usually intended? Perhaps not. The TAPS task is typically thought of as a laboratory method. Discussions of it sometimes raise the caution that having people think aloud during problem solving might cause interference. However, thinking aloud is a necessary part of the familiar task in a number of domains, such as radiological diagnosis and forensic analysis (i.e., autopsies), where practitioners think aloud and audio record their case analyses. Is interference inevitable, will it occur if thinking aloud is a highly practiced task, a part of the familiar task?

Because CTA in general has goals including training, decision making, and so on, and because cognitive work in complex contexts places expertise at a premium, anything we can learn about expert knowledge and reasoning can contribute to the broader agenda, whether that knowledge comes from clear-case experiments, clear-case CTA, or clear-case Cognitive Field Research.

Reasoning, in General

In one view of the mind, reasoning involves causally connected sequences of basic mental operations or processes. Furthermore, there must be a causal linkage between events at the cognitive level and events or operations at the task level of behaviors and utterances while a person is engaged in the task. One of the most venerable hypotheses about problem solving is that the process involves sequences of distinguishable operations, phases, or stages (cf. Duncker, 1945; Newell & Simon,

1972). Numerous studies of problem solving using a TAPS method have success-fully charted out reasoning sequences (e.g., Bailey & Kay, 1987; Claparéde, 1934; van Someren et al., 1994).

Strategies that have been observed and cataloged are also manifest in the reason-ing of experts. For instance, the "least effort" tactic has been observed in domains of expertise (Kusterer, 1978; Scribner, 1984, 1986). Experts also use analogical reasoning (Ross & Kennedy, 1990; Weitzenfeld & Klein, 1979). Experts certainly engage in deductive and inductive inference and hypothesis testing (Gordon & Gill, 1997; Johnson, Zualkerman, & Garber, 1987; Voss, Tyler, & Yengo, 1983).

Divide and Conquer

When people are confronted with problem-solving situations, they sometimes seem to follow some sort of "divide-and-conquer" problem simplification strategy (cf. Greeno, 1974; Hayes, 1965; Newell & Simon, 1972; Restle & Davis, 1962; Thomas, 1974). One such strategy is called "elimination by aspects," in which the problem solver generates the features of the desired solution(s) and then rules out consider-ation of all possible choices that do not have all of the desired features (Duncker, 1945) (e.g., in deciding which car to buy, start with a list of the features you want). Another divide-and-conquer strategy is called "means-end analysis" in which one identifies a goal state and attempts to reduce the difference between that goal and the current state. In the "method of simplification," there is an initial process of arriv-ing at a general understanding of the problem, which leads to a plan for breaking the problem into smaller parts. Each subproblem is then solved, working toward the final step of putting the partial solutions together. In Duncker's terminology, problem solving often consists of a number of phases, each of which has the character of being a problem plus its solution, with the solution being a "subspecies" of the main goal (see Newell, 1985).

Many of the tasks that are performed by experts sometimes rely on some form of divide-and-conquer strategy (Voss & Post, 1988). For example, software designers sometimes rely on an implicit divide-and-conquer strategy in which the program goal is achieved through the assembly of familiar functional subroutines (cf. Jeffries, Turner, Polson, & Atwood, 1981). The terrain analysis procedure in aerial photo interpretation involves separate, explicit, detailed analyses of landforms, fluvial fea-tures, vegetation patterns, cultural features, photo gray tones, and so on (Way, 1978). Overlays are made for each category, and specific kinds of features are noted. Finally, the separate analyses are combined into a final interpretation.

In decision analysis (e.g., Gardiner & Edwards, 1975; Raiffa, 1968), the problem solver deliberatively lists out the characteristics of a problem, the kinds of decisions that are possible, and the possible consequences of each of the decisions. The final result from the lists can be a decision tree not unlike those of Duncker (1945). Decision analysis has been used in the elicitation of experts' knowledge (Hart, 1985, 1986; Slovic, 1982). This is illustrated in Gardiner and Edwards's (1975) study of the decision-making deliberations of the Coastal Planning Commission in California. Hypothetical but realistic development requests were prepared, complete with infor-mation on relevant attributes. The judges' separate ratings on each attribute were combined using a multiattribute utility analysis. The results revealed the locus of disagreements and helped planners focus on the important issues.

Top-Down, Bottom-Up

Duncker (1945) presented word problems and mathematics problems to college students and had them think aloud during their attempts to solve the problems. Duncker observed that there were two general kinds of strategy or search, which he referred to as "suggestion from below" and "suggestion from above." In the modern literature on problem solving, a version of these two search concepts has been relied on extensively (cf. Chi, Glaser, & Rees, 1982; Larkin, 1981; Lesgold, 1984; Polya, 1957; Simon & Simon, 1978). In a "bottom-up search," one works from the premises, data, or initial state toward the goal or toward a hypothesis. This is also called a "forward-looking search," "forward chaining," and a "data-driven search." In a "top-down search" or processing, the assessment of data is guided by higher level knowledge, and one selects moves that go from the goal state closer to the initial state. This is also called a "concept-driven search" and "backward chaining" (from a hypothesis back to a data search and analysis). It makes sense to rely on such a search when there are more paths leading away from the goal and toward the premises or initial state than there are paths leading from the premises toward the goal. (All this is on the assumption of a "problem space" theory of problem solving.)

Some studies suggest that experts differ from novices in the frequency of reliance on these two types of reasoning strategies (e.g., Groen & Patel, 1985) though there is ongoing debate on this point (see Eva, Norman, & Brooks, 2002; Norman et al., 2006).

Deductive, Inductive, and Abductive Reasoning

Many theories of cognition and perception describe reasoning as a process in which people derive hypotheses from data, so-called hypothetico-deductive reasoning (e.g., Elstein, Shulman, & Sprafka, 1978). In the philosophy of science, the Hypothetico-Deductive Model (also called the Deductive-Nomological model and the Hempel-Oppenheim model) was one of the outstanding theories of how scientists reason, regarding scientific explanation (and prediction) as a form of deduction based on two kinds of premises: observations or empirical facts, and scientific laws (see Dunbar, 1995, 1999, 2000; Hemple, 1970).

It is clear that this is only part of the story. For instance, hypothetico-deductive reasoning does not distinguish experts from novices, because everyone engages in the deduction of hypotheses from data (G. R. Norman, personal communication, 2007). There is more to reasoning, especially expert reasoning, than inspecting data and forming a hypothesis. Specifically, there is a cycle in that one goes from the hypothesis back to the data, seeking to confirm or disconfirm the hypothesis. Furthermore, more than deductive inference is involved; so too is inductive inference (generalization) and abductive inference. Abduction is inference to the best explanation, that is, the selection of a hypothesis that would, if true, best explain the relevant evidence. According to Duncker's (1945) description of the reasoning cycle (see also Newell, 1985), problem solving involves the following cycle:

1. Understand the problem statement (i.e., inspect the data);
2. Form a mental model or conceptual understanding of the problem situation (induction, induction, abduction);
3. Generate tentative solutions (hypotheses), through deduction, induction, or abduction, that relate functionally to the goal;
4. Assess whether or why the tentative solutions might not work;
5. Recenter or reformulate the search for a "deeper" understanding of the problem based on reconsideration of the data, one's knowledge, and the premises; and
6. Return to Step 2.

Such a hypothesis-testing refinement cycle was proposed (in one form or another) by all of the experimental psychologists who pioneered the study of problem solving (e.g., Claparéde, 1934; Dewey, 1933, 1938; Selz, 1922; Wertheimer, 1945; see also Polya, 1957). Neisser (1976) defined perception as a kind of problem solving, in which there is a repeating cycle of anticipation and schema formation. On the basis of the work of the pioneers, Bransford and Stein (1984) generated what they called the "IDEAL" method for teaching creative problem solving, which consists of the following steps:

1. Identifying and Defining problems,
2. Exploring strategies for a solution,
3. Acting on the basis of the strategies, and
4. Looking at the effect.

This method was designed to facilitate transfer and is demonstrably effective in teaching problem solving to college students (Bransford, Franks, Vye, & Sherwood, 1989).

The hypothesis-testing cycle has been amply demonstrated in studies of experts. Geoff Norman and his colleagues (Barrows, Norman, Neufeld, & Feightner, 1982; Neufeld, Norman, Barrows, & Feightner, 1981; see also Elstein et al., 1978) engaged clinicians in a task in which they were presented live simulated patients, and they engaged in their clinical reasoning while thinking aloud. A key finding from this area of research is that clinical reasoning involves data interpretation followed by hypothesis formation, followed by a search for confirming (or disconfirming) evidence.

There are, of course, many variations on the Duncker theme. Discussions of the reasoning of intelligence analysts by Patterson, Roth, and Woods (2001) and Elm et al. (2005) have described these stages:

1. "Down collect" relevant data,
2. Construct interpretations, and
3. Explore the consequent hypotheses to build on the explanations.

The refinement cycle appeared in Lederberg and Feigenbaum's (1968) description of the goal for their expert system (DENDRAL) for the analysis of organic molecules:

Data somehow suggest an hypothesis, and deductive algorithms are applied to the hypothesis to make logically necessary predictions; these are then matched with the data in a search for contradictions. (p. 187)

Studies of critical thinking (in such domains as firefighting) such as those by Cohen, Freeman, and Wolf (1996) have suggested a process that is triggered when a proficient decision maker recognizes that a situation is atypical and problematic:

1. Detection of evidence that suggests that the situation is unusual,
2. Construction of a story,
3. Evaluation of the relations of the evidence to the story,
4. Critique of the story for completeness and inconsistency, and
5. Attempt to improve the story by collecting information and revising assumptions.

Many recent studies of experts at industrial design (i.e., Creativity and Cognition Studios, 2003) have used methods of case retrospection and think-aloud problem solving to reveal regularities of reasoning across individual expert designers, such as "reasoning from first principles" (as in the use of triangular structures for adding stability to a bicycle frame). Cross (2003) proposed a general model of design reasoning involving the following stagelike activities:

1. Realize the tension between the conflicting problem goals and the solution criteria (understand the problem),
2. Resolve the tension by matching the designer's "problem frame" (mental model) with possible solution concepts (generate tentative solutions), and
3. Achieve a matching by relying on first principles (deeper understanding).

Although expressed in terms of tensions, these ideas mirror those put forward by Duncker.

But this is by no means the end of the story. There is no single problem-solving process or critical-thinking process, and reasoning cannot be usefully or exhaustively taxonomized into types or stages based on some form of structural analysis of problems. Rather, there are supporting processes (such as mental model formation, sense making, deciding, envisioning, etc.) that are always highly parallel and interacting (see Dorst, 2003; Klein et al., 2003). In sum, all of the generic reasoning strategies and sequences observed in laboratory studies of nonexperts have also been observed in the skilled reasoning of professionals, ranging from waitresses, to inventory managers, to product assemblers (Scribner, 1986).

CTA research also shows that reasoning is domain and context dependent.

Reasoning, in Context

Although expert and everyday reasoning may rely on the same strategies, or even the same fundamental cognitive operations, the flow of expert reasoning is shaped by the tasks and contexts that are involved in the domain (Greeno, 1978; Scribner, 1984). It is the ways in which the generic strategies are contextualized that gives expert reasoning its power (Chi, Glaser, & Rees, 1982; Evans, 1988; Feigenbaum, 1977; Glaser, 1987; Kurzweil, 1985; Minsky & Papert, 1974; Scribner, 1984, 1986). As an example, let's return to the notion, mentioned earlier, that hypothetico-deduction does not distinguish experts from novices. What does distinguish experts from novices is that experts derive better hypotheses than novices, based on their knowledge and experience. Thus, even though experts may sometimes make errors in data gathering or data interpretation, their overall performance is better than that of novices (Groves, O'Rourke, & Alexander, 2003; G. R. Norman, personal communication, 2007).

One way in which expert reasoning is shaped is in terms of the sequences of reasoning operations, or we might say the relative emphasis on component operations, as opposed to the mere reliance on one or another individual process or mental operation. Larkin (1983) asked physics students and experienced physicists to solve mechanics problems (involving levers, weights, inclined planes, pulleys, forces, etc.) while thinking aloud. The results of a number of such studies on physics problem solving have shown that the basic reasoning operations or strategies can be applied in different orders and with different emphases for experts versus novices. In the initial stages of problem solving, experts spend proportionately more time than novices forming a conceptual understanding of the problem. Experts generate representations that are conceptually richer and more organized than those of the novices. Novices tend to use hastily formed "concrete" (i.e., superficial) problem representations whereas experts use "abstract" representations that rely on "deep" knowledge, that is, imaginal and conceptual understanding of functional relations and physical principles that relate concepts (in the case of the research on experts at mechanics, principles such as conservation of energy). Furthermore, experts are better able to gauge the difficulty of problems and know the conditions for the use of particular knowledge and procedures (e.g., if there is acceleration, use Newton's second law) (Chi, Glaser, & Rees, 1982).

Practice Effects: Recognition Priming

Experts become very adept at their usual or familiar tasks (Hoffman, Shadbolt, Burton, & Klein, 1995). In their study of expert radiologists, Myles-Worsely et al. (1988) found that experts were better than novices at recognizing chest X-rays but not at recognizing faces. Experts, in general, are good at what they are used to doing (Dawson, Zeitz, & Wright, 1989). Disruption of the experts' familiar task can cause experts' superior performance to decline markedly—in a disrupted task, they cannot form meaningful representations or solutions. For example, chess masters' memory for game positions is disrupted somewhat for scrambled games (Chase & Simon, 1973). Expert bridge players can be disrupted by meaningful rule changes (e.g., who leads each round) more than by superficial changes (e.g., the names of the suits) (Sternberg & Frensch, 1992). Expert programmers' memory for programs is disrupted if the programs are scrambled (McKeithen, Reitman, Reuter, & Hirtle, 1981).

A skill that comes with experience is recognition-primed decision making (Klein 1989a). Experts often size up a situation and immediately recognize it based on typicality or prototypicality. This leads to expectancies, and a commitment is made to a course of action without any deliberation over alternatives. One of the classic studies on radiology (e.g., Lesgold et al., 1988) concluded that reasoning depends on the recognition of schemata for normal and abnormal cases based on perceptible cues and cue constellations and that this recognition process is rapid and direct. This is an instance of recognition-primed decision making, a phenomenon we discuss in more detail in chapter 9. This phenomenon suggests that, for experts working routine cases, a divide-and-conquer-type strategy does not have to be used.

> If a novice were to consider buying a car, the decision-analytic technique would be to system-atically lay out the options and the evaluation dimensions. This would help clarify values, if nothing else. But one would not expect someone proficient, such as a used-car salesman, to go through the same exercise. (Klein, 1989a, p. 50)

Looking at subdomains of medical expertise, studies by Vimla Patel and her col-leagues (Patel, Evans, & Groen, 1988; Patel & Groen, 1986; Patel, Groen, & Norman, 1991) explored the diagnostic reasoning by clinicians. The TAPS task and protocol analysis showed that for routine cases, experts do not engage much in elaborate causal reasoning. Upon recognizing a case type, "encapsulated knowledge" (Boshuizen & Schmidt, 1992; Schmidt, Norman, & Boshuizen, 1990) is retrieved, with judgment following directly. Furthermore, a number of studies in medical diagnostic exper-tise have demonstrated experts' rapid visual diagnosis in representative tasks, such as studies by Geoff Norman and his colleagues on dermatologists, radiologists, and cardiologists (Allen, Brooks, Norman, & Rosenthal, 1988; Babcock, Norman, & Coblentz, 1993; Hatala, Norman, & Brooks, 1999b). Also, expert reaction time in diagnostic tasks shows a clear effect of diagnostic prototypes (e.g., diabetes is more typical of endocrine diseases than other forms of endocrine disease) (Bordage & Zacks, 1984; Bordage & Lemieux, 1991). For difficult cases, experts resort more to causal reasoning (Norman, Trott, Brooks, & Smith, 1994). All these findings fit with the notion of recognition-primed decision making.

In the literature on medical expertise, the idea that that reasoning involves either experiential knowledge or analytical-causal knowledge was referred to as the "two worlds hypothesis" (Patel & Groen, 1986). It is now fairly clear that reasoning episodes can involve both pattern-recognition-based reasoning and analytical, causal, or rule-based reasoning in some combination or degree, depending on the case at hand and the decision maker's experience (Barrows & Feltovich, 1987; Feltovich et al., 1997; Norman et al., 2006).

An important footnote to this is that for some problem types in some domains, it is by no means clear that experts are able to rely on any form of a divide-and-conquer strategy, as opposed to a recognitional strategy. Indeed, in time-pressured situations, experts cannot engage in lengthy deliberation of alternative courses of action and their relative costs and benefits (Orasanu & Connolly, 1993). Furthermore, there is some debate about the utility of decision analysis in actual business and manage-ment situations (Dreyfus & Dreyfus, 1986; Klein, 1998). Some studies have shown that when domain experts are forced to work their usual problems using decision analysis, their performance suffers (Fischhoff, Goitein, & Shapira, 1982; Fischhoff, Slovic, & Lichtenstein, 1979). In many domains of expertise, the tasks that experts usually perform do not require an explicit decompositional analysis of problems.

Case-Based and Analogical Reasoning

Analogical reasoning is a favorite topic of cognitive psychology and has been inten-sively studied in the laboratory, for example, in studies of how people understand electric circuits through a comparison to a plumbing system or understand atoms through a comparison to the solar system (e.g., Blanchette & Dunbar, 2000, 2001, 2002; Dunbar, 2001; Dunbar & Blanchette, 2001; Forbus, Gentner, Markman, & Ferguson, 1998; Gentner, 1989; Gentner & Gentner, 1983; Gentner, Holyoak, & Kokinov, 2001; Hofstadter, 2001; Holyoak, 1984; Holyoak & Koh, 1987; Holyoak, Novick, & Melz, 1994; Keane, Ledgeway, & Duff, 1994; Schunn & Dunbar, 1996; Spellman, Holyoak, & Morrison, 2001). This work has led to a considerable effort at creating computational models of analogical reasoning (e.g., Chalmers, French, & Hofstadter, 1992; Falkenhainer, Forbus, & Gentner, 1990; Forbus, Ferguson, & Gentner, 1994; Hoffman, 1995b; Hofstadter & the FARG, 1995; Holyoak & Thagard, 1989; Indurkhya, 1991; Keane & Brayshaw, 1988; Mitchell, 1993). Analogical reasoning has often been observed in studies of expert reasoning. Experts often refer to illustrative or prototypical examples of past cases when asked to justify or explain their decisions or actions. They like to "tell stories" (Crandall, Klein, & Hoffman, 2006). Sometimes it seems as if a great deal of experts' knowledge is remembered in the form of previously encountered cases. Hence, it has proved possible for developers of expert systems to elicit experts' knowledge by presenting them with sets of specially prepared "test cases" (Hart, 1985, 1986; McGraw & Harbison-Briggs, 1989). Indeed, there are domains of expertise wherein the primary method of reasoning involves explicitly comparing each given case to past cases. A clear example comes from avionics engineering (Weitzenfeld & Klein, 1979). The task of some avionics engineers is to predict the reliability and maintainability of new aircraft components or systems, and they do so on the basis of historical data about functionally or structurally similar components on older aircraft.

What this discussion of reasoning in context suggests is not just that expert reasoning depends on the domain but that the knowledge over which reasoning operates shapes the reasoning. The leads us to the notion of "mental models."

Mental Models

Many discussions of problem-solving strategies rely on the notion of the "mental model" (Anderson, 1983; Gentner & Stevens, 1983). Assuming that ongoing cognition, as well as problem solving and decision making, involves the understanding of information and events in terms of organized knowledge, the mental model concept is intended to capture the idea that people imaginally simulate events based on an understanding of concepts, lawful regularities, causal dynamics, and expectations, and then they test hypotheses that derive from the mental simulation (Beach, 1993; Hoffman, Trafton, & Roebber, 2008; Klein & Hoffman, 2007; Miller, 1984). The formation and refinement of a mental model is related to, but is more than, hypothetico-deductive reasoning. There, the focus is on the formulation and testing of individual hypotheses. Mental model formation and refinement is the broader explanatory envelope for this. The focus of the decision maker or problem solver is on developing richer, fuller mental representations that have explanatory and predictive value. The mental model refinement cycle notion has often been manifest in modern research and theory on expertise. The notion, or some variation of it, appears in numerous discussions of expert reasoning.

In a number of studies of expertise using CTA methods, researchers have observed the mental model refinement cycle (e.g., Anderson, 1982; Chi et al., 1982; Klein, 1998; Norman, 1987; Schumacher & Czerwinski, 1992; Voss et al., 1983). Experts usually "prethink" problems in an initial conceptual, strategic analysis (Glaser & Chi, 1988; McDermott & Larkin, 1978; Shanteau, 1989; Sternberg, 1977). Furthermore, the development of expertise involves an increase in flexibility—the ability to make adjustments and use feedback to modify initial decisions (Shanteau, 1989). A refinement cycle was observed in Kleinmuntz's (1968) early protocol analysis of problem solving by an expert neurologist. The cycle has been observed in other types of medical diagnosis (Groen & Patel, 1988; Kundel & Nodine, 1978) and in computer software design (Jeffries et al., 1981). Schön (1983) observed the refinement cycle, which he called "reflection in action" and "frame experimentation," in a number of professions: psychotherapy, engineering, architecture, town planning, and management. Recent research on the development of "job competence tests" has confirmed the existence of the cycle in the reasoning of expert business managers: "Planning/causal thinking is essentially hypothesis generation [and] diagnostic information seeking is the natural outcome" (Klemp & McClelland, 1986, p. 40).

An illustration of the mental model refinement cycle in a domain of expertise comes from studies of weather forecasters. "The verbal accounts of … their judgmental processes rarely contain statistical frequencies and Baysean algebra. They usually contain causal arguments" (Allen, 1982, p. 1). Maja-Lisa Perby (1989) conducted a CTA project on forecasting over a period of several years, using methods of observation and interviewing. She noted that the forecasters spend most of their time with pen in hand at traditional work methods intended to "assimilate information" (drawing isobars, areas of fog, etc.). However, these map preparation activities were all really in service of the formation of an "inner picture" that integrates background knowledge of principles and cause–effect relations, complications in the use of the principles when applied to specific dynamic circumstances, and some degree of "aesthetic consciousness" or a feeling of having achieved a coherent explanation.

> [This] inner weather picture gradually builds up in the minds of meteorologists and leads to understanding and the development of skill. … To make a forecast is not a distinct step in the work of a meteorologist: forecasts are made continuously, as an integrated part of elaborating an inner weather picture. (Perby, 1989, pp. 39, 46)

As one forecaster put it, "My first picture is quite abstract—I use a theoretical model of the strata of the atmosphere. During the work shift the abstractions disappear more and more. The picture is filled out by the weather as it actually is" (p. 46).

Hoffman (1987b) analyzed a number of the forecasting deliberations of small groups of expert meteorologists. Each deliberation had a leader, who would run through his or her forecast in a meteorological chart room, making frequent reference to various charts, satellite images, radar images, and tables of observational data. Hoffman took notes on the deliberator's comments and hypotheses and noted which of the available displays were referred to and for how long. The results showed the basic reasoning sequence that is typically involved in the weather forecasting task. The first step in the deliberations is essentially inductive and abductive hypothesis formation (bottom-up processing, category recognition, mental model formation). That is, one goes from an initial survey of data to an initial mental model and from that to some hypotheses. But the reasoning does not stop there—the actual forecast would come much later. Rather, there appeared a reasoning cycle involving a repeated (or continuing) loop.

Invariably, the first run through the mental modeling cycle begins with current regional observations (e.g., temperature, winds, etc.) and the most recent satellite images, which provide the "big picture." In the first cycle, weather data are scanned to form an initial mental model and derive a "ballpark" assessment of the current weather situation and the relevant atmospheric dynamics at a large scale (i.e., hemispheric scale and a period of many days). At that point, reasoning becomes top-down, with the mental model suggesting both predictions and testable hypotheses. The second cycle begins with a detailed inspection of particular data types (e.g., the output of mathematical forecasting models), with an eye toward refining or disconfirming the initial mental model and converging on local weather and a shorter time frame (i.e., days). For example, if the mental model suggests that thunderstorms are likely to occur, the meteorologist will almost certainly inspect half-hourly visible and infrared photographs of cloud cover. There are variations on the cycle theme, of course. For example, forecasting deliberations would occasionally get sidetracked into comparisons of the particular tendencies of different mathematical and statistical forecasting models. However, across all the forecasting deliberations, the cycle usually occurred at least twice, sometimes more for forecasting situations that were somehow tough.

Integrated Models of Reasoning

The literature on expertise, and expert–novice differences, has yielded two general models or frameworks for understanding expertise. One of these is a general (or macrocognitive) model of reasoning that characterizes experts; the other is a general model of reasoning that describes novices and apprentices (or learners) and obstacles to their achievement of expertise.

The "Base Model" of Expertise

The Base Model of expertise presented in Figure 8.2 is intended to capture a number of decision-making strategies. This integrative model regards the Duncker or mental model refinement cycle, recognition priming, and decision analysis as complementary and necessary to a full understanding of the richness of reasoning (Klein, 1989a, 1993b).

This model, or some variation on it, captures the core ideas from many discussions of problem solving, including expert problem solving. An example is a study by Daniel Serfaty, Jean MacMillan, and their colleagues (Serfaty, MacMillan, Entin, & Entin, 1997). The researchers were interested in investigating command-level decision making in the battlefield, and they proposed a general model involving the following sequence:

1. Mental modeling of the situation→
2. Schema recognition→

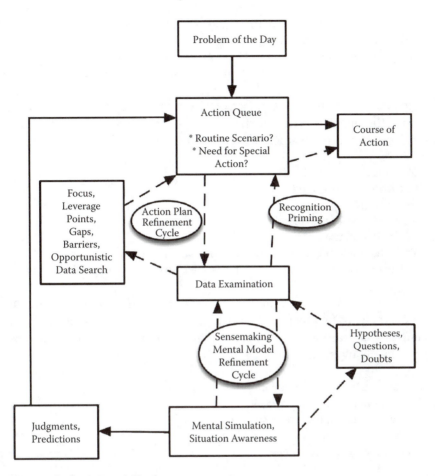

FIGURE 8.2 The "Base Model" of expert reasoning.

3. Formation of an initial plan→
4. Exploration of the plan→
5. Refinement of the plan→
6. Imaginary evaluation of plan effectiveness

The similarity to both the Duncker reasoning model and the Base Model of expertise is apparent.

Another instantiation of the Base Model can be found in the results from a study of expertise in medical diagnosis conducted by Benjamin Kuipers and his colleagues (Kuipers, Moskowitz, & Kassirer, 1988). In their study, the subdomain was medical diagnosis of pulmonary disease. From medical records, the researchers selected a case of preleukemia with complications (pneumonia, fever, respiratory fungus infection, loss of kidney function). Next, three specialists were asked to comment on the case, presented in the form of descriptions of events and indicators as the case proceeded over time. The experts were engaged in a TAPS task and an interview that was structured by probe questions. Statements in the transcripts were coded in terms of the following:

1. Expressions of the ontology of the domain (e.g., concepts),
2. Assertions of if–then relations,
3. Statements of reasoning processes in terms of goals or explanations, and
4. Statements of the likelihoods of alternative situations or outcomes.

In general, experts reasoned by "successive refinement of an abstract plan combined with the opportunistic insertion of steps" (Kuipers et al., 1988, p. 193). The steps in decision making that Kuipers et al. outlined are as follows:

1. Conceptualize the abstract→
2. Recognize the uncertainties of the case→
3. Treat or test?→
4. What's the risk of the treatment or the test?→
5. If you will test, use which test?→
6. What's the trade-off of risk versus the information gained?→
7. Review the plan as new data come in or under various hypothetical circumstances

In his discussions of human information processing (primarily focusing on decision support systems for process control), Cognitive Systems Engineer Jens Rasmussen (see Figure 8.3 in Rasmussen, 1986b; see chapter 7 of this book) described problem solving as involving the following:

1. Detect need for action→
2. Observe information and data→
3. Identify present state of the system→
4. Interpret consequences for current task→
5. Evaluate performance criteria

Rasmussen's "states of knowledge" would correspond to mental modeling—a "dynamic world model"—a concept that figures prominently in his theory (see Rasmussen, 1986b, chap. 10). In addition, Rasmussen indicated a number of "shunting paths," for example, a path going directly from an observation to a task procedure. This would be recognition priming. Note that both Kuipers's and Rasmussen's variations on the Base Model include some element of decision analysis.

The Base Model fits neatly with a model of the reasoning of expert industrial designers put forward by Kruger and Cross (2006; Cross, 2004) based on their studies using TAPS methods:

1. Gather and assess data and facts→
2. Identify constraints, define problems→
3. Generate partial solutions→
4. Evaluate solutions (loop back to Steps 2 and 3)→
5. Evaluate performance (loop back to Step 2)→
6. Assemble solution

To summarize, it is now fairly clear that expertise can be defined in terms of the development of proficient skill or performance. However, it is less clear that expertise can be defined in terms of any special reasoning processes that experts might possess, although experts within a domain do differ in terms of styles (which can be understood as variations on the Base Model). In terms of the general or basic problem-solving strategies, such as divide and conquer and means-ends analysis, experts seem to be "just plain folk." This begs the question of where experts get the good hypotheses that they infer (Norman, personal communication, 2007).

Cognitive Flexibility Theory

Research by Paul Feltovich, Rand Spiro, and their colleagues on expert–novice differences in domains of medicine investigated how people deal with difficult, challenging cases (e.g., Feltovich et al., 2001; Feltovich et al., 1989). That research identified characteristics of problems that cause cognitive difficulty for learners but not for experts. It also revealed how people respond to these elements of difficulty in learning and in the application of knowledge.

The research was initially driven by the identification of important biomedical science concepts that routinely cause difficulty among students for understanding and application. These concepts were identified by a large-scale polling of experts (medical school teachers) across the United States and Canada. Experts were asked to propose areas of basic biomedical science that were both important to the practice of medicine and also very difficult for learners to master (Dawson-Saunders, Feltovich, Coulson, & Steward, 1990; see also Patel, Kaufman, & Magder, 1991). The resulting compilation was used to guide the research on cognitive responses to difficulty, using CTA methods such as TAPS tasks. The research identified characteristics of subject matter or situations that cause difficulty for learners (Feltovich et al., 2001; Feltovich et al., 1989, 1993). The "dimensions of difficulty" that make tasks difficult and require mental effort on the part of learners, but that are less troublesome for experts, are presented in Table 8.1.

What this research revealed is expressed as an "if–then" conditional in Table 8.2. The if–then conditional expresses the "reductive tendency," the inclination for learners to construct understandings and categories that are overly simplistic. The reductive tendency is an inevitable consequence of how people learn (Feldman, 2003; Feltovich, Hoffman, & Woods, 2004). That is, when people are forming a new understanding or developing a new category, their knowledge is necessarily incomplete. It is only through additional experience and thought that distinctions come to be perceived, understood, and learned. So at any point in time, the human's understanding of anything that is at all complex, even some of the understandings held by domain experts, is bound to be simplifying at least in some respects. In the areas of complex cognition studied (e.g., the learning of clinical medicine), the reductive tendency has been shown to lead to significant misconceptions (e.g., Coulson, Feltovich, & Spiro, 1989; Feltovich et al., 2001; Spiro, Feltovich, Coulson, & Anderson, 1989) and in some instances to degraded medical care (Coulson, Feltovich, & Spiro, 1997). In addition, the misconceptions and errors that develop can be resistant to change, an obstacle to the achievement of expertise. When learners are confronted with evidence contrary to their views, they engage mental maneuvers to rationalize their faulty beliefs without fundamentally altering their views. These are the "knowledge shields." Twenty-three

TABLE 8.1 The Dimensions of Difficulty

Static versus dynamic

Are important aspects of a situation captured by a fixed "snapshot," or are the critical characteristics captured only by the changes from frame to frame? Are phenomena static and scalar, or do they possess dynamic vectorial characteristics?

Discrete versus continuous

Do processes proceed in discernable steps, or are they unbreakable continua? Are attributes describable by a small number of categories (e.g., dichotomous classifications like large–small), or is it necessary to recognize and use entire continuous dimensions (e.g., the full dimension of size) or large numbers of categorical distinctions?

Separable versus interactive

Do processes occur independently or with only weak interaction, or is there strong interaction and interdependence?

Sequential versus simultaneous

Do processes occur one at a time, or do multiple processes occur at the same time?

Homogeneous versus heterogeneous

Are components or explanatory schemes uniform (or similar) across a system, or are they diverse?

Single versus multiple representations

Do elements in a situation afford single (or just a few) interpretations, functional uses, categorizations, and so on, or do they afford many? Are multiple representations (e.g., multiple perspectives, schemas, analogies, case presidents, etc.) required to capture and convey the meaning of a process or situation?

Mechanism versus organicism

Are effects traceable to simple and direct causal agents, or are they the product of more systemwide, organic functions? Can important and accurate understandings be gained by comprehending just parts of the system, or must the entire system be comprehended for even the parts to be understood well?

Linear versus nonlinear

Are functional relationships linear or nonlinear (i.e., are relationships between input and output variables proportional or nonproportional)? Can a single line of explanation convey a concept or account for a phenomenon, or are multiple overlapping lines of explanation required for adequate coverage?

Universal versus conditional

Do guidelines and principles hold in much the same way (without the need for substantial modification) across different situations, or is there great context sensitivity in there application?

Regular versus irregular

Is a domain characterized by a high degree of routinizabilty or prototypicality across cases, or do cases differ considerably from each other even when they are called by the same name? Are there strong elements of symmetry and repeatable patterns in concepts and phenomena, or is there a prevalence of asymmetry and absence of consistent pattern?

"Surface" versus "deep"

Are important elements for understanding and for guiding action delineated and apparent on the surface of a situation, or are they more covert, relational, abstract?

TABLE 8.2 The Conditional Expression of the Reductive Tendency

IF the material to be learned or understood is characterized by the second alternative in each of the pairs in Table 8.1, that is,

- events are dynamic,
- event parameters are continuous,
- event parameters are highly interactive,
- events are simultaneous and parallel,
- events involve heterogeneous components or explanatory principles,
- events can best be understood by multiple representations,
- events are organic (evolving, emergent),
- events involve nonlinear dynamics,
- events involve multiple interdependencies,
- cases show asymmetries and irregularities; and
- underlying principles are abstract and nonobvious,

THEN

- learners will tend to interpret the situations as though they were characterized by the simpler alternatives;
- their understandings will tend to be reductive;
- they will tend to attempt to defend their simple understandings when confronted with facts that suggest that the situation is more complex than what they suppose—these "knowledge shields" will allow them to maintain their incorrect beliefs and understandings; and
- learners will need effort, practice, and experience (i.e., the achievement of expertise) to begin to overcome the knowledge shields.

of them have been identified (Feltovich et al., 2001), but just a few examples will be presented here.

One knowledge shield is called demean effect. When confronted with evidence contrary to their faulty view, learners using this shield acknowledge that the evidence may be true but dismiss it as trivial—"it's not a big deal."

> *Instruction:* As a vessel expands during the ascending phase of a pulse, it does not mean that all of the blood in the expanded vessel simply flows downstream through a now larger vessel, because some of it, for instance, flows into the expansion of the vessel itself.
>
> *Student response:* [long pause] Um, I'm going to agree. It sounds, it makes sense that some of it would flow into the expansion of the vessel, but I'm sure it is not a big part of it.

Another example demonstrates two knowledge shields. The first is the Argument From Faulty Causal Reasoning, in which the learner constructs a false causal explanation for anomalous evidence, consistent with his or her belief. The other is called Extirpation, in which the phenomenon to be explained is isolated from its real context. In the following example, both devices are used to avoid a real change in belief.

> *Instruction:* In the pulsing cardiovascular system, some of the energy produced by the heart is used up in making blood flow into and out of the expansion of vessel walls. Hence, factors associated with flow into and out of the vessel walls, such as stiffness and heart rate, contribute to opposition to blood flow.

Student response: And I agree with that, um, because when blood goes into the expanded area and then that expanded area contracts, the blood's gonna go both forward and backward, and this is going to create opposition to the other blood coming in.

Although this research first had its impact primarily in the domain of biomedical science as it relates to clinical medicine, it has found widespread application. Diverse areas where the research on the dimensions of difficulty and the reductive tendency have seen application and validation include biology (e.g., Patel, Kaufman, et al., 1991), complex systems (e.g., Hmelo-Silver & Pfeffer, in press; Resnick, 1996), laypeople's understanding of disease (Furze, Roebuck, Bull, Lewin, & Thompson, 2002), workplace error and mishap (Cook & Woods, 1994), military command and control (Leedom, 2001), and the process of design, especially the design of complex sociotechnical systems (e.g., Woods, 2002).

The knowledge shields and the reductive tendency are suggestive of human limitations, but the research led naturally to a broader theory of the flexibility of reasoning. Stephanie Boger-Mehall (2007) expressed this linkage in the following way:

Traditionally, instructors present information using a linear model. For example, a video may be shown from beginning to end or a textbook will be covered from chapter one to the next … cognitive flexibility theory suggests that this is not a problem when the information being presented is well-structured and simple. Often, however, as the difficulty of the material increases so does the ill-structuredness. When the knowledge domain to be taught is complex and ill-structured, the use of traditional linear instruction may be ineffective (Spiro, Feltovich, Jacobson, & Coulson, 1992; Spiro & Jehng, 1990). Straightforward, linear instruction in the form of tutorials, lectures, and many other formats will, according to cognitive flexibility theory, fail to accomplish important educational objectives in part because of oversimplification of the material presented. This oversimplification results in the inability to transfer knowledge across to new and varied domains. (Spiro et al., 1992)

The reductive tendency and knowledge shields combine to form a potent mix for both the development and the maintenance of misunderstandings of important and difficult subject matter, especially when misconceptions are reinforced by teachers and textbooks, as is often the case. But on the other hand, the studies of experts and expert–novice differences revealed that the achievement of proficiency depends on the learners' active, deliberative creation and refinement of their own knowledge. The Cognitive Flexibility Theory of Paul Feltovich, Rand Spiro, and their colleagues (Spiro et al., 1991, 1992; Spiro & Jehng, 1990) asserts that people (especially experts) have the ability to restructure their knowledge to adapt to complex, ill-structured problems. Cognitive flexibility is "the ability to represent knowledge from different conceptual and case perspectives and then, when the knowledge must later be used, the ability to construct from those different conceptual and case representations a knowledge ensemble tailored to the needs of the understanding or problem-solving situation at hand" (Spiro et al., 1992, p. 58). This ability hinges on experience with diverse problem types and on opportunities to understand the material from differing perspectives. This enables people to refine their understanding of concepts and the relations among concepts, in processes such as those discussed by Jean Piaget, i.e., assimilation and accomodation (e.g., Inhelder & Piaget, 1958) and David Ausubel (1968; Ausubel, Novak, & Hanesian, 1978). Flexibility theory also asserts that knowledge and knowledge-in-use are context dependent, and so instruction needs to be with reference to meaningful contexts.

The following entails some straightforward guidelines for effective instruction:

1. Learning activities must provide multiple representations of content.
2. Instructional materials should avoid oversimplifying the content domain and support context-dependent knowledge.
3. Instruction should be case based and emphasize knowledge construction, not transmission of information.
4. Knowledge sources should be highly interconnected rather than compartmentalized.

These guidelines have been widely and successfully applied since Cognitive Flexibility Theory was first published (e.g., Jonassen, Ambruso, & Olesen, 1992).

Cognitive Flexibility Theory bridges the gap between reasoning and knowledge, taking us from general models of expert reasoning to the research on expert knowledge and memory organization. One significant focus of Expertise Studies has stemmed from the empirical fact that experts can be distinguished by virtue of their knowledge.

What CTA Has Revealed About Expert Knowledge

In general, it does take a long time to become an expert, and by the time one has become an expert, one's knowledge is both specific to the domain and very extensive (Chase, 1983; Chiesi, Spilich, & Voss, 1979; Glaser, 1987; Scribner, 1984). Even though some experts may be said to "know it all," we are reminded by the reductive tendency that completeness per se is not an essential feature of knowledge organization, if only because knowledge is constantly evolving. One retired agronomy expert commented that he felt unqualified to judge a particular research project because he had not kept up with developments in that aspect of the discipline in the past few months, despite the fact that he had been a leading expert for 40 years (Gaeth, 1980).

It has been shown empirically that experts draw more complex conceptual distinctions than novices. For experts, the level of "basic objects" within their domain of expertise is more highly differentiated (Murphy & Wright, 1984). Estimates of the extent of expert knowledge put it anywhere from tens to hundreds of thousands of propositions and somewhere in the neighborhood of 50,000 concepts (Lenat & Feigenbaum, 1987; Simon & Gilmartin, 1973). For example, chess masters can recognize tens of thousands of game patterns.

But knowledge extent is not all there is to it.

Knowledge Organization

"The heart of any successful reasoning system for a complex domain is the proper *organization* [italics added] of knowledge" (Glaser, 1987, p. 83). Experts' performance undoubtedly relies on a number of psychological processes, such as problem recognition and decision making. Nevertheless, it has been hypothesized that "the outstanding performance of experts derives primarily from how their knowledge is structured for retrieval, pattern recognition, and inference" (Glaser, 1987, p. 90). Conversely, the poor performance of novices is often attributed to their inadequate knowledge representations (Chi et al., 1982; Murphy & Wright, 1984). Hence, a great deal of the research in Expertise Studies has focused on revealing the knowledge representations of novices and experts.

The driving hypothesis is that experts' domain-specific knowledge is highly complex, highly organized, and highly coherent or cohesive; that is, concepts are interrelated in meaningful ways organized according to categories and dimensions that are important and necessary and functional for their domain functions (Bordage, Connell, Chang, Gecht, & Sinacore, 1997; Bordage & Lemieux, 1991; Bordage & Zacks, 1984; Glaser, 1987; Mandler, 1967; Scribner, 1984). Experts' categories or schemas are "richer" (Chi, Feltovich, & Glaser, 1981; Chi et al., 1982; Chi & Koeske, 1983; Gregg, 1976; Lesgold, 1984; Posner, 1988; Voss & Post, 1988).

Experts are able to use their vast knowledge effectively and efficiently because they have larger "chunks." This shows when experts recall more from cases (Muzzin, Norman, Feightner, & Tugwell, 1983; Norman, Brooks, & Allen, 1989; Schmidt & Boshuizen, 1993a; Verkoeijen et al., 2004). Experts rely on conceptual categories that are principled (or more "abstract") (Voss et al., 1983), and experts know that conceptually different problem types may nonetheless manifest the same surface features (Murphy & Wright, 1984). This sort of finding is consistent across studies of diverse domains of expertise (cf. Popovic, 2003).

Such an organization would enable experts to distinguish relevant and irrelevant information and to "make order out of chaos" by simplifying what appears to the novice to be staggering complexity. Organization would also reduce or even eliminate the need for elaborate or time-consuming memory search: Even though knowledge is complex, one could "get directly at" the meaning. For example, the novice auditor is confronted by dizzying arrays of numbers, but the expert sees what is immediately relevant (Krogstad, Ettenson, & Shanteau, 1984).

Results from studies in which computer programmers comprehend and generate programs (while thinking aloud) have shown that experts represent programs in terms of the main functional processes that are needed to accomplish the goal of the program (Adelson, 1981, 1984; Jeffries et al., 1981; McKeithen et al., 1981). Experienced programmers are better able to identify bugs, especially those that can be found only after achieving a conceptual understanding of overall program function. Expert programmers recall a much greater amount of a program than initiates, even after a short exposure, hypothetically because their memory organization falls at a more conceptual level (see Sonnentag, Niessen, & Volmer, 2006).

Groen and Patel (1988) had expert medical diagnosticians and medical students read and recall descriptions of clinical cases. The results showed that experts tend to remember not the verbatim cases but their underlying "gist" or meaning, including their own inferences. Of course, this finding has its analogue in normal memory for short stories (Bartlett, 1932). A number of recent studies of experts' recall have shown this effect and, furthermore, that experts in diverse domains are better able to reorganize and make sense of scrambled information (Chase & Simon, 1973).

In a study of expert fighter pilots, Schvaneveldt et al. (1985) began by interviewing some experts to determine the basic elements involved in two particular scenarios, one simple and one complex. Example elements are "overtake," "accelerate," "the target is in range," and "the target is maneuvering." Next, some trainees and experts were presented with a list of the basic elements. Their task was to make pairwise comparisons and rate the items' similarity. For the experts, the concepts seemed to cluster into three groups: concepts that refer to events, concepts that refer to distances, and concepts that refer to orientation. Next, the scaling data were transformed into a graphical representation of concept nodes and relational links. The experts produced similar graphs, in which the important relations were made salient, whereas the initiates all produced different and less organized graphs.

Empirical studies of expert chemists, social policy makers, electronic circuit designers, clinical psychologists, nurses, mathematicians, radiologists, telephone system operators, and musicians have all produced similar demonstrations of the expert–novice difference in memory organization.

As we discussed earlier in this chapter, the knowledge of experts is often said to be manifested in the form of mental models, which are dynamic, concept-based, imaginal representations of entities, events, properties, and relations (Larkin, 1983; Miller, 1984; Schumacher & Czerwinski, 1992). The transformations or changes within a mental model represent the known cause–effect or principled relations among the modeled objects or events. A striking example of this would be the reports of Nikola Tesla's ability to imaginally design and test electric motors and other devices (Cheney, 2001; Johnson, 1982). (It has been reported that many engineers develop an ability to imaginally design and test structures.) Mental models resemble the modeled world perceptually—this is the imagery component. But they also represent abstract concepts and functional relations. There are some domains, such as government domestic policy making, where mental models are largely "abstract" (Voss et al., 1983). That is, they take the form of schemata that capture the essential features rather than the details and variabilities of concepts, categories, or situations (Adelson, 1981; Lesgold et al., 1988; Soloway et al., 1988).

Memory Interference?

We mentioned the notion of interference earlier in this chapter, in reference to CTA methodology, but interference manifests itself in another way in Expertise Studies. The organization of knowledge might help banish a counterintuitive "paradox of interference" that arises in the case of expertise. A long-standing hypothesis in the psychology of learning is that memory retrieval can fail because of interference. Access to memory (in such tasks as recognizing words that had been presented in lists) has been shown to be affected by semantic similarity or relatedness (cf. Schvaneveldt et al., 1985). Memories that are somehow similar to the to-be-recalled material (or close to it in a hypothetical memorial space or associative network) can be activated instead of, or in addition to, the target material. This causes retrieval interference, manifested as an omission or intrusion error in recall tasks or a false recognition error in recognition tasks. Numerous laboratory studies of learning have shown that reaction time to retrieve a particular fact about a concept increases as a person learns more facts about the concept. This is called the "fan effect" (Anderson, 1974, 1983). In theory, as a memory is activated or accessed, so too are memories or facts that are associated with it, causing a spread or fan of activation, interfering with the access of the target memory.

The interference hypothesis, and the hypothetical machinery that accompanies it, is one of the cornerstones of naive associationism. It seems to mean that expertise is impossible: The more one stores in memory, the less efficient one should be at storing or retrieving new memories and the more interference should occur on retrieval (Morris, 1988; Smith, Adams, & Schor, 1978). Fortunately for those who fret over paradoxes that are obviously a consequence of incomplete theories and of research that looks solely at artificial tasks and the performance of college-age "subjects," research has also shown that memory search for knowledge that is domain specific can become *more* efficient with repeated use. Specifically, Reder and Anderson (1980; Reder, 1987) have demonstrated that the fan effect does not occur when a domain of knowledge involves concepts and facts that are meaningfully or thematically integrated, as would be the case for expert knowledge

Indeed, knowledge that is semantically well integrated can be regarded as operating as a kind of mnemonic (Beach, 1988; Bellezza, 1992) in which meaning can be imposed (top-down) on complex data patterns (Egan & Schwartz, 1979; Vessey, 1985).

Myles-Worsley, Johnston, and Simons (1988) had expert (resident), journeyman (intern), and apprentice (medical student) radiologists examine and interpret a set of chest X-rays. Expertise led to faster recognition of distinguishing features and a reduced sensitivity to irrelevant features. Other studies of experts' memory and comprehension capabilities in domains as diverse as electronic circuit design, bird-watching, and sports have shown that experts benefit from their knowledge by being better able to assimilate new information into appropriate preexisting knowledge structures (Bellezza, 1992; Charness, 1976; Chiesi, Spilich, & Voss, 1979; Coltheart & Walsh, 1988; Dee-Lucas & Larkin, 1986; Ericsson & Polson, 1988). The more you know about a domain, the more and faster you can learn new things within that domain and the faster you can distinguish and categorize within-domain stimulus information (Lenat & Feigenbaum, 1987; Morris, 1988) Conversely, the learning of things outside of the domain is not facilitated by increasing within-domain expertise (Hatano & Osawa, 1983; Morris, 1988). In other words, memory interference does not occur for experts precisely because their within-domain memories are meaningfully integrated.

Experts can make memory errors, of course. For example, Dawson, Zeitz, and Wright (1989) had expert clinical psychologists recall test cases, and their recall showed an alteration of the order of presentation of information, reflecting their own categories and understanding in the chunking of information into conceptually meaningful units, a form of "gist recall" effect. Arkes and Freedman (1984) had baseball experts (college students) read stories about games and then attempt to recognize sentences from the stories. They were good at correctly recognizing sentences from the stories but also tended to falsely recognize synonym substitutions and inferences from the stories. Chiesi, Spilich, and Voss (1979) and Spilich, Vesonder, Chiesi, and Voss (1979) also asked baseball experts to remember sentences about game events. Some of the target sentences were accompanied by additional sentences that helped set the game context, and with that greater contextual information, the experts were better able to recognize and recall the target sentences. The context sentences helped them understand the game events, but this made them more likely to recall their own inferences and elaborations (see also Groen & Patel, 1988). In this research, the experts are showing that they remember their own conceptual understanding of the stories, not the verbatim stories. People "acquire an abstract relational concept which defines a class of events, not simply information about specific instances which they have experienced" (Shaw & Wilson, 1976, p. 208). The false recognition phenomena that occur as a consequence of conceptual-level learning have analogous results in studies of memory using the "depth of comprehension" paradigm (Craik & Lockhart, 1972) and the constructivist view of memory (Bransford, Barclay, & Franks, 1972).

We have referred to mental models, and we have alluded to the schema notion. On such matters, the boundaries between psychology and phenomenology get rather fuzzy, and debate can go on forever. But one issue involving the concept of knowledge relates rather directly to our topic of CTA.

The Issue of Different Kinds of Knowledge, in the Context of CTA

In the literature on expertise, a number of distinctions are used to talk about different kinds of knowledge (Glaser, 1987).

Factual knowledge: Factual knowledge consists of facts about objects, events, and concepts. It can be stated formally as propositions, which assert the existence of objects and the occurrence of events, and then predicate particular properties and relations of the objects or events (Popper, 1972).

Procedural knowledge: Procedural knowledge consists of procedures, rules, and strategies (Anderson, 1983; Rumelhart & Norman, 1978), including knowledge about what to do when conducting tasks. It also includes knowledge of what to do for exceptions to the standard rules and procedures. It has been argued that procedural knowledge is what makes it possible for experts to "act with good judgment in unique situations" (Josefson, 1988, p. 26). Experts often conceive of problems in terms of the procedures (strategies, goals, subgoals) they would use in solving them (Chi et al., 1982; Dreyfus & Dreyfus, 1986; Glaser, 1987; LaFrance, 1989; Pennington, 1987).

Metaknowledge: This is knowledge about how one knows and thinks, especially one's knowledge of one's own skills and capabilities and the skills of using knowledge. It includes the ability to plan and monitor ongoing problem-solving efforts, the ability to judge the difficulty of problems, the ability to use time and resources most efficiently, a sensitivity to relevant new information, a sensitivity to one's own capabilities, and an awareness of limitations in the breadth or depth of one's experience. Metaknowledge of these types is generally regarded as being an essential aspect of expertise (Chi, 1978; Chi et al., 1982; Clancey, 1988; Ericsson & Polson, 1988; Glaser & Chi, 1988; Larkin, 1983; Miyake & Norman, 1979; Simon & Simon, 1978). Indeed, it is possible to define the highest level of expertise (i.e., the master level) in terms of the ability to reason about intuitions and create new strategies for "tough cases" (Dreyfus, 1989; Dreyfus & Dreyfus, 1986; Kolodner, 1983). The metaknowledge category entails the interesting prediction that experts may sometimes perform more slowly than novices (Sternberg, 1977). It has been reported that experts often do "prethink" problems and decisions, taking time to form conceptually appropriate representations and considering many possibilities in advance. When confronted with test cases, experts spend time in an initial conceptual, strategic analysis; novices generally do not (Glaser & Chi, 1988; Larkin, McDermott, Simon, & Simon, 1980; Shanteau, 1989; Voss et al., 1983).

Of course, knowledge of these three different content–function types cannot be independent. For example, across development, a full understanding of declarative or propositional knowledge cannot be attained without practice at procedures and strategies (Gullers, 1988). It would take a lengthy philosophical discourse to do a full analysis of the notion of procedural knowledge and what it means to say that such knowledge qualifies as "knowledge." Complicating this is the hypothesis that knowledge can be "tacit." This notion brings to the forefront a hypothetical dimension of verbalizability, which can be effectively captured in terms of three levels:

Declarative or explicit knowledge: This is knowledge that can be verbally explicated. It is obviously true, if not definitive of the word *knowledge,* that some knowledge is of this kind. For example, performance at grammaticality judgments for stimuli in a mini artificial language can be correlated with the rules that participants deliberately, consciously derive during initial learning (Dulany, Carlson, & Dewey, 1984). It is typically asserted, or assumed, that factual knowledge is declarative knowledge.

Knowledge that cannot be easily verbalized: Sometimes better performance and verbalizability of knowledge go hand in hand (e.g., Anderson, 1987; Lewis & Anderson, 1985), but sometimes they do not (e.g., Broadbent, FitzGerald, & Broadbent, 1986; Rouse & Morris, 1986). Some knowledge is "sort of declarative," but special tasks must be used to help experts verbalize it or even think it through systematically and explicitly. For example, it might be difficult for me to describe precisely how I brush my teeth; nonetheless, I have a clear knowledge, which I can invoke by relying on visual, kinesthetic, and tactile imagery, of the routine I follow whenever I brush. If I were to go through it and think about it systematically, scaffolded by a CTA procedure, or be confronted with the challenge of doing it more efficiently, I could spell out my knowledge of how I brush my teeth and what my goals are for each component activity. Sometimes experts are aware of when they are having difficulty expressing their knowledge, and they deliberately work on this as a part of refining their skills (Crandall, Klein, & Hoffman, 2006; Josefson, 1988).

Knowledge that cannot be verbalized at all: Although this stretches the notion of knowledge well into a philosophical twilight zone, it has often been noted in the literature that experts can be highly verbal in personal conversations yet inarticulate about the strategic reasoning they employ in making their decisions (Cullen & Bryman, 1988; Josefson, 1988; Kidd & Welbank, 1984; Lawrence, 1988; Voss, Greene, Post, & Penner, 1983). "Experts in making a diagnosis are not necessarily experts in explaining the process" (Michalski & Chilausky, 1980, p. 63). When asked to describe their strategies, they may make vague statements such as, "That's just the way it is" (Dino & Shanteau, 1984). One expert firefighter attributed his rapid perceptual understanding of a novel fire situation to a "sixth sense" (Klein, Calderwood, & Clinton-Cirocco, 1986). Lusted (1960) reported that an acclaimed radiologist explained a difficult diagnosis by saying, "Because it looks like it." In the extreme form, it is sometimes claimed that experts possess knowledge that literally cannot be verbalized at all (see Gordon, 1992; Hoffman, 1992b).

Experts sometimes ascribe their complex reasoning to hunches or intuitions, when in fact the details of their reasoning can be spelled out through the application of systematic CTA procedures (Wagner & Sternberg, 1986; Waterman, 1986). Experts sometimes deny that they are working in a systematic fashion, when a properly designed and conducted knowledge elicitation procedure can show that they really are (Hartley, 1981; Ryan, 1970). But the claim underlying this knowledge category is that there is some "knowledge that is truly implicit … knowledge that can be demonstrated but not verbalized" (Berry, 1987, p. 147). Some developers of expert systems have observed that highly skilled experts can carry out tasks without being aware of how or why they do what they do (e.g., Kidd & Cooper, 1985). Thus, knowledge is variously called "perceptual," "tacit," "intuitive," or "unconscious" (cf. Broadbent et al., 1986; Dreyfus & Dreyfus, 1986; Evans, 1988; Feigenbaum, 1977; Sanderson, 1989). The belief here is the notion that some knowledge, or a kind of knowledge, is simply not "hooked up" to consciousness (Fowler, Wolford, Slade, & Tassinary, 1981). "Skill knowledge exists in industry, but cannot be coded, stored, or taught in school" (Gullers, 1988, p. 36). Hypothetically, such knowledge cannot be formalized as propositions or expressed as verbal rules but must be learned through practice and experience. As far as awareness is concerned, such knowledge can be hinted at only with metaphors (Gullers, 1988; Janik, 1988, 1990). And of course one wonders whether it should be called "knowledge," or something else.

By setting up a clever experiment such that the participants do not experience the full variation of the independent variables, social psychologists have found it possible to get people to do things with little or no verbalizable understanding of why they are doing what they are doing (Nisbett & Wilson, 1977). Some studies of concept formation have shown that performance can come to reflect the underlying rules, even though participants are apparently unaware of the rule they are following (Berry & Broadbent, 1984; Broadbent & Aston, 1978; Brooks, 1978b; Lewicki, 1986; Reber, Allen, & Regan, 1985; Reber & Lewis, 1977). Some research on chess masters has demonstrated that ability to recall game information can be unrelated to having made correct evaluations and moves (Holding & Pfau, 1985).

Taking this general notion further into the twilight zone, some researchers have argued that most of an expert's knowledge is tacit (e.g., Micciche & Lancaster, 1989; Sell, 1985), especially procedural knowledge and metaknowledge. Tacit (sometimes called "latent") knowledge is believed to be knowledge that people have but are not aware of at any given time. Expert weather forecasters, for example, may know all sorts of things about the internal structure and dynamics of supercell thunderstorms, but at the time they are looking for supercell development on the radar, their knowledge of things such as the principles of convection and vorticity are just not "on their minds" (in their working memory?). Yet, if asked, they can tell you all about supercell formation, and notions of convection and vorticity are bound to be involved in their explanation. So, at one time the knowledge was there and, in a sense, reasoning depended on it, but only at a later time was the knowledge declarative. (Presumably, tacit knowledge that was declared can become tacit again later when thoughts move on? This is yet another philosophical conundrum of the notions of kinds of knowledge.)

Experts, like people in general, may have difficulty expressing knowledge that was never conceived explicitly or declaratively in the first place. That is, some implicit knowledge is acquired through a process of implicit learning (Broadbent et al., 1986; Hayes & Broadbent, 1988; Reber, 1976). In learning to control complex systems (e.g., simulated economic models, models of a transportation system or an industrial process), an individual may achieve a high level of performance through lots of practice yet be unable to correctly answer questions about the system that is being controlled (Berry & Broadbent, 1984; Broadbent, 1977; Broadbent & Aston, 1978). Conversely, lots of explicit instruction can enable one to correctly answer questions but does not necessarily lead to improvement in task performance. There can be an increase in task performance without an increase in verbalizable knowledge or a drastic change in conceptual understanding and verbalizable knowledge without a corresponding change in task performance.

In the history of psychology, one finds many discussions of the notion of "automaticity" (James, 1890), that knowledge or skill undergoes a "declarative-to-procedural shift" or becomes "routinized" (Anderson, 1987). In a number of cognitive theories of the development of cognition, developmental levels are defined entirely in terms of the development of automaticity and a reliance on implicit knowledge, that is, procedural knowledge and perceptual skills rather than explicit or declarative knowledge (e.g., Benner, 1984; Charness & Campbell, 1988; Dreyfus & Dreyfus, 1986; Fitts, 1964; Fitts & Posner, 1967; Gordon, 1992; Norman, 1987; Rasmussen, 1986a, b). Dreyfus and Dreyfus (1986; Dreyfus, 1989) proposed a five-level theory that focuses exclusively on the development of "intuition" (i.e., nonverbalizable procedural knowledge and metaknowledge), which they regard as the essence of skill and expertise.

Most such theories have levels such as these:

> *Level One:* Practitioners at this level have knowledge that is declarative or propositional, and their reasoning is said to be explicit and deliberative. Problem solving focuses on the learning of facts, deliberative reasoning, and a reliance on general strategies.
> *Level Two:* The declarative knowledge of practitioners at this level has become procedural and domain specific. They can automatically recognize some problem types or situations.
> *Level Three:* At this level, procedures become highly routinized.
> *Level Four:* These practitioners are proficient and have a great deal of intuitive skill.
> *Level Five:* Practitioners at this highest level can deliberately reason about their own intuitions and generate new rules or strategies (what Dreyfus and Dreyfus called "deliberative rationality").

The essence of all such theories is the notion that reasoning or knowledge originates as an analytic, conscious, deliberative, stepwise process and evolves into rapid, automatic, nonconscious, understanding or immediate perceptual judgments.

Any particular bit of knowledge or particular reasoning strategy can theoretically be placed into one of the three categories of types of knowledge that we listed above and may fall somewhere on the dimension of accessibility. But out of all the combinations, only a few seem to be salient in discussions of expertise (Gordon, 1992). For instance, some researchers equate procedural knowledge with "knowledge that is not verbalizable in principle" (e.g., Anderson's "declarative to procedural shift") (Gammack, 1987; Gammack & Young, 1985; Gullers, 1988). Sometimes by "procedural knowledge" researchers seem to mean "knowledge about procedures that happens to be verbalizable." (Otherwise, it could not be elicited and included in an expert system, for example.) "Declarative knowledge" could be defined as "factual knowledge that happens to be verbalizable," but it is often taken for granted that all factual knowledge is verbalizable. To the contrary, experimental evidence suggests that experts' factual knowledge is sometimes highly proceduralized. That is, concepts are "bound" to procedures for their application and to conditions under which procedures are useful (Glaser, 1984). Such factual knowledge is verbalizable, but only with support (i.e., some sort of well-conducted CTA) or with the use of special tasks or materials. This phenomenon could be taken as an instance of "encoding specificity" (Tulving, 1983) or "transfer appropriate processing" (Bransford, 1979, chap. 3). Such phenomena have been demonstrated in the cognitive psychology laboratory and would belie the assumption that all factual knowledge is necessarily declarative (i.e., easily verbalized). The verbalizability or accessibility of knowledge may be highly cue, context, or task (CTA) dependent.

The early wave of comparative knowledge elicitation methodology research (Burton, Shadbolt, Hedgecock, & Rugg, 1987; Burton, Shadbolt, Rugg, & Hedgecock, 1988; Hoffman, 1987b) led to the "differential access hypothesis" that different kinds of knowledge might be more amenable to elicitation by particular CTA methods, and some studies suggested that differential access might occur (Cooke & McDonald, 1986, 1987; Evans, Jentsch, Hitt, Bowers, & Salas, 2001). For instance, tasks involving the generation of lists of domain concepts can in fact result in lists of domain concepts, and tasks involving the specification of procedures can in fact result in statements about rules or procedures. However, some studies have found little or no evidence for differential access (e.g., Adelman, 1989; Burton et al., 1987). We conclude that a strong version of the differential access hypothesis has not held up well under scrutiny. Many of the available CTA methods *can* say things about so-called declarative knowledge, so-called procedural knowledge, and so on. A recent project on expert weather forecasting (Hoffman, Coffey, & Carnot, 2000; see Hoffman, Trafton, & Roebber, 2008, compared a number of knowledge elicitation methods including protocol analysis, the Critical Decision method (see Hoffman, Crandall, & Shadbolt, 1998), the Knowledge Audit (Militello & Hutton, 1998), an analysis of "standard operating procedures" documents, the Recent Case Walkthrough method (see Crandall et al., 2006), a workspace and work patterns analysis (Vicente, 2000), and Concept Mapping. All methods yielded data that spoke to practitioner knowledge and to practitioner reasoning.

All knowledge elicitation and CTA methods can be used to identify leverage points—aspects of the work organization or work domain where even a modest infusion of supporting technologies might have positive results such as redesign of interfaces, redesign of the operations floor layout, creation of new functionalities for existing software, and ideas about entirely new software systems. (See the examples in chapter 12.)

Another lesson learned is that tacit knowledge is not a salient problem in applied contexts for expert knowledge elicitation of other kinds of CTA. A lingering concern has been the possibility that routine knowledge about procedures or task activities might become tacit, that is, so automatic as to be inexpressible via task reflection or any other form of verbal report. The empirical facts seem to mitigate the issue. For instance, in Concept Mapping interviews with domain experts, experience shows that almost every time, the experts will reach a point in making a Concept Map where they will say something like, *Well, I've never really thought about that, or thought about it in this way, but now that you mention it …* and what follows will be clear specification on some procedure, strategy, or aspect of subdomain knowledge that had not been articulated up to that point (Crandall et al., 2006). Good knowledge elicitation procedures are "effective scaffolds" (Crandall et al., 2006; Hoffman & Lintern, 2006).

Although there may be phenomena to which one could legitimately, or at least arguably, append the designation "tacit knowledge," there is no indication that such knowledge lies beyond the reach of science, in some unscientific twilight zone of intuitions or unobservables. Over and over again, the lesson is not that there is knowledge that experts literally cannot ever articulate, nor is it the issue of whether verbalization "interferes" with reasoning, but whether the knowledge elicitation or CTA procedure provides sufficient scaffolding to support the experts in articulating what they know. Support involves the specifics of the procedure (e.g., probe questions), but it also involves the fact that knowledge elicitation is a collaborative process. There is no substitute for the skill of the elicitor (e.g., in framing alternative suggestions and wordings). Likewise, there is no substitute for the skill of the participating practitioner, and some experts will have good insight but others will not. Although it might be possible for someone to prove the existence of "knowledge" that cannot be uncovered, we are not sure how such a demonstration proof might be engineered. Cognitive Systems Engineers face the immediate, practical challenges of designing new and better sociotechnical systems. They accomplish something when they uncover useful knowledge that might have otherwise been missed.

So far in this chapter we have discussed ideas from Expertise Studies concerning expert reasoning and knowledge. Naturally, a focus of the field of Expertise Studies is proficiency scaling and performance measurement. Research intended to explore the nature of expertise must be predicated on clear notions of what it means for someone to be called an "expert." This should include both conceptual and operational definitions (see Crandall et al., 2006; Hoffman, Trafton, & Roebber, 2008). Much of the research we have cited so far in this chapter involves tasks that can be regarded as instances of CTA (e.g., the TAPS task), although some of the research uses methods that are perhaps more properly considered psychological laboratory research methods (e.g., reaction-time tasks). In the next two sections of this chapter, we focus more squarely on knowledge elicitation as a form of CTA and methodological issues that have arisen in the study of expertise.

What Makes for a Good Method for Eliciting the Knowledge of Experts?

Given Expertise Studies' origins in psychology, it would be expected that preferred methods in Expertise Studies would resemble methods used in the experimental psychology laboratory (see Chi, 2006a, 2006b). Hoffman (1987b) referred to these as "limited information and constrained processing tasks."

Limited Information Constrained Processing Tasks

In the constrained processing method, the practitioner's familiar routines are constrained in some way. The experts may be explicitly instructed to adopt a particular strategy, for example. Conversely, the experts may be confronted with a task that challenges their usual strategy. For example, Hoffman (1986, 1987b) had expert terrain analysts inspect aerial photos for only 2 minutes—aerial photo interpretation ordinarily takes hours, even days. At first, the experts balked at the artificiality, but when encouraged to think of the task as a game rather than as a challenge to their expertise, they found the task to be interesting. Another curve ball that Hoffman introduced in the task was to capitalize on the participants' subdomain expertise. One participant, for instance, was a specialist in desert terrain, and he was presented with aerial photos of a tropical region. Following the 2-minute inspection period, the experts had to recall everything they could about the photos and provide their interpretation (e.g., "This region is an arid climate with shallow soils overlying tilted interbedded sandstone and limestone").

Results from this constrained processing task revealed the extent to which the experts achieve immediate perceptual understanding of terrain when viewing aerial photos (perhaps a form of recognition-primed decision making). For instance, after inspecting the tropical imagery for 2 minutes, one expert commented, "If you were to send troops there, they would have to be protected from bacterial infections." When asked how he knew that, the expert commented that he could tell from the ponds. The expert could see bacteria in a pond from 40,000 feet? No, but what the expert could see was flat interbedded limestone (in a homogeneous forest, the tree canopy informs about the terrain slope) in a tropical climate. Because the bedrock was lying flat, the distributaries led into ponds with no major tributary for an outlet. Stagnant water in a tropical climate means leguminous water plants, implying that the waterways would be laden with bacteria. This all seems like a long inference chain in retrospect, but in the image inspection task, it was more a matter of immediate perception built upon a refined knowledge base.

Hoffman (1998b) used another type of constrained processing task in an attempt to reveal the informational cues that expert weather forecasters use in interpreting satellite imagery. Participants were forecasters with the National Weather Service and the U.K. Meteorology Office. On a daily basis, weather forecasters inspect satellite imagery in the form of loops covering a span of time usually on the order of at least 24 hours. In the task Hoffman devised, a series of five infrared satellite images showing the eastern United States were taken from a loop. The first and second images were separated by a 1-hour interval, the second and third by a 1-hour interval, the third and fourth by a 6-hour interval, and the fourth and fifth by a 1-hour interval. The selection of the images was such that the 6-hour gap coincided with a merging of two low-pressure centers along a front. Unless the interpreter looked closely at a less salient weather feature—a small convective cell in the Gulf Coast—the interpreter might misinterpret the weather dynamics and hence become confused about the temporal ordering. In the task, the five images were presented in a random order and the participant's task was to determine the correct ordering. Most of the experts, unlike novices, were able to determine the correct ordering, although experts were not immune to the sequencing misinterpretation.

Following the sequencing task was a surprise recognition task. The participant was presented with a set of images and had to judge whether each image was one of those presented in the first task. The recognition set included the originals, plus some foils. The set of foils included images taken from an entirely different weather situation, images from the same loop but at different times from those in the original set, and also some visible-light images including ones that were from the same weather event as depicted in the original series. Both novices and experts tended to correctly label the visible-light images as "new," but for different reasons. The novices, upon seeing the visible images, would remark that they looked somehow different from the original set, the original set seeming pixelated or digitized. The experts, on the other hand, would immediately label a visible-light image as "new" because they knew, upon seeing the visibles, that all of the originals were all infrared. It was interesting that a few experts rapidly rejected the visibles but would then comment, "Oh, by the way, this image is of the same weather as the original set."

Both novices and experts found the recognition task to be confusing, but again for different reasons. The novices had to base their judgments on their literal understanding of the pictures and would sometimes correctly recognize an image because of literal features (e.g., "I remember seeing a cloud right over Long Island"). Experts, however, were confused because what they remembered was not the literal pictures but their understanding of the weather dynamics (fronts, high- and low-pressure systems, the location of the jet stream, etc.). This is another "gist recall" effect. Hence, they would sometimes falsely recognize a stimulus if it depicted the same weather dynamics as in the original set. This study revealed some of the cue configurations suggestive of such things as fronts and the jet stream—all those things that are rather invisible to the novice. This experiment, in sum, confirmed the finding that experts perceive dynamics based on complex configurations of cues and do not interpret images based on a literal understanding of isolated stimulus features (Chi et al., 1981; Hoffman & Fiore, 2007).

A constrained processing technique that has been recommended for use in knowledge elicitation involves combining online task performance with the use of probe questions, a technique called "interruption analysis" (Salter, 1988). During task performance, the expert can be asked, for example, "What were you just doing?" or "What was just going on?" or "What would you have done just then if ... ?" (see chapter 9; also Endsley, 1988).

A contrived technique illustrating both constrained processing and limited information is called "20 Questions" (Grover, 1983). The experts are provided with little or no information about a particular problem to be solved and must ask the elicitor for information needed to solve the problem. The information that is requested, along with the order in which it is requested, can provide the researcher with an insight into the experts' problem-solving strategy. The researcher needs a firm understanding of the domain to make sense of the experts' questions and provide meaningful responses on the fly. A way around this is to use two experts, one serving as the participant and the other serving as an interviewer's assistant (Hall, Gott, & Pokorny, 1995). The 20 Questions method has been used successfully in expert knowledge elicitation (Schweikert, Burton, Taylor, Corlett, Shadbolt, & Hedgecock, 1987; Shadbolt & Burton, 1990a, b).

Lessons Learned: TAPS as a Knowledge Elicitation Method

Many of the psychologists who became involved in Expertise Studies in the 1980s did so with a prior familiarity with the TAPS task. The TAPS task has a long track record, so it was a method of choice in the early days of Expertise Studies. It was used in the study of expertise in such domains as medical diagnostics (e.g., Feltovich, 1981), physics (e.g., Chi et al., 1981), computer programming (e.g., Jeffries et al., 1981), and process control (Bainbridge, 1979; Umbers & King, 1981).

The result of the TAPS task is a recording of a monologue (in problem solving) or a dialogue (in a knowledge elicitation interview), usually an audio recording. From that, a transcription is analyzed for its propositional content—a data analysis procedure called "protocol analysis" (Ericsson & Simon, 1984; van Someren et al., 1994). The primary purpose of the TAPS procedure, today as it has always been, is to use protocols to develop models of reasoning by revealing the moment-to-moment contents of working memory. Such models are usually expressed in the language of information processing flow diagrams showing causally linked patterns of memory access, strategic inference, and goal-directed reasoning that guide problem-solving behavior. In their magnum opus that helped pave the way for cognitive science and computer modeling of cognition, Newell and Simon (1972) described their program of research on human problem solving, which relied heavily on the TAPS task. Ericsson and Simon's (1993) treatise *Protocol Analysis* reviewed, integrated, and reinvigorated research on problem solving using the TAPS method.

The TAPS method has been used successfully in countless studies of problem solving (e.g., Belkin, Brooks, & Daniels, 1987; Benjafield, 1969; Johnson et al., 1987; van Someren et al., 1994). The TAPS procedure can indubitably yield information about the reasoning sequences and goal structures in experts' problem solving (e.g., Wielinga & Breuker, 1985; Wood & Ford, 1993). The TAPS task has been used extensively in cognitive research on medical diagnosticians (e.g., Johnson, Duran, et al., 1981; Kuipers & Kassirer, 1984; Kuipers et al., 1988; Patel & Groen, 1986), physicists (e.g., Chi et al., 1981; Chi et al., 1982), computer programmers (e.g., Jeffries et al., 1981), process controllers (Bainbridge, 1979; Umbers & King, 1981), and accountants (Dillard & Mutchler, 1987).

Expertise Studies has involved transporting the TAPS task into a new context and purpose—knowledge elicitation. Paul Johnson and his colleagues (Johnson, Duran, et al., 1981; Johnson, Hassebrock, Duran, & Moller, 1982) and Benjamin Kuipers and his colleagues (Kassirer, Kuipers, & Gorry, 1982; Kuipers & Kassirer, 1984, 1987; Kuipers et al., 1988) elicited the knowledge of expert medical diagnosticians using the TAPS task along with test cases, and have implemented the resulting protocols propositions in expert systems. In a study by Fox, Myers, Greaves, and Pegram (1987) (see also Kuipers & Kassirer, 1987), experts at diagnosing leukemia were presented with the records of a number of patients and were instructed to think aloud while coming to a diagnostic decision. From the experts' deliberations, a number of propositions were extracted, some of which referred to factual information and some referred to reasoning rules. These propositions were then used as the basis of a prototype expert system. (Although Fox et al.'s analysis of the performance records provided a great deal of information that could be used in building the knowledge base, they were able to see that some aspects of the diagnosis task were not elicited. A documentation analysis was needed to complete the prototype system.)

In a discussion of training and workforce issues in reference to the concept of expertise, Ernest Rothkopf (1986) beat up on TAPS rather severely, saying,

> What experts know has been determined largely through protocol analysis. This procedure is laborious, of unknown reliability, and at present, largely incapable of dealing with variability in results. ... Task analysis by the decomposition of protocols, is more useful as an art form than a reliable objective procedure ... multiple cross-validating analyses or replications are rarely undertaken [and] protocol analysis is largely insensitive to incompleteness ... protocol analysis, the current method of choice in analyzing expert knowledge, is insensitive to personal subject matter knowledge that is acquired inductively without analysis. It is also insensitive to holistic (i.e., multivariate) determinants of skilled performance. The precision of protocol analysis is not well known. (p. 287)

Although disagreeing with Rothkopf's claims about what protocol analysis can and cannot reveal, both Burton et al. (1987; Burton et al., 1988; Burton, Shadbolt, Rugg, & Hedgecock, 1990) and Hoffman (1987a) confirmed the claim that the TAPS task is very time-consuming and effortful *in the context of knowledge elicitation*, especially the process of transcribing the audiotape and coding the utterances according to some functional categories. In addition to the question of relative efficiency in knowledge elicitation is a question concerning the validity of the method: The task requirement of providing a verbal report may bias or alter mental processes, thus disturbing or distorting task performance (Ericsson & Simon, 1984; Porter, 1987; Wielinga & Breuker, 1984). We referred to this possibility of task interference earlier in this chapter, pointing out that things are not cut and dried, because we know of domains where the expert's familiar task involves thinking aloud.

Debate on the validity of verbal reports has been essentially continuous throughout the history of experimental psychology from its early days (e.g., Boring, 1913; Fernberger, 1937; Titchener, 1912, 1929) during the era of behaviorism (e.g., Woodworth, 1938), throughout the decades of cognitive psychology (e.g., Crutcher, 1994; Lieberman, 1979; Payne, 1994; Wilson, 1994), to today (e.g., Schooler, 2002). Much of the debate has circled around the argument that introspection and retrospection are tainted by unconscious processes, fabrications, and biases (e.g., Pollard & Crozier, 1989; Russo, Johnson, & Stephens, 1989; Wilson, 1994; Wilson & Schooler, 1991), taking this to the conclusion that introspective data are therefore always suspect and essentially useless (e.g., Melcher & Schooler, 1996; Nisbett & Wilson, 1977). Some researchers fault verbal reports (the TAPS task combined with the protocol analysis data analysis method) for resulting in incomplete or incorrect accounts of mental operations (Nisbett & Wilson, 1977) or for being of limited use in evaluating causal hypotheses (though useful in suggesting hypotheses). It has been argued that the process of providing a verbal report interferes with, or alters, the "normal" course of reasoning. Those of a different outlook site improvements in methods for obtaining and encoding protocols (e.g., Ericsson & Simon, 1980, 1984), arguing that "protocol data figure importantly in addressing major theoretical issues and advancing our understanding of the details of cognitive processes" (Crutcher, 1992, p. 242).

Ericsson and Simon (1980, 1984; see also Ericsson, 2006b; van Someren et al., 1994) reviewed research that addressed methodological issues of reliability, validity, and completeness (i.e., reasoning outside of awareness cannot be verbalized, or Rothkopf's "knowledge acquired inductively without analysis"). Anders Ericsson has made a strong case for the utility of verbal reports, a case that has had to be made to academic psychologists given (a) the historical baggage lingering from behaviorism (i.e., sometimes misguided attacks on the validity of introspective reports) and (b) the dominance of the information processing paradigm, which praised the precision and "objectivity" of microscale task decompositions by means of reaction-time studies (as in Rothkopf, 1986). As Ericsson and his colleagues have pointed out, it is important to keep in mind a subtle distinction between introspection and problem explication or task reflection. Classically, introspection is a process of thinking about (and attempting to verbalize) one's own thoughts, perceptions, beliefs, and so on. This is inward looking. In contrast, problem explication is outward looking and involves verbalizations about the problem described in terms of the problem elements rather than verbalizations that are about thoughts, perceptions, or beliefs. When experts think aloud as they solve problems, or when they reason about a particular case on the basis of a memory of similar cases (retrospection), they generally spend very little time introspecting; they spend most of their time reasoning about the problem at hand or the case being recalled (Benjafield, 1969; Claparéde, 1934; Deffner & Kempkensteffen, 1989; Ericsson & Simon, 1980, 1984; Evans, 1988; Woodworth, 1938, chap. 29).

A number of studies using simple puzzle tasks (e.g., anagrams, simple probability problems, etc.) have shown that the process of verbalizing strategies during problem solving can indeed interfere with solution finding (Russo et al., 1989; Schooler, Ohlsson, & Brooks, 1993). Researchers have been able to demonstrate that introspecting on or physically attempting to exert explicit conscious control over motor skills that rely on automatic processing can be detrimental to performance. On the basis of this literature on "automatic" processing, it might be posited that experienced domain practitioners should be unable to access automatic aspects of performance (cf. Anderson, 1982; Fitts & Posner, 1967).

Some research has demonstrated that the process of verbalization of descriptions of visual stimuli (e.g., faces) can interfere with subsequent performance on recognition memory tasks, a phenomenon called "verbal overshadowing" (Melcher & Schooler, 1996; Schooler, 2002; Wilson & Schooler, 1991), in which verbalization leads to a linguistically encoded memory that can interfere with performance at a perceptual recognition task conducted—after a significant delay. This finding has been replicated in studies in which participants (college students) have had to learn such things as (artificial) categories of mushrooms. However, even the early studies on this phenomenon hinted at an effect of experience. In a study comparing nondrinkers, nonexpert wine tasters, and wine experts, Melcher and Schooler (1996) found that verbalization during wine tasting interfered with performance at a memory task (recognizing previously tasted wines), but only for the nonexpert groups.

We are of course reminded here of the caution that most of the research in this area involves artificial tasks and relatively unpracticed participants. Indeed, Ericsson and Lehman (1996) argued that experts are likely to be *more* in touch (i.e., have better metacognitive skills such as monitoring) with their performance than nonexperts, because they are constantly critiquing their skills so as to better them and outperform their previous standards or the opposition. As one would predict from this, practitioners can be quite aware of this matter of interference. Here's a quote from an interview with an expert orienteer (the then European Orienteering Champion) (D. W. Eccles, personal communication, 2006; see Eccles, Walsh, & Ingledew, 2002), in which the researchers were considering what methods to use for investigations of orienteering: *So having to actually think about—to analyze what I'm doing [during orienteering]—I think I'm affecting the actual process … orienteering is quite difficult.*

The bulk of the research suggests that the process of verbalization does not typically cause dramatic interference; that is, it does not significantly affect the "normal" course of cognitive processes (Ericsson & Simon, 1993):

- The occurrence of interference is likely to be dependent on the context. World-class gymnasts try to "run on autopilot" during competition, which is what most of us see. But during *practice* (which consumes many, many more hours of effort), they attempt to enhance performance through explicit self- and coach-lead criticisms and feedback. Expert weather forecasters under time pressure might rely on their immediate judgments, but during everyday forecasting they attempt to self-critique so as to improve performance. Weather forecasting briefings are explicitly task reflective and critical (Hoffman, Trafton, and Roebber, 2008).
- The occurrence of interference is likely to be dependent on the proficiency levels of the participants. The research from the academic laboratory involves college students working at simple and often artificial problems in an artificial laboratory-task context. Of course, more research can be conducted to determine if verbalization (whether concurrent or retrospective) leads to interference on the part of apprentices and journeymen (versus experts) who are conducting their familiar tasks.
- The occurrence of interference is also likely to be dependent on the domain. As we have pointed out, in many domains of expertise, concurrent verbalization is actually a part of the familiar task (e.g., medical autopsy, X-ray interpretation, etc.), and in many domains, retrospective analysis is an aspect of the familiar task (e.g., weather forecasting case studies, aviation engineering case-based reasoning, etc.).

In their study demonstrating that the TAPS task can sometimes cause some interference in problem solving, Russo et al. (1989) asserted,

> Until a theory of protocol generation can fully specify the conditions of validity, the only assurance of [no interference] is empirical [i.e., experimentation using a] a silent control group … [but] we do not conclude that concurrent verbal protocols are invalid and should be avoided … we believe that nothing can match the processing insights provided by a verbal protocol. (p. 767)

The authors pointed out that of course there are limits to *all* research methods and trade-offs between assurances of validity and the achievement of the research goals. The experienced CTA researcher might sum this up in the following way: Although one should never take anything that domain experts say at face value, convergence and validation is always possible. Possibilities such as fabrication and interference are not a reason to forbid the use of TAPS-like CTA methods. Do not throw out the baby with the bathwater—you can often learn quite a lot by asking people questions and having them speak their minds.

The flip side of the issue of interference is the fact that sometimes participant explication is necessary to explain the so-called behavioral data. An example is the study by Bailey and Kay (1987), cited earlier in this chapter, in which adults built a lifting device using a child's construction set. Analysis in terms of literal, specific actions (e.g., bolting two parts together) was not enough to explain certain activities, such as putting a subassembly together but then taking it apart, showing that a participant had envisioned that the subassembly would not fit into another subassembly or would not quite work the intended way. Such actions could be made sense of *only* by categorizing verbalizations according to functional reference based on task explication (e.g., the goals of a particular action being planned or the evaluation of the outcome of a test of a component).

A final perspective on the issue of interference comes from evidence that having to think aloud during problem solving does not necessarily interfere with or disrupt the usual problem-solving process and may even facilitate problem solving by encouraging a systematic approach to problems (Bainbridge, 1979). In addition, the TAPS task can be useful in the teaching and practicing of knowledge and skills (Bereiter & Bird, 1985).

In the context of CTA, a problem with TAPS-like tasks that is more likely to be encountered than any issue of interference is individual differences in verbal expressiveness (Burton et al., 1990; Ericsson & Simon, 1993). Every Cognitive Systems Engineer who has conducted Cognitive Field Research has worked with experts who are an unstoppable font of knowledge, experts who are expressive but hard to keep on track, and experts from whom knowledge is elicited only in a manner not unlike the pulling of teeth (see, for example, Brown, 1989; Crandall et al., 2006). The moral is that the selection of participants for a TAPS task should be based on a positive interpersonal relationship between the domain practitioner and the knowledge engineer and on a full knowledge on the part of the knowledge engineer of the level of verbal expressiveness and interpersonal style of the domain practitioner.

This convergence of Expertise Studies in psychology with the practical problem of knowledge elicitation for expert systems gave rise to a branch of research aimed at exploring CTA methodological issues.

The Comparison of Knowledge Elicitation Methods

In the earliest days of expert systems, it seemed to take longer for computer scientists to elicit knowledge from experts than to write the expert system software. Almost at once, this "knowledge acquisition bottleneck" became a widely discussed problem (see Bramer, 1985; Buchanan, Sutherland, & Feigenbaum, 1969; Hart, 1986). The root cause of the knowledge acquisition bottleneck seemed to be the reliance on unstructured interviews by the computer scientists who were building expert systems (see Cullen & Bryman, 1988). It was conceivable that methods such as those used in the psychology laboratory might be brought to bear to widen the knowledge elicitation bottleneck, including methods of structured interviewing (long known to social psychology) and methods of studying learning and problem solving, such as the TAPS task.

Hoffman (1987b) conducted a study that compared a number of knowledge elicitation methods. The domain chosen was "terrain analysis," which is the evaluation of

aerial photographs to understand geological strata, terrain morphology, soils, vegetation, and so on. Terrain analysis has many purposes including waterways engineering,
land-use planning, habitat change detection, and military operations planning.
Hoffman compared four methods:

1. Documentation analysis was conducted to create a knowledge base of domain concepts and principles,
2. This was then used to add structure to an interview in which the expert commented
   on each of the propositions in the first-pass knowledge base, affirming or correcting
   propositions or adding additional propositions.
3. Experts were engaged in a TAPS task while working on a "tough case" of aerial radar
   interpretation. As the experts conducted their interpretation, they verbalized their
   judgments and hypotheses out loud, which the experimenter recorded.
4. The experts engaged in a constrained processing task in which they had to interpret
   aerial photographs but without benefit of maps or other data (limited information)
   and limited time to view the photos (constrained processing).

For comparison as a form of control, available to Hoffman were audio recordings of
unstructured interviews with experts in another domain: military airlift scheduling.
Those interviews had been conducted by researchers who were unaware of Hoffman's
purposes. This control allowed comparison of the relative efficiency of unstructured
interviews to those of the other methods.

Hoffman compared methods in terms of a yield metric referred to as "informative
propositions per total task minute" (IP/TTM). A proposition was regarded as being
informative if it was not already in the knowledge base of propositions that had been
formed on the basis of prior documentation analysis. "Total task minute" was the sum
of the task preparation time, the task time, and the data analysis time (i.e., the total
effort). The unstructured interview involved transcription of an audiotape and then
the culling of propositions from the transcript. This was time-consuming, having a
yield of about 0.10 IP/TTM. The structured interview yielded about 1.0 IP/TTM. The
constrained processing task and the analysis of tough cases were the most efficient,
yielding between 1.0 and 2.0 IP/TTM.

A similar study by Mike Burton, Nigel Shadbolt, and their colleagues (Burton et al.,
1987; Burton et al., 1988) involved advanced students of geology who were practiced in the
classification of igneous rocks. Burton et al. used four knowledge elicitation methods:

1. A structured interview about rock features and rock classification,
2. A TAPS task in which rock samples were examined and classified,
3. A task in which rock samples were rated on a number of pertinent dimensions, and
4. A task in which participants sorted domain concepts into categories.

Dependent measures included the time taken in the sessions, the time taken to
transcribe sessions into classification rules, the number of classification rules elicited,
and the complexity of the classification rules. A senior geologist provided a "gold
standard" rule set against which the session data could be compared.

It was hypothesized that the interview and think-aloud problem solving would yield
knowledge about procedures, whereas the techniques that seemed more contrived

(the rating task and the sorting task) would elicit knowledge about domain concepts. However, there was considerable overlap of knowledge elicited by each of the techniques; that is, there was no interaction of technique and knowledge type. A second experiment (Burton et al., 1988) studied experts' identification of the geographical features associated with glaciation, with results that closely resembled that of the first study. The next experiments (Burton et al., 1987; Shadbolt & Burton, 1990a, 1990b) involved the participation of eight senior experts (i.e., highly published academic and museum professionals) at the identification and classification of flint artifacts and pottery shards. The results suggested that interviews have to be used in conjunction with ratings and sorting tasks, because those contrived techniques elicit specific knowledge and do not yield an overview of the domain knowledge.

This early wave of applied cognitive research laid the foundation for the continued comparative evaluation of CTA methods for the study of expertise, a valuable area of work that continues today. The consensus that has stood the test of time is that in the study of expert knowledge and reasoning, it is valuable, if not critical, to always use more than one CTA or knowledge elicitation method, to be sure that one can fill in the gaps, and to make convergence and validation possible (Hoffman, 1987b; Hoffman, Shadbolt, Burton, & Klein, 1995).

Summary

The archives of psychology are rife with research that, in hindsight, involved the study of experts. This includes studies in the areas of decision making and psychometrics, on domains such as livestock judging, clinical nursing, and weather forecasting. Understanding individual differences has been a consistent theme in the history of psychology. Much of the research on expertise within experimental psychology has involved laboratory-like tasks, many of which might not ordinarily be thought of as CTA; however, the boundaries do get fuzzy. Whether a research procedure constitutes CTA or not depends on the relation of the materials and procedure to the expert's familiar tasks, although experiment-like tasks are also very useful in revealing expert knowledge and reasoning. Expertise Studies are critical for the formation of any general theory of cognition, which otherwise might be based largely on studies in the traditional academic laboratory using artificial tasks and materials and college-age "subjects." Furthermore, Expertise Studies has important implications for a range of applied questions having to do with personnel selection, training, and technology design.

The emergence of expert systems in the 1980s brought particular attention to the study of expertise and the challenges of knowledge elicitation. The creation of expert systems depends on knowledge bases and models of reasoning, and these have to be derived from CTA and knowledge elicitation procedures. The early work on expert systems revealed a "knowledge elicitation bottleneck"—it took longer for the system developer to elicit the knowledge than it took to create the expert system program (Hoffman, 1987b). This spurred experimental psychologists to develop and study alternative methods for knowledge elicitation in the search for effective and efficient methods, relative to the unstructured interviews that had been generally used by developers of expert systems.

This convergence of events and trends in psychology and computer science resulted in a field called Expertise Studies. (See chapter 5 for other historical threads that fed into this.) Expertise is now its own topic in cognitive psychology textbooks and a frequent topic in the experimental psychology literature.

CTA and Cognitive Field Research studies, in combination with experimental studies focusing on problem solving, have resulted in a growing understanding of expert reasoning in real-world problem-solving situations. A range of generic strategies has been identified, including the "least effort" tactic, analogical reasoning, deductive and inductive inference, and divide-and-conquer problem simplification strategies. Although experts may rely on such generic strategies, the flow of expert reasoning is shaped by the domain and the tasks the expert must accomplish. Experts become skilled at perceiving, comprehending, judging, and inferring in the context of a specific domain. For example, expert radiologists are very good at recognizing chest X-rays but not any better than novices at recognizing faces. Chess masters are very good at remembering game positions but not scrambled games.

Research suggests that experts often rely on their knowledge of prototypical examples, generally referred to as case-based or analogical reasoning. In addition, Expertise Studies have shown that experts often size up a situation and immediately recognize it. For the expert, recognition of the case or situation invokes expectancies about how the situation will unfold as well as awareness of the best course of action. This is referred to as recognition-primed decision making and contrasts with decision analysis or the deliberate generation of multiple options that are then compared analytically to select the best course of action.

The concept of a "mental model" figures heavily in the study of problem solving, including Expertise Studies. This is the idea that people build an imaginal representation of information and events and use that mental model to test hypotheses about the situation. The development of expertise seems to involve an increasing ability to make adjustments and use feedback to modify initial decisions.

Expertise Studies suggest that experts do not use "special" reasoning processes. Rather, a key difference between experts and novices seems to hinge on experts' knowledge organization and how they use their knowledge. An expert's knowledge, gained after years to decades of experience, tends to be specific to the domain, very extensive, and highly organized. This makes possible efficient retrieval, pattern recognition, and inference. Hence, a great deal of the research in Expertise Studies has focused on using CTA methods to explore the knowledge representations of experts and novices.

Expertise Studies indicate that experts are less susceptible to memory interference in their domain of expertise. Laboratory-based studies of memory have shown that when participants are asked to recognize a specific word embedded in a list of words, memories that are similar to the to-be-recalled word can be activated instead of or in addition to the target word. This has been explained in terms of "retrieval interference," which results in omission or intrusion error in recall tasks or false recognition error in recognition tasks. As a memory is activated, so too are memories or facts associated with it, interfering with the target memory. This interference hypothesis suggests that as experts' knowledge grows, so would their error rates. Performance would actually degrade as knowledge became more extensive and complex. Instead, experts seem to become *more* efficient as their domain-specific knowledge grows. The explanation for this is that the experts' knowledge is organized so that concepts and facts are meaningfully or thematically integrated.

All of these ideas have led to the development of a general "Base Model" of expert reasoning, which integrates notions of recognition-primed decision making, mental model refinement, and other notions. In addition, Expertise Studies contributed to the development of Cognitive Flexibility Theory, which proposes that the achievement of proficiency depends on the learners' active, deliberative creation and refinement of their own knowledge.

Expertise Studies have also explored the idea that there are different kinds of knowledge. Specifically, *factual knowledge* refers to knowledge of facts about objects, events, and concepts. *Procedural knowledge* consists of procedures, rules, and strategies, including knowledge about what to do when conducting tasks and knowledge of what to do in the case of exceptions. *Metaknowledge* is knowledge about one's cognitive capacities and how one knows and thinks, especially the skills of using knowledge. Metaknowledge is considered an essential aspect of expertise, including the ability to plan and monitor problem-solving efforts, the ability to judge the difficulty of problems, the ability to use time and resources most efficiently, a sensitivity to relevant new information, a sensitivity to one's own capabilities, and an awareness of limitations in the breadth or depth of one's experience.

Knowledge categories have also been proposed according to the ease in which different types of knowledge can be verbalized. This represents a significant linkage between Expertise Studies and CTA, especially knowledge elicitation. The hypothesized dimension of verbalizatility includes the following:

- *declarative or explicit knowledge* that can readily be verbally explicated;
- *knowledge that cannot be easily verbalized,* which includes knowledge that is declarative but requires the use of a special task to help experts verbalize it; and
- *knowledge that cannot be verbalized at all,* a concept that stretches the notion of "knowledge" altogether.

It has been noted that experts are sometimes inarticulate about the strategic reasoning they employ in making their decisions. In fact, experts sometimes attribute their complex reasoning to hunches or intuition. Researchers have used CTA methods to help scaffold experts in articulating knowledge that might initially have been attributed to hunches or intuition. This type of knowledge is variously referred to as perceptual, tacit, intuitive, or unconscious, suggesting that it is simply not "hooked up" to consciousness. Some researchers have argued that most of an expert's knowledge is tacit. The notion of "automaticity" is closely related to that of tacit knowledge. Theories of cognitive development suggest that knowledge or skill undergoes a "declarative-to-procedural shift" or becomes routinized as one becomes more expert. Development levels are considered in terms of the development of automaticity and a reliance on implicit knowledge rather than in terms of explicit or declarative knowledge.

Early work comparing knowledge elicitation methods sought to discover which types of methods would be most effective at eliciting which types of knowledge. The "differential access hypothesis" (Hoffman, Shadbolt, et al., 1995) has not received strong empirical support. Some studies have found little or no evidence for differential access. Furthermore, tacit knowledge has not proved to be a salient problem when studying experts in applied contexts. Good knowledge elicitation methods serve as effective scaffolds, supporting the interview in specifying procedures and strategies that may not have been previously articulated. Good knowledge elicitation is a collaboration, dependent on the interpersonal skill and verbal ability of both the interviewer and the interviewee.

Limited information and constrained processing tasks, forms of CTA, have been used to effectively elicit the knowledge and reasoning of experts. In the constrained processing method, the experts' familiar routines are constrained. For example, the experts may be asked to adopt a particular strategy, or they may be confronted with a task that challenges the usual strategy. In a limited information processing task, the experts conduct a procedure like their familiar task but under conditions of limited information. Another constrained processing task termed interruption analysis involves combining online task performance with the use of probe questions. Yet another task is called "20 Questions," in which the experts are provided with little or no information about a problem and must ask the elicitor for information needed to solve the problem. The information requested and the order in which it is requested provide information about the experts' problem-solving strategy. All of these experiment-like CTA methods can reveal phenomena of expert knowledge, reasoning, and reasoning strategies (Crandall et al., 2006).

TAPS has also been used extensively in the study of expertise. This method involves the recording and transcribing of a monologue of problem-solving activity or a dialogue of a knowledge elicitation interview. The transcript is analyzed using "protocol analysis," a qualitative analysis method in which verbalizations are categorized into functional categories. The continuing debate on the validity of verbal reports has pushed researchers to better understand what types of verbal reports are particularly problematic and which are less so. Task explication is distinguished from classical "introspection" and involves verbalizations about the problem and problem elements (rather than an introspective, inward focus on one's thought processes). The question of the validity of verbal reports has not seemed to be a salient issue in the practical context of applied Expertise Studies. For example, although some studies have shown that task interference is relatively easy to create in novices, it is less likely to occur with experts working within their own areas of expertise.

Studies comparing various CTA and knowledge elicitation methods indicate that structured interviews and constrained processing tasks are more efficient than unstructured interviews and that structured interviews used in conjunction with other kinds of CTA tasks (e.g., limited information, constrained processing, etc.) provide a better insight into knowledge and reasoning than individual tasks used alone. These comparisons of methods set the stage for continued examination of the strengths and weaknesses of various CTA methods in eliciting expert knowledge and reasoning.

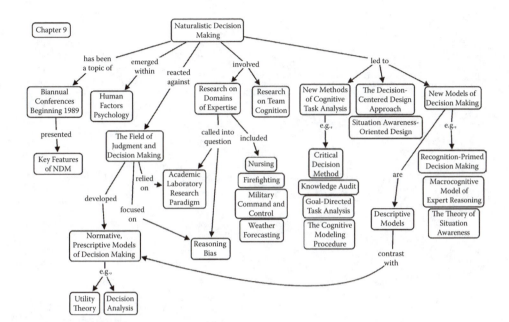

FIGURE 9.1 Chapter 9 Concept Map.

9

Naturalistic Decision Making

> During the past twenty-five years, the field of decision making has concentrated on showing the limitations of decision makers—that is that they are not very rational or competent. Books have been written documenting human limitations and suggesting remedies: training methods to help us think clearly, decision support systems to monitor and guide us, and expert systems that enable computers to make the decisions and avoid altogether the fallible humans. ... Instead of trying to show how people do not measure up to ideal strategies for performing tasks, we have been motivated by curiosity about how people do so well under difficult conditions.
>
> —Gary Klein (1998, p. 1)

Origins of This Community of Practice

Discussions of the origins of the Naturalistic Decision Making (NDM) paradigm appear in Klein, Orasanu, Calderwood, and Zsambok (1993); Moon (2002); and Ross and Shafer (2006). NDM as a community of practice has no formal society but is sustained by meetings and common interests. It began with the first conference in 1989 in Dayton, Ohio, at which a group of researchers who were studying different domains for different reasons found a common and seemingly distinctive set of goals and methods. At that meeting, Judith Orasanu, a leading human factors psychologist at NASA, laid out the key features of the NDM attempt to "redefine decision making" (Orasanu & Connolly, 1993) through the study of real-world decision making by domain experts working at challenging tasks that that are dynamic, ill structured, and high stakes. The 1989 meeting was intended as a workshop to allow sharing of results and interests, but it sparked demand for follow-on gatherings. The NDM community has met every 2 or 3 years since then, alternating between North American and European venues. Each of the NDM meetings has generated a book describing the research and the ideas of the conference participants (Flin, Salas, Strub, & Martin, 1997; Hoffman, 2007; Klein et al., 1993; Montgomery, Lipshitz, & Brehmer, 2005; Salas & Klein, 2001; Schraagen, 2008; Schraagen, Militello, Ormerod, & Lipshitz, 2007; Zsambok & Klein, 1997). Many NDM researchers gather every year as part of the Cognitive Ergonomics and Decision Making Technical Group within the Human Factors and Ergonomics Society and at meetings on situation awareness.

What triggered this?

A Study of Firefighters

In the mid-1980s, the U.S. Army Research Institute funded a research project to study decision making in time-pressured, high-risk settings. This led to a series of studies in which interviews were conducted with professional urban and forest firefighters (Calderwood, Crandall, & Klein, 1987; Klein, Calderwood, & Clinton-Cirroco, 1986). In these retrospective interviews, the participants recounted previously experienced cases that were rare or that involved tough, challenging decisions. Participants in these studies included individuals who had about a decade of experience (i.e., rank of captain or higher) and individuals who had only 1 or 2 years of experience as firefighters and no experience as fire-ground commanders (i.e., they were newly promoted lieutenants). In the knowledge elicitation task, the participants recalled cases from their past experience, described the events in terms of timelines, and answered probe questions about each decision point on the timeline (e.g., "What information did you need at that point?" "What were you seeing at that point?" and "What were your options at that point?").

The results included information about the experts' actions, goals, and plans. The probe questioning yielded information about the cues to which the experts attend and information about how the cues are linked to causal relations, actions, and plans. Investigators were able to specify many of the important cues in various types of firefighting situations—something that had not previously been done to such an extent. Some of the cues and cue patterns that were revealed were ones that the expert had never explicitly deliberated or specified. For example, in the initial description of one of his experiences, a firefighter initially explained that he had a "sixth sense" for judging the safety of a fire ground (i.e., a burning roof). Upon the subsequent sweep through the retrospective recall, using the probe questions, the expert "discovered" the perceptual pattern that he relied on, involving such things as smoke color and the feel of a "spongy" roof. Another finding was that the experts did not spend much time generating and evaluating options. Indeed, in this high-pressure decision-making situation, the deliberation of options is not an option: There's no time. Yet, the experts are able to make good decisions at small scale (e.g., where is the seat of the fire) and larger scale (e.g., when to call in extra tanker trucks).

A Study of Neonatal Intensive Care Nurses

The experience of nursing instructors had been that proficient nursing skill and knowledge are difficult for the expert to access and articulate. They operate tacitly in the course of decision making. In a study conducted by Beth Crandall and her colleagues (Crandall & Calderwood, 1989; Crandall & Gamblian, 1991), a group of 17 expert nurses performed detailed situation assessments for 24 cases of neonatal sepsis. From the nurses' accounts, Crandall et al. generated a description of assessment procedures and a list of indicators (perceptual cues and information from telemetry) of the physiological changes that occur in neonates over the course of sepsis. Cues included color change (pale tone, gray tone, paleness in extremities), apnea or brachycardia (frequency of episodes increases over time), and lethargy (sleepiness or listlessness, limp muscle tone, unresponsiveness). It was presumed that all of these important cues had already been spelled out and thoroughly analyzed in the textbooks used in clinical training. To test this hypothesis, the researchers examined the three leading texts and manuals and some of the associated literature in periodicals for their descriptions of neonatal sepsis in terms of its critical indicators. The finding was that many of the critical indicators discussed in the medical literature were not mentioned at all by the expert nurses during the situation assessment knowledge elicitation task (e.g., elevated temperature, vomiting, seizures, jaundice).

Conversely, some of the indicators that were important to the expert nurses were not mentioned in the medical literature (e.g., muscle tone, "sick" eyes, edema, clotting problems). Many of the discrepancies hinged on the clinical nurse's ability to detect early signs of sepsis that were manifested as cue configurations rather than as individual, salient cues. The medical literature focuses on advanced symptoms. Especially salient was the fact that clinical nurses are especially sensitive to certain symptom co-occurrences (e.g., the co-occurrence of pale skin tone with lethargy and apnea). Also, many of the critical cues on which the clinical nurses relied involved perceptual judgments and shifts in the patient's state: "A nurse would describe a growing concern as the infant became increasingly limp and unresponsive and as the infant's color changed from pink to pale to dingy grey over the course of the shift" (Crandall & Getchell-Reiter, 1993, pp. 47–48).

Crandall and Klein (1987a) obtained comparable findings in a study of paramedical treatment of heart attacks. Cue configurations that paramedics rely on in diagnosing heart attacks prior to the onset of the standard symptoms involve skin features (a blue-gray tone, or loss of pinkness, especially at the extremities; a cold, clammy feel), eye response (glazed, unfocused, dilated), breathing changes (rapid, shallow breathing), and changes in mental state (a confused or anxious mental state). In yet a third study modeled after Crandall's initial research, Militello and Lim (1995) identified individual cues and clusters of cues that experienced neonatal intensive care nurses rely on to assess an infant's risk for necrotizing enterocolitis. In this case, experienced nurses had learned to watch for indicators of gastrointestinal distress (i.e., increased girth, aspirates) coupled with early signs of infection (i.e., poor perfusion, change in activity level, temperature instability).

These and other findings set the stage for the initial motivation for the NDM paradigm—a reaction against a paradigm, or community of practice, called "Judgment and Decision Making" (JDM).

The Normative View of Judgment and Decision Making

JDM, a field with origins in the 1960s, focused on such domains as economics and business decision making and was concerned with discovering whether humans make decisions in accord with a logical standard for reasoning, such as the optimal strategies prescribed by probability theory or expected utility theory (Edwards, 1965b). A second line of research focused on the accuracy (or lack thereof) of judgments, including judgments made by experts (e.g., Hammond, McClelland, & Mumpower, 1980; Hoffman, 1960; Slovic, 1966). Another line of research focused on the flip side: reasoning biases and limitations in the human ability to evaluate the probabilities of events (Kahneman, Slovic, & Tversky, 1982; Kahneman & Tversky, 2000). One of the more consistent findings was that simple linear models perform as well as or better than humans, even experts with years of experience, on a wide variety of judgment tasks (Dawes, 1979; Dawes & Corrigan, 1974; Grove & Meehl, 1996; Swets, Dawes, & Monahan, 2000). If one takes the same information that the human has, apply an appropriate weight to each item of information, and add them up, one gets a result that is almost guaranteed to be as accurate as the human. If one provides the human with more information, the human does not necessarily get better and in fact can become more unreliable and less consistent (Stewart, 2001).

The Decision-Analytic Model

According to the Decision-Analytic Model, the "good" decision maker

1. Specifies all the objectives or the criteria for a solution→
2. Lays out all of the alternative actions→
3. Weighs the benefits versus the costs or risks of each alternative ("utility analysis")→
4. Conducts a multiattribute evaluation of the alternatives→
5. Orders the alternatives in terms of their satisfaction of the criteria→
6. Selects one option for implementation→
7. Engages in contingency planning

This model, or some variation of it, was widely prescribed as being the best method for conducting the decision-making process (e.g., Janis & Mann, 1977; Raiffa, 1986). The general Decision-Analytic Model is portrayed in Figure 9.2.

An example of decision analysis is a study by Kuipers, Moskowitz, and Kassirer (1988). Their study also illustrates one of the limitations of the Decision-Analytic Model. The domain under investigation was medical diagnosis. The medical records of the test case they used permitted a detailed traditional decision analysis, including the construction of a decision tree involving choice points, such as "perform lung biopsy," and the likelihoods of all of the possible scenarios based on the available data (e.g., the likelihood of the patient surviving a biopsy if a fungal infection were present). From the likelihoods (calculated on the basis of the medical literature), the utilities of alternative courses of action could be determined. The decision analysis was compared to results from think-aloud problem-solving protocols in which three experts analyzed the case.

The results showed that none of the physicians explicitly considered a particular alternative. That was included in the decision tree. Probe questioning revealed that the alternative in question would not have been considered because it was not clinically appropriate. Furthermore, the experts' reasoning never involved a sequence of laying out all the alternatives and then assessing the likelihoods or calculating the utilities. Rather, the experts "made an initial decision at an abstract level, and then went on to specify it more precisely" (Kuipers et al., 1988, p. 193). In the terminology of decision trees, they moved from the root to a main branch and only considered more specific alternatives as they proceeded along a particular path or course of action.

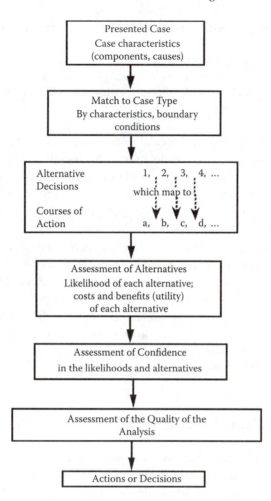

FIGURE 9.2 A depiction of the Decision-Analytic Model of decision making.

According to Janis and Mann (1977, p. 11), the failure to engage in a full formal decision-analytic process represents a "defect" in decision making (e.g., the failure to engage in this process as a consequence of time pressure will result in the ineffective use of all of the available information). However, a number of NDM researchers found the attempt to deliberately induce a decision-analytic procedure could actually interfere with decision making. Lipshitz (1987), for example, analyzed the decision-making protocols of military commanders in terms of the Decision-Analytic Model and found that forcing them to engage in a decision analysis distorted their usual strategies and reasoning sequences and failed to capture the recognitional aspects of command decision making.

The Rallying Point

In the 1980s, some researchers began to react against the JDM line of work, in part because the work was perceived as expressing a fairly negative view of human cognition.

- People tend to seek evidence that confirms hypotheses and do not look for discon-firming evidence.
- People are unreliable and inconsistent.
- People are said to consider only one or two hypotheses at a time.
- People's judgments of event likelihood are biased by recency, salience, and other factors.

The Decision-Analytic Model, especially its prescriptive nature, became a target for criticisms: "Decisions are not made after gathering all the facts, but rather constructed through an incremental process of planning by successive refinement" (Beach & Lipshitz, 1993, p. 21). Furthermore, the Decision-Analytic Model focuses on a final point in the problem-solving process, the moment of choice at which "a decision" is made (cf. Berkeley & Humphreys, 1982). Yet, a new wave of research, using what we would now say are CTA and CFR (Cognitive Task Analysis and Cognitive Field Research, respectively) methods, suggested that problem solving in real-world (versus academic laboratory) contexts involves a number of decision-like points along a timeline, points at which actions are taken and where options existed but there is no concurrent evaluation of options, no single "choice" (cf. Hoffman & Yates, 2005; Isenberg, 1984; Lipshitz, 1989). The only thing that "makes [an action] a 'decision' is that meaningful options do exist and that the decision maker can articulate them if necessary" (Klein, 1989a, p. 66).

Illustration of Naturalistic Decision Making

A study that illustrates how real-world decision making can rely on a strategy quite different from the decision-analytic strategy is a project conducted by Nancy Pennington and her colleagues (1981; Pennington & Hastie, 1981, 1988, 1993) on juror decision making. During the course of a trial, jurors are confronted with a great deal of information, information that can be rich in its implications. Pennington and her colleagues investigated what happens in the reasoning of jurors during trials and found that a majority of their time is spent creating storylike explanations of the causal events, integrating the evidence and the perceived intentions of the participants in the events—and this the jurors *must* do, because evidence is presented in a piecemeal, scrambled sequence. Sometimes jurors will conceive more than one possible story or schema, but they usually settle on one as being more coherent (complete, consistent, plausible). One of the consequences of this reasoning strategy could be tested empirically by engaging research participants (college students who participated in mock trials) in a recognition task involving statements that might, or might not, have actually been presented in evidence. Jurors were more likely to falsely recognize statements if they fit their own constructed story schemas (Pennington & Hastie, 1988).

A judge's final instructions to a jury present jurors with a set of mutually exclusive alternative decisions, and the task for the jurors is to attempt to match their story explanations to one of the permitted alternative decisions. Another implication of the juror decision strategy could be tested by comparing the verdict of a juror to that juror's story schema. Jurors who chose different verdicts had constructed different stories, and there was a distinct causal configuration to each story structure that mapped to each of the verdict categories. In another experiment, mock trials were composed such that witnesses would present evidence in according to the unfolding of the events, and the evidence could be presented as a coherent story rather than as piecemeal across witnesses or evidence categories. Participants were more likely to render a verdict of guilty if the prosecution's case had been presented in story order and were less likely to render a guilty verdict if the defense's evidence had been presented in story order. The model that Pennington adduced—which she called "explanation-based decision making"—places greater weight on the process of reasoning about evidence as it is gathered rather than on the evaluation of evidence in a decision-analytic fashion after it has all been gathered.

Additional Rallying Points

The blossoming research on expertise (see chapter 8) and Klein and Crandall's research on experts seemed to be painting a different picture from that painted by JDM.

Decision Making Under Pressure

The research suggested that the JDM approach was incomplete—the deliberation of options was simply not possible in time-critical domains, and in any event did not seem to describe what actually occurs in cognition during time-critical decision making. Experts rarely reported considering more than one option at a time (Klein et al., 1986). In domains involving time pressure, it is literally impossible for the decision maker to conduct a formal generation and evaluation procedure. Zakay and Wooler (1984) trained participants in a decision-analytic strategy and found that problem solving could proceed effectively using the strategy if there were no time pressure. But if even moderate time pressure was imposed, the strategy was not beneficial. Over trials, the decision-analysis strategy was truncated and adapted and eventually replaced by a more "heuristic" strategy (see also Payne, Bettman, & Johnson, 1988).

Decision Making on Unfamiliar Problems

Research suggested an explanation of why people are bad at decision analysis. Many studies have shown that people are not very good either at generating lists of options or at systematically evaluating options (e.g., Gettys, Fisher, & Mehle, 1978; Pitz & Sachs, 1984). Choices and decisions are not systematically based on the notions of utility and optimization (Fischhoff, Goitein, & Shapira, 1982; Simon, 1955). Furthermore, when people are forced to engage in a decision-analytic strategy, their evaluations can be subject to strong context effects, and judgments of uncertainty are insensitive to such things as the prior likelihoods of events or outcomes (Fischhoff, Slovic, & Lichtenstein, 1979; Lichtenstein, Fischhoff, & Phillips, 1982). The view of NDM was that such results are to be expected when people (mostly college freshmen) are confronted with artificial problem puzzles or probability-juggling tasks. The same sort of thing can occur when domain experts are presented with problems that fall out-side their domain. In a clever experiment by Tyzska (1985), experienced architects and car designers worked on two problems, one involving choosing an apartment and one involving choosing a car. The architects spent more time using a strategy reminiscent of decision analysis on the car choice problem, and the car designers did the same on the apartment choice problem. When confronted with problems outside their skill set, how could they do anything but a decision-analysis-like pro-cess, that is, an evaluation of individual courses of action and their values (costs or benefits) (Klein, 1989a)?

Missing the Forest for the Trees

Another debate arose concerning the assessment of proficiency in terms of the "hit rate" or correctness of final decisions, an approach common to studies in the para-digm of JDM (Hoffman, Shadbolt, Burton, & Klein, 1995). Part of the motivation for the study of hit rates is to support the use of statistical analysis, at least for purposes of diagnostic evaluation of decision-making skill. In linear statistical modeling, which we mentioned earlier in this chapter, the important features or dimensions of analysis are specified and their values mapped onto a simple measure of outcome. Analysis of cases reveals weightings for the variables, which serve to specify the regression equation. The predictions of the linear model are then compared with the predictions of domain experts for a set of test cases.

It has been argued that linear modeling ignores all the richness of proficient knowl-edge and skill. Whether statistical prediction outperforms human prediction can depend critically on the task, the experience level of the decision maker–participants, and the amount and kind of contextual information that is available to the deci-sion maker. A simple linear model, for example, cannot take "broken leg" cues into account. This interesting nomenclature comes from the example of the personality assessment device used to predict if a John Doe of some particular personality type or lifestyle would go to the movies some time during the next month. The model cannot take into account the consequences of John having just broken a leg. A human (expert or not) could. Whether hit rates are a useful measure for certain purposes (or not), the focus on hit rates, argue NDM researchers, ignores nearly everything else that is important about expertise—perceptual skills, knowledge, and context sensitivity and their relation to proficient performance.

The Inherent Predictability of Events

Some research has shown that linear regression equations can outperform a human expert (Dawes, 1979), even when the expert insists that the problems are complex. However, this finding has generally obtained for domains in which the expert's task is to predict either individual human behavior (e.g., diagnosis in clinical psychology, prediction of recidivism by parole officers) or stochastic aggregates of human behavior (e.g., the stock market, prediction of economic trends) and for tasks involving a lack of feedback, the assessment of dynamic situations, and a lack of decision aids (Shanteau,

1988, 1992). Stewart (2001) argued that the fallibility of judgment, including expert judgment, is linked to the inherent predictability of events:

> Predictability determines the maximum possible accuracy of judgments (either predictions, prognoses, or diagnoses), given currently available information. Predictability can be reduced either by inherent randomness or by inadequate or imprecise information, or both. Clearly, problems differ with regard to predictability. Predictability is important not only because it is a ceiling on the potential accuracy of judgment, but also because it affects the reliability of judgments. (Stewart, personal communication, 2004)

People tend to respond to less predictable environments by behaving less consistently (Brehmer, 1978; Camerer, 1981; Harvey, 1995). From this, Stewart predicted that there would be greater disagreement among expert judgments for less predictable events and that the performance gap between (perfectly reliable) mathematical models and (less reliable) human judgment will increase as inherent predictability decreases. These predictions were supported in a meta-analysis of studies that compared humans with linear predictive models. Stewart, Roebber, and Bosart (1997) found that for high-predictability tasks (e.g., weather forecasters' predicting precipitation or temperature), the performance of humans nearly equaled that of models, and there was close agreement among experts. For low predictability tasks—pathologists predicting survival time for patients who had ultimately died of Hodgkin's disease (Einhorn, 1972) and clinical psychologists judging psychosis or neurosis in patients (Goldberg, 1965)—the performance of the best judges nearly matched a linear model, but there was a greater downward range of performance, so most experts performed worse than linear models.

The NDM Paradigm Defined

NDM came to be defined as a paradigm involving the following:

1. A focus on the examination of decision making in "everyday" situations, both routine and nonroutine situations, both simple and complex;
2. A focus on decision making by experienced, knowledgeable individuals;
3. The examination of decision making in real-world job contexts in the study of decision making in domains that are especially important to business, government, and society at large.

These features distinguish NDM from traditional academic psychology, not because NDM work *must* take place in "the field" (although it often does); not because NDM work looks *only* at domains of practice that are important to business, government, and society (even though much of it does); not because laboratory research *must* eliminate all real-world complexity (it need not); and not because NDM research *always* involves looking at experts (though it often does). Rather, NDM is distinguished because traditional academic research tends to use simplified, artificial context-free problems, artificial tasks that occur only in the laboratory, and college undergraduates who serve, more or less willingly, as "subjects" in cognitive research.

Taken together, these foci serve to outline the interests of most NDM researchers, interests in such topics as ill-structured problems and domains, reasoning in uncertain and dynamic environments, reasoning in situations where goals come into conflict, reasoning under stress due to time pressure and high risk, and team or group problem solving (see, for example, Beach, Chi, Klein, Smith, & Vicente, 1997; Christiensen-Szalanski, 1993; Cohen, 1993a, c; Flin et al., 1997; Hammond, 1993; Klein, 1993a; Klein et al., 1993; Miller & Woods, 1997; Orasanu & Connolly, 1993; Woods, 1993; Zsambok & Klein, 1997). Hence, reports at the NDM conferences have involved, for example, studies of medical reasoning, of the skills of fighter pilots, of the use of CTA and other methods to reveal the knowledge and skills of experts, and so on. One goal of NDM research is to discover how people actually make real decisions in real situations. The goal is not to mold human decision making into normative or prescriptive models (such as the Decision-Analytic Model) (Cohen, 1993b).

Even the fundamental concept of the "decision" is brought into question (Hoffman & Yates, 2005). It is not regarded as a thing that is "made," as a single point that is somehow especially privileged in the analysis of problem solving. Rather, problem solving is described in terms of the dynamic assessment of situations and the incremental refinement of awareness and action plans. This resonates with the work of Jens Rasmussen and his colleagues (Rasmussen, Pejtersen & Goodstein, 1994), which regards decision making as a continuous control task rather than the resolution of individual conflicts (see chapter 10).

A goal of NDM research is to generate methods and technologies that will be useful in supporting the effective exercise of expertise and the preservation and dissemination of expertise. We turn now to a discussion of those methods.

CTA Methods That Have Emerged From the NDM Paradigm

Klein's early research (Klein, 1987; Klein & Weitzenfeld, 1982; Weitzenfeld & Klein, 1979) was on analogical problem solving by avionics engineers. In the "comparability analysis" procedure that the engineers follow, the reliability and maintainability of new aircraft components or systems are predicted on the basis of historical data about functionally or structurally similar components on older aircraft. Klein and Weitzenfeld had expert avionics engineers perform this familiar task for some test cases (e.g., the specifications for the hydraulics system on a new airplane). As the experts conducted a comparability analysis, they were prompted with a set of pre-planned interview questions. The results were clear: In this task, reasoning by analogy was built in. That is, new cases were solved by comparison to past cases.

Assuming that this style of reasoning would not be unique to avionics engineering, Klein and his colleagues went on to study other domains.

Evaluation and Refinement of the Critical Decision Method

Earlier in this chapter we summarized the seminal studies on fire-ground commanding and the key findings of those studies. In those and subsequent studies, the method of structured retrospection was refined and tested further. The method was related to the "critical incident method" that had been used for some time by human factors psychologists and others, especially in the retrospective analysis of accidents (e.g., Flanagan, 1954). Klein et al. found that asking for the recall of critical incidents tended to trigger the recall of cases in which lives or property had been lost, and did not necessarily involve situations in which expert skill or knowledge had been put to the test. Thus, refinements of the knowledge elicitation method involved focusing on critical *decisions,* because it appeared that the recall and analysis of nonroutine cases could be a rich source of data about proficient performance (Klein, Calderwood, & MacGregor, 1989, p. 465). Hence, Klein et al. dubbed their method the "Critical Decision Method" (CDM).

Unlike in the critical incident procedure, where the recall and the recalled events are relatively close in time, in CDM procedures events might be recalled well after they actually occurred. A study of forest firefighters (Taynor, Klein, & Thordsen, 1987) explored the effects of such delay. An elicitor conducted the interview procedure with a number of experts shortly after each of a number of critical incidents. A subset of the incidents was again assessed in a second interview procedure conducted 5 months later. A coder who was not present during the initial procedure conducted a detailed content analysis for the second run of the procedure. The resulting reliabilities across experts of the identified timeline decision points averaged at about 82%, with a range of 56% to 100% over elicitors. This finding suggested, as one would expect, that completeness and accuracy of event recall varies from expert to expert over time.

Another validity check involved having more than one coder specify a timeline based on selected transcripts from randomly selected event recall sessions. For the validity check in the study of urban firefighters, one coder had been the elicitor in the original sessions, and during those sessions he had developed his initial scheme for coding the decision points in the domain. The second coder was unaware of the scheme and had not been present during the initial interviews. The two judges agreed in their identification of between 81% and 100% of the decision points in four selected event recall transcripts. Disagreements reflected the tendency of the new coder to identify too many statements as decision points. This finding suggested that the method could be sensitive to the domain knowledge of the elicitor and coder. This too is to be expected and would obtain for any knowledge elicitation method, especially when the data are analyzed by a judge who is relatively unfamiliar with the domain.

The validity check involved assessing not just interjudge reliability in the identification of decision points but also reliability in the classification of decisions. Decisions in this domain had been classified into five basic categories, and the same two judges used this category scheme to independently code the decisions. The rate of agreement was about 67%, and although this was above statistical chance, it indicated that coders had difficulty in making unambiguous judgments at this level of detail. Recalculation of "essential agreement" was based on the fact that some categories of decisions were conceptually similar. This yielded an agreement rate of 87%.

A similar assessment of the reliability of the classification of decision strategies was conducted for the earlier forest firefighting study. Again, two independent judges, one of whom had been the elicitor, classified the decision strategies involved in 18 decision points. Overall, for five coding categories the rate of agreement was 74%, with essential agreement being 89%.

The findings concerning reliability in the classification of decisions suggest, as one would expect, that any highly fine-grained analysis of decisions or strategies will depend to some extent on the ontology preferred by the analyst. Another general conclusion is that experts love to tell stories. Indeed, in some cases practitioners learn on the job by sharing their war stories and even report they learn more that way than through their formal instruction (as illustrated by Orr's 1985 study of photocopier technicians). Providing structure and guidance to storytelling permits the interview process to flow more naturally, like a dialogue. Klein et al. reported that this is essential in maintaining the expert's cooperation and interest:

> Our goal was to focus the expert on those elements of the incident that most affected decision-making and to structure responses in a way that could be summarized along a specified set of dimensions while still allowing the details to emerge with the [expert's] own perspective and emphasis intact. (Klein et al., 1989, p. 465)

The CDM probe questions are designed to elicit information that is specific and meaningful: strategies and the basis for decisions, and the perceptual cues on which the decision maker relies on types of information that were not ordinarily the focus in either laboratory research on expertise or applied knowledge elicitation projects.

Although the CDM was created and refined during the era of expert systems and the rising interest in Expertise Studies, the CDM was not intended to be used solely for knowledge elicitation for the study of experts or for the development of expert systems. It was also envisioned as a technique to support training and instructional design and to support the preservation of corporate experience: "Organizations suffer when they do not properly value their own expertise and when they lose skilled personnel without a chance to retain, share or preserve the knowledge of people who retire or leave" (Klein et al., 1989, p. 471). Indeed, Klein (1992) carried this attitude over to knowledge-based systems, regarding the technology not just as a set of tools for use as decision aids but also as a tool to support the capture, preservation, and dissemination of the knowledge, skills, and experience of experts. Klein's seminal paper (1992) on "preserving corporate memory" helped usher in a wave of interest in what is now called knowledge management (cf. Brooking, 1999; O'Dell & Grayson, 1998).

The most detailed reviews of the CDM can be found in Crandall, Klein, and Hoffman (2006); Hoffman, Crandall, and Shadbolt (1998); Klein (1987, 1993a); and Klein et al. (1989). Crandall et al. (2006) provided a detailed protocol for conducting the CDM procedure.

A second empirical method that stemmed from the NDM research is called the "Knowledge Audit."

The Knowledge Audit

This procedure (Klein & Militello, 2004; Militello & Hutton, 1998) is based on the psychological research on expertise (see Chi, Feltovich, & Glaser, 1981; Ericsson & Smith, 1991b; Hoffman, 1991a; Klein & Hoffman, 1993), which has demonstrated the important cognitive factors or knowledge categories that distinguish novices from experts:

- Experts possess an extensive knowledge base that is conceptually organized around domain principles and that makes diagnosis and prediction possible.
- Experts are more effective at forming initial mental models of a problem situation and are more effective at achieving and maintaining a high level of situation awareness.
- Experts possess better metacognitive skills: They know how to manage information, what inferences to make, how and when to apply principles, how and when improvise, how to compensate for equipment or display limitations, how to recognize anomalies, and so on.
- Experts are more effective at prioritizing their activities during multitasking situations.

The Knowledge Audit interview attempts to get directly at these aspects of expertise. In other words, the purpose of the Knowledge Audit is to determine what distinguishes experts from nonexperts in a particular domain or task within a domain, including diagnosing and predicting, having situation awareness, improvising, having metacognition, recognizing anomalies, and compensating for technology limitations. The goal of the Knowledge Audit is not to demonstrate the importance of these factors but to identify the specific things that experts in a given domain need to know and skills they need to possess.

The Knowledge Audit procedure is useful as the very first interview in a cognitive engineering project, because it results in data that point the researchers to the important domain knowledge. Also, the incident analyses can point to possible differences between practitioners of differing levels of proficiency (i.e., expert–journeyman–trainee differences). The Knowledge Audit can also be used to study cognitive styles. An example is Pliske, Crandall, and Klein's (2004) study of U.S. Air Force weather forecasters. Like the CDM, Knowledge Audit probe questions focus on the recall of specific, lived experiences. They do not ask for reflection on generic knowledge or skills. Examples for the forecasting study appear in Table 9.1.

Pliske et al. interviewed a total of 65 forecasters (of varying degrees of experience). Next, the researchers engaged in a multitrial sorting task in which they reached a consensus on categories of the reasoning styles they had observed. These categories focused on the forecasters' overall strategic approach to the task of forecasting, their strategy in the use of computer weather models, their process in creating forecasts, their means for coping with data or mental overload, and their metacognition. The

TABLE 9.1 Probes Used in the Study of Weather Forecasting by Pliske, Crandall, and Klein (2004)

Probe	Knowledge or Skill of Interest
Can you recall and discuss some experiences where part of a situation just "popped" out at you, where you noticed things that others did not catch?	Skill at perceiving cues and patterns
Have there been times when you walked into a situation and knew exactly how things got there and where they were headed?	Skill at situation assessment
Can you recall past experiences in which you found ways of accomplishing more with less, noticed opportunities to do things better, and relied on experience to avoid being led astray by the equipment?	Metacognition skill, the ability to think critically about one's own thinking

categories they identified were dubbed "Scientist," "Proceduralist," "Mechanic," and "Disengaged." Features of the styles are presented in Table 9.2.

These categories were heuristic, intended to inform the creation of decision aids and other technologies, so that they may "fit" each of the styles that were observed. Pliske et al. did not claim that this set is exhaustive, that all practitioners will fall neatly into one or another of the categories, or that similar categories would be appropriate for any other given domain. The analysis of reasoning styles has to be crafted so as to be appropriate to the domain at hand.

Another method of CTA that is associated with the NDM community of practice is Goal-Directed Task Analysis (GDTA).

Goal-Directed Task Analysis

GDTA is a form of structured interview that uses probe questions to conduct a top-down analysis of work (see Endsley, 1993, 1995a, 1995b; Endsley, Bolté, & Jones, 2003). GDTA attempts to obtain detailed knowledge of the goals the decision maker must achieve and the information requirements for working toward those goals. As we will show, GDTA analyses are hierarchical in form, but even though GDTA might be seen as a form of Hierarchical Task Analysis (HTA) (see chapter 3), the historical origins are distinct, and the two approaches have slightly different focal points. HTA begins by stating a goal that a person has to achieve. This is redescribed into a set of subtasks and a plan (or plans) for conducting the tasks. The unit of analysis for HTA is the subtask specified by a goal, activated by an input, attained by an action, and terminated by feedback (Annett, 2000, 2004). In describing each subtask, many attributes of that subtask are laid out, including the goal. Thus, HTA is a goal-relevant analysis of tasks rather than an analysis of goals themselves (see also Kirwan & Ainsworth, 1992). In other words, HTA and GDTA highlight different but equally important aspects of decision making (R. Chow, personal communication, 2007). HTA primarily focuses on actions or behaviors, whereas GDTA primarily focuses on perceptions (of whether goal states are attained). HTA analyzes tasks in the context of the task goals, whereas GDTA analyzes the goals themselves (R. Chow, personal communication, 2007). (There is some circularity here, of course, because many descriptive statements of goals can be regarded as descriptions of high-level tasks and vice versa. As we pointed out in chapter 1, the word *task* is often understood as actions intended to achieve certain goals.)

A second key difference between HTA and GDTA is that in HTA it is assumed that higher level goals are typically achieved through teamwork and lower level goals are achieved through individual work (Annett, 2000, p. 34). In GDTA, the focus is generally on the individual worker, "determining what aspects of the situation are important for a particular operator's situational awareness. … In such analysis, the major goals of a particular job class are identified along with the major subgoals necessary for meeting each of these goals" (Endsley & Garland, 2000, pp. 148–149). This description suggests that the operator is identified first, followed by identification of the goals that are assigned to this operator. (In a third approach, which Renee Chow

TABLE 9.2 Features of the Four Main Reasoning Styles Observed in Weather Forecasting by Pliske, Crandall, and Klein (2004)

Affect	Skill	Activities
SCIENTIST: They tend to have had a wide range of experience in the domain, including experience at a variety of scenarios.		
They are often "lovers" of the domain.	They possess a high level of pattern-recognition skill.	They show a high level of flexibility.
They like to experience domain events and see patterns develop.	They possess a high level of skill at mental simulation.	They spend proportionately more time trying to understand the weather problem of the day and building and refining a mental model of the weather.
They are motivated to improve their understanding of the domain.	They understand domain events as a dynamic system.	
	Their reasoning is analytical and critical.	They possess skill at using a wide variety of tools.
	They possess an extensive knowledge base of domain concepts, principles, and reasoning rules.	They are most likely to be able to engage in recognition-primed decision making.
	They are likely to act like a mechanic when stressed or when problems are easy.	They spend relatively little time generating products, because this is done so efficiently.
	They can be slowed down by hard or unusual problems.	
PROCEDURALIST: Typically, they are younger and less experienced.		
Some are lovers of the domain.	They are less likely to understand domain events as a complex dynamic system.	They spend proportionately less time building a mental model and proportionately more time examining the computer model guidance.
Some like to experience domain events and see patterns develop.	They see their job as having the goal of completing a fixed set of procedures, but these are often reliant on a knowledge base.	They can engage in recognition-primed decision making only some of the time.
Some are motivated to improve their understanding of the domain.	Their knowledge base of principles of rules tends to be limited to types of events they have worked on in the past.	They are proficient with the tools they have been taught to use.
MECHANIC: They sometimes have years of experience.		
They are not interested in knowing more than what it takes to do the job; they are not highly motivated to improve.	They see their job as having the goal of completing a fixed set of procedures, and these are often not knowledge based.	They spend proportionately less time building a mental model and proportionately more time examining the guidance.
	They possess a limited ability to describe their reasoning.	They cannot engage in recognition-primed decision making.
	They are likely to be unaware of factors that make problems difficult.	They are skilled at using tools with which they are familiar, and changes in the tools can be disruptive.

continued

TABLE 9.2 (continued) Features of the Four Main Reasoning Styles Observed in Weather Forecasting by Pliske, Crandall, and Klein (2004)

Affect	Skill	Activities
DISENGAGED: They sometimes have years of experience.		
They do not like their job. They do not like to think about the domain.	They possess a limited knowledge base of domain concepts, principles, and reasoning rules. Knowledge and skill are limited to scenarios they have worked in the past. Their products are of minimally acceptable quality. They are likely to be unaware of factors that make problems difficult.	They spend most of the time generating routine products or filling out routine forms. They spend almost no time building a mental model and proportionately much more time examining the guidance. They cannot engage in recognition-primed decision making.

and her colleagues have referred to as "Hierarchical Goals Analysis," the first step is to identify and decompose goals for the entire system, before any goal is assigned to any one decision maker, team, and so on [Chow, personal communication, 2007].)

Unlike some forms of task analysis, GDTA does not assume that tasks can always be defined as strictly sequential or linear sequences actions. It does not assume that jobs can be defined as a lockstep series of procedures or even as hierarchies of branching dependencies. Rather, GDTA takes as its starting point the fact that in complex cognitive systems, situation awareness involves a constant juggling back and forth between multiple and sometimes conflicting goals, on one hand, and the processing of information in ongoing situations, on the other hand. In other words, the goals people work toward, and the action sequence alternatives they choose, are dependent on context.

In a GDTA, the major goals of a particular job class are identified first. When one asks domain practitioners what one of their main responsibilities is and what their immediate goals are in conducting it, the reply is often couched in terms of the technologies with which they have to work, the "environmental constraints" on performance (Vicente, 2000). Thus, as a hypothetical instance in weather forecasting, the practitioner might say,

> Well, I have to determine the valid interval of the model initialization, but to do that I have to access the last model run using the AWPIS system here, and then compare that to the following model run's initialization. Things might have gotten tweaked or biased.

At that point the analysts interjects, "No, what is it that you *really* are trying to accomplish?" and it invariably turns out that the "true work" that has to be accomplished falls at a more meaningful level, the knowledge level if you will, perhaps something like,

> Well, I want to know if COAMPS is the preferred model of the day or if the ensemble models are beating it up. That will tell me how much to trust the forecast low here in the southwest.

It is this clear focus on the meanings of goals and task activities that perhaps distinguishes GDTA analysis from some other forms of CTA. An example GDTA diagram appears in Figure 9.3.

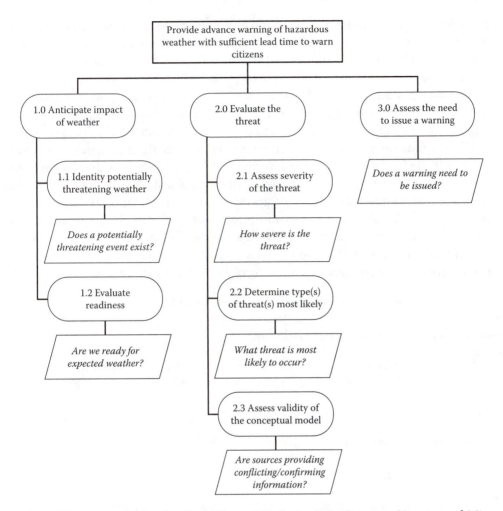

FIGURE 9.3 An example of a Goal-Directed Task Analysis diagram. (Courtesy of Mica Endsley, SA Technologies, Inc.)

The analysis then moves on to specify the major subgoals necessary for meeting each of the major goals. The major decisions that need to be made are identified for each subgoal. Also specified are the information requirements for decision making and the information needed for the human to maintain good situational awareness. Subgoal requirements often focus not only on what data the human needs but also on how that information is integrated or combined to address each decision. This provides a basis for determining what meanings the operator needs to derive from the data. In the example in Figure 9.3, information requirements for subgoal 1.1 (identify potentially threatening weather) would include the location of high and low pressure regions, the energy available for convection, winds at various heights in the atmosphere, evidence of lifting (sea breeze, surface heating), and so on.

One sees here that GDTA is similar to HTA, which we mentioned in chapter 3 and illustrated in chapter 5 (Figure 5.2) with respect to developments in task analysis and human factors from the 1960s through the 1980s. The advance over traditional task analysis represented by HTA was the realization by human factors psychologists that new jobs created by new technologies could not be described as liner sequences of activities. Rather, there are contextual dependencies and choice points, which mean that one needs hierarchical representations that describe task branchings or, stated in another way, goal–subgoal relationships (Drury, Paramore, Van Cott, Grey, & Corlett, 1987).

One way of understanding GDTA is to see it as a method that is complementary to the CDM procedure. In the CDM the domain practitioners are guided in retrospecting about particular past experiences and previously encountered tough cases. In the GDTA the practitioners are guided in discussing their goals in a generic sense, not necessarily tied to particular experiences or past cases. The GDTA does not seek to generate an event sequence according to a timeline, nor does it attempt to capture invariant goal priorities, because priorities change dynamically and vary across situations. In the CDM the practitioners will almost of necessity describe previous cases in terms of the actual work that was performed using the tools and technologies that were available. But both the CDM and GDTA seek to describe the "true work" divorced from particular technologies. For instance, one might ask a weather forecaster,

> What do you have to do when thunderstorms are approaching?

At which point the practitioner might say,

> I have to take data from the Warnings and Alerts System and reformat it to input it into the Pilot Information System because the data fields are different and have different parameters.

At which point the interviewer would say,

> No, what are your goals, what do you have to accomplish?

And at that point the practitioner might say,

> Well, I basically have to let the pilots know that they will be entering rough weather.

The idea is to cut through the actual work and perceive the true work in terms of the goals that have to be accomplished. The GDTA focuses on what information decisions makers would ideally like to know to meet each goal, even if that information is not available given current technology. In addition, the particular means a practitioner uses to acquire information are not the focus, because methods for acquiring information can vary from person to person, from system to system, from time to time, and with advances in technology. Once this information has been identified, current technology can be evaluated to determine how well it meets these needs, and future technologies can be envisioned that might better take these needs into account.

NDM research has contributed to theory as well as to method.

Theoretical Contributions of NDM

NDM has advanced many ideas about cognition and reasoning. We describe two main theoretical contributions. One extends the classical psychological notion of recognition into the analysis of cognitive work, and the other extends the classical psychological notion of attention.

From the Notion of Recognition to an Integrated Model of Proficient Reasoning: Recognition-Primed Decision Making

As we explained previously, the normative Decision-Analytic Model of decision making became a target for criticism because in domains involving time pressure it is impossible for the decision maker to conduct a procedure expressing the costs and benefits of all the alternative courses of action (cf. Beach & Lipshitz, 1993; Cohen, 1993a, b, c; Orasanu & Connolly, 1993). Through the 1980s a number of researchers in the NDM movement developed new models of decision making (for a review, see Lipshitz, 1993). A number of researchers who had been studying decision making in applied contexts for years (e.g., Ken Hammond, Jens Rasmussen) had also concocted models that were embraced by the NDM paradigm (Hammond, 1993; Rasmussen, 1983). These models converge in a number of respects (Lipshitz, 1993). They were all based on the following:

- appreciation for the fact that decision making in real-world contexts is not a single process but comes in a variety of forms involving differing strategies and differing sequences of mental operations,
- appreciation for the effects of context and the important role of situation assessment in problem solving in real-world situations,
- appreciation of the role of mental simulation in the medium of mental imagery or what cognitive scientists were calling "mental modeling,"
- rejection of the notion that real-world decision making culminates in a particularly critical event that can be isolated and called "the decision point," and
- the belief that prescriptions for effective problem solving and effective support for decision making come not from formal analytical idealizations but rather from a solid empirical descriptive base that comes from field research, including studies of experts, rather than the traditional academic laboratory.

Dovetailing with research on decision making under time pressure (e.g., Payne et al., 1988; Zakay & Wooler, 1984), Klein et al. found that most of the critical decisions were made within less than a minute from the time that important cues or information became available. (All of the longer decisions were for cases where the fire emergency lasted for days.) But the most striking finding was

> how rarely we found any evidence that the fireground commanders attempted to compare or evaluate alternatives at all. In only 19% of the decisions was there evidence of conscious and deliberated selection of one alternative from several. (Almost half of these were from an incident where [experience] was low and time pressure minimal.) ... Most commonly, the fireground commanders claimed that they simply recognized the situation as an example of something they had encountered many times before and acted without conscious awareness of making choices at all. Phrases such as "I just did it based on experience," and "It was automatic" were the most frequently encountered. (Klein, Calderwood, & Clinton-Cirocco, 1986, p. 577; Klein, 1989a)

The experts were probed repeatedly about alternative options, to no avail: "Look, we don't have time for that kind of mental gymnastics out there. If you have to think about it, it's too late" (expert quoted in Klein, Calderwood, & Clinton-Cirocco, 1986, p. 577). The experts seemed to make decisions on the basis of a process of matching a current situation to a course of action. Sometimes this could be expressed in terms of a comparison to previously encountered situations but only incidentally on anal- ogy to *particular* past cases (e.g., a fire involving a billboard on a rooftop brought to mind a past case involving a billboard). Rather, matching seemed to be what might be called action schemas, and when a given situation departed from the typical, the expert's situation assessment changed, and there was a change of plan. This had strong implications, for it suggested that problem solving and decision making are not always distinct or separate activities, as implied (if not mandated) by the tradi- tional Decision-Analytic Model, as depicted in Figure 9.2. Furthermore, it suggested that real-world decision making is not a process of "optimizing" or finding the best solution but a process of "satisficing" or rapidly finding an effective solution (after Simon, 1955).

Klein et al. referred to this as "recognition-primed decision making" (RPD). According to the RPD model, the decision maker spends most of his or her time evaluating situations rather than evaluating options. Acceptable courses of action are determined without conscious deliberation and evaluation of alternatives (or, at least, they are comprehended very rapidly). Commitments are made to courses of action even though alternative courses of action may exist. Experts performing under time pressure rarely report considering more than one option. Instead, their ability to maintain situation awareness provides the decision maker the important cues, provides an understanding of the causal dynamics associated with a decision problem, and directly suggests a promising course of action, which in turn generates expectancies (Klein et al., 1989, p. 463).

The initial RPD model is depicted in Figure 9.4.

According to Klein and his colleagues, the RPD model seemed to apply not only to their own results but to results of other research on decision making under time pressure. For example, even the classic on expertise in chess (de Groot, 1945, 1965)—regarded as a classic in cognitive science—converged with the criticisms of the Decision-Analytic Model. Chess masters, when confronted with game boards, usually, and rapidly, identify the best move or strategy as the first one they think of, whereas novices are more likely unable to generate the best options, let alone generate them first (Klein, 2003). Studies on what happens when a decision-analytic strategy is induced and the time pressure is brought to bear showed that the strategy breaks down and gives way to what some have called a more "intuitive" approach (Howell, 1984; Zakay & Wooler, 1984; see also Hammond, Hamm, Grassia, & Pearson, 1987). In a study of urban firefighters (Klein et al., 1986), both more (11 years) and less (1 year) experienced fire-ground commanders participated. Results from the CDM showed that

- both groups relied heavily on situation assessment and RPD, but it was the less expe- rienced practitioners who were more likely to deliberate over and evaluate alterna- tive options or courses of action;
- the recognition-priming strategy was more frequently used by the more proficient practitioners;

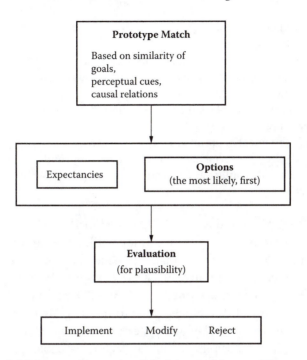

FIGURE 9.4 The initial recognition-primed decision-making model.

- the recognition-priming strategy was used more frequently even at nonroutine decision points, places where one would expect it to be more likely that one might find evidence of concurrent evaluation; and
- when experts did engage in deliberation, it was more likely to involve the deliberation of alternative situation assessments rather than alternative options.

The finding that less experienced decision makers were more likely to engage in an analytic process was striking, because it had been hypothesized (e.g., Beach & Mitchell, 1978; Hammond et al., 1987) that people with more experience would be *more* likely to rely on a decision-analytic strategy. So it seemed that the Decision-Analytic Model is less a model of actual expert problem solving than a model of apprentice (or junior journeyman) problem solving. If one is a novice, apprentice, or junior journeyman in a task domain (i.e., if one is still largely "in training"), then there is no way he or she can engage in a recognitional strategy. Some found these findings and conclusions to be disconcerting:

> Recognitional models may not be as satisfying as analytic models. One of the difficulties of coming to grips with a recognitional model is that so much of the important work is done out of conscious control. We are not able to become aware of how we access the memories or recognize patterns. This can be frustrating for applied researchers who would like to teach better decision-making by scrutinizing and improving each aspect of the process. In contrast, analytic models of decision-making offered the promise of bringing into the open the major tasks of evaluating options. The only thing hidden was the generation of the options themselves, and the antidote here was to generate them as exhaustively as possible. (Klein, 1989a, p. 80)

Klein (1989a, 1993b) described the human, domain, and problem features that would support, induce, or even require a decision-analytic or concurrent evaluation strategy, as opposed to an RPD strategy:

- less experienced decision makers;
- unfamiliar tasks;
- tasks involving data that are abstract or alphanumeric;
- tasks that include steps that depend on computation or involve a mandated formal analysis or stepwise procedure;
- the presence of conflict over how the situation, the options, or the goals are viewed;
- little time pressure;
- the explicit requirement of optimizing the outcome;
- the explicit requirement of having to justify the decision; and
- the need to reconcile conflict among individuals or groups who serve in different roles or capacities.

The research that converged on the RPD model made it clear that an outstanding problem in the analysis of expertise was (and still is) to capture and specify the process of perceptual learning, which makes possible the "immediate perception" of courses of action (Klein & Hoffman, 1993; Klein & Woods, 1993).

Subsequent research led to the refinement of the RPD model (Klein, 1997; Lipshitz & Ben Shaul, 1997). In fact, the model came to be integrated with the basic ideas about problem solving from Karl Duncker (see chapter 8) and also some new concepts that were emerging in the discipline of human factors psychology. As can be seen in Figure 9.3, the initial RPD model implicitly embraced the "refinement cycle" notion from the classic model of Duncker. That is, at the terminal decision point in the RPD, the options include "modify" and "reject" in addition to "implement." If a course of action is rejected, some other course of action must be determined. Thus, one must go back and reassess the situation (in RPD terminology) or reformulate one's mental model (in the Duncker approach).

On the other hand, the initial RPD model differed from the Duncker model in that there is no place for a process in which the decision maker takes (or can afford to take) the additional time to attempt to confirm or refute a mental model, judgment, or hypothesis. In the sorts of situations that were embraced by the initial RPD model (e.g., firefighting), the unfolding situation yields further cues or information about the effects of an implemented action.

Klein's initial research (Klein, 1987; Klein & Weitzenfeld, 1982; Weitzenfeld & Klein, 1979) focused on "comparability analysis" tasks in the domain of avionics engineering. In that domain it was natural for the experts to reason by analogy and comparison, that is, to solve new cases by comparison to a memory for past cases. Klein came to realize that case-based reasoning was only one possible problem-solving strategy, another important one being reasoning on the basis of a knowledge of causal relations and abstract principles—mental modeling (see Lipshitz & Ben Shaul, 1997). Within the span of a few years after the postulation of the initial RPD model and the refinement of the CDM procedure, Klein et al. had conducted a number of additional projects, involving over 150 CDM procedures with experts in diverse domains. The RPD model was elaborated on the basis of the findings.

One focus of the research that motivated the elaboration of the RPD was on the sampling of a variety of domains to assess the frequency with which experts relied on a recognition-priming decision strategy versus the concurrent evaluation of options.

One study used the CDM in the study of engineers who designed simulators (Klein & Brezovic, 1986). In that study, the researchers probed 72 design decisions involving cases in which ergonomic data were needed to decide about trade-offs in simulator design. Although the designers felt they were under time pressure, the decisions were actually made over a period ranging from weeks to months. Sixty percent of the decisions seemed to involve the recognition-priming strategy, but 40% involved concurrent evaluation of options. The elaboration of the RPD appeared in different forms circa 1989, appearing in Klein (1989a) and Klein et al. (1989) (for a review, see Klein, 1993b). The intent of the refinements was to capture differing strategies for decision making:

1. Matching of situations to actions,
2. The development of an "action queue" when simple matching fails or when the problem situation is highly dynamic,
3. A more complex decision process in which situation assessments and action queues must be evaluated and refined.

The initial RPD model emphasized the direct or serial linking of recognition with action. However, the initial RPD model did not explicitly capture the processes involved in situation monitoring: the refinement of goals across the decision-making process, a mental operation that de Groot (1965) called "progressive deepening":

> For some cases we studied the situational recognition was straightforward, whereas for other cases it was problematic and required verification, and yet for other cases there were competing hypotheses ... and these were the subject of conscious deliberation. (Klein, 1989a, p. 52)

Another focus of research was the elaboration of the RPD model to include a notion of mental model formation and refinement. In a study of the activities of nuclear power plant operators in simulated emergencies, Roth (1997a) saw evidence for recognition priming but also evidence for mental modeling, that is, the attempt of the operators to develop mental models of what was happening inside the power plant during the emergencies, supporting causal understanding. Roth referred to this as the "diagnostic and story-building" elements of decision making. The elaboration of the RPD (after Klein, 1989a, 1993b; Klein et al., 1989) incorporated a notion of progressive deepening as well as a path for decision-analysis-like activities. This is presented in Figure 9.5.

The "recognition" box in Figure 9.5 specifies the recognition of case typicality or prototypicality in terms of cues, expectancies, and goals. Following the leftmost path straight down the model, one finds the RPD strategy. Situation assessment, an emerging concept in human factors psychology, was adopted into the refined RPD model. By hypothesis, situation assessment permits the prioritizing of cues and thereby supports selective attention, explaining why experts do not feel overwhelmed whereas novices sometimes do. Cues come primarily in the form of information revealed by ongoing events. Thus, for example, in some urban firefighting situations, the commander must inspect flame or smoke color to make a decision or determine the timing for an action that follows from a decision.

One purpose of expectancies is to suggest ways of testing if a situation is correctly understood through the specification of events that should occur. If expectations are

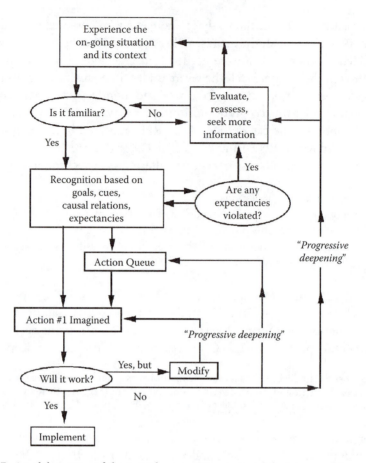

FIGURE 9.5 An elaboration of the initial recognition-primed decision-making model.

violated, this can create a shift in situation assessment and a consequent refinement or shifting of goals and actions. Here, "goal" refers not to the context-free types of goals expressed in Decision-Analytic Models but to the specific goals and outcomes that the domain expert wants to achieve. In time-critical decision making, goals are linked to an expectation of the timing of events. Also, the act of recognition of familiarity entails an action queue. In some situations the action queue is a single action. In other situations the queue involves a prioritization of a set of goals or subgoals, and in some situations the queue may involve the "timelining" of goals—actions may be "put on hold" pending the acquisition of additional information or the occurrence of certain events.

The action queue is potentially dynamic, as indicated by the progressive deepening loops in the elaborated RPD model. Like the initial RPD model, the elaboration of the RPD model maintained the emphasis on the fact that most decision making occurs without conscious deliberation of alternatives. The elaboration of the RPD model preserved an emphasis on the recognition of situations in terms of familiarity or prototypicality (Klein, 1989a) but takes this further by describing a process of mental simulation or "imagined action." This is clearly reminiscent of mental modeling in the Duncker model. According to Klein et al. (1989), the recognitional act suggests feasible goals, sensitizes the decision maker to important cues, suggests promising courses of action, and generates expectancies. But what makes the revised RPD model Dunckerian is the notion that the recognitional act makes all these things possible because it provides an understanding of the causal dynamics associated with a decision problem.

In the study of firefighters, Klein et al. found abundant evidence for a process of imaginal simulation. In one case of emergency services, a woman had jumped or fallen from a highway overpass but landed on a support strut for a highway sign. The woman was semiconscious, and the first task was to raise a ladder so that she could be held in place. Now, how should she be raised to safety? The commander considered a number of alternatives. He first imagined attaching her to a particular type of harness, but it would have to be snapped on from the back, and lifting her by it would put strain on her back. He imagined using a particular type of tied strap, but that would have a similar problem. Next he imagined using a ladder belt. He imagined lifting the woman up a few inches, sliding the belt under her, tying it to her waist, buckling and snapping it, and then lifting her away from the strut. This is the option he selected, and the rescue was successfully performed (Klein, 1989a). Across all the incidents that were analyzed using the CDM, "the experienced firefighters showed about three times more references to imagined future states, compared to the novices. … There is a steady increasing proportion of deliberations about situations as we move along the dimension from less experience to more experience" (Klein, 1989a, p. 68). One purpose of the first refinement of the RPD model was to acknowledge the role of imagery or the mental simulation of predicted or hypothetical future states (Klein, 1989a).

This emergency rescue example also illustrates the fact that decision making *can* involve the consideration of more than one alternative (as in the Decision-Analytic Model) but that the options are not generated, compared, or evaluated concurrently. Rather, they are considered and imaginally evaluated one at a time. The "evaluation" box is manifest in the first elaboration of the RPD, but the subsequent box that includes "implement," "modify," and "reject" options is replaced in the elaboration of the RPD by boxes and decisions indicating the modification and progressive deepening of plans.

Overall, the elaboration of the RPD seems to be a combination of aspects of the Duncker model (mental modeling, progressive deepening, and conscious deliberation), the Decision-Analytic Model (evaluation of alternatives under certain circumstances), and the RPD model (direct recognition leading to action plans) (Klein, 1993b; Klein & Zsambok, 1995). These ideas were all integrated into what we referred to as the "Base Model" of expertise in chapter 8 (Figure 8.2), which combines the notion of RPD, the Duncker refinement cycle, mental modeling, decision analysis, and the notion of situation awareness.

The Base Model of expertise is intended to capture a number of decision-making strategies; that is, a number of alternative submodels can be pulled out (Klein, 1993a). In the simplest case, experience of the situation (awareness of the problem of the day and data examination) leads to recognition based on typicality or prototypicality, which leads to expectancies and an implemented course of action taken right off the top of the action queue. This submodel, labeled as the "recognition-priming" ellipse in Figure 8.2, reflects the initial RPD, in which a commitment is made to a course of action without any deliberation over alternatives. This simplest case may also be one of the most frequent. Looking across three of the domains that have been investigated using the CDM—urban and forest firefighting, tank platoon commanding, critical care nursing, design engineering, and so on—Klein (1989a) found that expert decision making relied on recognition priming more than half of the time (range of 39% to 80% across all of the incidents). Concurrent evaluation tended to occur only about 40% of the time (range of 4% to 61%).

In a second submodel, situation recognition is followed by a process of evaluating the mental model and refining it prior to implementation, reflecting the Duncker model in that it involves the refinement of the initial assessment as supported by the reinspection of data or the search for additional data. This is indicated in the "Mental Model Refinement Cycle" ellipse.

The point of the RPD is to emphasize the belief that decision-analytic procedures either cannot or simply do not occur as a part of the expert's familiar routines. However, a third submodel of the elaborated RPD embraces the sort of situation described by the traditional Decision-Analytic Model. In this submodel, one goes from the initial situation assessment not to a single action that is to be implemented but to an "action queue." Through continued looping, indicated by the "Action Plan Refinement Cycle" ellipse, one can generate a set of alternative courses of action that might be assessed according to such things as costs versus benefits and likelihoods. Neither the elaborated RPD nor the Base Model precludes the sort of analysis that is involved in the traditional Decision-Analytic Model. Indeed, this integration regards the decision-analytic strategy, Dunckerian refinement cycles, and recognition priming as complementary (Klein, 1989a, 1993b). Examples such as where to locate airports and whether to elect for cosmetic surgery might benefit from analytical strategies, because the decision maker is faced with tasks that are so new or conflict laden that there is little opportunity for recognitional decision making. "If a novice were to consider buying a car, the decision-analytic technique would be preferred, to systematically lay out the options and the evaluation dimensions. This would help clarify values, if nothing else. But one would not expect someone proficient, such as a used-car salesman, to go through the same exercise" (Klein, 1989a, p. 50).

What Klein et al. have done is to argue that each of the core concepts of a number of models that all resonate with the NDM paradigm can be embraced by a single "synthesized process model." In concert with Rasmussen's (1983) approach to Cognitive Systems Engineering (see chapter 10), Klein et al. distinguish skill-based performance (i.e., recognitional skill), rule-based performance (i.e., the reliance on familiar procedures), and knowledge-based performance (i.e., reliance on conceptual principles, mental models, and conscious deliberation). The perception of typicality in the revised RPD model fits with a number of theories (e.g., Cohen, 1993c) emphasizing pattern recognition. The diagnosis and situation assessment boxes are in accord with Pennington and Hastie's (1993) model emphasizing the expert's attempt to generate causal explanations.

From the Notion of Attention to an Integrated Theory of Reasoning: Situation Awareness

The concept of attention has been central to psychology from its philosophical phase through to the late 1800s when it was established as a science (Boring, 1950). Attention is at once a phenomenon of consciousness (*Of what objects or events am I aware?*), a phenomenon of perception (*What am I seeing?*), and a phenomenon of categorization (*What kind of thing or event is that?*). Attention presents to consciousness an awareness of what we perceive, in terms of the concepts and categories we already know (memory). It thereby allows us make judgments and decisions (Ebbinghaus, 1908, chap. 8; Pillsbury, 1929). In traditional experimental psychology, attention was seen as a bridge between perception and memory—*What am I perceiving right now?* What one is sensing is related somehow to the concepts and categories residing in memory, allowing for perception or understanding. Numerous theories of attention have been proffered and heavily researched, beginning with the earliest studies of dual-task performance or "divided attention" that helped define psychology as a science and continuing to modern experimental psychology (Dember & Warm, 1979). Most models of attention have relied on the notion that human consciousness can "pay" attention to only a limited number of signals at a time. Attention is seen as a "filter," or as a "focusing" mechanism, or as a "limited resource," or as something that can be "captured." A number of detailed models have evolved from such metaphors and have been refined and debated over successive generations of experimental psychology (Hoffman, Cochran, & Nead, 1990).

In a classical view of cognition (i.e., Leibniz, Descartes, and many subsequent scholars), the process of sensation detects cues based on raw physical stimulus properties. These are then integrated—associations are activated and inferences are made—based on contact with memory, resulting in meaningful percepts. Attention guides or directs this sequence. But also in classical theory, there was a subsequent process of "apperception" involving contact with the sum total of one's knowledge (cf. Ebbinghaus, 1908, chap. 12; Moore, 1939). In more modern information processing terms, this would be seen as a "bottom-up" process. Wundt (1874) referred to this as *apperceptive Verbindungen,* or "apperceptive compounds." "All recall is controlled by apperception as well as by association. ... Apperception selects from the possible associates those which are in accord with the entire past of the individual as well as with the single connection" (Pillsbury, 1929, p. 185). Thus for instance, a pattern of colors, shapes, and movements might be detected or sensed, and with rapid contact with memory there would be the percept of "cat." Apperception would go beyond that to the sum of knowledge and such ideas as *I like cats* or *Cats are sometimes seen as a symbol of evil.* This is the "assimilation of ideas by means of ideas already possessed" (De Garmo, 1895, p. 32).

But there is also a "top-down" component. Johann Friedrich Herbart, a Leibnizian associationist, introduced the notion of apperception to refer not just to assimilation but to a process whereby the contents of consciousness determine what new impressions should enter. In the language of the early foundations of educational psychology, this was a mechanism for learning and the role of learning in subsequent behavior, referred to as the "education of attention" (Pillsbury, 1926; Ribot, 1890).

The concept of attention retains its centrality, and the concept of apperception reemerges today in applied cognitive science, in a theory of "situation awareness" (SA) developed by Mica Endsley and her colleagues (Endsley, 1995a, 1995b, 1997, 2001; Endsley, Bolté, & Jones, 2003). The point of this designation is that attention involves not just the detection of isolated signals, stimuli or cues, or even the perception of static objects but the ongoing awareness of one's environment, especially events that one must understand (apperceive). This, in turn, supports "projection," or the anticipation of events via mental simulation. Endsley posited three levels of ongoing situational awareness:

> *Level 1 SA* concerns the meaningful interpretation of data (i.e., perception), the process that turns data into information. Hence, what constitutes information will be a function of the operator's goals and decision requirements, as well as events within the situation that is being assessed.
>
> *Level 2 SA* concerns the degree to which the individual comprehends the fuller meaning of that information—a process akin to the classical notion of apperception, often referred to today as the formation of a "mental model" (see chapter 5). In complex domains, understanding the significance of information is nontrivial. It involves integrating many pieces of interacting information, forming another higher order of understanding, prioritized according to how it relates to achieving the goals.
>
> *Level 3 SA* is the mental or imaginal projection of events into a possible future. In complex domains, the capacity to apperceive is a key to the ability to behave proactively and not just reactively. SA is critical to successful operation in dynamic domains where it is necessary for the domain practitioner (e.g., controller of an industrial process, decision maker in a military unit, etc.) to accurately perceive and then understand and project (apperceive) actions and events in the environment (Endsley, 1995a, 1995b).

A look back at chapter 8 on Expertise Studies, and in particular the Base Model of expertise shown in Figure 8.2, includes a notion of a Sense-making Mental Model Refinement Cycle. This can be regarded as the process of maintaining situational awareness. This illustrates how there are some integrations of theoretical notions across the perspectives or communities of practice. As we show next, there are also integrations with regard to issues of design of information systems.

Implications for the Design of Information Technologies

NDM theories and research have approached the design of information technologies, in one case, to support SA and, in another case, to support decision making.

Situation Awareness-Oriented Design

The theory of SA has inspired an approach to the design of new information technologies referred to as Situation Awareness-Oriented Design (SAOD) (Endsley, 1995b; Endsley et al., 2003). In conducting SAOD, the researcher begins with the empirical study of SA. The levels of SA described previously form a coding scheme that is used in the Situation Awareness Global Assessment Technique (SAGAT) (Endsley, 1988, 1990, 1995a; Endsley & Garland, 2000). In SAGAT, a simulation employing a system of interest (e.g., a simulation of an air traffic controller's task) is briefly halted at randomly selected times, and the operators are queried as to their perceptions of the situation at that time. The system displays are blanked, and the simulation is sus-

TABLE 9.3 Examples of Situation Awareness Global Assessment Technique Probes, Adapted for a Study in Air Traffic Control

Level 1 SA: Perception of data	What is the aircraft's call sign? What is the aircraft's altitude?
Level 2 SA: Comprehension of meaning	Which aircraft are currently conforming to their assignments? Which aircraft are experiencing weather impact?
Level 3 SA: Projection into the future	Which aircraft must be handed off to another sector or facility within the next 2 minutes? Which pairs of aircraft have lost or will lose separation if they stay on their current (assigned) courses?

Note: SA = situation awareness.

pended while participants quickly answer questions about their current perceptions of the situation. SAGAT has been used in studies of avionics concepts, concepts for military command and control technology, and other display design and interface technologies (Endsley, 1995a). The SAGAT probes are illustrated in Table 9.3, which uses a scenario involving the aviation domain.

Research has shown that freezing can be done about a half a dozen times in a scenario trial lasting a total of 20 or so minutes without disrupting the flow of thought. Through SAGAT, the impact of design decisions on SA can be assessed via performance, giving one a window on the quality of the integrated system design when used within the actual challenges of the operational environment. The information derived from the evaluation of design concepts can then be used to iteratively refine the system design. SAGAT provides designers with diagnostic information on not only how aware operators are of key information but also how well they understand the significance or meaning of that information and how well they are able to think ahead to project what will be happening.

Generalizing across studies, we can achieve an understanding of some general principles of SAOD. For instance, the "Sacagawea Principle" (Endsley & Hoffman, 2002) asserts that human-centered computational tools need to support active organization of information, active search for information, active exploration of information, reflection on the meaning of information, and evaluation and choice among action alternatives. SAOD embodies three main steps or phases. SA requirements analysis, from SAGAT procedures and GDTA interview procedures, provides the leverage points for the design of systems to support SA. Next, SA design principles are brought to bear to translate SA requirements into ideas for system design. This process is illustrated in the Concept Map in Figure 9.6.

Historically, most interface design guidelines are focused at the level of the interfaces and graphical elements—fonts, how a menu should function or be placed, the best way to fill in information on a screen, and so on (Sanders & McCormick, 1992; Woodson, Tilman, & Tilman, 1992). Furthermore, most guidelines assume the "one person–one machine" scenario for human–computer interaction. With regard to such cognitive processes as attention and sensemaking, most guidance either remains silent on how to convey the meaning of the information that is to be displayed or offers unhelpful generalizations (e.g., "design an interface that is intuitive") (Kommers, Grabinger, & Dunlap, 1996, p. 127). SA-oriented design principles address issues including the

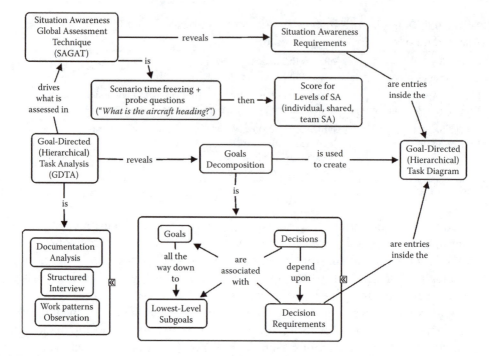

FIGURE 9.6 How Goal-Directed Task Analysis feeds into Situation Awareness-Oriented Design.

integration of information into knowledge and the guidance and direction of attention according to meaning, that is, how the operator manages information with the dynamically changing information needs associated with a dynamically changing situation. In some work contexts, a fixed task sequence can help constrain the layout of information. Yet for most systems flexibility is needed, allowing the operator to bounce between different goals as events change. Hence, a goal-oriented approach tries to take into account how people actually work.

A second example design principle is that *the human user of the guidance needs to be shown the guidance in a way that is organized in terms of their major goals. Information needed for each particular goal should be shown in a meaningful form and should allow the human to directly comprehend the major decisions associated with each goal* (Endsley & Hoffman, 2002). What we might call immediately interpretable displays need not necessarily present information in the same way it is presented in the real world. Displays of data from measurements made by individual sensors (e.g., airspeed indicators, altimeters) may be computationally integrated into goal-relevant higher order dynamic invariants (e.g., how a plane is flying in terms of its drag) presented as pictographic metaphors that may look fairly unlike anything in the world (see, for example, Still & Temme, 2006, and the discussion of the "OZ" display in chapter 10). In SAOD, displays are envisioned for supporting all three levels of SA including,

1. The display of information in such a way as to support perception of its meaning with respect to goals (Level 1 SA),
2. The display of information in such a way as to support mental model formation with respect to high-level goals and possible goal conflicts (Level 2 SA), and

3. The display of information in such a way as to support mental projection and the ongoing maintenance of "global SA"—a high-level overview of the situation across all the goals (Level 3 SA).

Decision-Centered Design

Decision-Centered Design (DCD) is so named as to focus the development of technologies on supporting decision making. Its focus reflects the same motivation that is expressed in the title of the CDM. In the evolution of the CDM, it was found that interviewing experts about their past decisions served as a good window to the identification of leverage points. Leverage points are aspects of cognitive work where an infusion of technology, however modest, might bring about a disproportionately large increase in the work effectiveness and quality. As the CDM evolved, it became clear that asking about decisions worked better than asking about other aspects of tasks or asking experts what they know. Likewise, focusing the design of new technologies on the support of decision making is the focus of DCD. "[Technology] should improve cognitive performance … [it should] make people smarter at what they do and their work easier to perform. Specifically, [technology] should support the cognitive activities of users and build upon and extend their domain expertise" (Stanard, Uehara, & Hutton, 2003, p. 1).

In the DCD process, the initial effort is aimed at identifying individuals who will be the "users" of the new technology, the practitioners in the domain at hand, and coming to a rich understanding of their needs and requirements. This goes beyond typical approaches to the development of new technologies in that the understanding of tasks and requirements is emphasized much more and is more than just a one-off interview procedure, after which the technology developers go off and write software that is subsequently presented as a finished "deliverable."

> [Such an] initial design estimate may be based on a naïve understanding of who the user is, but as the task domain is further explored, it can become more apparent that users really need help, and that there may actually be more than one user, each with a somewhat different set of requirements to be supported. (Stanard et al., 2003, p. 2)

The DCD approach also involves revealing and studying the really challenging and critical decision aspects of jobs. "Our working assumption is that 80% of the problems can be solved by understanding and improving the toughest 20% of the cognitive work" (Stanard et al., 2003, p. 2). This is put in contrast with certain other approaches to the design of information technologies, such as SAOD (Endsley, Bolté, & Jones, 2003) and work analysis (e.g., Vicente, 1999), which cover broad swaths of the cognitive work that is involved in particular jobs. Thus, in DCD the probe question categories of the CDM are carried over as implications for the design of things such as interfaces: For this given problem, what are the alternative strategies, and what are the critical cues and patterns that the expert perceives? What makes the problem difficult? What kinds of errors do less experienced practitioners typically make?

Although NDM has generated some integrated models of cognition and cognitive work, and has spawned approaches to design, it has recently dynamited the enterprise by invoking a distinction between models of "microcognition" and models of "macrocognition" (Klein et al., 2003).

The Emerging Notion of Macrocognition

Although NDM research and theory has contributed to the search for an integrated model of reasoning, the research has also dovetailed with an idea that was introduced by Erik Hollnagel and Pietro Cacciabue (Cacciabue & Hollnagel, 1995) to capture the phenomena of decision making that occur in natural settings as opposed to artificial laboratory settings.

> Although we might want to reveal specific causal sequences of various memory or attentional mechanisms, this turns out to be difficult. When we try to describe naturalistic decision making, we quickly realize that it makes little sense to concoct hypothetical information processing flow diagrams believed to represent causal sequences of mental operations, because they end up looking like spaghetti graphs. (Klein et al., 2003, p. 81)

This captures a major implication of CTA and CFR research. Specifically, it makes little sense to attempt to create any single model of how domain practitioners reason while conducting their tasks.

An example can be found in a study of weather forecasting (Hoffman, Coffey, & Ford, 2000; Hoffman, Trafton, & Roebber, 2008. The procedure that was used is now called the Macrocognitive Modeling Procedure (Crandall et al., 2006; Hoffman, Coffey, & Carnot, 2000; Klein & Hoffman, 2008). The purpose of the procedure is to generate refined and behaviorally validated models of reasoning, with less effort than that involved in the method that is more often used for this application—think-aloud problem solving combined with protocol analysis.

In the first step of the procedure, each participant was presented with two alternative "bogus" models of forecaster reasoning. These were based on the components of the Base Model (see Figure 8.2). One or the other of the bogus models included the idea of mental modeling, the idea of hypothesis testing, the idea of recognition priming, and the idea of situational awareness. One of the bogus models contained a loop, and the other was a linear sequence. In both models, the core concepts were expressed in domain-relevant terms. "Inspect satellite images to get the big picture" appeared in one of the bogus models instead of "Data Examination," for instance. Furthermore, the core concepts were not arranged and linked as they are in the Base Model, nor were they linked quite as one might expect them to be in the case of expert forecaster reasoning. For instance, in one of the bogus models, the forecaster's initial mental model was compared for agreement with one particular computer forecasting model, after which the forecast was adjusted to take local effects into account, after which the forecaster compared the forecast to another of the computer model forecasts. The intent was that the bogus models would have all the elements, using the right sort of language, would appear pertinent to the domain, and would seem not too unreasonable but not quite right either.

The participants were asked to select the one that they felt best represented their forecasting strategy. As expected, they found this an unacceptable choice, but then they could use the various elements and ideas from the bogus models to craft their own model, one that they felt better captured their reasoning in the forecasting procedure.

Next, the researchers observed the forecasters at their jobs. Some elements of each of the reasoning models could be validated observationally. For example, a forecaster could be observed to first inspect satellite images and other data and then look at one or another of the computer forecasts, as they said they did when they crafted their reasoning model. Elements of the reasoning models that could not be so easily validated were the subject of probe questions (e.g., "Did you watch the Weather Channel before you came in today?" "Why are you looking at that now?"). The results showed many convergences and many differences. The notion of mental modeling was salient in all of models, especially those of the experts. It turns out that the notion of mental modeling, as we defined it in chapter 4, is a comfortable notion to weather forecasters, because of the distinction, decades old, between the forecaster's conceptual understanding of the dynamics in a given weather situation versus the outputs of the computer forecasting models (Hoffman, Trafton, & Roebber, 2008).

Regarding differences and variations, some models from both experts and journeymen were simple, including only some core notions, and some were complex, including reference to individual computer forecast models. All of the models included what, in information processing terms, would be loops, such as the refinement cycle (e.g., if the output of a particular computer forecast model disagrees with the mental model, inspect such-and-such data and iterate until a resolution is found). In fact, all of the models included more than one loop. Some of the reasoning models had many loops or refinement cycles (as many as seven), reminiscent of "spaghetti graphs" in that everything connected to nearly everything else. Other reasoning models had just two or three loops. Some of the reasoning models showed the accommodation of local effects occurring after the formation of a mental model, and some had that accommodation occurring after the inspection of satellite images ("getting the big picture") and as a part of forming a mental model. Four of the five journeyman models, and none of the expert models, explicitly included the notion of "persistence," which is when weather dynamics are stable and a forecast can largely be a recapitulation of the previous forecast. This fits the idea that journeymen are more likely than experts to be more literal and procedure-oriented than experts (see chapter 5).

Four months after the reasoning models had been crafted, the researchers showed all of the various models to all of the participants, with an invitation to guess the owner of each of them. The results showed that the task was confusing, in part because all of the models expressed many of the same notions and did so in somewhat similar ways. Only 25% of the identifications were correct. As it turned out, the forecasters at this particular facility did not actually spend much time discussing their reasoning strategies with one another. Half of the participants did not correctly identify their own model. It turns out there was a reason beyond confusion. One forecaster, upon reflection, asserted,

> When this Bermuda High set up early a few years ago like now, the Eta and MM5 models did not handle it well, but NGM did. It is the same now, but we have COAMPS as well, and it does well too. This model of mine does not fit my reasoning now, since I am not using the [computer] models in the same way as I did when we made my [reasoning] model.

In other words, his diagram expressed a particular order of preference for examining each of the many computer model outputs in a strategy that was no longer appropriate. As Rasmussen said (1979, 1981; see chapter 10), the practitioner engages not in tasks but in context-sensitive, knowledge-driven choice among action alternatives.

Results of this exploration in CTA methodology showed that the sequence of reasoning operations and strategies that the expert engages in is a function of the weather situation. That includes effects of oscillations that affect seasonal trends (e.g., the El Niño and La Niña oscillation, among others) and whether the situation is a persistence situation. In other words, there is not, nor can there be, *a* model of the reasoning of weather forecasters. To depict even all of the most typical weather situations, one would need to construct many dozens of models just for one particular region or climate. Furthermore, forecasting is always a moving target—for instance, new radar algorithms might provide a new source of data for forecasting the size of hail.

The upshot of this sort of finding for the attempt to develop models of reasoning is profound. The implication is that in real-world problem solving, mental operations are parallel and highly interacting. The description of hypothetical "basic" mental operations in such sequences as the following might make sense if one is probing cognition at the millisecond level of causation (microcognition):

Attentional switching → Sensation → Memory contact → Recognition

But in the real-world context, it is far more appropriate to refer to processes such as problem detection, sensemaking, replanning, and mental simulation, which are continuous and interacting (macrocognition) and cannot be easily reduced to hypothetical building blocks placed into causal strings.

The studies of micro- and macrocognition are complementary. Macrocognitive functions—detecting problems, managing uncertainty, and so forth—are typically not studied in laboratory settings. To some extent, they are emergent phenomena. No amount of research on solving puzzles such as cryptarithmetic problems or logic problems or Tower of Hanoi problems is likely to result in inquiry about problem detection. However, once these macrocognitive phenomena are identified, it is possible to trace microcognitive aspects in them. Therefore, research on microcognition is needed in parallel with research on macrocognition:

> We must study these types of functions and processes, even though they do not fit neatly into controlled experiments. We must find ways to conduct cognitive field research that can improve our understanding of the functions and processes encountered at the macrocognition level. (Klein et al., 2003, p. 83)

This suggests a new perspective on the Base Model of expertise (see Figure 8.2), and the models presented in this chapter including Endsley's theory of situation awareness. Rather than regarding these as singular or single models that uniquely or completely capture proficient reasoning, researchers should regard them as macrocognitive models, ones that attempt, perhaps with only moderate success, to capture the parallelism and interactiveness of macrocognitive functions. What they fail to capture is how variations on the models can be appropriate for particular domains, particular times, particular local contexts, or particular proficiency levels—but that might not be the purpose of macrocognitive models. Furthermore, these are not the sorts of models that could be magically implemented in computer programs that would enable one to predict, for instance, how long in milliseconds it would take for a weather forecaster to predict fog. That is not the purpose of such models (Hoffman, Klein, & Schraagen, 2007).

The implications of the microcognition–macrocognition distinction extend to the design of technologies: The more detailed and bounded a task is, the more likely it can be cast in stone in software, but the more likely it will be that the task description will be brittle and fleeting with time and context.

Summary

NDM refers to the study of decision making in domains characterized by time stress, high stakes, vague goals, uncertainty, multiple players, organizational constraints, and dynamic settings. This approach to the study of decision making has had considerable applied impact as well as important theoretical contribution. In the 1980s studies of firefighters and neonatal intensive care nurses using retrospective interviews to explore actions, goals, and plans, as well critical cues that influenced decision making, were conducted. The outcomes of these studies had an impact on the firefighting and nursing communities that participated. Investigators succeeded in aiding interviewees in articulating cues and cue patterns that had not previously been documented and were subsequently integrated into training programs.

On a broader scale, these early studies also provided important evidence that the Decision-Analytic Model has important limitations. The Decision-Analytic Model had been developed and extensively applied in economics and business decision making within the JDM paradigm. The JDM paradigm focuses on issues such as optimal strategies prescribed by probability theory or expected utility theory, accuracy (or lack thereof) of judgments, reasoning biases, and limitations in the human ability to evaluate the probabilities of events. The Decision-Analytic Model was widely prescribed as being the best method for making decisions.

In the 1980s some researchers began to react against the JDM paradigm. Researchers reacted against the characterization of human cognition as limited and biased. The prescriptive nature of the Decision-Analytic Model became a target for criticism. Studies using CTA and CFR methods suggested that decision making in the real world is not reduced to a single moment of choice after all the facts had been gathered, but, constructed through an incremental process. CTA and CFR studies suggested a series of decisions-like points along a timeline in which actions are taken and options exist but no concurrent evaluation of options occurs.

A number of limitations of the JDM approach were articulated. Time-critical domains do not allow formal generation and evaluation procedures. Experts rarely report considering more than one option at a time. Furthermore, research has shown that people are not very good at either generating lists of options or systematically evaluating options. Another debate focused on the use of "hit rate" to assess proficiency. Studying hit rates allows for the use of statistical methods for diagnostic evaluation of decision-making skill. NDM researchers, however, take the perspective

that linear modeling and focusing solely on hit rates ignores all the richness of proficient knowledge and skill.

The NDM paradigm has come to be defined by three distinguishing characteristics: (a) a focus on examination of decision making in everyday situations, both
routine and nonroutine situations, both simple and complex; (b) a focus on decision making by experienced, knowledgeable individuals; and (c) the examination of
decision making in real-world job contexts. Given these foci, most NDM researchers
investigate ill-structured problems and domains, uncertain and dynamic environments, situations that involve goal conflict, scenarios involving time pressure and
high risk, and team or group problem solving.

CTA methods commonly used by the NDM community include the CDM, the
Knowledge Audit, and GDTA. The CDM was initially developed during studies of
decision making in fire-ground command. Researchers adapted Flanagan's (1954)
critical incident technique to focus on critical decisions. In a CDM interview, the
expert is asked to recall a critical incident, and the interviewer walks through the incident several times with the interviewee, unpacking more of the story and more detail
with each sweep. The method has been refined over time and explored for validity
from a range of perspectives.

The Knowledge Audit was developed to complement incident-based techniques
such as the CDM. Based on an understanding of human expertise, question probes
were developed to obtain examples of various aspects of expertise as they are instanti-
ated in a specific domain. Rather than eliciting one critical incident that is thoroughly
explored, as in the CDM, the Knowledge Audit elicits a series of incidents, illustrating
aspects of expertise such as diagnosis and prediction, situation awareness, improvisation, metacognition, recognition of anomalies, and compensation for technology
limitations. Often the Knowledge Audit is used early in a study to obtain an overview
of the knowledge and skills needed in a specific domain. The Knowledge Audit has
also been used to explore differing levels of proficiency.

GDTA is another interview technique used in NDM research. GDTA interviews
are organized around the goals the decision maker must achieve and the information
needed to achieve those goals. GDTA does not restrict task description to a linear,
sequential series of activities. GDTA is said to take into account the characteristics of
complex cognitive systems, including conflicting goals and the processing of information in ongoing situations. This method is similar to HTA in that goals and subgoals are elicited and represented in a graphical decomposition.

Two main theoretical contributions of the NDM community include the RPD
model and a theory of situational awareness. The RPD model was based on interview
data obtained from experienced firefighters and later refined and expanded based on
interview data collected from experienced critical care nurses and experts in a range
of other domains. RPD was articulated in reaction against analytic decision making.
Rather than generating a range of options and comparing those options to select the
best one at a specific decision point, firefighters reported that they rarely had time to
consider alternative options. Instead, they seemed to rely on matching the current
situation to a typical course of action based on internal prototypes or analogues. In
the RPD model, the decision maker spends most of the time available assessing the
situation rather than evaluating options.

In short, the expert recognizes the situation (generally as an analogue or prototype). By-products of the recognition include relevant cues, expectancies, plausible
goals, and a preferred course of action, all of which become activated based on the
recognition of the situation. In the simplest form of RPD, the course of action is
implemented without conscious deliberation. Variations include situations in which
the decision maker does not immediately recognize the situation as familiar. In this
case, the experienced decision maker is likely to engage in feature matching or story
building to assess the situation. After the expert assesses the situation, the same four
by-products, including a course of action, become evident, and the course of action
is implemented. In a third variation, if time is available, the expert may pause before
implementing the course of action to mentally simulate or imagine how events will
unfold. As a result of this mental simulation, the course of action may be refined
or rejected and another one selected. However, even in this third variation of RPD,
options are not compared but considered serially until an acceptable course of action
is generated.

A second theoretical contribution of NDM has been in moving from the notion
of attention to a theory of reasoning termed "situation awareness." The theory of
SA emphasizes that attention involves not just the detection of isolated signals,
stimuli, or cues, or even the perception of static objects, but the ongoing awareness
of one's environment. Three levels of SA have been posited: (a) meaningful interpretation of data, resulting in information; (b) comprehension of information, resulting
in a mental model or higher order understanding prioritized according to how it
related to achieving goals; and (c) the mental or imaginal projection of events into a
possible future.

Both of these theories have led to approaches to the design of information technologies. SAOD relies on GDTA and the theory of SA to form an approach to design that
is intended to support active organization of information, active search for information, active exploration of information, reflection on the meaning of information, and
evaluation and choice among action alternatives. In this approach, SA requirements
analysis is conducted using GDTA. Next, design principles are used to translate SA
requirements into ideas for system design. In the final step, the design is tested using
the SAGAT.

DCD is an approach motivated by the RPD perspective and is intended to focus
the development of technologies for supporting decision making. The DCD process
begins with the identification of individuals who will be users of the new technology. Ideally, these are experts in the domain at hand, and analysts are able to obtain
a rich understanding of their needs and requirements. The analysis portion of DCD
involves revealing and studying the challenging and critical aspects of jobs. There is
a working assumption that 80% of the problems can be solved by understanding and
improving the toughest 20% of the cognitive work.

Finally, it is important to mention the emerging notion of macrocognition, an
idea introduced to capture the phenomena of decision making that occur in natural
settings as opposed to artificial laboratory settings. The notion of macrocognition has
dovetailed with NDM research in the search for an integrated model of reasoning.
Macrocognition refers to the perspective that in a real-world context, it makes sense
to refer to processes such as problem detection, sense making, replanning, and mental

simulation, which are continuous and interacting. This is in contrast to microcognition, which attempts to reduce mental operations to hypothetical building blocks (i.e., attentional switching, sensation, memory contact, recognition) placed into causal strings. The microcognitive approach is perhaps most appropriate for probing cognition at the millisecond level of causation rather than in the larger context of on-the-job performance. The study of micro- and macrocognition are complementary. Lab-based studies of microcognition are needed in parallel with the study of emergent macrocognitive phenomena typically studied in field settings. Both micro- and macrocognitive research findings have implications for the design of technologies.

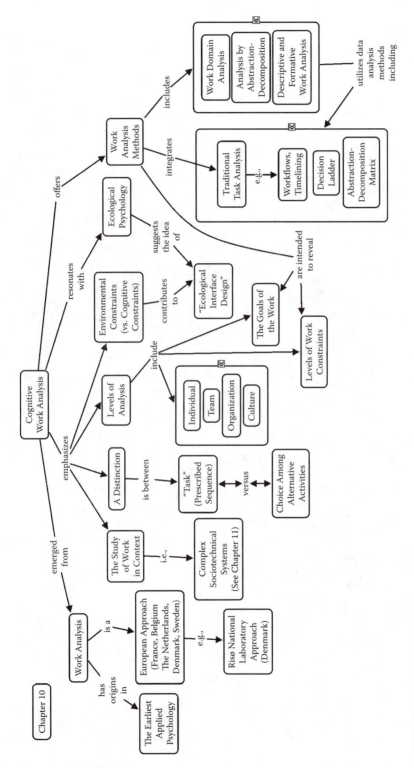

FIGURE 10.1 Chapter 10 Concept Map.

10

Work Analysis

> Work analysis should begin with the environment because that must be dealt with if there is any hope of achieving reliable and effective performance. Only once ecological compatibility has been obtained is it useful to ensure that cognitive compatibility is also achieved.
>
> —Kim Vicente (1999, pp. 114–115)

Origins of This Community of Practice

The paradigm of Work Analysis has its origins primarily in ergonomics in France, Belgium, and Denmark (see Leplat, 1993), which historically has referred to "work analysis" and "activity analysis" rather than to "task analysis," because the term *task* has connotations in English that are different from those in European languages and traditions.

Primarily in France and Belgium, the "Francophone Ergonomics" community of practice represents the traditions of European industrial psychology dating back to the late 1800s and early 1900s (see chapter 2), amplified by concerns about worker health, safety, and productivity that became salient starting in the 1960s. In their review of this framework, De Keyser, Decortis, and Van Daele (1988; see also Nyssen & De Keyser, 2000) pointed to clear overlap and linkages to international literatures (i.e., North American human factors) and the influence of cybernetics, information theory, and systems theories and models. De Keyser et al. also pointed to the defining feature of Francophone Ergonomics: an emphasis on field studies involving in-depth observations and analyses of work in context, with the goal of contributing to the design of workplaces and technologies to avoid creating a gap between the envisioned operations versus "what actually happens" in the workplace activity.

> This interest in studying work situations … can be explained by observing the gap between real situations and laboratory simulations … operators must be familiar with certain rhythms and the duration of certain operations because they use these data to plan and coordinate actions and develop strategies. … For example, the speed of operation of a machine will be linked to the time needed to refill a steel-casting ladle. The characteristics of a product will determine how long it will take for a tool to wear out … this temporal dimension, which is the cornerstone of experience, is often absent from simulations. (De Keyser et al., 1988, p. 153)

The emphasis on field studies of cognitive work in context would make it reasonable to include a discussion of Francophone Ergonomics within the broader discussion of

211

sociological perspectives and ethnographic methodologies (chapter 11). Indeed, one thing that distinguishes Francophone Ergonomics from North American Human Factors psychology is the realization that the concept of the "man–machine system" is too narrow to describe the work situation (De Keyser et al., 1988, p. 152). Much more than North American human factors, Francophone Ergonomics studies include a perspective on the organization and the social context, what Jaques Leplat called the "constraints" or "work conditions." Thus, work is described as involving anticipation and adaptation to cope with uncertainty. Furthermore, "the social components of the situation influence the cognitive aspects because, even in highly automated jobs, the work is teamwork; the transmission of information and the creation of collective knowledge depend on these components" (De Keyser et al., 1988, p. 153).

Some ideas that are regarded as having been influential in Francophone Ergonomics are strikingly similar to ideas developed in the North American Cognitive Engineering community (chapters 6 and 7). For instance, Russian ergonomicist D. A. Ochanine (1964) (writing in French) proposed that workers create "operating images" of the machines they work with, abstracting a simplified representation that emphasizes the functions that the worker knows about and relies on. This image develops over time, in a process of assimilation and accommodation (Piaget is also cited as having influenced the ideas of Francophone Ergonomics). This notion that workers attempt to form mental models of the technologies with which they work is salient in Cognitive Systems Engineering, perhaps even qualifying as a law of cognitive work (cf. Hollnagel & Woods, 2006). For instance, one would predict that when workers are faced with a novel situation and have difficulty using tools or machines or computers, they will revert to an earlier stage in the development of knowledge and attempt manipulations and experimentation because the necessary conceptual understanding is lacking (see Leplat & Pailhous, 1981).

Another distinguishing feature is that Francophone Ergonomics places more emphasis on seeing work from a developmental perspective, indicated by our reference to Piaget. Worker knowledge and other competencies are not regarded as static. Both knowledge and reasoning adapt as a result of technological change. This has implications for how one evaluates worker reliability, because "the worker" is a moving target. The analysis of reliability has involved a focus on studies in incidents and errors, using measures such as gaze shifts, reaction time to alarms, and so on, in such domains as air traffic control.

The goal of contributing to design has been successfully achieved by Francophone Ergonomicists, largely to the tradition of including ergonomic analysis in industrial contexts (i.e., design of machines such as lathes and other industrial equipment) (see Société d'Ergonomie de Langue Française, 2008). De Keyser et al. (1991) noted, however, that new challenges have arisen, not unlike challenges discussed by North American Cognitive Systems Engineers and Human Factors psychologists. Researchers in all these communities of practice see a need for early input into design decisions, they seek to develop new information technologies to support processes of decision making, and they seek to conduct research to support allocation of tasks and workload in new and dynamic work contexts. This is one reason, and not the only reason, why a discussion of Francophone Ergonomics could be placed within a discussion of the Cognitive Systems Engineering perspective. Another reason is the interest on the part of Francophone ergonomicists to go from field studies to predictions about the nature of cognitive work in envisioned worlds (cf. Daniellou, 1985).

Francophone ergonomicists also see challenges that are same as ones addressed in Expertise Studies (chapter 8), including the challenge of developing models of expert reasoning. Hence, Francophone ergonomicists refer to Guy Boy's method of cognitive function analysis (1983, 1998), which includes descriptions of practitioner knowledge into the "design rationale" of design documents, and Rasmussen's analysis of expert knowledge in terms of the levels of skills, rules, and knowledge (Rasmussen, 1979, 1983), which we discuss later in this chapter. This is one, but not the only, reason why Francophone Ergonomics could be placed within a discussion of the Expertise Studies perspective.

References to Francophone Ergonomics, and ideas about field research, appear throughout the chapters of this book. Three things tipped the scales in our decision to have this short discussion of Francophone Ergonomics to introduce the work analysis perspective: (a) the shared historical roots of Francophone Ergonomics and the work analysis framework of Jens Rasmussen; (b) the shared emphasis on understanding cognitive work from multiple perspectives, including social and organizational perspectives; and (c) the shared view that cognitive work cannot be understood solely as a closed system or as a sequences of steps. There are "different patterns within a complex web of actions rich in meaning ... [that] provide a springboard for the study of interruptions and activity planning, which is continually restarted by the operator ... [there is a] need to consider stories, or semantic fields, which we call activity-organizing principles" (De Keyser et al., 1988, p. 157).

Jens Rasmussen and his colleagues at the Risø National Laboratory in Denmark have been especially influential in articulating a Work Analysis framework, applying it to real-world problems and sharing their experiences with the scientific community (cf. Pejtersen & Rasmussen, 1997; Rasmussen, 1986b, 1992). Concepts from work analysis have had an impact in the discipline of human factors psychology, especially on topics such as the design of graphic interfaces for decision support systems in industrial process control. One result has been an integrated approach to work analysis called Cognitive Work Analysis (CWA). Kim Vicente of the University of Toronto and Penelope Sanderson of the University of Queensland have provided valuable summaries and integrations of the Risø work (Sanderson, 2002; Vicente, 1999) and have advanced the CWA framework. They have also integrated the work analysis notions with some ideas from Ecological Psychology (Burns & Hajdukiewicz, 2004; Pejtersen & Rasmussen, 1997). Most recently, Neelam Naikar of the Defense Science and Technology Organisation of Australia has taken the work analysis principles articulated by Rasmussen, Vicente, and others and elaborated the methods and methodology for applying these principles (Naikar, Hopcroft, & Moylan, 2005).

Defining CWA

Vicente (1999, 2000) defined CWA as the analysis of work with the goal of giving designers insights into how to create tools that effectively support human work. Effectiveness is defined in terms of increased safety (reduced risk of accidents and errors), increased productivity, and improved quality of life. Effectiveness is also defined in terms of adaptability. The technology should support the continual adaptation of the state and structure of the sociotechnical system to local and contextual contingencies, which, in turn, should lead to increased safety, productivity, and improved quality of life.

Pejtersen and Rasmussen (1997) defined CWA as a framework that

> separates a representation of the work domain, its means and ends, its relational structure, and the effective task strategies among which the user may choose, from a representation of the user's general background, resources, cognitive style, and subjective preferences. The aim is to design work support systems that leave the freedom open to a user to choose a work strategy that suits the user in the particular situation. (p. 316)

The key point here hinges on the meaning of the word *task*. One definition is that a task is a specific sequence of actions, perhaps hierarchical or conditional, but a sequence nonetheless. Rasmussen's argument, one that is difficult to deny because it has been empirically demonstrated, is that in complex cognitive work contexts, workers do not engage in tasks; they engage in context-sensitive, knowledge-driven choice among alternative activities (see Rasmussen, 1979). It sometimes appears as if workers are conducting tasks, but that happens when action sequences are mandated or situations are routine and no choice is needed. But the "human in the loop" becomes critical precisely in nonroutine situations. An example might be the weather forecaster who is challenged with predicting where and when afternoon thunderstorms will crop up, just as the uplink to the radar goes down. Using other sources of data and refined reasoning strategies, the forecaster can work around such problems (see Hoffman, Trafton, & Roebber, 2008).

CWA Versus Cognitive Task Analysis

Although CWA and Cognitive Task Analysis (CTA) share many goals, they are in many ways distinct (Vicente, 2000). Specifically, CWA is described as a philosophy or "framework" for studying work, whereas CTA is generally considered to be a set of particular, specified methods for understanding the cognitive aspects of a task. In fact, some would describe CTA as a designation for some of the methods that can be used in pursuit of CWA. A second important distinction is that of constraint-driven design versus design based on cognitive requirements. CTA techniques are generally aimed at identifying cognitively complex aspects of a task so that training, technology, and processes can be designed to accomplish such system goals as reduced mental workload, increased efficiency, and fewer errors. CWA, in contrast, focuses on identifying constraints, environmental as well as cognitive, that shape work. Both CWA and CTA, however, consider work in the work settings and are not anchored to the academic laboratory. The research does not study workers engaged in isolated, pensive activities. Rather, research focuses on experienced professionals doing complex jobs in "real-world" settings.

CWA and Ecological Psychology

CWA resonates with Ecological Psychology. Ecological Psychology evolved from the work of James Gibson and his colleagues (see Burns & Hajdukiewicz, 2004, chap. 1;

Gibson, 1979). Gibson's work on perception involved a reaction against the traditional theory put forth in the 1800s by such pioneering psychologists as Herman Helmholtz (1856–1866). Helmholtzian theory stated that perception is a process in which stimulus information provides impoverished cues (e.g., retinal images presented to the two eyes) that must be integrated in the brain through processes of inference, resulting in a complete percept of the world (e.g., fused depth perception). In contrast, Gibson proposed laws of "ecological optics," which specify how the perceiver can directly perceive objects and events. Gibson also suggested that perception involves the awareness objects and events at a meaningful level rather than the level of isolated physical features and cues such as size, shape, and color.

> A key concept behind ecological psychology is that environments and information should be described in terms that reveal their functional significance for an actor rather than being described in objective actor-free terms. ... A further concept is the idea of affordances. The affordances of an object are the possibilities for action with that object, from the point of view of a particular actor. (Sanderson, 2002, p. 237)

The Ecological Approach is characterized by the view that there exists a reciprocity between the human and the environment (Flach, Hancock, Caird, & Vicente, 1995; Hancock, Flach, Caird, & Vicente, 1995; Vicente, 2002). From an Ecological Approach, the environment is as much a determinant of human behavior as any mentalistic phenomenon (e.g., mental representations). Gibson saw little need for postulates concerning mental causality within a theoretical explanation of perception. This is in contrast to the cognitivist approach that regards mental phenomena as the major causal determinant of behavior. Vicente stated that in traditional human factors research, there is a "widely held belief that it is always important to identify a worker's mental model of the work domain and then design a human–computer interface to be compatible with that model" (1999, p. 49). A key feature of the application of the work analysis is that designers do not elicit or rely on understandings of workers' mental models, strategies, and preferences as starting points for interventions, because mental models can be incomplete and erroneous (e.g., Vicente, 2001, 2002). This may seem ironic given the designation *Cognitive* Work Analysis, but it is a matter of emphasis, or rather, priorities. CWA concentrates initially on the physical and social constraints that are inherent to a given task or within a given work domain.

Thus, CWA is driven more by environmental constraints than worker characteristics, in that work analysis sets out to describe the possibilities for action that are inherent in the worker's environment rather than the workers' action itself (Vicente, 1999, p. 155). For example, Vicente (1999) asserted that human factors approaches to aviation systems design should move away from a focus on how pilots and other crew think about entities such as aircraft function and conduct "Work Domain Analysis" by focusing first on how those entities actually work.

Complex Sociotechnical Systems

As with many of the approaches described in this book, CWA arose as a response to increased complexity in the workplace. The Work Analysis community generally refers to this in terms of "complex sociotechnical systems" (e.g., Vicente, 1999). These are

TABLE 10.1 Characteristic Features of Complex Sociotechnical Systems

1. Problem Features

  - Large problem spaces involving multiple strategies and multiple cognitive activities
  - A need to engage in different activities to achieve the same goal at different times or in different situations
  - Dynamic problem spaces with longtime constants
  - Problem spaces that include uncertainty in systems and data
  - Problem spaces that involve indirect or mediated access to information
  - Problem spaces that include hazards and risks, and frequent and sometimes radical disturbances or perturbations in the form of unexpected events

2. Workplace Features

  - A great deal of automation, requiring a great deal of compensatory problem solving during routine situations and ad hoc problem solving during abnormal situations
  - Many people who must work together in cooperation and collaboration
  - People who have heterogeneous perspectives, goals, and value structures
  - People who work in distributed physical locations

3. Complex Interactions of Problem and Workplace Features

  - Those interactions that must all be considered at the same time and that involve diverging propagation paths, cascade failures, and potential communication breakdowns

defined as systems composed of psychological (cognitive), social, and technological elements, all embedded in a broader team, organizational, and social context. A complex sociotechnical system is characterized by certain problem and workplace features. Specifically, work within the system is generally accomplished using a range of strategies, including multiple cognitive activities. Tasks or activities usually must be maintained over time, accommodating and adapting to changes in a dynamic environment. There is uncertainty in the data available, which is complicated by indirect or mediated access to information. The operation of complex sociotechnical systems often involves hazards and risks, which must be managed in the face of unexpected events.

The workplace associated with a complex sociotechnical system generally includes automation over which humans have some degree of supervisory control. As a result, the human must engage in compensatory problem solving even during routine situations, and in ad hoc problem solving during abnormal situations. There are typically many people with different perspectives, expertise, goals, and values who must collaborate and cooperate for the system to operate successfully. However, individuals working together are sometimes not colocated. All of these elements interact within the context of the sociotechnical system. Those working within the system, as well as those responsible for improving or designing new sociotechnical systems, must consider these interactions and the resulting diverging propagation paths, cascade failures, and potential communication breakdowns. These characteristic features of complex sociotechnical systems are summarized in Table 10.1.

The Risø Framework of Work Analysis

Rasmussen and his colleagues (Pejterson & Rasmussen, 1997; Rasmussen, 1979, 1981, 1983, 1985, 1986a, 1986b, 1988, 1992, 2000) began by distinguishing traditional work environments (e.g., manufacturing assembly) from newer, computer-reliant contexts for cognitive and collaborative work. They saw cognitive work, in contrast with routine work, as a form of exploration within a space of constraints:

> The options for action will be defined by the work environment and the users are faced with a space of possibilities defined by the limits of functionally-prescribed work performance, by limits of acceptable efficiency and, finally, by the knowledge and experience of the particular user. ... Within this space of work performance, many action possibilities are left for the individual to explore and learn. User's opportunities to learn and plan in a new territory depend on their knowledge of goals, work requirements and constraints, action possibilities and functional properties of the work environment. User knowledge is in particular critical for the initial planning of an activity and for the exploration of action possibilities ... the view taken here is to regard work and work organization in a dynamic environment to be a self-organizing and learning process. (Pejtersen & Rasmussen, 1997, p. 316)

Critical to the analysis of cognitive work, Rasmussen emphasized the dynamics of the workplace, in which there is a continuous flux of technological changes that challenge the worker to learn and adapt. "The effects of one drastic technological change will not have stabilized before another change appears and the many influences of the technological development can no longer be considered separately" (Pejtersen & Rasmussen, 1997, p. 317). Furthermore, there are challenges to those who design new tools and technologies: Design cannot be a sequence of processes conducted by different systems engineering subteams but must be simultaneous, integrated activities that rely on an analysis of future needs as much as on immediate user needs.

Seeing that the problem is to design not merely human–computer interfaces but also human–work interfaces, Rasmussen and his colleagues developed a framework for analyzing work domains, one that is said to differ from traditional task analysis: "A typical task sequence will not normally exist in a modern, advanced work setting. In consequence, generalization cannot be made in terms of work procedures found by a classical task analysis" (Pejtersen & Rasmussen, 1997, p. 319). Methods adopted by Rasmussen et al. are essentially ethnographic (interviews and observation) (see Rasmussen, 1992). (But the researcher is also challenged to acquire some degree of expertise in the domain being studied and a familiarity with pertinent areas of psychology such as decision theory and cognitive psychology.) Ethnographic field studies include the following:

1. Activity analysis to generate a repertoire of activities and strategies;
2. Actor analysis aimed at describing roles, resources, the preferences of individual workers, and patterns and content of communications; and
3. A mapping of the activities to the actors, expressed in psychological terms, which allows, for example, the alignment of the possible strategies with the individual's preferences and resources and with information requirements and decision requirements.

Work is examined at a number of "levels," ranging from the highest level system purposes, down to lower levels of work activities and functions, and finally down to the lowest level of the physical form of particular tools. The analysis, called "Abstraction-Decomposition," involves describing the many-to-many mapping of the means-end relations that cut across the levels of abstraction—the "functional territory within which the actors will navigate" (Pejtersen & Rasmussen, 1997, p. 319; see also Naikar, 2005a, 2005b; Rasmussen, 1986b, chap. 4). As one moves up the levels, one sees the purposes and intentions that constrain activity (i.e., why something is done). As one moves down the levels, one gets closer to implementation (i.e., how something is done).

Let's use an example of weather forecasting. The activities of the weather forecaster are of course constrained by the ways that the weather works, the dynamics of the atmosphere. This is a domain constraint that influences all aspects of the work and also shapes the workplace. The activity of the forecaster has high-level purposes, such as to issue forecasts that are valuable to the public. The creation of quality forecasts depends on conducting a host of activities that contribute to the forecaster's achievement of a good understanding of what is going on in the atmosphere, such as inspecting satellite images. At this level, activities are still described in domain terms (e.g., identify high- and low-pressure systems, locate the subpolar jet stream). At the next lower level are a variety of specific activities (e.g., determine the lowest air pressure in a given area), at which point the particular constraints of the workplace enter into the picture (e.g., the ways for calling up various kinds of data for display and analysis), as do the particular constraints of the worker (knowledge, experience, skills, etc.). Description at this level uses the languages of task (go to such-and-such URL to get the latest observations from weather buoys) and reasoning (plan for issuing a severe weather alert later in the day). All of this allows for the identification of the key cognitive functions (e.g., sense making, planning, etc.), the decision requirements (what has to be decided, when, and by whom), and the information requirements (what data are needed, when, and why).

As Rasmussen and colleagues showed in a number of case studies, this analysis is useful in the design of technologies for diverse domains:

- It is useful in the design of an iconic or graphic object interface to a retrieval system for a public library. For such "loosely coupled intentional systems," the environment includes man-made tools and artifacts, actions are reversible, and trial and error is acceptable. The interface used a variety of metaphors and symbols (e.g., clicking on a globe would allow the user to select a location, clicking on a pair of eyeglasses would allow the user to specify readability, and so on).
- It also is useful in the design of a graphic object interface for process control in power plants. For such "tightly coupled technical systems," users have to cope with rare events, and the work domain structure must be based on system processes and their causal structure (Pejtersen & Rasmussen, 1997, p. 344). Thus, the graphic objects represented such things as valves and tanks, along with numerical indicators of the values of the key process parameters and a graphical depiction of the ways the parameters interacted in the power plant functioning.

To again use our own weather forecasting example, if one knows the constraints of the work domain (e.g., the ways in which aviation forecasting is different from marine forecasting) and the ways that the domain and organization have allocated roles (e.g., the aviation forecaster versus the marine forecaster), one can begin to specify the content of the communications and knowledge sharing that would be needed for the individuals to act in concert (e.g., when the marine forecaster sees a developing tropical storm out at sea that might influence air travel over land the following day). In this way, goals and intentions link to decisions about the design of information systems (e.g., who sees what displays), including methods and formats for communication.

The analysis of the individual worker, in terms of cognition, is critical to work analysis in the Risø framework, so much so that Rasmussen and colleagues (as well as other European ergnomicists) see no need to include the word *cognitive* in the framework title. We need merely recap the statement by Erik Hollnagel that we used near the beginning of chapter 4:

> The functional analysis of the machine is … not sufficient for making a task analysis since that would require that the human was completely under the control of, or subsumed by, the machine. This state of affairs seemed attractive for the task analyses made in the first decades of the century. But it is neither attractive nor possible with the complex systems we have now. … This indicates that a task analysis must be made along two different dimensions. One is the engineering analysis of the functional requirements of the machine. Another is an analysis of the performance characteristics of the operator, i.e., a cognitive analysis of the basis for human performance. This is so obvious that no further arguments are needed. (1982, p. 3)

Within the Risø framework, reasoning is seen as being based on either skills, rules, or knowledge (Rasmussen, 1986b, chap. 10). Skills are highly learned activities that link intentions to smooth, "automatic" behaviors. Proficient skill depends on an ability to form good mental models of the world (or process being controlled), which also derives from experience and practice. Rule-based behavior relies on a recognition of previously encountered similar situations and the use of procedures that worked in the past. We admit that the skills–rules distinction can be fuzzy, as when a worker recognizes that a situation is novel and therefore that an automatized skill is not applicable. In such a case, new rules may have to be composed.

> For an expert in a familiar situation the rule-based performance may roll along without the person's conscious attention, and she will typically be unable to make explicit the cues consulted. … For a less trained person in an unfamiliar situation, some higher level, rule-based coordination is based on explicit knowledge, and the rules are consciously used and can be reported by the person. (Pejtersen & Rasmussen, 1997, p. 329)

Knowledge-based behavior relies on mental models. The mapping of situations to procedures, in rule-based behavior, differs from knowledge-based behavior, because the situations–actions rules would, by themselves, not allow the worker to anticipate the future, which is a key functionality of mental models (see chapter 8). Rasmussen's description of reasoning at this level conforms generally to the description of the mental model refinement cycle we presented in chapter 8. Especially when the worker encounters an unfamiliar situation, activity is driven primarily by goals, and taps into domain knowledge and causal reasoning, and involves generating and testing plans.

This skills–rules–knowledge breakdown, and its accompanying treatment of expert–novice differences, is critical to design of information technologies because, according to the Risø framework, cognitive work in complex domains is typified by learning and exploration. Thus, good technologies must support the progression of proficiency from the novice level to the expert level. Among other things, this suggests the possibility that interfaces might have to be different depending on the level at which the work is being conducted. Skill-based and rule-based strategies will depend on interfaces that present the critical cues, patterns, and affordances ("signs") that trigger recognition ("direct perception interfaces"), and knowledge-based strategies will depend on interfaces that present meanings ("symbols") that describe situations ("externalized mental model interfaces"). At the same time, interfaces must support work at all levels, "because users with different levels of training may use the same system, and because learning to meet new requirements will require different interactions between cognitive levels" (Pejtersen & Rasmussen, 1997, p. 330). "Learning through experiments is necessary for system users in order to be able to develop knowledge and optimize skills. Thus, interface design should aim at a 'learning' work system, making the relational work domain structure and/or boundaries and limits of acceptable performance visible to the users, while the effects are still observable and reversible" (p. 344). Reasoning strategies "should be visible and directly represented in the interface" (p. 345).

This presentation is something of a simplification, for introductory purposes to kick off this chapter. We describe the Abstraction-Decomposition method in more detail later in this chapter, because, as a method, it is common to both the Risø framework and the Vicente–Ecological Framework.

The Vicente–Ecological Framework of CWA

The CWA process can be described in terms of three important steps. First, the designer identifies a "constraint space" and support for agent control. Based on this, the interface is designed so as to show the constraint boundaries and local data for ongoing situations in a way to support choice among activities. After the display is integrated into work, the end user finishes the design based on local information, knowledge, and expertise.

Vicente's (1999) presentation of CWA includes traditional task analysis (i.e., decomposition in terms of information input and output, activity flow, timelining, etc.) but combines it with the European Work Analysis approach. Also, in concert with the Ecological Approach, CWA is about "the need to model the environment, or ecology, in which work takes place as much as to model human activity in that environment" (Sanderson, Eggleston, Skilton, & Cameron, 1999, p. 323). Thus, CWA seeks to model work activity in terms of various constraints that shape human activity rather than in terms of the literal action sequences of the human (Sanderson, Eggleston, et al., 1999).

Researchers in the Work Analysis tradition have made a case that multiple perspectives need to be engaged for the researcher to come to a rich understanding of human factors and engineering design issues. (This dovetails with the approach of the sociological perspectives; see chapter 11.) Following the work of Rasmussen, Vicente described five layers of constraints inherent in complex sociotechnical systems (Sanderson, Eggleston, et al., 1999; Vicente, 1999). The *work domain* layer refers to constraints associated with the system. The *control task* layer refers to constraints associated with goals to be achieved (often obtained using constraint-based task analysis). The *strategies* layer refers to constraints associated with processes used to achieve the control tasks. The *social organizational* layer refers to constraints associated with the relationships between and among actors. The *worker competencies* layer refers to generic human capabilities and limitations as well as to the knowledge, rules, and skills needed to fulfill a specific job. The five layers or sources of constraint are summarized in Table 10.2.

TABLE 10.2 Sources of Constraint on Work in Complex Sociotechnical Systems

Domain Constraints	These constraints are inherent in the system that is being controlled or environment that is being acted upon. They occur independently of any particular worker, task, goal, or interface. No matter what control task is being pursued, what strategy is being used, or what agents are conducting the strategy or the competencies of the agents, the functional structure of the domain imposes constraints: • the capabilities of the system that is being controlled or environment that is being acted upon, and • the information required to understand the state of the system that is being controlled, which includes the information that has to be sensed and the ways it has to be manipulated into derived forms and organized meaningfully.
Control Tasks ("Goals")	These are constraints on what needs to be accomplished in or done to the work domain; the goals that are to be achieved, independently of how they are to be achieved or by whom. Following Rasmussen's work, Vicente (1999) referred to these as control tasks: • which actions are meaningful; • the order of action; • the goals that need to be satisfied for situations and situation classes and the constraints on those goals, independently of how they are to be achieved or by whom; and • the information and relations that are relevant for particular classes of situations suggest context-appropriate interfaces, ones that present the right information at the right time.
Strategies	These are the practices that emerged historically in a culture of a particular application domain and shape the ways in which work is allocated across individuals, how individuals are organized into groups or teams, and how groups or teams communicate. These constrain how goals can be achieved. For each control task, or goal, there will be a variety of possible activities, but specific strategies impose particular flows or processes: • how it can be done—mechanisms or processes by which goals can be achieved, • the work that is to be allocated, • specification of strategies entails a specification of human–computer dialog modes and the process flows within modes. Cognitive Work Analysis seeks to identify new, effective strategies.
Social Organizational	These constrain the relationships among agents (workers, computers), allocation of responsibilities, allocation of control tasks, distribution of strategies across agents, and coordination of activities. A variety of possible collectives and organizations of agents could conduct any particular strategy. Each organization will impose its own constraints: • who can do it—the relationships between agents (workers, computers), • allocation of responsibilities, • allocation of control tasks, • distribution of strategies across agents, • coordination of activities, and • allocation of roles, defining the job content and responsibilities of the agents, and means for effective organization and communication.
Worker Competencies	These are basic human capabilities and limitations, required knowledge, and also acquired skills and competencies: • basic human capabilities and limitations; • required knowledge, skills, and competencies; and • specifications for selection and training.

Two features of these layers of constraint are especially important. One is their invariance.

> Constraints remain invariant in the presence of context-conditioned variability. As a result, they provide a basis for reconciling formative modeling (by specifying boundaries on action) and worker adaptation (by giving workers the flexibility to adapt within those boundaries). This one idea is, without a doubt, the single most important prerequisite to understanding Cognitive Work Analysis. (Vicente, 1999, p. 122)

The other important feature is "successive narrowing." Degrees of freedom are reduced with each layer of constraint, moving from the work domain to worker competencies. Changes to one layer of constraint propagate to other layers of constraint but only in a downward direction. For example, if the work domain is changed (say, a new theory of tornado formation leads to discovery of a new method for predicting tornados from radar data) then all the subsequent layers may be affected. New control tasks may be required, and older ones may be discarded. Furthermore, changes in control tasks may require changes in strategy, and so on.

Vicente (1999) distinguished three purposes for studying work. He described the first as *normative,* because the purpose is to identify or prescribe an optimal way to complete a task. This category encompasses traditional task analysis methods, as well as constraint-based task analysis (described later), which is more closely identified with the Work Analysis philosophy. The second purpose is *descriptive,* referring to techniques that are aimed at describing actual practice. Many CTA methods fall within this category. The third purpose is called the *formative* approach, because the goal is to identify intrinsic work constraints with the goal of designing a (new or better) system that provides workers the flexibility to make situation-specific decisions as needed. Vicente suggested that all three purposes (normative, descriptive, and formative) are useful and necessary in conducting work analysis within the CWA framework. However, the goal is often formative design, the design of new sociotechnical systems, what Cognitive Systems Engineering refers to as "envisioned worlds" (see chapter 7). Therefore, a primary utility of normative and descriptive approaches is in informing the formative work analysis process.

Normative Task Analysis

As F. W. Taylor showed in the early 1900s, task analysis in manufacturing settings has proved to be a powerful methodology. This normative approach, in which an optimal way of conducting a task is identified via careful task analysis, has resulted in increased efficiencies and safety improvements in industrial settings for many decades. However, the modern workplaces are quite different from those Taylor encountered in the early 1900s. Researchers in the Work Analysis community have been some of the most articulate in describing changes in the modern workplace where tasks are less repetitious and predictable than in traditional manufacturing settings. These researchers have described the need for not just new methods but a new framework for studying work. Traditional task analysis decomposes the flow of activity in jobs into particular tasks, each having well-defined beginnings and endings and well-defined and sequential subtasks, or modular events, that can be specified in terms of singular sequences of physical and cognitive actions and procedures and that result in the achievement of well-defined goals. Task analysis enables one to identify "what the operator must or can do [to complete the task] and how s/he naturally thinks about the domain ... when, how and with what priority information will be needed to perform expected tasks ... [and] the full set of factors which will influence operator behavior" (Miller & Vicente, 1999, p. 331). Thus, task analysis is well suited for developing detailed procedures for dealing with routine and anticipated events.

Work on a production assembly line can sometimes be typified by sequences of specific, standardized, stable, and routine actions, typically carried out on physical work objects in relatively well-structured and nondynamic environments (Rasmussen, Pejtersen, & Schmidt, 1990). Furthermore, in traditional work, only a few feasible alternative actions would achieve work goals, and often even fewer would ordinarily be considered by operators. In addition, work environments and methods can remain unchanged over relatively long time periods. As a consequence of these task and workplace characteristics, it was quite appropriate to identify a "one best way" of undertaking a task, as Taylor and Gilbreth had done, with the goal of training staff so that they became specialized and maximally efficient in this way of working (Rasmussen, 2000).

Many modern jobs have characteristics that are different from characteristics of traditional jobs. There is an ever-increasing pace of change in technology and communications. Work environments have become more complex in terms of size, distribution, control, and regulation (see Goodstein, Andersen, & Olsen, 1988; Rasmussen, 2000). New jobs are characterized by more dynamism, openness, instability, and multiple degrees of freedom than traditional work (Naikar, Sanderson, & Lintern, 1999; Rasmussen, 2000). For example, network management is a "highly distributed, highly shared, and high speed complex work domain" (Chow & Vicente, 2001, p. 356; see also Burns, Barsalou, Handler, Kuo, & Harrigan, 2000). Workers are required not to be specialists in a limited range of routine tasks, as are workers in traditional work, but to posses a broader range of cognitive abilities that include the flexibility required to meet dynamic and unanticipated work demands (Rasmussen et al., 1990).

In the modern era, many routine tasks, such as those conducted on a production line, have been implemented mechanically so that they can be performed automatically by machines. Similarly, many routine cognitive tasks have been reduced to a set of rules or algorithms so that they can be undertaken automatically by computers (Vicente, 2002). Typically (or ideally) such automation does not require human intervention in the control of normal functions. Instead, the human is sometimes left with the job of overseeing such systems to ensure that production and workflow is smooth and efficient.

Although abnormal events can sometimes be predicted and thus prepared for, it is unanticipated events and those that "have never been seen before" that pose the greatest challenge to complex systems (Sanderson, 2002). Because modern systems are characterized by openness, they are much more susceptible to system-external factors and thus to perturbations and disturbances.

> There are … factors that cannot be reliably anticipated because the relevant information is only available during operation. … Workers must deal with the contingency online in real time because the relevant information is only available locally … the more open a system is, the more these unanticipated factors are likely to occur. (Vicente, 1999, p. 125)

Automation cannot account for all eventualities, and unanticipated and non-routine events, such as "when things go wrong," have to be handled by humans (Naikar et al., 1999; Naikar et al., 2005). Having humans in the control loop is necessary, because one characteristic of humans, when compared to computers, is their ability to adapt and improvise, that is, to create work-arounds or solutions "on the fly" (Vicente, 2001, 2002). Thus, as Rasmusssen and Rouse (1981) proposed, humans effectively "finish off the design" of many work systems through their responsibility for handling the unanticipated and nonroutine events. This shows clearly when workers create "kluges" and "work-arounds" (Koopman & Hoffman, 2003).

With these considerations in mind, advocates of work analysis have argued that task analysis has, over time, become less appropriate as a tool for analysis and design of complex sociotechnical systems. Five specific limitations of traditional forms of task analysis have been highlighted (see Miller & Vicente, 1999).

1. *Task analyses can be conducted only for anticipated tasks; it is not possible to begin a task analysis if an event or situation is unanticipated.* Donald Norman (1998) observed that it is not possible to write a work procedure for every work scenario that comes along, yet every work domain seems to have procedures and rules books. The irony is that even for procedures that one might be able to prespecify because circumstances can be anticipated, there can be variability and hidden dependencies. As Sanderson (2002) commented,

   > Verbal protocols of electronics technicians diagnosing faults in laboratory equipment showed that the technicians used a variety of problem-solving strategies, often jumping between different strategies (Rasmussen, 1981; Rasmussen & Jensen, 1973, 1974). … Each time a strategy was carried out it was different in its details. (p. 246)

   This limitation of task analysis is important because the greatest threats to safety in many work domains are posed by situations that have not been anticipated or encountered previously (Vicente, 2002). Sanderson, Naikar, Lintern, and Goss (1999) argued that a design intervention must support adaptation and flexibility inherent in modern work if the negative consequences of unanticipated situations are to be avoided.

2. *Task analyses tend to be prescriptive or are too easy to be used as prescriptions.* The task analytic approach tends to be normative. The designer creates an optimal plan in advance through task analysis, the automation is designed to enforce certain procedures, and then the human executes the designer's plan. Norm-based systems tend to be applicable only to the tasks that have been identified and the particular ways of conducting them that have been specified. In fact, in complex sociotechnical systems, workers do not follow prescriptions. Indeed, work-arounds and kluges are par for the course (Koopman & Hoffman, 2003). Analyses that focus on routine procedures cannot accommodate the adaptation of those procedures by workers. Such adaptation always happens necessarily in response to changes in the work environment that occur over time. Workers are often in situations in which they *cannot* follow prescriptions.

3. *Even though task analyses can be complex (e.g., hierarchies of conditional branchings), task analyses are always context bounded.* They cannot cope well with goal conflicts or other forms of unanticipated, emergent circumstances—circumstances in which workers should not follow prescriptions. Vicente offered an example from the nuclear power industry:

> At one [nuclear power] plant, operators would not always follow the written procedures when they went to the simulator for recertification. They deviated from them for one of two reasons. In some cases, operators achieved the same goal using a different, but equally safe and efficient, set of actions. In complex sociotechnical systems, like nuclear power plants, there is rarely one best way of achieving a particular goal. In other cases, the operators would deviate from the procedures because the desired goal would not be achieved if the procedures were followed. It is very difficult to write a procedure to encompass all possible situations. A small change in context might require different actions to achieve the very same goal. In either case, the operators' actions seemed justifiable, particularly in the latter set of circumstances. The people who were evaluating the operators in the simulator did not agree, however. They criticized the operators for "lack of procedural compliance." Despite this admonishment, the operators got their licenses renewed. This happened several times. Eventually, the operators became frustrated with the evaluators' repeated criticism because they felt it unwarranted. The operators decided that, the next time they had to go into the simulator for recertification, they would do exactly what the procedure said—no matter what. One team of operators followed this "work-to-rule" approach in the simulator and became stuck in an infinite loop. At one point, an emergency procedure told operators to switch back to another procedure, but then that procedure eventually sent operators back to the first one. The operators dutifully followed the procedures, and thus wound up in a cycle, repeating the same set of actions several times. The evaluators were not amused. … Later, the evaluators wrote a letter to the utility that employed this group of operators. In that letter, the evaluators criticized the operators yet again, this time for "malicious procedural compliance." (Vicente, 1999, p. xiii)

4. *The finer the detail of the task analysis, the more transient and fragile it will be.* One could analyze a given task, say the things a weather forecaster does in trying to predict how and when a thunderstorm might develop. One could examine specific activities right down to the level of individual keystrokes, individual acts of attentional shifting, adding in fractional seconds for long-term memory access, and so on. (See the analysis of the toaster example in chapter 2.) One could then design a protocol for the task and even perhaps make a specialized series of data displays and forms to fill out to support the forecaster's work at this one task. The problem is that the specific activities are highly contingent on the locale, the season, and so forth. So, one might then generate task protocols for the thunderstorm task in different locales and in different seasons. It is at that point when the major problem starts to become clear. There is a fundamental disconnect between the time scale for detailed task analytic work and the time scale of change in the sociotechnical workplace. By the time all those detailed protocols have been created, the methods and technologies that forecasters rely on will have changed. The more detailed and specific the task analysis, the longer it takes to derive it, the less useful it will be in the long run, and the more fragile it will be in the face of unanticipated or emergent complexities.

5. *Task analyses are based on a false premise.* The false premise is that jobs can be broken down into well-defined and sequential subtasks that can be specified in terms of sequences of individual, basic physical and cognitive actions and that result in the achievement of well-defined goals. In the weather forecasting example, what if the weather radar communications link goes down? Is the forecaster blocked from evaluating if a thunderstorm might occur? No, of course not. He or she will find

other data sources or types to support his or her understanding of the dynamics in the atmosphere. This is a fundamental and critical insight from Jens Rasmussen and his colleagues (Rasmussen et al., 1990): *Workers in sociotechnical systems do not, in fact, conduct "tasks." They engage in context-sensitive, knowledge-driven choice among action alternatives. Only in hindsight can these be composed as a linear, sequential story. When it appears as if a worker is engaged in tasklike behavior, that is because either the task sequence is mandated or the worker is in a situation that does not require any choice.*

The Work Analysis approach encourages us to call into question the traditional notion of a "task." The goal of work analysis is to create a meaningful environment that presents the human with a "resource envelope" (Rasmussen, 2000) that provides workers with the following:

- the ability to explore and select from among of the multiplicity of action alternatives that are available,
- the ability to adapt to unforeseen circumstances,
- the discretion to generate action sequences and to express their preferences, and
- the ability to recover from errors and cope with context-conditioned variability.

Work analysis recognizes that workers in complex systems have multiple degrees of freedom in performing their work. Hence, rather than concentrating on specific trajectories of behavior, work analysis focuses on boundaries or constraints inherent to a work domain that shape human behavior. Constraints that define the functional structure of a domain are independent of particular events and circumstances. Thus, a system designed through such an analysis should be able to accommodate a wide variety of responses or actions to both routine and unpredictable events. Furthermore, such a design should allow for each operator's own style of response to various events (Mitchell & Sundstrom, 1997).

In spite of the limitations of traditional task analysis, normative task analysis can be of value in the context of CWA. To illustrate how and which normative approaches may be useful, Vicente discussed three levels of normative task analysis, from which both constraint-based and instruction-based task analyses derive. (Table 10.3 summarizes the key ideas of normative task analysis.) The three levels involve an increasing degree of specificity:

Level 1: Input–Output
Level 2: Flow Sequence
Level 3: Time Line

Constraint-based task analysis addresses Level 1 only. This can be understood as describing the general constraints on worker action. It involves the identification of the information requirements that will help workers achieve anticipated task goals in a flexible, situated manner. It does not specify the actions the workers take, their sequence, or how long each will take. Indeed, the analysis can be couched in terms that are largely device independent. It identifies the inputs that are required to perform a task, including the information requirements that allow workers to achieve anticipated

TABLE 10.3 Key Ideas of Normative Task Analysis

<table>
<tr><td colspan="2" align="center">Normative Task Analysis</td></tr>
<tr><td colspan="2">Constraint-Based Task Analysis</td></tr>
<tr><td colspan="2">

- These techniques specify what actions should NOT be performed if the goal is to be achieved.
- They identify the information requirements that will help workers achieve anticipated task goals in a flexible, situated manner.
- They yield task specifications that are more device independent than instruction-based task analysis—they describe properties of the task rather than properties of how to do the task with a particular device.
- They give workers the greatest discretion—the worker must decide what actions to take, their sequence, and how long each will take.
- They are more likely to foster learning through variability in action and the consequent feedback and, by implication, enhance the ability to deal with novelty.
- They are suitable for open systems because they can accommodate to the demands associated with unanticipated events (i.e., context-conditioned variability).

</td></tr>
<tr><td>Level 1:
Input–Output Task Analysis</td><td>

- Identifies the inputs that are required to perform a task and the outputs that are achieved after the task is completed but NOT the specific actions that should be taken to reach the goal,
- Specifies the constraints that must be taken into account in selecting the actions that are required to achieve the goal, that is, actions that should be avoided, and
- Identifies the information requirements that allow workers to achieve anticipated task goals in a flexible, situated manner.

</td></tr>
<tr><td colspan="2">Instruction-Based Task Analysis</td></tr>
<tr><td colspan="2">

- These techniques specify the actions (including cognitive operations) that should be performed or are required to be performed if the goal is to be achieved.
- They give workers less discretion (more detailed guidance).
- They yield more detailed task specifications, which are more likely to be more device dependent—the task content and form changes as a function of the interface and automation.
- They are limited in the ability to comprehensively identify the information requirements in complex sociotechnical systems.
- They are suitable for closed systems and not well suited to the demands associated with unanticipated events.

</td></tr>
<tr><td>Level 2:
Sequential Flow Task Analysis</td><td>

- Identifies the temporally ordered sequence of actions that are required to achieve the goal, and
- Sequential flow task analysis is usually device dependent because it is more detailed.

</td></tr>
<tr><td>Level 3:
Time Line Task Analysis</td><td>

- Identifies the temporally ordered sequence of actions that are required to achieve the goal, with duration estimates for each action

</td></tr>
</table>

task goals in a flexible, situated manner. It describes the outputs or results that are achieved after the task is completed but *not* the specific actions that should be taken to reach the goal. These two elements, the input requirements and output goals, represent important constraints that must be taken into account in selecting the actions that are required to achieve the goal and actions that should be avoided. Another way of looking at constraint-based normative task analysis is to say that the only thing the analysis really specifies is the actions that workers should *not* perform if the goal is to be achieved. Vicente (1999) suggested that this sort of analysis is most useful for open systems subject to unpredictable disturbances from the environment.

Instruction-based task analysis, on the other hand, provides a much more detailed description of how the task should be accomplished. This includes specification of the goals that are to be achieved and the ideal way in which they should be achieved—prescriptions for how a human and a machine should behave; a rational benchmark for worker behavior in different situations. Some instruction-based techniques address Level 2, others Level 3, and still others both Levels 2 and 3. Starting with Taylor's Time and Motion Study, and the many variants that evolved, the type of task analysis that Vicente dubbed instruction-based task analysis has often been used in courses and instruction manuals. The resulting job descriptions take the form of sequential flows or timelines that describe temporally ordered sequences of actions and their durations. Such task descriptions provide workers more detailed guidance but less discretion. The job descriptions are more likely to be more device dependent, because the task content and form change as a function of the interface and automation. Task analyses having this purpose can be limited in the ability to comprehensively identify the information requirements in complex sociotechnical systems. They are suitable for closed systems and not well suited to the demands associated with unanticipated events.

Both forms of normative task analysis—constraint-based task analysis and instruction-based task analysis—assume that the goals of the system can be defined beforehand. The methods are event dependent—they require a specification of a class of initiating events before the analysis can even get off the ground. Otherwise, the precise goal to be pursued cannot be identified. The focus here is on the actions (including cognitive operations) that should be performed or are required to be performed if the goal is to be achieved. Although Vicente concluded that constraint-based task analysis is more suitable for open systems subject to unpredictable influences, constraint-based task analysis is not sufficient. Event-independent work analysis techniques are needed to fill in the gaps left by event-dependent task analysis.

Descriptive Work Analysis

The purpose of descriptive work analysis is to generate descriptions of how an existing system (humans and machines) behaves. In this application, the specification of work constraints (as in Table 10.2) will show why existing devices are ineffective or how workers' activities have evolved over time. The analysis can identify work-arounds, which point to functionalities that should be properly supported. It can point to tasks that should be performed but that are not currently being performed.

The Naturalistic Decision Making community has been quite active in exploring descriptive techniques, in terms of both data collection and knowledge representation (see chapter 9). In fact, several edited volumes have been published examining methodological issues, reporting descriptive studies, and proposing descriptive models of decision making (Klein, Orasanu, Calderwood, & Zsambok, 1993; Montgomery, Lipshitz, & Brehmer, 2005; Salas & Klein, 2001; Zsambok & Klein, 1997). Table 10.4 summarizes the key ideas of descriptive work analysis.

The framework of CWA goes beyond normative work analysis and descriptive work analysis to formative work analysis, which hinges on Vicente's distinction between the "actual work" and the "true work."

TABLE 10.4 Key Ideas of Descriptive Work Analysis

Descriptive Work Analysis

- The goal is to generate descriptions of how a system (humans and machines) behaves.
- It is useful in determining why existing tools are ineffective or how workers' activities have evolved over time.
- Descriptive work analysis is useful but not sufficient for systems design. It is just one method for investigating work constraints—it can suggest novel strategies that could be adopted by workers.
- For instance, it can identify work-arounds, which point to functionalities that should be properly supported. It can point to tasks that should be performed but that are not currently being performed.
- This is a good starting point for collecting data to inform a Cognitive Work Analysis, but it is insufficient for the design of complex sociotechnical systems. It is inadequate because it does not include a model of the "true work."

Strategies	Analysis of effective strategies is required to identify the mechanisms that can generate the practices that have emerged historically in a culture of a particular application domain.
Social and Organizational Factors	Analysis must address the issue of how work can be allocated across individuals, how individuals can be organized into groups or teams, and how groups or teams can communicate. Technological change must be coordinated with organizational change.
Worker Competencies	The analysis must identify the various demands that the application domain imposes on individual worker's competencies (i.e., expertise). Designed systems need to facilitate the acquisition of skill and support expert action.

Formative Work Analysis

Formative work analysis focuses not on the details of what people or machines do—the "actual work" that has been shaped by their current work technologies and systems—but on the "true work," the work that really needs to be accomplished by the envisioned sociotechnical system. Here is an example of the actual work–true work distinction.

Weather forecasters whose job it is to provide weather data to pilots have to fill out a particular form, filled in according to the pilot's flight plan, indicating the weather forecast pertinent to the flight. This form includes checklist categories of significant weather, such as the potential for turbulence in the upper atmosphere, the potential for icing, and so on. The form is a legacy of older technology, in which one had to cram as much information as possible onto a single side of a single piece of paper. Hence, the form has many rows and slots and check boxes. It relies on cryptic symbology (e.g., graphical shapes such as diamonds, clovers, etc.) to indicate types of weather and weather severity. Only the experienced pilots were familiar with and comfortable with the form. Hoffman, Coffey, and Ford (2000) referred to the form as an instance of the "lucky charms theory of information display"—one is lucky if meanings can be directly apprehended. Hoffman et al. reviewed many of the completed forms, for easy flights and complex ones and for cases of complex and simple weather, and found that in most cases most of the slots and boxes were unfilled. They concluded that in the attempt to create a "one size fits all" form, the result was "one size fits few." Next, they interviewed a number of pilots and observed pilot–forecaster interactions, showing that what pilots really needed was to be able to see the "big picture" (i.e., satellite images, radar images). When pilots interacted face-to-face with the forecasters, they often did not refer to the completed form. Rather, they would ask meaningful questions such as "How rough will the turbulence really be when I fly over the Rockies?" These findings suggested an entirely new form, one better suited to pilot needs. For instance, it included a screen shot of the national satellite image and a graphical depiction that coordinated the flight path with iconic indications of the predicted significant weather. Subsequently it was learned that a very similar form had already been developed and was in use in the United Kingdom.

Traditional task analysis often focuses on existing work practices, and so there is a tendency to accept those practices rather than query them (see Hollnagel & Cacciabue, 1999, p. 3). The purpose of formative work analysis is to specify the requirements that must be satisfied so that a new system can be created or so that an existing system can re-created so as to support the true work. The challenge for the researcher is to use CTA to get a "window into the true work." Unlike descriptive work analysis, formative work analysis does *not* specify many of the things that are the focus in traditional task analysis: sensors, databases, current automation, function allocations, interfaces, and so on. In the design of new systems, or the redesign of existing systems, all of these things can be up for grabs. Specific control tasks, the specific strategies used, and the social context are all fair game for redesign. They are, at least to some extent, device independent, as the aviation weather forecasting example shows.

Thus, formative work analysis seeks to identify the intrinsic domain and work constraints without specifying a detailed design; it specifies the boundaries on action, a range of action sequence alternatives. Within that range, workers must be free to adapt and free to choose different trajectories to achieve goals in different ways.

Although no data collection methods are prescribed for conducting formative work analysis, documentation analysis often proves a valuable source of data (Naikar et al., 1999; Naikar et al., 2005). The key ideas of formative work analysis are presented in Table 10.5.

Normative, descriptive, and formative approaches all fall within the CWA framework. These approaches are used opportunistically over the course of a project, guided by the CWA framework. Much of our discussion in this chapter focuses on the notion that CTA in general, and CWA in particular, is aimed at the creation of new systems. But this is not always the case. CWA can be used in analysis at all stages in the "system life cycle," from the initial specification of requirements, to performance analysis in the operational setting, to analysis intended to support the process of decommissioning (see Sanderson Naikar, et al., 1999). More often than not, the efforts of CTA researchers are aimed at fixing existing systems that seem to be incomplete, inadequate, user hostile, and so on. Cummings and Guerlain (2003) argued that the full set of steps in CWA (as described in Vicente, 1999) can be applied only in the redesign of existing systems "since it assumes an existing organizational structure, an existing infrastructure, existing users, and clearly defined boundaries" (p. 5). Legacy systems are systems that are in place in the operational context and cannot be altered except in selected, sometimes even superficial, ways (e.g., better interfaces). Rather than having all design decisions emerge as outputs of a work analysis sequence, some of the decisions are inherited. The levels of constraint—domain, goals, strategies, social

TABLE 10.5 The Key Ideas of Formative Work Analysis

Formative work analysis seeks to identify the intrinsic work constraints. It does not specify a design. Although the "window to the true work" suggests possible design notions, formative work analysis does NOT prespecify:

- the existing sensors used to obtain information,
- the content or structure of the database that organizes the information in the information system,
- the functionality of the automation that is currently in place,
- the allocation of functions among people and machines,
- the allocation of job responsibilities among individuals or groups,
- the appearance or structure of the interface, and
- worker's competency and training requirements.

The goals of formative work analysis are to specify the requirements that must be satisfied so that the system can behave in a new or desired way and to develop novel systems to support new and more effective means of performing work.

Formative work analysis focuses not on what people or machines actually do but on the work that needs to be accomplished by the sociotechnical system.

The activities in which workers engage emerge from a confluence of constraints—the work domain, the control tasks, the strategies used, the social context, and worker competencies.

Formative work analysis focuses on activity-shaping constraints rather than on particular tasks or actions conducted with particular pieces of technology.

Activity-shaping constraints include constraints that remain invariant over context-conditioned variability. They specify boundaries on action but do not specify actions—workers have flexibility to adapt within the boundaries.

These constraints on work must to some extent be device independent. They do not uniquely specify the actions of workers or automation. Rather, they specify a range of activity alternatives.

It is that range that defines the requirements that a design must satisfy if it is to effectively support the work. Within that range, workers must be free to adapt and free to choose different trajectories to achieve goals in different ways.

factors, and worker competencies—can be used to represent the frozen decisions (e.g., the social organization as it is rather than as it should be). Propagation toward design decisions can continue, however. For example, although a social organization is frozen, work analysis might reveal new ways of training to permit more effective work within that organization.

CWA Methods

Vicente (2002) described how the analysis of a work domain and the analysis of tasks are qualitatively different: "A task is something you do (a verb), whereas a work domain is something you act on (a noun)" (p. 63). CWA of domains identifies the functional structure of the work domain, and results in work domain representations that are independent of particular events and technologies. It describes the capabilities of the system (i.e., that workers will be acting upon), and specifies the information workers need to generate an appropriate action sequence. It identifies the information requirements that will allow workers to deal with unfamiliar and unanticipated events. Work Domain Analysis seeks to employ event-independent analysis techniques, the relevance and utility of which are not tied to a specific set of anticipated events. (For a discussion of Work Domain Analysis methods, see Naikar [2005a, 2005b].)

To better understand task analysis versus Work Domain Analysis, and their associated advantages and disadvantages, Vicente used an analogy of way finding. Work Domain Analyses are like maps used as way-finding tool because they are event independent: The map does not provide specific route-finding information for a given event (such as getting from one location to another). Task analysis descriptions of work are like directions used as specific way-finding methods because they are event dependent. They provide specific route-finding information for a specific navigational path. The advantage of being provided with directions when traveling from one location to another is that this method does not require the navigator to read a map, and thus mental workload can be reduced. The disadvantage is that the directions are brittle. If the navigator experiences disturbances, such as being deviated from the route owing to an obstacle or a failure to see a sign that is mentioned in the directions, the directions are no longer useful. By contrast, being provided with a map means that flexibility is afforded. If the navigator is deviated from the route, a new route can be planned because "it shows the lay of the land independently of any particular activity on that land" (Vicente, 1999, p. 113). However, the disadvantage is that map interpretation is required.

> The only way to adapt to disturbances is to leave some decisions about how a task should be performed to the worker. ... [Work Domain Analysis does this by identifying] the information and relationships that actors can use to reason under virtually any situation, including those that have not been anticipated by designers. (Vicente, 1999, p. 154)

This approach is described more abstractly by Sanderson, Naikar et al. (1999) in the following excerpt:

> We can support operator adaptation and flexibility if we design systems that are based not on supporting typical or normal work trajectories, such as specific sequences of actions, but instead based on models of the constraints and possibilities for functional action (affordances) in the work domain. If a computer based interface to a complex work domain is designed so that operators can see the constraints, boundaries, and affordances of that work domain, then they are much more likely to respond appropriately if something unusual happens. (p. 318)

Although Vicente's scheme for dividing task analysis into functional categories (descriptive, normative, formative) seems logical, the approach to methodology is less specific. Indeed, as long as the analysis of the work results in good systems, the particulars of the method do not matter. According to Vicente (1999), the conduct of CWA is opportunistic:

> If the analysis framework is to have a systematic basis, the conceptual perspective should be logical and rational (i.e., very orderly and coherent) because the concepts that are proposed for analysis should be clearly defined, internally-consistent and well integrated. In contrast, the methodological perspective is much less orderly because the methods that are chosen are eclectic and the activities that analysts actually engage in while conducting an analysis are very opportunistic, chaotic, non-linear, and iterative. (Vicente, 1999, p. 35; see also Vicente, Burns, & Pawlak, 1997)

Thus, it matters less to Vicente what particular method or methods one uses than whether one successfully achieves a complete functional understanding of the work domain and the constraints on the cognitive work.

As our own discussion shows, treatments of CWA projects often include statements in which the word *analysis* is used quite repeatedly, as in a description of how a Work Domain Analysis was followed by a sequential flow analysis, and so on. This can make the CWA program somewhat abstract, especially to those who are just learning about it. In practice, CWA relies most heavily on documentation analysis (especially for Work Domain Analysis; see Naikar, 2005a, 2005b), combined with interviews and field observations of actual work (e.g., Mumaw, Roth, Vicente, & Burns, 2000). Thus, CWA seems to differ little from CTA as utilized. In addition, in the CWA framework, laboratory-based methods are considered to be ill-suited to studies of complex systems. "To be useful for understanding and designing effective human interaction with complex systems, research must be directed to much more complex work situations, rather than historical, well-defined laboratory experiments" (Rasmussen, 1988, pp. 1–3, cited in Mitchell & Sundstrom, 1997; see also Rasmussen et al., 1990).

Furthermore, Vicente (1999) has been critical of the focus of traditional human factors research on laboratory-based methods of work systems study. Instead, he advocated a multistage research approach that begins with qualitative, descriptive field studies. Such studies are effective for the determination of "pressing, significant problems" (p. 326) in the work domain of interest. The second stage examines such problems under closer scrutiny and more controlled conditions, including laboratory studies. Although the ecological validity of the research might be affected negatively by the introduction of laboratory methods, representative conditions for testing in the laboratory can be identified from the qualitative studies conducted in the first stage. The third stage comprises tests of the generalizability of any causal relations identified in the second stage. This is achieved by trading off some of the experimental control inherent to the testing undertaken in the second stage, for the introduction of more complex and thus representative conditions during testing in the laboratory. In the final stage, converging findings from the previous stages can be used to inform work design interventions undertaken in the field, that is, in the work domain itself. Thus, a full circle of research is achieved through the four stages that begins and ends in field settings.

Other advocates of CWA, and many advocates of CTA in general, are also in favor of applying multiple methods to systems design. For example, Schaafstal, Schraagen, and van Berlo (2000) brought a number of methods to bear during their CWA of structured troubleshooting by the Royal Netherlands Navy's Weapon Engineering Service. In their study, Schaafstal et al. made use of documentation analysis, interviews, work observations accompanied by concurrent think-aloud protocols, and controlled experiments. However, the controlled experiments were not the traditional "laboratory experiments with artificial tasks" but "experiments under naturalistic conditions with the stimuli [which were faults with weaponry] ... under control" (p. 85).

Although data collection methods are not prescribed by CWA, representation techniques or modeling tools guide each level of analysis. Two particular methods of representing analytical results are advocated, and relied upon heavily, by practitioners of work analysis and CWA. One is the Decision Ladder, and the other is the Abstraction-Decomposition Matrix. Of these, the Abstraction-Decomposition Matrix has been used most extensively. Vicente (1999) and others (e.g., Burns & Hajdukiewicz, 2004; Naikar, 2005a, 2005b) adopted it as the core method, and so our treatment of it is more extensive than that for the Decision Ladder. According to Vicente (1999),

- domain constraints are revealed by interviews and observations, and are represented by Abstraction-Decomposition Matrices;
- control tasks ("goals") are revealed by interviews and represented in Decision Ladders;
- strategies are revealed by interviews and are represented using Information Flow Diagrams;
- social factors are revealed by observations and interviews and are represented using the Abstraction-Decomposition Matrix, the Decision Ladder, and Information Flow Diagrams; and
- worker competencies are revealed through interviews and observations, consolidating requirements generated in the CWA phases with existing knowledge of human cognition using Rasmussen's taxonomy of skills, rules, and knowledge.

The Decision Ladder

Rasmussen (1979) developed the Decision Ladder method for representing human information processing and decision-making activities, and used it in the analysis of decision-making strategies in the area of process control. Decision laddering has subsequently been used in many applications by European ergonomicists as well as Australian and North American human factors psychologists. A Decision Ladder is a graphical depiction of nodes and links that is used to represent decompositions of individual tasks. It might be thought of as a breakout of the lowest level of analysis within a hierarchical task analysis, that is, the finest grain of the subtasks or the specific goals (e.g., one subtask within the forecasting of severe weather is to issue a severe weather warning). In the Decision Ladder diagram, the course of action is broken down into a series of component actions or activities.

Decision Ladders are derived from protocols or interviews in which domain practitioners describe their tasks to a fine level of detail (see Rasmussen, 1986b, chap. 2). In interviews with process control operators in power plants, Rasmussen and his colleagues found that the domain practitioners did not describe what they did in terms of mental operations or strategies, but the task, and specifically the changes in their states of knowledge—what they knew about situations and the task activities they engage in. Thus, in Decision Ladder diagrams, there are two types of nodes: one type refers to states of contents or knowledge, and the other type refers to particular activities.

Rasmussen's theory of reasoning (human information processing) fits the Base Model of expertise (see chapter 5), although his description is of a stepwise process, whereas the Base Model is more macrocognitive in that processes are parallel. According to Rasmussen, the decision maker must first *observe* something that requires action, then *analyze the evidence* to come to an understanding of the situation, then *evaluate the consequences* of the situation, then *determine a course of action* for achieving the target state, and then *plan and execute the proper procedure*. Thus, the Decision Ladder is a "map" of the structure of a particular decision-making process,

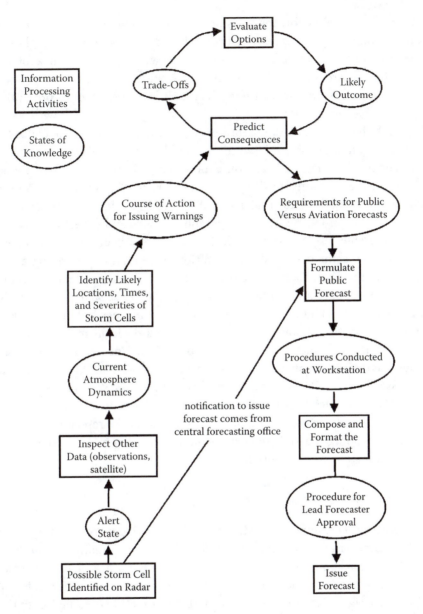

FIGURE 10.2 An Example Decision Ladder.

and it helps to identify the requirements of decision making (Rasmussen, Pejtersen, & Goodstein, 1994). The creation of a Decision Ladder usually focuses on expert performance, not so much with the goal of describing how a system *should* act but with the goal of suggesting how a system *could* act if given a flexible problem space. Thus, Decision Ladders include a representation of the analysis of options, consequences, and trade-offs.

An example is presented in Figure 10.2. This example concerns a specific task in weather forecasting. A first glance shows why the Decision Ladder is called a ladder: It has two "legs." The upward-pointing branch on the left refers to the processes required to reach a judgment (e.g., sense making, situation awareness), and the downward leg describes how the decision is implemented. At the pinnacle is an evaluation of options, consequences, and trade-offs. In this case, options might include a decision to wait on issuing a forecast. A consequence might be issuing a forecast that goes bust (i.e., severe weather does not occur). A trade-off might be that between the issuance of a forecast that goes bust versus the issuance of a forecast promptly in the hope of possibly saving lives.

Although the Decision Ladder represents the fundamental knowledge-based decision processes, it is possible that within the ladder, an expert would be able to skip certain rungs of the ladder based on experience and familiarity with the system. Representing these "shunts" or shortcuts (see Figure 10.2) makes the Decision Ladder a flexible tool that allows for understanding of different levels of decision making; that is, the Decision Ladder can represent both novice and expert decision-making processes (Vicente, 1999) as well as reflect possible users' heuristics (Rasmussen et al., 1994). When an actor takes a shortcut, various information processing actions are bypassed, but the desired results are still achieved. The Decision Ladder not only displays these shortcut relationships but also highlights those states of knowledge that are bypassed if a shortcut is taken (Nehme, Scott, Cummings, & Furusho, 2006). This is reminiscent of the notion of recognition-primed decision making (see chapters 5 and 9). In the case of systems with computer-based decision support tools, the Decision Ladder represents the decision process and states of knowledge that must be addressed by the tool whether a computer or a human makes the decision (Nehme et al., 2006). Thus, Decision Ladders also point to places where automation can be introduced, also a form of "shunting," if the purpose of the research is to determine how automation might better support the human decision maker and what kinds or levels of automation are appropriate.

The Abstraction-Decomposition Matrix

The Abstraction-Decomposition Matrix also evolved in the research of Rasmussen et al. The matrix is a way of creating a model of the work domain. The model constitutes information about the constraints of the work domain, and, in turn, this information can be used in a design intervention to support work. In interface design specifically, designers strive to integrate all the information obtained from the work analysis. The interface can then serve as an externalized model of the work domain constraints for the operator and, in turn, support the cognitive work (see Pejtersen & Rasmussen, 1997; Rasmussen & Pejtersen, 1995; St-Cyr & Burns, 2001), including the work involved in the achievement of expertise (Burns & Hajdukiewicz, 2004, chap. 1).

This is accomplished by using a two-dimensional diagram of the sort in Figure 10.3 (adapted from Naikar, 2005a, 2005b; Naikar et al., 2005). The rows refer to the levels of abstraction for analyzing the aspect of the work domain that is under investigation. The columns refer to the decomposition of the important functional components.

The second example, in Table 10.6 (adapted from Rasmussen, 1979), expresses in a general way the content of the cells at each level of abstraction and decomposition.

Levels of Abstraction ↓

Levels of Decomposition →

	Whole System	Subsystem	Component
Goals			
Values and priority measures			
Purpose-related functions			
Object-related processes			
Physical objects			

FIGURE 10.3 An Abstraction-Decomposition Matrix.

TABLE 10.6 A General Description of the Meanings Expressed in Each of the Cells in an Abstraction-Decomposition Matrix

	Structure	Elements	Relations	Data
Functional Meaning	Related to properties of environment	Physical variables, processes, or objects of environments	As required by system's environment	Magnitude of variables or states of objects, processes
Abstract Function	Topology of overall causal structure of system	Abstract variables related to state in causal net	General laws, conservation laws; logic relations	Symbolic, quantitative variables; truth values; related to modeling language
Functional Structure	Network of relations ordered in sets, that is, typical functions	Physical variables	Sets of physical laws and empirical relations; equations, graphs, and tables related to typical functions and processes	Magnitude of variables
	Set of "objectivized" typical functions	Typical processes or functions	Potential for interaction among processes and functions	States of functions; events
Physical Function	Sets of variables related to typical objects	Physical variables	Input–output relations of typical components, equations, graphs, and tables	Magnitude of physical variables
	Sets of interacting objects or components	Typical components	Potential for interaction between objects	States of objects; events
Physical Form	Topographic map: "landscape of typical objects"	Objects, technical components	Spatial distance	Form and spatial position of objects
	Distributed spatial maps	Fields of uniform surface or matter	Spatial arrangement	Location of fields of sense data; visual, tactile, auditory

TABLE 10.7 An Abstraction-Decomposition Analysis of a Hospital

	Patient		Hospital		
	Social	Biological	Cure	Care	Administration
Goals and Constraints	Patient relation with family Patient's commitments	Effects of illness and treatment on patient's goals	Patient cure Legal, ethical, economic constraints	Patient well-being	Laws, unions, public opinion
Measures of the Goals	Patient's finances and employment	Probability of cure, side effects	Disease categories Treatment cost Patient suffering	Patient flow Staff workload	Distribution of funds Flow of resources and personnel
General Functions and Activities	Patient's employment, living conditions, family relations	General state of health, disease category	Diagnosis, treatment, medication, research	Lodging, feeding, social services, etc.	Human resources administration, accounting, etc.
Specific Functions and Activities	Patient's work, leisure activities	Specific disorders and their possible treatments	Treatment plan Patient monitoring Functioning of equipment	Specific procedures in feeding, cleaning, etc.	Specific procedures in administration, planning, etc.
Configuration	Age, address, education, etc.	Patient weight, height, etc.	Personnel Inventory of equipment, medications	Facilities, inventories	Facilities, inventories

To understand this Abstraction-Decomposition Matrix, it helps to see how it is manifested in particular instances. Table 10.7 is an Abstraction-Decomposition analysis of a hospital (adapted from Rasmussen et al., 1990; Vicente, 1999).

Note that the names given to the levels of abstraction are different from the matrices in Tables 10.6 and 10.7. This is deliberate. It reflects the fact that different researchers compose their Abstraction-Decomposition Matrices in different ways, adapting the basic idea to the problems at hand. In this sense, Abstraction-Decomposition can be regarded as a class of related analytical representations, although there is some disagreement within the Work Analysis community about whether there should be canonical forms for the matrices. (See Naikar et al. [2005] for a discussion of important variations in the Abstraction-Decomposition Matrix.)

This being said, the subtle wording differences in the matrices that appear here can be seen as superficial relative to the more important analytical goals; the underlying meaning of each level is largely same. For example, when analyzing a work domain, data at the "physical form" level would constitute the form and spatial location of objects in the environment. An example from a work domain might be the location of a store of coal in a coal-fired power station. A less decomposed view is possible at the physical form level of abstraction. For example, structure at the physical form

Functional Structure	F/A -18 Abstraction Hierarchy			
Functional Purpose		Security of sovereign airspace	Initiation of offensive action	
Priorities and values	Operation within procedural and physical constraints	Reduction of enemy combat effectiveness	Minimization of collateral damage	Nullification of enemy air and surface attack
Purpose-Related Functions	Flight	Communication and coordination	Evaluation of tactical information	Weapons delivery to air and surface targets
Physical Functions	Supersonic cruise	Exchange of information	Level of hostility	Weather
Physical form	Displays	Data link	VHF/UHF/HF Radio channels	Air and surface threats

FIGURE 10.4 An example of an Abstraction-Decomposition Matrix.

level would constitute a topographic map of objects in the work domain. An example from the power station might be a topographic map that would provide information about spatial interrelationships between different coal supplies and other facilities. In addition, a more abstract view of the work domain is possible. For example, a relation at the functional structure level might include the rate of change in the ratio of the weight of coal burnt to energy produced.

Each level of abstraction is related to the one above by a means–end relation. The contents of cells in a level are *means* to achieving the content of the cells in the level above, which are the *ends*. This excerpt from Naikar et al. (1999) explains these relations further:

> Within the boundaries defined by the properties, workers can engage in numerous activities as they explore the multiple means (resources) available to them for achieving multiple system ends (purposes). … If one focuses attention on a particular function, links to higher levels of abstraction indicate "why" that function is performed (ends). Conversely, links to lower levels of abstraction indicate "how" that level is performed (means). (p. 1129)

Naikar et al. (1999) provided examples of means–end relations in their analysis of the work system of an F/A-18 aircraft. A simplified version of their analysis is presented in Figure 10.4. Naikar et al. (1999) modified the Abstraction-Decomposition procedure for their own purposes by using only the abstraction levels. The table shows that communication and coordination in the aircraft work domain is a means to achieving the end that is operation within procedural and physical constraints. Similarly, communication and coordination relies on an adequate exchange of information, which in turn is supported by data link and VHF/UHF/HF radio channels.

Abstraction-Decomposition can also be used as a scheme for coding interviews and think-aloud problem-solving sessions. An Abstraction-Decomposition Matrix for protocol analysis is intended to show in a single stroke both the category of each proposition and how each proposition fits into the participant's strategic reasoning process and goal orientation (see Rasmussen, 1986b, chap. 10; Rasmussen et al., 1990).

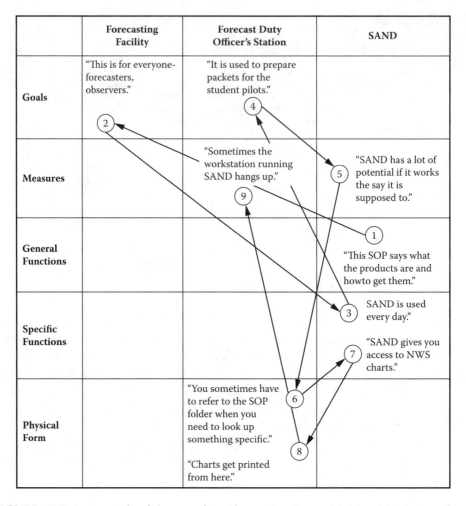

FIGURE 10.5 An example of the use of an Abstraction-Decomposition Matrix to code an interview protocol.

Note: SAND = Satellite, Alphanumerics, NEXRAD, and Difax Display System.

Details of the procedure are described in Crandall, Klein, & Hoffman (2006; see also Hoffman & Lintern, 2006). In Figure 10.5 we present an example from an interview with a weather forecaster concerning the Satellite, Alphanumerics, NEXRAD, and Difax Display System (SAND) workstation, which is used by the U.S. Navy (Hoffman, Coffey, & Ford, 2000).

Figure 10.6 illustrates the use of the method to describe the place of the SAND system within the forecasting organization context.

An Example Study

One of the most well-documented applications of the principles of Work Domain Analysis, and the Abstraction-Decomposition method in particular, is in interface design. This area has become known as Ecological Interface Design (EID) (Pejtersen

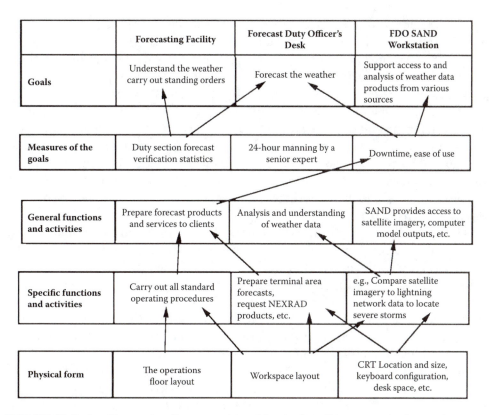

	Forecasting Facility	Forecast Duty Officer's Desk	FDO SAND Workstation
Goals	Understand the weather carry out standing orders	Forecast the weather	Support access to and analysis of weather data products from various sources
Measures of the goals	Duty section forecast verification statistics	24-hour manning by a senior expert	Downtime, ease of use
General functions and activities	Prepare forecast products and services to clients	Analysis and understanding of weather data	SAND provides access to satellite imagery, computer model outputs, etc.
Specific functions and activities	Carry out all standard operating procedures	Prepare terminal area forecasts, request NEXRAD products, etc.	e.g., Compare satellite imagery to lightning network data to locate severe storms
Physical form	The operations floor layout	Workspace layout	CRT Location and size, keyboard configuration, desk space, etc.

FIGURE 10.6 An Abstraction-Decomposition Matrix describing a particular workstation in terms of the total work domain context.

Note: SAND = Satellite, Alphanumerics, NEXRAD, and Difax Display System.

& Rasmussen, 1997; Vicente & Rasmussen, 1992; see Burns & Hajdukiewicz, 2004, for an overview and examples), reflecting the resonance that CWA has with Ecological Psychology. (There is also a resonance with Human-Centered Computing. Chapter 10 includes a striking example of EID, the "OZ" cockpit display.) Pejtersen and Rasmussen (1997) described the resonance of CWA and Ecological Psychology in the following way:

> According to Gibson (1979), the basis for direct perception is … invariant combinations of variables that demand or invite appropriate behaviors … an affordance represents attributes of the environment that are relevant to the organism's purposes. … Thus, perception is viewed as a means of selecting the appropriate action to attain a goal. … Gibson provides some examples to explain how the world is actually composed of a hierarchy of affordances … the relations between levels are means–ends relations … [In the interface] the information in the relational means–ends structure would be perceived as affordances that would specify what actions to take … [D]isplaying the invariant structure and the affordances of the work domain is a more effective way to support discretionary tasks than procedural guides … skilled actors in work are not subject to information input, they are actively asking questions to the environment. (p. 322)

This is clearly a conceptual match with the core notion of Abstraction-Decomposition as a representation of many-to-many means–ends relations across levels of abstraction.

A poorly designed interface can distance operators from the feeling that they are actually interacting directly with the target system or process that they are trying to control (Sanderson, 2002). The objective of EID is to provide the information about the work domain that supports operator work and do so at the least possible "cognitive cost" (Sanderson, 2002). Vicente (2002) argued that it is a violation of Ecological Psychology principles not to do so in display design. If perception is of affordances and events, then good displays are ones that support direct perception of the affordances and events. The EID process involves integrating in the interface the information about functions and goals obtained from the Abstraction-Decomposition. The interface can then serve as an externalized model of the work domain constraints for the operator and, in turn, support the cognitive work (Rasmussen & Pejtersen, 1995; St-Cyr & Burns, 2001).

Kim Vicente and his colleagues (Bisantz & Vicente, 1994; Burns & Hajdukiewicz, 2004; Christoffersen, Hunter, & Vicente, 1996; Vicente, Christoffersen, & Pereklita, 1995) showed how the methods of work analysis and the principles of the Ecological Approach could be applied to inform interface design. They described a system known as DURESS II, which is a simulation of a complex thermo-hydraulic industrial process. The simulation was designed to be representative of the complex work domains found in many modern workplaces such as nuclear power stations, air traffic control stations, and military command and control centers.

In the research task, the participants were presented with preplanned scenarios and interacted with a display in the attempt to understand and control the industrial process. The DURESS II system constituted two streams of water that could be manipulated so as to supply either, both, or neither of two reservoirs. Users had access to eight valves that controlled water flow. Participants were required to keep water reservoirs at a constant temperature and to satisfy reservoir output demand.

The researchers constructed two different interfaces for system control. The interfaces were designed by obtaining information about the inherent constraints of the work domain through the application of the Abstraction-Decomposition procedure and then representing this information within the interface. The first interface was based on concrete, specific domain information obtained from the physical form level (i.e., a low level) of the Abstraction-Decomposition analysis. As a consequence, this interface contained information about the state of physical components and goal variables. For example, the open–closed state of a given reservoir inlet valve was indicated on a scale ranging from 0 to 10. This level of information provision—individual indicators for individual actuators and sensors—was regarded as typical of traditional interface design.

The second interface contained the same physical form level information as the first but also contained more abstract domain information obtained from the abstract function level (i.e., a higher level) of the Abstraction-Decomposition analysis. As a consequence, this interface contained information about the state of the *functions* that the physical components were intended to achieve. For example, the mass inflow–outflow rates of a given reservoir were each displayed as bars, like a bar graph. The bars were separated in the display, but the tops of the bars were linked by a line. Thus, the height of the start of the line displayed the open–closed state of the input valve, and the height of the end of the line displayed the open–closed state of the output valve.

As a consequence, the angle (steepness) of the line constituted higher order functional information in the form of the rate of change of the volume of the reservoir.

This sort of informational display is regarded as ecological in that it depicts invariant relations that represent cofunctions. In controlling an industrial process, the operator needs to know not just the individual values of individual sensors or actuators but also how to directly perceive how the controlled process is functioning as the variables interact. In the ecological display Vicente et al. created, the operator could rapidly perceive the status of reservoir filling and emptying. Changes in lower level variables, such as the open–closed state of a given valve, were the *means* for achieving the *ends,* such as the satisfaction of reservoir output demand (other examples of EID are presented in Burns & Hajdukiewicz, 2004, and Pejtersen & Rasmussen, 1997).

By including more of the functional level information that lay between physical variables and the higher order purposes of the system, the researchers hoped that the operator would be provided with critical information about how his or her changes in the physical variables would help achieve system purposes. In effect, the interface was intended to make available a detailed externalized mental model of the work domain and, in doing so, provide robust cognitive support for the operator work (St-Cyr & Burns, 2001).

Vicente et al. trained one group of participants to use the first interface and another group to use the second. The participants were asked to use the interface to control various system tasks such as starting up, tuning, shutting down, and repairing faults. The results showed that there was very little difference in average performance between the groups. However, the group using the ecological interface, which included both physical and functional information, exhibited more consistent performance compared with the group using the first interface, which included just the physical information. In addition, participants in the group using the first interface occasionally took up to twice as long to complete their tasks, even after extensive training.

Subsequently, Ham and Yoon (2001a, 2001b; Ham, Yoon, & Han, 2008) extended these studies to include tests of interfaces that provided function, generalized function, and abstract function levels of the abstraction hierarchy analysis of a nuclear power plant system. Overall, these studies show that EID can lead to interfaces that support better human performance under truly unanticipated and complex conditions. The best levels of performance are seen only when all the information from the Abstraction-Decomposition Matrix is included in the interface and interface enhancements expose the structural means–ends relations in the work domain (Sanderson, 2002, p. 256).

Abstraction-Decomposition and CTA

On one hand, the Abstraction-Decomposition method has a track record of successful applications in diverse domains. The Abstraction-Decomposition is regarded by research agencies worldwide as being an important, if not necessary, component of research and development efforts. Questions about the method have been raised, mirroring concerns and questions that have been raised about other methods of CTA and Cognitive Field Research (see Hoffman & Woods, 2000) (e.g., method reliability, validity, replicability, generalizability across applications and across coders, etc.). Among the most challenging concerns are the claims that Abstraction-Decomposition diagrams do not really involve "abstraction" and that the meaning of "decomposition" is vague and misleading.

Some refer to the "Abstraction Hierarchy" and to the "Abstraction-Decomposition Matrix" when decomposition is included with the hierarchy (e.g., Bisantz et al., 2002; Hoffman and Lintern, 2006). Jens Rasmussen would probably be the first person to want to see his ideas extended, refined, and adapted and the last person to want to see his ideas cast in stone, for example, the notion that some particular five levels of abstraction are the only right way to do the analysis (see Naikar et al., 2005, for a discussion of variations in the Abstraction-Decomposition Matrix). In our view, the matrix it is not a hierarchy in either a taxonomic or a graph-theoretic sense; that is, it is not an "is a" tree. Second, the levels of abstraction are arguably not levels of abstraction (e.g., an "object-related" process is not an abstraction over objects). What is said to cross the levels of abstraction are means–ends analyses, and this can reasonably be taken to mean that the so-called levels are indeed levels. Some have found the ambiguity about the concepts to be placed in the Abstraction-Decomposition Matrix a severe limitation (Lind, 1999). As the framework has been generalized from process control systems to "intentional systems," some have found the Abstraction-Decomposition Matrix insufficient for representing key aspects of the work such as time and cause-and-effect tracings for unanticipated events (Cummings, 2005, 2006). Although the analysis of work domains and the specification of control tasks that are governed by natural laws allow one to specify strategies for decision making, in intentional systems, such as military command and control operations, the work activity is dominated by human intent and goals and involves dynamic and ill-defined problems and interdependent decisions. Thus, it is argued that the general progression from ecological analysis (domain constraints, control strategies) to cognitive analysis (social and organizational factors, demands on worker competencies) is in need of extension, adaptation, and refinement for use in the analysis of intentional systems. Instances of the adaptations can be seen in reports by Burns, Bryant, and Chalmers (2005); Cummings (2006); and Naikar (2006).

This is all a matter of current debate, and our discussion is by no means the final word on the matter. And to be sure, all methods have strengths and weaknesses, uses and limitations. These point CTA researchers to new territories in methodology.

Summary

Early forms of work analysis arose in France, Belgium, and Denmark, becoming particularly salient in the 1960s in response to concerns about worker health, safety, and productivity. Of the various European research threads, Francophone Ergonomics is perhaps the most relevant to a discussion of work analysis. Francophone Ergonomics has similar elements to many of the perspectives described in other chapters of this book but is most closely linked to Work Analysis. Francophone Ergonomics emphasizes field studies using in-depth observations and analyses of work in context, similar to sociological perspectives (chapter 11). Francophone Ergonomics also includes notions that overlap with North American Cognitive Systems Engineering (chapter 7), such as the idea of mental models or workers' "operating images" of the machines they use. Francophone Ergonomics places emphasis on seeing work from a developmental perspective in that worker knowledge and reasoning adapt as a result of technological change. Francophone Ergonomics also involves research aimed at developing models of expert reasoning, with clear links to Expertise Studies (chapter 8). However, we included Francophone Ergonomics in our discussion of Work Analysis because of the shared roots of these two traditions in the framework of Jens Rasmussen, the shared emphasis on understanding cognitive work from multiple perspectives, and the shared view that cognitive work cannot be understood solely as a closed system or as a sequence of steps.

The most widely cited definition of CWA was offered by Kim Vicente (1999, 2000): CWA is the analysis of work with the goal of giving designers insight into how to create tools that effectively support human work. "Effectively" refers to increased safety, increased productivity, improved quality of life, and adaptability. An earlier definition offered by Pejtersen and Rasmussen (1997) emphasizes the separation of the representation of the work domain from the user's general background, resources, cognitive style, and subjective preferences as the defining characteristic of CWA. They described the aim of CWA as the design of a work support system that allows the user to select a work strategy to fit the situation.

CTA and CWA are in many ways distinct. In particular, CTA generally refers to a set of methods for understanding the cognitive aspects of a task. CWA, in contrast, is a philosophy or framework for studying work. In fact, some researchers use CTA methods in pursuit of CWA. CTA and CWA can be seen as complementary. CTA methods are aimed at identifying cognitively complex aspects of a task, whereas CWA is aimed at identifying constraints that shape work. Both, however, focus on studying experienced professionals doing complex jobs in real-world settings.

CWA has strong links to Ecological Psychology. The Ecological Approach advocates the view that there exists a reciprocity between the human and the environment, in which the environment determines human behavior as much as mentalistic or cognitive activity. This perspective resonates strongly with CWA, which concentrates initially on physical and social constraints inherent to a given task or work domain. CWA is driven more by environmental constraints than worker characteristics.

The CWA framework is generally applied in the context of "complex sociotechnical systems." This term refers to systems that are made up of psychological (cognitive), social, and technological elements, all embedded in a broader team, organizational, and social context. Work within a sociotechnical system requires a range of strategies. Tasks require accommodation and adaptation to the environment over time. There is uncertainty in the data available, and access to information is often indirect or technology mediated. Sociotechnical systems often involve hazards and risks, which must be managed in the face of unexpected events.

The Risø framework of work analysis distinguishes traditional work environments from new, computer-reliant contexts for cognitive and collaborative work, and sees cognitive work as a form of exploration within a space of constraints. This perspective emphasizes the dynamics of the workplace, including the continuous flux of technological change that requires the worker to learn and adapt.

In addition, the Risø framework is designed to analyze work domains using ethnographic methods rather than traditional task analysis techniques designed to example simpler human–computer interaction in isolation. A type of analysis termed "Abstraction-Decomposition" is used to examine work at several levels, ranging from high-level system purposes down to the lowest level of physical form of particular tools. At the higher levels, the purposes and intentions that constrain activity are represented. At lower levels, implementation, or how something is accomplished, is represented.

The analysis of the cognitive activity of individual worker is critical to work analysis in the Risø framework. Reasoning is described as being based on skills, rules, or knowledge. Skills are highly learned activities that link intentions to smooth, automatic behaviors. Experience and practice are required to develop skills. Rules rely on recognition of previously encountered similar situations and the solutions that were successfully applied in the past. Knowledge-based activity relies on mental models. These different types of reasoning are seen as key to the design of information technologies. Within the Risø framework, cognitive work is typified by learning and exploration, thus information technologies must support these types of activities and all three types of reasoning. Interfaces must support work at all levels, because users with different levels of expertise and reasoning strategies may be using the same system.

The Vicente–Ecological framework of CWA could be described a direct descendant of the Risø framework, as Vicente studied and worked with Rasmussen at the Risø National Laboratory. Vicente's articulation of CWA describes three important steps: (a) the designer identifies a constraint space and support for agent control, (b) the interface is designed to show the constraint boundaries and local data for ongoing situations with the goal of providing the user choice among action sequences, and (c) the end user finishes the design based on local information, knowledge, and expertise.

Following the work of Rasmussen, CWA seeks to model work activity in terms of various constraints that shape human activity rather than in terms of the literal action sequences of the human. This is accomplished via analysis of five levels of constraints: the *work domain,* the *control task,* the *strategies* or processes used to achieve the control tasks, the *social organizational* layer, and *worker competencies.* A key concept within CWA is that the constraints at each of these levels remain invariant across a range of contexts. Thus the analyst seeks to identify these invariant constraints that specify boundaries of action and allow the design to support worker adaptation by giving the workers the ability to adapt within these boundaries. Another important feature is that degrees of freedom are reduced with each layer of constraint, moving from the work domain to worker competencies. This is referred to as "successive narrowing."

Vicente distinguished three purposes for studying work. *Normative* refers to strategies for studying work aimed at identifying or prescribing an optimal way to complete the task. This category includes traditional task analysis methods designed for use in work environments in which work is highly predictable and often repetitive. *Descriptive* refers to techniques aimed at describing actual practice. Many CTA methods fall within this category. *Formative* refers methods for which the aim is to identify intrinsic work constraints. Although the goal of CWA is formative design, all three approaches for studying work are useful and necessary in conducting CWA.

Normative and descriptive approaches are useful in informing the formative analysis and design process.

The normative approach is perhaps best exemplified by Taylor's Time and Motion Study (1911). This method evolved in the context of industrial settings with the goal of increasing efficiency and safety. This decomposition of tasks into a sequential flow with well-defined beginnings and endings and well-defined goals is less relevant to many work settings today. Modern sociotechnical systems are more complex in terms of size, distribution, control, and regulation. Jobs are more dynamic, open, and instable and include multiple degrees of freedom. Rather than specializing in a limited range of routine tasks, workers possess a broader range of cognitive abilities that include the flexibility to meet dynamic and unanticipated work demands. Because of these changes in the work environment, advocates of work analysis have argued that task analysis has become a less appropriate tool for analysis of complex sociotechnical systems. Limitations include the following:

1. Task analysis can be conducted only for anticipated tasks; it is not possible to begin a task analysis if the event or situation is unanticipated.
2. Task analyses tend to be prescriptive or too easy to be used as prescriptions.
3. Even though tasks can be complex, task analyses are always context bound.
4. The finer the detail of the task analysis, the more transient and fragile it will be.
5. Task analyses are based on the false premise that jobs can be broken down into well-defined and sequential subtasks that result in the achievement of well-defined goals.

In spite of these limits, normative task analysis can be of value in the context of CWA. Vicente described three levels of normative task analysis: Level 1 is input–output, Level 2 is flow sequence, and Level 3 is timeline. *Constraint-based task analysis* addresses Level 1 only by describing the general constraints on user action. The only thing this analysis specifies is the actions the workers should *not* perform. *Instruction-based task analysis* provides a much more detailed description of how the task should be accomplished. Some instruction-based techniques address Level 2, others address Level 3, and still others address both Levels 2 and 3. Both of these forms of normative task analysis assume the goals of the system can be defined beforehand. One must anticipate initiating events to conduct these types of task analysis. Vicente described this approach as insufficient. Event-independent work analysis techniques are needed to fill in the gaps and design for unanticipated events.

Descriptive work analysis is used to generate descriptions of how an existing system behaves. Many CTA methods fall within this category. The Naturalistic Decision Making community has been quite active in exploring description techniques (see chapter 9). Vicente considered descriptive techniques to be a good starting place for CWA, but they are insufficient in that they do not include a model of "true work."

Formative work analysis focuses on the "true work" that must be accomplished by the envisioned sociotechnical system, in contrast to the "actual work" that has been shaped by the current work technologies and systems. It specifies boundaries on action and a range of action sequence alternatives. Although no data collection methods are prescribed for conducting formative work analysis, documentation often provides a value source of data.

Normative, descriptive, and formative approaches are used opportunistically over the course of a project, guided by the CWA framework. Vicente advocated a multistage approach that begins with qualitative, descriptive field studies to identify "pressing, significant problems," which are subsequently examined more closely via controlled laboratory studies. After scrutiny of these significant problems in a highly controlled setting, more complex and representative conditions are introduced into the laboratory testing to examine generalizability. In the final stage, converging findings from the previous stages are used to inform work design interventions undertaken in the work domain.

These analyses are informed by a generic model of information processing represented by the Decision Ladder. The Decision Ladder is a graphical depiction of nodes and links that is used to represent decompositions of individual tasks. It has been used in the analysis of decision-making strategies in the area of process control. Two types of nodes are used. One type refers to states or contents of knowledge, and the other refers to particular activities. The Decision Ladder represents the fundamental knowledge-based decision processes in a generic form, but it can also be used to depict how an expert might be able to skip certain steps based on experience and familiarity with the system. It can be used to describe both novice and expert decision-making processes.

The Abstraction-Decomposition Matrix is the most commonly used method within CWA, focused primarily on representing the first level of constraints: the work domain. Within the matrix, levels of abstraction (i.e., goals, values and priority measures, purpose-related functions, object-related functions, physical objects) are represented on the vertical axis, and the levels of decomposition (whole system, subsystem, and component) are shown on the horizontal axis. The matrix is tailored within each project. The number of levels as well as the labels for the levels of abstraction for each dimension can vary. However, analysts strive to retain the underlying meaning of each level across projects. A key component of the matrix is that levels of abstraction represent means–end relationships.

As with other methods of CTA and Cognitive Field Research, questions about method reliability, validity, replicability, generalizability, and so on have been raised with regard to the Abstraction-Decomposition Matrix. In considering these issues, researchers need to keep in mind that the Abstraction-Decomposition Matrix has a track record of successful application in diverse domains. Debate continues about how to best describe and bound the Abstraction-Decomposition Matrix. Some have found the ambiguity associated with the method to be a severe limitation. Some argue for more rigid definition and application of the method. Others argue that the method is in need of extension, adaptation, and refinement for use in analysis of intentional systems.

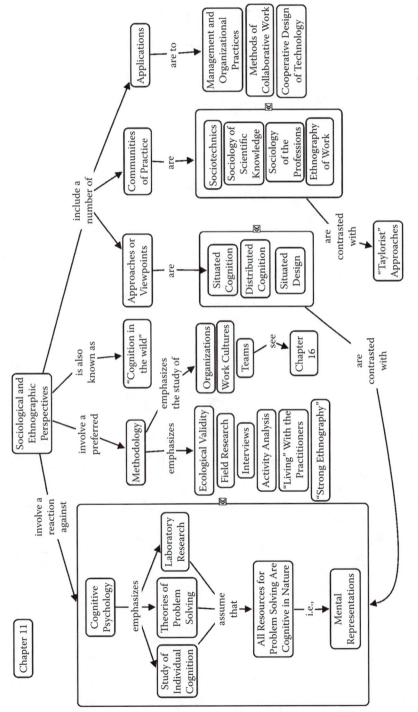

FIGURE 11.1 Chapter 11 Concept Map.

11

Sociological and
Ethnographic Perspectives

If sociology could not be applied in a thoroughgoing way to scientific knowledge, it would mean that science could not scientifically know itself.

—David Bloor (1976, p. 40)

There is an injunction in social studies of science to eschew interest in the validity of the products of science, in favor of an interest in their production. While I generally agree with this injunction, my investigation of one of the prevailing models of human action in cognitive science is admittedly and unabashedly interested. That is to say, I take it that there is a reality of human action, beyond either the cognitive scientist's models or my own, to which both are trying to do justice. In that sense, I am not just examining the cognitive science model with the dispassion of the uncommitted anthropologist of science, I am examining it in light of an alternative account of human action to which I am committed, and which I attempt to clarify in the process.

—Lucy A. Suchman (1987, p. x)

Introduction

In recent decades, a number of ethnographers, sociologists, and philosophers of science have begun to study "communities of practice" (Lave, 1993; Lave & Wenger, 1991; Wenger, 1998). This paradigm has been referred to as the study of "everyday cognition," "cognition in the wild," "situated cognition," "distributed cognition," and "business ethnography" (Clancey, 1995; Hutchins, 1995a; Kirsch, 2001; Lave, 1988; Nardi, 1997; Scribner, 1984; Suchman, 1987). Within this perspective we place "ethnomethodology" (Garfinkel, 1967, 1982). Although ethnomethodology relies on ethnographic methods, it differs from traditional sociology by focusing on the methods (hence, "-methodology") used by individuals and society (hence, "ethno-") to make sense of things and achieve social order.

Researchers have studied a broad range of domains of proficiency, including traditional farming methods used in Peru, photocopier repair, the activities of military command teams, the social interactions of collaborative teams of industrial designers, artists, financiers, climatologists, physicists, engineers, and so on (Collins, 1985; Creativity and Cognition Studios, 2003; Cross, Christiaans, & Dorst, 1996;

Ehn, 1988; Fleck & Williams, 1996; Greenbaum & Kyng, 1991; Hutchins, 1990, 1995b; Lynch, 1991; Mieg, 2001; Nardi, 1997; Orr, 1985; Rogoff & Lave, 1984; Suchman, 1987). Classic studies in this paradigm include the following:

- Edwin Hutchins's studies of navigation by both individuals and teams, by both culturally traditional methods and modern technology-based methods, focusing on the interplay of navigation tools and collaborative activity (Hutchins & Hinton, 1984);
- Edwin Hutchins's (1990) study of flight crew collaboration and teamwork;
- Julian Orr's (1996) study of how photocopier repair technicians acquire knowledge and skill by sharing their "war stories" with one another; and
- Jean Lave's (1988, 1993, 1997) ethnographic studies of traditional methods used in crafts such as tailoring, the nature of skills used in everyday life (e.g., math skills used during supermarket shopping), and the nature of learning and apprenticeship activities in diverse cultures.

Within this perspective we place research in the area of the "Sociology of Scientific Knowledge" and "Sociology of the Professions" (also known as Science and Technology Studies) (e.g., Collins, 1983, 1997; Fleck & Williams, 1996; Garfinkel, 1982; Gorman, Tweney, Gooding, & Kincannon, 2005; Hakkarainen, Palonen, Paavola, & Lehtinen, 2004; Knorr-Cetina, 1981; Knorr-Cetina & Mulkay, 1983; Kurz-Milcke & Gigerenzer, 2004; Latour, 1983, 1992; Latour & Woolgar, 1979; Mieg, 2001). The field of the "sociology of knowledge" (a term coined by David Bloor, 1976) emerged following the impact of Thomas Kuhn's *The Structure of Scientific Revolutions* (1962), in which Kuhn argued that social and psychological factors were critical in scientific progress. This contrasted with the prevailing approach in the philosophy of science, which was to understand science primarily as a rational and logical enterprise. Kuhn's work stimulated further thinking in the philosophy of science, specifically the notion that science could be understood through the application of social scientific methods, to understand not only the process of science but the rational content of science as well, a view called "social constructivism" (e.g., Bijker, Hughes, & Pinch, 1987; Fuller, 1993; Knorr-Cetina, 1983; Merton, 1977). This led to detailed analyses of science and scientific discourse as it is (and has been) practiced, for example, the relations of research to broader issues of economics and public policy, the role of consensus in decisions about what makes for proper practice, breakdowns in the attempt to transmit skill from one laboratory to another, failures in science or in the attempt to apply new technology, and so on. (For a discussion of the history of this community of practice, see Knorr-Cetina and Mulkay [1983, chap. 1].) Given this, it is not surprising to see a dovetailing with ethnomethodology, which had special impact in the sociology of scientific knowledge. For instance, the dependence of meaning on context has implications for the view that scientific knowledge is "objective."

We might also place within sociology and ethnography much of the European work on Activity Analysis for the design of information technologies, especially the contributions of Scandinavian researchers Pele Ehn (1988), Anne-Sophie Nyssen (2000), Joan Greenbaum and Morten Kyng (1991), and Veronique De Keyser and her colleagues (e.g., De Keyser, Decortis, & Van Daele, 1988), in which system design is understood as embedded within a social context. As is the case for Cognitive Systems Engineering (chapter 6) and Cognitive Work Analysis (chapter 8), here we see the cross influences of European and North American work. Indeed, Activity Theory has become foundational to the ethnographic study of the modern workplace in such organizations as Apple Computer (De Keyser & Samercay, 1998; Marti & Scrivani, 2003; Nardi, 1996).

To some it may seem not quite right to gather sociological, ethnographic, and anthropological approaches under one umbrella. Nardi (1997, p. 361) pointed out that "the chief ethnographic methods are anthropological"; that is, the main methods are shared (and include interviewing, participant observation, surveys, and Activity Analysis) (see Blomberg, Giacomi, Mosher, & Swenton-Wall, 1993; Clancey, 2001, 2006; Nardi, 1996). As we show in this chapter, this commonality emerges when one looks at the details of actual research methods in the literatures of the communities and disciplines. Few researchers in these disciplines would find comfort in the claim that their methods could be called Cognitive Task Analysis (CTA). Some of the scientists we have cited in this chapter would wonder at the term *cognitive work*. They would ask, What work is *not* cognitive in some respect? Who put the word *cognitive* on the front, and why? Is this perhaps a throwback to the emphasis on laboratory research on expertise or the view of cognition as reliant on as stored knowledge? Researchers in the sociological and ethnographic communities of practice emphasize the social nature of work; this is a common thread at the level of theory. The focus in these areas is different from that of cognitive scientists in that emphasis is not placed on individual cognition. Rather, the emphasis is more on the study of work practices in their social and cultural contexts.

A Research Example

The primary ethnographic methods are observations (including video analysis), interviews, documentation analysis, and their combinations (Blomberg, Burrell, & Guest, 2003). These methods have been applied in the study of diverse domains of practice and types of workplaces, but especially offices. Examples are Kirsch's (2001) ethnographic studies of how people arrange and use their offices, giving us the now-familiar distinction between "neats" and "scruffies," and the studies by Jeanette Blomberg and her colleagues (Blomberg et al., 1993) at Xerox PARC on the ways in which workers process electronic and paper documents. These studies introduced the notion of "Participatory Design." Blomberg et al. (1993), Blomberg et al. (2003), and Clancey (2001, 2006) provided excellent overviews of ethnographic field research methods, with advice about the conduct of observations, note taking, interviewing, and video analysis.

An example study is one by Rachel Carkett (2003), who used ethnographic methods to study expert designers in the aerospace industry, with a focus on identifying barriers to creativity within the team, group, and organization environment. By tracking and interviewing 13 designers over an 8-week period and building "interview diaries," Carkett was able to identify a number of important factors in design, such as the importance of information sharing and the importance of the development of social networks within which people could accomplish two critical things: they could achieve trust, and they could share their individual expertise. Business barriers to creativity included a new corporate training program that made it difficult for the experienced designers to work in mentor–apprentice dyads and thereby sustain and build the organization's knowledge base. Carkett also noted some downsides to technology, including the demise of the traditional white board and face-to-face meetings and the constraints imposed by the use of a new software tool to manage the team's activities (it was seen as too formal, it undermined group processes, and it took away from "free thinking"). True to the ethnographic point of view (e.g., Lave, Scribner, Schön, etc.) throughout her discussion, Carkett emphasized the fact that creativity is a social ("situated" and "distributed") process, not an individual process. (Additional papers by Creativity and Cognition Studios [2003] illustrate the use of ethnographic interviews and observations in the study of experts and expert teams in the area of technology design.)

Dekker and Nyce (2004) provided an extended example of the ethnographic approach to the analysis of the cognitive work of air traffic controllers, comparing studies that used ethnographic methods of observation and interviewing with studies that used experimental methods. Their opening empirical question, one still under debate, is whether air traffic control can work without paper flight strips (e.g., Mackay, 2000). The paper flight strip is a small slip that contains flight plan data about each controlled aircraft's route, speed, altitude, times over waypoints, and other characteristics. It is used by controllers in conjunction with a radar representation of air traffic. New air traffic control systems are being developed without flight strips, which has generated concern on the part of some regulators, because it creates largely unknown future work.

Dekker and Nyce began by pointing out the limitations of the experimental approach when it comes to understanding the current work and designing future work:

> Experimental steps into the future are of necessity narrow, affecting the generalizability of research findings. The mapping between test and target situation may also miss important factors. Albright et al. (1996) employed a number of measures to find out if controllers perform just as well with strips as they do without them [e.g., number of conflict alerts activated, mean time to grant pilot requests, number of unable requests, number of requests ignored, number of controller-to-center requests, etc.]. In experimental work, such number and diversity of measurements may substitute for (or be taken as evidence of) the strength of the epistemological claim. But each empirical encounter is of necessity limited. In the case of Albright et al., 20 air traffic controllers participated in two simulated airspace conditions (one with strips and one without strips) for 25 min each. One of the results was that controllers took longer to grant pilot requests when they did not have access to flight strips, presumably because they had to assemble the basis for a decision from other information sources. That finding, however, seemed anomalous compared to other results, which showed no significant difference between workload and ability to keep control over the traffic situation across strip/no strip conditions. Apparently, the compensatory behaviors were sufficient to maintain effective control at what controllers perceived to be a comparable workload. Albright et al. explained the anomaly as follows: "Since the scenarios were only 25 minutes in length, controllers may not have had the opportunity to formulate strategies about how to work without flight strips, possibly contributing to the delay." This led Albright et al. to conclude that the presence or absence of strips had no effect on either performance or perceived workload. Their explanation admits that the correspondence between the experimental setting and the future system and setting may be weak. Designers may, or perhaps should, wonder what 25 min of undocumented struggle tells them about a future system that will replace decades of accumulated practice. The ultimate resolution of the fundamental constraint on empirical work is that more research is always necessary. The idea is that more of

the same, eventually, will lead to something different; that a series of similar studies over time will produce a knowledge incrementally useful to the literature and useful to the consumers of the research. (paraphrased from pp. 1626–1628)

Dekker and Nyce contrasted this experimental approach with an ethnographic approach, which began not by presuming a use of flight strips (i.e., merely a memory aid that can be easily removed or replaced) but by seeing the use of strips as something that is open to negotiation, disagreement, or multiple interpretations. Through qualitative inquiry (also called Contextual Design; see Beyer & Holtzblatt, 1998; Holtzblatt, 2003), one tries to "see the world through the eyes of the workers." What role do tools play for people in the accomplishments of their tasks? How do tools affect their expression of expertise? Qualitative research interprets the ways in which people make sense of their work experiences by examining the meanings and categories people use and construct in light of their own situation.

In an ethnographic study of air traffic control (Harper, 2000; Hughes, Randall, & Shapiro, 1993), researchers spent many months observing and documenting air traffic control. During this time, the researchers developed an understanding of flight strips as an artifact whose multiple functions derive from controlling work: "The strip is a public document for the members of the (controlling) team; a working representation of an aircraft's control history and a work site of controlling. Moving the strips is to organize the information in terms of work activities and, through this, accomplishing the work of organizing the traffic" (Hughes et al., 1993, pp. 132–133). However, in the view of Dekker and Nyce (2004), Hughes et al. do not "excavate the significance of controller remarks for their design implications." Hughes et al. left user statements unpacked and largely unanalyzed, and hence they did not derive design implications. Hughes et al. acknowledged this bridge-building problem:

> Ethnography can serve as another bridge between the users and the designers. In our case, controllers have advised on the design of the display tool with the ethnographer, as someone knowledgeable about but distanced from the work, and able to appreciate the significance of the controllers' remarks for their design implications, and on the other hand, familiar enough with the design problems to relate them to the controllers' experiences and comments. (Hughes et al., 1993, p. 138)

However, in attempting to build a bridge, Hughes et al. offered suggestions that fall prey to the substitution myth that work is partitionable such that machines can swap out for people without consequences. Hughes et al. asked questions such as, What characteristics of the existing manual system are unimportant and need not be supported in a computerized system? What characteristics of the manual system must be replicated without change in a computerized system? This led Dekker and Nyce to the question of what kind of ethnography is needed to provide meaningful design guidance.

> Hughes et al. (1993) have confused ethnography with what informants tell us, and the result is designers are left to pick and choose among informant statements to justify what they are going to do. So flight strips help controllers "get the picture." This kind of statement is obvious to controllers. If ethnographic analysis cannot take us beyond common sense, it offers designers no way to make analytic sense of what end users regard as natural and logical, and it is no wonder that designers often think they can do better themselves (e.g., Forsythe, 1999). (paraphrased from Dekker & Nyce, 2004, p. 1632)

Strong Ethnography

To Dekker and Nyce, the work of Hughes et al. constitutes "weak ethnography" in that it equates ethnography with something like natural history—an enterprise strong on description and data collection but weak on analysis and interpretation.

> Ethnography must involve more than interviewing and observing if the field research (observations and interviews) is to take a step into the future and connect to designers (Forsythe, 1999). Finding out what users think is not enough. Qualitative inquiry has to unpack informant meanings and categories, otherwise it hardly provides designers with helpful input for the creation of future work. To connect to designers, then, qualitative researchers need to see informant statements as starting points, not as conclusions. Researchers must engage in second-order analysis, transforming informant statements about present work into terms designers can use in building future work. (paraphrased from p. 1630)

Dekker and Nyce described "strong ethnography" as an approach that does not aim for a single definitive description of the target system. Rather it is a continuous, progressive reinterpretation and enrichment of the successive layers of data mined from the field observations and interviews (see also Blomberg et al., 1993). Methods are applied "in the context of a distinctive philosophical stance ... [researchers should take] as little as possible for granted. This stance promotes the conceptual distance necessary for systematic comparison of multiple perspectives on events and processes" (Forsythe, 1999, p. 129).

A number of ethnographers have commented on some myths concerning ethnographic methodology that are assumed by scientists in other "hard" disciplines and practitioners in domains on information technology where ethnographic and anthropological methods are seen as a path to system design. Dianna Forsythe (1993, 1999) compiled and refuted these myths.

Anyone can do it—it is just a matter of common sense. "Field research takes talent, training and practice to become competent, and careful data collection and analysis to produce reliable results" (Forsythe, 1999, p. 129). Ethnography runs counter to common sense because it requires the researcher to identify things that workers take for granted and tend to overlook. This includes detecting tacit knowledge, which is generally invisible to insiders.

Being insiders qualifies insiders to do ethnography in their own work setting. Insiders tend to view their own assumptions as obvious truths. Ethnography works best when conducted by an outsider who has gained significant and deep insider experience. The ethnographer's job is not to replicate the insider's perspective but to analyze it through systematic comparison of insider perspective and multiple alternative outsider perspectives.

Ethnography does not involve preformulated study designs or systematic methods— anything goes. Ethnography does not assume that the only path to scientific knowledge is controlled experimentation, but at the same time it does involve systematic methods with a deep concern about issues of reliability and validity. In interviewing, for example, questions are refined and changed as the work proceeds, with "midcourse correction" being part and parcel of field research. "The interpretation of the more improvisational ethnographic approach as a complete absence of method may reflect the intentional unobtrusiveness of ethnographic inquiry" (Forsythe, 1999, p. 131).

To find out what people do, all you have to do is ask them. "Because the uninitiated see only the fieldworker's interaction with her respondents and do not see the analytical expertise being deployed, they may assume that they already have the skills to carry out ethnographic fieldwork" (Forsythe, 1999, p. 131). Ethnographic interviews are what domain practitioners see when ethnographers do their thing; they do *not* see the selectivity of question answering and observation and processes of inferential data analyses that underlie the data collection procedures. Also, ethnographers do not take what practitioners say at face value. A transcript of an interview is data, not results. Think-aloud protocols and cognitive walk-throughs, often taken as basic data in cognitive science studies of problem solving, are not treated by ethnographers as prima facie valid data about behavioral patterns. To make this point, Forsythe gave an example of an expert neurologist's reconstruction of a typical doctor–patient dialog concerning headaches. The neurologist's reconstruction departs from the reality of actual doctor–patient dialogs in significant ways, including the omission of the meanings conveyed in nonverbal cues, the vivid and emotional imagery used by patients to describe symptoms, and other key features. Because verbal reports are partial, and sometimes incorrect, ethnographers also engage in extensive observation, sometimes spanning months or even years.

Behavioral and organizational patterns exist "out there." Research is just a matter of looking and listening to detect the patterns. "To imagine that behavioral patterns become visible and self-explanatory in a videotape is analogous to believing that a photograph reveals the diagnosis of a patient's illness … what this common misconception fails to grasp is the selectivity and interpretation that goes into the process of gathering careful ethnographic data, writing useful field notes, and analyzing the data in an appropriate and systematic way" (Forsythe, 1999, p. 132; see also Sanjek, 1990). Forsythe told the story of a project in which she tape-recorded hospital work rounds, with the resulting transcript being a largely undecipherable babble. In contrast, her typed field notes were rich with information about tacit hospital practices. Upon seeing this, a physician blithely asserted that the ethnographer was merely a "better sort of tape recorder," failing to realize the skillful observation and analysis that went into the creation of the field notes—work that was invisible to the hospital staff.

Forsythe (1999) cited a number of studies of how "do-it-yourself ethnography" goes wrong, especially when the ethnography consists solely of short periods of observation and a mere handful of interviews. The researchers fail to study individual workers over time and in different settings; they do not look for disparities and do not compare what workers say about each other with what they do. According to Forsythe, in domains of work in which superficial ethnography has been conducted, both domain practitioners and informaticians hold a view that equates research with experimentation and analysis with quantification. They take their own expertise seriously but believe that good ethnographic research can be conducted by amateurs, in some cases after having simply read one or two articles about ethnographic methodology. "Researchers [have] no way of knowing whether they [had] really understood anything of their informants' world view or simply [have] projected then 'discovered' their own assumptions in the data" (p. 126).

In Forsythe's experience in the application of ethnography to software systems design, technologists also commonly hold a view that equates research with experimentation and analysis with quantification. This sets the stage for a clash of worldviews.

> [Although] designers welcome ethnographic insights into users' assumptions and expectations [they are] less happy when the ethnographic gaze is turned on them ... designers consistently discount those aspects of their own work that involves social interactions or maintenance activities, such as teaching, planning, discussion at meetings, reading and sending email, or backing up their computers. ... They dismiss these tasks as "pseudowork." Such activities were not included when I asked people to describe their work ... their "real" work was the technical job of system building, which they saw as restricted to sitting in front of a monitor and writing computer code ... this deletion [of social phenomena] is carried over into system design. (pp. 142–143)

It is not surprising then that do-it-yourself ethnography can culminate in the design of information systems that do not serve the real needs of users.

We can contrast this with Ross's (1995) survey-based study of flight strips in Australia, an example of strong ethnography. Surveys are sometimes derided by qualitative researchers, because surveys can risk imposing the researcher's understanding of the work onto the data. The survey results Ross gathered included respondent commentaries, and these were analyzed, coded, and categorized but then recategorized from multiple perspectives until the masses of context-specific controller remarks began to form sensible, generalizable themes that could meaningfully speak to designers. Ross moved down from conceptual descriptions of controller work and up again from the context-specific details. In line with characterizations of epistemological analysis through abstraction hierarchies (Hollnagel, Pedersen, & Rasmussen, 1981; Xiao & Vicente, 2000; see chapter 8), each step from the bottom up is more abstract than the previous one; each is cast less in domain-bound terms and more in concept-dependent terms than the one before.

Our example from Ross (1995) concerns domain-specific controller activities such as "entering a pilot report" and "composing a flight plan amendment." These low-level, context-specific activities are not without semantic load. With Ross's data, however, readers can question what informs otherwise taken-for-granted events such as "entering" a pilot report. What does a "pilot report" mean for the controller in a particular context (e.g., weather related), and what does "entering" a report mean for the controller's ability to manage other traffic issues in the near future (e.g., avoiding sending aircraft into severe turbulence)? Although permitting a finer grained analysis of apparently basic tasks, Ross's data also support a higher order analysis. "Entering a report" could be thought of as a transformation or translation of information that could be grouped under a label "coding," together with other information strategies. Part of the coding used in controller reports is symbolic in that it uses highly condensed markings on flight strips (red underlining, black circles) to represent for controllers what is going on. The highly intricate nature of even one flight (where it crosses versus where it had planned to cross a sector boundary, what height it will be leaving when, whether it has yet contacted another frequency, etc.) can be collapsed by simple symbolic notation—one line or circle around a code on the strip that stands for a complex, multidimensional state that other controllers can easily recognize. Unable to keep all the details of what a flight would do in their head, the controller compresses complexity by letting one symbol stand for complex concepts and inter-relationships, some even temporal.

Similarly, "recognizing a symbol for a handoff" (on a flight strip), while allowing further unpacking (e.g., What do you mean by "recognize"?), is an instance of a tactic that transforms information. This in turn represents a larger controller competency of "decoding," which is also part of a strategy to use symbolic notation to collapse complexity. From "recognizing a symbol for a handoff" to the collapsing of complexity, there are four steps, each more abstract and less couched in domain terms than the one before. Inspired by Ross's analysis, Dekker and Nyce surmised that controllers rely on flight strips for collapsing complexity, supporting coordination, and anticipating dynamics. All of these make preplanning, continuous adapting, and replanning possible.

Whatever designers want to build, they will have to take into account how controllers use their artifact(s) to help them deal with complexity, to anticipate dynamic futures, and to support their coordination with other controllers. These three high-level categories of controller flight strip work derived from Ross (1995) could tell designers how air traffic controllers have developed strategies for dealing with the communication of complexity to other controllers and for predicting workload and planning future work. Flight strips play a central role, but the research account is written up so that status quo does not preempt any number of alternatives: tools other than flight strips could conceivably help controllers deal with complexity, dynamics, and coordination issues. The categories listed previously are in a language that developers can begin to look at as a designable future.

These (no longer so large) jumps to the highest level of abstraction identify the role the flight strip has in making sense of workplace and task complexity; they are not so much a leap of faith any longer, because the various layers of abstraction in between can be tracked. At each step, alternative interpretations are always possible. This is why strong ethnography does not always lead to a definitive analytic or descriptive statement (Batteau, 2001). The main criterion by which we should judge results and interpretation is not so much accuracy as plausibility: whether these statements make sense given what the literature and other fieldworkers have had to say about the same issue. This helps explain the continuous, cyclical nature of ethnographic analysis: reinterpreting results that have been interpreted once already and gradually developing and confirming an explanation of why flight strips help controllers know what is going on—an explanation derived from a researcher's evolving understanding of his or her informants' work and their world.

> Qualitative research … can claim legitimacy because of its authentic encounters with the field where people actually carry out the work. Such research can speak meaningfully to design issues because it allows users to express their preferences and choices. [However] when communicating qualitative research results, designers must not be given a license to equate (or confuse) what informants say with the results of qualitative analysis. (Dekker & Nyce, 2004, p. 1636)

> The study takes shape as the work proceeds. People are such surprising creatures that it is impossible to know what may be of interest in a research setting before the work is done … unlike an experiment interesting material can and should be explored when it is encountered. … [Furthermore] testing is not "user testing" in a laboratory but careful study of what happens after the installation of the prototype into a setting where the real users of the system can use it … it is useful to

follow an ethnographic study with a quantitative study focusing on particular questions. ... A good qualitative study provides "ecological validity" to a quantitative study, giving wider latitude for interpreting numerical data. (Nardi, 1997, p. 362)

Strong Ethnography and Technology Design

Strong ethnography was also discussed by Robert Anderson (1994) and Jeanette Blomberg et al. (1993), who focused on the role of ethnography in the establishment of requirements for the design of complex information systems. Ethnographic methodology became a topic of interest on the part of system developers in the early 1990s. This was because software engineering had encountered a situation in which "formal methods" of requirements specification seemed inadequate to capture the orientations, understandings, and needs of the end users (e.g., Luff, Heath, & Greatbach, 1992). Ethnographic methods came to be regarded as data collection methods that could be used to capture end-user needs and working knowledge. Indeed, ethnographic methods of observing and interviewing came to be widely used in software and systems design (Forsythe, 1993, 1999; Hughes & King, 1992; Nyce & Lowgren, 1995).

Blomberg et al. (1993) listed some ways in which ethnographic research is pertinent to design:

1. Ethnographic methods yield rich descriptions of the work and the workplace and are necessary for designers so that they can understand the work.
2. Ethnographic methods yield rich descriptions of the work and the workplace and help one envision how the new technologies will shape the work.
3. The ethnographic approach helps one avoid the trap of Designer-Centered Design, so the designer's worldview is not imposed on the users.
4. Understanding the work can identify new work opportunities and refine the designs.
5. Ethnographic work in context (i.e., interviewing, participant observation, perspective taking) supports mutual understanding on the part of designers and workers, providing workers with scaffolding to help them envision new work possibilities for radically new technologies.
6. Ethnographic study and analysis is necessary because work is influenced by its broader context, and traditional methods and analyses (i.e., the performance of the one person–one machine dyad) are limited.

In regard to this latter rationale, Anderson (1994, p. 153) argued, the computer-supported cooperative work and human–computer interaction communities had misconstrued the character of ethnography.

This is not to say that getting to know users and their knowledge and practices is unnecessary or irrelevant or that observational fieldwork and impressionistic reportage can be of no value ... far from it! It is simply that you do not need ethnography to do that; just a minimal competency in interactive skills, a willingness to spend time, and a fair amount of patience ... it is difficult, skillful, and requires certain orders of talents that most "system people" do not possess. (pp. 155, 160)

Blomberg et al. (1993, p. 146) provided a roster of limitations of some of the traditional methods used to support design, especially methods such as surveys and focus groups:

1. Traditional methods have the limitation of being conducted away from the context of work. Thus, "the quality of the information is limited by the designer's ability to represent the concept in relation to some imagined workplace and the users' ability to envision themselves using the product."
2. Traditional approaches are technology driven: "The focus is on obtaining answers to specific questions about the acceptability of a particular technology concept."
3. Traditional approaches do not involve users as true collaborations in design and the evolution of designs. "Traditional approaches depend on the users' ability to verbalize their needs or expose design inadequacies in isolated tests." Thus, ethnography places emphasis on what it calls "Participatory Design" (Blomberg et al., 1993).

In Anderson's (1994) description of strong ethnography, and fitting with other discussions of strong ethnography, ethnography is primarily a method of analysis, not a method of data collection. "Data, observations, stories are important only as means to working through and working out the analytic possibilities" (p. 155). The implication is that software engineers might engage in ethnographic fieldwork to describe organizations and work without ever actually conducting "analytic ethnography" found in the social sciences. Ethnography is much more than "typed up, spell-checked, anonymized, field notes" (p. 158) or a description of behavioral episodes; it is a search for deeper patterns and regularities.

The search for patterns, according to Anderson, often involves the use of analogy. Anderson illustrated this in an exercise comparing software customization with a traditional mode of marriage. Based on a study by Mackay (1990), customization involves three participant roles: systems programmers, end users, and "mediators"— individuals who broker between the creators of customizations and others who come to use the customizations. On the analogy to marriage, this process of brokering is understood as the development of mutual obligations for gift giving, the exchange or flow of value in which "individuals gain a sense of self-esteem, the knowledge that others respect their technical competence, the chance to solve tricky problems, all in exchange for creating and sharing customizations" (p. 164). This aspect of software development and use might be overlooked without considering the work activity from some alternative perspective—"decentering of the familiar through its juxtaposition with the bizarre"—such as the comparison of software customization to marriage brokering. (Another example of such analytical decentering is in Latour [1992].)

> What ethnography may offer designers … is not just a detailed description of work routines and daily life with which to fix the features of the design, but an opportunity to open up the overall problem–solution frame of reference. … Seeking to evaluate practices against a single or narrow range of formal criteria may cause designers to miss much of what is vital to the lived work of the technology in use. Hence, designers' solutions may even make things worse not better. It may be suggested, for instance, that when more closely inspected, apparent inefficiencies usually turn out to be not problems but precisely shaped (and therefore effective) solutions to exigencies to which individuals in a working order are subject. In other words, the contribution that ethnography may make is to enable designers to question the taken-for-granted assumptions embedded in the conventional problem–solution design framework … apparently inefficient and unproductive behavior … is often exquisitely designed for the practicalities of organizational life with which individuals have to deal. A decontextualized, globalized approach to determining and assessing the fit of means to ends, effort to outcome, behavior to goals, would in all likelihood be blind to this. (Anderson, 1994, p. 170)

Anderson gave a number of examples of apparently inefficient social behaviors that workers use to "keep their organization at bay" and cope with the complexity and unpredictability of work, such as playing phone tag when e-mail would do or using ploys such as, "It was on my desktop just now ... come back a bit later and I will have found it." Anderson contrasted such various forms of coping with the software tools that are created on the theory that they would make work more efficient: work-flow tools, collaborative calendar systems, document management systems—by which designers end up forcing the work to take very different directions. The tools prevent workers from exploiting time by managing when documents arrive and jug-gling schedules, which help workers preserve some degree of local order. Tools that override the "natural viscosity of events" wind up creating "organizational amnesia with ever diminishing structural half-lives" (p. 175).

In these discussions of strong ethnography, we get a feel for the intended purposes of ethnographic methods, which go beyond methodological strictures concerning methods of observing and interviewing to deeper issues about understanding work. As well as sharing this methodological stance on the value of field research, which we will illustrate further in this chapter, the communities of practice we group in this chapter share certain points of view on other matters. These involve three communi-ties of practice that have a shared approach to methodology, an overlapping focus, and a shared agenda. These are as follows:

- Sociotechnics,
- the "situated cognition" community of practice,
- the "distributed cognition" community of practice,
- the Sociology of Scientific Knowledge, and
- the Sociology of the Professions.

Sociotechnics

In chapter 2 we discussed the work of the Industrial Fatigue Research Board in the United Kingdom and its important contributions to industrial psychology in the years following World War I. Another important contribution, made in the 1940s, to industrial-organizational psychology in the United Kingdom was work conducted by the Tavistock Institute of Social Relations, with the support of the Human Factors Panel of the Committee on Industrial Productivity and the Medical Research Council. A goal was to disseminate new approaches to social organization, but the Tavistock activities included a series of studies of how social and technological factors interact to influence work and productivity.

A classic study by Trist and Bamforth (1951) was subtitled "Social and Technological Content of the Work System," and it is from that that we derive our current notion of the "sociotechnical system" (as in Vicente, 1999). Trist and Bamforth examined how psychological factors, social factors, and legacy work methods interacted with new technology to fundamentally change the work of coal miners. The method of study that Trist and Bamforth used was, we would say today, a combination of participant observation with a multiyear series of in-depth, semistructured interviews with a group of informants, in this case interviews with 20 experienced miners over a period of about 2 years. This is essentially the same as many modern studies in the ethnography of work, the sociology of work, or CTA.

In the traditional method ("hand-got mining"), miners worked as teams with designated roles and skill sets (with such names as "hewer" and "trammer"). Mining was regarded as a craft. Coal seams could be thin, hard, or uneven. Significant expertise and experience were involved in perceiving seams and knowing for a given type of seam how to proceed in mining it. The teams operated in a system of "responsible autonomy" that contributed to work quality and lifestyle (for the individual), cohesion (at the team level), and organization (at the level of management). When powered machines for cutting large seams of coal and conveying the coal to the surface ("long-wall mining") came into use, the mining methods changed completely. The old crafts and skills were gone. Rather than working in primary pairs, the primary work group was larger and more spread out. The opportunity for miners to work together and communicate directly with one another was severely restricted; roles were fractionated. Workers were functionally tied but socially separated. The way work shifts were composed and coordinated changed completely, and new kinds of problems emerged for management (e.g., greater levels of external supervision, a totally new scheme for payment of miners).

> The associated characteristics of mechanized complexity, and of largeness as regards the scale of the primary production unit, created a situation in which it was impossible for the method to develop as a technological system without bringing into existence a work relationship structure radically different from that associated with hand-got procedures. The artisan type of pair, composed of the skilled man and his mate, assisted by one or more labourers, was out of keeping with a model for the type of work group required. Need arose for a unit more of the size and differentiated complexity of a small factory department. A structure of intermediate social magnitude began therefore to emerge. (Trist & Bamforth, 1951, p. 9)

The new mining technology involved a new method, and this created a disconnect in that new roles segregated people (workers were socially isolated by being spread out along the long wall), and new shift work methods segregated entire groups (back shifters are either coming from or going to work in the evening and so are segregated from normal community activities during the entire week). New forms of disputes and resentments broke out, with management perceiving a lack of support from the miners and miners feeling they were being tricked and driven by management.

Nearly every page in the Trist and Bamforth report carries a passage that can be applied with full force today, in reference to the computerized workplace rather than to coal mining. In the following series of passages, we bracketed the references to mining and invite the reader to mentally insert a reference to any modern sociotechnical domain.

> The small group capable of responsible autonomy, and able to vary its work pace in correspondence with changing conditions, would appear to be the type of social structure ideally adapted to the [underground] situation. It is instructive that the traditional work systems, evolved from the experience of successive generations, should have been formed on a group with these attributes. (p. 7)

In the pre-mechanized pattern, the pair-based primaries [hewer–trammer teams] and the large relatively undifferentiated collectivities [group action as, for instance, in a mining danger or accident] composed a dynamically interrelated system that permitted an enduring social balance. (p. 8)

The [long-wall mining] method will be regarded as a technological system, expressive of the prevailing outlook of mass-production engineering as a social structure consisting of the occupational roles that have been institutionalized in its use. These interactive technological and sociological patterns will be assumed to exist as forces having psychological effects in the life-space of the worker. (p. 5)

The consequence was a conflict between the demands of the new situation and the resources available from past experience. (p. 10)

The relationship between the various aspects ... the social and the psychological, can be understood only in terms of the detailed engineering facts and of the way the technological system, as a whole behaves. (pp. 10–11)

Occupational roles express the relationship between a production process and the social organization of the group. In one direction, they are related to tasks, which are related to each other; in the other, to people, who are also related to each other ... roles are related to their component tasks [forming] interrelated technological and social structures. (p. 14)

Bad conditions tend to instigate bad work. When they occur, the smooth sequence of tasks is more likely to be disturbed by faulty performance. Bad work can, and does, arise when conditions are good; from persona shortcomings and social tensions, in themselves independent of bad conditions ... but difficulties are more readily and more conveniently expressed when the additional difficulty and excuse of bad conditions is also present. The result is a tendency for circular causal processes of a disruptive character to be touched off. ... The system is therefore always to some extent working against the threat of its own breakdown, so that tension and anxiety are created. (p. 21)

The [mining] skill of attending to [underground] conditions, and of maintaining a high level of performance when difficulties arise, is developed only as a result of several years of experience. ... A work-system basically appropriate to the [underground] situation requires to have built into its organization the findings of this experience. (p. 23)

The badness of both the group and the individual are exclusively effects of the system that the group is compelled to operate without having the power to change. (p. 33)

The benefits [of increased mine productivity] are not realized in the work activities of the group. They lie outside the work system, which is tolerated as a means to external ends [i.e., wages] rather than accepted also as an end in itself, worthy of whole-hearted pursuit in virtue of the internal satisfactions it affords. (p. 33)

The Trist and Bamforth study is a clear case of the consequences of mechanization and mass production.

It was the introduction of machines that caused the appearance of a new order, changing the scale to mass production and bringing fractionation of tasks, extension of sequence, role and shift segregation, small group disorganization, and inter-group dependence. (p. 37)

However, Trist and Bamforth included some more general guidance that is directly pertinent to team cognitive work and CTA. For good work, the primary work groups (or teams) must have responsible autonomy, satisfying tasks or partial tasks to the work as a whole, and some scope for flexibility in the work and its pace. Another salient aspect of the Tavistock studies of the 1950s was the involvement of the workers in assessing the problems caused by new technologies and new work methods and creating solutions to the problems' causes. This was precedent for "Participatory Design" (also known as "participatory ergonomics") and for greater worker involvement in organizational decision making.

The notions stemming from the Tavistock studies led to an emerging community of practice, (largely in North American and Scandinavia) that is referred to as "Sociotechnics" (Applebaum, 1997; Clegg et al., 1997), a sociological approach to the design of work systems, and especially organizations (Davis, 1982). It is no accident that this phrase was coined, in the United Kingdom, because the term *psychotechnics* was used to name the earliest form of industrial psychology, which had flourished in Europe for decades (see chapter 2).

The goal of Sociotechnics is to create new work systems that optimize the organization's goals and also the goals, motivation, and welfare of the workers. This is accomplished by creating "self-regulating work groups" rather than by building new technologies and then forcing the humans to adapt. This approach has been put to use by organizations including Amoco and General Electric (Cummings, 1994; Cummings & Worley, 1993). Classic studies in this area, including studies in which researchers empirically and functionally analyzed literally hundreds of businesses and organizations, are summarized in Applebaum (1997).

Sociotechnics is concerned with optimizing the capacity of organizations to achieve their goals, but it is also concerned with the social and social-psychological aspects of work, including worker motivation and social support. Sociotechnicians have discussed a number of principles or checklist considerations for the design of organizations that are effective and adaptive and yet at the same time compatible with sociological and social-psychological considerations in organizational design (Applebaum, 1997; Badham, Clegg, & Wall, 2000; Carayon & Smith, 2000; Cherns, 1976, 1987; Clegg, 2000; Clegg et al., 1997; Klein, 1994; Thorsrud, 1972).

Engage workers in constructive participation. This will support adaptation and will leverage the creativity of the workers.

Impose minimal critical specification of tasks. It is important to prevent rigid task specifications from promoting premature closure of options and paths to goals. "Users, as local experts, should be allowed to solve their own problems and develop their own methods of working" (Clegg, 2000, p. 472).

Support "equifinality," in which there are multiple paths to the same goal. Together with the principle of task specification, this principle resonates with an idea from Work Analysis (chapter 10) that in complex cognitive systems, people do not conduct tasks but rather engage in context-sensitive, knowledge-driven choice among activities.

> A careful observer of people in their work situation will learn how people contrive to get the job done in spite of the rules. As the railwaymen in Britain have demonstrated, the whole system can be brought to a grinding halt by "working to the rules." Many of the rules are there to provide protection when things go wrong for the man who imposed them; strictly applied, they totally inhibit adaptation or even effective action. (Cherns, 1987, p. 155)

Control the variances close to their point of origin. When there is some unexpected event, breakdown, failure, or error, the work system should enable the individuals to evaluate their own work and learn from their mistakes.

> The advantages [of variants control] are: motivational (people like to have control over the problems they face); cognitive (people learn to perform better through exerting control and by anticipating and solving problems); logistical (it is quicker to solve a problem locally than to wait for an "expert" to visit); and resource-based (the company can use the "experts" elsewhere). (Clegg, 2000, p. 471)

Locate the responsibility for coordination with those who must remain coordinated. The work system should not departmentalize the work so as to prohibit the sharing of knowledge and experience.

Currently, Sociotechnics offers many dozens of principles of work and work design (Clegg, 2000, lists about 40 of them) that entail guidance in deciding when teamwork would serve better than individual work (a checklist having 20 entries is in Clegg, 2000), conditions for successful teamworking (Clegg, 2000, lists 15), and criteria for the design or selection of information technology in support of new work methods (Clegg, 2000, lists 15). Taken together, these checklists show that Sociotechnics advocates a process that is referred to by participants in other communities of practice as Work-Centered Design, Goal-Oriented Design, and Use-Centered Design. As the following passage shows, the descriptions offered in the Sociotechnics literature are nearly identical to similar presentations in the literature in such communities of practice as Cognitive Systems Engineering:

> The information system should be designed after the goals of a system have been determined, and in parallel with the work organization. The system components should be consistent with one another. The information should support those who need to take action. ... The information should be available to the appropriate person at the right time and in a usable format. (Clegg, 2000, p. 470)

Within Sociotechnics, no less than in other communities of practice, this stance serves as part of the foundational justification for the empirical approach—a fundamental dependence on CTA, we would say.

The Sociotechnics literature is chock full of case studies in work system design that illustrate its principles and approach. For example, Ainger (1990) developed a shop floor production scheduling system for use in small-batch manufacturing. Rather than have the computers work out the "optimum" production schedule, the operators (with computer support) were responsible for making scheduling decisions. The reasoning was that the production system was highly variable and uncertain. Since many automated scheduling systems are based on assumptions and data that quickly become out of date, the design philosophy was that the operators should draw on their local knowledge updated in real time. The underlying values were that the operators are the experts in the system and that they need computers as tools to support them in their work.

The Sociotechnics literature also includes cases that parallel the "best practice" in human factors and Cognitive Systems Engineering. Specifically, the literature shows the benefit of basing designs for new technologies and new work systems on a foundation of empirical evidence from CTA (in this case, a largely ethnographic approach). Some refer to this as User-Centered Design, and some refer to it as Participatory Design, the key idea being the involvement of end users in the design process. Here is one example, a case where a manager might have made decisions for innovation based on presuppositions about worker needs and knowledge of existing technologies but instead took an empirical approach, with good result:

> A confectionery company wished to improve the quality and speed of information flow from its customers. The company manufactured and delivered a range of products for sale in a wide range of independent retail outlets. Unfortunately, it experienced significant delays and inaccuracies in the feedback of information from the shops via its drivers. The national sales manager thought a system involving the use of hand-held computers by the drivers would improve speed and accuracy. However, rather than simply select the apparent best option from a range of available technical products, he first considered how the whole system should work. Thus, he worked with drivers, depot managers, members of his area sales teams, IT specialists, and staff from accounts and sales administration at the head office to design how the work would be organized. For example, his team considered whether the drivers would work in a delivery role only, or as salespeople, or as franchise holders. He wanted to make these choices before selecting the technical system he would purchase, in part because these organizational choices (for how the system would work) would affect what functionality should be built into the technical systems. (Clegg, 2000, p. 466)

In chapter 15 we will point out additional ways in which the views held within this community of practice dovetail with views of other perspectives, including Work Analysis, Cognitive Systems Engineering, and human factors.

Situated Cognition

We also place under the sociology and ethnography umbrella the viewpoint or community of practice called "situated cognition," which emerged in ethnography and spread to computer science (see Clancey, 1993, 1997; Cole, Engeström, & Vasquez, 1997; Nardi, 1997; Salomon, 1993). This view holds that cognitive processes cannot be analyzed in isolation from their contexts of learning and use. Cognition is, invariably, situated within a given context of learning and use and cannot be analyzed without considerations of this context (e.g., Brown, Collins, & Duguid, 1989; Cole et al., 1997; Lave, 1988; Nardi, 1997; Resnick, Levine, & Teasley, 1996; Salomon, 1993; Suchman, 1987; Woolgar, 1987; Wortham, 2001).

> Learning is neither wholly subjective nor fully encompassed in social interaction, and it is not constituted separately from the social world. ... This recommends a de-centered view of the locus and meaning of learning, in which learning is recognized as a social phenomenon. (Lave, 1993, p. 64)

The Background of Situated Theory

Within psychology, a source of the situated cognition notion is held to be the classic work of Sir Frederic Bartlett (1932), in which he proposed that learning is a social process (see Weldon, 2001). Another early treatment of the social aspects of remembering is sociologist Émil Durkheim's (1915) discussion of cultural memory (i.e., religion as a repository of belief systems and knowledge), arguing (among other things) that logic has its origins in human understanding of social groupings and categories. In other words, the categories of individual thought have their origins in society and culture.

Bartlett began the experimental study of remembering with a reaction to the work of pioneer Herrmann Ebbinghaus (1885), which reported experiments on the memorization of lists of syllables. Bartlett questioned whether such highly controlled and artificial experiments could provide a true window to remembering and the ways in which remembering interacts with other processes such as perception and imagination. Bartlett's studies of how people of different cultures frame and remember stories showed clearly that culture and society provide the individual with schemas that are used in remembering and in the understanding of events. Bartlett (1932) cited the example of African herdsmen who could remember details of cattle transactions over spans of years. Culture and society also shape the ways in which memory manifests itself. Rogoff and Mistry (1985) cited the example of Mayan children who appear to have poor storytelling recall when in fact the apparent poor recall is due to the fact that Mayan culture is one in which children are not to speak freely to adults.

The example of the African herdsmen can be linked to the topic of expert knowledge and organization (see chapter 8). That example and the example of the Mayan children also involve moving beyond the controlled laboratory into methodologies from anthropology and sociology. The literature on social cognition makes frequent reference to the ideas of Lev Vygotsky (1962).

> Vygotsky's social learning theory has been adopted, developed, and modified in many sociocultural approaches to cognition that have taken inspiration from him, including "activity theory" and theories of "situated learning." In general, the important assumption of these cultural-historical perspectives is that there is interdependency among the individual, activity, society, culture, and their respective histories, and they are mutually constituted in ongoing processes. Therefore, the individual cannot be studied in isolation because to do so would separate these component processes from their normal integrated functioning. (Weldon, 2001, pp. 74–75)

Situated Theory Versus Information Processing Theory Versus Behaviorism

For decades, psychology as a whole has been focused on the information processing metaphor and its assumption that cognition was completely covered by notions of symbol manipulation and memory storage within individuals (see Gardner, 1985), setting aside considerations of such things as emotion, social relations, and cultural influences. Within cognitive science and computer science, the proposal of situated cognition was the result of a growing dissatisfaction with this traditional cognitive psychology approach. Researchers became especially dissatisfied when attempting to reconcile the results of studies of real-world problem solving in natural field-based settings with the traditional problem-solving theories of the cognitive sciences (e.g., problem space theory; Newell & Simon, 1972).

> If one relegates all of cognition to internal mental processes, then one is required to pack all the explanatory machinery of cognition into the individual mind as well, leading to misidentification of the boundaries of the cognitive system, and the overattribution to the individual mind alone all of the processes that give rise to intelligent behavior. (Weldon, 2001, p. 76)

The academic cognitive psychology approach adopts an essentially Cartesian position by considering knowledge as an abstract entity that represents "the world outside" of the human mind (Lave, 1988). This view can be traced to the origins of modern cognitive psychology, itself a reaction against behaviorist psychology. The naive behaviorist paradigm did not consider mentalistic phenomena to play any causal role in behavior and instead relied solely on the environment (operant and respondent conditioning) as the causal agent. Naive behaviorism, attributed to John Watson, went so far as to explain away mental phenomena (e.g., thinking is merely "subvocal" speech) and insisted that mentalism has no place in a scientific psychology. So-called radical behaviorism of B. F. Skinner acknowledged the occurrence of mental phenomena but saw them as just one more thing to be explained in terms of such notions as reinforcement and stimulus-response association. Neither naive behaviorism nor radical behaviorism was willing to ascribe a causal (explanatory) role to mental events. (The literature on this is, of course, extensive. A short counter-argument to the behaviorist view is presented in Hoffman [1979].)

By contrast, the cognitive paradigm has relied heavily on mentalistic phenomena in causal explanations. As we pointed out in discussing the origins of Cognitive Systems Engineering and its reaction against "traditional" human factors, new emerging paradigms are typically highly antagonistic to the established paradigm paradigms (Kuhn, 1977). Thus, one of the situated theorist's criticisms of the cognitive paradigm is that the legacy of behaviorist psychology has caused cognitive theorists to become *overly* individualistic and mentalistic in their focus, resulting in theories that treat the environment as if it is only acted upon rather than interacting with the individual. For example, Lave (1988) highlighted a taken-for-granted conceptualization in the cognitive sciences of a divide between "cognitive processes and the settings and activities of which they are part" (p. 76).

Hutchins (1995a) approached this matter in his discussion of a parable offered by Simon (1981) to demonstrate the cost of assuming that all resources for problem solving are solely mentalistic in origin:

> As we watch the complicated movements of an ant on a beach, we may be tempted to attribute to the ant some complicated program for constructing the path taken. In fact, Simon says, that trajectory tells us more about the beach than about the ant. (p. 169)

Hutchins described how well-worn paths and chemical trails created over time by the ant colony effectively guide the individual ant to food stores. Thus, many of the resources for ant cognition during navigation lie not in the individual ant's head but in its environment. By contrast, the notion proposed in traditional cognitive theories is that the cognitive resources required for problem solving are carried around in the head like a box of tools that can be unpacked when needed so that the individual can act upon the world. Proponents of situated theories present evidence suggesting that the moment-to-moment relations between individuals and the sociocultural context of their lives structure problem-solving behavior as much as any mentalistic tools formulated prior to the problem.

Here we see an interesting pendulum swing, in which a reaction against cognitive psychology has resulted in a view that is reminiscent of radical behaviorism, emphasizing as it does the role of the environment while acknowledging the occurrence of mental phenomena.

The assertion within the situated cognition approach is that not all behavior is deliberately coordinated or structured using preformulated mental representations (Lave, 1988; Sierhuis, 2001; Suchman, 1987, 1988). To elaborate, Suchman (1987) wrote,

> The circumstances of our actions are never fully anticipated and are continuously changing around us. As a consequence our actions, while systematic, are never planned in the strong sense that cognitive science would have it. (p. viii)

Suchman asserted that many problems are solved "on the hoof" and use resources that are inherent in the problem context. In contrast to notions that problem-solving behaviors are structured solely by preformulated mental representations, such as plans (cf. Miller, Galanter, & Pribram, 1960), situated cognition theorists advocate a view that such representations are "best viewed as a weak resource for what is primarily ad hoc activity [i.e., problem solving]" (Suchman, 1987, p. ix).

> Probably the most common approach is what might be called a *cognition plus* view. According to this view, researchers [studying] cognitive processing, representations, memory, and problem solving, and cognitive theory should now attend to other factors as well ... researchers should extend the scope ... to include everyday activity and social interaction ... social factors become conditions whose effects on individual cognition are then explored. But cognition ... is not itself the subject of reconceptualization in social terms. A proponent of this position is likely to argue that a person thinking alone in a forest is not engaged in social cognition. The *interpretive view* locates situatedness in the use of language and/or social interaction ... the first position postulates a fixed Cartesian external world in which words have fixed referential meaning and in which rational agents ("scientists" or "experts"), devoid (ideally) of feelings or interests, are engaged in linear communication of "information" without integral relations of power and control (Rommetveit, 1987). In the interpretive view, meaning is negotiated, the use of language is a social activity rather than a matter of individual transmission of information, and situated cognition is always interest-relative. (Lave, 1993, p. 66)

Thus, argued Lave, and others, neither cognition nor the social world can be "bracketed off" as objects of study. "Learning, thinking, and knowing are relations among people engaged in activity in, with, and arising from the socially and culturally structured world" (Lave, 1993, p. 67). This leads ethnographers to emphasize the study of apprenticeship activities—the interactions of "newcomers" and "old-timers"—rather than the study of learning as conceived by psychologists (e.g., Becker, 1972; Jordan, 1989; Lave & Wenger, 1991; Willis, 1977). Using interviews and observational methods, ethnographers study how "evaluation of apprentices' progress is intrinsic to their participation in ongoing work practices. Hence, apprenticeship usually involves no external tests and little praise or blame, progress being visible to the learner and others in the process of work itself ... access for the apprentice to ongoing work and participation in that work are important conditions for learning" (Lave, 1993, p. 68).

In addition to blurring the distinction between cognition and social aspects of work, the literature of ethnography blurs another distinction. Bruno Latour (1992) described how even mundane objects, such as locks, hinges, and seat belts, cannot be adequately described in terms of their functions without considering social context: "Every time you want to know what a human does, simply imagine what other humans ... would have to do were this character not present" (p. 229). Fitting with Situated Theory and distributed cognition, Latour attempted to collapse the sociology–technology dichotomy, referring to the "ascriptions" of artifacts—what psychologists would refer to as designed-in affordances. Perhaps Latour's clearest example is the "Berlin key," a key with groves at both ends of the shank. It cannot be removed from the lock once it is unlocked. Meant for use in front gates, it forces the key bearers to lock the gate behind them.

A final strong claim of Situated Theory that we note, a claim that gets at issues of methodology in the study of cognition, is that people possess tacit knowledge that cannot be articulated, that is, converted into descriptive form by inventorying facts, procedures, and rules. Situated Theory holds that tacit knowledge is not verbal and is coupled to perceptual-motor coordinations, including conceptualizations that are not enumerable into terms, propositions, or inferential rules. The reason for this is that "knowledge and skill develop in a process—and as an integral part of the process—of becoming like master practitioners within a community of practice" (Lave, 1993, p. 71).[1] This is the claim that CTA is limited because there exists a form of knowledge that cannot be verbalized "in principle" (see chapter 5, and also Crandall, Klein, & Hoffman, 2006).

Situated Cognition Versus Cognition in the Laboratory

Situated theorists have argued that the nature of cognition during problem solving in real-world settings is qualitatively different from that which occurs in the comparatively context-poor, artificial "puzzle-solving" laboratory settings typically employed in traditional or academic cognitive psychology (Lave, 1988; Suchman, 1987, 1988). Thus, the claim of Situated Theory is not just that the study of cognition or memory is incomplete unless it takes contextual factors into account by treating sociocultural influences as yet another independent variable to be controlled or manipulated. Rather, the claim is a stronger one: that theories of cognition are fundamentally flawed by the attempt to study and understand cognitive processes without simultaneously accounting for the social and historical influences that shape learning and collaborative activity. Lave (1993) presented a number of examples of ethnographic studies showing how apprenticeship takes on different forms and meanings in different domains and in different cultures (e.g., African crafts, Yucatese Mayan midwives). "Learning [is not just a process of] socially shared cognition that results in the internalization of knowledge by individuals, [but a] process of becoming a member of a sustained community of practice. Developing an identity as a member of a community and becoming knowledgeably skillful are part of the same process, with the former motivating, shaping, and giving meaning to the latter" (Lave, 1993, p. 65).

Mary Weldon (2001) provided an example in her review of the recent work on cross-cultural cognition and cognitive styles (Nisbett, 2003). The studies involve bringing the social and cultural factors into the traditional laboratory, showing differences, for instance, in the recall and recognition memory for focal versus background features of scenes, between Japanese students and American students.

The approach (a) employs standard experimental methods and design; (b) uses the individual as the unit of analysis; (c) implies that cultural influences can be conceptualized and described within a traditional factorial structure, in which culture is independent from other factors; ... and (d) models cognition as an information processing system, within the individual. In this approach culture is simply added on as an additional factor in a factorial design and, as the logic of this approach goes, if culture is an important factor in cognitive functioning then it should produce at least a main effect, but hopefully an interaction. (Weldon, 2001, pp. 80–81)

Weldon (2001) described studies in which small groups had to collectively recall some material, in fact one of the short stories that Bartlett had used (other studies used a collaborative map reconstruction task). In such group remembering, one thing that might happen is group facilitation, whereby recall of part of the story by one group member might cue recall of other story elements by another member or trigger comments to the effect that the recalled story element was not quite correct. Another possibility is group interference, where recall of a story element by one individual may interfere with recall by another group member because the recalled material does not match up with the memory organization of other individuals. In comparing group recall versus recall by a "nominal group" (pooled recall by a set of individuals who did not participate as a group in the recall task), the findings showed this "collaborative inhibition" effect. (To rule out such possibilities as "social loafing" and timidity, the researchers had motivated the participants by offers of reward.) In another study, dyads were tasked with recalling words, and for each word in the to-be-recalled list, the dyad had to agree on a word associate that would be used as a recall cue. In this case, one in which the individuals engaged in shared memory encoding, the collaborative inhibition effect disappeared.

What these studies show is how memory phenomena and effects (interference, facilitation, encoding specificity, etc.) that originated in the study of individual learning and theories of individual memory could be discovered as operating within the group context and that activities of collaborative remembering can have significant and complex effects on what individuals do and do not recall.

The work on cross-cultural cognition and on social remembering is exciting and important. One might consider these avenues of study to be a culmination of ideas hearkening back to Sir Frederic Bartlett. But in the situated cognitive view, they do not go far enough in rethinking the nature of cognition or expanding the methods used to study cognition. Likewise, analyses of group problem solving in terms of information processing metaphors do not go far enough (see Hinsz, Tindale, & Volrath, 1977; Hutchins, 1990, 1995a). Weldon (2001) contrasted information processing lines of inquiry (calling them "conservative") with studies that have taken a more "adventurous" approach. For instance, Hutchins analyzed collaborative activity in terms of information processing metaphors but regarded sociocultural processes as constituting cognitive activity. Thus, ethnographic field study methods are used, and data take the form of descriptions of activities and dialogs.

Proponents of the situated cognition approach offer many examples of why one should define "the cognitive system" as persons acting in coordination with a social group to conduct activities using tools and practices that have evolved within a culture.

Case Study in Situated Cognition

Lave (1988) described a study involving the comparison of everyday math use with formal math learned in school. Lave posited that the objective of learning math in school is to formulate abstract mental representations of mathematical operations so as to allow for their general application in future problem scenarios. However, in her study of everyday math use by people attending a Weight Watchers program, Lave observed qualitative changes over time in the way foodstuffs were quantified to structure food preparation for dieting. In the early stage of the program, dieters were observed to use formal math as a method of measuring and quantifying their foodstuffs, including the use of measuring cups and spoons and weighing scales. However, this method required extra time and energy to prepare food. Most dieters were under time pressure to produce meals for their families and so the formal math method proved inconvenient. Lave observed that, over time, participants noticed how a given quantity of liquid would look or feel in a particular circumstance and thus contrived their own units of quantity to measure foodstuffs that were situated within their everyday experiences of food and that did not require recourse to traditional methods. For example, participants would pour liquid "up to just below the circle of blue flowers [on an everyday drinking vessel]" (p. 128) and also gained knowledge that a given number of swallows of liquid was equivalent to a given number of fluid ounces.

Thus, math activity in dieting became less an interpolation of formal math methods into the problem scenario and more an integration of the "structuring of quantitative relations into ongoing cooking activity" (p. 130). Scribner (1984) observed the use of "situated" metrics in a variety of domains: The cup is the canonical unit of measurement among Liberian rice farmers, the volume of a canoe is used to establish a scale by the expert boat builders in the Palawan Islands, bartenders use glass shape and position as memory cues, and dairy inventory workers use the "case stack" as a unit for counting.

Lave (1988) also proposed that the results of laboratory-based investigations of cognition typical of cognitive psychology have little relevance to cognition in the real world. It might be speculated that a laboratory investigation of math use during dieting would have been unlikely to include a consideration for the real-world issue of time pressure during meal preparation, and thus different conclusions might have been made about cognition in this instance. Lave argued that problem solving, such as in the dieting example, is always determined to some extent by multiple "structuring resources" inherent in real-world contexts and that these resources are not always present in the comparatively context-poor environment of the laboratory. Lave described an example of this phenomenon from her everyday life:

> I can read and knit. Sometimes the process of knitting gives shape to the reading. I might read while knitting a row, but wait to turn the page until the row is finished, or stop reading in order to pick a dropped stitch. At other times I read to the end of the page before starting a new row, knitting faster if the plot thickens, slightly tighter when it gets tense. Knitting projects look more promising if they don't require constant attention, hard-cover books appeal partly because their pages stay open better. Knitting is a structuring resource for the process of reading and reading provides structuring resources that give shape and punctuation to the process of knitting. They shape each other, but not necessarily equally. Usually one is the ongoing activity, the other is given shape more than it shapes the first. (1988, pp. 98–99)

From a situated cognition approach, problem-solving behaviors are not specified wholly by the problem-solving theories typical of cognitive psychology; a more holistic analysis of the activities by which problem solving is undertaken is required.

Distributed Cognition

Within the social and ethnographic perspectives, as in the Cognitive Systems Engineering perspective (see chapter 7), it has been argued that cognition in practice is not isolated in the minds of individuals but distributed across individuals and their context of work (e.g., Agnew, Ford, & Hayes, 1997; Hollan, Hutchins, & Kirsh, in press). As we described in the previous section, this is a core claim of the situated cognition view. Knowledge creation and other cognitive activities (e.g., remembering) are regarded as value-laden, social processes (see Weldon, 2001). It is argued that expertise is not a property of individuals but a social attribution that is context bound. Although highly similar in spirit to Situated Theory, the emphasis here is on collaborative work, both human–human and human–machine collaboration. (For a discussion of the implications of Situated Theory for organizational psychology and organizational change, see Clancey [1995].)

As we have explained, traditional cognitive psychology has been concerned primarily with the individual human, investigating how mental processes are used to structure the individual's behavior (Hutchins, 1995a). However, as Olson (1994) proposed, in collaborative work "the resources and constraints that affect cognitive activity have a very different profile than those associated with traditional models of individual cognition" (p. 991). Because the traditional cognitive psychology approach considers the unit of analysis as the individual, the locus of resources for problem solving is also considered to lie within the individual. However, the notion of distributed cognition directs the researcher to think outside of the "skin and skull" of the individual so as to consider how individuals working in groups solve problems collaboratively. Typical questions that researchers studying distributed cognition attempt to address are as follows (paraphrased from Hollan et al., in press):

- How are the cognitive processes normally associated with an individual mind implemented in a group of individuals?
- How do the cognitive properties of groups differ from the cognitive properties of the people who act in those groups?
- How are the cognitive properties of individual minds affected by participation in group activities?

Thus, in addition to the intramental processes considered by the traditional cognitive science approach, the distributed cognition approach acknowledges the role of a variety of extramental structures and processes in cognition (Wortham, 2001). Constituents of extramental structures and processes include the nature of social and communicative interactions within work groups, the sociohistorical context at large, and elements of the external, physical environment (e.g., external memory and reminding aids). As a consequence, some researchers studying collaborative work from a distributed cognition approach have proposed that work studies should employ a "work systems" perspective by considering the entire cognitive system as the unit of analysis, within which individual cognition is of interest to researchers but, in contrast to traditional cognitive science, is not *the* interest of researchers. Cognitive systems are considered to process information pertaining to real-world phenomena in a distributed manner, both across individuals within groups and across cultural artifacts in the environment. As a consequence of a change of focus from the individual to the system, researchers have proposed that expertise and skilled performance are not fixed properties of individuals but a dynamic property of the systems in which individuals operate (Agnew et al., 1997; Hutchins, 1995a, 1995b; see also Bateson & Bateson, 2000).

Hutchins (1995a) provided an example of distributed cognition in the collaborative work of maritime personnel. Hutchins observed how a maritime navigation team undertakes its work. One task of a navigation team is to plot and record the position of the ship every 3 minutes. This process is known as obtaining a fix.

> While simultaneously watching a fishing boat that crossed close under the bow of the ship and discussing the watch bill for the remainder of the day, the plotter and recorder missed a fix time. This problem was caught by the keeper of the deck log about 2 minutes late.
> Deck log: Chief, you're going to have another call. Missed at 3. Your round at 3.
> Plotter: I'll get one here in a minute.
> Recorder: Stand by to mark.
> Plotter: Time is 5, yeah 5; we'll just kind of space this one out.
> Even though timing the fixes is not part of the keeper of the deck log's job, he is a participant at the chart table and in this case, happens to have noticed that a scheduled fix was missed. (p. 221)

Hutchins referred to this aspect of distributed cognition as "overlapping knowledge" and proposed that this is a characteristic of cooperative work. Flexibility in the system was afforded because the knowledge of the individuals in the group overlapped; that is, there was redundancy in the system. This flexibility facilitated rapid adaptation by the group to work disruptions. Thus, system redundancy has a function as a "safety net." When demands on human resources (e.g., physical effort, attention, and memory) change within areas of the system, redundant resources can be distributed and redistributed accordingly. As a consequence, in Hutchins's words, work systems can be conceived of as malleable and adaptable (1995a, p. 219).

Another important task required for ship navigation is to record the spatial relations between the ship and the world. One such relation is the angular position of the ship at sea relative to a landmark. Hutchins described how this information is first represented within a sighting compass on board the ship (called an alidade). He then described how the information is transformed through various representational states on the route to its final destination, the navigational chart, where it is integrated with other representations of spatial relations to produce a navigational "fix" on the position of the ship. Hutchins showed how the information is propagated across various media on its route that include different individuals within the team and the physical artifacts they use.

Hutchins wrote that the space in which the ship and the landmark are located is a macrospace, but the angular relationship between these two entities is captured for navigational purposes through its reproduction in a microspace, that is, the eyepiece of the alidade. This reproduction is achieved by aiming the alidade eyepiece such that the hairline within the eyepiece superimposes the landmark image. The alidade is constructed in such a way that when the hairline of the sighting mechanism is aligned with the landmark feature, the angular relationship between the ship and the landmark will be reproduced in a third space: the angular relationship between the center of a compass card, located within the alidade and marked along the edge with degrees of angle, and the point on the edge of the compass card over which the hairline falls. This permits the angular relationship of the ship to the landmark to be represented in a digital mode, that is, as a numerical angle.

The next transformation of this representation, on its route to the chart, depends on the maneuvers of the ship. When the position of the ship is distal to potential hazards, such as land, the frequency with which bearing recordings are taken decreases. As a consequence, fewer personnel are required for navigation, and the same person can operate the alidade and record the bearing at the navigation chart. However, the operator must physically transport the bearing information between the alidade and the navigation chart: The alidade is located outside of the bridge, and the chart is located inside. Thus, the alidade operator would obtain the digital representation of the angular relationship from the alidade and then walk to the chart. The representation must be remembered while being transported, and thus the operator might choose to represent it internally using mental rehearsal or represent it externally even by writing it down on his or her hand.

However, when the ship is proximal to hazards, the frequency of bearing recordings increases, and more personnel are brought to bear on the work. One person operates the alidade, and others conduct operations at the chart. In this situation, the digital representation would be obtained from the alidade by the operator and then transmitted over a closed circuit to the chart room. In this situation, the advantage of representing the angular relationship in a digital form is that it is transmissible over a restricted-bandwidth channel. Hutchins asked the reader to imagine that the angular relationship could be represented only in an analogue format. This would require a device that could represent the angle not only analogically but also semipermanently to transfer the information to the chart. For example, a two-arm protractor could be used, but such a system would be more labor intensive and time-consuming than the radio and thus potentially impracticable when hazards are proximal.

The digital representation of the angular relationship is subsequently written into the record log inside the bridge. The log entry serves as a permanent and space-efficient external digital representation of the bearing information. This digital representation is then converted back to an analogue representation in the form of an angle on a one-arm protractor called a hoey. The hoey is adjusted to a position that embodies the correct representative state and is finally placed on the chart where it serves, with other information, in the process of obtaining a fix.

Hutchins's objective in providing this description was to show that it is as much the artifacts that shape the way in which information is represented and processed as it is the individual. Furthermore, Hutchins showed that a noteworthy description of the flow of information and, more broadly, the system can be explained without significant recourse to individual cognition. Elements of the external, physical environment are important components of cognitive systems because they effectively extend human cognitive capabilities. As a consequence, systems can exhibit capabilities that individuals cannot. For example, cultural artifacts can be used to embody knowledge that would be difficult to represent mentally or used as external memory devices to reduce demands imposed by work on working memory.

Hutchins (1995b) also investigated the cognitive work conducted in aircraft cockpits and, specifically, how the system remembers information about flight speeds. Hutchins concluded,

> The cockpit system remembers its speeds [but] ... the memory of the cockpit ... is not made primarily of pilot memory. A complete theory of individual human memory would not be sufficient to understand that which we wish to understand because so much memory function takes place outside the individual. In some sense, what the theory of human memory explains is not how the system works, but why this system must contain so many components that are functionally implicated in cockpit memory, yet are external to the pilots themselves. (p. 286)

Given the role artifacts play in cognitive systems, and how individual cognition has been argued to be interrelated inextricably with contextual elements such as the physical environment, any change to these artifacts will affect the way people work and, ultimately, the work domain at a more general level. Thus, any work system interventions or novel artifacts need to be regarded as hypotheses about how they shape the domain and domain practices. Research studies need to trace how individuals and teams change strategies and other activities in response to new work systems and artifacts (see Clancey, 1998). This is, of course, in close accord with the "envisioned world problem" put forth by Cognitive Systems Engineers. (See chapter 7.)

Another community of practice that falls into the sociology and ethnography group is one called the Sociology of Scientific Knowledge.

Sociology of Scientific Knowledge

Following an argument similar to that of the situated theorists, Harry Collins (1997) reacted to the failures of so-called intelligent machines in artificial intelligence research. Collins wrote that artificial intelligence, like cognitive psychology, fails to consider the idea that "knowledge" is not situated in human bodies. Collins argued that cognitive science and artificial intelligence had "disembedded" knowledge from its social and cultural contexts and that the "neglect of the social embeddedness of both humans and computers" is what limits the capabilities of intelligent machines: "Much of the abilities of computers lies not inside the case but in the way we interact with them when we use them; we continually 'repair' the deficiencies of computers" (p. 303). Collins proposed that computer development is constrained because computers are limited to acting only *on* the world in a disembedded way as opposed to interacting *in* the world in the socially situated or embedded way that is inherent in human life.

Collins (1992) argued that computers are not intelligent because they are not social agents, and social embeddedness is needed for intelligence because society is the locus of knowledge and understanding. Only recently have computer scientists tried to tackle this problem of making computers act as "team players" (see Klein, Woods, Bradshaw, Hoffman, & Feltovich, 2004). Furthermore, computers and other machines can nevertheless act as "social prostheses" (Collins, 1992). That is to say, the computer does not do intelligent things on its own but is embedded in a social network of activities. Just as an artificial heart does not have to do exactly the same job as a natural heart because the rest of the body will make up for its failings, so will computers and the social group. A spell checker is a good example—it alerts the writer to problems, but the writer or human editor chooses the solution.

In the field of Sociology of Scientific Knowledge, investigations range from historio-graphic-philosophical analyses (e.g., Barnes, 1974) to the use of ethnographic methods of observation, participant observation, work-space analysis, and interviewing. (For a detailed example of methods and results, see the in-depth studies of scientific practice at the Salk Institute for Biological Science, conducted by Latour and Woolgar [1979].) Researchers have focused on the study of science (both inside and outside the laboratory), the acquisition and dissemination of scientific knowledge, and other topics (e.g., Barnes, 1974; Bijker et al., 1987; Collins, 1997; Fleck & Williams, 1996; Garfinkel, 1982; Knorr-Cetina, 1981; Knorr-Cetina & Mulkay, 1983; Leigh, 1992; Lynch, 1991, 1993; Lynch & Edgerton, 1988). Researchers within this approach have proposed that the acquisition of scientific knowledge is as much a social accomplishment as a process of individual experience and, thus, have argued that science is a largely "constructive" process that cannot be analyzed without considerations of the historical, cultural, and social context in which it occurs. "There is a trend away from regarding science as the earthly embodiment of some Platonic universal; instead it is being treated more and more as a human activity like any other, or as a sub-culture routinely interacting with other areas of society" (Barnes, 1974, p. 155). The literature on the sociology of professions abounds with illustrations of this.

For example, Collins (1985) provided detailed descriptions of efforts in laser development and other scientific endeavors and presented evidence that experimentation, far from being an objective tool for scientific inquiry, is a largely social process. Collins (1985, chap. 4) discussed how gravitational waves, predicted by Einstein, are incredibly difficult to detect. The force of a light beam on a 100-kilogram mass of metal would move the metal more than any gravity wave reaching the Earth from distant bodies. The basic gravity wave detector is a bar of metal, often weighing tons. An effect of gravity waves should be to cause slight variations in the length of the bar, but only on the order of the radius of a single electron. The alternative approach is to try to detect gravity waves by the ringing or oscillations caused by gravity waves, triggering minute shape changes in piezo-electric crystals that are glued along the bar. The bar must of course be isolated from all other disturbances. Gravity waves register as oscillations over the vibrational "thermal noise" caused by the atoms in the bar, which are always in motion because their temperature is well above absolute zero. An initial, and reportedly successful, attempt to measure gravity waves came into disrepute, because the measurements suggested gravitational radiation far above what would be expected on the basis of cosmological theories. The ensuing difficulties of interpretation and experimentation led to what Collins called the "experimenter's regress": The correct outcome for gravity wave detection depends on whether there are gravity waves hitting the earth at detectable levels, but one cannot know if one has a good detector until one has been built and detected gravity waves. In other words, the debate concerned what is, and what is not, a good gravity wave detector, in the absence of an independent criterion for success.

Resolution of this issue occurred within the society of physicists, not within the laboratory. Referring to an experimental report, one scientist commented, "I am not really impressed with his experimental capabilities so I would question anything he has done more than I would question other people's" (Collins, 1985, p. 85). Many researchers built detectors but perceived the differences among detectors differently. Some scientists saw certain differences as important, and others saw the differences as insignificant. Even when researchers found coincident signals from two detectors separated by large distances, some researchers doubted the claim that gravity waves had been detected. On the basis of his interviews, Collins generated a list of nonscientific reasons that physicists had for their beliefs (or disbeliefs): faith in experimental capabilities, personality, intelligence, reputation for running large labs, academic versus industrial situation of the researchers, previous history of failures, style or presentation of results, prestige of the university, and even nationality. Meetings on gravity waves were full of discussions of secondhand reports, rumors, and debates over whose detectors were good and whose were not good. One scientist commented, "At that point, it was not doing physics any longer. It is not clear that it was ever physics, but it certainly wasn't by then [1972] … there is just no point in building a detector of the type that x has" (Collins, 1985, p. 94).

The strong argument by sociologists is that scientific "facts" are social constructions. Another study (also based on interview data) that illustrates the social construction of knowledge is one by sociologist Michael Lynch (1991; see also Lynch & Edgerton, 1988; Lynch, Livingston, & Garfield, 1983), who interviewed a number of expert astronomers about the "representation craft" of generating false-color displays based on multispectral data.

The raw data from space probes and satellites can be portrayed using a variety of color palettes, some of which can be misleading (Hoffman & Markman, 2001). False-color multispectral satellite images that cover a range of visible and nonvisible bandwidths (infrared, radar, X-ray, etc.) can create special problems for display design and interpretation. A clear example is the photographs of the planets that NASA produced from Voyager data. Contrary to those brilliant and colorful depictions, most of the planets look rather like dirty tennis balls; they are not colored vividly. The "Great Red Spot" is not red; the moon Io does not look like a pepperoni pizza (see Young, 1985). For public relations purposes, astronomers orient explicitly to the aesthetic aspects of their images and are unashamed to talk about the "pretty pictures" that adorn the hallways of their research facilities. For publications in popular outlets, experts sometimes change their figures to match the goals of their text and the figure captions rather than write captions to really explain the figures. Even for technical publications, images are tailored to show the features that are being discussed (e.g., for an article about radio-emitting nebulae, an image may be recolorized to make the apparent emission pattern match a visible-light image).

The primary or scientific goal of image processing is to support scientists' accurate perception and comprehension. As one expert astronomer put it, "Through a complex series of adjustments and modifications of an image … [a display should] enable researchers to *see* the physics" (quoted in Lynch, 1991, p. 73). To make this point, Lynch attempted to show that the aesthetic judgments are not so distinct from the scientific ones. Most of the expert astronomers insisted that their actual scientific work involves working with raw, quantitative data, perhaps depicted graphically but even then using a more "boring" gray scale rather than fancy colors. However, Lynch probed the experts about what it was that made some of their color graphic products especially pleasing:

> E (expert): This is one that starts out red and then goes through yellow and white. Here's some radio data that's multi-color. I like these maps that have sort of one color, they start out dim, then go brighter, then go white. I think those are prettier than these that have many different colors.
>
> I (interviewer): Is it strictly a matter of liking one color?
>
> E: The reasons are artistic rather than scientific.
>
> I: Other people told me they like a more uniform thing because it is not misleading.
>
> E: Yes, there's that too. You show this picture to someone and you say, "This is what it looks like." Now, you can't really see it, it doesn't really look like anything. But this does seem to be more realistic.
>
> I: Choice of color would have some relation if it were an extension of the spectrum.
>
> E: Right. At one time I thought I wanted to make the X-ray purple and the radio red because it gives you an idea that this is a higher energy photon. (Lynch, 1991, p. 75)

The experts' "aesthetic" judgments clearly play a role but do not do so in any arbitrary way—they are driven by their foundational scientific knowledge and their goals.

In Collins's (1993) words, "Most of what we once thought of as the paradigm case of 'unsocial' knowledge—science and mathematics—has turned out to be deeply social; it rests on agreements to live our scientific and mathematical life a certain way" (p. 102). Collins (1983; 2004) made a case that although our lay perceptions of physical laws are that they are universal, they are in reality more a reflection of what is the received view of the world at a given time in history and in a given social and cultural context (see also Bloor, 1976).

Similarly, Latour and Woolgar (1979), in studying the science of neuroendocrinology, concluded that although the layperson might perceive a marked contrast between scientific and, for example, political processes, there is no evidence for such a premise. Latour and Woolgar argued that negotiation between scientists about what can be accepted as proof is no different from any argument between politicians or lawyers. Likewise, Lynch (1993) stated, "The once unquestionable conviction that science must be different from 'mere' political opinion, untested speculation, and commonsense belief has recently taken a beating" (p. xi). Consistent with these assertions, philosophers of science have observed a paradox in the scientific process in that the subjective and highly personal activity of science is purported to result in objective and impersonal knowledge (Ravetz, 1971, cited in Gooding, 1986, p. 206).

Collins (1985) described a number of social processes in scientific endeavors that are characterized primarily by the need to maintain a perceived orderliness of the world: "Without order there can be no society. Communication, and therefore the whole of culture in its broadest sense, rests on the ability of human beings to see the same things and respond to them in the same ways" (p. 5). For example, Collins demonstrated that the competence with which an experiment is replicated will not be questioned so long as the results uphold the received view of the phenomenon being studied and thus social order. This was also asserted by Barnes (1974), who reported that in science, "the conditions under which existing beliefs would be abandoned are never specified, and often they are retained in the face of apparently strong disconfirming evidence" (p. 46). Furthermore, Collins (1984) described how scientists who might interpret experimental findings from a radical standpoint actually choose to interpret the findings from a more commonly received standpoint to avoid the risks of challenging the social order.

Pinch (1985) elaborated this point after studying the scientific practice of physicists. He argued that the scientist, when reporting research findings, is faced with a trade-off between acceptability and profundity. Pinch provided an example of the study of solar neutrinos, which are believed to be a by-product of the nuclear fusion reactions thought to occur in the core of the Sun. He described how the physicist might interpret "splodges" observed on an image of particle tracks as either splodges on a graph, Ar^{37} atoms, or solar neutrinos (p. 9). Each interpretation has an increased level of what Pinch called externality. The scientist can choose to interpret findings at a low level of externality, that is, report findings that are proximal to the observing agent. For example, "splodges on a graph" is the literal description of the information provided by the observing agent. As an alternative, the scientist can choose to interpret findings at a high level of externality, that is, report findings that are distal to the observing agent and more reflective of the broader observational situation. In this particular case, interpreting findings at a high level of externality includes a proposal that the splodges on a graph represented solar neutrinos. Interpreting findings at a high level of externality might have profound implications for science but is risky because bold interpretations often threaten previous theories and thus attract challenges. Interpreting findings as having low externality (interpreting splodges simply as splodges) is less risky and thus is more likely to be acceptable because such interpretations are relevant to many contexts. However, a high degree of relevance also carries its own risks, because the investigation could be criticized as being trivial, in that there is no contribution to science. Therefore, the scientist must consider carefully how to interpret findings based on the given social context.

This is one of many social phenomena that have led researchers to propose about scientists that "the better politicians and strategists they are, the better the science they produce" (Latour & Woolgar, 1979, p. 213).

To demonstrate how culture, as much as carefully conducted research, might determine "good" science and scientific expertise, Bernstein (1982), a physics professor, described the following example. He reported that he receives calls from members of the public who claim to have made major scientific breakthroughs. Typically, he dismisses these callers as "cranks" but adds that he reflects occasionally on the following fantasy:

It is the year 1905 and I am a professor of physics at the University of Bern. The phone rings, and a person I have never heard of identifies himself as a patent examiner in the Swiss National Patent Office. He says that he has heard I give lectures on electromagnetic theory and that he has developed some ideas which might interest me. "What sort of ideas?" I ask a bit superciliously. He begins discussing some crazy sounding notions about space and time. Rulers contract when they are set in motion; a clock on the equator goes at a slower rate than the identical clock when it is placed at the North Pole; the mass of an electron increases with its velocity; whether or not two events are simultaneous depends on the frame of reference of the observer; and so on. How would I have reacted? Well, a great many of Albert Einstein's contemporaries would have hung up the phone. After all, in 1905, Einstein didn't even have an academic job! (p. 311)

Einstein was not well known within the scientific community that investigated these specific topics in physics, what Collins (1984) called the "core set." The core set refers not to the scientific establishment or a core group but to a locus of scientific discussion and debate. Einstein might have found difficulty in being accepted as a member of the core set because of his lowly status, but if he had high status his heterodox ideas might well have been grist to the mill of a core set; that is, he would have been "admitted to the game" of science (Latour & Woolgar, 1979, p. 208). In addition, Einstein's ideas were radical and contrasted with the socially ordered world of the core set (Collins, 1984).

Knorr-Cetina (1981) proposed that judgments about scientific claims may depend on where the work was completed, who completed it, and how it was completed, such that the results of a study are often identified with the context of their production. Similarly, Latour, and Woolgar (1979) wrote, "Sociological elements such as status, rank, award, past accreditation, and social situation are merely resources utilized in the struggle for credible information and increased credibility" (p. 213). They described how the perusal of a scientist's résumé reveals examples of such elements and how these elements can vary in their contribution to credibility: For example, multiple journal publications afford more credibility than a few conference abstract publications, and membership in a world-renowned research group affords more credibility than working independently for a less respected institution. By the criteria proposed by Knorr-Cetina (1981) and Latour and Woolgar (1979), Einstein would have had limited credibility in Bernstein's fantasy, and thus his claims would not have been taken seriously.

To return to our primary topic—CTA—we hope that our discussion of this rich literature on the sociology of science has driven home an important point: You can learn a great deal simply by asking people questions. Of course, the CTA researcher can and should seek confirmation and not always take anyone's word for anything. Sociologists and ethnographers are, of course, aware of this issue. For instance, in Collins's work on gravity waves, he interviewed dozens of practitioners, repeatedly over many years, and analyzed the interview data in waves of interpretation and reinterpretation that permitted the exploration of hypothesis, in an approach that some have called "strong ethnography" (see Dekker, Nyce, & Hoffman, 2003). Furthermore, this research shows clearly what it means for the CTA researcher to "bootstrap" into the domain of study, all the way to achieving journeyman levels of proficiency.

The final community of practice that we place within the sociology and ethnographic perspectives is one that has strong links to Expertise Studies but evolved from within other traditions.

Sociology of the Professions

The Sociology of the Professions has emerged within recent decades and has clear links to topics in Expertise Studies (Abbott, 1988; Evetts, Mieg, & Felt, 2006; Kurz-Milcke & Gigerenzer, 2004). This includes conceptual analyses, interviews, and survey studies of the ways in which experts are perceived by society (i.e., as an elite group), ways in which experts understand their role within organizations and society, ways in which experts perceive their relations with their clients, and ways in which expertise is managed as a resource, both within organizations and by society at large.

One way of approaching this topic, and for present purposes maintaining our focus on CTA, is to begin with a seminal contribution to the Sociology of the Professions by psychologist James Shanteau (1992). He surveyed the literature on expert performance within the field of judgment and decision making, noting professions where there are clear performance metrics allowing one to specify what "superior performance" means: domains such as weather forecasting, livestock judging, piloting, chess, accountancy, nursing, and others. For instance, a weather forecast can be compared to the actual weather, yielding what is called a "skill score," showing the value added by the human forecaster over and above the accuracy of the computer model forecasts. It is not uncommon for the most senior forecasters to reach levels of 85% correct or more (in forecasting such things as precipitation, high and low temperatures, winds, etc.) (see Hoffman Trafton, & Roebber, 2008). For other domains, it is less clear that the designation of "being an expert" can be tied to clear performance measures: clinical psychologists, judges, counselors, parole officers, stockbrokers, and others. Shanteau concluded that researchers are more likely to encounter difficulty in nailing down what it means for someone to be an expert in domains where the primary task of the professional involves predicting individual or aggregate human behavior.

Here we see a link to sociology. If for some domains it is difficult, or even impossible, to define expertise in terms of measures of performance (e.g., astrologers), how then is expertise to be defined? Shanteau's conclusion was an impetus for sociologist Harald Mieg (2001, 2006) to conduct surveys of the literature on two contrasting domains of professional practice, stockbrokering, and climatology. The study of stockbrokering focused on how brokers cope with risk and uncertainty, asking the question, *Can there be expertise in forecasting financial markets?* According to Schwager (1989), most top traders begin their career with large losses. On the other hand, according to a study in which experienced investors competed against a "dartboard" prediction, 58% of the stocks selected by the investors outperformed the Dow average (Sundali & Atkins, 1994). According to Mieg, the disparity in results (some brokers do poorly, others do OK) are accounted for by the fact that the best performing brokers work in brokering houses that make their investment decisions according to plans, that have good research resources, and that have good sources of information. In other words, brokering expertise lies in the ways the organization works: "[Individual] experts are blind in that they can only try to follow some hypothesis, but lack insight in the complexity that drives the market" (Mieg, 2001, p. 122). This certainly fits Shanteau's generalization.

Although climate change prediction is also a field in which professionals have to cope with risk and uncertainty, the situation for climatology is different from that of brokering, although it too shows how expertise is relative to organizations. Atmospheric dynamics are highly nonlinear and involve multiple causation. Nevertheless, there is significant technical expertise in creating computer models of atmospheric circulation, energy dynamics, and chemistry. Global computer models can be tested by application to scenarios for climate change, which have been produced by the International Panel on Climate Change since 1990. The scenarios lay out predictions for changes in greenhouse gases, population density, and other factors, but these factors are expressed in terms of policy decisions, for example, whether in accord with international treaties on greenhouse gas emissions. Thus, the scenarios have to link climate change, which is incremental, to dramatic changes in policy and politics, and so climatologists are embroiled in policy, consensus seeking, and mediation. Although the International Panel has been successful at "bridging science and politics at an international level ... [and] creating a consensus that can be communicated as the scientific knowledge base" (Mieg, 2001, p. 134), "the problem in predicting climate change cannot be solved by improving the model projections and parameter estimations ... the logic of the work of the [International Panel] is driven by linear thinking that is misleading when it comes to understanding the nonlinear climate system" (p. 132).

> A clear conclusion from all this is that the role of the expert remains socially contingent: what is judged is not so much the content of the evidence or advice, as the credibility or legitimacy of the person giving the evidence or advice; if we trust the expert, we must trust their advice. (Williams, Faulkner, & Fleck, 1998, p. 4)

Mieg, like Williams et al., presented a view of expertise as a social attribution, regarding expertise as a role that is defined relative to organizations. In this view, expertise is created by society as a whole, in which a demand creates a market. Mieg referred to this as the "cognitive economics" of expertise. Mieg's focus was on how individuals and organizations conceive of the role of expert, how organizations use experts as resources or "heuristics" in decision making, and how practitioners deal with conflicts that arise between the role of the expert and the organization or bureaucracy within which they work. For example, the kinds of explanations or opinions that an expert provides depend on the status of the expert relative to the person to whom they are providing advice or opinion (e.g., a physician providing an opinion to another physician versus to a patient versus to a hospital manager). For these reasons, Mieg and other sociologists advocate the use of sociometric and social network analysis methods for identifying experts (e.g., Hakkarainen et al., 2004; Stein, 1992, 1997). Individuals within organizations are surveyed (e.g., "To whom do you go for advice about x?") to reveal the organization's knowledge network (i.e., who talks to whom, how often, and about what) and identify individuals in terms of their unique knowledge and capabilities.

Another seminal contribution to the Sociology of the Professions was Donald Schön's (1982, 1987) studies of professional practice in a variety of domains, including town planning, management, engineering design, teaching, psychiatry, and others. His method involved interviewing and detailed analyses of transcripts (e.g., 1982, chap. 7). From the analyses he was able to draw out the similarities in the reasoning of practitioners in domains that one would think are quite different, such as psychotherapy and architectural design. Salient among the similarities is the activity of thinking about one's own professional activities by reference to *situations*. Here is an example from Schön's interview with a town planner, concerning the way in which the planner manages meetings with developers who have submitted proposals:

> The planner is an individual who likes to reflect on his practice. Indeed, his willingness to participate in our research grew out of this interest. … He mentioned in the interview, for example, that he spends time experimenting with such rhetorical devices as delivery, intonation, and eye contact. He reflects on the strategies by which he tries to create the desired impressions in others, but he does not reflect on the role frame, problem setting, or theory of action which lead him to try to create one impression rather than another. Indeed, his balancing act and his strategy of mystery and mastery are bound together in a system of knowing-in-practice which tends, in several ways, to make itself immune to reflection. Since the planner is doing one thing while appearing to do another, he cannot easily make his assumptions public or subject them to public testing. His sense of vulnerability discourages reflection. And he is so busy managing the balancing act, manipulating the impressions he makes on others and defending against vulnerability to exposure, that he has little opportunity to reflect on the problem settings that drive his performance. Moreover, he is unlikely to detect errors of interpretation which might provoke broader and deeper reflection. (1982, p. 229)

From these studies of "reflective practitioners"—revealing what they do and what they do not reflect on, revealing when they do and when they do not reflect on their actions, and revealing the values that drive their activity—Schön developed a view of expert performance that hinges on notions of intuition and tacit knowledge, relying less heavily on notions of formal or rational-analytic thinking. That is, Schön's theory is not so much a theory of expertise but a claim about all knowledge or, more broadly, the role of tacit understanding as a requirement for action.

In his "demystification of professional practice"—the elitist view that professionals lay claim to extraordinary knowledge and skill—Schön compared two kinds of skilled practitioners in terms of their motivations, sources of satisfaction, and values. Table 11.1 summarizes this contrast, in which Schön uses the designation of "expert" to refer to professionals who maintain an elitist stance (see also Kurz-Milcke & Gigerenzer, 2004).

Thus, Schön's theory of professional practice is contrasted with "rationalist" approaches, such as that of Herbert Simon (e.g., Simon, 1972), that emphasize deliberative cognition and statistical decision theory more than tacit knowledge, which is ordered by conceptualization of the social context (Schön, 1982, chap. 2).

TABLE 11.1 Schön's Contrast Between "Experts" and "Reflective Practitioners"

Experts	Reflective Practitioners
I am presumed to know, and I must claim to do so regardless of my own uncertainty.	I am not the only one to have relevant and important knowledge. My uncertainties may be a source of learning for others and for me.
I keep my distance from the client and preserve my role. I give the client a sense of my expertise but convey a feeling of sympathy.	I allow the client's respect for my knowledge to emerge in the situation.
I look for deference and status in the client's responses.	I seek a real connection to the client and do not try to maintain a professional facade.

What's at issue is the nature of knowledge. Simon believed that you don't know something if you haven't articulated a domain theory. Real knowledge is a descriptive model; anything else is just "intuition," many disparage. Some believed that such terms are cop-outs—attempts to stop theorizing about the nature of knowledge, to say "it's tacit" so we can't study it, or worse, it's some kind of mystical process that can't be understood because it's not a mechanism. (W. J. Clancey, personal communication, 2006)

In a resonance with the notion of situated cognition, discussed previously, Schön also emphasized that some knowledge cannot be easily articulated but is nonetheless manifested in the activities of practitioners, including interactions among mentors and their students.

Even if reflection-in-action is feasible, however, it may seem dangerous. The baseball pitcher who claims never to think about his pitching in the middle of a game, and the famous story of the centipede paralyzed by the attempt to explain how he moves, suggest that reflection interferes with action. It may seem to do so for different reasons. ... There is no time to reflect when we are on the firing line; if we stop to think, we may be dead. When we think about what are doing, we surface complexity, which interferes with the smooth flow of action. The complexity that we can manage unconsciously paralyzes us when we bring it to consciousness. ... These arguments admit the possibility of reflecting *on* action ... but they point to the dangers of reflection *in* action ... we have observed how practitioners like architects, musicians, and therapists construct virtual worlds in which the pace of action can be slowed down and iterations and variations of actions tried. Indeed, our conception of the art of practice ought to give a central place to the ways in which practitioners learn to create opportunities for reflection-in-action. (1982, pp. 277–279)

Although one could model tacit knowledge in formal constructs, as Schön's example points out, it is not useful for the practitioner to carry this to the extreme attempted by cognitive modelers, artificial intelligence researchers or roboticists. Schön's argument hearkens to the notion of "recognition-primed decision making" that emerged in the paradigm of Naturalistic Decision Making (see chapter 9 of this volume). Schön's latter point in the previous quotation leads to suggestions for education (Schön, 1982, chap. 10, 1987), showing a clear influence of the ideas of educator John Dewey (1974). Ideas include the institutionalization of programs to train "reflective teachers," a reliance on case-based learning ("learning by doing"), and an emphasis on coaching and mentoring.

Clancey (1997) offered a restatement of Schön's logic of inquiry and his categories of reflective thinking, which we recapitulate here in Table 11.2, because it may make Schön's concepts more accessible to people who are familiar with conventional cognitive or modeling terminology.

Research Approach

As we pointed out in the introduction to this chapter, few of the individuals we have cited would say that their methods are CTA. Indeed, it would be argued that lumping work practice analysis (also called Activity Analysis) with task analysis (or CTA) is incorrect because these are different analytical frameworks (see Clancey, 2002; Nyssen, 2000; Turner & McEwan, 2004). Task analysis uses an ontology including such notions as goals, procedures, tasks, functions, and expertise. Activity Analysis

TABLE 11.2 A Description of Schön's Logic of Inquiry

Doing (knowing-in-action)	Attentive but automatic action.
Adapting (reflection-in-action)	One is caught short momentarily but easily continues. We "glitch" on something unexpected but respond immediately, proceeding from another conceptual coordination.
Framing ("conversations" with the situation)	The deliberate attempt to generate appropriate descriptions of the situation.
History telling (reflection on knowledge or action)	Reflecting on past actions and descriptions to generate new theories or new ways of understanding.
Designing	Creating and carrying out an activity that carries the previous four components to some productive end.

Note: Adapted from Clancey (1997).

uses an ontology including motives, emotions, practices, activities, scripts, and work, adding such anthropological concepts of setting, activity, rhythm, ritual, norm, and identity. Advocates of Activity Analysis wonder why the word *cognitive* is tacked on to the phrase "task analysis," because it is impossible to imagine some kind of task analysis that would *not* be cognitive. Lave, Schön, Sachs, Scribner, Wenger, and others we have cited were distinctly and explicitly claiming to have a perspective that task analysis cannot capture. They have argued that task analysis is framed by the study of expertise, whereas Activity Analysis is framed by the study of work or work practices.

Our view is that both sets of core concepts are appropriate and have intersecting application in most situations (specifically, activities give rise to problems that are resolved through the methods articulated by task analysis). Also, the notions of 'goal,' 'patterned (rule-like) behavior,' and 'operator' are common to both ontologies. Ethnographic and sociological approaches, such as Cognitive Work Analysis (chapter 10) and Cognitive Systems Engineering (chapter 7), hold that certain kinds of methods need to be brought to bear in the study of complex sociotechnical domains. Although there are differences in the "methods palette" used in the three paradigms, all three rely on some of the same basic ideas of observation and interviewing. Some researchers in ethnography and Sociology of the Professions might bristle, however, if their methods were to be regarded as CTA.

> The view of action that ethnomethodology recommends is neither behavioristic, in any narrow sense of that term, nor mentalistic. It is not behavioristic in that is assumes that the significance of action is not reducible to uninterpreted bodily movements. Nor is it mentalistic, however, in that the significance of action is taken to be based, in ways that are fundamental rather than secondary or epiphenomenal, in the physical and social world. The basic premise is twofold: first, that what traditional behavioral sciences take to be cognitive phenomena have an essential relationship to a publicly available, collaboratively organized world of artifacts and actions, and secondly, that the significance of artifacts and actions, and the methods by which their significance is conveyed, have an essential relationship to their particular, concrete circumstances. (Suchman, 1987, p. 50)

Cognitive variables are not directly investigated in a way like that of Expertise Studies, for example. On the other hand, some traditional cognitive science methods are employed such as protocol analysis, which has been used to analyze the interplay of people within groups and with technology in the observed situations (Cross et al.,

1996). However, cognitive variables are not singled out as being somehow uniquely (or solely) cognitive in nature. Rather, they are regarded as part of a complex and dynamic mix, which includes social, cultural, and historical aspects. These aspects too are not regarded as "isolated" variables or "factors."

Thus, the communities of practice we have discussed in this chapter adopt methods that differ in some ways from those used in Expertise Studies and Cognitive Engineering but in some ways resemble methods advocated in those communities as well. For example, they all hold that the good researcher is immersed in the domain. The research approach involves the following features:

- Actual situations are taken as natural laboratories—investigators shape the conditions of observation through scenario design and through artifact based methods.
- Studies in actual situations are taken as a starting point for the creation of laboratory studies, but laboratory studies are required to be ecologically valid.
- Researchers "live" in the domain.
- Researchers collaborate with one or more domain practitioners whose role is more than that of a mere "informant." They are regarded as a part of the research team.
- Research relies on direct observation, sometimes involving detailed analysis of videotaped events during actual practice and during simulations.
- Protocol analysis (or "thinking out loud") is sometimes used to analyze the interplay of people and technology in the observed situations.
- Advances in recording technology are exploited to observe more than one activity at a time. For example, Clancey (2001) used time-lapse photography to capture activity in one area of the work domain while he observed activity in another. From the data elicited through the application of such methods, activities can be modeled and evaluated, and patterns of activity can be identified. These patterns can be used to inform work system design (Clancey, 2006).
- Interviews are often used to analyze the interplay of people and technology in the observed situations.
- Technological interventions or changes are regarded as hypotheses. Studies trace how individuals and teams change strategies and other activities in response to new technology.

Methods of investigation used in the communities of practice that we grouped in this chapter share many more commonalities than differences. The methods could be described generally as ethnographic in nature. Ethnography is the scientific study of a human society and makes great use of fieldwork to study the behaviors and activities of humans in their environments. There is a large social–psychological and ethnomethodological literature on interviewing techniques (e.g., Benfer & Furbee, 1989; Garfinkel, 1967; Spradley, 1979). An objective of ethnographic research is to gain a deeper appreciation of how skilled actions depend on their context through a broad and holistic consideration of the work undertaken. This consideration is extended beyond the individual to consider work as a system that includes groups of individuals, the space they work in, and the tools they work with. It is extended beyond the individual to a consideration of the social networks of communities of practitioners and the ways in which people create, share, and manage their knowledge (e.g., Hakkarainen et al., 2004). Furthermore, considerations are extended to the details and activities of work that are essential for getting the job done. These considerations might be missed during traditional process descriptions of "on-task" work that might concentrate on sources of work information such as written procedures, policy manuals, job descriptions, business process models, and work-flow models. The investigation would also consider broader social factors, such as the ways in which expertise might be socially determined, how expertise relates to power politics, the ways it may or may not give rise to successful technological innovation, the ways in which expertise may or may not relate to effective social policy making, and the implications of all this for such things as the management of technological change (see Fleck & Williams, 1996; Kurz-Milcke & Gigerenzer, 2004; Mieg, 2001).

In the ethnographic approach, actual situations are taken as "natural laboratories" wherein investigators shape the conditions of observation through scenario design. A variety of methods can be used that allow the direct experience, observation, and recording of a given work domain by researchers. For example, Suchman (1988) conducted a detailed analysis of audiovisual recordings to reveal the ways in which team members used white boards in their collaborative design of software. Ethnographic researchers are likely to be involved in the study of a domain for a considerable length of time. For her report on the use of metaphors in the scientific laboratory, Knorr-Cetina (1995) drew on 5 years of ethnographic research conducted in physics and biology laboratories. Harry Collins (Collins, Evans, Ribeiro, & Hall, 2006) spent decades studying physicists who were developing gravity wave detectors.

The research methods used within this approach include observational analyses, but the method scoffs at any notion of "unobtrusive" observation. (The argument is that no observation can be unobtrusive.) Practitioners are observed and their actions documented, although there are detailed analysis of videotaped events of behavior. Structured and unstructured interviews are conducted with domain participants (for examples, see Ball & Ormerod, 2000; Clancey, 2001; Knorr-Cetina, 1981). However, the researcher may shadow, or actually work with, the people being studied. As Knorr-Cetina (1981) argued, a good understanding of a domain, and the operatives who work within it, is unlikely "to be gained from observation alone. We must also listen to the talk [by operatives] about what happens, the asides and the curses, the mutterings of exasperation, the questions they ask each other, the formal discussions and lunchtime chats" (p. 21).

These methods can be applied during actual practice and during simulations. Frequently, a suite of these methods will be brought to bear on investigations of practice in domains. An example is the study by Latour and Woolgar (1979). In this study, Latour spent 21 months observing endocrinologists in the laboratory. He made field notes throughout and analyzed research papers produced out of work undertaken in the laboratory and documents relevant to the daily activities of the scientists. Formal interviews were conducted with members of the laboratory teams and with staff from other laboratories. Latour also worked within the laboratory as a technician and, therefore, was able to learn about laboratory life from within the culture by listening to, and partaking in, conversations between scientists and by actually experiencing the nature of the work. Latour was given his own office space in a prominent area of the work domain, and he proposed that his physical proximity to the work being undertaken aided the research process. (See also Knorr-Cetina [1981] for details of the application of similar methods in the domain of science.)

Collins et al.'s study (2006) of physicists' work on gravity wave detectors, which we mentioned earlier, shows that researchers in the ethnographic domains do not just observe and interview—they also conduct experiments. The study also shows how the distinction between field studies and experimentation can become blurred. And it also drives home the importance of social factors in the determination of expertise. After studying the domain for many years, Collins began playing an "imitation game." A set of questions about gravitational physics was sent to a physicist, and his answers, along with Collins's own answers, were presented to nine other gravity physicists. When asked to spot the "real" physicist, seven of the nine were unsure. Only two chose Collins. Collins had gone beyond participant observation of physicists at work to the point of actually fooling some physicists into believing that he might be a physicist, not so much on the basis of his knowledge of physics but on the basis of the knowledge he had acquired about how the physicists interact, communicate, and collaborate. (Collins's experiments on "interactional expertise" can be found at http://www.cf.ac.uk/socsi/expertise.)

> Outsiders can develop a kind of expertise in a scientific field … this could affect the argument about whether an outsider, such as an anthropologist, can properly understand another group … the debate was part of the science wars, when some scientists claimed that sociologists studying science could not understand the disciplines involved, in part because they did not practise them. (Giles, 2006, p. 8)

Here we see a parallel to a point made in the field of Expertise Studies: As researchers study a domain, they try to achieve at least a journeyman-level of understanding (Hoffman, 1987b). However, Collins (1981, 1984, 2004) took this a step further, referring to what he called "participant comprehension" and "participatory field research."

> The idea is that you sojourn in the field long enough to gain the same understanding of their world as the natives have. You can then write about their world without doing anything like "observing" or "interviewing" since you might as well interview yourself. Interviews are still useful, however, because they provide better illustrative material than you could provide yourself. (H. M. Collins, personal communication, July 2006)

Another example of innovative methodology in Activity Analysis is a study by Marti and Scrivani (2003) on air traffic control. Their goal was to conduct an analysis that captured the role of organizational and social factors in air traffic control operations while at the same time contributing to the design of new work methods and technologies.

> The literature on accidents and incidents in safety-critical systems suggests that the usability of a control system and its ability to tolerate variances are strictly related to an adequate distribution of knowledge, and the consequent correct interaction and cooperation between humans and tools. In order to simulate and analyze these interactions, it is necessary to adequately represent the context and to have a high-level analysis. In this respect, task analysis is not adequate since it tends to focus fine granularity on specific human tasks, and is weak in analyzing high-level communication tasks and cooperative activities. (p. 38)

Their method of "shadow-mode simulation" involved having a prototype for a new system situated in the workplace. Off-duty air traffic controllers worked using the new system, using actual real-time data, at the same time that the "real" controllers conducted their work using their current workstation technology and work systems, affording a comparison and the "non-interfering use of a new system in a real environment" (p. 37). By studying the transcripts of controller-to-controller and controller-to-pilot communications, it was found that a new software and workstation system failed to adequately support the handoff procedure, "driving back the human activity from an organizational ritual to a memory task that consistently increased the controller's mental workload" (p. 43). The researchers concluded, "The shift of attention to the larger context of interaction among controllers and pilots ... allows one to analyze a hierarchy of goals that exist beyond the specific situation of controller–system interaction (e.g., a clearance issued by a mistake, that traditional approaches would categorize as 'human error')" (p. 43).

Applications

Like the other perspectives on CTA that we describe in the chapters of this book, the social and ethnographic studies have been framed by practical concerns; that is, they are oriented toward changing and improving practices and tools. This links to the historical influence of European Work Analysis and work-oriented design, which is the topic of chapter 10. Emphasizing the merger of design and practice, in which practitioners play a central role in the design process (Anderson, 1994), researchers have advanced methods for cooperative design of performance support systems, for example, by prototyping by means of mock-ups of alternative forms of representations, in such areas as clinical dentistry and newspaper production (see the chapters in Greenbaum & Kyng, 1991). Other applications involve the relation of expertise to successful innovation, the importance of tacit knowledge even in such domains as the design of nuclear weapons, the importance of strategic thinking in the creation of electronic funds transfer networks, and the improvement of methods of apprenticing in the control of computer-driven printing presses (see the chapters in Williams, Faulkner, & Fleck, 1998). Clancey's research at NASA has implications for the design of space exploration work systems, which broadly includes operations, automation, facilities, tools, and automated systems such as software agents. The overarching goal is to design "total systems" by studying authentic work in analogue settings such as the habitats established at remote locations on Earth. By applying ethnographic techniques, one can understand how people do their work in natural and analogue settings on Earth and thus reveal what must be replaced or augmented or might become a problem in space (e.g., for a geologist in a space suit, how does the inability to taste rocks onsite affect their work?).

Social and ethnographic studies have also been framed by practical concerns at a larger scale: methods of management, organization, policy, and cultural differences. For example, Harald Mieg (2001) also pointed out implications of the "cognitive economics" view for organizational management. The nature of organizations is such that managers are limited in their ability to achieve expertise concerning their own organization (e.g., lack of process feedback). Thus, Mieg recommended that managers include their organization's experts in their management procedures. He also strongly advocated programs of "knowledge management" so that organizations can preserve and reuse their expertise.

Clancey (1995) contrasted rational or formal models of work and of organizations with a situated ("interactional") view. Rather than regarding plans as road maps that are created before acting and that describe deliberate choice at every step, the interactional view regards plans as emerging in the activity of work, a "process of constructing new ways of coordinating" (p. 23). As Clancey pointed out, this view has implications for how organizations are understood and how organizations are changed by practices that occur in everyday work. "The ongoing process of perceiving how we are doing, finding patterns, and justifying developments through new theories, is a process of inquiry and discovery. The manager, like the architect, the writer, and the programmer, must be open to serendipity and unashamed by unexpected interactions. What happens in practice is always one step ahead of theory" (p. 43).

The sociology of cognitive work involves the study of many work domains, and this includes the particular work domain in which information technologies are created. The collectives of people and machines (forming teams, organizations, etc.) who work with the goal of creating new decision aids and other systems and work methods are themselves a complex sociotechnical system (Feltovich, Hoffman, & Woods, 2004). Ethnographic methodology became a topic of interest on the part of developers of information systems, primarily because ethnographic methods could be taken as being data collection methods. Indeed, methods of observing and interviewing are widely used in systems design (Anderson, 1994). In reference to this work domain, the importance of sociological and ethnomethodological ideas and methods has been emphasized by Joseph Goguen (Oxford University and the University of California–San Diego). His wide-ranging interests and influences left a mark in the areas of programming languages, logic, software engineering, and also consciousness studies. In the 1990s Goguen (1992, 1994, 1997) spoke of the "culture" of computer science as one that emphasizes formal, context-insensitive information and information processing, pointing out the importance of social and contextual (or situated) information. His main focus was on the implications for requirements engineering. The formal languages of computer science are, in Goguen's view, only one language used in requirements engineering. Although formal languages provide a path to specification of the requirements for software, they do not help much in determining whether requirements are correct or good. For this, another language is used, a social language that allows project managers, system developers, programmers, and users collaborate in software development.

> [There is a need for] methods from the social sciences, particularly during the requirements phase of large system development projects. A significant difficulty with this, however, is that few computing scientists know very much about the social sciences; indeed, many computing scientists have little sympathy with the social sciences, and prefer the relative certainties of hardware and software ... to ambiguities, conflicts and vagueness. (1992, p. 4)

Goguen and his colleagues used a taxonomy of social theories of organizations to categorize approaches to requirements specification, on the assumption that those methods assume a tacit social theory. In observing what seems to actually happen in the processes of procurement (design and creation of technology), Goguen distinguished requirements (specific properties and behaviors a system must have) from "needs" (the desirability of certain kinds of system functionalities). In Goguen's view, not enough attention is paid to the latter, resulting in inappropriately designed and executed software and wholesale failures in the procurement of large-scale information systems (Goguen, 1994, p. 165).

> It is interesting that most of the effort for typical large systems goes into the maintenance phase. Some … have argued that this is because not enough effort has been put into being precise in the earlier phases, particularly specification, but I believe the reason is that much more is going on in the so-called maintenance phase than meets the eye … in real projects, there is no orderly progression from one stage to the next (contrary to the so-called waterfall model) but rather, there is a continual process of projection forward and backward … reassessment of requirements, specification, and code is very much a part [of it] … procurement processes attempt to rigidly separate phases with contractual barriers, in the name of competition. (Goguen, 1992, p. 5)

> A linear ordering imposed on events is itself the result of the retrospective reconstruction of causal chains to explain events (i.e., to give them significance in relation to shared values) (Goguen, 1997, p. 37)

In other words, there is more to design than listing requirements. Requirements specification is a process, not a one-off activity conducted only at the beginning of system development projects. "Requirements are emergent, in the sense that they do not already exist, but rather emerge from the interactions between analysts and the client organisation" (p. 5) (see also Hoffman & Elm, 2006). Requirements are not preestablished things but things that emerge in social interactions and achieve stability only in retrospect.

> [This] explains why it can be so difficult to manage the requirements of a large system: it only becomes clear what the requirements really are when the system is successfully operating in its social and organizational context. Thus, a reasonably complete and consistent set of requirements for a large, complex system can only emerge from a retrospective reconstruction … [this] also explains why it can be so difficult to enforce process models on actual system development projects: it is difficult even to know what phase a given action fits into until some coherence has emerged retrospectively. … We can now understand why it is impossible to completely formalize requirements: it is because they cannot be fully separated from their social context … the activities that are necessary for a successful system development project cannot always be expected to fit in a natural way into any system of pre-given categories, and practising software engineers often report (informally) that they have to spend much of their time circumventing "the system." (1994, p. 194).

Because errors made during a requirements phase can end up being costly and difficult to correct, Goguen proposed that system development be based on "hyper-requirements" as well as on some process of requirements specification. Goguen's hyper-requirements allow system developers to approach requirements specification as a process, generating easily accessible traces of the processes through which requirements were identified, the decisions that were made, and their rationale. Software tools to support system development must enable people to track requirements, and progress in implementation, but also support "retrospective revision." As Hoffman and Elm (2006) described it, the usual sentiment about "requirements creep" in the field of software engineering is that creep is a bad thing. Rather, Hoffman and Elm argued, it is an inevitable empirical fact and something to be accommodated in the procurement process, because it is a key to how software is actually created.

Furthermore, the usual procedure of requirements elicitation does not always dig down to the tacit knowledge: "Simply asking managers what they want often works poorly" (Goguen, 1994, p. 166), an issue widely discussed in the literature on expert knowledge elicitation methodology (see chapter 7). "In order to build a system that effectively meets a real business need, it may be necessary to find out what workers, clients, and managers really do" (Goguen, 1994, p. 166). "[It] is usually best to go where the work is actually done, and carefully observe what actually happens" (Goguen, 1997, p. 33). This is a theme of CTA. Goguen and his colleagues approached this methods issue by noting the limitations and weaknesses of certain widely used methods. Questionnaires and surveys were seen as limited because they decontextualize reasoning and leave no room for negotiation. Focus groups, often used in requirements specification, were seen as likewise limited and vulnerable to issues of politics, interpersonal conflicts, historical baggage, and the like. Think-aloud problem solving was seen as limited because it disengaged the participant from the social context of problem solving, critical to system development in teams. Finally, all of these methods were seen as limited in their ability to reveal tacit knowledge. Hence, Goguen and his colleagues recommended the appropriate use of combinations of methods, including ethnomethodological methods.

> [It] is usually good idea to start with an ethnographic study to uncover basic aspects of social order, such as basic concept systems used by members, the division into social groups, etc. ... After this one might use questionnaires or interviews to explore what problems members see as most important, how members place themselves in various classifications schemes, etc. Then one might apply conversation, discourse, or interaction analysis to get a deeper understanding of selected problematic aspects. (Goguen, 1997, p. 50)

Workplace observation combined with conversation analysis of social interactions is recommended to reveal such things at the conceptual categories used to shape interactions, and the value systems that drive organizations, and use that empirical knowledge to help inform processes of technology development (i.e., determining the importance or precedence of requirements, identifying the trade-offs when requirements are in conflict). This recommendation of a palette of methods, rather than some single method, is a theme to discussions of CTA in both Expertise Studies (see chapter 8) and Cognitive Systems Engineering (see chapter 7).

Summary

In this chapter we grouped several related communities of practice that have focused on the idea that cognition (and cognitive work) is not an isolated construct that resides solely within an individual. Proponents of situated cognition reacted against the idea that the environment is simply acted upon rather than interacting with the individual. Studies of cognition in the context of society and work have supported the idea that cognition in a real-world setting looks quite different from cognition in an academic laboratory. Those studying distributed cognition have taken these ideas even further, suggesting that expertise is not a property of an individual but distributed across individuals and their context of work. The Sociology of Scientific Knowledge has focused on the acquisition and dissemination of scientific knowledge, arguing that acquisition of scientific knowledge is as much a social accomplishment as an individual experience. The Sociology of the Professions has investigated social and economic issues related to professional domains and expertise.

Although few people working within the communities of practice we covered in this chapter would see much value added in referring to their methods as CTA, as opposed to ethnographic in nature, one key element in common is that interviews and observations are often used to analyze the interplay of people and technology. The research demonstrates how such methods can be taken to great depths of analysis and understanding of cognitive work. It also shows how some researchers bootstrap themselves to the journeyman level in the domain(s) being studied. The communities of practice reviewed in this chapter also share the view that cognitive processes cannot be analyzed in isolation from their organizational and social contexts.

Ethnographic methods include observations, interviews, documentation analysis, and combinations of all three. They have been used to study a broad range of domains including navigation (Hutchins, 1995a), flight crew collaboration (Hutchins, 1990, 1995a), photocopier repair (Orr, 1996), tailoring (Lave, 1988), expert designers in the aerospace industry (Carkett, 2003), and air traffic controllers (Dekker & Nyce, 2004; Mackay, 2000). As with many of the other perspectives discussed in this book, ethnographers have pointed out limitations of the experimental approach when it comes to understanding work and designing future work, including generalizability of research findings and the likelihood of missing important factors when relying solely on experimental methods.

Some make a distinction between strong and weak ethnography (Dekker & Nyce, 2004). Weak ethnography is something like a natural history, strong on description and data collection but weak on analysis and interpretation. Strong ethnography is described as a continuous, progressive reinterpretation and enrichment of the successive layers of data mined from the field observations and interviews. A philosophical stance is required that allows systematic comparison of multiple perspectives on events and processes.

Myths about ethnography include the following:

- Anyone can do it—it is just a matter of common sense.
- Being insiders qualifies insiders to do ethnography in their own work setting.
- Ethnography does not involve preformulated study designs or systematic methods—anything goes.
- To find out what people do, all you have to do is ask them.
- Behavioral and organizational patterns exist "out there." Research is just a matter of looking and listening to detect the patterns.

Each of these myths was addressed by Forsythe (1993, 1999), who carefully refuted each oversimplification, describing the reality of ethnography as a careful, systematic set of methods that require significant training and skill to apply properly. He also offers examples of "do-it-yourself ethnography," highlighting where inexperienced ethnographers often go wrong.

Strong ethnography has been discussed in the context of requirements for the design of complex information systems (Anderson, 1994). Anderson made the point that ethnography is primarily a method of analysis, not a method of data collection. There is a tendency to think about ethnography as "typed up spell-checked, anonymized, field notes" rather than a search for deeper pattern and regularities. This search for patterns often involves the use of analogy. Ethnography can offer more than a detailed description of work routines. It can help in changing the frame of reference. By considering the problem in terms of analogy, issues previously considered to be problems can become precisely shaped solutions that workers have evolved to deal with the challenges of the workplace.

Situated cognition is a view that arose within ethnography and spread to computer science. The core of this view is that cognition is "situated" within a given context of learning and use and cannot be analyzed without considerations of this context. Early contributors to this view include psychologist Sir Frederic Barlett (1932), who proposed that learning is a social process, and Émile Durkheim (1915), who discussed cultural memory ("collective conscience").

More recently, situated cognition was proposed in the context of growing dissatisfaction with the information processing metaphor espoused by the traditional cognitive psychology approach. Researchers became especially dissatisfied when attempting to reconcile the results of studies of real-world problem solving in natural field-based settings with traditional problem-solving theories of the cognitive sciences. The academic cognitive psychology approach considers knowledge an abstract entity that represents "the world outside" the human mind. This was a reaction against the behaviorist paradigm that did not consider mentalistic phenomena to play any causal role in behavior. The cognitive paradigm in contrast relied heavily on mentalistic phenomena in causal explanations. Situated theorists criticized the cognitive paradigms for becoming overly individualistic and mentalistic in their focus. Cognitive theories treated the environment as if it were only acted on rather than interacting with the individual.

Situated theorists argue that neither cognition nor the social world can be "bracketed off" as objects of study. Ethnographers emphasize the study of apprenticeship activities rather than isolated learning as conceived by psychologists. In addition, ethnographers blur the distinction between sociology and technology, claiming that the function of even mundane objects such as locks, hinges, and seat belts cannot be adequately described without considering social context. A final strong claim of Situated Theory is that people possess tacit knowledge that cannot be articulated. From this claim follows the conclusion that CTA is limited because there exists a form of knowledge that cannot be verbalized. (See chapter 8.)

Situated theorists have argued that the nature of cognition in real-world problem solving is qualitatively different from that which occurs in context-poor laboratory settings. It thus follows that situated theorists consider theories of cognition to be fundamentally flawed by the attempt to study cognitive processes without accounting for the social and historical influence that shape learning and collaborative activity. Proponents of situation cognition offer many examples illustrating why one should consider "the cognitive system" as a person acting in coordination with a social group to conduct activities using tools and practices that have evolved within a culture.

Distributed cognition is a term used to describe the notion that cognition in practice is not isolated in the minds of individuals but distributed across individuals and their context of work. Because traditional cognitive psychology considers the unit of analysis as the individual, the locus of resources for problem solving is also considered to lie within the individual. Distributed cognition directs the researcher to think outside the "skin and skull" of the individual to consider how individual working groups solve problems collaboratively. Thus, researchers are encouraged to consider "extramental" structures such as the nature of social and communicative interactions within work groups, the sociohistoric context at large, and the elements of the external, physical environment. In shifting the focus from the individual to the system, researchers have proposed that expertise and skilled performance are not fixed properties of individuals but a dynamic property of the system in which individuals operate.

Sociotechnics is a form of applied sociology that was introduced in the United Kingdom at the Tavistock Institute in the 1950s. Classic studies of the sociology of industrialized work introduced the notion of the "sociotechnical system," which is widely used in modern communities of practice to designate the research focus and is sometimes used to define the focus of CTA (e.g., Vicente, 1999; see chapter 10). The Tavistock research, and subsequent Sociotechnics work, demonstrated the links of psychological, sociological, and technological factors in determining the goodness of work. The goal of Sociotechnics is to develop new work systems that optimize the achievement of the goals of the organization and the individual workers. Sociotechnicians have proposed a number of principles for guiding the design of good work methods, principles for good teamwork, and principles for technology design. In Sociotechnics we see parallels to many ideas in Cognitive Systems Engineering. (Team cognitive work and team CTA are the special focus of chapter 16.)

The *Sociology of Scientific Knowledge* represents another related view considered in this chapter. Harry Collins (1996) reacted to the failures of so-called intelligent machines. He claimed that artificial intelligence research fails to consider the idea that knowledge is not situated in human bodies. Because of this attempt to "disembed" knowledge from its social and cultural context, the capabilities of intelligent machines are severely limited. Collins (1992) argued that computers are not intelligent because they are not social agents, and social embeddedness is needed for intelligence. Society is the locus of knowledge and understanding. Only recently have designers tried to tackle this problem of making computers act as "team players."

In the field of *Sociology of Knowledge*, investigations range from historiographic–philosophical analysis to the use of ethnographic observation, participant observation, work-space analysis, and interviewing. Researchers have focused on the study of science, the acquisition and dissemination of scientific knowledge, and other topics. Researchers within this approach argue that science is a largely "constructive" process that cannot be analyzed without considerations of the historical, cultural, and social context in which it occurs. Furthermore, this approach suggests that experimentation, far from being an objective tool for inquiry, is largely a social process. Sociologists also argue that "facts" are social constructs. Latour and Woolgar (1979) argued that negotiation between scientists about what can be accepted as proof is not different from any argument between politicians or lawyers. Latour and Woolgar went on to propose with regard to scientists that "the better politicians and strategists they are, the better the science they produce."

The final community of practice discussed in this chapter is the *Sociology of Professions*. This community has clear links to Expertise Studies (chapter 8). This includes conceptual analyses, interviews, and survey analyses of the ways in which experts are perceived by society (i.e., as an elite group), ways in which experts understand their role within organizations and society, ways in which experts perceive their relations with their clients, and ways in which expertise is managed as a resource, both within organizations and by society at large. Researchers are likely to encounter difficulty nailing down what it means for someone to be an expert in domains where the primary task of the professional involves predicting individual or aggregate human behavior (Shanteau, 1992). Researchers within this community present a view of expertise as a social attribution, regarding expertise as a role that is defined relative to organizations. Expertise is created by society as a whole, in which a demand creates a market, referred to as the "cognitive economics" of expertise.

In a study of professionals across a range of domains, Schön (1982, 1987) drew out similarities in the reasoning of practitioners in disparate domains. From these studies, Schön developed a view of expert performance that hinges on notions of intuition and tacit knowledge rather than on formal or rational-analytic thinking. Schön differentiated the use of the term *expert* to refer to professionals who maintain an elitist stance, versus *reflective practitioners,* who do not try to maintain a professional façade at the expense of knowledge sharing and connection. Schön also emphasized that some knowledge cannot be easily articulated but can be observed in the activities of practitioners.

With regard to methods, some would claim that it is inappropriate to group work practice analysis or Activity Analysis with CTA because they are different analytical frameworks. Task analysis methods refer to goals, procedures, tasks, functions, and expertise. Activity Analysis refers to motives, emotions, practices, activities, scripts, and work, in addition to anthropological concepts such as setting, activity, rhythm, ritual, norm, and identity. Some have argued that task analysis is framed by the study of expertise, whereas Activity Analysis is framed by the study of work or work practices. We suggest that both sets of core concepts are appropriate and have intersecting applications. Although there are differences in the "methods palette" used, Cognitive Work Analysis (chapter 10), Cognitive Systems Engineering (chapter 7), and the ethnographic and sociological approaches discussed in this chapter all rely on some of the same basic ideas of observation and interviewing for studying work in natural settings. Ethnographers tend to spend more time in the domain than do researchers in many of the other perspectives discussed in this book. Some ethnographers advocate participatory field research, in which the investigator becomes immersed in the study of domain until the investigator has nearly the same depth of understanding of the world as the natives have.

Ethnographic methods have been applied effectively in the cooperative design of work systems in areas such as clinical dentistry and newspaper production, in relating expertise to innovation in the design of nuclear weapons, in the importance of strategic thinking in the creation of an electronic funds transfer network, and in importing methods of apprenticing in the control of computer-driven printing presses. Ethnographic research at NASA has had implications for the design of space exploration work systems. Social and ethnographic studies have also examined methods or management, organization, policy, and cultural differences. Finally, considerations from sociology have played a role in reshaping how some computer scientists think about the process of "requirements specification" for the procurement of information systems.

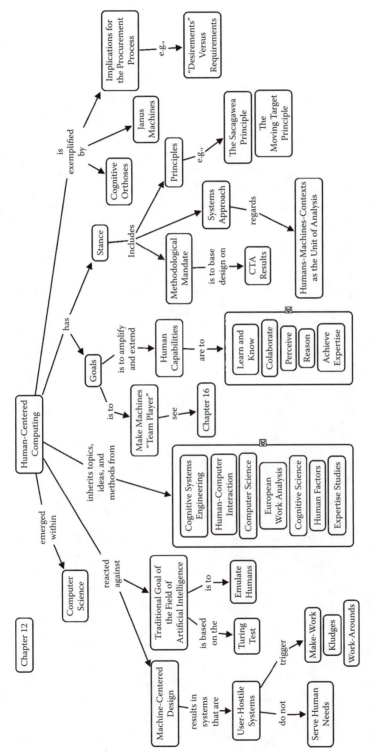

FIGURE 12.1 Chapter 12 Concept Map.

12

Human-Centered Computing

> Human-Centered Intelligent Systems, like motherhood and apple pie, is a warm snugly term that anyone would find hard to feel negative towards.
>
> —Paul Attewell (1997, p. 305)

Introduction

As we have indicated throughout the chapters in this volume, a main application of Cognitive Task Analysis (CTA) is in the design of new technologies. Many CTA practitioners program computers to create decision aids and interfaces. For example, the various alternative approaches to decision aiding studied by Stephanie Guerlain, Phil Smith, and their colleagues at Ohio State (see chapter 7) all involved programming and interface design activities on the part of the researchers. On the main, however, computer scientists, programmers, engineers, and other technologists are the ones who actually "bend the metal." A perspective on computer science that emerged in recent decades not only embraces CTA methodology but underscores its importance. Thus, we have reserved a discussion of the "Human-Centered Computing" (HCC) perspective for last. HCC emerged within computer science but as an approach to design, its stance mandates a methodology in which design is based on CTA, welcoming any and all specific methods that might be employed, ranging from the methods of the psychology laboratory to the methods of the field ethnographer. In other words, HCC pulls it all together by focusing on applications of CTA.

HCC is integrative of many of the ideas we have relayed in the earlier chapters. Discussions of HCC as a viewpoint show many of the reactions and "pendulum swings" we have noted in discussions of other perspectives—ways in which emerging communities of practice define themselves in terms of what they are *not*.

What HCC Is *Not*

In a traditional approach to the design of information processing technology, system developers specify the requirements for machines via methods of task analysis; they then implement or prototype the requirements; and finally they produce devices and software. Although this process is intended to ensure that important environmental and user components are captured during the requirements phase, too often the focus has been on technological and organizational requirements. Experience has shown that devices that are designed according to the "design then train" philosophy "force users to adapt to the system. The user is entangled with the system terminology and jargons that are the designer's view of the world" (Ntuen, 1997, p. 312). Many lessons learned over recent decades have pointed toward a new approach. The lessons span a range including insights from significant accidents caused by differences between the intentions of designers and the understanding and cognitive capabilities of the users (e.g., the Three Mile Island incident). But the lessons also come much closer to home (see Norman, 1988). We have all experienced, for example, the frustrations of learning to use upgraded software, advertised for its new capabilities by those who designed it and are therefore familiar with it. The new capabilities, however, usually require significant relearning, backpeddling, kludging, finding work-arounds, and so on. Bells and whistles often go unused and even unnoticed.

Human-Centered Computing is the term used to designate a new approach that is distinguished from what might be called Machine-Centered Design (see chapter 7), but in this case involves a reaction within computer science, paralleling the reaction of Cognitive Systems Engineers against Machine-Centered Design within traditional human factors psychology.

What HCC Might, or Might Not, Be

A report to the National Science Foundation (NSF) (Flanagan, Huang, Jones, & Kasif, 1997) presented proceedings from a workshop on "Human-Centered Systems," which included position papers from 51 researchers spanning many disciplines including electronics, psychology, medicine, and the military. Diverse opinions were presented about precisely what HCC is all about:

- To some, HCC is a philosophical–humanistic position regarding the ethics and aesthetics of the workplace.
- To some, an HCC system is any system that enhances human performance.
- To some, an HCC system is any system that plays any kind of role in mediating human interactions.
- To some, HCC is a software design process that results in interfaces that are *really* user friendly.
- To some, HCC is a description of what makes for a good tool: the computer does all the adapting.
- To some, HCC is an emerging interdiscipline, requiring institutionalization and special training programs.

Complicating the matter is that some of the statements offered as being definitional of HCC seem like old wine in new bottles:

The first thing to note is that many Artificial Intelligence efforts in the past did exhaustively map human experts' knowledge and tried to model it. They were certainly Human-Centered in that respect. How then are future Human-Centered Intelligent Systems supposed to be more Human-Centered than the old? The term clearly suggests a change in direction for AI research, but is there a real commitment to a change in direction or is this just a new way of re-packaging the existing approach, a way of putting past disappointments behind us, while arguing for a new wave of funding? (Attewell, 1997, p. 305)

An instance of old wine might be the following:

To be human-centered, a [computer] system should be based on an analysis of the human tasks that the system is aiding, monitored for performance in terms of human benefits, built to take account of human skills, and adaptable easily to changing human needs. (Flanagan et al., 1997, p. 12)

This idea, some would say, has *always* been a goal in human factors engineering. And what seemed like old wine continued to pour:

Human-centered design recognizes that technology structures social relationships and takes into account the various ways in which actors and organizations are interconnected via social relationships, information flow, and decision making authority. (Flanagan et al., 1997, p. 12)

This idea, some would say, is old wine in organizational psychology. And more old wine continued to pour: "Technology is often based on human-centered intentions" (Flanagan et al., 1997, p. 64). But this is a weak sense of HCC; that is, a system is human centered if it is intended to satisfy some need.

To ergonomicists who have developed technologies in the European tradition of work analysis (see chapter 10), the entire notion of an HCC paradigm is thoroughly old wine:

The concept of "human centered systems" has been extensively utilized by the European Commission in its research programs, during the eighties. A whole program was totally focused on this topic. It was an attempt to develop a precompetitive research strategy in Europe driven by the users' needs, and not pushed by the technology market. (De Keyser, 1997, p. 261)

So if the foundational ideas of HCC are old wine in new bottles, and the new crop of HCC advocates can get away with casting traditional approaches as straw men, is there anything to HCC that is really new?

What HCC *Is*

HCC entails a shift in thinking about information technology, including intelligent systems. HCC recognizes the fact that the design and use of new information processing tools must be couched in systems terms (Hoffman, Hayes, Ford, & Hancock, 2002; Hollnagel & Woods, 2005; Woods & Hollnagel, 2006). That is, the human workers and the information processing device are regarded as a coupled, coadapting system nested within a context to which they have adapted and in which they are functional. Furthermore, the design of systems must regard the human (traditionally referred to as the "end user") as one aspect of a larger and dynamic context, including the worker's team, the organization, and the organization's clients and sponsors. In other words, the fundamental unit of analysis is not the machine, not the human, not the one human–one machine interaction, and not the context and domain of work but the collective of all of these. The capabilities of the human are contingent on the support provided by the machine and are conditional on the context in which they are exercised. The capabilities of the machine are contingent on the support provided by the human and are conditional on the context in which they are exercised.

HCC can be defined as the design, development, and evaluation of technology that amplifies and extends human perceptual, cognitive, and collaborative activities (Hoffman, Hayes, & Ford, 2001). HCC research focuses on all aspects of human–machine integration—humans with software, humans with hardware, humans with work spaces, and humans with humans—as well as on aspects of machine–machine interaction insofar as they affect total system performance. The HCC vision inherits all the complexity of software engineering and systems integration (e.g., issues of "user friendliness") plus the additional complexity of understanding and modeling human–human and human–organization interactions in the work context. Thus, HCC provides a new research outlook, with new research agendas and goals.

The HCC approach contrasts with a traditional view of artificial intelligence. This traditional view is based on the goal or challenge of the "Turing Test," named after pioneer Alan Turing. That goal for computer science is to create machines that emulate human capabilities. This is an ancient dream of humanity, with links to the Pygmalion myth, the concept of the Golem, Frankenstein, and other legends (Hoffman, Klein, & Laughery, 2002). Across the ages there has been considerable discussion of the "man as machine" metaphor, from Julian Offray de la Mettrie's (1709–1751) view that the human body is nothing but a machine, to Rene Descarte's (1596–1650) argument that no machine could adequately emulate humans:

> It is indeed conceivable that a machine could be so made that it would utter words, and even words appropriate to the presence of physical acts or objects which cause some change in its organs; as, for example, if it is touched in some spot it would ask what you wanted, it in another that it would cry that it was hurt, and so on for similar things. But it could never modify its phrases to reply to the sense of whatever was said in its presence, and even the most stupid men can do ... although such machines could do many things as well as, or perhaps better than men, they would infallibly fail in certain others, by which we would discover that they did not act by understanding or reason, but only by the disposition of their organs. For while reason is a universal instrument which can be used in all sorts of situations, the organs have to be arranged in a particular way for each particular action. From this it follows that is it morally impossible and clearly incredible that there should be enough different devices in a machine to make it behave in all the occurrences of life as our reason makes us behave. (Descartes, 1637/1964, pp. 52–57)

This line of argument continues even to the present, manifested in such things as competitions between human and machine chess players. HCC does not advocate that we give up the dream of creating the intelligent machine, though it does share Descartes's sense of caution. Rather, HCC advocates an alternative approach to thinking about the creation of new technologies.

HCC research is regarded as being inherently interdisciplinary, combining research in cognitive science, computer science, and the social sciences. An ensuing difficulty, however, is that there are perhaps as many definitions of HCC as there are agencies in the federal government.

Why HCC?

There emerged from the NSF Workshop some pointed consensus on the new ideas, which included the following.

HCC is not just old wine in new bottles. Confusion on this has arisen perhaps because HCC does inherit ideas and issues from the past decades of Cognitive Systems Engineering:

> This effort expands and substantially generalizes existing notions of human–computer interaction and user interface design as core activities of Human-Centered Systems. This initiative also includes many fundamental topics in computing, communications, epistemology, and language that emerge from the need to develop complex computational/communication frameworks for supporting diverse human activities. (Flanagan et al., 1997, p. 35)

Having "seen the light," many advocates of HCC find themselves in a state of considerable frustration:

> The most extensive attempt to think out a new, more human-centered approach to informatics, is found in Thomas Landauer's book *The Trouble With Computers* (1995). ... He contrasts Human-Centeredness with computer automation, and blames past failures on computer researchers' repeated efforts to replace human skills and decisions rather than trying to augment human skills. Landauer's image is of computer as tool for human use rather than as machine. Central to achieving that is the development of Human-Centered Design: research and development of techniques which focus on how people do their work, identify where bottlenecks to performance exist, and chart out the possibilities for computer augmentation. I note that most of the discourse in the current AI and human–computer interaction literatures continues the old approach. It starts with the machine, not the work-system. The changing capacities of computers, not the needs of working humans, continue to direct where research goes. So parallel processing and neural nets evoke new attempts at replacing human decision-making. There are calls for more research on speech recognition. And so on. It is not that these are bad directions, but we should be honest and admit they fall squarely in the traditional AI philosophy of using the latest technologies to model/simulate and then replace what humans do. Even current work on Virtual Realities, fascinating as it is, follows the logic of increasing the envelope of technological capacity and then afterwards seeing what humans can use the technology for. These are not Human-Centered in any new or different sense. (Attewell, 1997, p. 305)

The HCC approach is being forced on us by the rapid pace of technological advancement. The introduction of poorly designed technology has led to countless accidents. In aviation, for instance (Billings, 1997), accidents have been caused by pilot mental overload and loss of situation awareness due to system complexity, lack of feedback, misplaced trust in automation, and imposed system autonomy. Aviation automation systems have been designed such that "there is little to do when things are going well, but the computer demands more activity on the part of the human at times when workload is already high" (Billings, 1997, p. 131).

Likewise in other domains, a new approach is being forced on us:

> In many businesses, computerized accounting systems appear like the layers of an archaeological dig, with newer systems built upon older systems. ... There is often no central rationale or architecture ... and systems developers, analysts, managers and employees feel themselves caught in a web of overly complicated and redundant accounting schemes. Such legacy systems can take on a fragile inflexible quality: changing any part of them is fraught with problems, not only because one is changing archaic code, but also because what seem to be harmless modifications

of one part may prove to have unexpected, and occasionally disastrous effects on other parts of the system. (Flanagan et al., 1997, p. 94)

I study how people work around computer technology in real workplaces. In such settings it is often quite clear that information technologies, while facilitating some activities, create numerous burdens and bottlenecks for employees which fritter away potential productivity gains. Even in large wealthy high-tech corporations, one sees little evidence that system design has improved or become markedly more user-friendly in recent years. Learning how to cope with systems flaws and idiosyncrasies—a knowledge of kludges and work-arounds remains a large part of an employees skill. These are all symptoms or indicators that information technologies in the work world fall far below their potential. (Attewell, 1997, p. 305)

And in aviation:

The introduction of a machine expert can alter users' cognitive and decision processes in ways that lead to worse performance than if the person were working unaided. There have been several empirical studies that have compared the performance of individuals performing cognitive tasks with and without the aid of a decision-aid that generated a problem solution for the user. A consistent finding is that the availability of this type of decision-aid alters people's information gathering activities, and narrows the set of hypotheses that they consider, increasing the likelihood that they will miss critical information or fail to generate the correct solution in cases where the intelligent system's recommendation is wrong. As example a recent study of airline pilots and dispatchers showed that in a scenario where the computer's recommendation was poor, the generation of a suggestion by the computer early in the person's own problem solving produced a 30 percent increase in inappropriate plan selection over users of a version of the system that provided no recommendation (Layton et al., 1994). (Roth, 1997b, p. 248)

Analyses of trends in work productivity have shown that the introduction of computers actually leads to *declines* in productivity. This trend has been referred to as the "productivity paradox" (see Harris, 1994; Landauer, 1995). Not mincing words, Flanagan et al. (1997) referred to a "sense of crisis in current system design practice":

that there is a lag in the development of analytical approaches and institutions, which can safely manage the greater complexity of today's information systems, and in a way that will be more effectively human-centered. For others, the need for change is demonstrated by spectacular failures of some very large systems which can be attributed to the combination of human and technological factors: The Challenger disaster; the failures of air-traffic control systems, and long costly delays in the development of systems for agencies such as the Social Security System and the IRS; problems with the implementation of private enterprise-wide information retrieval systems are all examples. (p. 94)

In general, the new HCC approach is being forced on us because

we are moving towards an era of ubiquitous computing (anyone, any time, any place, anywhere). We must provide effective means for humans to generate new creative environments and knowledge/communication infrastructures that support activities that were not possible before (e.g., Web-based education, electronic commerce, virtual travel). ... We are experiencing unprecedented leaps in technological power which is manifested as computer speed, memory, disk capacity, miniaturization, and universally accessible networks. These advances present unparalleled opportunities for expanding the ubiquitous use of computers in fundamental human activities such as communication, interaction, collaboration, decision making, knowledge creation and dissemination, and creative work. (Flanagan et al., 1997, pp. 4, 11)

Traditional approaches to systems design have resulted in tools that are user hostile. As Woods (1994b, p. 3) put it, "The road to technology-centered systems is with human-centered intentions." Typically, computer systems force the worker to adapt, require make-work (e.g., lots of window housekeeping), and are annoyingly brittle. We should be careful here to not sell systems designers too short: "All designers in some sense believe they are taking a 'human-centered' approach" (Roth, 1997b, p. 250). Nevertheless, there is an urgent need to set a much higher standard for systems design. Systems need to be flexible and transparent (easily understood by the user). They need to support the worker and not force the worker to conform to predesigned tasks. They need to make the work engaging and enjoyable.

> Technologies that cannot take interactive direction from humans make the joint human–machine system vulnerable to a variety of miscommunications, misassessments, and miscoordinations that can and have lead to failures. Thus, human-centered systems need to fit into the context of use, uphold human authority, and be open, inspectable, and intelligible. (Flanagan et al., 1997, pp. 4, 11)

Recognizing this, a number of computer scientists are beginning to cut through older traditions.

> The current graphic user interfaces are still quite primitive and poorly designed to take advantage of the remarkable human visual perceptual system. ... It seems increasingly archaic to see 40–60 icons on the screen, deal with the cluttered desktop of overlapping windows, and waste time with unnecessary window housekeeping, when appealing alternatives are beginning to appear in research prototypes. ... The future of user interfaces is in the direction of larger, higher resolution screens, that present perceptually rich and information-abundant displays. Human perceptual skills are quite remarkable and largely underutilized in current information and computing systems. (Schneiderman, 1997, pp. 208–209)

Shneiderman and his colleagues have created a number of new interfaces that leverage human cognitive capabilities, including such ideas as coupled windows, synchronized scrolling, and multiwindow operations.

The levels and scales for systems design and analysis have to undergo a major shift. This is from a focus on "one person–one machine" to an inclusion of the social and organizational contexts. Indeed, organizers of the NSF Workshop realized that this factor was of such importance that it merited its own breakout group. Here are two participants' expressions of the core idea:

> The information science literature lends studies of the multiple paths that information converges along—such as colleague networks, personal collections, community practices. To these, we are adding that convergence is a process in which status, cultural and community practices, resources, experience, and infrastructure work together. ... The greatest issue for the creation of intelligent systems is that these processes are invisible to traditional requirements analysis; they can only be seen through the analysis of work. (Bowker, 1997, p. 308)

> Human-centered systems should engage the richness of people's work practices, social lives, etc. ... people's work relationships are not simply cooperative, and may also sometimes be conflictual, competitive, coercive, or convivial. Human-Centered Systems have to help people and groups under the wide gamut of plausible work relationships. We need to develop ways of modeling systems use under a wide variety of social relationships. (Kling, 1997, p. 310)

There needs to be a merger of traditionally separate realms of science. Information sciences (knowledge representation and management, visualization, etc.), collaboration sciences (distributed learning, collaboration, team cognition, etc.), and social sciences (social and organizational aspects of computing), merge into a Science of Design. This entails a significant change for computer science:

> A [new] science of design is needed; that is, design methodologies in which the unit of analysis is the joint human–machine system, where particular attention is paid to the ways in which technological change transforms cognitive and collaborative activities in a field of practice. It is insufficient to study and model people in isolation from technology or technology disconnected from a field of human activity. Both perspectives are needed in a fundamentally integrated way. An implication of this view is the centrality of field work to provide real data on real activity in real contexts. (Flanagan et al., 1997, p. 4)

> All engineering and design activities call for the management of tradeoffs. In classical engineering disciplines, the tradeoffs can often be quantified: material strength, construction costs, rate of wear, and the like. In [new] design discipline, the tradeoffs are more difficult to identify and to measure because they rest on human needs, desires, and values. The designer stands with one foot in the technology and one foot in the domain of human concerns, and these two worlds are not easily commensurable. As well as being distinct from engineering, interaction design is not covered by the existing design fields either. If the computer user just looked at software, rather than operating it, traditional visual design would be at the center. If the spaces were actually physical, rather than virtual, then traditional product and architectural design would suffice. But computers have created a new medium—one that is both active and virtual. Designers in this new medium need to develop principles and practices that are unique to the computer's scope and fluidity of interactivity. (Winograd, 1997, p. 286)

The NSF report went on to lay out dozens of open avenues for research in topics including data mining, virtual reality, natural language interfaces, ontologies for adaptive information systems, the preservation of organizational memories, collaborative scientific computation, dynamic multimedia documents, management systems, ubiquitous access for special populations, the modeling of dynamic databases, the prediction of the cognitive complexity of systems with long design cycles, the modeling of the impact of technologies on social relationships in the workplace, and so on.

> Key topics for research include knowledge representation and exchange, interaction with a sea of unstructured information, ability to cope with ambiguity and uncertainty, adaptive environments, learning, user and organizational models, collaborative environments, data visualization, summarization and presentation, universal access to complex hybrid digital libraries, and distributed knowledge networks. Communication network issues, including standards, accessibility, and dynamic resource allocation methods, also are a part of the picture. (Flanagan et al., 1997, p. 4)

So far, so good. We have a definition of HCC (in terms of what it is and what it is not) and a mandate for its application. But how does HCC pull it all together?

Integrative Principles of HCC

In a series of essays,[1] Hoffman, Pat Hayes, Kenneth Ford, and their colleagues have discussed a number of proposed "principles" of HCC. These tap into all of the literature we have discussed in the chapters of this volume, integrating ideas from Donald Norman, Mica Endsley, David Woods, Erik Hollnagel, Gary Klein, Emilie Roth, and others. Table 12.1 lists some of these principles.

TABLE 12.1 Some Principles of Human-Centered Computing

The Aretha Franklin Principle	Do not devalue the human to justify the machine. Do not criticize the machine to rationalize the human. Advocate the human–machine system to amplify both.
The Sacagawea Principle	Human-centered computational tools need to support active organization of information, active search for information, active exploration of information, reflection on the meaning of information, and evaluation and choice among action sequence alternatives.
The Lewis and Clark Principle	The human user of the guidance needs to be shown the guidance in a way that is organized in terms of their major goals. Information needed for each particular goal should be shown in a meaningful form and should allow the human to directly comprehend the major decisions associated with each goal.
The Envisioned World Principle	The introduction of new technology, including appropriately human-centered technology, will bring about changes in environmental constraints (i.e., features of the sociotechnical system or the context of practice). Even though the domain constraints may remain unchanged, and even if cognitive constraints are leveraged and amplified, changes to the environmental constraints will impact the work.
The Fort Knox Principle	The knowledge and skills of proficient workers is gold. It must be elicited and preserved, but the gold must not simply be stored and safeguarded. It must be disseminated and used within the organization when needed.
The Pleasure Principle	Good tools provide a feeling of direct engagement. They simultaneously provide a feeling of flow and challenge.
The Janus Principle	Human-centered systems do not force a separation between learning and performance. They integrate them.
The Mirror–Mirror Principle	Every participant in a complex cognitive system will form a model of the other participant agents as well as a model of the controlled process and its environment.
The Moving Target Principle	The sociotechnical workplace is constantly changing, and constant change in environmental constraints may entail constant change in cognitive constraints, even if domain constraints remain constant.

These principles express cautionary tales that have been learned in such disciplines as Cognitive Systems Engineering, Expertise Studies, and human factors. But they are not entries in a cookbook that allow one to go directly to good system designs. They're not a substitute for empirical inquiry via CTA, design creativity, or proper software development. Rather than being formulas, the principles imply design challenges. Looking back on the essays, we find one challenge expressed directly. For example, an implication of the Fort Knox Principle is what Hoffman and Hanes (2003) called the "Tough Nut Problem": How can we redesign jobs and processes, including workstations, computational aids, and interfaces, in such a way as to get knowledge elicitation as a "freebie" and at the same time make the usual tasks easier? Designers or project managers may choose to adopt the principles as policies, if their goal is to create good complex cognitive systems. Thus, the stance of HCC has implications for the procurement process by which new technologies are designed and implemented.

There is wide recognition that the development of information technologies hinges on the interaction of users, systems designers, and systems developers (including systems analysts, computer scientists, engineers, etc.) (Green, 1989). The designers need to understand the user's needs and the goals for the system that is being created (Holtzblatt & Beyer, 1995). However, the process for the designer–user interactions is not currently grounded in the empirical methodologies of CTA. The result of mis-communication is misinterpretation of user needs (Kim & March, 1995). This leads to design glitches that force the user to create work-arounds and cope with user-hostile features such as brittleness and automation surprises when the machine does things the user does not understand. As a consequence, it is the rare system that does not have to go through redesigns, often costly ones (Scott, 1988).

This critique made Hoffman and Elm (2006) wonder about the assumption that requirements *should* be fixed, especially in a world that is not.

> It would seem that change in the world vastly outpaces our current ability to build and adequately test large-scale decision-aiding and performance support systems. Yet, the default belief seems to be that the world can be frozen, and that requirements must be frozen, otherwise nothing would get built. The result of technological backlash is to always a blame game seeking simple, clear-cut "human errors" or "human limitations," or putting blame on a contractor, when the root cause is systemic. "Requirements creep" is not a nasty thing to be eradicated, but an empirical inevitability to be accommodated. (p. 76)

Hoffman and Elm proposed a new notion of "desirements," which is contrasted with requirements, similar to Goguen's ideas (1997) we discussed in chapter 11.

> Users not only have immediate, definite needs (that should be captured as requirements), but they also have "desirements" … desired functionalities that cannot be included as system requirements, but might be at some future time. These are not "bells and whistles" to be scratched off the project accounting ledgers because managers think the users do not *really* need them, or because budget constraints preclude expending time and effort. While appreciating the trade-offs that are involved here, we are also guided by the common finding from studies of expertise in context, that domain practitioners' candid statements about what they *really* need are often not given due consideration. (p. 79)

To build for desirements, technology must be created from the start so as to antici-pate, and not merely allow for, subsequent modifications. Modifiability is generally thought of in terms of common operating systems, interoperability, and modularity. A new software bundle might plug and play, making the technology adaptable from an engineering point of view. But there is also a largely neglected human-centering and human–machine system aspect. Because of the complex interactions and con-textual dependencies that are always involved in complex cognitive and collaborative work, adding on a new capability module, based on a desirement, might alter the work demands of an existing system capability; for example, it might lead to goal conflicts. This requires CTA.

We now concretize the discussion by presenting a capsule view of some examples of human-centered systems.

Examples of Human-Centered Systems

Example 1: A Janus Machine

This example illustrates what it means for a system to be human centered by pursuing the Janus Principle listed in Table 12.1. The U.S. Navy's Naval Air Warfare Center sponsored the creation of a software and display tool to help train oceanographers about sonar oceanography. The Interactive Multisensor Analysis Trainer is based on a graphic-object, perspectival display that portrays a volume of ocean in horizontal view, with a ship at its surface. Sonar beams are depicted as ray tracings. Within the volume of water are colorized layers, representing different layers of temperature and salinity. These cause deflections in sonar beam paths, which the learner can see after manipulating layer parameters (see Hoffman, Lintern, & Eitelman, 2004). The first cohort of sailors who trained using this system found it very useful and helpful as a training aid. Indeed, the sailors found it so helpful that they took it with them when they deployed to the fleet, and they attempted to use it to visualize actual conditions of operation. The users had realized that the system worked as a performance support tool. This is a case in which the training aid was well designed as a training aid, and as a consequence it also supported performance—and, interestingly enough, it was the users who discovered that.

Example 2: A "Cognitive Orthosis"

Following the definition of HCC as technologies that amplify and extend human abilities, Ford, Glymour, and Hayes (1997) proposed that such tools be called "cognitive orthoses." The orthosis metaphor implies the importance of designing systems that fit the human and machine components together in ways that synergistically exploit their respective capacities. One such device is the Tactile Vision Substitution System. Studies have demonstrated that visual information (which leads to the subjective qualities of seeing) can be obtained tactually using a sensory substitution system (Bach-y-Rita & Kercel, 2003; Sampaio, Maris, & Bach-y-Rita, 2001). This is made possible by "sensory plasticity," the capacity of the brain to reorganize when there is (a) functional demand, (b) the sensor technology to fill that demand, and (c) the training and psychosocial factors that support the functional demand. To constitute such a system, it is only necessary to present environmental information from an artificial sensor in a form of energy that can be mediated by the receptors at the human–machine interface and through a motor system (e.g., a head-mounted camera under the motor control of the neck muscles) to determine the origin of the information.

The most recent advance in tactile substitution uses the tongue. The tongue is extremely sensitive and highly mobile. Because it is in the protected environment of the mouth, the sensory receptors are close to the surface. The presence of an electrolytic solution (saliva) ensures good electrical contact. Electrotactile stimuli are delivered to the dorsum of the tongue via electrode arrays placed in the mouth, with connection to the stimulator apparatus via a flat cable passing out of the mouth. The tongue electrode array and cable are made of a thin (100 μm) strip of polyester material onto which a rectangular matrix of gold-plated copper circular electrodes

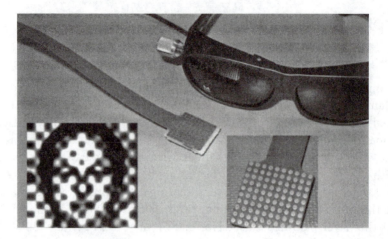

FIGURE 12.2 A view of the interface that uses the tongue to convey visual information, showing the eyeglasses-mounted camera, the tongue stimulator, and a simulated view the wearer "sees" with the tongue. (Photograph courtesy of Anil Raj, Institute for Human and Machine Cognition.)

has been deposited by a photolithographic process similar to that used to make printed circuit boards.

The results obtained with a small electrotactile array demonstrated that perception with electrical stimulation of the tongue is somewhat better than with fingertip electrotactile stimulation, and the tongue requires only about 3% of the voltage (5–15 V) and much less current (0.4–2.0 mA) than the fingertip. In what is perhaps the most striking demonstration, blind individuals can, after some training, use the tongue display to play a game of "catch." After sufficient training, people report experiencing the image in space, and they learn to make perceptual judgments using visual means of analysis, such as perspective, parallax, looming and zooming, and depth judgments. A view of this technology is presented in Figure 12.2.

Example 3: A Human-Centered Cockpit Display

Using conventional "dials-based" displays, pilots are required to engage in protracted understanding of the status of the aircraft. The pilot must scan the instruments, looking at or near each of a number of instruments in succession to obtain information (Harris, Glover, & Spady, 1986; Temme, Woodall, & Still, 1998). It is not unusual for even trained pilots to spend as much as 0.5 seconds viewing a single instrument, and durations of 2 seconds or more are to be expected even from expert pilots in routine maneuvers. Thus, the delay imposed by the requirement to sequentially gather information can be substantial, severely limiting the pilot's ability to cope with rapidly changing or unanticipated situations and emergencies. Furthermore, the pilot must constantly monitor instruments to ensure that the aircraft is performing as intended. Further complicating the pilot's task, current instrument displays use many different frames of reference, with information in a variety of units: degrees, knots, feet, rates of change, etc. This means that the pilot must integrate these different units into a common frame of reference to create an overall state of situational awareness.

The traditional solutions to these problems have been to severely limit flight procedures, emphasize instrument scan training, and require extensive pilot experience (U.S. Department of Transportation, 2000).

An ideal cockpit instrument display should do many things, including showing the direction and degree of turn in a normal manner, showing angle of bank in a normal manner, and showing climb and glide by position of the "nose" of aircraft. It should require little special training to use and allow the pilot to use the controls in an easy manner (Ocker & Crane, 1932). The following should be added to Ocker and Crane's list on the basis of modern avionic capabilities: the ideal cockpit display should

Enable pilots to fly as aggressively and as effectively on instruments as in visual flight conditions,

Adapt to changes in aircraft configuration and environment,

Show real-time aircraft capability,

Mitigate spatial disorientation and loss of situational awareness by providing a visually compelling 360° frame of reference as a true 6 degrees-of-freedom directly perceivable link to the outside world,

Fly aircraft without deficit while simultaneously studying a second display (i.e., radar, forward-looking infrared, or map), and, finally,

Be realized with a software change in any aircraft with a glass cockpit. This is a tall order.

"OZ" is the name given to a system designed by going back to "first principles" of vision science, aerodynamics, and the principles of HCC to converge on a control system that meets the requirements of an ideal cockpit display. The name "OZ" is not an acronym but rather a nickname. Early in the project, the display used a large rear projection screen. Prior to a demonstration, one of the inventors would go behind the screen to set up the instrumentation. Visitors were told to "pay no attention to the man behind the curtain." We now see OZ as an appropriate metaphor for the HCC approach. That is, effective technology should amplify and extend the human's perceptual, cognitive, and performance capabilities while at the same time reducing, and in some cases eliminating, mental workload. The controlling software (i.e., the calculations ordinarily imposed on the pilot) should run "behind the curtain."

Research on vision and cognition suggested ways to eliminate the fundamental speed barrier of traditional displays, the "instrument scan." One important factor is functional differences between the focal (closely related to central or foveal vision) and the ambient visual fields (Simoneau, Leibowitz, Ulbrecht, Tyrrell, & Cavanagh, 1992; Turano, Herdman, & Dagnelie, 1993). The focal channel is used for tasks such as reading, which require directed attention. The ambient channel is used primarily for tasks such as locomotion, which can be accomplished without conscious effort or even awareness. In the normal environment both of these channels are simultaneously active. It is significant that the design of conventional instruments requires that the focal channel be directed sequentially to each instrument, producing the "instrument scan" (Naval Air Training Command, 1993), whereas the part of the visual system that is optimized for processing locomotion information, the ambient channel, is largely ignored.

To harness the power of both focal and ambient channels, OZ display elements are constructed using visual perceptual primitives—luminance discontinuities that are

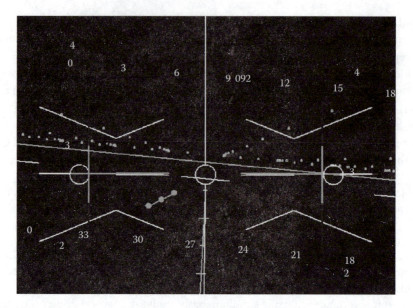

FIGURE 12.3 A screen shot of the OZ cockpit display.

resilient to one- or two-dimensional optical and neurological demodulation (i.e., dots and lines). The resilience of the perceptual primitives to demodulation allows them to pass information through both the ambient and focal channels' optical and neurological filters (Thibos, Still, & Bradley, 1996). OZ organizes these perceptual primitives into meaningful objects using well-known principles from visual perception. These principles include figure-ground, pop-out, chunking, texture, effortless discrimination, and structure-from-motion. These principles organize the graphic primitives into the objects that constitute OZ symbology, objects that have perceptual meaning and are quickly understood. OZ combines and reduces different data streams into proportionately scaled symbology that the pilot can immediately apprehend and use. For example, information on aircraft configuration, altitude, and location are integrated into a directly perceivable picture of the aircraft's present capability.

A screen shot of the OZ display is shown in Figure 12.3 (for color views and details, see Temme et al., 1998; Thibos et al., 1996; also http://www.ihmc.us/research/projects/OZ_UCAV/). The display uses a "star field" background. The stars are projections of real-world horizontal and vertical displacements. The stars are layered and flow as the aircraft moves, creating apparent altitude planes and heading streams. The display also uses an aircraft metaphor: a stylized triplane composed of lines and circles whose location within the star field metaphor is used to show attitude and flight path information. The size and interrelationship of the triplane's parts map the aircraft's configuration, airspeed, engine output, and flight envelope. For example, the spanwise location of the struts connecting the wings (the vertical lines in Figure 12.3, which appear as blue and green in the actual display) is proportional to airspeed. The length of the struts indicates power available. The struts are scaled so that power equals demand when the green of the struts reaches the upper and lower wings. In this way, the wings and struts depict the complex interrelationship among power, drag, airspeed, configuration, and performance. (In addition to such elements, OZ can also display waypoints, other aircraft, obstructions, and thunderstorms.)

Using a flight simulator, experiments have demonstrated superior flight performance for both experienced pilots and practiced nonpilots, for both turbulent and slow flight conditions (where altitude and airspeed are harder to maintain), as well as for simple conditions, and even when flying involves the dual task of reading text. Trained pilots execute straight and level flight equally well with OZ as with a conventional display, despite the fact that the pilots had far more experience with conventional displays. In fact, with OZ, heading was not at all affected by turbulence. OZ is not only easier to fly but easier to learn. OZ enables flight with significantly more precision than conventional instrumentation and is currently being adapted for application in hovercraft and the control of unmanned aerial vehicles and in contexts other than aviation. OZ researchers have recently demonstrated that trained pilots can work using two OZ displays and actually fly two simulators *simultaneously* under severe turbulence conditions, executing different maneuvers.

OZ has to be experienced to really be appreciated. OZ reduces the cognitive workload of instrument flight by using a single frame of reference that can be clearly and quickly understood. Depicting aerodynamic relationships by the size and interaction of structure, as illustrated by the wings and struts, is a general concept carried throughout OZ. As a consequence of this design approach, OZ produces an explicit graphic depiction of aircraft performance, which the pilot would otherwise have to construct and maintain as a mental model. We cannot fail to note that the OZ display would serve as a very good example of an "ecological interface" (see chapter 10) because of its reliance on a notion of direct perception of dynamic, functional relations (see Flach & Warren, 1995).

Example 4: Going From CTA to a Human-Centered System

A project on expertise in weather forecasting (Hoffman, Coffey, & Ford, 2000; Hoffman, Coffey, et al., 2002) involved applying and comparing a number of CTA methods, including the Critical Decision Method, workplace observations, protocol analysis, a variety of structured interviews, and other methods. The research relied on the participation of expert, journeyman, and apprentice weather forecasters at the Naval Training Meteorology and Oceanography Facility at Pensacola Naval Air Station. The methods were compared in terms of (a) their yield of information that was useful in modeling expert knowledge, (b) their yield in terms of identification of leverage points (where the application of new technology might bring about positive change), and (c) their efficiency. Efficiency was gauged in terms of total effort (time to prepare to run a procedure, plus time to run the procedure, plus time to analyze the data) relative to the yield (number of leverage points identified, number of propositions suitable for use in a model of domain knowledge). CTA and Cognitive Field Research methods supported the identification of dozens of leverage points and also yielded behaviorally validated models of the reasoning of expert forecasters. Knowledge modeling using Concept Mapping resulted in thousands of propositions covering domain knowledge. The Critical Decision Method yielded a number of richly populated case studies with associated Decision Requirements Tables.

The leverage points that were identified ranged all the way from simple interventions (e.g., a "tickle board" to remind the forecasters of when certain tasks need to be conducted) to very complex ones (e.g., an artificial-intelligence-enabled fusion box to support the forecasters' creation of a visual representation of their mental models of atmospheric dynamics). All of the leverage points were affirmed as being leverage points by one or more of the participating experts. Furthermore, all of the leverage points were confirmed by their identification in more than one method. The leverage points were placed into broad categories (e.g., decision aids for the forecaster, methods of presenting weather data to pilots, methods of archiving organizational knowledge, etc.). No one of the CTA methods resulted in leverage points that were confined to any one category. The observational methods had a greater yield of identified leverage points. On the other hand, acquiring those leverage points took more time. For example, the researchers observed 15 weather briefings that were presented to pilots or to other forecasters, resulting in 15 identified leverage points. But the yield was only 15/954 minutes = 0.016 leverage points per observed minute.

The need for the forecasting facility to preserve and share local weather forecasting expertise was identified as an organizationally relevant leverage point for a prototyping effort. The main way in which the knowledge and reasoning heuristics of the senior forecasters had been preserved was in the form of videotapes of briefings. Although they might have captured expert knowledge and reasoning, a video archive is of limited usefulness and usability, as, for example, when an apprentice might need to find advice about some particular forecasting problem. With this as a starting point, the researchers created a model of expert knowledge using Concept Maps (not unlike those that we use to introduce the chapters of this volume). Details of the CTA methodology are presented in Crandall, Klein, and Hoffman (2006); Hoffman, Coffey, Ford, and Novak (2006); and Hoffman and Lintern (2006).

An example Concept Map appears in Figure 12.4. This is the "Top Map" in the knowledge model, the first thing one sees when entering the knowledge model. Nodes refer to the main concepts that are elaborated in more detail in the other Concept Maps in the model.

The knowledge model contains 24 Concept Maps, which themselves contain a total of 1,129 propositions and 420 individual multimedia resources that are directly accessible from the clickable icons that are appended to many of the concept-nodes. These include satellite images, charts, and digitized videos allow the apprentice to "stand on the expert's shoulders" by viewing minitutorials, a feature of this knowledge model that makes it human centered.

Also appended to concept-nodes are Concept Map icons that take one to the Concept Map indicated by the concept-node to which the icon is attached. The Top Map serves as a "Map of Maps" in that it contains concept-nodes that designate all of the other Concept Maps (e.g., cold fronts, thunderstorms, etc.). At the top node in every other Concept Map is an icon that takes one back to the Top Map and to all of the immediately associated Concept Maps. For example, the Top Map contains a concept-node for hurricanes, and appended to that are links to both of the Concept Maps that are about hurricanes (i.e., hurricane dynamics and hurricane developmental phases). Through the use of these clickable icons, one can *meaningfully* navigate from anywhere in the knowledge model to anywhere else, in two clicks at

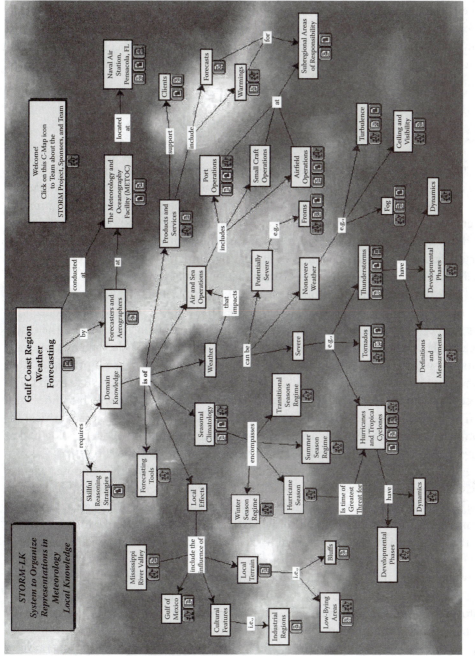

FIGURE 12.4 An example Concept Map from the "System to Organize Representations in Meteorology."

most. Disorientation in Web space becomes a nonissue. This is another way in which this knowledge model is human centered.

The knowledge model contains all of the information in the "Local Forecasting Handbook," and because the Concept Maps are Web-enabled, they allow real-time access to actual weather data (radar satellite, computer forecasts, charts, etc.)—within a context that provides the explanatory glue for the weather understanding process. Thus, the knowledge model can be used in distance learning and collaboration, acceleration of the acquisition of expertise, and knowledge preservation at the organizational level.

Summary

HCC emerged in recent decades within the computer science community, providing a voice for many of the philosophies found more commonly in the human factors and Cognitive Systems Engineering communities. Computer science has traditionally been a technology-driven field, pushing forward computer capabilities and envisioning future technological benefits, but it has also anchored itself in the Turing Test vision for artificial intelligence: the goal of emulating human cognition. HCC encourages designers of intelligent systems to expand their vision beyond the technological issues and base development efforts on an empirical footing, relying on CTA. Although the "humans–machines systems" approach to design is not an entirely new concept, it has not been emphasized until recently in the design of intelligent systems. The emergence of HCC from within the computer science community has led to a new research outlook, with new research agendas and goals. This includes proposed "principles" that can be used to guide design and also a mandate to base designs on results from CTA. Recent system development efforts illustrate a number of ways in which technologies can be human centered. This involves not merely acknowledging that it is critical for computer systems to be usable and useful but also attempting to build technologies that amplify and extend human abilities to learn, perceive, and collaborate.

HCC echoes many of the ideas relayed in earlier chapters. Within computer science, HCC represents a reaction against Machine-Centered Design (see chapter 7). A report to the NSF in 1997 presented a range of opinions about what HCC is all about. Positions from 51 researchers showed only partial agreement about how to define HCC. In fact, many of the statements seem like old wine in new bottles, repackaging views that have been stated previously. More recently, researchers have articulated what is new about HCC. HCC entails a shift toward thinking about information technology in systems terms. This includes the characterization of the human workers and the information processing device as a coupled, coadapting system. This system functions within a dynamic context to which it continually adapts. The context includes the worker's team, the organization, and the organization's clients and sponsors.

HCC can be defined as the design, development, and evaluation of technology that amplifies and extends human perceptual, cognitive, and collaborative activities. This is in contrast to the traditional view of artificial intelligence, in which the ultimate goal was to create machines that emulate human capabilities.

HCC is not old wine in new bottles. It does inherit ideas and issues from past decades of Cognitive Systems Engineering, but it seeks to apply them in new contexts and applications. As with other perspectives in this book, HCC seems to represent a new approach being forced on us by the rapid pace of technological advancement. For HCC, the era of ubiquitous computing has been the impetus for a change in approach. Poorly designed information systems result in accidents, sometimes catastrophic accidents. Examples abound in aviation and business accounting systems. Analysis of trends in work productivity has shown that the introduction of computers actually leads to declines in productivity. In spite of good intentions, traditional approaches lead to technologies that are user hostile.

Hoffman, Hayes, Ford, and their colleagues proposed a number of principles of HCC, tapping into literatures discussed in other chapters of this volume. These principles are listed in Table 12.1. They represent cautionary tales that have been learned in related disciplines such as Cognitive Systems Engineering, Expertise Studies, and human factors. They are not intended as a cookbook or a substitute for empirical inquiry via CTA, for design creativity, or for proper software development. Rather, these principles imply challenges that must be addressed in the design of information systems. Researchers have also raised the issues of whether system requirements should be fixed given the dynamic world in which system will function. Instead it may make sense to think in terms of "desirements" or desired functionalities that may be available in the future. Anticipating system modifications may be an important factor in effective design.

Examples of HCC systems include a software and display tool design to help train oceanographers about sonar oceanography. This project, sponsored by the U.S. Navy, exemplifies the Janus Principle in that the technology not only supports training but also supports real-time performance by helping sonar operators visualize actual conditions of operations. The Tactile Vision Substitution System is a second example of an effective HCC system. This system could be considered a "cognitive orthosis" in that it allows humans to obtain visual information via tactual stimulus using a sensory substitution system. A third example is the human-centered cockpit display called OZ, which goes back to "first principles" of vision science, aerodynamics, and the principles of HCC to create an ideal cockpit display. This cockpit design is intended to amplify and extend the human's perceptual, cognitive, and performance capabilities while at the same time reducing, and in some cases eliminating, mental workload. Using a flight simulator, experiments have demonstrated superior flight performance with the OZ cockpit design for both experience and practiced nonpilots and for turbulent and slow conditions, as well as for simple conditions. A fourth example offered in this chapter describes the transition from CTA data to the design of an HCC system to support weather forecasting. The resulting knowledge model presents an expert knowledge model that is available real-time within an explanatory context. The knowledge model can be used in distance learning and collaboration, acceleration of the acquisition of expertise, and knowledge preservation at the organizational level.

Part 3

Synthesis

13

Introduction to Section 3
Synthesis

A theme of convergences and divergences is the one we use in section 3 to integrate and summarize the chapters of this book. The perspectives we have discussed share key elements but also have important differences. Some perspectives include detailed descriptions of the methods they use as Cognitive Task Analysis (CTA). Others do not, but they have important points of convergence that have informed and shaped the way CTA methods are used. Some perspectives define themselves in terms of what they are not—the ideas and perspectives they are reacting against. Some perspectives naturally resonate with others, to the extent of "discovering" similar ideas and methods. Other perspectives seem more like oil and water.

The chapters on the perspectives (section 2) discussed the following key points of each of the perspectives:

Cognitive Systems Engineering (CSE): Investigations and "lessons learned" have provided important cautionary tales about the broader contexts for cognitive work. This perspective has expanded the horizons of traditional human factors engineering to a systems approach. It has provided a number of principles and challenges for the design of information technologies. CSE advocates a process in which new technologies are evaluated for their usefulness, usability, and impact on the workplace. Finally, CSE raises important open questions concerning the utility, validity, and reliability of methods of CTA and Cognitive Field Research.

Expertise Studies: Research by cognitive and educational psychologists has contributed many ideas to our understanding of the nature of expertise, including ideas about reasoning, knowledge, and knowledge organization. This has invigorated academic cognitive psychology. The research has also spawned ideas about knowledge elicitation and proficiency scaling, as forms of CTA.

Naturalistic Decision Making: Research has enriched our understanding of decision making in complex, real-world contexts. It has yielded new models of reasoning. It has spawned challenging new ideas, such as the notion of "macrocognition." It has yielded new methods for the CTA methods palette.

Work Analysis: Research has shown the importance of studying work domains from a number of perspectives and the value of developing a rich understanding of the "true work" prior to designing new information technologies. The research has also spawned ideas about CTA, drawing distinctions between constraint-based and instruction-based task analytic techniques. This perspective also emphasizes the usefulness of mapping important elements of the work domain using the Abstraction-Decomposition Matrix.

Sociology and Ethnography: Research has shown the value of embracing an anthropological or ethnographic approach in the study of real-world domains of practice. Researchers have challenged traditional notions from cognitive psychology by discussing ways in which cognition is "situated" and "distributed."

Human-Centered Computing: Lessons learned about the ways in which new technologies can be user hostile has spawned this new approach, which seeks to amplify and extend human cognitive, perceptual, and collaborative technologies rather than attempt to build artificial intelligences that might replace humans. A number of principles for design have emerged. In addition, Human-Centered Computing is integrative in that its basic principles mandate that information technologies be built on the basis of an empirical foundation derived from CTA.

Each of the perspectives has moved us closer to the concept of CTA as it exists today. As researchers within these different communities have found venues to share and debate ideas, methods, and philosophies, the concept of CTA has been refined, stretched, and challenged. Key elements of modern CTA that have emerged include the following:

- the study of complex cognition in real-world settings;
- the attempt to describe, study, model, and design new technologies;
- the study of how experts and teams of practitioners confront significant problems, aided by technology and other types of artifacts; and
- the shared approach to capture and apply concepts about cognition in response to challenges created by the transformation of the workplace to place greater emphasis on cognitive and collaborative work.

In the following chapters we discuss the ways in which the perspectives diverge, clash, and disagree; the ways in which the perspectives converge and agree; and, finally, some outstanding challenges for CTA methodology that cut across all of the perspectives.

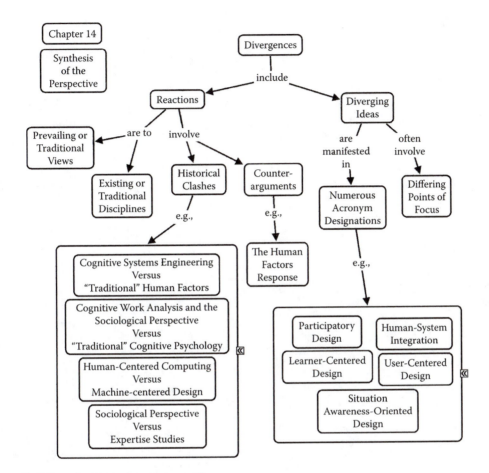

FIGURE 14.1 Chapter 14 Concept Map.

14

Synthesis
Divergences of the Perspectives

The danger for a movement that regards itself as new is that it may try to embrace everything that is not old.

— Lee Roy Beach, Michelene Chi, Gary Klein, Philip Smith, and Kim Vicente (1997, p. 29)

Fighting is fiercest among like-minded thinkers in rival disciplines.

—Steve Fuller (1993, p. 13)

Introduction

As our discussion has made clear, each of the perspectives examined in this book has involved a reaction against one or more traditions. This is usually the case in the emergence of new scientific paradigms (Kuhn, 1977). These reactions are summarized in Table 14.1. We go into more detail on selected reactions in this chapter.

In chapter 11 we discussed in some detail the reactions of the sociological perspectives against the ideas of cognitive psychology—to motivate and explain such notions as situated cognition and distributed cognition. We could continue the exploration of any of the divergences listed in Table 14.1, but here we highlight just a few of the more salient divergences.

Work Analysis Versus Human Factors and Cognitive Psychology

Tables 14.2 and 14.3 illustrate the reactionary views of work analysis—in particular, the reactions against traditional human factors psychology and traditional cognitive psychology that have shaped the development of Cognitive Work Analysis. In the titles of both of these tables, we used scare quotes to suggest that at least some of the individuals who might count themselves as traditionalists would regard the reactionaries as setting up straw arguments. As our presentation of the history of task

TABLE 14.1 Each Perspective Is a Reaction Against Something

Perspective	Reacts Against
Expertise Studies	• The limitations of the traditional academic psychology laboratory, including the reliance on brief and artificial tasks • The attempt to build models of cognition based on studies of college-age "subjects"
Cognitive Systems Engineering	• Traditional human factors psychology • Machine-Centered Design • Designer-Centered Design
Sociology and ethnography	• Traditional cognitive psychology • Traditional human factors psychology
Cognitive Work Analysis	• Traditional human factors psychology • Traditional cognitive psychology
Naturalistic Decision Making	• Traditional judgment and decision making • The limitations of the traditional academic psychology laboratory
Human-Centered Computing	• Machine-Centered Computing that typifies traditional computer science • The traditional procurement process, which results in user-hostile systems

TABLE 14.2 The Contrast of Work Analysis and "Traditional" Human Factors

Cognitive Work Analysis Approach	"Traditional" Human Factors Approach
In the work analysis design process,	The traditional approach is normative,
1. the designer identifies a constraint space and support for agent control, 2. the computer is designed so as to show the constraint boundaries and local data for ongoing situations in a way to support choice among action sequences, and 3. the end user finishes the design based on local information, knowledge, and expertise.	1. the designer creates an optimal plan in advance through task analysis, 2. the automation is designed to enforce certain procedures, and 3. the human executes the designer's plan.
Tools should be designed so as to give workers the ability to adapt to unforeseen circumstances.	Norm-based systems tend to be brittle because of their prescriptive nature.
Tools should be designed so as to give workers the discretion to generate action sequences and to express their preferences.	Norm-based systems tend to be applicable only to the tasks that have been identified and the particular ways of conducting them that have been specified.
Tools should be designed so as to give workers an ability to recover from errors and cope with context-conditioned variability.	Norm-based systems are limited because of their inability to cope with context-conditioned variation.

analysis shows (chapters 2–4), researchers of years and decades past were quite aware of many of the issues that drive current trends and debates.

As is often the case in the emergence of a new paradigm, the proponents of the new view set up a "straw man" view of the tradition against which they are reacting. The straw man often represents an extreme depiction that is useful in exploring boundaries and limitations of the existing paradigm. This extreme depiction, however, is often viewed as an overreaction by researchers who are less involved in developing the new paradigm. Thus, although some researchers in the area of Expertise Studies

TABLE 14.3 The Contrast of Work Analysis and "Traditional" Cognitive Psychology

Cognitive Work Analysis Approach	Cognitive Psychology Approach
It is assumed that work involves constraints coming from the domain dynamics and the larger work context and that these constraints will be primary determiners of work activity, including cognitive activity.	Behavior is believed to be primarily driven by the workers' cognitive characteristics. Thus, the information system and interface should be designed so as to make them compatible with that mental model.
Workers rarely engage in isolated, pensive activities. They rely on external artifacts to reduce the burdens on cognitive resources.	It is assumed that work involves just the worker and the computer. Problem solving depends on isolated, unaided cognition.
Normative procedures are an ideal that is seldom achieved.	Problem solving should proceed through adherence to normative procedures for rational choice.

are reacting against the limitations of the traditional academic psychology laboratory, many see Expertise Studies as a broadening of the horizons of academic experimental psychology. Although some Cognitive Systems Engineers are reacting against the perceived limitations of traditional Cognitive Engineering and human factors psychology, many see Cognitive Systems Engineering as a broadening of the horizons of those perspectives. Although Work Analysis involves reactions to perceived limitations of traditional views, many human factors researchers see it as a broadening of the horizons of human factors psychology.

We also note that this paradigm shift characteristic of scientific change comes on what seems to be a terribly short timescale. So, for instance, Cognitive Systems Engineering reacts against "traditional" Cognitive Engineering given the emphasis of the latter on the study of the one person–one machine context. However, "traditional" Cognitive Engineering is barely 25 years old.

One thing that most of the perspectives share is a reaction against "traditional" cognitive psychology. To those less immersed in the paradigm shift, this appears to be an overreaction or, as some might say, an instance of throwing out the baby with the bathwater. Table 14.4 provides an example of a point–counterpoint involving Cognitive Work Analysis (i.e., Vicente, 1999) and cognitive psychology.

Human Factors Replies

Cognitive Work Analysis is not the only perspective that reacts against "traditional" human factors. So too does Cognitive Systems Engineering, and this also can be viewed as an overreaction. For instance, many reports on studies that claim to use Cognitive Task Analysis (CTA) methods begin by saying something about the perceived differences between CTA and "traditional" task analysis, often referred to as "behavioral task analysis." But as we showed in chapter 2, task analysis was always to some extent cognitive, and the clearest example of what might be called microscale analysis of task behavior (e.g., Time and Motion Study) included the study of expert performance. How might a "traditional" human factors psychologist respond to the claims of the new perspectives? Table 14.5 provides a point–counterpoint.

TABLE 14.4 Counterarguments to the Cognitive Work Analysis Reaction Against "Traditional" Cognitive Psychology

Claim Against Traditional Cognitive Psychology	Counterargument
Workers' mental models get shaped by the technology and are not good representations of the work domain.	How could it be otherwise? One can take this into account.
Workers' mental models may be incomplete and inaccurate. Designs based on bad mental models can reinforce misconceptions.	As a point of fact, there are domains in which experts possess refined and accurate mental models and render judgments that are nearly always correct. Aside from that, how could the claim not be true? By definition, the knowledge of anyone, even an expert, is incomplete at any one time. This is the "reductive tendency" (Hoffman, Feltovich, & Woods, 2004). The question to be asked about a worker is, in what way is his or her mental model functional? Going from the claim that it is sometimes useless to study mental models to the conclusion that one should not ever study them would lead to paralysis.
Workers are usually unaware of the deficiencies and incompletenesses of their mental models.	Top experts are usually very aware and explicit on this, and they desire to continually improve.
Deficiencies in mental models are most likely to be manifest, and lead to breakdowns, during rare, abnormal, or time-critical situations.	This is unavoidable. Top experts can recognize rare or tough cases and develop strategies de novo. If technology keeps the worker from recognizing that a situation is critical, it does not mean that it is a problem with the worker's mental model.
Design that focuses on capturing the mental model of an exceptionally skilled worker is likely to be flawed, because in complex systems, workers will all have different mental models (and accompanying inaccuracies and incompletenesses). A design based on a single (albeit proficient) worker's mental model may not fit other workers.	This is a straw man argument. Consensus in the design community for some time has been that designs should never be based on analyses of single end users. Individual differences in models entail differences in styles and learning stages, and one has to acquire that information for the design of both training aids and decision aids.
Compatibility of a system or interface with worker cognition is of little use if it is not compatible with the work ecology.	This is a non sequitur. Compatibility with worker cognition is of little use if it is not compatible with the ecology of the workplace, but this does not mean that systems should not be compatible with workers' mental models.

Sociology and Ethnography Versus Expertise Studies

Work in the Sociology and Ethnography perspective has confirmed a number of the findings from the research in Expertise Studies:

- Whether one is investigating domains of the sort that are typically the focus for technological interventions (e.g., aviation, medicine, military command and control, etc.) or "everyday" kinds of expertise, it does take a long time to become an expert, and by the time one has become an expert, one's knowledge is both specific to the domain and very extensive (Scribner, 1984).

TABLE 14.5 Human Factors Counterargues the Claims of Cognitive Systems
Engineers and Cognitive Work Analysis Researchers

Claim Against "Traditional" Human Factors	Counterargument
The "traditional" human factors approach is too prescriptive or normative.	There will always be trade-offs between ease of use and prescriptiveness. In some domains, certain fixed sequences are mandated, sometimes by highly entrenched traditions and sometimes even by law.
"Traditional" task analysis is of limited value, because it does not take a systems approach. It focuses on specific actions conducted by individuals who are performing particular, well-specified tasks with well-specified goals.	Human factors engineering emerged in the context of cybernetics in the years during and immediately after World War II, so it can hardly be argued that the systems approach is new. Indeed, the systems approach was part of the definition of human factors from the very beginning. The claim about particularity is well taken, but this is because we are in a whole new ballgame in which computers have entered the workplace. The world has changed.
Human factors treats the machine as an artifact that can be designed independently of the needs and capabilities of the human operator.	Human Factors never involved building devices apart from considerations of the human (see Chapanis, 1999). The truth can be traced, for instance, to the design of lathes and machine tools in the years following World War I, when such human capabilities as strength were taken into consideration in the design of control mechanisms (e.g., spring-loaded foot pedals).
Systems that are built according to the traditional approach are brittle in that they do not support recovery from error. Normatively designed devices are applicable only to the tasks that have been identified and the particular ways of conducting them that have been specified. Normatively designed devices are limited because of their inability to cope with context-conditioned variation.	It can be argued that all systems must include some narrowly applicable, prescriptive components or component tasks, but that does not mean that all of the components or component tasks must be narrowly applicable. It is condescending to assert that human factors engineers sought systems that limited workers' abilities to adapt. If a system limits the ability to cope with and recover from error, that is a problem with the particular system and not with the human factors paradigm.
Cognitive Work Analysis researchers argue that the traditional notion of "task" has to be totally discarded in favor of the notion of action sequence alternatives.	The idea of action sequence alternatives just raises the stakes in the face of system complexity and does not fundamentally change the nature of the analysis. Rather than describing fixed linear sequences, one just makes the analysis more complex by capturing multiple strategies and options in terms of multiple specifications including parallelisms rather than singular linearities. Indeed, this is what hierarchical task analysis is supposed to do (see Stanton, 2004).

- One might expect that wholesale delivery truck drivers, warehouse inventory managers, office clerks, and product assemblers would mostly rely on routine procedures and tasks, rather like the airline pilot's checklist. However, anthropological investigations of such domains has revealed that many of the reasoning strategies and sequences observed in laboratory studies (e.g., goal decomposition, problem reformulation, etc.) have also been observed in the highly skilled reasoning of professionals (Scribner, 1986).

- In conducting their familiar tasks, experts show a great "economy of effort." Scribner (1984, 1986) presented highly experienced workers with some test cases and revealed a great deal of reasoning flexibility in service of efficiency and economy (see also Schön, 1982).

Expertise Studies has focused on the study of the cognition of individuals (although team cognition has recently become a topic of interest; see chapter 16). However, sociological approaches focus on showing how expertise is context dependent and culturally relative. Scribner (1984) illustrated this by noting the domain dependence of metrics: The cup is the canonical unit of measure among Liberian rice farmers, the volume of a canoe is used to establish a scale by the expert boat builders in the Palawan Islands, bartenders use glass shape and position as memory cues, dairy inventory workers use the "case stack" as a unit for counting, and so on. The Sociology and Ethnography perspective has led to a deeper appreciation of how individual skilled actions depend on their broader context, the ways in which expertise relates to agendas (individual, cultural, political) and politics, the ways it may or may not give rise to successful technological innovation, the ways in which expertise may or may not relate to effective social policy making, and the implications of all this for such things as the management of technological change (see Fleck & Williams, 1996).

Once we cut through the misunderstandings, many of which seem from an inadequate appreciation of the richness of history, we begin to see how the perspectives have more commonalities than they have disagreements. We will return to this in the next two chapters. But we cannot pass comment on the fact that forces are at work that essentially put people in the position of having to distinguish themselves and their ideas.

The Acronym Soup

Research is highly competitive. Scientists are intrinsically motivated to contribute new and important findings and ideas. They are under pressure to get grants and publications. They can be just as insecure as any other flavor of humanity; they need to be appreciated and respected for their unique skills and contributions. They have to "sell" themselves and present themselves as standing out from the crowd. Through the chapters of this book, we have referred to a great many acronyms that are used to designate approaches, each with a slightly different focus but all that involve the use of one or more CTA methods. We have a chapter on Human-Centered Computing (chapter 12), and we have referred to Decision-Centered Design (chapter 9) and Designer-Centered Design (chapter 12), and other "X-Centered-X" designations. One way of approaching an integration of perspectives on CTA is to survey these designations—to ferret out the factors that apparently make approaches, perspectives, and methods different from one another. Figure 14.2 presents this "acronym soup" (or at least a good part of it—new "X-Centered-X" designations appear all the time).

In the next synthesis chapter, we look at this acronym soup from another viewpoint, that of the ways in which the perspectives and communities of practice converge.

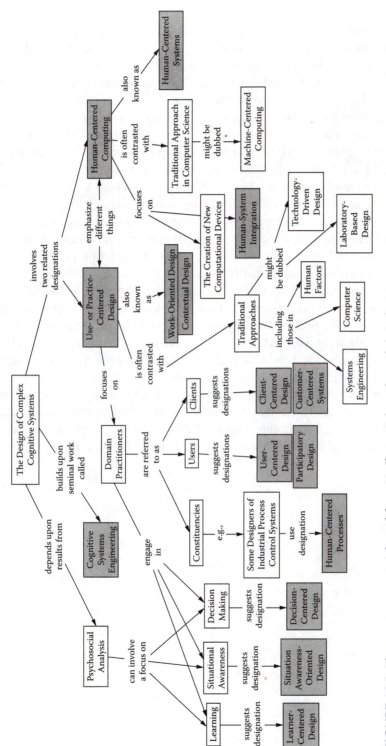

FIGURE 14.2 The acronym soup. Adapted from Hoffman, Feltovich, et al. (2002).

Summary

Each of the perspectives discussed in this book has included a reaction against one or more traditions, including the academic psychology laboratory, traditional human factors psychology, Machine-Centered Design, Designer-Centered Design, traditional cognitive psychology, traditional judgment and decision-making research, and the entrenched procurement process. Most have also included an attempt to address new challenges presented by a changing world. Each has seemed somewhat revolutionary. However, a less reactionary analysis reveals that characterization of "traditional" approaches has often been extreme and might be regarded as straw argument. Tables 14.2, 14.3, 14.4, and 14.5 illustrate how various traditional approaches might respond to the many criticisms—highlighting ways in which some of these characterizations might be considered misrepresentations or distortions. Although many of these perspectives have been perceived as controversial, in hindsight one can see continuous threads linking these new perspectives to traditional approaches.

A second synthesis involves a look across perspectives. Examination of the many acronyms and labels discussed in this volume reveals much commonality and even redundancy across approaches. This is not completely surprising, as research is highly competitive and scientists are rewarded for generating new and important findings and ideas. In fact, the ability to distinguish one's own ideas from others is rewarded in the form of grants and opportunities to be published. The social context of science encourages researchers to label and package their findings in a way that seems revolutionary and different rather than as an extension of existing ideas. One way to begin to integrate the various perspectives on CTA is to survey the many labels and acronyms to search out the factors that make approaches, perspectives, and methods appear different from one another. Figure 14.2 presents a Concept Map depicting the "acronym soup" of ideas, methods, and frameworks related to CTA.

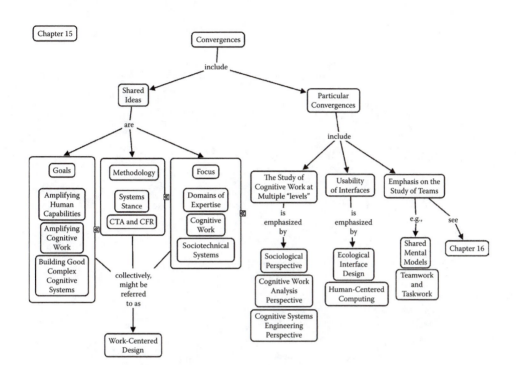

FIGURE 15.1 Chapter 15 Concept Map.

15

Synthesis
Convergences of the Perspectives

The real world has a deplorable tendency to go beyond artificial imposed boundaries.

—Erik Hollnagel, Jean-Muchel Hoc, and Pietro Carlo Cacciabue (1995, p. 283)

The myth of stability is essential to enable us to cope with the demands of change.

—Albert Cherns (1987, p. 159)

As the final figure in chapter 14 shows, the perspectives define themselves in terms of their divergences and reactions to each other's views, but they also converge. This "common ground" is shown in Figure 15.2.

1. *A shared goal:* All the approaches have as a goal the development of ideas, methods, and tools to enhance human capabilities.
2. *A systems stance:* All of the research and development activities regard the subject matter as one involving complexity, necessitating a systems approach.
3. *A method:* All of the research and development activities adopt a core empirical methodology, using methods that could be considered Cognitive Task Analysis (CTA) and Cognitive Field Research (CFR).
4. *A focus on cognition:* All of the research and development activities concern themselves with the understanding of cognition on the part of individuals, teams, organizations, and so forth.
5. *A focus on cognitive work:* All of the research and development activities focus on complex sociotechnical workplaces or domains of "significant" expertise—domains that are important to society, government, and business.

One way of thinking about CTA is that it necessitates the formation of hybrids. In the community of practice known as "Computer-Supported Cooperative Work" (which we describe in chapter 16), Monarch et al. (1997) argued that participatory design for technologies to support group collaboration requires the invention of a "sociologist–engineer hybrid." A similar sentiment is expressed by CTA practitioners in all of the perspectives and communities of practice we have discussed in the chapters of this book. To conduct CTA on the reasoning of forecasters, the psychologist must

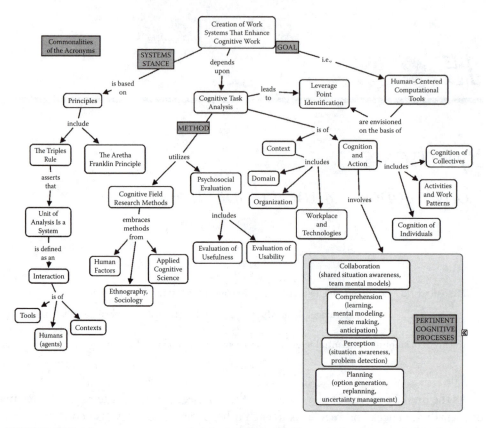

FIGURE 15.2 The common ground. Adapted from Hoffman, Feltovich, et al. (2002).

become highly conversant in the language and concepts of weather forecasting. To understand how medical practitioners could benefit from changes in their diagnostic technologies, the Cognitive Systems Engineer must become thoroughly conversant in the field of health care, and so on. Hybridization also involves significant overlap in the people, ideas, and issues that are the focus in each community of practice. Acronyms such as User-Centered Design, Participatory Design, Human-Centered Design, and Work-Centered Design, etc. crop up in all of the communities of practice (although each community has its preferred clarions) (Hoffman, Feltovich, et al., 2002). Leaders and champions in each community of practice contribute to the literatures of other communities of practice.

In looking across the perspectives, and the acronyms in the soup, we find a number of particular and interesting convergences.

An Example Convergence: Sociotechnic, Cognitive, and Computational Perspectives

In chapter 11 (Sociological and Ethnographic perspectives) we discussed the emergence of the notion of the "sociotechnical system" in the field of human relations, pointing out that research in "Sociotechnics" (Sociotechnical Design for organizations) depended on our familiar suite of CTA methods (i.e., observations, interviews, documentation analysis). The principles of Sociotechnics amount to an approach that in Cognitive Systems Engineering is referred to as Goal-Oriented Design and as Use-Centered Design and in computer science is known as Human-Centered Computing.

Sociotechnicians ask many, if not most, of the same questions that are raised by the other communities of practice we have discussed in this book:

> Are more complex jobs always "better" than simplified ones? Are there cultural differences? Are more complex jobs especially beneficial under conditions of uncertainty? Under what conditions is teamworking a better solution than individual working? What forms of teamworking are optimal under what circumstances? How should teams be configured? (Clegg, 2000, p. 469)

At the same time, Sociotechnical Design, as a point of view, transcends the typical focus of Cognitive Systems Engineering. Although Cognitive Systems Engineering is concerned with issues of cognitive work at team and organizational levels, the focus tends to be on the design of technologies for work methods (tasks). The sociotechnical approach focuses more on the design of organizations (e.g., Cherns, 1976) and the sociology of design (Clegg, 2000). That being said, Sociotechnical Design certainly resonates with Cognitive Systems Engineering, Human-Centered Computing, and other perspectives on CTA. Cherns (1976) contrasted the Sociotechnics approach with a traditional "Taylorist" approach, which assumes the following:

> People are unpredictable. If they are not stopped by the system design, they will screw things up. It would be best to eliminate them completely; but since this is not possible, we must anticipate all the eventualities and then program them in to the machines. The outcome is the familiar pattern of hierarchies of supervision and control to make sure that people do what is required of them, and departments of specialists to inject the "expert" knowledge that may be required by the complexities ... but is equally often required to make the elaborate control, measurement, and information systems work ... if the [designer of an organization or work system] does not take the absolute requirements of a social system into account, he will find that they will be met in some way or other, quite probably in ways that will do as much to thwart as to facilitate the functions for which he has not planned ... organizational objectives are best met not by the optimization of the technical system ... but by the joint optimization of the technical and social aspects. (pp. 783–784)

The Sociotechnical principle of task specification (see chapter 11) resonates with an idea from Work Analysis (chapter 10) that in complex cognitive systems, people do not conduct tasks but engage in context-sensitive, knowledge-driven choice among activities. Cherns (1976) expressed this in terms of the concept of "equifinality," where there can be many paths to the same goal.

Sociotechnical Design also presents its own version of the notion of "common ground" that is important in the study of team cognitive work (Klein, Woods, Bradshaw, Hoffman, & Feltovich, 2004). In Sociotechnical Design this is referred to as "congruence" of attitudes and goals among the stakeholders in an organization (workers, managers, supervisors, unions, etc.).

A third resonance we can use to exemplify the convergence of perspectives involves the humanist inclination of Sociotechnical Design in a resonance with human factors engineering. This is with regard to the hedonomics of cognitive work (see Hoffman, Marx, & Hancock, 2008) and what it means for a job to be "good":

- the need for the content of the job to be reasonably demanding of the worker in terms other than sheer endurance and yet to provide a minimum of variety (not necessarily novelty),
- the need to be able to learn on the job and go on learning (again it is a question of neither too much nor too little),
- the need for some minimal area of decision making that the individual can call his own,
- the need for some minimal degree of social support and recognition in the workplace,
- the need for the individual to be able to relate what he does and what he produces to his social life, and
- the need to feel that the job leads to some sort of desirable future (not necessarily just promotion).

A fourth resonance we can use to exemplify the convergence of perspectives involves the empirical foundation of Sociotechnical Design. In chapter 11 we pointed out that Sociotechnics seeks to guide the creation of new technologies on the basis of an understanding of the goals and information requirements of the workers. This empirical attitude extends further, to the issue of evaluation. On this matter, Sociotechnics resonates with essentially all of the communities of practice, in pointing out the track record of failure for new information technologies. The *Wall Street Journal* reported that 50% of software projects fail to meet CEO expectations, and 42% of corporate information technology projects are discontinued before completion (cited by Coyle, 1999). A 1995 Department of Defense study estimated that 46% of funded system development efforts result in products that are delivered but not successfully used, and 29% never even produce a product (cited by Leishman & Cook, 2002). These statistics translate into workers who lose out, because they don't have the systems they need to perform their work effectively, not to mention billions of dollars squandered. For example, the Internal Revenue Service (IRS) has spent $4 billion on computer systems that, in the words of an IRS official, "do not work in the real world" (Marketplace, 1997), and the U.S. Federal Bureau of Investigation more recently spent $170 million on a problem-riddled software development effort before abandoning it (Eggen, 2005).

In the field of human factors, this often takes the form of concern over the inadequate funding for evaluation and follow-on, compared to the funding for prototyping.

Organizations so rarely undertake systematic evaluations of their investments against their original goals. There may be many reasons for this. The original estimates of performance may have been over-optimistic. The estimates may have been political statements to persuade senior managers to release capital for investment. There may have been little expectation that the goals would actually be met. Project champions and managers may not want to have subsequent evaluation since they do not wish to have any failures exposed ... it may be more exciting to plan new projects and new ideas than to get buried in the detail of past hopes and intents. In other words, there are many good human, political and organizational reasons why evaluation appears not worth the effort. Nevertheless, evaluation is a requirement for learning. This applies both within particular projects, and also across projects over time. ... A sociotechnical perspective explicitly assumes a commitment to evaluating the performance of new systems against the goals of the organization and the people in it, and includes the explicit inclusion of social, technical, operational and financial criteria. The emphasis is on pluralistic evaluation. (Clegg, 2000, p. 473)

An entire set of resonances involves the Sociotechnics view of design activity (Clegg, 2000). This is a view largely in accord with that of Cognitive Systems Engineering and Human-Centered Computing, regarding design as an activity, a form of cognitive work (Hoffman, Roesler, & Moon, 2004; Hoffman & Woods, 2005).

> Design is an arena of conflict. It has to satisfy an array of objectives, each represented by some organizational element ... the design team has to work on its own process and principles of operation. ... Members must reveal their assumptions and reach decisions by consensus. Joint "optimization" of technical and social systems is often wrongly interpreted as modification of a technical design for social considerations. It is joint design in which each decision is reached for both technical and social reasons. Experts too are required to reveal their assumptions ... for some experts, this is a shock. How they deal with it is at least partly a function of how well the team has prepared them. (Cherns, 1987, p. 155)

Furthermore, the Sociotechnics view regards design as an extended process. Within the Human-Centered Computing and Cognitive Systems Engineering communities of practice, this is referred to under the banner of macrocognition (see chapter 9), which regards the primary cognitive functions as parallel and highly interacting, often with no clear-cut beginning and end points:

> Design is extended over lengthy periods of time. It is not a one-off that has a clear end. Design continues beyond implementation and throughout use, for example, as the people using the new system interpret it, amend it, massage it and make such adjustments as they see fit and/or are able to undertake. In part this reflects the attempts by people to take ownership of, and control over, the systems they manage and use. Whilst designers are clearly involved, so too are the people involved in implementation, use, management, evaluation, maintenance and upgrade. Thus the system gets (re-)configured as it goes along. Such changes may be formally negotiated in, or may just happen in practice as people start to use and tailor a system in a way that suits them. (Clegg, 2000, p. 467)

Like Cognitive Systems Engineers (see chapter 7), Sociotechnicians are sensitive to the consequences of technologies that are created through a process of Designer-Centered Design in which technical and social systems are disconnected:

> The designers of some new technology, method of working or information system, may not be able to anticipate the impacts of their design efforts on other aspects of the system, and may experience difficulty planning changes that make their operation consistent. Put another way, there may be unintended consequences of various change initiatives. Some of these consequences may only become obvious when the system is in operation. Furthermore, some of the knock-on effects may have political consequences for others. ... A sociotechnical perspective encourages one to challenge two related sets of views: First, that human beings are error-prone, unreliable agents, resistant to change, that ideally should be designed out of systems as soon as this is technically feasible and can be afforded; and second, that when they cannot be designed out, humans need to be managed exclusively through Tayloristic systems of command and control. Of course, such views may not be articulated explicitly, but they do appear widespread ... the "Charge of the Byte Brigade" is the continuing overemphasis on technological solutions to system design. (Clegg, 2000, pp. 465–466)

Sociotechnics also presents its own version of the Envisioned World Problem (see chapter 7): "Design is a re-iterative process. ... As soon as design is implemented, its consequences indicate a need for re-design" (Cherns, 1976, p. 792). When organizations are in transition, they have to support the current work methods while at the same time preparing the workers to conduct work in a new context using new work methods and technologies. This is reminiscent of the "Moving Target Principle" of Human-Centered Computing (see Table 12.1): "The transitional organization is both different from and more complex than the old" (Cherns, 1987, p. 159). Like Human-Centered Computing, Sociotechnics has proposed a solution in which retraining is folded into the design of the new work system: "Start-up and its debugging should be planned and designed to enhance training" (Cherns, 1987, p. 159).

Like Cognitive Systems Engineers (see chapter 7), Sociotechnicians are sensitive to the necessity of having multiple disciplines and perspectives represented on design teams.

> Pluralism is the norm, and this implies that they share their views and expertise. They need to educate one another in the opportunities that may exist for the design of a new system and what they have to offer the design process. The intent here is not to argue that the holders of one perspective should try to educate others in the correctness of one view (and thereby the inappropriateness of others). Rather, views of the kind articulated in [sociotechnical] principles need to be incorporated into design thinking and design practice as worthy of debate. The goal is to educate one another in the complexities of design, and in the need for a more multi-disciplinary understanding. A further potential benefit exists: a multidisciplinary approach to design is more likely to foster creative and innovative solutions. Whilst this may seem obvious, a sociotechnical approach explicitly assumes that design needs to draw upon the expertise of both social and technical domains. (Clegg, 2000, p. 473)

A final resonance of Sociotechnics and Human-Centered Computing with regard to design is the understanding that the collectives of people and machines that have the goal of creating new work technologies and new work methods are themselves a sociotechnical system. Thus, all of the principles pertinent to cognitive work in complex contexts apply equally to the cognitive work of the developers of cognitive technology. For instance, when understanding complex systems (such as the circulatory system), humans have a tendency to generate simplifying assumptions and mental models (Feltovich, Hoffman, & Woods, 2004). This "reductive tendency" has negative consequences in the design of new technologies intended to support cognitive work, when processes that involve multiple causation are understood as involving simple causation (continuous things are thought of as being discrete, things that are interacting are thought of as being separable, and so on). The emergent theme here is, of course, complexity—a hornet's nest of issues with which all of the communities of practice are grappling.

An Example Convergence: Ethnographic and Cognitive Perspectives

Many of the basic ideas in the Ethnographic and Sociological perspectives dovetail with the ideas of Cognitive Work Analysis and Cognitive Systems Engineering. Indeed, these perspectives have cross-fertilized one another to a considerable extent. For instance, there seems to be general convergence at the level of methodology, and in particular there is a multimethod approach combining field studies with experimental investigations. For instance,

[T]he study takes shape as the work proceeds. People are such surprising creatures that it is impossible to know what may be of interest in a research setting before the work is done ... unlike an experiment, interesting material can and should be explored when it is encountered. ... [Furthermore] testing is not "user testing" in a laboratory but careful study of what happens after the installation of the prototype into a setting where the real users of the system can use it ... it is useful to follow an ethnographic study with a quantitative study focusing on particular questions. ... A good qualitative study provides "ecological validity" to a quantitative study, giving wider latitude for interpreting numerical data. (Nardi, 1997, p. 362)

Both Cognitive Systems Engineering and the Ethnographic and Sociological perspectives hold that new technology should be regarded as a hypothesis about how cognitive work will be shaped (Suchman, 1987). Cognitive Systems Engineering, Cognitive Work Analysis, and Sociotechnics all hold that sociotechnical systems need to be studied from a variety of perspectives or levels (individuals, teams, organizations, etc.).

All of the perspectives hold the view that knowledge and skill are (at least partly) contextually defined and constituted. The Sociology and Ethnography perspectives dovetail to some extent with Cognitive Systems Engineering and Cognitive Work Analysis because they regard problem solving as situated within the context in which it occurs. The specification and uniformity of work processes and skills for the workplace is necessary to some degree, but variation in the way in which jobs get done and in how problems are solved should not be regarded negatively (see Clancey, 1998). Work can be prescribed, configured, facilitated, and organized for operatives, but the way in which work is ultimately undertaken cannot be and should not be completely controlled. Thus, there is an imperative in work systems design to leave room in the work environment for creativity and improvisation, as well as the freedom required for adaptation, and to allow the discovery of work rules and methods of bending them so that operatives can work more effectively and enjoyably.

With the exception of the Sociological perspective, which has a thread involving social criticism on the notion that "expertise" is an elitist concept (see chapter 11), all of the perspectives converge in recognition of the importance of expertise, not just to cognitive work and teamwork but also as a concept central to the methodology of CTA and the focus of CTA research. For example, an article aptly subtitled "I Have a Feeling We're Not in Kansas Anymore," written from the perspective of Cognitive Systems Engineering, Hollnagel, Hoc, and Cacciabue (1995) stated,

Why does technology require that we are experts? The answer is that we must be experts to cope with the complexity that the technology carries with it. ... High usability at one point in the system will require high complexity in other parts. ... When something goes wrong the full complexity of the system strikes back—and pity the user who is not an expert. (p. 285)

Another example of a convergence of otherwise differing perspectives is Thomas Sheridan's treatment (1997) of the problem of task allocation. Sheridan's view, situated within the tradition of human factors psychology, converges on the notion of the "envisioned world problem" in Cognitive Systems Engineering (chapter 7) and the notion of the "actual work–true work gap" that emerged within the tradition of work analysis, especially the idea of formative work analysis (chapter 10).

> There is a tendency to fall into the trap of analyzing the task as a series of steps for a human to look at particular existing displays and operate particular existing controls—the very displays and controls which constitute the present interface one seeks to improve upon or automate. The correct way to analyze the task is with each named step, to specify the information to be obtained and/or stored, the decisions to be made, and the actions to be taken, independent of the human or machine means to achieve those steps. (Sheridan, 1997, p. 90)

Among all the perspectives and historical trends we find some surprising convergences. For instance, there is the matter of "behavioral task analysis." As we showed in chapters 2 and 3, task analysis was never completely devoid of cognition even in the case of what some might regard as behavioral task analysis: the microscale "time and motion" studies of pre-World War II industrial psychologists. In the modern literature on ethnographic analysis of cognitive work, we find the method of "Activity Analysis" (see chapter 11), which has been described thusly:

> While situated cognition and activity theory share many perspectives, situated action is more readily differentiated. It is committed to the study of moment-by-moment interactions, usually involving the study of segments of videotape. ... In these studies it is interactions between study participants that are the focus of the investigator's attention. (Nardi, 1997, p. 365)

Activity Analysis is distinguished also because situated cognition is more focused on the distribution and regulation of knowledge and beliefs. These two distinguishing notions, one involving method (we measure action) and the other involving subject matter (we do not investigate cognition), conspire such that Activity Analysis seems to present itself as behavioral in flavor. Of course there is no direct linkage to, let alone avowal of, behaviorism. In the pendulum swings of perspectives and reactions, ideas seem to sometimes demand themselves into existence, or back into existence.

Another somewhat surprising convergence involves the idea of Ecological Interface Design in the Cognitive Work Analysis perspective (chapter 10) with the notion of Human-Centered Computing. In chapter 12 we discussed what might be regarded as a prototypical example of Ecological Interface Design—the OZ cockpit display. OZ was based on "first principles" in vision science, aviation science, and Human-Centered Computing, not on ideas from Ecological Psychology. Yet OZ converged on the key features of Ecological Interface Design, specifically the notion of "naturalness" of representation and the representation of coupled functional relationships, which serve to support direct perception (see Flach & Warren, 1995).

The notions of Human-Centered Computing dovetail in spirit and in many details with the notions of Cognitive Systems Engineering. Don Norman (1993), for instance, offered many ideas and principles that have been carried over into the principles of Human-Centered Computing (Endsley & Hoffman, 2002; Hoffman, Coffey, & Ford, 2000; Hoffman & Hayes, 2004):

1. Tools for reflection must support the exploration of ideas. They must make it easy to compare and evaluate and to explore alternatives.
2. The tools must be "invisible"—they must not get in the way. The human should be enabled to work on problems, not struggle with the technology.
3. Tools should provide a sense of direct engagement. They should provide feedback and motivate the human. They should instill a continual feeling of challenge, neither so difficult as to cause hopelessness or frustration nor so easy as to promote boredom.

4. Tools should be created by a process of user involvement. The design team should start by considering the tasks that the artifact is intended to serve and the people who will use it. To accomplish this, the design team must include expertise in human cognition, in social interaction, in the task that is to be supported, and in the technologies that will be used.

Appropriate tools are designed by starting off with human needs, working with those who will be using the tools to fashion them into the most effective instruments for the task. Above all, such tools allow people to be in control: This is an appropriate use of an appropriate technology. (Norman, 1993, p. 252)

Norman also described the envisioned world problem:

The trick in designing technology is to provide situations that minimize error, that minimize the impact of error, and that maximize the chance of discovering error once it has been committed. ... Changing the equipment may accidentally destroy the information communication channels that make work proceed smoothly, synchronized among a group of workers without the need for direct verbal communication. (Norman, 1993, pp. 138)

Furthermore, Norman sees human–computer interaction in systems terms, a hallmark of both Cognitive Systems Engineering and Human-Centered Computing (Hoffman, Hayes, Ford, & Hancock, 2002):

Shared communication may at first seem unnecessary, exposing people to irrelevant messages. But, the messages carry information about the activities of others, information that is at times essential to the smooth synchronization of the task or, as in the case of the ship navigators, information that serves as an efficient training device for the entire crew, regardless of their level of expertise. (Norman, 1993, p. 153)

Technology tends to be unyielding, demanding, coercive. Social groups require flexibility, cooperation, and resilience, allowing diverse personalities, interests, and work styles to interact. (Norman, 1993, p. 215)

Automation works best when conditions are normal. When conditions become difficult—say, there is a storm and an engine, a radio, an electrical generator fails—then the automation takes over when it is least needed, gives up when it is most needed. When the engine fails, often with no advance warning, people are suddenly thrust into the process, suddenly asked to figure out the current state of the system, what has gone wrong, and what should be done. (Norman, 1993, p. 223)

When people work on the factory floor, they can tell what is happening by sounds, vibrations, even by smells. In computer-controlled factories ... the people moved to be with the automation, thus changing their interaction with the machinery. ... Some representations impoverish their users, providing insufficient information to understand the entire problem, reducing the richness of the sensory information, isolating the users from the situation. (Norman, 1993, p. 225)

Finally, both the Cognitive Systems Engineering and Human-Centered Computing views lament the problems in overcoming inertia in the design and development of new information technologies:

Any large change [in a sociotechncal system] must be accompanied by massive alteration of the supporting infrastructure. It is the infrastructure and the inertia of the existing technologies and customs that slow down the introduction of new ones. One problem is called the "established base." If a new technology is to supplant an old one, then people must somehow be convinced to give up the old technology. We live with many outmoded, inefficient technologies because the potential gain does not appear to be worth the pain and cost of change. (Norman, 1993, p. 192)

What about convergence with regard to the acronyms in the soup, such designations as "User-Centered Design," "Contextual Design," and the like (see Figure 14.2)?

Convergence on Design: Work-Centered Design

Apart from a shared dependence on methods of CTA, if there is one single thing that the perspectives converge on with regard to approach and goals, it is *design*. Some communities of practice focus on the design of interfaces, and usability testing, whereas others focus, for example, on the design of work methods, the design of teams, and so on—but all focus on design of something. All of the communities of practice advocate particular design strategies, each with particular designations:

> Scenario-Based Design (Carroll, 1995; Rosson & Carroll, 2003)
> Contextual Design (Holtzblatt, 2003)
> Participatory Design (Mueller, 2003)
> Decision-Centered Design (Crandall, Klein, & Hoffman, 2006)
> Ecological Interface Design (Vicente, 2002)
> User-Centered Design (Klein, Kaempf, Wolf, Thordsen, & Miller, 1997)
> Use-Centered Design (Flach & Dominguez, 1995)
> Work-Oriented Design (Ehn, 1988)
> Work-Centered Design (Eggleston, 2003)
> Work-Centered Support Systems (Scott, Roth, Deutsch, Kuper, et al., 2005)

Some of these are fairly specific procedural guidelines (e.g., Scenario-Based Design for the envisioning of new technology), whereas some seem more like general approaches or viewpoints (e.g., Contextual Design) (though they too come wrapped with preferred design methods and procedures). Given this plethora, it is little surprise that the designations churn up discussions of differences and contrasts. Lots of semantic deboning.

For example, the idea of Decision-Centered Design from the Naturalistic Decision Making perspective (chapter 9) was met with concern because work in this area was by no means restricted to the study of decision making. Indeed, the focus was on revealing the ways in which domain practitioners accomplish cognitive work. Likewise, some were concerned with the designation of User-Centered Design (as in Klein et al., 1997). The notion of User-Centered Design had two aspects to it. One was the idea of building information technologies (and interfaces) that were adapted to, or adaptable to, the reasoning styles of knowledge levels of individual human end users. That is an important topic, of course, and a considerable amount of research has been conducted on adaptive interfaces (cf. Allen, 1997). The second aspect to the User-Centered Design designation, the one that was of concern to some, was the implication that good technologies for supporting cognitive work must be designed with a focus on the cognitive work of particular individual workers. John Flach of Wright State University, among others, argued that the focus needs to be on the work itself, and so he coined the designation "Use-Centered Design" (Flach & Dominguez, 1995). One can run through the entire roster of acronyms and raise similar concerns.

One way of understanding all of the various "X-Centered Design" designations is in terms of a convergence on the general notion of creating technologies that support the cognitive work *in context*. Holtzblatt (2003) defined this as

> a full front-end design process that takes a cross-functional team from collecting data about users in the field, through interpretation and consolidation of that data, to the design of product concepts and a tested product structure. (p. 942)

Holtzblatt advocated using such methods as field interviews, diagramming, and storyboarding. All this could be taken as a fair description of activities of the practitioners who follow any of the acronyms in the acronym soup, but in this case the reference was to Contextual Design. This designation emerged as a reaction on the part of researchers having a background in ethnography to what was perceived as a misguided focus in the field of human–computer interaction, that is, a focus on the one person–one machine interaction. Thus, Contextual Design broadened the activity to include attempts to model not just tasks but also work and communication flows, organizational culture, and other higher level factors.

Work-Centered Design is a designation that seems to cover most of the variations. It emerged in the collaboration of Emilie Roth (Roth Technologies) and Robert Eggleston and other researchers at the U.S. Air Force Human Effectiveness Directorate (Eggleston, 2003; Eggleston & Whitaker, 2002; Eggleston, Young, & Whitaker, 2000; Scott et al., 2005, 2006; Whitaker et al., 2005).

Research conducted under the Work-Centered Design umbrella has included studies of military command and control units and weather forecasting operations. Methods of study include observations of the work and interviews with practitioners. A core argument is that cognitive work in complex contexts requires support technologies that are flexible and adaptable (Roth et al., 2006). Adaptability is required because work teams in complex sociotechnical contexts confront change constantly—change in priorities, goals, team roles, information sources, and so on. The modern sociotechnical workplace is a moving target.

> While some of the changes were anticipated, others were not. Further, even in the case of anticipated changes, their impact on team roles and work structure were not necessarily foreseeable…. While they anticipated an increase in scale, the management of the organization had not determined what changes would be needed in organizational structure to accommodate the increased number of missions…. With the increase in scale there turned out to be a shift in team member roles and tasks…. Among the consequences of the various changes we observed was a growing mismatch between the support provided by the information systems in place, WCSS-GWM included, and the requirements of work…. As a consequence, we observed users turn to development of informal artifacts including 'home-grown' software to compensate for system–work mismatches. (Scott et al., 2005, p. 245)

To paraphrase Scott, Roth, Deutsch, Kuper, et al. (2005, p. 244), technology must change in ways that are responsive to the user's changing requirements. This represents a somewhat radical departure from the traditional notion of software engineering, which regards requirements as a sort of specification of all features (functions, interfaces, etc.) that are to be created. Ideally, these specifications are largely "cast in stone" before the technology is created. They provide software developers a clear and usable description of what the software has to do. From this perspective, "requirements creep"—when design specifications change even as the technology is being created (i.e., as the software is being written, user comments suggest that a prototype interface needs major fixing)—is a bad thing indeed. But experience with information technology shows that change in requirements is an empirical fact, and it forces software developers to design for "desirements" as well as requirements (Hoffman & Elm, 2006). More than that, the Work-Centered Design philosophy is that technology must be created so that it is capable of adapting even after it comes off the assembly line. This approach raises entirely new research questions, such as the following: Can users and developers be provided with the tools to rapidly adapt their systems to changing workplace demands? Can test and evaluation procedures be developed that adequately support the process for rapid change in software capabilities?

A Case Study in Work-Centered Design

Complicating matters further, if workplace change is continuous, this means that one must design for change even while the workplace under study is itself changing.

> At the time the study was initiated (February 2001), Flight Managers and weather forecasters worked closely to determine the potential impact of predicted weather on the viability of upcoming flights. If hazardous weather conditions were forecasted (e.g., high turbulence or lightning) then the Flight Manager and weather forecaster worked collaboratively to identify alternative routing that would avoid the problematic weather areas. However, they had limited software tools to support their collaborative decision-making processes. While the weather forecasters had various displays available for actual and predicted weather in different parts of the world, the information came from multiple sources and was presented on separate displays. Further, there were no graphics depicting the planned flight paths of upcoming missions making it necessary for forecasters and Flight Managers to mentally fuse the various sources of disparate information to assess the potential impact of weather on a mission. (Whitaker et al., 2005, p. 6)

These problems were solved in the creation of a map display that allowed the description of routes and significant weather events and that also allowed the user to create "software agents" that could scan for emerging weather and send alerts to the Flight Manager.

By the second year of the Whitaker et al. Work-Centered Design project, the prototype was situated in a workplace and was being used with good result. So far, so good. But by then the workplace was changing: Different missions on a larger scale of operations required new team members and new roles.

> While initially forecasters worked one on one with a Flight Manager to produce a "tailored forecast" for each flight managed mission, the nature of the collaboration between forecaster and Flight Manager changed as the number of Flight Managers and flight managed missions increased. (Whitaker et al., 2005, p. 9)

There were new information sources for weather data:

> A new weather forecasting software system came on-line for forecasters to use in preparing forecast hazard charts. While the new system provided much more detailed weather information, it had no capability to overlay flight plans on the same map as weather data. This led to a new requirement on [our system]—the import of forecast chart data produced by the new on-line weather forecasting system and the overlay of it on [our] map. (Whitaker et al., 2005, p. 9)

And there were changes in the workplace which actually distanced the forecasters from the flight managers. With airlift resources stretched, the forecaster and flight managers now needed additional support in identifying and managing a set of "high-risk" missions to focus on, treating those differently from the more routine missions.

As the project drew to a close, the researchers looked back at all the change requests and asked whether they could have been anticipated. Where there any requirements that might have been understood from the start? What kinds of software changes were needed to make the requirements changes?

> The lesson learned … is that the bulk of system change requests, at least for this system, arise from changes in how the system is to be used, what other systems this one needs to communicate with, or other environmental changes surrounding this system. These are all changes that cannot be anticipated during the original design process. (Whitaker et al., 2005, p. 11)

With regard to the sorts of software changes that were needed to accommodate the changing work demands, the most scary, from a software engineering point of view, would be changes in such things as data formats, map layers, network configurations, and security protocols. Such software infrastructure changes can be handled only the hard way, by heavy software engineering work. Changes in the alerts system were relatively easy (i.e., adding new rule-based software agents). However,

> more than half of the system change requests involved changes to the user interface. … The impact of designing a Work-Centered Support System that could easily accommodate these changes by the end-user organization would be high. We estimate that more than half of the system change requests were of types that could be satisfied by the end-user organization operating an evolvable work-centered system. (Whitaker et al., 2005, p. 13)

What usually happens in work domains where work change is not matched by functional adaptation of the technology? Users create kluges and work-arounds (Koopman & Hoffman, 2003). Though "cheat sheets" and "sticky notes" are commonly used tools, work-arounds can be clever and sophisticated "homegrown software" as well:

> The display, as designed, focused on displaying the number of aircraft scheduled to land at an airfield as the primary indicator of the viability of current landing schedules. However, there were additional important factors … that were not visible in the display as designed. These were the operating hours of the airfield, which could change on short notice, and whether the scheduled landing time was during night or day since there could be restrictions on whether planes could take off and land during those periods. The users came up with an ingenious way to graphically depict these important types of information on the airfield displays. They defined "pseudo-planes" that did not actually exist and scheduled them to be at the airfield during the critical times in question (i.e., when the airfield was supposed to be closed; or when planes were not allowed to fly in or out). By entering these "pseudo-planes" into the display system, they were able to create graphic visual indicators of information critical to their decision-making that was not anticipated as important in the original system design. (Whitaker et al., 2005, pp. 14–15)

We highlight this project on Work-Centered Design to suggest that some integration of perspectives on CTA has been occurring, because the work conducted under each of the acronyms in the acronym soup shares the same goals, stance, method, and focus of work. Nothing could better show how the perspectives on CTA converge than to point out a couple of not entirely coincidental coincidents:

- "Work-Oriented Design" is the designation used by Pele Ehn (of the School of Art and Communication, Malmoe University, Sweden) to designate his studies of technology design from a sociological perspective of activity analysis (see chapter 7; Ehn, 1988). Ideas sometimes seem to demand themselves into existence.
- The workplace as a moving target is recognized as a key challenge by researchers in the Work Analysis perspective (see chapter 10). Pejtersen and Rasmussen (1997) argued that information technology should be designed to support continual learning and adaptation to change. The moving target challenge is also recognized in Human-Centered Computing (Ballas, 2007) (see chapter 12). In the case of the Work-Centered Design work on weather forecasting, the new or envisioned work system was to replace a legacy method and older set of technologies.
- An important convergence of the perspectives on CTA, the communities of practice, and the designations of "X-Centered Design" is the sensitivity to context. Entire communities of practice rally around the idea that it is necessary to understand cognitive work in the context of teams, organizations, cultures, and societies as a whole (see chapter 11). Examples abound of how CTA, conducted in context, reveals critical information; examples abound of how cognitive work needs to be understood in context. Here is just one more example to add to others that appear across the pages of this book:

  > I was performing a requirements analysis in a police department and observing police officers using a system of standardized forms. … I learned a lot about how users worked around the forms with their own format, that helped in designing better online forms. A traditional systems analysis would typically not involve studying users using paper forms in their actual work but would instead have taken the paper forms themselves as a description of the work to be automated. (Mahew, 2003, p. 920)

There are not only convergences of ideas that we can find across the perspectives but also convergences of particular topics. Perhaps the most salient of these is the study of teamwork and team cognition. Because this is such an important area, and shows convergence by cutting across all of the perspectives and communities of practice that we have discussed in the chapters of this book, we now devote a chapter just to this topic.

Summary

This chapter opened with a Concept Map depicting commonalities across perspectives (Figure 15.2). Specifically, all the approaches considered in this book have a shared goal of developing ideas, methods, and tools to enhance human capabilities. Each takes a systems stance, focusing on the complexity of work in context. All share a core set of methods that could be considered CTA and CFR. All focus on cognition from the perspective of individuals, teams, and organizations. All focus on cognitive work, examining sociotechnical workplaces and domains of "significant" expertise.

Convergence exists at many levels. For example, the Ethnographic and Sociological perspectives dovetail with the ideas of Cognitive Work Analysis and Cognitive Systems Engineering. These approaches advocate a combination of field studies and experimental investigation, regard technology as a hypothesis about how cognitive work will be shaped, and suggest that sociotechnical systems should be studied from a variety perspectives or levels. In addition, these approaches share the ideas that knowledge and skill are (at least) partially contextually defined and constituted and that problem solving is situated within the context in which it occurs. Furthermore, these approaches agree that work can be prescribed, configured, facilitated, and organized, but the way in which work is undertaken cannot and should not be completely controlled. They view expertise as important to cognitive work and teamwork and central to the methodology of CTA. These approaches raise issues related to the envisioned world problem and the actual work–true work gap.

Other examples of convergence include the notion of "naturalness" of representation and the representation of coupled functional relationships in support of direct perception found in both Ecological Interface Design and Human-Centered Computing. Human-Centered Computing and Cognitive Systems Engineering share similar goals for the design of information tools. Specifically, tools must make it easy to compare and evaluate, as well as explore, alternatives. Tools should enable humans to work on problems, not struggle with the technology. Tools should provide a sense of direct engagement, providing feedback and motivating the human. Tools should be created via a process of user involvement. In addition, these approaches share an interest in the exploring the envisioned world problem, they express human-centered interaction in systems terms, and they lament problems in overcoming inertia in the design and development of new technologies.

Another point of convergence is in the context of design. In spite of the many "X-Centered Design" designations, most converge on the general notion of creating technologies that support the cognitive work. Work-Centered Design is a recent framework proposed to leverage the strengths of other X-Centered Design designations in pursuit of designing work-centered support systems. Work-Centered Design suggests that technologies must be flexible and adaptable to be effective in constantly changing sociotechnical contexts. This is in contrast to traditional software engineering, in which requirements are seen as a specification of all features that are to be created. Traditionally, requirements creep has been considered a bad thing rather than an empirical reality. Work conducted under each of the X-Centered Design designations shares the same goals, stance, method, and focus of work.

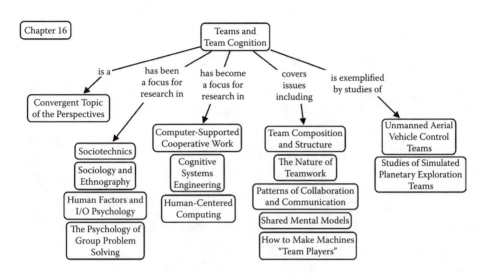

FIGURE 16.1 Chapter 16 Concept Map.

16

Synthesis

Convergence on the Topic of Teamwork and Team Cognition

> Although it can be exciting to find a new source of information and a new audience, it can be frustrating when the other group is ignorant of work that you assume to be basic shared knowledge. The groups ... are not always aware of the extent to which they have relied on different conferences, journals, and books.
>
> —Johnathan Grudin (1994, p. 23)

Those who are familiar with the communities of practice that we have covered in this book, and the diverse research that is being conducted, may have noted a salient topic that we have not yet singled out for discussion. This is the topic of team cognition and team cognitive work. Using methods ranging from ethnographic Activity Analysis to experiment-like procedures using simulators, researchers have studied teams in diverse domains: surgical teams, military command and control teams, air traffic control teams, air crews, nuclear power plant controllers, and many other domains (e.g., see Salas & Klein, 2001; Schraagen, Chipman, & Shalin, 2000; Serfaty, MacMillan, Entin, & Entin, 1997). The importance of teams, and team cognition, to the modern workplace and modern organization has made it into the popular press, in books such as that by Boynton and Fischer (2005), in which they presented analyses of some "virtuoso teams" (e.g., the Manhattan Project, Thomas Edison's invention factory, Sid Caesar's team that produced *Your Show of Shows* in the 1950s, and others). The authors derived lessons for good team management, including a process they called "DeepDive," which aids managers in creating virtuoso teams. (As one might guess, the process involves activities such as identifying expertise and engaging people in brainstorming.)

Although this topic is deserving of a review of its own, certainly a book-length one, we saved it for this synthesizing chapter for a simple yet important reason: The study of team factors shows how Cognitive Task Analysis (CTA) methods and research topics cut across all of the perspectives. Team cognition represents a topic, and a set of research challenges, on which all of the perspectives converge.

In chapter 7 we discussed the notion that machines need to be designed such that they can be "team players," and in chapter 12 we elaborated on this notion in

357

a discussion of the idea of the "Basic Compact" and the notion of machines that can act as team players. In chapter 11 we discussed the idea of "distributed cognition" and illustrated some ethnographic Activity Analyses of team collaboration (i.e., Ed Hutchins's research on team navigation of ships). In chapter 9 we discussed the interest on the part of the Naturalistic Decision Making (NDM) community to understand the cognitive and collaborative work of teams that have to work in dynamic, high-stakes, time-pressured circumstances.

Teamwork and team design have been a long-standing focus of research and theorizing within human factors and organizational-industrial psychology (e.g., Medsker & Campion, 1997; West, 1996). The topic of team cognition and team cognitive work leverages what is known about group problem solving and decision making from the fields of social psychology and sociology (e.g., Hirokawa & Poole, 1996).

In the following sections of this chapter, we present capsule views of the ideas and research on teams from a number of communities of practice. We begin with an example from ethnography.

Ethnography

From a situated cognition approach, problem-solving activities are not specified wholly by the problem-solving theories typical of cognitive psychology; a more holistic analysis of the activities by which problem solving is undertaken is required. For example, the notion of a goal in the situated cognition approach is different from that in psychological problem-solving theories in that, although all human activity is considered purposeful, not every goal is considered a problem to be solved and not every activity is considered a goal-oriented task (Clancey, 2001). Bill Clancey's study of the activities of crews on simulated planetary exploration missions showed that activities that would be categorized as "off task" or "nonoperations" in traditional problem-solving theories are often an integral part of how teamwork is undertaken. The studies are being conducted at a simulated Mars habitat facility at Houghton Crater, a relatively uneroded 23.4-million-year-old impact structure, located near the western end of Devon Island in the Canadian Arctic Archipelago. In one scenario, operatives were required to wait to receive help in removing their space suits. The activity of waiting would not traditionally be conceived of as an "on-task" problem-solving behavior; it is more likely to be seen as a disruption. However, as Clancey argued, people's minds do not go into stasis during waiting. To the contrary, operatives used waiting time to plan upcoming tasks. Thus, planning and collaboration were facilitated by waiting.

In another example, Clancey described how a water tank at a camp needed filling regularly to supply personnel with fresh water. The valve for the supply line to the tank originated a half mile from the camp, and a team member was required to travel to the valve to open and shut the supply line. A second team member was needed to look into the tank and inform the first when the tank was full. A radio was available in the camp to communicate to the valve operator about when the valve needed to be opened and shut. However, the radio was not physically accessible to the team member at the tank because the tank was located 8 feet above the floor of the camp.

Thus, a third team member was required as a radio operator to convey messages from the person at the tank to the valve operator. However, even more than those three people were actively engaged in the task—others were observing the operatives and learning about tank-filling operations as they watched the operatives go about their task. In addition, other team members who were directly concerned with *other* tasks remained aware, at least tacitly, of the tank-filling task. If a problem had arisen during the tank-filling process, such as the radio breaking, the extra demands placed on the team members could have been met by help from the colocated operatives, who were more or less cognizant about tank-filling procedures owing to their observations and close proximity.

Interpreted from a traditional task analysis approach, the water-filling activities were far from optimal in terms of the allocation of human time and resources: some people were engaged in the task but were not directly contributing to its accomplishment. More people were actively involved than were needed. Indeed, a traditional argument might be that the tank-filling process could have been automated and thus all of the human resources allocated more appropriately elsewhere. Clancey's view is that this misses the point. Automating this task would reduce the opportunity for critical facets of work such as coordination to achieve common ground. Traditional task analysis approach would have overlooked these key components of work.

Clancey (2001) cautioned researchers conducting studies of teamwork against relying on easy categorizations of activities, such as "work related" or "nonwork related," because such a dichotomy may gloss over aspects of team cognition and collaboration. Perceptions based on categories that are assumed a priori to the observation of the teamwork can bias the observer's judgment about whether activities are salient to work. For example, researchers might judge some activities as inefficient or even time wasting, but in actuality these activities might contribute to work in a variety of ways. For example, they may be necessary to make work more "tolerable, interesting, learnable, [and] shareable" than it would be otherwise (Clancey, 2006). Throughout this process of "taking practice seriously" (Wynn, 1991), Clancey's approach is to conduct microanalyses of behavior but over long time periods (several hours at minimum). Furthermore, the caution about simplifying categories for work or Activity Analysis reminds us of the notion of strong ethnography: Analysis proceeds best if observational (or interview) data are analyzed in waves using multiple conceptual schemes and categories.

Sociotechnics

In chapter 11 we discussed the idea of "distributed cognition," and we illustrated some ethnographic Activity Analyses of team collaboration (i.e., Ed Hutchins's research on team navigation of ships). Also in that chapter we presented a capsule view of the community of practice known as Sociotechnics, which introduced the notion of the "sociotechnical system" in research conducted beginning in the 1940s at the Tavistock Institute in the United Kingdom. Much of the emphasis in Sociotechnics is on the sociology of organizations, leading to a focus on teams and teamwork. "We place a great deal of emphasis on the training of operating teams; not only have they

TABLE 16.1 A Checklist for Making Decisions About Teaming

Would interdependence enhance the efficiency or quality of the work?

Do the tasks require a variety of knowledge, skills, and abilities such that combining individuals with different backgrounds would make a difference in performance?

Would breadth of skills and workforce flexibility be valuable to the organization?

Would increased communication, information exchange, and cooperation improve performance rather than interfere with it?

Are individual evaluation and rewards difficult or impossible to make, or are they mistrusted by workers? Could common measures of performance be developed and used?

Is it technically possible to group tasks in a meaningful, efficient way?

Can teams be defined as meaningful units of the organization with identifiable inputs, outputs, and buffer areas, which allow the teams to develop an identity?

Would the amount of time taken to reach decisions, consensus, and coordination not be detrimental to performance?

Would individuals be willing to work in teams?

Do the workers have the interpersonal skills needed to work in teams? If not, would team members have the capacity and willingness to be trained in interpersonal and technical skills required for teamwork?

Would teamwork be compatible with cultural norms, organizational policies, and leadership styles?

Would labor–management relations be favorable to team job design?

Note: Adapted from Clegg (2000) and Medsker and Campion (1997).

to learn the appropriate operating skills, they have to learn to operate *as a team*" (Cherns, 1987, p. 160).

The field of Sociotechnics has contributed to our analysis of team cognitive work some lengthy considerations of teamwork issues, including checklists for deciding whether teamwork is advantageous relative to individual work, and criteria for evaluating teamwork. These are summarized in Tables 16.1 and 16.2.

Bringing about a team-based reorganization involves many challenges, especially if the change is from a more individual-centered organization. Thus,

> supervision will require major restructuring to support teamworking. Since the team takes on many of the responsibilities traditionally allocated to supervisors, the role of supervisors will change quite radically, moving from a controlling role to one facilitating effective team performance. … This will involve "boundary management," such as liaising with other teams or other parts of the organization and procuring resources from the organization for the team. This means that supervisors will need extensive training in these skills, which will be quite different from the skills used in a traditional supervisory role. Supervisors may feel that their authority is being removed, or that their jobs are under threat, and they may find their new role quite stressful or frustrating. This can lead to resistance or inappropriate actions, which may adversely affect team performance. … Other groups may also feel threatened by expanded operator roles. For example, engineers and quality inspectors may feel that their jobs are being taken away. However, they may be reassured by the fact that the new work organization may help them to be more proactive in their work. Wider organizational structures and systems also need to be congruent with a team-based work organization, and failure to take these into account is a frequent reason for a lack of success of teamworking. For example, many team-based organizations find it necessary to change the payment structure from seniority-based to skill-based and team-based. (Clegg, 2000, p. 470)

TABLE 16.2 Conditions for Successful Teamwork

Functional grouping	A team should be an intact group with clear boundaries, it should have interdependent members and differentiated roles, and it should be congruent with employees' mental models about how work should be done.
Good composition	The team needs to have all the skills necessary to perform each task. It is necessary to ensure that each team member is capable of a number of different tasks.
Size	The size of the team will vary according to the exact nature of the work, but it should always be of a manageable size (typically not more than 10 or 12 members).
Autonomy	The team should be empowered to plan and manage all aspects of its own work. This includes taking responsibility for planning and scheduling the work, organizing rest breaks, and ensuring that quality standards are achieved.
Meaningful goals	The team should have challenging performance goals that foster motivation. These goals should cover the full range of team task goals rather than just one measure such as short-term work efficiency.
Self-determination of task design	Teams should be empowered to shape the procedures by which the work is done, understanding that there will be constraints to meet performance targets and the need to adhere to codes or regulations.
Effort sharing	No one person is assigned tasks that are less desirable or enjoyable.
Teamwork skills	Training has been provided in planning skills, team and interpersonal skills, and technical skills.
Communication	There must be an effective information system that provides team members access to relevant information to enable them to make decisions.
Feedback	Teams should receive feedback at the team performance level. (However, individual team members may at times face problems with which they need help, and the feedback system should include a way of identifying such occasions in a way that is not threatening to individuals.)

Note: Adapted from Clegg (2000).

Interest in teams, teaming, and group collaboration emerged along with the Internet and the World Wide Web, and in parallel there emerged an international community of practice in the mid- to late 1980s, calling itself "Computer-Supported Cooperative Work" (CSCW).

Computer-Supported Cooperative Work

The term *Computer-Supported Cooperative Work* (CSCW) was introduced at a conference in 1976 by Irene Grief (Grief, Seliger, & Weihl, 1976). Participants in this community of practice include computer scientists (especially in the fields of management information systems and office automation), social scientists, and also Cognitive Systems Engineers (Grudin, 1994). Attendance at meetings showed heavy representation by industry, which fueled the community out of a desire to move beyond single-user applications (Grudin, 1994). Through annual conferences sponsored by the Association for Computing Machinery (the 10th such conference was in 2006;

[http://www.acm.org/conferences]), conference proceedings (e.g., Shen, Chao, Lin, Barthès, & James, 2006), and the CSCW journal (www.springer.com), this community takes a broad view of technologies such as groupware, blogs, wikis, videoconferencing, and so on. It considers multiple levels: the psychological, the social-interpersonal, and the organizational aspects of using information technology to support group and teamwork (Brehmer, 1991; Grudin, 1994). The research addresses all of the "three Cs" with respect to various forms of group organization: communication, cooperation, and collaboration. Some reviews and compendia are Baecker (1992); Beaudoin-Lafon (1999); Bowker, Star, Turner, & Gasser (1997); Carstensen & Nielsen (1997); Galegher, Kraut, & Egido (1990); Grief (1988); O'Donnell, Hmelo-Silver, and Erkens (2006); Olson, Malone, & Smith (2001); Stahl (2006); and Wilson (1991). Grudin (1994) presented a capsule view of the history of CSCW, including discussions of the international mix in the community (North America, Japan, and Europe) and the subtle differences in focus and emphasis.

Diverse domains of work are studied, including science, product development, hardware and software engineering, bibliotechnics, architecture, and so on. Diverse hypotheses are explored in the research, such as the development of working relationships, the effects of colocation versus distance cooperation, the challenge of designing technology to fit the nature of the group work, the challenge of supporting the work of ad hoc groups, the challenge of developing good models of collaboration, ways in which information technology can support collaborative learning and knowledge creation, and so on. As one might expect, many studies in CSCW analyze patterns in e-mail and voice messaging (e.g., Rice & Shook, 1990). However, in many studies the primary research methods are observations, participant observations, and interviews—the basic palette of ethnographic methods. Additional methods used in the research include surveys and workspace analyses (e.g., Kraut, Egido, & Galegher, 1990). Many studies on the effects of technology on group work have been laboratory based. For example, Boland and Tenkasi (2001) had physicians make "causal maps" diagrams of their understanding of the health care system and factors influencing the quality of medical care. Field experiments are also conducted in which new technology is introduced and changes in group work are studied (e.g., Bikson & Eveland, 1990). Thus we see in the research of this community of practice a full range of the broader palette of CTA methods.

As one might expect, there is considerable overlap (of people, topics, goals, issues) of this community of practice with the distributed cognition, situated cognition, and Sociotechnics communities of practice (see, for instance, Blomberg, Suchman, & Trigg, 1997; Boland & Tenkasi, 2001; Monarch et al., 1997). Also shared with other perspectives on CTA is a focus on design, specifically the design of technology (e.g., Hmelo-Silver, 2006; Shen et al., 2006; Stahl, 2006). Common reference is made in the CSCW literature to notions of user involvement in design and the perspective of Work-Centered Design (see, for instance, Blomberg et al., 1997; Bowker et al., 1997, section II; Ehrlich, 1999).

We next present a capsule view of ideas about teaming developed within the Human-Centered Computing (HCC) community of practice.

Making Machines Team Players

An outstanding challenge within the HCC community of practice is the challenge of making machines "team players." This phrase captures a high-level goal also for Cognitive Systems Engineering (CSE), entailed by the ironies of automation and the reaction of CSE to Designer-Centered Design. Many researchers have been looking for ways to make automated systems team players (Christoffersen & Woods, 2002). A great deal of the current work within the software and robotic-agent research communities involves determining how to build automated systems with sophisticated team-player qualities (e.g., Allen & Ferguson, 2002; Bradshaw, Feltovich, et al., 2004; Tambe et al., 1999). In contrast to previous research in computer science that focused almost exclusively on how to make machines more autonomous, much current research, especially the work on intelligent "software agents" and on autonomous vehicles, seeks to understand and satisfy requirements for the basic aspects of joint activity, either within multiagent systems or as part of human–agent teamwork. Software agents are functional computer programs. One might think of them as computer viruses, but software agents do good things, such as control an unmanned aerial vehicle (UAV) or go out on the World Wide Web to search for particular kinds of information. In the computer science (intelligent systems) literature, humans, robots, decision support systems, unmanned vehicles, and software agents are all referred to as "agents," meaning that they can do things and have goals and intentions.

When humans collaborate in teams, they enter into a Basic Compact that they intend to work together. This is an agreement (often tacit) to facilitate coordination, work toward shared goals, and prevent breakdowns in team coordination. The Basic Compact is not a once-and-for-all prerequisite to be satisfied but rather something that has to be continuously reinforced or renewed. It includes an expectation that all parties will be to some extent predictable so that individuals can plan their individual and their coordinated activities. It includes an expectation that all parties will be to some extent directable. Individual parties will deliberately assess and modify the actions of the other parties in a joint activity as conditions and priorities change (Christoffersen & Woods, 2002). It includes an expectation that the parties will repair faulty knowledge, beliefs, and assumptions when these are detected. This is all a process of building and maintaining "common ground." Common ground includes the pertinent knowledge, beliefs, and assumptions that are shared among the involved parties (Clark, 1996). Common ground enables each party to comprehend the messages and signals that help coordinate the joint actions. Team members must be alert for signs of possible erosion of common ground and take preemptive action to forestall a potentially disastrous breakdown of team functioning. Part of achieving coordination is investing in those actions that enhance the integrity of the compact, and remaining sensitive to and counteracting those factors that could degrade it.

No form of automation today or on the horizon is capable of entering fully into the rich forms of Basic Compact that are used among people. Klein, Woods, Bradshaw, Hoffman, and Feltovich (2004) outlined a number of challenges for making automation components into effective team players in cognitive work. To be a team player, an intelligent machine must fulfill the requirements of a Basic Compact. Looking beyond current research and machine capabilities, not only do machines need to be able to enter into a Basic Compact but they must also "understand" and accept the joint goals of the enterprise, understand and accept their roles in the collaboration and the need for maintaining common ground, and be capable of signaling if they are unable or unwilling to fully participate in the activity.

To be an effective team player, intelligent machines must be able to adequately model the other participants' intents and actions relative to the state and evolution of the joint activity; for example, are they having trouble? Are they on a standard path proceeding smoothly? What impasses have arisen? How have others adapted to disruptions to the plan? In the limited realm of what today's machines can communicate and reason about among themselves, there has been some success in the development of theories and implementations of multiagent cooperation. This usually involves some notion of shared knowledge, goals, and intentions that function as the glue that binds the agents' activities together (Cohen & Levesque, 1991). By virtue of a largely reusable explicit formal model of shared "intentions," multiple software agents attempt to manage general responsibilities and commitments to each other in a coherent fashion that facilitates recovery when unanticipated problems arise.

To be a team player, an intelligent machine or software agent—like a human—has to be reasonably predictable and has to have an ability to predict the actions of others. Thus it should act neither capriciously nor unobservably, and it should be able to observe and correctly predict future behavior of teammates. Currently, however, the intelligence and autonomy of machines directly work against the confidence that people have in their predictability. Although people will rapidly assign tasks to simple deterministic mechanisms whose design is artfully made transparent, they are usually reluctant to trust complex agents to the same degree (Bradshaw, Beautement, et al., 2004). It is ironic that by making agents more adaptable, we may also make them less predictable, as Lisanne Bainbridge pointed out in 1983. The more a system takes the initiative in adapting to the existing working style of its operator, the more reluctant operators may be to adapt their own behavior, because of the confusions these adaptations might create (e.g., Klein, 2003; Klein et al., 2004).

To be a team player, an intelligent machine must be directable. The nontransparent complexity and inadequate directability of machines can be a formula for disaster. In response to this concern, software agent researchers have increasingly focused on developing means for controlling aspects of software agent autonomy in a fashion that can both be dynamically specified and easily understood. "Policies" are a means to dynamically regulate the behavior of a system without changing code or requiring the cooperation of the components being governed (Bradshaw, Beautement, et al., 2004; Bradshaw, Feltovich, et al., 2004). Through policy, people can precisely express bounds on autonomous behavior in a way that is consistent with their appraisal of a machine agent's competence in a given context. The machine's behavior becomes more predictable in respect to the actions controlled by policy. Moreover, the ability to change policies dynamically means that poorly performing agents can be immediately brought into compliance with corrective measures.

To be a team player, an intelligent machine must participate in the management of attention. As a part of maintaining common ground during coordinated activity, team members direct each other's attention to the most important signals, activities, and changes. They must do this in an intelligent and context-sensitive manner, so as not to overwhelm each other with low-level messages containing minimal signals mixed with a great deal of distracting noise. In human teams, individuals rely on their mental models of each other. They expend effort to appreciate what each other needs to notice, within the context of the task and the current situation (Sarter & Woods, 2000).

To be a team player, a machine must be able to make pertinent aspects of its status and intentions obvious to its teammates. Classic results have shown that the highest levels of automation on the flight deck of commercial jet aircraft often leave commercial pilots baffled in some situations, wondering what the automation is currently doing, why it is doing it, and what it is going to do next (Woods & Sarter, 2000). To make their actions sufficiently predictable, machines need to make their own targets, states, capacities, intentions, changes, and upcoming actions obvious to the people and other agents that supervise and coordinate with them (Feltovich, Bradshaw, Jeffers, Suri, & Uszok, 2004). This challenge runs counter to the advice that is sometimes given to automation developers to create systems that are barely noticed. People need to have a model of the machine as an agent participating in the joint activity (Norman, 1990). People can often effectively use their own thought processes as a basis for inferring the way their teammates are thinking, but this self-referential heuristic is not usually effective in working with machines.

It takes continuous effort to maintain common ground. The processes of understanding, problem solving, and task execution are necessarily incremental, subject to negotiation, and forever tentative (Bradshaw, Acquisti, et al., 2004). The Basic Compact commits people to coordinating with each other and to incurring the costs of providing signals, improving predictability, monitoring the others' status, and so forth. All of these take time and energy. These coordination costs can easily get out of hand, and therefore the partners in a coordination transaction have to do what they reasonably can to keep coordination costs down. This is a tacit expectation—to try to achieve economy of effort. Achieving coordination requires continuous investment, hence the power of the Basic Compact—a willingness to invest energy and to accommodate others rather than just to perform alone in one's narrow scope and with one's subgoals. Coordination doesn't come free and, once achieved, does not allow one to stop investing. Otherwise the coordination breaks down.

It will push the limits of technology to get the machines to communicate as fluently as a well-coordinated human team. The automation will have to signal when it is having trouble and when it is taking extreme action or moving toward the extreme end of its range of authority. Such capabilities will require interesting relational judgments about agent activities: How does an agent tell when another team member is having trouble performing a function but is not yet failing to perform? How and when does an agent effectively reveal or communicate that it is moving toward a limit of capability? Charles Billings (1996) and David Woods (2002) argued that an inherent asymmetry in coordinative competencies between people and machines will always create difficulties for designing human–machine teams. Nevertheless, some researchers are exploring ways to stretch the performance of software agents to reduce this asymmetry as far as possible. Similarly, a few research efforts are taking seriously the agent's need to interpret the physical environment. If they accomplish nothing more, efforts such as these can help us appreciate the difficulty of this problem.

Human Factors, Cognitive Systems Engineering, and Naturalistic Decision Making

Interest in team cognition, team expertise, and related topics also emerged within the fields of human factors and Cognitive Systems Engineering, beginning in the 1980s, but it accelerated in recent years because of the impact of world events (e.g., the increasing emphasis on multicultural teams, changes in military organizations and teaming schemes, etc.). As Eduardo Salas and Steve Fiore's reviews of CSE and NDM research on team cognition show, a number of important issues have been explored (Fiore & Salas, 2007; Salas & Fiore, 2004), some of which stretch our core notions of cognition.

- How do teams come to acquire the strategic knowledge that makes the whole greater than the sum of the parts and that makes the teamwork smooth and efficient (see Smith, Ford, & Kozlowski, 1997)? Teams must master both task work and teamwork. Task work skills are those that team members must understand and acquire for actual task performance, whereas teamwork skills are those that team members need to function effectively as a part of a team (Gersick, 1988; Rouse & Morris, 1986; Salas, Rosen, Burke, Goodwin, & Fiore, 2006).
- How do we identify good teams in the first place through performance measures (see Cooke, Salas, Cannon-Bowers, & Stout, 2000; Cooke, Salas, Kiekel, & Bell, 2004)? How do we distinguish expert from nonexpert teams, or, more broadly, how do we scale the proficiency level of teams? Surely this entails doing more than measuring the proficiency of the individual team members (see Blickensderfer, Cannon-Bowers, Salas, & Baker, 2000; Salas, Burke, & Stagl, 2004).
- How do teams make decisions? Research on teams conducted by scientists within the NDM perspective has shown that normative rational models of decision making are not descriptive of how teams make decisions, paralleling the finding for the decision making of individual experts (Klein, 1993a; Lipshitz, Klein, Orasanu, & Salas, 2001; Salas & Klein, 2001). Teams can make "intuitive" decisions, just as individuals can (see Kline, 2005).
- How is it that individual team members can come to have a *shared* mental model or *shared* situation awareness of the situation or problem case that the team is working on (see Cooke et al., 2000)? There is ample evidence showing that when team members have shared mental models, the team performance is best (Orasanu, 1990).
- How do teams develop a *team* mental model? This refers to the fact that each individual on a team develops mental models of the other team members—what they know, what their skills are, and what their information requirements are. Something like this seems necessary to explain how team members can anticipate the needs of other team members, providing them with just what they need even moments before they need it (see Cooke et al., 2004; Kiekel, Cooke, Foltz, Gorman, & Martin, 2002; Orasanu & Salas, 1993).
- How do teams develop metaknowledge about the task work, for example, the knowledge that certain team procedures are appropriate for certain conditions (see Salas et al., 2006)?
- How do teams acquire a common vision, shared goals, and mechanisms for cooperation and coordination; in other words, how do teams establish and maintain "common ground" (see Pearce & Ensley, 2004; van Berlo, Lowyck, & Schaafstal, 2007)?

- How do teams develop mutual trust and confidence (see Cooke et al., 2004; Salas, Burke, et al., 2004)?
- In many domains and circumstances, teams are composed on an ad hoc basis or have to adapt to novel circumstances. If an expert team is one that is adaptive and flexible, how is this achieved (see Burke et al., in press; Edmondson, Bohmer, & Pisano, 2001; Hatano & Inagaki, 1983?
- What are the effects of stress on the decision making of expert teams (see Entin & Serfaty, 1999; Kleinman & Serfaty, 1989)?
- There are significant training issues and challenges, which have been summed up in the question "How do we turn a team of experts into an expert team?" (Salas, Cannon-Bowers, & Johnson, 1997; also see Brun et al., 2005; Salas, Bowers, & Edens, 2001; Salas, Cannon-Bowers, & Blickensderfer, 1993; Salas et al., 2006; Zsambok, 1997). What are the lessons learned by the experiences of "virtuoso teams" (Boynton & Fischer, 2005)?

These, and more topics besides, have been a focus of considerable research over the past two decades, having significant overlap with work in CSCW. To be sure, the empirical study of teams is no less difficult than the study of other aspects of cognitive work, with teams adding many dimensions to the mix for consideration, such as interpersonal interaction and style issues (Salas, Stagl, Burke, & Goodwin, 2007), as well as factors of leadership and team member status (Fleishman et al., 1991; Salas, Burke, et al., 2004).

Researchers have studied team cognitive work using a variety of methods, including the retrospective analysis of critical incidents and critical decisions (e.g., Carroll, Rudolph, Hatakenaka, Widerhold, & Boldrini, 2001; Zsambok, 1997), field observations of team activities (e.g., Edmondson et al., 2001), analysis of transcripts of team communications (e.g., Patel & Arocha, 2001), and research in which teams work on scenarios in laboratory-like settings having multiple workstations (e.g., Cooke et al., 2004; Orasanu & Fischer, 1997).

An Example From Cognitive Systems Engineering

The many challenges facing teams are compounded when the individuals composing the team are located in different places. This precludes ordinary interpersonal (face-to-face) communication, which is rich with cues, and replaces it with media such as telephones, videophones, and networked computers. Although intended to make "distance collaboration" possible, the computer-mediated technologies add complexities and opportunities for communication breakdowns (e.g., we have all sent at least one e-mail message that we would like to take back) (Fiore, Salas, Cuevas, & Bowers, 2003; Hedlund, Ilgen, & Hollenbeck, 1998). As businesses have internationalized, educational systems have come to rely more on "distance learning," and military operations have become more "Net-centric," a clear need has arisen for a foundation for "team science" based on empirical study—we would say, "team CTA" (Kleinman & Serfaty, 1989).

The Cognitive Engineering Research on Team Tasks Lab (CERTT Lab) at Arizona State University was established by Nancy Cooke and her colleagues to be an environment in which teamwork and task work could be empirically studied at a facility including multiple workstations (for team members and leaders) and additional workstations and accoutrements that support the observers—the CTA researchers who study such things as team performance and team communications. Using simulated tasks, the researchers at CERTT have studied a number of kinds of teams, in domains including emergency response, NASA Mission Control operations, airport operations, and the like (see http://www.certt.com).

A recent study (Cooke, Gorman, Pedersen, & Bell, 2007) looked at the effects of "geographical distribution" on teams having the task of controlling reconnaissance UAVs. Such military teams are composed of individuals having differing degrees of experience and skill. Such teams are also sometimes composed on an ad hoc basis. In this case, the team members must be experienced enough at *teamwork* (i.e., making the team work as a team, building shared mental models, etc.) to allow the *task work* to ramp up quickly—even though the dispersed team members may never actually see each other's work space or meet face to face. When a team member is assigned a role, he or she needs to know immediately not only what to do but what the key communication and coordination channels will be. The military's reliance on a standard division of labor and distinct specializations helps in team formation and teamwork, but the challenges to team members remain. This is all complicated by the fact that the task work involves coping with world situations that are dynamic, sometimes unpredictable, and high risk. Hence, the task work nearly always involves real-time synchronization and coordination among team members.

Precisely how does geographical distribution, as opposed to colocated work, affect team performance and team cognition in these settings? The answers will almost certainly have implications for training and technology design in the support of distributed work.

With the participation of college students, Cooke et al. (2007) composed 20 three-person teams consisting of a designated pilot (who controls the UAV), a payload operator (who works the cameras, takes photos, etc.), and a navigator (who overviews the mission with a concentration on the flight path). Half of the teams worked in a single room (colocated) and could see each other and could see one another's workstation computer screens (though, as in military settings, their communication was over headsets). The members of the "geographically" distributed teams were in different rooms or were separated by partitions. All the participants received training, which involved study of training modules followed by practice at individual tasks (e.g., change altitude and airspeed, take a photo, etc.).

The teams then worked in seven 40-minute sessions, easier ones at first and harder ones later on. Each session involved a reconnaissance mission scenario. Missions involved the pilot flying a UAV along a route designated by the navigator for the payload operator to take photographs. Camera settings depended on the relation of altitude and airspeed, and thus the determination of camera settings required the interaction of the pilot and payload operator. Typical low-workload missions involved nine targets to be photographed. High-workload missions involved 20 targets and additional constraints on the route (i.e., tighter altitude restrictions). Missions were also salted with critical incidents, such as low camera battery or low fuel.

A host of measurements was taken, including measures of individual team members' situation awareness and subjective mental workload. Of particular interest were measures of team performance and team knowledge at the "holistic" level. Team performance involved time spent in an alarm or warning state (off course, low camera battery, etc.), efficiency of reaching the waypoints, and number of successful missions (i.e., photos taken and UAV returned).

Researchers evaluated team process by observing teams and analyzing communications at points when the teams encountered critical events. Observers looked to see, for example, whether the team members discussed their plans before a mission or discussed their performance during or after critical events. Team knowledge— the shared mental model—will not simply be some sort of summation of the mental models of the individual team members (Cooke et al., 2000).

> Metrics of team cognition applicable at the group or team level should also be relevant in terms of a holistic view of team cognition. For example, team members in a military aviation setting may *individually* have information about an impending threat, but without adequate communication that helps to produce the integration or fusion of the pieces of information at a very global level, the *team's* knowledge would be lacking and the *team* would fail to act on the impending threat. In this case, collective knowledge metrics would inaccurately represent the team as having knowledge about the impending threat, whereas holistic metrics would better reflect the team's actual knowledge. (Cooke et al., 2007, p. 150).

How can research get at this? Individual knowledge was assessed by having each participant rate the "relatedness" of pairs of task-relevant terms (e.g., "altitude–focus," "airspeed–fuel," "restricted operation zone–fuel"). The ratings were used to form semantic networks, a way of representing mental models (Schvaneveldt, 1990). But ratings were also generated by the teams, who made group ratings based on a consensus discussion. All of the networks were referenced to one that had been created by a domain expert, as the gold standard.

In theory, being colocated makes it easier for team members to learn how to anticipate what other team members need or will do (Entin & Serfaty, 1999; Stout, Cannon-Bowers, Salas, & Milanovich, 1999), enhancing team process and enabling them to coordinate their activities appropriately. However, the overall performance of the two types of team—colocated versus geographically distributed—was nearly equivalent, and both types of teams showed effect of steadier improvement across the easier scenarios.

For team members in all three roles, distributed teams engaged in less communication overall compared to the colocated teams—less communication to coordinate and plan prior to missions and less discussion of their performance after the missions, even though the colocated teams, like the distributed teams, communicated over headsets. The communications seem to have had an impact on team knowledge, and not just process, because the communications of the colocated teams facilitated the achievement of a shared mental model of the task. In addition, in terms of task knowledge, the colocated teams acquired more knowledge about the tasks of their fellow team members. In other words, the colocated teams were better at teamwork, though both those and the distributed teams performed about as well at the task work.

Based on this research, it seems counterintuitive that the colocated teams suffered a somewhat greater decline in performance than the distributed teams upon encountering the shift from the initial easier scenarios to the subsequent more difficult ones.

One explanation may be that being colocated increases team members' arousal (i.e., fears of being evaluated) and makes distractions more likely (Penner & Craiger, 1992), with effects of these factors showing up only in higher workload conditions. There was some evidence for this in the measures of subjective mental workload. However, it is just as reasonable to speculate that the achievement of a shared mental model mitigates the effects of increased stress or workload in teamwork (Stout et al., 1999). But then there must be some other explanation for the relatively poorer performance of the colocated teams on the more difficult scenarios. Cooke et al. (2007) suggested that there is a principle of "equifinality": Distributed and colocated teams adapt differently given the constraints of their work environments, entailing differences in team behavior and team cognitions, leading them along different routes to what comprises qualitatively the same outcome, that is, comparable levels of overall team performance.

> Distributed teams interact only as the task necessitates. … We might think of this form of adaptation as developing a much more rigid but efficient team cognition, whereas co-located teams have more "play" in the system, from which they can develop expectancies about what it means to play a different role on the team. However this was clearly not always adaptive, given the findings of performance decrement [for the colocated teams] under high workload. Indeed, the distributed modes of interaction seemed to be most impervious to the demands of high workload compared with the more easy going interaction of co-located teams … teams with different knowledge structures [may] not differ in terms of team performance … team members who [are] allowed to freely share knowledge [have] more accurate taskwork knowledge than those who were restricted from information sharing. (p. 163).

This study, as many studies, leads to further questions. In light of the fact that the participants in the Cooke et al. study were college students, it is an open question as to how the effects and subtle interactions that Cooke et al. found will manifest themselves in similar studies with individuals who are experienced at distributed and colocated teamwork.

The findings point to an immediate conclusion about distributed teamwork: One need not expect that a distributed team will perform less well than a colocated team. "In this task the benefits of using distributed teams appear to outweigh any minor costs of geographic distribution, [but in other tasks] in which communication is hampered … the costs may be significant" (Cooke et al., 2007 p. 165). But also in light of the nature of the Cooke et al. participants, the study has implications for training. Specifically, individuals being trained for distributed teams might benefit by scaffolding or encouragement to engage in coordination in terms of more pre- and postmission communications about teamwork and team process.

Future research should be directed at identifying factors that facilitate or inhibit the adaptiveness of certain team process behaviors as well as team members' knowledge. Team members' knowledge about the tasks of other team members may not always be critical if the work involves a highly specialized division of labor. However, at the other extreme in which team members are highly interchangeable, communication restrictions of distributed work environments (such as requiring team members to communicate by computer messaging or restricting the amount of communication allowed) may produce a greater decline in performance compared to colocated teams, who presumably can develop expectancies about the needs of other team members.

A final note on this study concerning CTA methodology that returns us to the theme of this section of the book—the synthesis of the perspectives. This one study involved the use of methods that have their origins in human factors (the subjective rating scale of mental workload), origins in Expertise Studies (the semantic network models of knowledge), origins in ethnography (the observations and probe questioning during task performance), and origins in NDM (the measure of situation awareness). In a sense then, this study presents CTA as a "wrapped package."

An Example From Naturalistic Decision Making

Ad hoc teams have also been studied in the context of emergency response command and control (Militello, Patterson, Bowman, & Wears, 2007; Militello, Patterson, Wears, & Snead, 2005; Militello, Quill, Patterson, Wears, & Ritter, 2005). Research conducted at the University of Dayton Research Institute has explored team issues from the perspective of the emergency operations center, which consists of a colocated command and control cell that coordinates with a set of distributed teams, including an incident command post, an on-scene command post, and other emergency response centers. These exploratory studies used CTA interviews in combination with ethnographic observation of exercises to better understand the barriers to collaboration that exist and generate potential solutions.

Observations took place over a 3-year period and included both military and civilian exercises, as well as one integrated military–civilian exercise. Interviews were conducted with representatives from the emergency operations center, including local government officials, firefighters, bioenvironmental personnel, health care personnel, and crisis action planners. In addition, lessons-learned documents from real-world incidents were reviewed.

Findings suggest that the emergency response community is a particularly rich domain of study, because the community is engaged in a "reinvention" of itself as it prepares for challenges of modern-day terrorism. Many municipalities are creating emergency operations centers for the first time. Others are expanding existing centers. This includes the hiring of new personnel, the development of new facilities, the acquisition of new equipment, and the formation of new policies and procedures. Furthermore, across the United States there are deliberate efforts to standardize organizational structures and procedures. In this context, the emergency response community is very open to reflection. This community is aggressively pursing input that will guide it in leveraging the resources available to create an increasingly well-designed emergency response system, which includes flexible and adaptable technological support to be used by ad hoc human teams to deal with novel, high-risk, and unpredictable situations.

Although several of the issues identified in this investigation may be considered common challenges for teams regardless of the domain, examining specific examples within emergency response led to important insights. For example, nearly every team must find strategies for developing and maintaining shared situation awareness. To do this effectively and efficiently, highly functioning teams rely on predetermined symbology, software, or language to communicate important status and priority information. Representatives in the emergency response center, however, come from a broad range of backgrounds and have highly variable levels of expertise with respect to emergency response. Depending on the nature of the incident, representatives in the emergency operations center might include a fire chief with 25 years of experience in dealing with emergencies and a newly appointed county representative who has never participated in a disaster exercise before. Furthermore, diverse agencies are likely to be present, including local government, private companies (i.e., hospitals), nongovernmental agencies (i.e., the Red Cross), and military organizations. As a result, there are no culturally shared or agreed-on conventions for communicating status and priority information. This difficulty is compounded by the fact that the types of disasters about which the group might be communicating varies widely, including anything from a snow emergency to a flu pandemic to the release of a toxic chemical agent to a hurricane.

It is important to note that software tools do exist that are intended to support shared situation assessment in emergency operations centers. Observations suggest that these tools are not currently used effectively, due no doubt to the convergence of new elements this community is contending with, including new personnel, new procedures, and new facilities. Personnel have not yet had time to learn to comfortably use the software, so during a fast-paced exercise, these tools are quickly abandoned for tried-and-true paper maps and handwritten notes.

Related issues include the implementation of conventions and tools for managing information flow in chaotic and unpredictable situations. Again, lack of protocol (or lack of training on existing protocol) for passing along information is exacerbated by the sheer volume of information and the range of media via which it is transmitted (cell phones, landlines, radios, e-mail, instant messenger, television, fax). Emergency operations centers must also contend with differences in decision-making styles across organizations. Military organizations tend to use command style, whereas civilian organizations tend toward consensus-based decision making. Conflict across agencies can greatly hinder emergency response efforts. Another challenge for emergency operation centers is the ever-present need for creative problem solving. Although having standard operating procedures in place will continue to be critical, emergency response teams will also be forced to look beyond the plans in place, as every disaster has novel and unanticipated elements that must be addressed. Personnel must be trained to develop creative problem-solving skills, and information technology must support real-time innovation.

These studies have highlighted key challenges that should serve as guiding elements in the design of technologies, facilities, and training exercises for the emergency response community. It is likely that conventions will emerge and be refined over the next few years as the emergency response community works through this reinvention of itself and begins to instantiate and institutionalize many of the procedures and strategies that are currently under development. In addition, as personnel become more experienced and the first generation of software tools becomes better tailored to this dynamic setting, we expect to see more effective use of software tools in promoting shared situation awareness and information flow across the team. The insights gained from these exploratory studies will provide direction as design teams and emergency response personnel iterate and explore how to best instantiate and refine tools and procedures to better support shared mental models, shared situation awareness, and shared goals, as well as team collaboration and trust.

Codicil

Although we have painted a picture of topical convergence among perspectives (here and also in chapter 15), we would be remiss were we not to point out that the desire to approach topics from multiple disciplines and create hybrid researchers does not always meet with smooth success. This can be ironic, as is illustrated in the literature on teamwork and in particular the work in CSCW. One might expect that the community of practice of CSCW would, as a whole, engage in cooperation and collaboration. But this is not always the case, as is suggested in the quotation from Johnathan Grudin (1994) with which we began this chapter. Grudin continued,

> Will the different priorities of the active researchers and organizations in Europe and the US persevere? ... Conferences have had limited success in drawing from both groups simultaneously. Philosophically oriented European submissions often strike empirically oriented American reviewers as lacking in content. American contributions strike European reviewers as unmotivated or shallow. Differences in terminology block understanding. For example, I listened to a European CSCW researcher criticize an American group's understanding of "task analysis." The Americans used the term to describe a cognitive task analysis based on experimental interface testing, a standard practice in human–computer interface studies. To the European, "task analysis" meant an organizational task analysis based on mapping the flow of information from person to person. He thought the term was "nonsensical" in an experimental setting. ... Some writers describe CSCW as an emerging field or discipline, but what we see today resembles a forum, an undisciplined marketplace of ideas, observations, issues, and technologies. We expect to find shared or overlapping interests, but we should anticipate differences in interests and priorities. (pp. 23, 25)

It could hardly be any other way, for, as we have shown in the chapters of this book, communities emerge, in part, from reactions against and within existing disciplines, perspectives, and communities. And so it goes.

In the next and final chapter, we take one more stab at laying out convergences, bringing us back to the unifying theme of this book. Transcending the perspectives, challenges, and even the ironies, it all comes back to CTA methods and methodology at the foundations of the sciences.

Summary

A major point of convergence of the perspectives is on the topic of team cognition and team cognitive work. Specific topics such as strategies for team formation, performance measures for assessing teams, and team decision making are considered. Shared mental models of the situation, as well as team mental models or awareness of other team members' knowledge, skills, and information requirements, are studied. How teams acquire metaknowledge about task work, a common vision, shared goals, and mechanisms for coordination and cooperation are examined. Other topics include the development of mutual trust and confidence, the assembly of adaptive and flexible ad hoc teams, and the transformation of a team of experts into an expert team. The different perspectives also converge in terms of methods, the study of team cognition using retrospective analysis of critical incidents and critical decisions, field observations, analysis of transcripts of team communications, and scenario-based studies in laboratory-like settings.

Examination of team studies conducted within the perspectives of Ethnography, Sociotechnics, Cognitive Systems Engineering, and CSCW illustrate the synthesis of perspectives, drawing from and adapting methods developed within human factors and Expertise Studies to explore teams in a range of applied work settings. Within the Sociotechnics perspective, the emphasis on the sociology of organizations naturally leads to a focus on teams and teamwork. Issues such as determining when teamwork might offer advantages over individual work, as well as how to restructure an organization to better support teamwork, have been carefully researched. The CSCW community cuts across several of the perspectives discussed in this volume to explore teams, teaming, and group collaboration as they are facilitated (and hindered) by the Internet and the World Wide Web. Diverse domains are studied, addressing issues such as the development of working relationships, the effects of colocation versus distance cooperation, the design of technology to fit the nature of the group work, strategies for supporting ad hoc groups, the development of models of collaboration, and so on.

An outstanding challenge for the HCC community is to design machines that operate as "team players." Although historically the field of artificial intelligence has focused on creating autonomous machines, a great deal of current work focuses on developing systems in which automated technology acts a team member, working in concert with humans. Human-to-human collaboration has been described as a "Basic Compact." This often implicit agreement includes efforts to facilitate coordination, work toward shared goals, and prevent breakdowns in team coordination. The Basic Compact must be continuously reinforced and renewed if teams are to function smoothly.

No form of automation today or on the horizon is capable of entering fully into the rich forms of Basic Compact that are used among people. To be an effective team player, intelligent machines must be able to understand and accept the joint goals of the enterprise, understand and accept their roles in the collaboration and the need for maintaining common ground, and be capable of signaling if they are unable or unwilling to fully participate in the activity. Intelligent machines must be able to adequately model the other participants' intentions and actions relative to the state and evolution of the joint activity. Intelligent machines must be reasonably predictable and have an ability to predict the actions of others, and they must be directable. Intelligent machines must participate in the management of attention and be able to make pertinent aspects of their status and intentions obvious to teammates. It will push the limits of technology to get machines to communicate fluently in the context of a complex sociotechnological system.

Human factors and Cognitive Systems Engineering communities have framed team research around the concept of team cognition, exploring both how cognitive activities such as team decision making and shared mental models, common goals, and team trust happen and how to measure these aspects of team cognition. Issues of how to train teams so that they transition from a team of experts to an expert team have also been addressed.

In spite of the many common research questions and methods that span research communities in examining teams, progress is not always smooth. As with any new perspective, this emphasis on studying teams emerges, in part, from reactions against and within existing disciplines, perspectives, and communities.

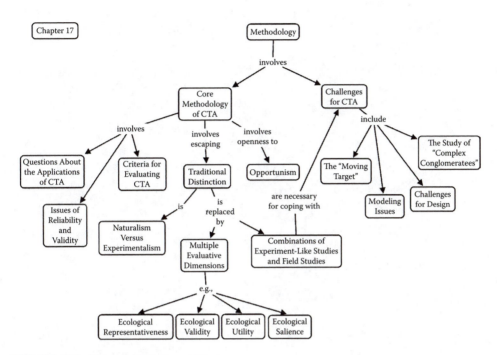

FIGURE 17.1 Chapter 17 Concept Map.

17

Synthesis
Methodological Challenges for Cognitive Task Analysis

*Robert R. Hoffman and Laura G. Militello,
with contributions by David D. Woods*

> We have not succeeded in solving all your problems. The solutions we have found only serve to raise a whole new set of problems. We are as confused as ever, but we believe we are confused on a higher level and about more important things.
>
> Clayton Mullen (2006)

In this chapter, like the previous two chapters, we overview and integrate by looking across the disciplines and perspectives. Here, we focus on synthesis in terms of the outstanding challenges and issues for Cognitive Task Analysis (CTA) methods and methodology.

As the previous chapters show, CTA and Cognitive Field Research (CFR) can focus on a description of the "as is" world, or it can try to capture or predict processes of transformation and adaptation. CTA can be thought of as an investigation of fields of practice or as a tool to support innovation of new tools, collaborative structures, or organizational roles. CTA may address distributed cognitive work as a public phenomenon, or it may address cognition as a private, individual phenomenon. CTA may be more empirical or more analytical, based on some sort of model of the domain or of practitioners or the interaction of the two. Research can focus locally, to understand and help in some particular setting, or more globally, to understand larger (macrocognitive) dynamics of cognitive work. CTA can focus on the activities of practitioners or on characteristics of the domain—properties such as coupling, variations in tempo including rhythms of self-paced and event-driven activity, or what makes problems difficult. CTA can be a modeling process based on a series of reinforcing or converging yet diverse investigations (Potter et al., 2000). It can develop a model of the problem space practitioners can face, the factors that make problems difficult, or the demands that any practitioner or set of practitioners need to meet. CTA can be aimed at uncovering how practitioners achieve expertise and succeed in the face of difficulties and complications, but it can also focus on uncovering how practice breaks down and risks failure. All of these are aspects of studying cognitive systems in context (Mumaw, Roth, Vicente, & Burns, 2000; Schaafstal, Schraagen, & van Berlo, 2000; Woods & Patterson, 2000).

Naturalism Versus Experimentalism

CTA research methods may be an adaptation of ethnographic methods, that is, direct observation in "the field." Many times, a CTA procedure seems like natural history. Practitioners are observed in a case, or they describe cases they have experienced, either in situ (e.g., in the operational setting or in simulations) or ex post facto (e.g., via retrospection). The investigation creates a collection or corpus of cases. We presume the corpus is sufficiently large to permit the informed analysis of individual cases and, especially to permit the comparison and contrast of cases that have been observed under various conditions (e.g., critical versus routine, successful versus unsuccessful, and so on). It remains a challenge for researchers to move past descriptions of what happened in particular cases to capture more general phenomena or patterns.

CTA sometimes looks, as an alternative, like an adaptation of experimental methods, such as interventions to control a situation through scenario design or through the evaluation of prototypes. We find it useful to think of this as a span of possibilities:

- *laboratory:* a machined environment (an environment in which there is interaction with tools), designed to include artifacts necessary for the conduct of research;
- *artificial laboratory:* a laboratory in which participants have experiences with little or no reference to the human ecology;
- *naturalistic laboratory:* a laboratory in which participants have experiences similar to those had in the human ecology;
- *natural laboratory:* research conducted in a human ecology that has been partly machined to conduct research; and
- *field laboratory:* research methods from ethnography or methods adapted from the artificial laboratory are used in the human ecology or in a nonlaboratory-designed environment.

For the researcher who is undaunted by claims that CTA is not the stuff of "real" science, we see people following a path not unknown to psychologists (e.g., Bartlett, 1932) that combines naturalistic and experimental research, including observations of ongoing activities in situ and other natural history techniques. Cognitive Systems Engineers believe that it is time to move beyond the artificial choice posed in traditional discussions of the merits of field-oriented research versus laboratory-based research (Hoffman & Deffenbacher, 1993; Woods, 1993). We do not simply face a choice between either a precise and controlled but sterile, artificial, simplified laboratory method from experimental psychology versus a relevant, multifactor but less controlled, subjective anthropological or historical method. Rather, field settings can function as natural laboratories, and CFR can include controls and the manipulation of variables (Crandall, Klein, & Hoffman, 2006; Hoffman & Woods, 2000).

Winograd and Woods (1997) argued that breaking down traditional barriers that exist in thinking about investigations is necessary for the study of cognitive work

TABLE 17.1 Some Possible Dimensions on Which the Research Materials and Tasks Used in Cognitive Task Analysis Methods Might Be Evaluated, and Ways in Which the Research Results Might Be Evaluated

The Relation of Methods to the Ecology of Cognitive Work	
Ecological validity	Materials, tasks, and settings present events in a way that preserves their natural forms and the natural covariation of dimensions or cues.
Ecological relevance	Materials or tasks involve things that people actually perceive or do.
Ecological salience	Materials or tasks involve important things that people actually perceive or do.
Ecological representativeness	Materials or tasks involve things that people often perceive or do.
The Relation of Methods to Scientific Understanding	
Epistemological validity	Materials and tasks make sense in terms of available theories and accepted methodologies.
Epistemological relevance	Materials and tasks link to current theoretical or methodological issues.
Epistemological salience	Materials and tasks link to theoretical concepts or research issues that are generally regarded as important.
Epistemological representativeness	Materials and tasks rely on theoretical and methodological concepts that scientists often rely on.
The Relation of Results to Action	
Ecological utility	The results help you do important things.
Ecological novelty	The results help you do new things.
Ecological generality	The results help you do things in diverse contexts.
The Relation of Results to Scientific Understanding	
Epistemological utility	The results lead to refinements in hypotheses and theories.
Epistemological novelty	The results suggest new theoretical concepts or hypothetical mechanisms.
Epistemological generality	The results have implications for diverse theories or hypotheses.

in context to progress. Some of those barriers exist between technology and behavior (consider the machine–agent mutuality), individual and society (consider how the individual is influenced by organizational, cultural, and societal factors), and laboratory and field (consider how field studies can be used as natural laboratories). Table 17.1 provides some specification on what it means to escape the "applied versus basic" and "naturalism versus experimentalism" dichotomies (after Hoffman & Deffenbacher, 1993).

Ecological Dimensions

Among the many issues that CTA raises, ecological ones seem especially salient, especially as a defining feature of the research (e.g., the goal of creating new and better complex cognitive systems). Thus, one focus for CTA concerns the cluster of ecological validity, relevance, salience, and representativeness, as these pertain to the coordination of field- and lab-oriented studies (see Xiao & Vicente, 2000). For example, one can consider the question of how to use fieldwork results to develop scaled world simulations that capture what is believed to be the critical, deeper aspects of the situations of interest (see De Keyser & Samercay, 1998; Ehret & Gray, 2000).

In natural laboratories, randomization and participant sampling may be limited or impossible, but other methods for creating meaningful comparisons exist. Investigators can design test scenarios and contrast performance across interrelated sets of scenarios that are representative of the real world (Woods, 1993). Particular attention can be paid to the recreation within the scenario of the vulnerabilities and challenges of the domain. In addition, the experts or operatives in the domain can be given the opportunity to bring their domain-specific knowledge to bear in the scenario. At the same time, various kinds of controls and validity checks can be embedded within the CFR.

Investigators also can probe the nature of practice by changing the kinds of artifacts practitioners use to carry out their activities (see Watts-Perotti & Woods, 1999, for one example). Artifact-based methods have great potential, because new technology is an experimental intervention into fields of ongoing activity (Carroll & Campbell, 1988; Flores, Graves, Hartfield, & Winograd, 1988). Prototypes of new systems are not simply partially refined final products; they also can function as a kind of experimental probe to better understand the nature of practice and to help discover what would be useful (Hoffman, Roesler, & Moon, 2004; Woods, 1998a).

Different field studies can become part of a larger series of converging observations and operations that overcome or mitigate the limits of individual studies. This could be based on using different techniques to examine a single field of practice or on examining the same theme across different natural laboratories.

As we consider how to examine cognitive systems in natural and naturalistic laboratories, perhaps astronomy or evolutionary biology is a better model for us than the laboratory model of science (Klein et al., 2003; Kugler & Lintern, 1995). In astronomy, experimenters cannot in general manipulate variables (e.g., the properties of stars) or create microworlds to falsify a hypothesis about a specific cause–effect relation. Yet astronomers are able to select and shape conditions of observation and use models to form expectations about what one might see to discover and understand more about the processes at work. These are areas that have, in Neisser's words, demonstrated the enormous power of functional analysis coupled with naturalistic observation (Neisser, 1991, p. 35).

Issues of Validity and Reliability

CTA research has also triggered debate and discussion over methodology (Hoffman & Woods, 2000). In counterpoint to the concerns of CTA researchers on issues of ecological validity, salience, and so on are concerns about the corresponding dimensions of epistemological validity, relevance, salience, and representativeness. How can the validity, reliability, and utility of CTA methods be evaluated (see Hoffman, Crandall, & Shadbolt, 1998; Prietula, Feltovich, & Marchak, 2000)? How do CTA techniques warrant the conclusions drawn? Researchers believe that CTA yields valid information—it seems to be taken for granted that the CTA data really do capture knowledge and reasoning. However, most of the applications of CTA have been driven by concrete project goals and have been constrained by practical considerations. CTA methods have largely been evaluated only in terms of a "satisficing" criterion; that is, the method seems to have worked to someone's satisfaction. We need to know not just what CTA and CFR are but what it means to do them well. How can one empirically approach issues of reliability, validity, and efficiency? We need to know how one can build an empirical anchor to justify CTA and CFR methods.

One way of understanding the validity–reliability question is to rephrase it at a higher level: How do we tell the difference between a poor-quality CTA and a high-quality CTA? How can you discriminate a competent investigation from an incompetent investigation given the uncertainties and limits of any particular study? (For in-depth discussion of this, see Ehret and Gray [2000] and Fowlkes, Salas, Baker, Cannon-Bowers, and Stout [2000].) Efficiency and effectiveness of CTA might be measured in terms of yield of useful information, time or effort required, and so on. But here we begin to see how foundational questions about methods (e.g., reliability, validity) quickly lead to higher issues. So, for instance, how might one gauge overall project success at capturing the "true work" and creating an authentic and veridical description of what it is like to function in the field of practice? One possibility is to look for CTA to uncover cognitive complexity not previously articulated. Another possibility is to see how well CTA identifies leverage points where change, however modest or resource limited, might produce relatively large positive impact.

One thing about the issue of CTA validity that sometimes raises eyebrows is that the research is often opportunistic, adapting methods "on the fly" as new things are learned about cognitive work or in response to practical constraints of conducting research in the field setting.

Opportunistic Methodology

An example of opportunistic methodology comes from a study of weather forecasting (see Hoffman, Coffey, Ford, & Novak, 2006; Hoffman, Trafton, & Roebber, 2008). Weather forecasters, it turns out, are rather comfortable with the psychologist's notion of the "mental model," because for years they have distinguished the forecaster's "conceptual model" of weather situations from the various numerical or computer models for generating forecasts. In one study of weather forecasting (Hoffman, Coffey, et al., 2006), a forecaster who was acting as a collaborator or informant for the researchers was shown the "Base Model" of expertise (see Figure 8.2) and was asked if this seemed to describe forecaster reasoning. He asserted that it did, to some extent, and offered suggestions about how it might be better adapted to the forecasting domain (e.g., the *Data Examination* box in Figure 8.2 would be labeled as *Inspect data including satellite imagery, local observations, radar*, etc.). Hoffman realized that he had stumbled on a new method, which is now called the Macrocognitive Modeling Procedure (MMP) (Crandall et al., 2006; Hoffman, Coffey, & Carnot, 2000; Klein & Hoffman, 2008). We referred to this procedure in chapter 9 to make a point about cognitive models—that generic models may serve as useful guides and research tools but cannot always be thought of as good models of actual strategies in use. Here we refer again to this procedure to make a general point about CTA methodology.

In the first step of this three-step procedure, the participants describe their reasoning by creating a flow-diagram-like model of their strategies and procedures, scaffolded by a diagram like that in Figure 8.2. They are invited to use the diagram elements (e.g., the hypothesis-testing cycle) as elements for their own description, adding flesh as they go (e.g., specifying the weather forecasting computer models and data types they prefer to rely upon). In Step 2, conducted weeks later, the forecasters were observed from the moment they arrived at the beginning of their period of watch. It was possible to validate some of the claims expressed in their reasoning diagram. For instance, some forecasters might have said in Step 1 that they begin their work by observing the sky as they walked across the parking lot, that the first thing they do on arrival at the facility is inspect the satellite loop to get the "big picture," or that after examining satellite and radar data, they inspect the outputs of their preferred computer model. Other claims in the reasoning model could not be so validated (e.g., the Duncker refinement cycle—hypothesis testing based on the forecaster's mental model of the weather situation), but these could be subject to the judicious use of probe questions (e.g., "What are you doing or thinking now?"). The MMP resulted in validated, high-level (or "macrocognitive") models of reasoning generated with less time and effort than usually required by the most commonly used procedure that cognitive scientists use to study problem solving, the "think-aloud problem-solving" method combined with protocol analysis (Ericsson & Simon, 1984; Hoffman, Coffey, & Carnot, 2000, Hoffman, Coffey, et al., 2002).

The MMP was also used to study the ways in which forecasters discussed their reasoning with one another. In a third step of the MMP, each forecaster was shown the diagrammatic models of all of the other forecasters (along with a couple of bogus models as controls) and were asked to play a "guess who" game. It was relatively easy for the more experienced forecasters to pick out the models of reasoning that had been made by the less experienced forecasters, because the latter group tended to indicate that they created forecasts by relying most heavily on the computer-generated forecasts (rather than on their own Dunckerian reasoning). In general, however, it turned out that the forecasters were not very good at identifying other forecasters by viewing diagrammatic depictions of how they reasoned. The MMP had revealed a leverage point for this forecasting organization: the need for more and more systematic ways of knowledge sharing and mentoring.

The MMP had yet another valuable result. One of the most experienced forecasters failed to recognize his own model. Upon being told of this error, he looked again at his model and said, *Oh, yeah. We made this months ago. I do not think like that now, because we are in a different weather regime. The computer model I looked at first back then is not the preferred model now.* What this showed is that there is no such thing as *a* model of expert reasoning. Hoffman et al. estimated that to describe the reasoning of weather forecasters in one particular locale, one would need on the order of many dozens of diagrammatic representations like that of Figure 8.2 but crafted for particular seasonal tendencies, events, and regional effects.

It takes some measure of experience for the researcher to be ready, willing, and able to adapt research methods on the fly and conduct such ad hoc procedures, refining them as one proceeds. To paraphrase Orville Wright's comment about discovering the secret of flight, doing a CTA is like trying to learn the secret of a magic trick.

Once you know the trick and know what to look for, you see things that you did not notice when you did not know exactly what to look for.

We are in the midst of a wave of interest in cognitive work, which has reawakened and broadened the need for CTA (see Crandall et al., 2006; Schraagen, Chipman, & Shalin, 2000). Across all of the perspectives we have described in the chapters of this book, researchers are asking such questions as the following:

- What is the predictive power of CTA in revealing how developments in information technology can cause changes in roles, changes to expertise, new forms of error, and so on?
- What is the effectiveness of CTA in design innovation to lead to tools that are usable, useful, and understandable; that help in the avoidance of errors; and so on?
- Are the results of CTA useful in the software and product development process?
- Does the reliance on CTA in project development result in systems that are more cost-effective in the long run in that they truly support cognitive work?

These and related challenges remain at the forefront of CTA research conducted within all of the perspectives.

Challenges for CTA

The study of cognitive systems in context is a process of discovering how the activities and strategies of practitioners are adapted to the various purposes and constraints of the field of activity (e.g., Dominguez, Flach, Lake, McKellar, & Dunn, in press; Hutchins, 1995b; Nyssen & De Keyser, 1998; Patterson et al., 1998). Although great strides toward this goal have been made in the past 25 years, many challenges remain for the field of Cognitive Systems Engineering and the CTA methods it employs (Mumaw et al., 2000; Schaafstal et al., 2000; Woods & Patterson, 2000). Many have called for the means to make Cognitive Systems Engineering more scientific (i.e., more anchored to laboratory experimentation rather than to CFR), more repeatable, or more generalizable.

The history of multiple threads in CTA reflects responses to the same basic needs and driving forces. Focusing on and expanding the common ground in response to these challenges will spur the constructive growth of knowledge and benefit all, regardless of the particular historical route to this place at the intersections between technological and behavioral sciences, individual and social perspectives, the laboratory and the field, design activity and empirical investigation, and theory and application. There are a number of broad challenges for CTA methodology.

Coping With the Moving Target

Fields of practice are complex and dynamic; artifacts, demands, strategies, and coordination are mutually interconstrained. Transformation and change is the rule; the workplace is always a moving target (Ballas, 2007). People who work in a sociotechnical workplace are changed by the systems with which they work. The machines are changed by their interactive experience. How can one design new technologies for a world that is ever-changing? How can data collected at one time ever be applicable to actions taken at a subsequent time? How does one envision performance in a changing world? New technology is an experimental investigation into fields of ongoing activity. An example would be efforts at designing new weather forecasting workstations even while the operational systems are undergoing modification and testing (Hoffman, 1991a). Changes in systems mean changes in what it means for someone to be an expert. How can both *expert* and *error-full performance* be defined or gauged in a changing workplace?

If new systems are dependent on cognitive components, then we must understand cognitive systems if we are to develop designs that enhance performance. The psychological experimenter must function as designer, and the engineer or designer must function as experimenter. If we are to enhance the performance of operational systems, we need conceptual looking glasses that enable us to see past the unending variety of technology and the diversity of domains.

Are the Results of a CTA Bound Only to That Specific Setting?

Fieldwork occurs in a specific context—these practitioners in these situations in this work domain. But as research, CTA needs to establish means for facilitating generalizability. What is this activity or setting or scenario a case of? What other cases or situations does this apply to? How can the results obtained in that setting speak to more general regularities of cognitive and collaborative work? What are the bounds for those links to other people and situations (see Xiao & Vicente, 2000)?

Field settings cannot be natural laboratories alone; they are at the same time a meaningful world with their own purposes. This creates the challenge of how to balance the needs of the stakeholders and actors in that specific setting and specific project or programmatic goals, with the broader goals of adding to the research base about dynamics of people, technology, and work. Whenever one does CTA, one needs to balance the demands of research goals and the demands of stakeholders in substantive fields of practice. Rather than seeing the local goals as simply exacting a "cost of doing business" or a "corrupting" influence that limits the ability to carry out otherwise "ideal" methods, they must be taken as meaningful in themselves in the research enterprise and as a test of a deeper understanding of the factors at work (Woods, 1998a).

What Is the Relation of Models to Data?

Research over the past decade that has involved examination of cognitive work, or work in complex sociotechnical contexts (Vicente, 1999), has relied to a greater or lesser extent on theory, depending on the discipline (e.g., the work in ethnomethodology as compared with that in Ecological Interface Design). Some research has had as a primary goal the creation of models of reasoning, such as that presented in Figure 8.2. But we know that formal models can be brittle, unable to deal with complex problems at the level of meaning and knowledge, context bound, and limited in terms of the sorts of things that they compute. Where do the theoretical notions (that shape the CFR and CTA methods) come from? Prior data? Models emerging from the academic psychology laboratory? Are the models representations of the human head bone or tools that we can use to explore and lay out alternative reasoning sequences? Do we really need to compute how long it will take a human to conduct some particular sequence of actions, down to the millisecond, and determine whether there will be an overload of short-term memory capacity limitations?

The point here is that the perspective of the theorist plays a determining role in modeling. For the design of complex cognitive systems, models, and theories must be developed to account for how new technology shapes cognition and to account for how people adapt around new technology. A model can suffer from the reductive tendency, in which the researcher misconceives or overly simplifies the domain, creates artificial distinctions, or misinterprets domain concept-terms (Feltovich, Hoffman, & Woods, 2004; Feltovich, Spiro, & Coulson, 1993). A result can trigger ontological drift; that is, the systems that are built are not the ones that the end user had envisioned (Bannon & Bødker, 1991). How can one facilitate the researcher's perception of the distinctions that practitioners make or understand the practitioner's culture from the insider's perspective?

Coping With the Wild Card of Design

Advancing our understanding is not the only purpose for studying cognitive systems in context. That understanding must be instrumental; that is, it must contribute to the process of design. The usually separate roles of researchers and designers converge and become complementary because artifacts embody hypotheses about how technology shapes cognition and collaboration in general and in that setting (Carroll & Campbell, 1988; Woods, 1998a). The researcher functions as a designer because "if we truly understand cognitive systems, then, as a test of that understanding, we should be able to develop designs that enhance cognition and collaboration in operational settings" (Woods, 1998a, p. 169). The designer functions as a researcher because the artifacts they develop embody hypotheses about what will be useful and about how the field of practice will be transformed by new artifacts.

But when people begin to study cognitive systems in context as part of a practice-centered design process, a new challenge emerges—the envisioned world problem (Smith et al., 1998). How do the results of a CTA characterizing the current domain inform or apply to the design process, *because the introduction of new technology will transform the nature of practice*? New technology introduces new error forms, new representations change the cognitive activities needed to accomplish tasks and enable the development of new strategies, and new technology creates new tasks and roles for people at different levels of a system (Flores et al., 1988). Changing artifacts, and the process of organizational change it is a part of, can change what it means for someone to be an expert and the kinds of breakdowns that will occur. An example is efforts at designing new weather forecasting workstations even while the operational systems are undergoing modification and testing and local kludging (Hoffman, 1991a).

Coping with the envisioned world problem will require our methods to meet new challenges of predicting the evolution of a dynamic process. How does one envision or predict the relation of technology, cognition, and collaboration in a domain that doesn't yet exist or is in a process of becoming? How can we predict the changing nature of expertise and new forms of failure as the workplace changes? Even on a smaller scale, how can we predict the impact of new technology when it is introduced into an established sociotechnical system?

Each perspective has wrestled with how CTA can be used as a prerequisite for design—how to link CTA results to design and how to link understanding to innovation. For all of the perspectives, CTA is a means to a larger end of developing useful support and enhancing effectiveness of human and team performance. If artifacts are hypotheses about how technology shapes cognition, collaboration, and performance (Woods, 1988), they are subject to empirical jeopardy and can be wrong. In other words, CTA needs to serve as a guard against design error where the system built is not useful or creates new burdens for practitioners—a problem that seems ubiquitous in system development. This leads to CTA studies that attempt to find the holes in the designers' work by, for example, drawing out the implications of a design for cognition and coordination; and it leads to CTA studies of the process of transformation and adaptation to be able to predict these dynamics in other cases of technological change.

There are a number of broad challenges in applying CTA to design (Dekker & Nyce, 2004; Hoffman & Woods, 2000; Woods & Hollnagel, 2006). Ultimately, the purpose of studying complex cognitive systems is to inform design—to help in the search for what is promising or what would be useful in changing fields of practice (Woods & Roesler, 2007; Woods, 1998a). Thus, methods for studying cognitive work are the means to stimulate innovation and not just ways to build up the pattern base (Woods, 2002). In many ways, the impact of design on studies of how cognitive systems work is a reminder that in closed loop or cyclical processes such as research, a cycle can rotate in two directions. What you want to do next (influence design and innovation) rotates back to influence how you study and model a cognitive system, especially when previously designed artifacts are part of the system under study and are undergoing change.

Studies of complex cognitive systems usually occur as part of a process of organizational and technological change spurred by the promise of new capabilities, dread of some paths to failure, or continuing pressure for higher levels of performance and greater productivity (systems under "faster, better, cheaper" pressure). This means that investigators, through observing and modeling practice, are participants in processes of change in those fields of practice. To become integral to the generation of possibilities for the future of a complex cognitive system, CTA methods must be extended to meet the challenges of design. There are five challenges design imposes on how to study complex cognitive systems at work:

- *The leverage problem*—How do studies of complex cognitive systems at work help decide where to spend limited resources to have significant impact (because all development processes are resource limited)?
- *The innovation problem*—How do studies of complex cognitive systems at work support the innovation process (the studies are necessary but not sufficient as a spark for innovation)?

- *The envisioned world problem*—How do the results that characterize cognitive and cooperative activities in the current field of practice inform or apply to the design process, because the introduction of new technology will transform the nature of practice (a kind of moving target difficulty)?
- *The adaptation through use problem*—How does one predict and shape the process of transformation and adaptation that follows technological change?
- *The problem of "error" in design*—Designers' hypotheses, as expressed in artifacts, often fall prey to William James's Psychologist's Fallacy, which is the fallacy of substituting the designer's vision of what the impact of the new technology on cognition and collaboration might be for empirically based but generalizable findings about the actual effects from the point of view of people working in fields of practice (Woods & Dekker, 2000).

How to Study Complex Conglomerates?

Although research focuses on activity in a domain with its particular technical constraints, it also involves aspects of the psychology of the practitioners who are embedded in that field of practice. Although it might reveal individuals' strategies and knowledge, those individuals are constantly engaged in coordinated and cooperative activity. In the study of cognitive systems in context, it is not enough to note specific activities or tease out the strategies of individual practitioners. Complex cognitive systems come as a "wrapped package" (Woods, 1993). This poses a major scientific challenge and points directly to the relation of naturalistic research to experimental research (Klein et al., 2003).

One way that humans deal with complexity is to try to bind the world into manageable units (Woods & Roth, 1988a). Techniques for discovery and investigation that are reductionistic would simplify wrapped packages into units for experimental manipulation by slicing dynamic processes into static snapshots and by converting multiple factors and physically coupled and interconnected processes into the assessment of a few separable variables (Woods & Roth, 1988b; Woods & Tinapple, 1999). However, Cognitive Systems Engineers have been critical of these techniques, suggesting that they lead to oversimplified fallacies. Research by Feltovich, Spiro, and Coulson (1997) on complex reasoning (e.g., medical diagnosis) revealed a human tendency to see phenomena that are "continuous, dynamic, simultaneous, organic, interactive, conditional, heterogeneous, irregular, nonlinear, deep, [and] multiple" as being "discrete, static, sequential, mechanistic, separable, universal, homogenous, regular, surface, [and] single" (p. 134). This human tendency applies equally to those who would design and build new technologies (Feltovich, Hoffman, et al., 2004).

Woods and Roth (1988a) proposed that the act of transposing cognitive work into the laboratory can eliminate the very phenomena of interest, in the process of simplification: "In reducing the target world to a tractable laboratory or desktop world in search of precise results, we run the risk of eliminating the critical features of the world that drive behavior" (p. 418). In turn, these techniques would retard understanding. For example, human problem solvers in fault diagnosis must deal with "multiple failures, misleading signals, [and] interacting disturbances" that often occur in parallel (Woods, 1993, p. 229). However, Woods (1993) reported that nearly all research in the area of fault diagnosis has focused on static scenarios with single faults and thus falls foul of oversimplifying the true problem domain.

An additional argument is that the time frame for effective laboratory experimentation (i.e., the "nailing down" of hypotheses about cause–effect relations and interactions) is far outstripped by the time frame of technological change and change in the workplace. If the only legitimate science—the only way of disconfirming hypotheses about cause–effect relations—is the controlled experimentation of the laboratory, then the laboratory scientist confronts the argument that the science is incapable of dealing with unique events. And in the arena of complex cognitive systems, unique events abound.

Woods (1998a) argued that no single CTA method can be sufficient in informing the design process. This matches the long-standing recommendation in the field of Expert Systems that multiple methods be used to reveal expert knowledge and reasoning, combining structured interviews, observational methods, and case-structured problem-solving tasks (Hall, Gott, & Pokorny, 1995; Hoffman, 1987b; Hoffman, Shadbolt, Burton, & Klein, 1995). Furthermore, there is a need for research methods to be flexible, and this is another idea that challenges the perceived view that research must be carefully planned and the plan rigorously executed. Studying cognitive systems in context is concerned with discovery, not simply with compiling a list of the tasks, data, knowledge, causal variables, or linkages involved in handling a specified situation (Klein & Militello, 2001). There is no such thing as unobtrusive observation: What one seeks to reveal is *authentic* activity, not behavior unaffected by the researcher (Woods, 1993). As a discovery process, the question becomes, How do we prepare to immerse ourselves in the domain of practice and be ready to see, notice, and recognize something fresh, something we did not know to look for?

We conclude this chapter with a summary of a study that illustrates the wrapped package notion and at the same time illustrates how methods adopted from across the perspectives can be effectively combined.

A Wrapped Package

Many of the various methods, ideas, and themes that we have discussed in this book can also be integrated by looking at some single studies. The synthesis of perspectives is not just a matter of ideas and "X-Centered X" frameworks but a matter of action. This is aptly illustrated in a study by Ann Bisantz et al. (2002). This single study involved the following:

- the use of Abstraction-Decomposition, a technique developed within the work analysis community (chapter 10);
- the use of the Critical Decision Method, a technique developed within the Expertise Studies and Naturalistic Decision Making communities (chapters 8, 9);
- the appreciation of how cognitive work must be understood as contextually bound (or situated) and distributed among teams of humans and machines, a focus of the Sociological and Ethnographic perspectives (chapter 11);

- the challenges of designing for envisioned worlds, a focus of the Cognitive Systems Engineering perspective (chapter 7);
- the notion of opportunism of methodology, a theme to both sociological and ethno-graphic approaches (chapter 11) and the Cognitive Systems Engineering approach (chapter 7); and finally
- the drive to develop information processing tools that are useful and usable, a prime concern of the Human-Centered Computing perspective (chapter 12).

Their project was motivated by the U.S. Navy's program to develop next-generation surface ships with a highly reduced crew complement. This entails eliminating any jobs that might be eliminated, merging jobs that can be merged, automating jobs that can be automated, and, of the remaining tasks, reducing crew complement through new human–machine partnerings based on new software tools, interfaces, and so on. Hence, the Navy program is called "Human–Systems Integration" (HSI). This is a situation in which the Cognitive Systems Engineer has to define human roles and human–computer interfaces requirements early in the design process, yet the overall humans–machines system is not yet pegged down and, indeed, is continually evolving.

> Many of the tools-of-the-trade (e.g., sequential task analysis, interface design guidelines, usability testing) often depend on having a well-defined system for which to create and test a user interface. ... Analyses had to be conducted and recommendations made in parallel with, and as inputs to, design regarding system purposes, functionality, automation capabilities, and staffing levels. (Bisantz et al., 2002, p. 177)

Following the pattern set by Vicente (1999) and Rasmussen, Pejtersen, and Goodstein (1994), Bisantz et al. conducted a work domain analysis to reveal the complexities and constraints of the work domain, independently from the actual work, tools, and legacy systems. Bisantz et al. (2002) noted, however, that they were faced with a challenge, because the track record of successful use of Cognitive Work Analysis has involved mostly the design of technologies for work contexts that are either legacy systems (which would involve what Vicente called "Descriptive Task Analysis") or reasonably well defined at the outset (e.g., known properties of physical systems such as in indus-trial process control, which would involve what Vicente called "Constraint-Based Task Analysis"). Furthermore, the Navy HSI program used a rapid design cycle (sometimes on the order of a few weeks), limiting the opportunity for in-depth data collection and analysis.

> We could not wait for particular design decisions to be made before proceeding ... it was neces-sary to select and adapt cognitive work analysis methods and models as appropriate, to fit the demands of an information-limited and time-limited situation ... this required explicit links to be made between the concepts and constructs regarding the ship systems, operator tasks, and design recommendations developed during the cognitive work analysis and the functional breakdowns and system models being developed concurrently by the system engineering design teams. (p. 179)

Bisantz et al. concentrated the work domain analysis at the ship bridge and com-mand control center, involving core ship functions and certain "watchstander" roles (navigation, weapons control, communication with other ships, situation assessment, etc.). Given the Navy's goal of manpower reduction, the work analysis had to reveal possibilities for task reassignment, combination, and automation relative to legacy naval operations but also possibilities for new watchstander roles for the new functionalities in an envisioned world. Thus, "a detailed mapping of ship goals to system functions, task responsibilities and operator actions was impossible" (p. 180). Instead, what Bisantz et al. did was attempt to map higher level information needs to potential functions and then make recommendations regarding function allocation (human versus machine) based on human-centering considerations. This is where Abstraction-Decomposition came in.

The three primary sources of data were domain experts, design documents being produced by other teams within the larger project, and Navy design requirements. The primary methods were as follows:

- interviews with 13 officers who had an average of 26 years of experience at watchstanding and commanding and who were also working on the ship design teams, and
- documentation analysis (e.g., textual and graphical representations of potential design concepts); documents also included some functional decompositions based on Navy requirements for operational functionalites.

The interviews were semistructured in that they were informal but relied on preplanned probe questions that complemented those used in methods including the Critical Decision Method (Hoffman et al., 1998). They fell into four main categories: ship and mission goals to be accomplished, the many-to-many mapping between goals and available systems, choice points and complications in decision making, and collaborative activities. Examples are "What are the goals of this mission of the ship?" "What if the systems we talked about were disabled?" and "What communication of information is needed between these watchstanders?"

An Abstraction-Decomposition Matrix was created on the basis of the data. Levels of abstraction included system purposes, system processes, and physical form (see chapter 10). The focus was on two possible scenarios, one involving land attack and the other involving undersea warfare, so most of the nodes referred to those concrete situations. In addition, the linkages among nodes (connecting nodes across the rows of the matrix) were not restricted to means-ends relations as they are in classical Rasmussen-type matrices but also included relations of constraint. The full final matrix was large, consisting of over 100 nodes (or filled cells). An example submatrix is presented in Figure 17.2.

A software aid was used for creating the matrix, the Work Domain Analysis Workbench (Sanderson, Eggleston, et al., 1999). Using a highlighting function, one could pull out from the full matrix portions that pertained, for instance, to one or the other of the scenarios or to one or another of the possible linkage patterns (e.g., means-ends linkages or constraint linkages).[1] As for any such matrix, moving up and down across the rows shows the linkages among the physical components of the ship (e.g., sensors such as radar) and the highest level purposes of the ship (e.g., maintain awareness of the battle space).

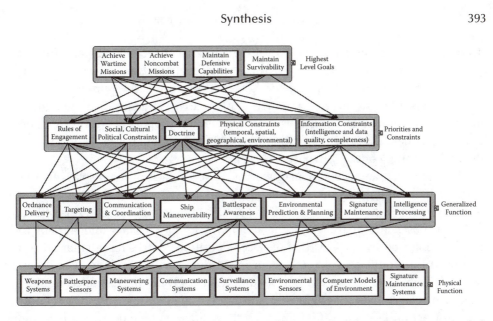

FIGURE 17.2 An example Abstraction-Decomposition Matrix, adapted from Bisantz et al. (2002).

> The representation explicitly showed how functions could be related to multiple ship goals, and how multiple functions could rely on the same sub-system … for example, one would maneuver the ship to facilitate sensing of undersea contacts (supporting a defensive goal) while at the same time impeding the maintenance of the ship's signature (adversely affecting a defensive goal). Maneuvering could also restrict the use of some weapons systems, affecting both offensive and defensive goals … executing one mission could delay the execution of another. … These relationships … were not captured in the decompositions created by the system engineering teams. (p. 11)

Showing both constraints on design and opportunities for design, the matrix was used to guide further knowledge elicitation interviews with the experts about how goals could be decomposed (e.g., how a radar system is managed and directed). It was also used to inform the design of display prototypes (e.g., multiple ship goals for a single weapons system) and communication channels (e.g., the need for bridge watchstanders to communicate to sonar operators).

In addition to the decomposition according to goals, there was a functional decomposition from the perspective of systems engineering, and a cognitive decomposition expressing the cognitive tasks required of watchstanders (e.g., high-level goals such as monitoring progress toward mission objectives). Watchstanders responsible for land attack warfare needed to be able to see over 10 different display fields (e.g., task schedules, tactical picture, etc.), each having clear linkages to ship functions and ship goals. "Cognitive functions (such as planning and monitoring) were absent from the system engineering decomposition of the ship itself" (p. 12).

Eventually, it all had to come together. "A substantial portion of our effort was spent developing principled mappings between system functional decompositions being provided by the system engineering design teams, the cognitive analysis team, information needs, automation requirements, and concepts for displays" (p. 12). The full final multimatrix analysis was complex, as one might imagine. (The functional decomposition for land attack warfare alone consisted of over 300 different functions and subfunctions.) But the mapping of the multiple matrices was critical: "Completion of these matrices provided inputs to design teams regarding the appropriate operator role vis-á-vis different possible automation alternatives and specified the high-level information requirements which would allow human support of system function as well as more detailed information that watchstanders should have access to based on the understanding of ship purposes" (p. 12).

Here we see an additional benefit worthy of note—each of the displays that were entailed by the analysis (the information requirements and description of cognitive tasks) came wrapped along with the design rationale stated in terms of higher order purposes and goals. Thus, the requirements for displays and human roles were rationalized by the Abstraction-Decomposition Matrix representation of the data, and this could be used by system integrators as a part of the overall design rationale. For instance, one might assume that a given watchstander would not need a display showing activities in some other area of responsibility. However, the Abstraction-Decomposition analyses showed the potential for conflict among certain ship functions and goals, leading to specific recommendations for which area of responsibility displays different watchstanders should be able to view.

This study could be considered a success story in CTA, one that coped with the practical constraints of time pressure and the challenge of designing for an envisioned world, a large-scale system when system elements had not been fully specified. This integrative study and the integration we saw in chapter 15 on Work-Centered Design show how designations are perhaps less important than how we devise and blend techniques to focus the research, advance our understanding, and address scientific challenges, while at the same time coping with various practical constraints and leveraging emerging opportunities.

Where the Rubber Meets the Road

As we look across all the perspectives, and all of the acronyms in the acronym soup, we see many important differences but we also see some fundamental commonalities among CTA methods and methodology.

Practitioners in all the perspectives see their overarching methodological goal as that of perceiving the true work and gathering rich and useful data concerning the authentic activity, knowledge, and reasoning of practitioners.

There are nearly boundless ways of combining and applying particular CTA methods. The Critical Decision Method (to generate models of reasoning) can be combined to good effect with Concept Mapping (to generate models of knowledge) (Hoffman, Coffey, et al., 2002). Rehak, Lamoureaux, and Bos (2006) used Critical Decision Method procedures (see chapter 9) to populate Abstraction-Decomposition Matrices in a Cognitive Work Analysis (see chapter 10). Methods can be combined and conformed into procedures that are more experiment-like, more like experiments conducted in the field, or more like field observations or interviews. One might conduct a task–goal hierarchical analysis through an interview conducted in the workplace, or one might have participants think aloud while they work using a prototype interface in the laboratory. And so on.

Where the rubber meets the road, in the study of cognitive work one can (a) study existing documentation or other records, (b) observe performance, or (c) ask people questions.

- Researchers in the field of Expertise Studies study the domains of interest intensively and then observe expert performance at domain tasks. They probe expert knowledge and reasoning by using methods such as think-aloud problem-solving and Concept Mapping knowledge elicitation interviews. They ask experts questions about reasoning by having experts retrospect about past experiences.
- Cognitive Systems Engineers observe the ways in which people interact with technology, and they observe patterns of communication and coordination in workplaces (such as NASA Mission Control). They ask practitioners questions about what they know and how they reason. They inject prototypes to conduct experiment-like procedures in the field setting to study envisioned worlds.
- Sociologists and ethnographers immerse themselves for long periods of time in the setting of interest. They observe workplaces and work patterns, and they ask people questions about how they share knowledge and collaborate. As data emerge, waves of analysis are predicated on the deliberate attempt to view the data from differing perspectives.
- Practitioners of Cognitive Work Analysis conduct elaborate analyses of background documentation and other records, and they observe workplaces and work patterns. They interview practitioners to generate models of goals and models of human–machine system functions within their larger organizational context. They generate new technologies and then seek to determine the system performance gains.
- Advocates of Naturalistic Decision Making observe workplaces and work patterns; they ask practitioners questions about reasoning, past experiences, and so on. They build multiple in-depth case studies into larger pictures of macrocognitive processes.
- Advocates of Human-Centered Computing, by tradition mostly computer scientists, have relied heavily on the study of end users to generate ideas for technologies that are user friendly and not user hostile or, beyond that, technologies that amplify human capabilities. That reliance involves asking people questions and observing performance, borrowing methods as appropriate from the other perspectives.

This being said, of course each perspective carries a particular focus and preferred methods palette. The training and skill of the researcher greatly influences which methods will be used and how they will be adapted to address any given domain of study. The Critical Decision Method, for instance, is used most often by practitioners in Naturalistic Decision Making, but it has also been applied in the creation of human-centered systems. Think-aloud problem solving has been used mostly by those who study expertise, from a cognitive psychology background, but methods of thinking aloud and protocol analysis have also been used by Cognitive Systems Engineers. Sociometric analysis (who talks to whom) has mostly been used by practitioners in

Sociology and Ethnography but has also be used in Expertise Studies to generate proficiency scales for determining who is, and who is not, an expert. And so on.

Final Implications

It is important that the phrase "complex sociotechnical systems" includes the word *complex*. Complexity is what this book is all about, and not just the complexity of cognitive work. The teams of people, and machines, that conduct CTA are themselves a complex sociotechnical system (Feltovich, Hoffman, et al., 2004), one that has the goal of designing new complex sociotechnical systems or fixing existing ones. Those who are considering an attempt to conduct CTA may feel overwhelmed by the variety of approaches and communities of practice, the variety of perspectives and strongly held views, the complexity of theoretical and methodological issues, and the practical constraints on research. We hope therefore that it is of some comfort to know that the complexity can be rough on us old hands as well.

We may be repeating a variant on an old saw, but it is one that deserves repeating. New information processing technologies for complex sociotechnical contexts are best created, and good ones can be created *only* when disciplines work together, combining their perspectives, methods, and strengths. Indeed, every one of the perspectives we have discussed is, in its own way, a merger of earlier perspectives and approaches. For complex cognitive systems to be truly human centered, there must be full involvement of designers, technologists, and computer scientists with Cognitive Systems Engineers, Ethnographers, and so on, as well as deep involvement of domain practitioners. Thus, we conclude with a paraphrase of the quotation from Samuel Fernberger (1937) that opened chapter 2:

> *The present book is an attempt to reveal and reconcile some of the differences between the proponents of the different points of view in the hope that researchers will realize that all of us are working toward the same ends and that we are all working in the same scientific universe.*

Summary

This chapter examines synthesis across perspective in terms of challenges and issues for CTA methods and methodology. As previous chapters show, CTA and CFR can be applied from a range of perspectives, each of which represents an aspect of studying cognitive systems in context.

The first challenge discussed is the naturalism versus experimentation dichotomy. CTA can be an adaptation of ethnographic methods, as well as an adaptation of experimental methods. This combination of naturalistic and experimental research leads some to claim that CTA is not the stuff of "real science." However, many suggest that it is time to move beyond the artificial choice posed in traditional discussions of field-oriented research versus laboratory-based research. It is a question not of either–or but of how to leverage the strengths of different approaches. Breaking down barriers that exist in thinking about investigations is necessary for the study of cognitive work in context. We must escape the "applied versus basic" and "naturalism versus experimentalism" dichotomies if we are to progress.

The second set of challenges includes ecological dimensions such as ecological validity, relevance, salience, and representativeness. These issues might be considered in terms of how to use findings from field research to develop scaled world simulations. They might also be considered in terms of natural laboratories, where traditional strategies of randomization and participant sampling may be impossible. Instead, researchers focus on the representativeness of scenarios, the ability to re-create the vulnerabilities and challenges of the domains, and whether the scenarios provide experts an opportunity to employ their domain-related expertise. In addition, controls and validity checks can be embedded within the CFR. Investigators can also probe the nature of practice by changing the kinds of artifacts practitioners use to carry out their activities. Different field studies can become part of a larger series of converging observations and operations that overcome or mitigate the limits of individual studies.

The third set of challenges address issues of validity and reliability. How can the validity, reliability, and utility of CTA methods be evaluated? Most applications of CTA have been driven by concrete project goals and have been constrained by practical considerations. Thus issues such as what it means to conduct CTA and CFR have not yet been thoroughly examined. No clear empirical anchor to justify CTA and CFR methodologies has been articulated. These issues are complicated by the fact that CTA and CFR research is often opportunistic, including adaptations on the fly based on previous learning and practical constraints.

The MMP described in this chapter represents a clear example of method adaptation that resulted in increased understanding of reasoning in the weather forecasting domain. In addition to revealing rich and specific details about problem solving for specific types of weather forecasting problems, investigators also learned important information about the variability of reasoning strategies, even with the same expert during different weather regimes.

In spite of successful CTA and CFR projects, questions related to validity and reliability remain. Specifically, what is the predictive power of CTA for anticipating changes in roles, expertise, new forms of error, and so on when new information technology is introduced? How effective is CTA in supporting design innovation resulting in tools that are usable, useful, and understandable? Are the results of CTA useful in the software and product development process? Does the reliance on CTA in project development result in systems that truly support cognitive work and are therefore more cost-effective in the long run?

Yet another challenge discussed in this chapter is that the topics of study for CTA and CFR are generally moving targets. Fields of practice are dynamic; artifacts, demands, strategies, and coordination are mutually constrained. Researchers are generally designing new technologies even as existing systems are undergoing modification and change. If we are to enhance the performance of operational systems, we need to be able to see beyond the unending variety of technology and the diversity of domains.

Generalizability is a challenge for all researchers, and no less for those who use CTA and CFR methods. Field research occurs within a specific context. Questions such as how the results obtained in a specific setting speak to more general regularities of cognitive and collaborative work must be addressed.

Field settings are not just natural laboratories; they are at the same time meaningful worlds with their own purposes. One must constantly balance the demands of research goals and the demands of stakeholders in fields of practice.

Many of the perspectives discussed in this book rely to a greater or lesser extent on theory to drive the methods. Some research has had as the primary goal the creation of models of reasoning. For the design of complex systems, models and theories must be developed to account for how new technology shapes cognition and to account for how people adapt around new technology. However, a model can suffer from the reductive tendency, resulting in ontological drift. It is important that models facilitate rather than hinder the researcher's ability to understand the practitioner's culture from the insider's perspective.

In addition to developing models and increased understanding, CTA studies must contribute to the process of design. The usually separate roles of researcher and designer begin to merge as artifacts embody hypotheses about how technology shapes cognition and collaboration. Furthermore, the issue of how results from CTA describing the current system apply to the design of future systems must be addressed. Given that the introduction of new technology will transform the nature of work, this is a particularly salient challenge.

Another challenge is that of how to study complex conglomerates. It is not enough to study an individual's strategies and knowledge. One must examine the entire wrapped package of coordinated and cooperative activity. Often, to study a phenomenon, humans try to chop the world into manageable units. In the extreme, transposing cognitive work into laboratory settings can eliminate the very phenomena of interest. We must balance this tendency to reduce and simplify if we are to be successful in understanding work in context and designing systems to support it.

The case study of a Cognitive Systems Engineering approach to the design of a new Navy ship illustrates the synthesis of many perspectives, as well as many of the challenges associated with studying and designing for complex sociotechnical systems. This study is considered a success story in CTA. This study coped with the practical constraints of time pressure and the challenges of designing for an envisioned world.

Finally, in terms of synthesis, we see many commonalities across CTA methods and methodologies. Although the underlying theory or perspective certainly influences how methods are adapted and applied, making the variations seem infinite, there are really only three key strategies for studying cognitive work. One can study existing documentation, observe performance, and ask people questions. Each of the methods considered in this volume uses these three strategies, developing methods that build on these fundamental elements and then adapting them to answer specific questions and study particular domains. Perhaps the most unifying element is that all approaches are working toward the same ends and in the same scientific universe.

Notes

Chapter 2

1. In addition to observing the movements of schoolchildren while at their studies, Lindley conducted a survey of students in G. Stanley Hall's psychology course concerning the movements they found themselves engaged in (e.g., fiddling with pencils) during his lectures.
2. Dvorak was so enamored of Gilbreth that he presented many of his ideas about the skills and reasoning of expert typists in the form of a hypothetical dialog between the reader (referred to as a "typist") and someone named "Gilbreth." See Dvorak, Merrick, Deals, and Ford (1936).
3. In the historical context, the elimination of jobs and the push toward efficiency seems inhumane. However, apologia are easy to come by. Books on industrial psychology emphasized job satisfaction, loyalty, relaxation, pleasure, and similar factors and not just raw efficiency on the production line (see Scott, 1921). Taylor's work was motivated in part by his sympathy with workers and the oppressions of the "piece work" system (see Gies, 1991). Many workers damned the "force approach." However, as a movement, Taylorism was doomed because "of the refusal to include the human element in the whole situation from any other respect than rate of production" (Moore, 1942, p. 308). At congressional hearings in 1912, Taylor was heckled (especially by auto-assembly-line workers) to the point of igniting his temper. Taylor's testimony was stricken from the record and "scientific management" was prohibited in appropriation bills. Years later, the Gilbreths advocated a set of practical methods, not a grander theory of management, but found themselves still having to be on the defensive. In 1934 Lilian Gilbreth felt compelled to argue that TMS "looks upon man as the center of creative activity, and thinks of tools, machines, and power as enabling him to accomplish more, and with less effort and fatigue, and with more interest in his work and what it accomplishes … it thinks in wholes as well as in parts" (p. 35).
4. One cannot fail to note that similar things are said today about the need for trained and uniquely capable cognitive systems engineers!
5. A full listing of the IFRB reports appears in Osier and Wozniak (1984).

Chapter 3

1. In his classic 1959 text on human engineering, Chapanis used the wartime studies of radar primarily to illustrate concepts in experimental design, such as the computation of the Pearson product-moment correlation coefficient, the "treatments × subjects" experimental design, and the need for randomizations and other control procedures.

2. This may seem a bit quaint today, but the selection of "Battle Telephone Talkers" was an important issue early in the war because many recruits had never used a telephone (see Bray, 1948, chap. 5; Hunter, 1946, p. 486).

3. Important exceptions include the following: (a) a few citations of industrial psychology research on human and instrument error in the reading of measurements (i.e., from dials and other indicators) (see Behar, 1940; Lawsche & Tiffin, 1945, as cited in Chapanis, 1951), and (b) a report by Paul Fitts (1953) on an Air Force study of response coding, in which reference is made to the research of Dvorak on the design of typewriter keyboards. Dvorak relied heavily on TMS in his design of alternative (today we would say ergonomic) keyboard arrangements (see Dvorak, Merrick, Deals, & Ford, 1936).

Chapter 7

1. Classic results have also shown the converse—that the highest levels of automation on the flight deck of commercial jet aircraft often leave commercial pilots baffled in some situations, wondering what the automation is currently doing, why it is doing it, and what it is going to do next (D. D. Woods & Sarter, 2000).

2. In addition to being an approach that is advocated within the field of Cognitive Systems Engineering, Human-Centered Computing designates a community of practice that has emerged within the field of computer science. This is the focus of chapter 12.

Chapter 11

1. This leads to some rather scathing criticisms of formal educational systems (see Becker, 1972). "Standardization of curricula and examinations, evaluation through grading, the deskilling of teaching, relations between the composition of school knowledge by teachers and their control over students in classrooms, and forms of student stratification and classification in schools all serve to reduce the meaning and even the possibility of engaging in ... knowledgeably skilled activity in the classroom. ... This [is a] view of learning as ingestion (with teaching as feeding)" (Lave, 1993, pp. 78, 79).

Chapter 12

1. Dekker, Nyce, & Hoffman, 2003; Endsley & Hoffman, 2002; Feltovich, Hoffman, & Woods, 2004; Flach & Hoffman, 2003; Hoffman, Bradshaw, Hayes, & Ford, 2003; Hoffman & Elm, 2006; Hoffman, Feltovich, et al., 2002; Hoffman & Hanes, 2003; Hoffman & Hayes, 2004; Hoffman, Hayes, & Ford, 2001; Hoffman, Hayes, Ford, & Hancock, 2002; Hoffman, Klein, & Laughery, 2002; Hoffman, Lintern, & Eitelman, 2004; Hoffman, Roesler, & Moon, 2004; Hoffman & Woods, 2005; Hoffman & Yates, 2005; Klein, Moon, & Hoffman, 2006; Klein et al., 2003; Klein, Woods, Bradshaw, Hoffman, & Feltovich, 2004; Koopman & Hoffman, 2003. All are downloadable at http://ihmc.us/research/projects/EssaysOnHCC/.

Chapter 17

1. The discipline of thinking through specific linkages and linkage types in diagrams such as this is a critical exercise for the achievement of skill at this sort of analysis. Space does not permit us the luxury of working through examples, so the reader is referred to the Bisantz et al. (2002) report.

References

Abbott, A. (1988). *The system of professions: An essay on the division of expert labor.* Chicago: Chicago University Press.

Abelson, R., et al. (14 others) (1976). "A Proposed Particular Program on Cognitive Science." Report, Sloan Foundation, New York, NY.

Adelman, L. (1989). Management issues in knowledge elicitation. *IEEE Transactions on Systems, Man, and Cybernetics, 19,* 483–488.

Adelson, B. (1981). Problem solving and the development of abstract categories in programming languages. *Memory & Cognition, 9,* 422–433.

Adelson, B. (1984). When novices surpass experts: The difficulty of a task may increase with expertise. *Journal of Experimental Psychology: Learning, Memory, & Cognition, 10,* 483–495.

Adler, M. H. (1973). *The writing machine.* London: George Allen and Unwin.

Agnew, N. M., Brown, J. L., & Lynch, J. G. (1986). Extending the reach of knowledge engineering. *Future Computing Systems, 1,* 115–141.

Agnew, N. M., Ford, K. M., & Hayes, P. J. (1997). Expertise in context: Personally constructed, socially selected, and reality-relevant? In. P. J. Feltovich, K. M. Ford, & R. R. Hoffman (Eds.), *Expertise in context* (pp. 219–244). Cambridge, MA: MIT Press.

Agre, P. (1997). The decline of "command-and-control" computing. In J. Flanagan, T. Huang, P. Jones, & S. Kasif (Eds.), *Human-centered systems: Information, interactivity and intelligence* (pp. 303–304). Washington, DC: National Science Foundation.

Ainger, A. (1990). *Aspects of an experimental industrial application of human-centred CIM systems.* London: IEE Colloquium.

Akerstrom-Hoffman, R. A., & Smith, N. W. (1994). Mariner performance using automated navigation systems. In *Proceedings of the 38th Annual Meeting of the Human Factors and Ergonomics Society.* Santa Monica, CA: Human Factors and Ergonomics Society.

Albright, C. A., Truitt, T. R., Barile, A. B., Vortac, O. U. & Manning, C. A. (1996). *How controllers compensate for the lack of flight progress strips* (Report DOT/FAA/AM-96/5). Washington, DC: Department of Transportation.

Allee, V. (1997). *The knowledge evolution: Expanding organizational intelligence.* Boston: Butterworth-Heinemann.

Allen, G. (1982). Probability judgment in weather forecasting. In *Proceedings of the 9th Conference on Weather Forecasting and Analysis* (pp. 1–6). Boston: American Meteorological Society.

Allen, J. F., & Ferguson, G. (2002). Human-machine collaborative planning. In *Proceedings of the NASA Planning and Scheduling Workshop.* Houston, TX: NASA.

Allen, R. B. (1997). Mental models and user models. In M. Helander, T. K. Landauer, & P. Prabhu (Eds.), *Handbook of human–computer interaction* (pp. 49–63). Amsterdam: Elsevier.

Allen, S. W., Brooks, L. R. Norman, G. R., & Rosenthal, D. (1988). Effect of prior examples on rule-based diagnostic performance. In *Research on medical education: Proceedings of the 27th Annual Conference* (pp. 9–14). Chicago: American Association of Medical Colleges.

Alluisi, E. A. (1967). Methodology in the use of synthetic tasks to assess complex performance. *Human Factors, 9,* 375–384.

Alvarado, G. (2006, August). *Demonstration session: Capturing expert's knowledge using concept mapping.* Paper presented at the Second International Conference on Concept Mapping, San Jose, Costa Rica.

Amirault, R. J., & Branson, R. K. (2006). Educators and expertise: A brief history of theories and models. In K. A. Ericsson, N. Charness, P. Feltovich, & R. Hoffman (Eds.), *Cambridge handbook on expertise and expert performance* (pp. 69–86). New York: Cambridge University Press.

Anastasi, A. (1979). *Fields of applied psychology* (2nd ed.). New York: McGraw-Hill.

Anderson, J. R. (1974). Retrieval of propositional information from long-term memory. *Cognitive Psychology, 5,* 451–474.

Anderson, J. R. (1982). Acquisition of a cognitive skill. *Psychological Review, 89,* 369–406.

Anderson, J. R. (1983). *The architecture of cognition.* Cambridge, MA: Harvard University Press.

Anderson, J. R. (1987). Skill acquisition: Compilation of weak method problem solutions. *Psychological Review, 94,* 192–210.

Anderson, J. R. (1990). *The adaptive character of thought.* Hillsdale, NJ: Erlbaum.

Anderson, J. R. (1991). Cognitive architectures in a rational analysis. In K. VanLehn (Ed.), *Architectures for intelligence* (pp. 1–24). Mahwah, NJ: Erlbaum.

Anderson, J. R. (1993). *Rules of the mind.* Hillsdale, NJ: Erlbaum.

Anderson, J. R., & Lebiere, C. (1998). *The atomic components of thought.* Mahwah, NJ: Erlbaum.

Anderson, R. J. (1994). Representations and requirements: The value of ethnography in system design. *Human–Computer Interaction, 9,* 151–182.

Andre, A. D., Wickens, C. D., Moorman, L., & Boschelli, M. M. (1991). Display formatting techniques for improving situation awareness in the aircraft cockpit. *International Journal of Aviation Psychology, 1,* 205–218.

Andreas, B. G., & Weiss, B. (1954). *Review of research on perceptual-motor performance under varied display-control relationships* (Scientific Report No. 2, Contract No. AF 30(602)–200). Rochester, NY: University of Rochester.

Andriole, S. J., & Adelman, L. (1995). *Cognitive systems engineering for use—Computer interface design, prototyping, and evaluation.* Hillsdale, NJ: Erlbaum.

Annett, J. (2000). Theoretical and pragmatic influences on task analysis methods. In J.-M. Schraagen, S. Chipman, & V. Shalin (Eds.), *Cognitive task analysis.* Mahwah, NJ: Erlbaum.

Annett, J. (2003). Hierarchical task analysis. In E. Hollnagel (Ed.), *Handbook of cognitive task design* (pp. 17–36). Mahwah, NJ: Erlbaum.

Annett, J. (2004). Hierarchical task analysis. In D. Diaper & N. A. Stanton (Eds.), *The handbook of task analysis for human-computer interaction* (pp. 67–82). Mahwah, NJ: Erlbaum.

Annett, J., & Duncan, K. D. (1967). Task analysis and training design. *Occupational Psychology, 41,* 211–222.

Annett, J., Duncan, K. D., Stammers, R. B., & Gray, M. J. (1971). *Task analysis.* London: Her Majesty's Stationery Office.

Annett, J., & Kay, H. (1956). Skilled performance. *Occupational Psychology, 30,* 112–117.

Anonymous. (1949). *A study of plotting techniques* (Report No. 11). Cambridge, MA: Systems Research Laboratory, Harvard University.

Ansbacher, H. L. (1941). German military psychology. *Psychological Bulletin, 38,* 370–392.

Ansbacher, H. L. (1944). German industrial psychology in the fifth year of the war. *Psychological Bulletin, 41*, 605–614.

Applebaum, S. H. (1997). Socio-technical systems theory: An intervention strategy for organizational development. *Management Decision, 35*, 452–463.

Aquinas, T. (circa 1267/1945). *Summa theologica*. A. Pegis (trans). New York: Random House.

Ark, T. K., Brooks, L. R., & Eva, K. W. (2006). Giving learners the best of both worlds: Do clinical teachers need to guard against teaching pattern recognition to novices? *Academic Medicine, 81*, 405–409.

Arkes, H. R., & Freedman, M. R. (1984). A demonstration of the costs and benefits of expertise in recognition memory. *Memory & Cognition, 12*, 84–89.

Atkinson, M. L. (2003). Contract nets for control of distributed agents in unmanned air vehicles. *Proceedings of the 2nd AIAA Unmanned Unlimited Conference* (pp. 1–7). Reston, VA: AIAA.

Atkinson, M. L. (2005). Adding an operator into a task auction paradigm. *Proceedings of the AIAA InfoTech Conference, Workshop and Exhibit* (pp. 1–9). Reston, VA: AIAA.

Atkinson, R. C. & Shiffrin, R.M. (1968). Human memory: A proposed system and its control processes. In K. W. Spence & J. T. Spence (Eds.), *The psychology of learning and motivation (vol. 2)* (pp. 89–195). London: Academic Press.

Attewell, P. (1997). Position paper. In J. Flanagan, T. Huang, P. Jones, & S. Kasif (Eds.), *Human-centered systems: Information, interactivity and intelligence* (pp. 305–306). Washington, DC: National Science Foundation.

Ausubel, D. P. (1968). *Educational psychology: A cognitive view*. New York: Holt, Rinehart and Winston.

Ausubel, D. P., Novak, J. D., & Hanesian, H. (1978). *Educational psychology: A cognitive view* (2nd ed.). New York: Holt, Rinehart and Winston.

Avrahami, J., Kareev, Y., Bogot, Y., Caspi, R., et al. (1997). Teaching by examples: Implications for the process of category acquisition. *Quarterly Journal of Experimental Psychology, 50A*, 586–606.

Baars, B. J. (1986). *The cognitive revolution in psychology*. New York: Guilford Press.

Babcock, C. J., Norman, G. R., & Coblentz, C. L. (1993). Effect of clinical history on the interpretation of chest radiographs in childhood bronchiolitis. *Investigative Radiology, 28*, 214–217.

Bach-y-Rita, P., & Kercel, S. W. (2003). Sensory substitution and the human–machine interface. *TRENDS in Cognitive Sciences, 7*, 541–546.

Badham, R. J., Clegg, C. W., & Wall, T. D. (2000). Sociotechnical theory. In W. Karwowski (Ed.), *International encyclopedia of ergonomics and human factors* (pp. 1370–1373). New York: Taylor & Francis.

Baecker, R. M. (Ed.). (1992). *Readings in groupware and computer-supported cooperative work: Assisting human–human collaboration*. San Francisco: Morgan-Kaufman.

Bailey, A. A. (1932). *From intellect to intuition*. London: Lucis Press.

Bailey, W. A., & Kay, D. J. (1987). Structural analysis of verbal data. In J. M. Carroll & P. Tanner (Eds.), *Human factors in computing systems and graphics interfaces* (pp. 297–301). London: Academic Press.

Bain, A. (1879). *Education as science*. New York: D. Appleton.

Bainbridge, L. (1979). Verbal reports as evidence of the process operator's knowledge. *International Journal of Man–Machine Studies, 11*, 411–436.

Bainbridge, L. (1981). Mathematical equations or processing routines? In J. Rasmussen & W. B. Rouse (Eds.) *Human detection and diagnosis of system failures.* (NATO Conference Series III: Human Factors, Vol. 15), (pp. 259–286). New York: Plenum Press.

Bainbridge, L. (1983). Ironies of automation. *Automatica, 19,* 775–779.

Bainbridge, L. (1989). Development of skill, reduction of workload. In L. Bainbridge & S. A. Ruiz-Quintanilla (Eds.), *Developing skills with information technology* (pp. 87–116). New York.

Bainbridge, L. (1992). Mental models in cognitive skill : the case of industrial process operation. In Y. Rogers, A. Rutherford, & P. Bibby (Eds.) *Models in the mind* (pp. 119–143). London: Academic Press.

Bakan, D. (1954). A reconsideration of the problem of introspection. *Psychological Bulletin, 51,* 105–118.

Ball, L. J., & Ormerod, T. C. (2000). Putting ethnography to work: The case for a cognitive ethnography of design. *International Journal of Human–Computer Studies, 53,* 147–168.

Ballas, J. A. (2007). Human centered computing for tactical weather forecasting: An example of the "Moving Target Rule." In R. R. Hoffman (Ed.), *Expertise out of context: Proceedings of the Sixth International Conference on Naturalistic Decision Making.* Mahwah, NJ: Erlbaum.

Banaji, M. R., & Crowder, R. G. (1989). The bankruptcy of everyday memory. *American Psychologist, 44,* 1185–1193.

Bandura, A. (2000). Exercise of human agency through collective efficacy. *Current Directions in Psychological Science, 9,* 75–78.

Bannon, L., & Bødker, S. (1991) Beyond the interface: Encountering artifacts in use. In J. M. Carroll (Ed.), *Designing interaction* (pp. 227–250). New York: Cambridge University Press.

Barber, P. (1988). *Applied cognitive psychology.* London: Methuen.

Barley, S. & Orr, J. E., (Eds.) (1997). *Between craft and science: Technical work in US settings.* Ithaca, NY: IRL Press.

Barnard, P., Wilson, M., & MacLean, A. (1987). Approximate modeling of cognitive activity: Towards an expert systems design aid. In *Proceedings of CHI 1987* (pp. 21–26). New York: Association for Computing Machinery.

Barnes, B. (1974). *Scientific knowledge and sociological theory.* London, UK: Routledge and Kegan Paul.

Barnes, R. M. (1949). *Motion and time study* (3rd ed.; first edition 1937). New York: Wiley.

Barrows, H. S., & Feltovich, P. J. (1987). The clinical reasoning process. *Medical Education, 21,* 86–91.

Barrows, H. S., Norman, G. R., Neufeld, V. R., & Feightner, J. W. (1982). The clinical reasoning process of randomly selected physicians in general medical practice. *Clinical Investigative Medicine, 5,* 49–56.

Barry, D. (2000). There is no plane, but your flight is still on schedule. *The Pensacola News Journal,* p. 4G.

Bartlett, F. C. (1932). *Remembering: A study in experimental and social psychology.* Cambridge: Cambridge University Press.

Bartlett, F. C. (1947). The measurement of human skill. *British Medical Journal, 1,* 835–838, 877–880.

Bascones, J., & Novak, J. D. (1985). Alternative instructional systems and the development of problem-solving skills in physics. *European Journal of Science Education, 7,* 253–261.

Bateson, G., & Bateson, M. C. (2000). *Steps to an ecology of mind: Collected essays in anthropology, psychiatry, evolution, and epistemology.* Chicago: University of Chicago Press.

Batteau, A. W. (2001). The anthropology of aviation and flight safety. *Human Organization, 60,* 201–210.

Bauer, M. I., & Johnson-Laird, P. N. (1993). How diagrams can improve reasoning. *Psychological Science, 4,* 372–378.

Beach, K. D. (1988). The role of external mnemomic symbols in acquiring an occupation. In M. M. Gruneberg, P. E. Morris, & R. N. Sykes (Eds.), *Practical aspects of memory: Current research and issues, Vol. 1* (pp. 342–346). Chichester, England: John Wiley.

Beach, L. R. (1990). *Image theory: Decision-making in personal and organizational contexts.* Chichester, UK: Wiley.

Beach, L. R. (1993). Image theory: Personal and organizational decisions. In G. Klein, J. Orasanu, R. Calderwood, & C. Zsambok (Eds.), *Decision making in action: Models and methods* (pp. 148–157). Norwood, NJ: Ablex.

Beach, L. R., Chi, M. T. H., Klein, G., Smith, P., & Vicente, K. (1997). Naturalistic decision making research and related lines. In C. E. Zsambok & G. Klein (Eds.), *Naturalistic decision making* (pp. 29–36). Mahwah, NJ: Erlbaum.

Beach, L. R., & Lipshitz, R. (1993). Why classical decision theory is an inappropriate standard for evaluating and aiding most human decision making. In G. Klein, J. Orasanu, R. Calderwood, & C. Zsambok (Eds.), *Decision making in action: Models and methods* (pp. 21–35). Norwood, NJ: Ablex.

Beach, L. R., & Mitchell, T. R. (1978). A contingency model for the selection of decision strategies. *Academy of Management Review, 3,* 439–449.

Beaudoin-Lafon, M. (Ed.). (1999). *Computer supported co-operative work.* New York: Wiley.

Becker, H. (1972). A school is a lousy place to learn anything in. *American Behavioral Scientist, 16,* 85–105.

Behar, M. F. (1940). The "accuracy" and other measuring properties of temperature instruments. *Instruments, 13,* 240–242.

Behforooz, A., & Hudson, F. J. (1996). *Software engineering fundamentals.* Oxford: Oxford University Press.

Belkin, N. J., Brooks, H. M., & Daniels, P. J. (1987). Knowledge elicitation using discourse analysis. *International Journal of Man–Machine Studies, 27,* 127–144.

Bellezza, F. S. (1992). Mnemonics and expert knowledge: Mental cueing. In R. R. Hoffman (Ed.), *The psychology of expertise: Cognitive research and empirical AI* (pp. 204–217). New York: Springer-Verlag.

Benfer, R. A., & Furbee, L. (1989, November). Knowledge acquisition in the Peruvian Andes. *AI Expert,* pp. 22–29.

Benjafield, J. (1969). Evidence that "thinking aloud" constitutes an externalization of inner speech. *Psychonomic Science, 15,* 83–84.

Benner, P. (1984). *From novice to expert: Excellence and power in clinical nursing practice.* Menlo Park, CA: Addison-Wesley.

Berbaum, K. S., Franken, E. A., Dorfman, D. D., Rooholamini, S. A., Kathol, M. H., Barloon, T. J., et al. (1990). Satisfaction of search in diagnostic radiology. *Investigative Radiology, 25,* 133–140.

Bereiter, C., & Bird, M. (1985). Use of thinking aloud in identification and teaching of reading comprehension strategies. *Cognition and Instruction, 2,* 131–156.

Berg-Cross, G., & Price, M. E. (1989). Acquiring and managing knowledge using a conceptual structures approach: Introduction and framework. *IEEE Transactions on Systems, Man, and Cybernetics, 19,* 513–527.

Berkeley, D., & Humphreys, P. (1982). Structuring decision problems and the "bias heuristic." *Acta Psychologica, 50,* 201–252.

Bernstein, J. (1982). *Science observed: Essays out of my mind.* New York: Basic Books.

Berry, D. C. (1987). The problem of implicit knowledge. *Expert Systems, 4,* 144–151.

Berry, D. C., & Broadbent, D. E. (1984). On the relationship between task performance and associated verbalizable knowledge. *Quarterly Journal of Experimental Psychology, 36A,* 209–231.

Berry, D. C., & Broadbent, D. E. (1988). Interactive tasks and the implicit–explicit distinction. *British Journal of Psychology, 79,* 251–272.

Beyer, H. R., & Holtzblatt, K. (1998). *Contextual design: Defining customer-centered systems.* San Diego, CA: Academic Press.

Bias, A. D., & Mahew, D. J. (1994). *Cost-justifying usability.* Boston: Academic Press.

Biegel, R. A. (1931). Eine Eignungsprüfung für Funkentelegraphischen. *Psychotechnik, 6,* 41–45.

Bijker, W. E., Hughes, T. P., & Pinch, T. J. (Eds.). (1987). *The social construction of technological systems: New directions in the sociology and history of technology.* Cambridge, MA: MIT Press.

Bikson, T. K., & Eveland, J. D. (1990). The interplay of work group structures and computer support. In J. Galegher, R. E. Kraut, & C. Egido (Eds.), *Intellectual teamwork: Social and technological foundations of cooperative work* (pp. 245–290). Mahwah, NJ: Erlbaum.

Billings, C. E. (1996). *Aviation automation: The search for a human-centered approach.* Hillsdale, NJ: Erlbaum.

Billings, C. E. (1997). Issues concerning human-centered intelligent systems: What's "human-centered" and what's the problem? In J. Flanagan, T. Huang, P. Jones, & S. Kasif (Eds.), *Human-centered systems: Information, interactivity and intelligence* (pp. 125–135). Washington DC: National Science Foundation.

Bills, A. G. (1927). The influence of muscular tension on the efficiency of mental work. *American Journal of Psychology, 38,* 227–251.

Bills, A. G. (1931). Blocking: A new principle of mental fatigue. *American Journal of Psychology, 43,* 230–240.

Birmingham, H. P., & Taylor, F. V. (1954). A design philosophy for man–machine control systems. In *Proceedings of the IRE, 17,* 1748–1758.

Bisantz, A. M., Roth, E., Brickman, B., Gosbee, L. L., Hettinger, L., & McKinney, J. (2002). Integrating cognitive analyses in a large-scale system design process. *International Journal of Human–Computer Studies, 58,* 117–206.

Bisantz, A. M., & Vicente, K. J. (1994). Making the abstraction hierarchy concrete. *International Journal of Human Computer Studies, 40,* 83–117.

Black, A. (1990). Visible planning on paper and on screen: The impact of working medium on decision-making by novice graphic designers. *Behavior and Information Technology, 9,* 283–296.

Blanchette, I., & Dunbar, K. (2000). How analogies are generated: The roles of structural and superficial similarity. *Memory and Cognition, 28(1),* 108–124.

Blanchette, I., & Dunbar, K. (2001). Analogy use in naturalistic settings: The influence of audience, emotion and goals. *Memory and Cognition, 29,* 730–735.

Blanchette, I., & Dunbar, K. (2002). Representational change and analogy: How analogical inferences alter target representations. *Journal of Experimental Psychology: Learning, Memory, and Cognition, 28,* 672–685.

Blickensderfer, E. L., Cannon-Bowers, J. A., Salas, E., & Baker, D. P. (2000). Analyzing requirements in team tasks. In J. M. Schraagen, S. F. Chipman, & V. L. Shalin (Eds.), *Cognitive task analysis* (pp. 431–450). Mahwah, NJ: Erlbaum.

Blomberg, J., Burrell, M., & Guest, G. (2003). An ethnographic approach to design. In J. A. Jacko & A. Sears (Eds.), *The human–computer interaction handbook* (pp. 964–986). Mahwah, NJ: Erlbaum.

Blomberg, J., Giacomi, J., Mosher, A., & Swenton-Wall, P. (1993). Ethnographic field methods and their relation to design. In D. Schuler & A. Namioka (Eds.), *Participatory design* (pp. 123–155). Mahwah, NJ: Erlbaum.

Blomberg, J., Suchman, L., & Trigg, R. H. (1997). Reflections on a work-oriented design project. In G. C. Bowker, S. L. Star, W. Turner, & L. Gasser (Eds.), *Social science, technology, and cooperative work: Beyond the great divide* (pp. 189–216). Mahwah, NJ: Erlbaum.

Bloom, B. S. (1956). *Taxonomy of educational objectives—The classification of educational goals.* New York: David McKay.

Bloor, D. (1976). *Knowledge and social imagery.* London, UK: Routledge and Kegan Paul.

Blumenthal, A. L. (1997). Wilhelm Wundt. In W. G. Bringmann, H. E. Lück, R. Miller, & C. E. Early (Eds.), *A pictorial history of psychology* (pp. 117–125). Chicago: Quintessence.

Boger-Mehall, S. R. (2007). *Cognitive flexibility theory: Implications for teaching and teacher education.* Retrieved June 6, 2007, from http://www.kdassem.dk/didaktik/l4–16.htm

Bogner, M. S. (Ed.). (1994). *Human error in medicine.* Hillsdale, NJ: Erlbaum.

Boland, R. J., & Tenkasi, R. V. (2001). Communication and collaboration in distributed cognition. In G. M. Olson, T. W. Malone, & J. B. Smith (Eds.), *Coordination theory and collaboration technology* (pp. 51–66). Mahawh, NJ: Erlbaum.

Bonaceto, C., & Burns, K. (2007). A survey of the methods and uses of cognitive engineering. In R. R. Hoffman (Ed.), *Expertise out of context* (pp. 29–78). Boca Raton, FL: CRC Press.

Bonar, J. (with 14 others). (1985). "Guide to Cognitive Task Analysis." Report under contract No. F41689-83-C-0029 from the Air Force Human Resources Laboratory. Learning Research and Development Center, University of Pittsburgh, Pittsburgh, PA.

Bonnardel, R. (1943). *The adaptation of man to his job.* Paris: PUF.

Book, W. F. (1908). *The psychology of skill with special reference to its acquisition in typewriting* (University of Montana Studies in Psychology, Vol. 1). Missoula: University of Montana Press.

Book, W. F. (1924). Voluntary motor ability of the world's champion typists. *Journal of Applied Psychology, 8,* 283–308.

Boose, J. H. (1985). A knowledge acquisition program for expert systems based on personal construct psychology. *International Journal of Man–Machine Studies, 23,* 495–525.

Bordage, G., Connell, K. J., Chang, R. W., Gecht, M. R., & Sinacore, J. M. (1997). Assessing the semantic content of clinical case presentations: Studies of reliability and concurrent validity. *Academic Medicine, 72,* S37–S39.

Bordage, G., & Lemieux, M. (1991). Semantic structures and diagnostic thinking of experts and novices. *Academic Medicine, 66,* S70–S72.

Bordage, G., & Zacks, R. (1984). The structure of medical knowledge in memories of medical students and practitioners: Categories and prototypes. *Medical Education, 18,* 406–416.

Boring, E. G. (1913). Introspection in dementia praecox. *The American Journal of Psychology, 24,* 145–170.

Boring, E. G. (1950). *A history of experimental psychology.* Boston: D. C. Heath.

Boring, E. G. (1953). A history of introspection. *Psychological Bulletin, 50,* 169–189.

Boshuizen, H. P. A., & Schmidt, H. G. (1992). Biomedical knowledge and clinical expertise. *Cognitive Science, 16,* 153–184.

Bowker, G. C. (1997). Information convergence. In J. Flanagan, T. Huang, P. Jones, & S. Kasif (Eds.), *Human-centered systems: Information, interactivity and intelligence* (pp. 307–308). Washington, DC: National Science Foundation.

Bowker, G. C., Star, S. L., Turner, W., & Gasser, L. (Eds.) (1997). *Social science, technical systems, and cooperative work: Beyond the great divide.* Mahwah, NJ: Erlbaum.

Boy, G. A. (1983). Le systeme MESSAGE: un premier pas vers l'analyse assistée par ordinatur des interactions Homme-Machine. *Le Travail Humain, 46,* 2.

Boy, G. A. (1998). *Cognitive function analysis.* Stamford, CN: Ablex.

Boynton, A., & Fischer, B. (2005). *Virtuoso teams: Lessons from teams that changed their worlds.* New York: Prentice Hall.

Bradford, G. C. (1915). An experiment in typewriting. *Pedagogical Seminary, 22,* 445–478.

Bradshaw, G. (2000). *The sand-reckoner.* New York: Forge Books.

Bradshaw, J. M., Acquisti, A., Allen, J. F., Breedy, M., Bunch, L., Chambers, N., et al. (2004). Teamwork-centered autonomy for extended human-agent interaction in space applications. In *Proceedings of the AAAI Spring Symposium* (pp. 136–140). Stanford, CA: The AAAI Press.

Bradshaw, J. M., Beautement, P., Breedy, M., Bunch, L., Drakunov, S. V., Feltovich, P. J., et al. (2004). Making agents acceptable to people. In N. Zhong & J. Liu (Eds.), *Intelligent technologies for information analysis: Advances in agents, data mining, and statistical learning* (pp. 355–400). Berlin: Springer-Verlag.

Bradshaw, J. M., Feltovich, P., Jung, H., Kulkarni, S., Taysom, W., & Uszok, A. (2004). Dimensions of adjustable autonomy and mixed-initiative interaction. In M. Nickles, M. Rovatsos, & G. Weiss (Eds.), *Agents and computational autonomy: Potential, risks, and solutions* (Lecture Notes in Computer Science, Vol. 2969, pp. 17–39). Berlin, Germany: Springer-Verlag.

Bramer, M. (Ed.) (1985). *Research and development in expert systems.* Cambridge: Cambridge University Press.

Bransford, J. D. (1979). *Human cognition: Learning, understanding and remembering.* Belmont, CA: Wadsworth.

Bransford, J. D., Barclay, J. R., & Franks, J. J. (1972). Sentence memory: A constructive versus interpretive approach. *Cognitive Psychology, 3,* 193–209.

Bransford, J. D., Franks, J. J., Vye, N. J., & Sherwood, R. D. (1989). New approaches to instruction: Because wisdom can't be told. In S. Vosniadou & A. Ortony (Eds.), *Similarity and analogical reasoning* (pp. 470–497). Cambridge: Cambridge University Press.

Bransford, J. D., & Stein, B. S. (1984). *The IDEAL problem solver.* San Francisco: W. H. Freeman.

Bray, C. W. (1948). *Psychology and military proficiency.* Princeton, NJ: Princeton University Press.

Brehmer, B. (1978). Response consistency in probabilistic inference tasks. *Organizational Behavior and Human Decision Processes, 22,* 103–115.

Brehmer, B. (1991). Distributed decision making: Some notes on the literature. In J. Rasmussen, B. Brehmer, & J. Leplat (Eds.), *Distributed decision making: Cognitive models for cooperative work* (pp. 3–14). Chichester, England: Wiley.

Breuker, J. A., & Wielinga, B. J. (1984). *Techniques for knowledge elicitation and analysis* (Report 1.5, ESPRIT Project 12). Amsterdam: University of Amsterdam.

Breuker, J., & Wielinga, B. (1987). Use of models in the interpretation of verbal data. In A. L. Kidd (Ed.), *Knowledge acquisition for expert systems: A practical handbook* (pp. 17–44). New York: Plenum Press.

Broadbent, D. E. (1957). A mechanical model for human attention and immediate memory. *Psychological Review, 64,* 205–215.

Broadbent, D. E. (1977). Levels, hierarchies, and the locus of control. *Quarterly Journal of Experimental Psychology, 29,* 181–201.

Broadbent, D. E., & Aston, B. (1978). Human control of a simulated economic system. *Ergonomics, 21,* 1053–1043.

Broadbent, D. E., FitzGerald, P., & Broadbent, M. H. P. (1986). Implicit and explicit knowledge in the control of complex systems. *British Journal of Psychology, 77,* 33–50.

Brooking, A. (1999). *Corporate memory: Strategies for knowledge management.* London: International Thomson Business Press.

Brooks, L. R. (1978a). Decentralized control of categorization: The role of prior processing episodes. In U. Neisser (Ed.), *Concepts and conceptual development* (pp. 141–174). Cambridge: Cambridge University Press.

Brooks, L. R. (1978b). Nonanalytic concept formation and memory for instances. In R. Rosch & B. Lloyd (Eds.), *Cognition and categorization* (pp. 169–211). Hillsdale, NJ: Erlbaum.

Brooks, L. R., Norman, G. R., & Allen, S. W. (1991). The role of specific similarity in a medical diagnostic task. *Journal of Experimental Psychology: General, 120,* 278–287.

Brown, B. (1989). The taming of an expert: An anecdotal report. In C. R Westphal & K. L. McGraw (Eds.), *Special Issue on Knowledge Acquisition, SIGART Newsletter,* No. 108, pp. 133–135.

Brown, C. W., & Ghiselli, E. E. (1953). The prediction of proficiency of taxicab drivers. *Journal of Applied Psychology, 37,* 437–439.

Brown, G. S., & Campbell, D. P. (1948). *Principles of servomechanisms: Dynamics and synthesis of closed-loop control systems.* New York: Wiley.

Brown, J. S., Collins, A., & Duguid, P. (1989). Situated cognition and the culture of learning. *Educational Researcher, 18,* 32–42.

Brozek, J., & Hoskovec, J. (1997). Academic psychology in Prague. In W. G. Bringmann, H. E. Lück, R. Miller, & C. E. Early (Eds.), *A pictorial history of psychology* (pp. 562–567). Chicago: Quintessence.

Brule, J. F., & Blount, A. (1989). *Knowledge acquisition.* New York: McGraw-Hill.

Brun, W., Eid, J., Johnsen, B. H., Laberg, J. C., Ekornas, B., & Kobbeltvedt, T. (2005). Bridge resource management training: Enhancing shared mental models and task performance? In H. Montgomery, R. Lipshitz, & B. Brehmer (Eds.), *How professionals make decisions* (pp. 183–193). Mahwah, NJ: Erlbaum.

Bryan, W. L. (1892). On the development of voluntary motor ability. *American Journal of Psychology, 5,* 125–204.

Bryan, W. L., & Harter, N. (1897). Studies in the physiology and psychology of the telegraphic language. *Psychological Review, 4,* 27–53.

Buchanan, B. G., Davis, R., & Feigenbaum, E. A. (2006). Expert systems: A perspective from computer science. In K. A. Ericsson, N. Charness, P. Feltovich, & R. Hoffman (Eds.), *Cambridge handbook on expertise and expert performance* (pp. 87–104). New York: Cambridge University Press.

Buchanan, B. G., Sutherland, G. L., & Feigenbaum, E. A. (1969). Rediscovering some problems in artificial intelligence in the context of organic chemistry. In B. Meltzer & D. Michie (Eds.), *Machine intelligence 4* (pp. 209–254). Edinburgh: Edinburgh University Press.

Buchanan, B. G., & Wilkins, D. C. (Eds.). (1993). *Readings in knowledge acquisition and learning: Automating the construction and improvement of expert systems.* San Mateo, CA: Morgan Kaufmann.

Bültmann, W. (1928). *Psychotechnische Berufsprüfung von Geissereifacharbeiten.* Berlin: Verlag von Julius Springer.

Burke, C. S., Stagl, K. C., Salas, E., Pierce, L., & Kendall, D. (in press). Understanding team adaptation: A conceptual analysis and model. *Journal of Applied Psychology.*

Burke, F. (1989). From fundamental to accessory in the development of the nervous system and of movements. *Pedagogical Seminary, 6,* 4–64.

Burns, B. D. (2004). The effects of speed on skilled chess performance. *Psychological Science, 15,* 442–447.

Burns, C. M., Barsalou, E., Handler, C., Kuo, J., & Harrigan, K. (2000). A work domain analysis for network management. *Proceedings of the Human Factors and Ergonomics Society 44th Annual Meeting* (pp. 469–472).

Burns, C. M., Bryant, D. J., & Chalmers, B. A. (2005). Boundary, purpose and values in work domain models: Models of naval command and control. *IEEE systems, Man, and Cybernetics, Part A: Systems and Humans, 35,* 603–616.

Burns, C. M., & Hajdukiewicz, J. R. (2004). *Ecological interface design.* Boca Raton, FL: CRC Press.

Burton, A. M., Shadbolt, N. R., Hedgecock, A. P., & Rugg, G. (1987). A formal evaluation of a knowledge elicitation techniques for expert systems: Domain 1. In D. S. Moralee (Ed.), *Research and development in expert systems* (Vol. 4, pp. 35–46). Cambridge, UK: Cambridge University Press.

Burton, A. M., Shadbolt, N. R., Rugg, G., & Hedgecock, A. P. (1988). A formal evaluation of knowledge elicitation techniques for expert systems: Domain 1. In *Proceedings, First European Workshop on Knowledge Acquisition for Knowledge-Based Systems* (pp. D3.1–D21). Reading, UK: Reading University.

Burton, A. M., Shadbolt, N. R., Rugg, G., & Hedgecock, A. P. (1990). The efficacy of knowledge elicitation techniques: A comparison across domains and levels of expertise. *Journal of Knowledge Acquisition, 2,* 167–178.

Burtt, H. E. (1929). *Psychology and industrial efficiency.* New York: Appleton.

Burtt, H. E. (1957). *Applied psychology.* Englewood Cliffs, NJ: Prentice Hall.

Butler, K. E., & Corter, J. E. (1986). Use of psychometric tools for knowledge acquisition: A case study. In W. A. Gale (Ed.), *Artificial intelligence and statistics* (pp. 295–319). Cambridge, MA: Addison-Wesley.

Bylander, T., & Chandrasekaran, B. (1987). Generic tasks for knowledge-based reasoning: The "right" level of abstraction for knowledge acquisition. *International Journal of Man–Machine Studies, 26,* 231–243.

Cacciabue, P. C., & Hollnagel, E. (1995). Simulation of cognition: Applications. In J. M. Hoc, P. C. Cacciabue, & E. Hollnagel (Eds.), *Expertise and technology: Cognition and human-computer cooperation* (pp. 55–73). Hillsdale, NJ: Lawrence Erlbaum Associates.

Calderwood, R., Crandall, B., & Klein, G. (1987). *Expert and novice fireground command decisions* (Report MDA903-85-C-0327). Alexandria, VA: U.S. Army Research Institute.

Camerer, C. (1981). General conditions for the success of bootstrapping models. *Organizational Behavior and Human Performance, 27,* 411–422.

Campbell, R. L., Brown, N. R., & DiBello, L. A. (1992). The programmer's burden: Developing expertise in programming. In R. R. Hoffman (Ed.), *The psychology of expertise: Cognitive research and empirical AI* (pp. 269–294). Mahwah, NJ: Erlbaum.

Cañas, A. J. (1997, November). *Colaboración en la Construcción de Conocimiento Mediante Mapas Conceptuales.*[Collaboration in the construction of knowledge through Concept Maps.] Proceedings of the VIII Congreso Internacional sobre Tecnología y Educación a Distancia, San José, Costa Rica.

Cañas, A. J. (1999, November). *Algunas Ideas sobre la Educación y las Herramientas Computacionales Necesarias para Apoyar su Implementación.* [Some ideas about education and the necessary computaional toolbox to support implementation.] Revista RED, Educación y Formación Profesional a Distancia, Ministry of Education, Spain.

Cañas, A. J., Coffey, J. W., Carnot, M. J., Feltovich, P., Hoffman, R., Feltovich, J., et al. (2003). *A summary of literature pertaining to the use of concept mapping techniques and technologies for education and performance support.* Report to the Chief of Naval Education and Training, prepared by the Institute for Human and Machine Cognition, Pensacola, FL.

Cañas, A. J., Coffey, J., Reichherzer, T., Suri, N., & Carff, R. (1997, May). *El-Tech: A performance support system with embedded training for electronics technicians*. Paper presented at the 11th Florida Artificial Intelligence Research Symposium, Sanibel Island, FL.

Cañas, A. J., Ford, K. M., Brennan, J., Reichherzer, T., & Hayes, P. (1995, July). *Knowledge construction and sharing in quorum*. Paper presented at the Seventh World Conference on Artificial Intelligence in Education, Washington, DC.

Cañas, A. J., Leake, D. B., & Wilson, D. C. (1999). *Managing, mapping and manipulating conceptual knowledge* (AAAI Workshop Technical Report WS-99-10). Menlo Park, CA: AAAI Press.

Cañas, A. J., & Novak, J. D. (2006). Re-examining the foundations for effective use of concept maps. In A. J. Cañas & J. D. Novak (Eds.), *Proceedings of the Second International Conference on Concept Mapping* (pp. 494–502). San Jose, Costa Rica: University of Costa Rica.

Cannon, M. D., & Edmondson, A. C. (2001). Confronting failure: Antecedents and consequences of shared beliefs about failure in organizational work groups. *Journal of Organizational Behavior, 22,* 161–177.

Carayon, P., & Smith, M. J. (2000). Work organization and ergonomics. *Applied Ergonomics, 31,* 649–662.

Card, S. K., Moran, T. P., & Newell, A. (1980a). Computer text editing: An information processing analysis of a routine cognitive skill. *Cognitive Psychology, 12,* 32–74.

Card, S. K., Moran, T. P., & Newell, A. (1980b). The keystroke-level model for user performance time with interactive systems. *Communications of the ACM, 23,* 396–410.

Card, S. K., Moran, T. P., & Newell, A. (1983). *The psychology of human–computer interaction*. Hillsdale, NJ: Erlbaum.

Carkett, R. (2003). "He's different. He's got 'Star Trek' vision:" Supporting the expertise of conceptual design engineers. In Creativity and Cognition Studios (Ed.), *Expertise in design*. Sydney, Australia: Creativity and Cognition Studios, University of Technology. Retrieved September 29, 2006, from http://research.it.uts.edu.au/creative/design/

Carmody, D. P., Kundel, H. L., & Toto, L. C. (1984). Comparison scans while reading chest images: Taught but not practiced. *Investigative Radiology, 19,* 462–466.

Carroll, J. B. (1953). *The study of language: A survey of linguistics and related disciplines in America*. Cambridge, MA: Harvard University Press.

Carroll, J. M. (1995). *Scenario-based design: Envisioning work and technology in system development*. New York: Wiley.

Carroll, J. M., & Campbell, R. L. (1988). *Artifacts as psychological theories: The case of human–computer interaction* (IBM Research Report RC 13454). Yorktown Heights, NY: Watson Research Center.

Carroll, J. M., & Rosson, M. B. (1992). Getting around the task-artifact cycle: How to make claims and design by scenario. *ACM Transactions on Information Systems, 10,* 181–212.

Carroll, J. S., Rudolph, J. W., Hatakenaka, S., Widerhold, T. L., & Boldrini, M. (2001). Learning in the context of incident investigation: Team diagnoses and organizational decisions at four nuclear power plants. In E. Salas & G. Klein (Eds.), *Linking expertise and naturalistic decision making* (pp. 349–366). Mahwah, NJ: Erlbaum.

Carstensen, P. H., & Nielsen, M. (1997). Towards computer support for cooperation in time-critical settings. In G. Salvendy, M. J. Smith, & R. J. Koubek (Eds.), *Design of computing systems: Cognitive considerations* (pp. 101–105). Amsterdam: Elsevier.

Cattell, J. M. (1886). The time taken up by cerebral operations. *Mind, 11,* 220–224, 377–392, 524–538.

Chalmers, D. J., French, R. M., & Hofstadter, D. R. (1992). High-level perception, representation and analogy: A critique of artificial intelligence methodology. *Journal of Experimental and Theoretical Artificial Intelligence, 4,* 185–211.

Chandrasekaran, B. (1983, Spring). Towards a taxonomy of problem solving types. *AI Magazine, 11,* 9–17.

Chandrasekaran, B. (1986). Generic tasks in knowledge-based reasoning: High-level building blocks for expert system design. *IEEE Expert, 1,* 23–30.

Chapanis, A. (1946). *Speed of reading target information from a direct-reading counter-type indicator versus conventional radar bearing-and-range dials* (Report No. 166-I-3). Baltimore: Johns Hopkins University.

Chapanis, A. (1947). *The relative efficiency of a bearing counter and bearing dial for use with PPI presentations* (Report No. 166-I-26). Baltimore: Johns Hopkins University.

Chapanis, A. (1949). *Some aspects of operator performance on the VJ remote radar indicator* (Report No. SDC 166-I-91). Port Washington, NY: Office of Naval Research.

Chapanis, A. (1951). Theory and methods for analyzing errors in man–machine systems. *Annals of the New York Academy of Sciences, 51,* 1179–1203.

Chapanis, A. (1959). *Research techniques in human engineering.* Baltimore: Johns Hopkins University Press.

Chapanis, A. (1996). *Human factors in systems engineering.* New York: Wiley Interscience.

Chapanis, A. (1999). *The Chapanis chronicles: 50 years of human factors research, education, and design.* Santa Barbara, CA: Aegean.

Chapman, J. C. (1919). The learning curve in typewriting. *Journal of Applied Psychology, 3,* 252–268.

Charlin, B., Roy, L., Brailovsky, C., Goulet, F., & van der Vleuten, C. (2000). The Script Concordance Test: A tool to assess the reflective clinician. *Teaching and Learning in Medicine, 12,* 189–195.

Charness, N. (1976). Memory for chess positions: Resistance to interference. *Journal of Experimental Psychology: Human Learning and Memory, 2,* 641–653.

Charness, N., & Campbell, J. I. D. (1988). Acquiring skill at mental calculation in adulthood: A task decomposition. *Journal of Experimental Psychology: General, 117,* 115–129.

Chase, W. G. (1983). Spatial representations of taxi drivers. In D. R. Rogers & J. H. Sloboda (Eds.), *Acquisition of symbolic skills* (pp. 391–405). New York: Plenum.

Chase, W. G., & Simon, H. A. (1973). Perception in chess. *Cognitive Psychology, 5,* 55–81.

Cheney, M. (2001). *Tesla: Man out of time.* New York: Touchstone Books.

Cherns, A. (1976). The principles of sociotechnical design. *Human Relations, 29,* 783–792.

Cherns, A. (1987). Principles of sociotechnical design revisited. *Human Relations, 40,* 152–162.

Cherry, E. C. (Ed.). (1955). *Information theory.* London: Butterworths.

Chi, M. T. H. (1978). Knowledge structures and memory development. In R. Siegler (Ed.), *Children's thinking: What develops?* (pp. 73–96). Hillsdale, NJ: Erlbaum.

Chi, M. T. H. (2006a). Laboratory methods for assessing experts' and novices' knowledge. In K. A. Ericsson, N. Charness, P. Feltovich, & R. Hoffman (Eds.), *Cambridge handbook on expertise and expert performance* (pp. 167–184). New York: Cambridge University Press.

Chi, M. T. H. (2006b). Two approaches to the study of experts' characteristics. In K. A. Ericsson, N. Charness, P. Feltovich, & R. Hoffman (Eds.), *Cambridge handbook on expertise and expert performance* (pp. 21–20). New York: Cambridge University Press.

Chi, M. T. H., Feltovich, P. J., & Glaser, R. (1981). Categorization and representation of physics problems by experts and novices. *Cognitive Science, 5,* 121–152.

Chi, M. T. H., Glaser, R., & Farr, M. J. (Eds.). (1988). *The nature of expertise*. Mahwah, NJ: Erlbaum.

Chi, M. T. H., Glaser, R., & Rees, E. (1982). Expertise in problem solving. In R. J. Sternberg (Ed.), *Advances in the psychology of human intelligence* (Vol. 1, pp. 7–75). Hillsdale, NJ: Erlbaum.

Chi, M. T. H., & Koeske, R. D. (1983). Network representation of a child's dinosaur knowledge. *Developmental Psychology, 19*, 29–39.

Chiesi, H., Spilich, G. J., & Voss, J. F. (1979). Acquisition of domain-related information in relation to high and low domain knowledge. *Journal of Verbal Learning and Verbal Behavior, 18*, 257–283.

Chiles, W. D. (1967). Methodology in the assessment of complex performance: Discussion and conclusions. *Human Factors, 9*, 385–392.

Chomsky, N. (1957). *Syntactic structures*. The Hague: Mouton.

Chomsky, N. (1959). A review of Skinner's verbal behavior. *Language, 25*, 26–58.

Choo, C. W. (1998). *The knowing organization: How organizations use information to construct meaning, create knowledge and make decisions*. New York: Oxford University Press.

Chow, R., Christoffersen, K., Woods, D. D., Watts-Perotti, J. C., & Patterson, E. (2000). *Communication during distributed anomaly response and replanning* (Institute for Ergonomics/Cognitive Systems Engineering Laboratory Report, ERGO-CSEL 00-TR-02).

Chow, R., & Vicente, K. J. (2001). A field study of collaborative work in network management: Implications for interface design. *Proceedings of the Human Factors and Ergonomics Society 45th Annual Meeting*, 356–360.

Christensen-Szalanski, J. J. (1993). A comment on applying experimental findings of cognitive biases to naturalistic environments. In G. Klein, J. Orasanu, R. Calderwood, & C. E. Zsambok (Eds.), *Decision making in action: Models and methods* (pp. 252–264). Norwood, NJ: Ablex.

Christiansen, J. M. (1949). Arctic arial navigation: A method for the analysis of complex activities and its application to the job of the arctic aerial navigator. *Mechanical Engineering, 71*, 11–16, 22.

Christiansen, J. M. (1950). A sampling technique for use in activity analysis. *Personnel Psychology, 3*, 361–368.

Christoffersen, K., Hunter, C. N., & Vicente, K. J. (1996). A longitudinal study of the effects of ecological interface design on skill acquisition. *Human Factors, 38*, 523–541.

Christoffersen, K., & Woods, D. D. (2002). How to make automated systems team players. *Advances in Human Performance and Cognitive Engineering Research, 2*, 1–12.

Clancey, W. J. (1988). Acquiring, representing, and evaluating a model of diagnostic strategy. In M. T. H. Chi, R. Glaser, & M. J. Farr (Eds.) *The nature of expertise* (pp. 343–418). Hillsdale, NJ: Erlbaum.

Clancey, W. J. (1993). The knowledge level reinterpreted: Modeling socio-technical systems. In K. M. Ford & J. M. Bradshaw (Eds.), *Knowledge acquisition as modeling* (Pt. 1, pp. 33–49). New York: Wiley.

Clancey, W. J. (1995). Practice cannot be reduced to theory: Knowledge, representations and change in the workplace. In C. Zuccermaglio, S. Bagnara, & S. U. Stucky (Eds.), *Organizational learning and technological change* (pp. 16–46). Berlin: Springer.

Clancey, W. J. (1997). *Situated cognition: On human knowledge and computer representations*. Cambridge: Cambridge University Press.

Clancey, W. J. (1998). Developing learning technology in practice. In C. Bloom & R. Loftin (Eds.), *Facilitating the development and use of interactive learning environments* (pp. 3–20). Hillsdale, NJ: Erlbaum.

Clancey, W. J. (1999). *Conceptual coordination: How the mind orders experience in time.* Hillsdale, NJ: Erlbaum.

Clancey, W. J. (2001). Field science ethnography: Methods for systematic observation on an expedition. *Field Methods, 13,* 223–243.

Clancey, W. J. (2002). Simulating activities: Relating motives, deliberation, and attentive coordination. *Cognitive Systems Research, 3,* 471–499.

Clancey, W. J. (2004). Roles for agent assistants in field science: Understanding personal projects and collaboration [Special issue]. *IEEE Transactions on Systems, Man and Cybernetics, Part C: Applications and Reviews, 34,* 125–137.

Clancey, W. J. (2006). Observation of work practices in natural settings. In K. A. Ericsson, N. Charness, P. J. Feltovich, & R. R. Hoffman (Eds.), *Cambridge handbook on expertise and expert performance.* New York: Cambridge University Press.

Clancey, W. J. (in press-a). Participant observation of a Mars surface habitat mission simulation. *Habitation.*

Clancey, W. J. (in press-b). Simulating activities: Relating motives, deliberation, and attentive coordination [Special issue]. *Cognitive Systems Review.*

Clancey, W. J., Lee, P., Cockell, C. S., & Shafto, M. (2006). To the north coast of Devon: Navigational turn-taking in exploring unfamiliar terrain. In J. Clarke (Ed.), *Mars analogue research* (Vol. 111). American Astronautical Society Science and Technology Series. San Diego, CA: AAS Publications.

Clancey, W., & Shortliffe, E. (Eds.). (1984). *Readings in medical artificial intelligence: The first decade.* Reading, MA: Addison-Wesley.

Claparéde, E. (1917). *La psychologie de l'intelligence. Scientia, 22,* 353–368.

Claparéde, E. (1934). La genese de l'Hypothese: Etude experimentelle. Archiv de Psychologie, 24, 1–154.

Clark, H. (1996). *Using language.* Cambridge: Cambridge University Press.

Clark, R. E., & Estes, F. (1996). Cognitive task analysis for training. *International Journal of Educational Research, 25,* 403–417.

Clark, W. L. G. (1954). The anatomy of work. In W. F. Floyd & A. T. Welford (Eds.), *Symposium on human factors in equipment design.* London: Lewis.

Cleaves, D. A. (1987). Cognitive biases and corrective techniques: Proposals for improving elicitation procedures for knowledge-based systems. *International Journal of Man–Machine Studies, 27,* 155–166.

Clegg, C. W. (2000). Sociotechnical principles for system design. *Applied Ergonomics, 31,* 463–477.

Clegg, C. W., Axtell, C. M., Damodaran, L., Farbey, B., Hull, R., Lloydjones, R., et al. (1997). Information technology: A study of performance and the role of human and organizational factors. *Ergonomics, 40,* 851–871.

Clot, Y. (Ed.). (1996). *The histories of work psychology: A multidisciplinary approach.* Toulouse, France: Octares.

Cochran, E. L., Bloom, C. P., & Bullemer, P. T. (1990). Increasing end-user acceptance of an expert system by using multiple experts: Case studies in knowledge acquisition. In C. R. Westphal & K. L. McGraw (Eds.), *Readings in knowledge acquisition: Current practices and trends* (pp. 73–89). London: Ellis Horwood.

Coderre, S., Mandin, H., Harasym, P. H., & Fick, G. H. (2003). Diagnostic reasoning strategies and diagnostic success. *Medical Education, 37,* 695–703.

Codesman, A. H., & Wagner, A. R. (1996). *The lessons of modern war, Vol. 4: The Gulf War.* Boulder, CO: Westview.

Cofer, C. N. (Ed.) (1961). *Verbal learning and behavior.* New York: McGraw-Hill.

Coffey, J. W. (1999). *Institutional memory preservation at NASA-Glenn Research Center* (Tech. Rep.). Cleveland, OH: NASA-Glenn Research Center.

Cohen, G. (1989). *Memory in the real world*. Mahwah, NJ: Erlbaum.

Cohen, M. S. (1993a). The bottom line: Naturalistic decision aiding. In G. Klein, J. Orasanu, R. Calderwood, & C. E. Zsambok (Eds.), *Decision making in action: Models and methods* (pp. 265–269). Norwood, NJ: Ablex.

Cohen, M. S. (1993b). The naturalistic basis of decision biases. In G. Klein, J. Orasanu, R. Calderwood, & C. E. Zsambok (Eds.), *Decision making in action: Models and methods* (pp. 51–102). Norwood, NJ: Ablex.

Cohen, M. S. (1993c). Three paradigms for viewing decision making processes. In G. Klein, J. Orasanu, R. Calderwood, & C. E. Zsambok (Eds.), *Decision making in action: Models and methods* (pp. 36–50). Norwood, NJ: Ablex.

Cohen, M. S., Freeman, J. T., & Wolf, S. P. (1996). Metarecognition in time-stressed decision making: Recognizing, critiquing, and correcting. *Human Factors, 38,* 206–219.

Cohen, P. R., & Howe, A. E. (1989). Toward AI research methodology: Three case studies in evaluation. *IEEE Transactions on Systems, Man, and Cybernetics, 19,* 634–646.

Cohen, P. R., & Levesque, H. J. (1991, March). *Teamwork* (Technote 504). Menlo Park, CA: SRI International.

Cole, M., Engeström, Y., & Vasquez, O. (1997). *Mind, culture, and activity*. Cambridge: Cambridge University Press.

Collins, H. M. (1981). What is TRASP: The radical programme as a methodological imperative. *Philosophy of the Social Sciences, 11,* 215–224.

Collins, H. M. (1983). An empirical relativist programme in the sociology of scientific knowledge. In K. D. Knorr-Cetina & M. Mulkay (Eds.), *Science observed: Perspectives on the social study of science* (pp. 85–114). London: Sage.

Collins, H. M. (1984). Concepts and methods of participatory fieldwork. In C. Bell & H. Roberts (Eds.), *Social researching* (pp. 54–69). Henley-on-Thames: Routledge.

Collins, H. M. (1985). *Changing order: Replication and induction in scientific practice*. Beverly Hills, CA: Sage.

Collins, H. M. (1992). *Artificial experts: Social knowledge and intelligent machines*. Cambridge, MA: MIT Press.

Collins, H. M. (1993). The structure of knowledge. *Social Research, 60,* 95–116.

Collins, H. M. (1996). Embedded or embodied: Hubert Dreyfus's What computers still can't do. *Artificial Intelligence, 80,* 99–117.

Collins, H. M. (1997). RAT-tale: Sociology's contribution to understanding human and machine cognition. In P. J. Feltovich, K. M. Ford, & R. R. Hoffman (Eds.), *Expertise in context* (pp. 293–311). Cambridge, MA: MIT Press.

Collins, H. M. (2004). *Gravity's shadow: The search for gravitational waves*. Chicago: University of Chicago Press.

Collins, H. M., Evans, R., Ribeiro, R., & Hall, M. (2006). Experiments with interactional expertise. *Studies in the History and Philosophy of Science, 37A,* 656–674.

Coltheart, V., & Walsh, P. (1988). Expert knowledge and semantic memory. In M. M. Gruneberg, P. E. Morris, & R. N. Sykes (Eds.), *Practical aspects of memory: Current research and issues, Vol. 1* (pp. 459–465). Chichester, England: John Wiley.

Cook, R. I. (1998, May). Being bumpable. *Proceedings of the Fourth International Conference on Naturalistic Decision Making*. Fairborn, OH: Klein Associates Inc.

Cook, R. I. (2006). Being bumpable: Consequences of resource saturation and near-saturation for cognitive demands on ICU practitioners In D. D. Woods & E. Hollnagel (Eds.), *Joint cognitive systems: Patterns in cognitive systems engineering* (pp. 23–35). Boca Raton, FL: CRC Press.

Cook, R. I., & Woods, D. D. (1994). Operating at the sharp end: The complexity of human error. In M. S. Bogner (Ed.), *Human error in medicine* (pp. 255–310). Hillsdale, NJ: Erlbaum.

Cook, R. I., & Woods, D. D. (1996). Implications of automation surprises in aviation for the future of total intravenous anesthesia (TIVA). *Journal of Clinical Anesthesia, 8,* 29–37.

Cook, R. I., Woods, D. D., & Miller, C. (1998). *A tale of two stories: Contrasting views of patient safety.* Chicago: National Patient Safety Foundation at AMA.

Cook, T. D., & Campbell, D. T. (1979). *Quasi-experimentation: Design and analysis issues for field settings.* New York: Rand McNally.

Cooke, N. J. (1992). Modeling human expertise in expert systems. In R. R. Hoffman (Ed.), *The psychology of expertise: Cognitive research and empirical AI* (pp. 29–60). Mahwah, NJ: Erlbaum.

Cooke, N. J. (1994). Varieties of knowledge elicitation techniques. *International Journal of Human–Computer Studies, 41,* 801–849.

Cooke, N. J., & Durso, F. (2007). *In the aftermath of tragedy: Cognitive engineering solutions.* Boca Raton, FL: CRC Press.

Cooke, N. J., & Rowe, A. L. (1994). Evaluating mental model elicitation methods. In *Proceedings of the Human Factors and Ergonomics Society 38th Annual Meeting* (pp. 261–265). Santa Monica, CA: Human Factors and Ergonomics Society.

Cooke, N. J., Salas, E., Cannon-Bowers, J. A., & Stout, R. J. (2000). Measuring team knowledge. *Human Factors, 42,* 151–173.

Cooke, N. J., Salas, E., Kiekel, P. A., & Bell, B. (2004). Advances in measuring team cognition. In E. Salas & S. M. Fiore (Eds.), *Team cognition: Understanding the factors that drive process and performance* (pp. 83–106). Washington, DC: American Psychological Association.

Cooke, N. J., Gorman, J. C., Pedersen, H., & Bell, B. (2007). Distributed mission environments: Effects of geographical distribution on team cognition, process, & performance. In S. M. Fiore & E. Salas (Eds.), *Toward a science of distributed learning and training* (pp. 147–167). Washington, DC: American Psychological Association.

Cooke, N. J., & McDonald, J. E. (1986). A formal methodology for acquiring and representing expert knowledge. *Proceedings of the IEEE, 74,* 1422–1430.

Cooke, N. J., & McDonald, J. E. (1987). The application of psychological scaling techniques to knowledge elicitation for knowledge-based systems. *International Journal of Man–Machine Studies, 26,* 533–550.

Coover, J. E. (1923). A method of teaching typewriting based on a psychological analysis of expert typists. In *Proceedings of the National Education Association* (pp. 561–567). Washington, DC: National Education Association.

Copley, F. B. (1923). *Frederick W. Taylor: Father of scientific management.* New York: Harper and Brothers.

Cordingley, S. (1989). Knowledge elicitation techniques for knowledge-based systems. In D. Diaper (Ed.), *Knowledge elicitation: Principles, techniques, and applications* (pp. 89–175). Chichester, England: Ellis-Horwood.

Coughlin, L. D., & Patel, V. L. (1987). Processing of critical information by physicians and medical students. *Journal of Medical Information, 62,* 818–828.

Coulson, R. L., Feltovich, P. J., & Spiro, R. J. (1989). Foundations of a misunderstanding of the ultrastructural basis of myocardial failure: A reciprocation network of oversimplifications [Special issue]. *Journal of Medicine and Philosophy, 14,* 109–146.

Coulson, R. L., Feltovich, P. J., & Spiro, R. J. (1997). Cognitive flexibility in medicine: An application to the recognition and understanding of hypertension. *Advances in Health Sciences Education, 2,* 141–161.

Couvé, R. (1925). *Der Prüfungswagen der Psychotechnischen Versuchsstelle bei der Reichs-bahndirektion Berlin.* [Examination Papers for the Psychotechnical experimental station at the administration office of the State railroad of Berlin]. *Industrielle Psychotechnik, [Industrial Psychotechnics],2,* 382–383.

Cox, P. A., & Balick, M. J. (1994, June). The ethnobotanical approach to drug discovery. *Scientific American,* 82–87.

Coyle, P. E. (1999, May). *Simulation based acquisition for information technology.* Paper presented at the 1999 Academia, Industry, Government Crosstalk Conference, Washington, DC.

Craik, K. J. W. (1944a). *Handwheel designs in C.R.S.I. mock-up* (Report 44/164). Cambridge, England: Applied Psychology Unit, Medical Research Council.

Craik, K. J. W. (1944b). Medical Research Council Unit for Applied Psychology. *Nature, 154,* 476–479.

Craik, K. J. W. (1947). Theory of the human operator in control systems: 1. The operator as engineering system. *British Journal of Psychology, 38,* 56–61.

Craik, F. I. M., & Lockhart, R. S. (1972). Levels of processing: A framework for memory research. *Journal of Verbal Learning and Verbal Behavior, 11,* 671–684.

Crandall, B. (1989). A comparative study of think-aloud and critical decision knowledge elicitation methods. *SIGART Newsletter, 108,* 144–146.

Crandall, B., & Calderwood, R. (1989). *Clinical assessment skills of experienced neonatal intensive care nurses.* Yellow Springs, OH: Klein Associates.

Crandall, B., & Gamblian, V. (1991). *Guide to early sepsis assessment in the NICU.* Yellow Springs, OH: Klein Associates.

Crandall, B., & Getchell-Reiter, K. (1993). Critical decision method: A technique for eliciting concrete assessment indicators from the intuition of NICU nurses. *Advances in Nursing Science, 16,* 42–51.

Crandall, B., & Klein, G. (1987a). *Critical cues for MI and cardiogenic shock symptoms.* Yellow Springs, OH: Klein Associates.

Crandall, B., & Klein, G. (1987b). *Key components of MIS performance.* Yellow Springs, OH: Klein Associates.

Crandall, B., Klein, G., & Hoffman, R. R. (2006). *Working minds: A practitioner's guide to cognitive task analysis.* Cambridge, MA: MIT Press.

Crane, G. W. (1938). *Psychology applied.* Chicago: Northwestern University Press.

Creativity and Cognition Studios. (Ed.). (2003). *Expertise in design.* Sydney, Australia: Creativity and Cognition Studios, University of Technology. Retrieved September 29, 2006, from http://research.it.uts.edu.au/creative/design/

Cronbach, L. (1953). *A consideration of information theory and utility theory as tools for psychometric problems* (Report to the Bureau of Educational Research). Urbana, IL: University of Illinois.

Cross, N. (2003). The expertise of exceptional designers. In Creativity and Cognition Studios (Ed.), *Expertise in design.* Sydney, Australia: Creativity and Cognition Studios, University of Technology. Retrieved September 29, 2006, from http://research.it.uts.edu.au/creative/design/

Cross, N. (2004). Expertise in design: An overview. *Design Studies, 25,* 427–441.

Cross, N., Christiaans, H., & Dorst, K. (Eds.) (1996). *Analyzing design activity.* Chichester, England: Wiley.

Crossman, E. (1956, February). Perception study: A complement to motion study. *The Manager*, pp. 141–145.

Crutcher, R. J. (1992). The effects of practice on retrieval of vocabulary learned using the keyword method. Doctoral dissertation. University of Colorado, Boulder, CO.

Crutcher, R. J. (1994). Telling what we know: The use of verbal report methodologies in psychological research. *Psychological Science, 5*, 241–244.

Cullen, J., & Bryman, A. (1988). The knowledge acquisition bottleneck: Time for reassessment? *Expert Systems, 5*, 216–225.

Cummings, M. L. (2005). *The applicability of CWA to command and control decision support*. Manuscript in preparation.

Cummings, M. L. (2006). Can CWA inform the design of networked intelligent systems? In J. Plats (Ed.), *Proceedings of Moving Autonomy Forward 2006* [CD]. Lincoln, UK: Muretex.

Cummings, M. L., & Guerlain, S. (2003). *The tactical tomahawk conundrum: Designing decision support systems for revolutionary domains*. Paper presented at the IEEE Systems, Man, and Cybernetics Society Conference, Washington, DC.

Cummings, T. G. (1994). Self-regulating work groups. In W.L. French, C. Bell, & R. A. Zawacki (Eds.), *Organizational development and transformation* (pp. 268–277). Burr Ridge, IL: Irwin.

Cummings, T. G., & Worley, C. G. (1993). *Organizational development and change*. Minneapolis, MN: West.

Daniellou, F. (1985). *La modélisation ergonomique de l'actitivé de ravail dans la conception industrielle: Le cas des industries de processus continu*. Unpublished doctoral thesis, Conservatoire National des Arts et Métiers, Paris.

Davenport, T. H., & Prusak, L. (1998). *Working knowledge: How organizations manage what they know*. Cambridge, MA: Harvard Business School Press.

Davis, L. E. (1982). Organizational design. In G. Salvendy (Ed.), *Handbook of industrial engineering* (pp. 2.1.1–2.1.29). New York: Wiley.

Dawes, R. (1979). The robust beauty of improper linear models in decision making. *American Psychologist, 34*, 571–582.

Dawes, R. M., & Corrigan, B. (1974). Linear models in decision making. *Psychological Bulletin, 81*, 95–106.

Dawson, V. L., Zeitz, C. M., & Wright, J. C. (1989). Expert-novice differences in person perception: Evidence of experts' sensitivity to the organization of behavior. *Social Cognition, 7*, 1–30.

Dawson-Saunders, B., Feltovich, P. J., Coulson, R. L., & Steward, D. E. (1990). A survey of medical school teachers to identify basic biomedical concepts medical students should understand. *Academic Medicine, 7*, 448–454.

Day, S. C., Norcini, J. J., Webster, G. D., Viner, E. D., & Chirico, A. M. (1988). The effect of changes in medical knowledge on examination performance at the time of recertification. In *Proceedings of the 27th Annual Conference on Research on Medical Education* (pp. 139–144). Washington, DC: Association of American Medical Colleges.

Dee-Lucas, D., & Larkin, J. H. (1986). Novice strategies for processing scientific texts. *Discourse Processes, 9*, 329–354.

Deffner, G., & Kempkensteffen, J. (1989, November). "The effect of different instructions to think aloud." Paper presented at the meeting of the Psychonomic Society, Atlanta, Georgia.

De Garmo, C. (1895). *Herbart and the Herbartians*. New York: Scribner.

de Greef, P., & Breuker, J. (1985). A case study in structured knowledge acquisition. In A. Joshi (Ed.), *Proceedings of the 9th International Joint Conference on Artificial Intelligence* (pp. 390–392). Los Altos, CA: Kaufman.

de Greef, P., Breuker, J., Schreiber, G., & Wielemaker, J. (1988). StatCons: Knowledge acquisition in a complex domain. In *ECAI-88: Proceedings of the 8th European Workshop on Artificial Intelligence*. London: Pitmann Publishing.

de Greef, P., Breuker, J., & Wielinga, B. (1986). *Statcons-1 Design Document. ESPRIT Deliverable E2.2*. Amsterdam: University of Amsterdam.

de Groot, A. D. (1945). *Het denken van der schaker*. [The thinking of the chess player.] Unpublished doctoral thesis, University of Amsterdam.

de Groot, A. D. (1965). *Thought and choice in chess*. The Hague: Mouton.

De Keyser, V. (1991) Work analysis in French language ergonomics: Origins and current research trends. *Ergonomics, 34*, 653–669.

De Keyser, V. (1992). Why field studies? In M. G. Helander & N. Nagamachi (Eds.), *Design for manufacturability: A systems approach to concurrent engineering and ergonomics* (pp. 305–316). London: Taylor & Francis.

De Keyser, V. (1997). "Shallow" versus "in-depth" work analysis in human-centered design. In J. Flanagan, T. Huang, P. Jones, & S. Kasif (Eds.), *Human-centered systems: Information, interactivity and intelligence* (pp. 261–266). Washington, DC: National Science Foundation.

De Keyser, V., Decortis, F., & Van Daele, A. (1988). The approach of Francophone ergonomy: Studying new technologies. In V. De Keyser, T. Qvale, B. Wilpert, & S. A. Ruiz-Quintallina (Eds.), *The meaning of work and technological options* (pp. 148–163). New York: Wiley.

De Keyser, V., & Samercay, R. (1998). Activity theory, situated action and simulators. *Le Travail Humain, 61*, 305–312.

Dekker, S. W. W. (2005). *Ten questions about human error*. Mahwah, NJ: Erlbaum.

Dekker, S. W., & Nyce, J. M. (2004). How can ergonomics influence design? Moving from research findings to future systems. *Ergonomics, 47*, 1624–1639.

Dekker, S. W. A., Nyce, J. M., & Hoffman, R. R. (2003, March–April). From contextual inquiry to designable futures: What do we need to get there? *IEEE Intelligent Systems*, pp. 74–77.

Dekker, S. W. A., & Woods, D. D. (1999a). To intervene or not to intervene: The dilemma of management by exception. *Cognition, Technology, and Work, 1*, 86–96.

Dekker, S. and Woods, D.D. (1999b). Extracting data from the future: assessment and certification of envisioned systems. In S. Dekker and E. Hollnagel (Eds.), *Coping with computers in the cockpit* (7-27). London: Ashgate.

Dember, W. N., & Warm, J. S. (1979). *Psychology of perception* (2nd ed.). New York: Holt, Rinehart and Winston.

Descartes, R. (1637/1964). Discourse on method. In *Descartes: Philosophical essays* (L. J. Lafleur, Trans.). Upper Saddle River, NJ: Prentice Hall.

Dewey, J. (1933). *How we think*. Boston: D. C. Heath.

Dewey, J. (1938). *Logic: The theory of inquiry*. New York: Henry Holt and Company.

Dewey, J. (1974). *John Dewey on education: Selected writings* (R. D. Archambault, Ed.). Chicago: University of Chicago Press.

Dhaliwal, J. S., & Benbasat, I. (1990). A framework for the comparative evaluation of knowledge acquisition tools and techniques. *Knowledge Acquisition, 2*, 145–166.

Diamond, J. (1997, April). The curse of QWERTY. *Discover Magazine*, pp. 34–42.

Diaper, D. (Ed.). (1989a). *Knowledge acquisition: Principles, techniques, and applications*. New York: Wiley.

Diaper, D. (Ed.). (1989b). *Task analysis for human–computer interaction*. London: Ellis Horwood/Halsttead Press.

Diaper, D., & Stanton, N. (Eds.). (2004). *The handbook of task analysis for human–computer interaction*. Mahwah, NJ: Erlbaum.

Dietze, A. G. (1954). Psychology in industry: Work and efficiency. In J. S. Gray (Ed.), *Psychology applied to human affairs* (pp. 330–364). New York: McGraw-Hill.

Dijksterhuis, E. J. (1987). *Archimedes*. Princeton, NJ: Princeton University Press.

Dillard, J. F., & Mutchler, J. F. (1987). Expertise in assessing solvency problems. *Expert Systems, 4,* 170–179.

Dino, G. A., & Shanteau, J. (1984, November). "What skills do managers consider important for effective decision making?" Paper presented at the meeting of the Psychonomic Society, San Antonio, TX.

Dixon, T. R., & Horton, D. L. (Eds.). (1968). *Verbal behavior and general behavior theory*. Englewood Cliffs, NJ: Prentice Hall.

Dockeray, F. C., & Isaacs, S. (1921). Psychological research in aviation in Italy, France, England, and the American expeditionary forces. *Comparative Psychology, 1,* 115–148.

Dodson, D. C. (1989). Interaction with knowledge systems through connection diagrams: Please adjust your diagrams. In B. Kelly & A. L. Rector (Eds.), *Research and development in expert systems: V* (pp. 33–46). Cambridge: Cambridge University Press.

Dominguez, C., Flach, J., Lake, P., McKellar, D., & Dunn, M. (in press). The conversion decision in laparoscopic surgery: Knowing your limits and limiting your risks. In J. Shanteau, K. Smith, & P. Johnson (Eds.), *Psychological explorations of competent decision making*. New York: Cambridge University Press.

Dorst, K. (2003). The problem of design problems. In Creativity and Cognition Studios (Ed.), *Expertise in design*. Sydney, Australia: Creativity and Cognition Studios, University of Technology. Retrieved September 29, 2006, from http://research.it.uts.edu.au/creative/design/

Drever, J. (1921). *The psychology of industry*. New York: E. P. Dutton.

Dreyfus, S. E. (1989, Spring). Presentation. *The AI Magazine,* pp. 64–67.

Dreyfus, H., & Dreyfus, S. E. (1986). *Mind over machine*. New York: Free Press.

Drury, C. G., Paramore, B., Van Cott, H., Grey, S. M., & Corlett, E. N. (1987). Task analysis. In G. Salvendy (Ed.), *Handbook of human factors* (pp. 370–401). New York: Wiley.

Dulany, D.E., Carlson, R. A., & Dewey, G. I. (1984). A case of syntactical learning and judgment: How conscious and how abstract? *Journal of Experimental Psychology: General, 113,* 541–555.

Dunbar, K. (1993). Concept discovery in a scientific domain. *Cognitive Science, 17,* 397–434.

Dunbar, K. (1995). How scientists really reason: Scientific reasoning in real-world laboratories. In R. J. Sternberg & J. Davidson (Eds.), *Mechanisms of insight* (pp. 365–395). Cambridge, MA: MIT Press.

Dunbar, K. (1999). Scientific thinking and its development. In R. Wilson & F. Keil (Eds.), *The MIT encyclopedia of cognitive science* (pp. 730–733). Cambridge, MA: MIT Press.

Dunbar, K. (2000). What scientific thinking reveals about the nature of cognition. In K. Crowley, C. D. Schunn, & T. Okada (Eds.), *Designing for science: Implications from everyday, classroom, and professional settings* (pp. 115–140). Hillsdale, NJ: Erlbaum.

Dunbar, K. (2001). The analogical paradox: Why analogy is so easy in naturalistic settings, yet so difficult in the psychology laboratory. In D. Gentner, K. J. Holyoak, & B. Kokinov (Eds.), *Analogy: Perspectives from cognitive science* (pp. 313–334). Cambridge, MA: MIT Press.

Dunbar, K., & Blanchette, I. (2001). The in vivo/in vitro approach to cognition: The case of analogy. *Trends in Cognitive Sciences, 5,* 334–339.

Dunbar, K., & Fugelsang, J. (2005a). Causal thinking in science: How scientists and students interpret the unexpected. In M. E. Gorman, R. D. Tweney, D. Gooding, & A. Kincannon (Eds.), *Scientific and technical thinking* (pp. 57–79). Mahwah, NJ: Erlbaum.

Dunbar, K., & Fugelsang, J. (2005b). Scientific thinking and reasoning. In K. J. Holyoak & R. Morrison (Eds.), *Cambridge handbook of thinking and reasoning* (pp. 705–726). Cambridge: Cambridge University Press.

Dunbar, K., & Fugelsang, J. (2006). Problem solving and reasoning. In E. E. Smith & S. M. Kosslyn (Eds.), *Cognitive psychology: Mind and brain* (pp. 411–450). New York: Prentice Hall.

Duncker, K. (1945). On problem solving. *Psychological Monographs, 58*(270), 1–113. (L. S. Lees, Trans.)

Dunlap, K. (1919). Psychological research in aviation. *Science, 49,* 94–97.

Dunlap, K. (1930). Response in psychology. In C. Murchinson (Ed.), Psychologies of 1930 (pp. 309–323). Worcester, MA: Clark University Press.

Dunlap, K. (1932). Knight Dunlap. In C. Murchison (Ed.), *A history of psychology in auto-biography* (Vol. 2, pp. 35–61). Worcester, MA: Clark University Press.

Durkheim, É. (1915). *The elementary forms of the religious life.* New York: Macmillan.

Dvorak, A., Merrick, N. I., Deals, W. L., & Ford, G. C. (1936). *Typewriting behavior.* New York: American Book.

Easter, J. R. (1991). The role of the operator and control room design. In J. White & D. Lanning (Eds.), *European nuclear instrumentation and controls* (Report PB92-100197). Baltimore: World Technology Evaluation Center, Loyola College.

Eastman Kodak Company. (1983). *Ergonomic design for people at work.* New York: Van Nostrand Reinhold.

Ebbinghaus, H. (1885). *On memory: A contribution to experimental psychology* (H. Ruger & C. Busenius, Trans.). New York: Teacher's College, Columbia University.

Ebbinghaus, H. (1908). *Psychology: An elementary text* (M. Meyer, Trans.). Boston: D. C. Heath.

Eccles, D. W., Walsh, S. E., & Ingledew, D. K. (2002). A grounded theory of expert cognition in orienteering. *Journal of Sport and Exercise Psychology, 24,* 68–88.

Edmondson, A. C., Bohmer, R. M., & Pisano, G. P. (2001). Disrupted routines: Team learning and new technology implementation in hospitals. *Administrative Science Quarterly, 46,* 685–716.

Edwards, J., & Fraser, K. (1983). Concept-maps as reflectors of conceptual understanding. *Research in Science Education, 13,* 19–26.

Edwards, W. (1965a). Men and computers. In R. M. Gagné (Ed.), *Psychological principles in system development* (pp. 75–113). New York: Holt, Rinehart and Winston.

Edwards, W. (1965b). Optimal strategies for seeking information: Models for statistics, choice reaction time, and human information processing. *Journal of Mathematical Psychology, 2,* 312–329.

Egan, D. E., & Schwartz, B. J. (1979). Chunking in the recall of symbolic drawings. *Memory & Cognition, 7,* 149–158.

Eggen, D. (2005, June 6). *FBI pushed ahead with troubled software.* Retrieved from Washingtonpost.com

Eggleston, R. G. (2003). Work-centered design: A cognitive engineering approach to system design. In *Proceedings of the Human Factors and Ergonomics Society 47th Annual Meeting* (pp. 263–267). Santa Monica, CA: Human Factors and Ergonomics Society.

Eggleston, R. G., & Whitaker, R. D. (2002). Work centered support system design: Using organizing frames to reduce work complexity. In *Proceedings of the Human Factors and Ergonomics Society 46th Annual Meeting* (pp. 265–269). Santa Monica, CA: Human Factors and Ergonomics Society.

Eggleston, R. G., Young, M. J., & Whitaker, R. D. (2000). Work-centered support system technology: A new interface client technology for the battlespace infosphere. In *Proceedings of the IEEE National Aerospace Electronics Conference (NAECON), 2000.* Retrieved April 2, 2007, from http://ieeexplore.ieee.org/Xplore/dynhome.jsp

Ehn, P. (1988). *Work-oriented design of computer artifacts.* Stockholm, Sweden: Arbetslivcentrum.

Ehn, P. (1997). Seven "classical" questions about Human Centered Design. In J. Flanagan, T. Huang, P. Jones, & S. Kasif (Eds.), *Human-centered systems: Information, interactivity and intelligence* (pp. 266–268). Washington, DC: National Science Foundation.

Ehret, B. D., & Gray, W. D. (2000). Contending with complexity: Developing and using a scaled world in applied cognitive research. *Human Factors, 42,* 8–23.

Ehrlich, K. (1999). Designing groupware applications: A work-centered design approach. In M. Beaudoin-Lafon (Ed.), *Computer supported co-operative work* (pp. 1–24). New York: Wiley.

Einhorn, H. J. (1972). Expert measurement and mechanical combination. *Organizational Behavior and Human Performance, 7,* 86–106.

Einhorn, H. J. (1974). Expert judgment: Some necessary conditions and an example. *Journal of Applied Psychology, 59,* 562–571.

Elieson, S. W., & Papa, F. J. (1994). The effects of various knowledge formats on diagnostic performance. *Academic Medicine, 69,* S81–S83.

Elm, W., Potter, S. S., Tittle, J., Woods, D. D., Grossman, J., & Patterson, E. S. (2005). Finding decision support requirements for effective intelligence analysis tools. In *Proceedings of the Human Factors and Ergonomics Society 49th Annual Meeting* (pp. 297–301). Santa Monica, CA: Human Factors and Ergonomics Society.

Elmore, W. K., Dunlap, R. D., & Campbell, R. H. (2001). Features of a distributed intelligent architecture for unmanned air vehicle operations. In *Proceedings of the 2001 Unmanned Systems International* (pp. 1–15). Arlington, VA: AUVSI.

Elstein, A. S., Shulman, L. S., & Sprafka, S. A. (1978). *Medical problem solving: An analysis of clinical reasoning.* Cambridge, MA: Harvard University Press.

Endsley, M. R. (1988). Situation Awareness Global Assessment Technique (SAGAT). In *Proceedings of the National Aerospace and Electronics Conference* (pp. 789–795). New York: IEEE.

Endsley, M. R. (1990). Predictive utility of an objective measure of situation awareness. In *Proceedings of the Human Factors and Ergonomics Society 34th Annual Meeting* (pp. 41–45). Santa Monica, CA: Human Factors Society.

Endsley, M. R. (1993). A survey of situation awareness requirements in air-to-air combat fighters. *International Journal of Aviation Psychology, 3*(2), 157–168.

Endsley, M. R. (1995a). Measurement of situation awareness in dynamic systems. *Human Factors, 37,* 65–84.

Endsley, M. R. (1995b). Toward a theory of situation awareness in dynamic systems. *Human Factors, 37,* 32–64.

Endsley, M. R. (1997). The role of situation awareness in naturalistic decision making. In C. E. Zsambok & G. Klein (Eds.), *Naturalistic decision making* (pp. 269–284). Mahwah, NJ: Erlbaum.

Endsley, M. R. (2001). "Designing for situation awareness in complex systems." Invited presentation in *Proceedings of the Second International Workshop on Symbiosis of Humans, Artifacts and the Environment* (pp. 175–190). Kyoto: Japan Society for the Promotion of Science.

Endsley, M., Bolté, B., & Jones, D. G. (2003). *Designing for situation awareness.* New York: Taylor & Francis.

Endsley, M. R., & Garland, D. J. (Eds.). (2000). *Situation awareness analysis and measurement*. Mahwah, NJ: Erlbaum.

Endsley, M. R., & Hoffman, R. (2002, November/December). The Sacagawea Principle. *IEEE Intelligent Systems*, pp. 80–85.

Entin, E. E., & Serfaty, D. (1999). Adaptive team coordination. *Human Factors, 41*, 321–325.

Ericsson, K. A. (2006a). Introduction. In K. A. Ericsson, N. Charness, P. Feltovich, & R. Hoffman (Eds.), *Cambridge handbook on expertise and expert performance* (pp. 3–20). New York: Cambridge University Press.

Ericsson, K. A. (2006b). Protocol analysis and expert thought: Concurrent verbalizations of thinking during experts' performance on representative tasks. In K. A. Ericsson, N. Charness, P. Feltovich, & R. Hoffman (Eds.), *Cambridge handbook on expertise and expert performance* (pp. 223–242). New York: Cambridge University Press.

Ericsson, K. A., Charness, N., Feltovich, P. J., & Hoffman, R. R. (Eds.). (2006). *Cambridge handbook on expertise and expert performance*. New York: Cambridge University Press.

Ericsson, K. A., Krampe, R. Th., & Tesch-Römer, C. (1993). The role of deliberate practice in the acquisition of expert performance. *Psychological Review, 100*, 363–406.

Ericsson, K. A., & Lehman, A. C. (1996). Expert and exceptional performance: Evidence on maximal adaptations on task constraints. *Annual Review of Psychology, 47*, 273–305.

Ericsson, K. A., & Polson, P. G. (1988). A cognitive analysis of exceptional memory for restaurant orders. In M. T. H. Chi, R. Glaser, & M. J. Farr (Eds.), *The nature of expertise* (pp. 23–70). Hillsdale, NJ: Erlbaum.

Ericsson, K. A., & Simon, H. (1980). Verbal reports as data. *Psychological Review, 87*, 215–251.

Ericcson, K. A., & Simon, H. A. (1984). *Protocol analysis: Verbal reports as data* (1st. ed.). Cambridge, MA: MIT Press.

Ericsson, K. A., & Simon, H. (1993). *Protocol analysis: Verbal reports as data* (2nd ed.). Cambridge, MA: MIT Press.

Ericsson, K. A., & Smith, J. (1991a). Prospects and limits in the empirical study of expertise: An introduction. In K. A. Ericsson & J. Smith (Eds.), *Toward a general theory of expertise* (pp. 1–38). Cambridge: Cambridge University Press.

Ericsson, K. A., & Smith, J. (Eds.). (1991b). *Toward a general theory of expertise*. Cambridge: Cambridge University Press.

Erikson, F., & Schultz, J. (1982). *The counselor as gatekeeper*. New York: Academic Press.

Essens, P., Fallasen, J., McCann, C., Cannon-Bowers, J., & Dorfel, G. (1995). *COADE-A framework for cognitive analysis, design, & evaluation* (Tech. Rep. AC/243 of the Panel on Decision Aids in command and Control). Brussels, Belgium: NATO Defence Research Group.

European Coal and Steel Community. (1976, October 26–27). *Human factors evaluation at Hoogovens No. 2 Hot Strip Mill*. Report of the meeting Ijmuiden (Amsterdam, NL). Secretariat of Community Ergonomics Action, European Coal and Steel Community, Luxembourg.

Eva, K. W. (2003). On the generality of specificity. *Medical Education, 37*, 587–588.

Eva, K. W. (2005). What every teacher needs to know about clinical reasoning. *Medical Education, 39*, 98–106.

Eva, K. W., Neville, A. J., & Norman, G. R. (1998). Exploring the etiology of content specificity: Factors influencing analogical transfer and problem solving. *Academic Medicine, 73*, S1–S6.

Eva, K. W., Norman, G. R., & Brooks, L. R. (2002). Forward reasoning as a hallmark of expertise in medicine: Logical, psychological, phenomenological inconsistencies. *Advances in Psychological Research, 8*, 25–40.

Evans, A.W., Jentsch, F., Hitt, J. M., Bowers, C. A., & Salas, E. (2001). Mental model assessments: Is there a convergence among different methods? In *Proceedings of the Human Factors and Ergonomics Society 45th Annual Meeting*, pp. 293–296. Santa Monica, CA: Human Factors and Ergonomics Society.

Evans, D. A., & Patel, V. L. (1989). *Cognitive science in medicine: Biomedical modeling.* Cambridge, MA: MIT Press.

Evans, J. (1988). The knowledge elicitation problem: A psychological perspective. *Behavior and Information Technology, 7,* 111–130.

Evetts, J., Mieg, H. A., & Felt, U. (2006). Professionalization, scientific expertise, and elitism: A sociological perspective. In K. A. Ericsson, N. Charness, P. Feltovich, & R. Hoffman (Eds.), *Cambridge handbook on expertise and expert performance* (pp. 105–126). New York: Cambridge University Press.

Fairchild, M. (1930). Skilled specialization. *Personality Journal, 9,* 28–71, 128–183.

Falkenhainer, B., Forbus, K. D., & Gentner, D. (1990). The structure-mapping engine: Algorithm and examples. *Artificial Intelligence, 41,* 1–63.

Farmer, E. (1921). *Time and motion study* (Report No. 14, Industrial Fatigue Research Board). London: His Majesty's Stationery Office.

Farmer, E., & Chambers, E. G. (1929). *A study of personal qualities in accident proneness and proficiency* (Report No. 55, Industrial Health Research Board). London: His Majesty's Stationery Office.

Feigenbaum, E.A. (1977). The art of AI. In *Proceedings of the Fifth International Joint Conference on Artificial Intelligence.* New York: International Joint Conferences on Artificial Intelligence.

Feldman, J. (2003). The simplicity principle in human category learning. *Current Directions in Psychological Science, 12,* 227–232.

Feltovich, P. J. (1981). Knowledge-based components of expertise in medical diagnosis. Pittsburgh, PA: University of Pittsburgh.

Feltovich, P. J., Bradshaw, J. M., Jeffers, R., Suri, N., & Uszok, A. (2004). Social order and adaptability in animal and human cultures as analogues for agent communities: Toward a policy-based approach. In A. Omacini, P. Petta, & J. Pitt (Eds.), *Engineering societies in the agents world IV* (Lecture Notes in Computer Science Series, pp. 21–48). Heidelberg, Germany: Springer-Verlag.

Feltovich, P., Coulson, R. L., & Spiro, R. J. (2001). Learners' (mis)understanding of important and difficult concepts: A challenge to smart machines in education. In K. D. Forbus & P. J. Feltovich (Eds.), *Smart machines in education.* Menlo Park, CA: AAAI/MIT Press.

Feltovich, P. J., Hoffman, R. R., & Woods, D. P. (2004, May–June). Keeping it too simple: How the reductive tendency affects cognitive engineering. *IEEE Intelligent Systems,* pp. 90–95.

Feltovich, P., Johnson, P., Moller, J., & Swanson, D. (1984). LCS: The role and development of medical knowledge in diagnostic expertise. In W. Clancey & E. Shortliffe (Eds.), *Readings in medical artificial intelligence: The first decade* (pp. 275–319). Reading, MA: Addison-Wesley.

Feltovich, P. J., Prietula, M. J., & Ericsson, K. A. (2006). Studies of expertise from psychological perspectives. In K. A. Ericsson, N. Charness, P. Feltovich, & R. Hoffman (Eds.), *Cambridge handbook on expertise and expert performance* (pp. 41–68). New York: Cambridge University Press.

Feltovich, P. J., Spiro, R. J., & Coulson, R. L. (1989). The nature of conceptual understanding in biomedicine: The deep structure of complex ideas and the development of misconceptions. In D. A. Evans & V. L. Patel (Eds.), *Cognitive science in medicine* (pp. 115–171). Cambridge, MA: MIT Press.

Feltovich, P. J., Spiro, R. J., & Coulson, R. L (1993). Learning, teaching and testing for complex conceptual understanding. In N. Frederiksen, R. J. Mislevy, & I. I. Bejar (Eds.), *Test theory for a new generation of tests* (pp. 181–217). Hillsdale, NJ: Erlbaum.

Feltovich, P. J., Spiro, R. J., & Coulson, R. L. (1997). Issues of expert flexibility in contexts characterized by complexity and change. In P. Feltovich, K. Ford, & R. Hoffman (Eds.), *Expertise in context* (pp. 125–146). Menlo, CA: AAAI Press/MIT Press.

Fernberger, S. W. (1937). A psychological cycle. *American Journal of Psychology, 50,* 207–217.

Fernberger, S. W. (1941). Perception. *Psychological Bulletin, 38,* 432–468.

Fetterman, D. M. (1998). *Ethnography: Step by step.* Thousand Oaks, CA: Sage.

Fiore, S. M., & Salas, E. (Eds.). (2007). *Toward a science of distributed learning and training.* Washington, DC: American Psychological Association.

Fiore, S. M., Salas, E., Cuevas, H. M., & Bowers, C. A. (2003). Distributed coordination space: Toward a theory of distributed team process and performance. *Theoretical Issues in Ergonomic Science, 4,* 340–364.

Fischhoff, B. (1989). Eliciting knowledge for analytical representation. *IEEE Transactions on Systems, Man, and Cybernetics, 19,* 448–461.

Fischhoff, B., Goitein, B., & Shapira, Z. (1982). The experienced utility of expected utility approaches. In N. Feather (Ed.), *Expectations and actions: Expectancy value models in psychology.* Hillsdale, NJ: Erlbaum.

Fischhoff, B., Slovic, P., & Lichtenstein, S. (1979). Subjective sensitivity analysis. *Organizational Behavior and Human Performance, 23,* 339–359.

Fisher, R. P., & Geiselman, R. E. (1992). *Memory-enhancing techniques for investigative interviewing: The cognitive interview.* Springfield, IL: Charles C. Thomas.

Fitts, P. M. (1946). German applied psychology during WWII. *American Psychologist, 1,* 151–161.

Fitts, P. M. (1951). Engineering psychology and equipment design. In S. S. Stevens (Ed.), *Handbook of experimental psychology* (pp. 1287–1340). New York: Wiley.

Fitts, P. M. (1953). The influence of response coding on performance in motor tasks. In B. McMillan, D. A. Grant, P. M. Fitts, F. C. Frick, W. S. McCulloch, G. A. Miller, et al. (Eds.), *Current trends in information theory* (pp. 47–75). Pittsburgh, PA: University of Pittsburgh Press.

Fitts, P. M. (1954). The information capacity of the human motor system in controlling the amplitude of movement. *Journal of Experimental Psychology, 47,* 381–391.

Fitts, P. M. (1964). Perceptual-motor skill learning. In A. W. Melton (Ed.), *Categories of human learning.* New York: Academic Press.

Fitts, P. M., Chapanis, A., Frick, F. C., Garner, W. R., Gebbard, J. W., et al. (1951). *Human engineering for an effective air navigation and traffic control system.* Washington, DC: National Research Council.

Fitts, P. M., and Jones, R. H. (1947). Analysis of factors contributing to 460 "pilot error" experiences in operating aircraft controls. Report TSEAA-694-12, Aero-Medical Laboratory, Wright Patterson Air Force Base, OH. Reprinted in W. H. Sinaiko (Ed.) (1961). *Selected papers on human factors in the design and use of control systems* (pp. 332–358). New York: Dover.

Fitts, P. M., & Posner, M. I. (1967). *Human performance.* Pacific Palisades, CA: Brooks Cole.

Flach, J. M., & Dominguez, C. O. (1995). Use-centered design: Integrating the user, instrument, and goal. *Ergonomics in Design, 3,* 19–24.

Flach, J. M., Hancock, P., Caird, J., & Vicente, K. J. (1995). *Global perspectives on the ecology of human machine systems.* Hillsdale, NJ: Erlbaum.

Flach, J. M., & Hoffman, R. R. (2003, January–February). The limitations of limitations. *IEEE Intelligent Systems,* pp. 94–97.

Flach, J. M., & Warren, R. (1995). Low altitude flight. In P. A. Hancock, J. M. Flach, J. K. Caird, & K. J. Vicente (Eds.), *Local applications of the ecological approach to human machine systems* (pp. 65–103). Hillsdale, NJ: Erlbaum.

Flanagan, J. C. (1954). The critical incident technique. *Psychological Bulletin, 51,* 327–358.

Flanagan, J., Huang, T., Jones, P., & Kasif, S. (Eds.). (1997). *Human-centered systems: Information, interactivity and intelligence.* Washington, DC: National Science Foundation.

Fleck, J., & Williams, R. (Eds.). (1996). *Exploring expertise.* Edinburgh, Scotland: University of Edinburgh Press.

Fleishman, E. A. (1967). Performance assessment based on an empirically derived task taxonomy. *Human Factors, 9,* 349–366.

Fleishman, E. A. (1975). Toward a taxonomy of human performance. *American Psychologist, 30,* 1127–1149.

Fleishman, E. A., Mumford, M. D., Zaccaro, S. J., Levin, K. Y., Korotkin, A. L., & Hein, M. B. (1991). Taxonomic efforts in the description of leader behavior: A synthesis and functional interpretation. *Leadership Quarterly, 4,* 245–287.

Flin, R., Salas, E., Strub, M., & Martin, L. (Eds.). (1997). *Decision making under stress: Emerging themes and applications.* Aldershot, UK: Ashgate.

Flores, F., Graves, M., Hartfield, B., & Winograd, T. (1988). Computer systems and the design of organizational interaction. *ACM Transactions on Office Information Systems, 6,* 153–172.

Floyd, W. F. (1958). Ergonomics and industry. *Proceedings of the Institution of Mechanical Engineers, 172,* 75–78.

Foley, M., & Hart, A. (1992). Expert–novice differences and knowledge elicitation. In R. R. Hoffman (Ed.), *The psychology of expertise: Cognitive research and empirical AI* (pp. 233–244). Mahwah, NJ: Erlbaum.

Forbus, K. D., Ferguson, R. W., & Gentner, D. (1994). Incremental structure mapping. In A. Ram & K. Eiselt (Eds.), *Proceedings of the Sixteenth Annual Conference of the Cognitive Science Society* (pp. 313–318). Atlanta, GA: Erlbaum.

Forbus, K., Gentner, D., Markman, A., & Ferguson, R. (1998). Analogy just looks like high-level perception. *Journal of Experimental and Theoretical Artificial Intelligence, 10,* 231–257.

Ford, J. W., Coffey, J., Cañas, A., Andrews, E. J., & Turne, C. W. (1996). Diagnosis and explanation by a nuclear cardiology expert system. *International Journal of Expert Systems, 9,* 499–506.

Ford, K. M., & Adams-Webber, J. R. (1992). Knowledge acquisition and constructivist methodology. In R. R. Hoffman (Ed.), *The psychology of expertise: Cognitive research and empirical AI* (pp. 121–136). Mahwah, NJ: Erlbaum.

Ford, K. M., & Bradshaw, J. M. (Eds.). (1993). *Knowledge acquisition as modeling.* New York: Wiley.

Ford, K. M., Cañas, A., Jones, J., Stahl, H., Novak, J., & Adams-Webber, J. R. (1991). ICONKAT: An integrated constructivist knowledge acquisition tool. *Knowledge Acquisition, 3,* 215–236.

Ford, K. M., Glymour, C., & Hayes, P. J. (1997, Fall). Cognitive prostheses. *AI Magazine,* p. 104.

Forsythe, D. E. (1993). Engineering knowledge: The construction of work in artificial intelligence. *Social Studies of Science, 23,* 445–477.

Forsythe, D. E. (1999). "It's just a matter of common sense": Ethnography as invisible work. *Computer Supported Cooperative Work, 8,* 127–145.

Fowler, C. A., Wolford, G., Slade, R., & Tassinary, L. (1981). Lexical access with and without awareness. *Journal of Experimental Psychology: General, 110*, 341–362.

Fowlkes, J. E., Salas, E., Baker, D. P., Cannon-Bowers, J. A., & Stout, R. J. (2000). The utility of event-based knowledge elicitation. *Human Factors, 42*, 24–35.

Fox, J., Myers, C. D., Greaves, M. F., & Pegram, S. (1985). Knowledge acquisition for expert systems: Experience in leukemia diagnosis. *Methods of Information in Medicine, 24*, 65–72.

Fox, J., Myers, C. D., Greaves, M. F., & Pegram, S. (1987). A systematic study of knowledge base refinement in the diagnosis of lukemia. In A. Kidd (Ed.), *Knowledge acquisition for expert systems: A practical handbook* (pp. 73–90). New York: Plenum Press.

Fraser, J. M., Smith, P. J., & Smith, J. W. (1992). A catalog of errors. *International Journal of Man–Machine Studies, 37*, 265–307.

Freeman, G. L. (1931). The facilitative and inhibitory effects of muscular tension in mental work. *Psychological Bulletin, 27*, 687–688.

Frenz, G. (1920). *Kritik der Taylor-System*. Berlin: Verlag von Julius Springer.

Fryer, D. H., & Henry, E. R. (Eds.). (1950). *Handbook of applied psychology* (Vol. 1). New York: Holt, Rinehart.

Fuller, S. (1993). *Philosophy of science and its discontents*. New York: Guilford Press.

Furze, G., Roebuck, A., Bull, P., Lewin, R. J. P., & Thompson, D. R. (2002). A comparison of the illness beliefs of people with angina and their peers: A questionnaire study. *BioMed Central Cardiovascular Disorders, 2*. Retrieved February 19, 2004, from http://www.pubmedcentral.nih.gov/articlerender.fcgi?artid=88998

G. and C. Merriam Company. (1979). *Webster's new collegiate dictionary*. Springfield, MA: Author.

Gadlin, H., & Ingle, G. (1975). Through the one-way mirror: the limits of experimental self-reflection. *American Psychologist, 30*, 1003–1009.

Gaeth, G. J. (1980). "A comparison of lecture and interactive training designed to reduce the influence of interfering materials: An application to soil science." Master's Thesis, Department of Psychology, Kansas State University, Manhattan, KS.

Gagné, R. M. (1965). Human functions in systems. In R. M. Gagné (Ed.), *Psychological principles in system development* (pp. 35–73). New York: Holt, Rinehart and Winston.

Gagné, R. M. (1968). Learning hierarchies. *Educational Psychologist, 6*, 1–9.

Gagné, R. M. (1974). Task analysis—Its relation to content analysis. *Educational Psychologist, 11*, 11–18.

Gagné, R. M., Mayor, J. R., Garstens, H. L., & Paradise, N. E. (1962). Factors in acquiring knowledge in a mathematical task. *Psychological Monographs,* Whole No. 526.

Gaines, B., & Boose, J. H. (Eds.). (1988). *Knowledge acquisition for knowledge based systems*. London: Academic Press.

Galegher, J., Kraut, R., & Egido, C. (Eds.). (1990). *Intellectual teamwork: Social and technical bases of cooperative work*. Mahwah, NJ: Erlbaum.

Gallagher, J. P. (1979). Cognitive/information processing psychology and instruction: Reviewing recent theory and practice. *Instructional Science, 8*, 393–414.

Gammack, J. G. (1987). Different techniques, and different aspects of declarative knowledge. In A. L. Kidd (Ed.), *Knowledge acquisition for expert systems: A practical handbook* (pp. 137–164). New York: Plenum Press.

Gammack, J. G., & Anderson, A. (1990, February). Constructive interaction in knowledge engineering. *Expert Systems, 7*, 19–26.

Gammack, J. G., & Young, R. M. (1985). Psychological techniques for eliciting expert knowledge. In M. Bramer (Ed.), *Research and development in expert systems* (pp. 105–112). Cambridge: Cambridge University Press.

Gardiner, P. C., & Edwards, W. (1975). Public values: Multi-attribute utility measurement in social decision making. In M. Kaplan & S. Schwartz (Eds.), *Human judgment and decision processes.* New York: Academic Press.

Gardner, H. (1985). *The mind's new science: A history of the cognitive revolution.* New York: Basic Books.

Garfinkel, H. (1967). *Studies in ethnomethodology.* Englewood Cliffs, NJ: Prentice Hall.

Garfinkel, H. (Ed.). (1982). *Ethnomethodological studies of work in the discovering sciences* (Vol. 2). London: Routledge and Kegan Paul.

Garg-Janardan, C., & Salvendy, G. (1987). A conceptual framework for knowledge elicitation. *International Journal of Man–Machine Studies, 26,* 521–531.

Garrett, H. E. (1922). A study of the relation of accuracy and speed. *Archives of Psychology,* Whole No. 56.

Gebhard, J. W. (1948). *Some experiments with the VF aided tracking equipment* (Report No. 166-I-53). Baltimore: Johns Hopkins University.

Geddes, N., & Lee, J. (1998). Intelligent control for automated vehicles: A decision aiding method for coordination of multiple uninhabited tactical aircraft. In *Proceedings of the 1998 Unmanned Systems International* (pp. 755–764). Arlington, VA: AUVSI.

Geiwitz, J., Klatzky, R. L., & McCloskey, B. P. (1988). *Knowledge acquisition techniques for expert systems: Conceptual and empirical comparisons* (Report No. DAAB07-87-C-A405). Fort Monmouth, NJ: U.S. Army Communications Electronics Command.

Gentner, D. (1989). Mechanisms of analogical learning. In S. Vosniadou & A. Ortony (Eds.), *Similarity and analogical reasoning* (pp. 199–241). Cambridge: Cambridge University Press.

Gentner, D., & Gentner, D. R. (1983). Flowing waters or teeming crowds: Mental models of electricity. In D. Gentner & A. Stevens (Eds.), *Mental models* (pp. 99–130). Hillsdale, NJ: Erlbaum.

Gentner, D., Holyoak, K. J., & Kokinov, B. N. (Eds.). (2001). *The analogical mind: Perspectives from cognitive science.* Cambridge, MA: Bradford Books.

Gentner, D., & Stevens, A. L. (Eds.). (1983). *Mental models.* Mahwah, NJ: Erlbaum.

George, G. C. (1932). Typing plateaus. *Journal of Business Education, 7,* 17–18.

Gersick, C. J. (1988). Time and transition in work teams: Toward a new model of group development. *Academy of Management Journal, 31,* 9–41.

Gettys, C. F., Fisher, S. D., & Mehle, T. (1978). *Hypothesis generation and plausibility assessment* (Tech. Rep. No. 15-10-78). Norman: University of Oklahoma.

Geuter, U. (1992). *The professionalization of psychology in Nazi Germany.* Cambridge, MA: Cambridge University Press.

Geuter, U. (1997). German military psychology. In W. G. Bringmann, H. E. Lück, R. Miller, & C. E. Early (Eds.), *A pictorial history of psychology* (pp. 553–556). Chicago: Quintessence.

Gibson, J. J. (1979). *The ecological approach to visual perception.* Boston: Houghton Mifflin.

Gick, M. L., & Holyoak, K. J. (1980). Analogical problem solving. *Cognitive Psychology, 12,* 306–355.

Gies, J. (1991, Winter). Automating the worker. *Invention and Technology,* pp. 56–63.

Giese, F. (1927). *Methoden der Wirtschaftspsychologie.* Berlin: Urban and Schwartzenberg.

Gilbreth, F. B. (1911). *Motion study.* New York: Van Nostrand.

Gilbreth, F. B., & Gilbreth, L. M. (1919). *Fatigue study: The elimination of humanity's greatest unnecessary waste.* New York: Macmillan.

Gilbreth, L. M. (1934). Time and Motion Study techniques. *Occupations, 12,* 35–38.

Gilbreth, L. M., & Gilbreth, F. B. (1917a). *Applied motion study.* New York: Sturgis and Walton.

Gilbreth, L. M., & Gilbreth, F. B. (1917b). Problem of the crippled soldier. *Scientific American Supplement*, No. 83, 260–261.

Giles, J. (2006). Sociologist fools physics judges. *Nature, 442*, 8.

Glaser, R. (1976a). Cognitive psychology and instructional design. In D. Klahr (Ed.), *Cognition and instruction* (pp. 303–315). Mahwah, NJ: Erlbaum.

Glaser, R. (1976b). Components of a psychology of instruction: Toward a science of design. *Review of Educational Research, 46*, 1–24.

Glaser, R. (1984). Education and thinking. *American Psychologist, 39*, 93–104.

Glaser, R. (1987). Thoughts on expertise. In C. Schooler & W. Schaie (Eds.), *Cognitive functioning and social structure over the life course* (pp. 81–94). Norwood, NJ: Ablex.

Glaser, R., & Chi, M. T. H. (1988). Overview. In M. T. H. Chi, R. Glaser, & M. J. Farr (Eds.), The nature of expertise (pp. xv–xxviii). Mahwah, NJ: Erlbaum.

Glaser, R., Lesgold, A. M., & Lajoie, S. (1985). *Toward a cognitive theory for the measurement of achievement.* Pittsburgh, PA: University of Pittsburgh.

Glaser, R., Lesgold, A. M., Lajoie, S., Eastman, R., Greenberg, L., Logan, D., et al. (1985). *Cognitive task analysis to enhance technical skills training and assessment.* Pittsburgh, PA: University of Pittsburgh.

Glaser, R., & Pellegrino, J. W. (1979). Cognitive process analysis of aptitude: The nature of inductive reasoning tasks. *Bulletin de Psychologie, 32*, 603–615.

Glaser, R., & Resnick, L. B. (1972). Instructional psychology. *Annual Review of Psychology, 23*, 207–276.

Gluck, K. A., & Pew, R. W. (Eds.). (2005). *Modeling human behavior with integrated cognitive architectures: Comparison, evaluation.* Mahwah, NJ: Erlbaum.

Goguen, J. A. (1992). The dry and the wet. In E. Falkenberg, C. Rolland, & El-S. El-Sayed (Eds.), *Information systems concepts* (pp. 1–17). Amsterdam: Elsevier North-Holland.

Goguen, J. A. (1994). Requirements engineering as the reconciliation of technical and social issues. In J. A. Goguen & M. Jirotka (Eds.), *Requirements engineering: Social and technical issues* (pp. 165–199). London, UK: Academic Press.

Goguen, J. A. (1997). Towards a social, ethical theory of information. In L. Star & W. Turner (Eds.), *Social science research, technical systems and cooperative work: Beyond the great divide* (pp. 27–56). Mahwah, NJ: Erlbaum.

Goldberg, L. R. (1965). Diagnosticians vs. Diagnostic Signs: The Diagnosis of Psychosis vs. Neurosis from the MMPI. *Psychological Monographs, 70*, 1–28.

Gooding, D. (1986). How do scientists reach agreement about novel observations? *Studies in History and Philosophy of Science, 17*, 205–230.

Goodstein, L. P., Andersen, H. B., & Olsen, S. E. (Eds.). (1988). *Tasks, errors, and mental models.* London: Taylor & Francis.

Gorden, R. L. (1987). *Interviewing: Strategy, techniques, and tactics* (4th ed.). Chicago: Dorsey Press.

Gordon, J. L. (2000). Creating knowledge maps by exploiting dependent relationships. *Knowledge-Based Sysytems, 13*, 71–79.

Gordon, S. E. (1988). Pitfalls of keeping the human out of the loop. *AI Applications in Environmental Science, 2*, 44–46.

Gordon, S. E. (1992). Implications of cognitive theory for knowledge acquisition. In R. R. Hoffman (Ed.), *The psychology of expertise: Cognitive research and empirical AI* (pp. 99–120). New York: Springer-Verlag.

Gordon, S. E. (1994). *Systematic training program design: Maximizing effectiveness and minimizing liability.* Englewood Cliffs, NJ: PTR Prentice Hall.

Gordon, S. E., & Gill, R. T. (1997). Cognitive task analysis. In C. Zsambok & G. Klein (Eds.), *About naturalistic decision making* (pp. 131–149). Mahwah, NJ: Erlbaum.

Gordon, S. E., Gill, R. T., & Dingus, T. A. (1987). Designing for the user: The role of human factors in expert system development. *AI Applications in Environmental Science, 1,* 35–46.

Gordon, S. E., Schmierer, K. A., & Gill, R. T. (1993). Conceptual graph analysis: Knowledge acquisition for instructional system design. *Human Factors, 35,* 459–481.

Gorman, M. E., & Carlson, W. B. (1990). Interpreting invention as a cognitive process: The case of A. G. Bell, T. Edison, and the telephone. *Science, Technology, and Human Values, 15,* 131–164.

Gorman, M. E., Tweney, R. D., Gooding, D. C., & Kincannon, A. P. (Eds.). (2005). *Scientific and technological thinking.* Mahawh, NJ: Erlbaum.

Gray, J. S. (1954). *Psychology applied to human affairs* (2nd ed.). New York: McGraw-Hill.

Gray, W. D., John, B. E., & Atwood, M. E. (1993). Project Ernestine: Validating a GOMS analysis for predicting and explaining real-world task performance. *Human–Computer Interaction, 8,* 237–309.

Green, G. I. (1989). Perceived importance of systems analysts' job skills, roles, and non-salary incentives. *Management Information Systems Quarterly, 13,* 115–133.

Greenbaum, J., & Kyng, M. (1991). *Design at work: Cooperative design of computer systems.* Hillsdale, NJ: Erlbaum.

Greeno, J. G. (1973). Theory and practice regarding acquired cognitive structures. *Educational Psychologist, 10,* 117–122.

Greeno, J. G. (1974). Hobbits and Orcs: Acquisition of a sequential concept. *Cognitive Psychology, 6,* 270–292.

Greeno, J. G. (1976). Cognitive objectives of instruction: Theory of knowledge for solving problems and answering questions. In D. Klahr (Ed.), *Cognition and instruction* (pp. 123–160). Hillsdale, NJ: Erlbaum.

Greeno, J. G. (1978, March). *Some examples of cognitive task analysis with instructional implications.* Paper presented at the ONR/NPRDC Conference, San Diego, CA.

Greeno, J. G. (1980). Some examples of cognitive task analysis with instructional implications. In R. E. Snow, P.- A. Federico, & W. E. Montague (Eds.), *Aptitude, learning and instruction: Cognitive process analyses of learning and problem solving* (pp. 1–22). Hillsdale, NJ: Erlbaum.

Greeno, J. G. (1989). Situations, mental models, and generative knowledge. In D. Klahr & K. Kotovsky (Eds.), *Complex information processing: The impact of Herbert A. Simon* (pp. 285–318). Hillsdale, NJ: Erlbaum.

Gregg, L. W. (1976). Methods and models for task analysis in instructional design. In D. Klahr (Ed.), *Cognition and instruction* (pp. 109–116). Hillsdale, NJ: Erlbaum.

Grief, I. (Ed.). (1988). *Computer-supported cooperative work.* San Francisco: Morgan Kaufman.

Grief, I., Seliger, R., & Weihl, W. (1976). Atomic data abstractions in a distributed collaborative editing system. In *Proceedings of the 13th Annual Symposium on Principles of Programming Languages* (pp. 160–172). New York: Association for Computing Machinery.

Griffith, C. R. (1934). *An introduction to applied psychology.* New York: Macmillan.

Groen, G. J., & Patel, V. L. (1985). Medical problem solving: Some questionable assumptions. *Medical Education, 19,* 95–100.

Groen, G. J., & Patel, V. L. (1988). The relationship between comprehension and reasoning in medical expertise. In M. T. H. Chi, R. Glaser, & M. J. Farr (Eds.), *The nature of expertise* (pp. 287–310). Hillsdale, NJ: Erlbaum.

Grove, W. M., & Meehl, P. E. (1996). Comparative efficiency of formal (mechanical, algorithmic) and informal (subjective, impressionistic) prediction procedures: The clinical/statistical controversy. *Psychology, Public Policy, and Law, 2,* 293–323.

Grover, M. D. (1983). A pragmatic knowledge acquisition methodology. In A. Bundy (Ed.), *IJCAI-83: Proceedings of the 8th International Joint Conference on Artificial Intelligence* (pp. 436–438). Los Altos, CA: Kaufmann.

Groves, M., O'Rourke, P., & Alexander, H. (2003). The clinical reasoning characteristics of diagnostic experts. *Medical Teaching, 25,* 308–313.

Grudin, J. (1994). Computer-supported cooperative work: Its history and participation. *IEEE Computer, 27,* 19–26.

Gruppen, L. D., & Frohna, A. Z. (2002). Clinical reasoning. In G. R. Norman, D. I. Newble, & C. van der Vleuten (Eds.), *International handbook of research in medical education* (pp. 205–230). Dordrecht, the Netherlands: Kluwer.

Guerlain, S. (1995). Using the critiquing approach to cope with brittle expert systems. In *Proceedings of the Human Factors and Ergonomics Society 39th Annual Meeting* (pp. 233–237). Santa Monica, CA: Human Factors and Ergonomics Society.

Guerlain, S., & Bullemer, P. (1996). User-initiated notification: A concept for aiding the monitoring activities of process control operators. In *Proceedings of the Human Factors and Ergonomics Society 40th Annual Meeting* (pp. 283–287). Santa Monica, CA: Human Factors and Ergonomics Society.

Guerlain, S., & Smith, P. (1996). Decision support in medical systems. In R. Parasuraman & M. Mouloua (Eds.), *Automation and human performance: Theory and application* (pp. 385–406). Mahwah, NJ: Erlbaum.

Guerlain, S., Smith, P., Obradovich, J. H., Rudman, S., Strohm, P., Smith, J. W., et al. (1999). Interactive crtitiquing as a form of decision support: An empirical evaluation. *Human Factors, 41,* 72–89.

Guest, C. B., Regehr, G., & Tiberius, R. G. (2001). The lifelong challenge of expertise. *Medical Education, 35,* 78–81.

Gullers, P. (1988). Automation-skill-apprenticeship. In B. Goranzon and I. Josefson (Eds.), *Knowledge, skill, and artificial intelligence* (pp. 31–38). London: Springer-Verlag.

Gundlach, H. U. K. (1997). The mobile psychologist: Psychology and the railroads. In W. G. Bringmann, H. E. Lück, R. Miller, & C. E. Early (Eds.), *A pictorial history of psychology* (pp. 506–509). Chicago: Quintessence.

Hadley, J. M. (1944). The relation of personal data to achievement in radio training school. *Psychological Bulletin, 41,* 60–63.

Hakkarainen, K., Palonen, T., Paavola, A., & Lehtinen, E. (2004). *Communities of networked expertise.* Amsterdam: Elsevier.

Hall, E. P., Gott, S. P., & Pokorny, R. A. (1995). *A procedural guide to cognitive task analysis: The PARI methodology* (Report No. AL/HR-TR-1995-0108). Human Resources Directorate, Manpower and Personnel Research Division, Air Force Materiel Command, Brooks AFB, TX.

Ham, D.-H., & Yoon, W. C. (2001a). The effects of presenting functionally abstracted information in fault diagnosis tasks. *Reliability Engineering and System Safety, 73,* 103–119.

Ham, D.-H., & Yoon, W. C. (2001b). Design of information content and layoug for process control based on Goal-means domain analysis. *Cognition, Technology, & Work, 3,* 205–233.

Ham, D.-H., Yoon, W. C., & Han, B.-T. (2008). Experimental study on the effects of visualized functionally abstracted information on process control tasks. *Reliability Engineering and System Safety, 93,* 254–270.

Hammond, K. R. (1966). Clinical inference in nursing: II. A psychologist's viewpoint. *Nursing Research, 15,* 27–38.

Hammond, K. R. (1993). Naturalistic decision making from a Brunswikian viewpoint: Past, present, future. In G. Klein, J. Orasanu, R. Calderwood, & C. Zsambok (Eds.), *Decision making in action: Models and methods* (pp. 205–227). Norwood, NJ: Ablex.

Hammond, K. R., Hamm, R. M., Grassia, J., & Pearson, T. (1987). Direct comparison of the efficacy of intuitive and analytical cognition in expert judgment. *IEEE Transactions on Systems, Man, and Cybernetics, 17,* 753–770.

Hammond, K. R., Kelly, K. J., Schneider, R. J., & Vancini, M. (1966). Clinical inference in nursing: Information units used. *Nursing Research, 15,* 236–243.

Hammond, K. R., McClelland, G. H., & Mumpower, J. (1980). *Human judgment and decision making: Theories, methods, and procedures.* New York: Praeger.

Hancock, P., Flach, J., Caird, J., & Vicente, K. J. (1995). *Local applications of the ecological approach to human-machine systems.* Hillsdale, NJ: Erlbaum.

Hancock, P. A., Pepe, A. A., & Murphy, L. L. (2005, Winter). Hedonomics: The power of positive and pleasurable ergonomics. *Ergonomics in Design,* pp. 8–14.

Hancock, P. A., & Scallen, S. F. (1998). Allocating functions in human-machine systems. In R. R. Hoffman, M. F. Sherrick, & J. S. Warm (Eds.), *Viewing psychology as a whole* (pp. 509–539). Washington, DC: American Psychological Association.

Hanson, C. F. (1922). Serial action as a measure of motor capacity. *Psychological Monographs, 31,* 320–382.

Harper, R. H. R. (2000). The organisation in ethnography: A discussion of ethnographic fieldwork programs. *Computer-Supported Cooperative Work, 9,* 239–264.

Harrell, T. W. (1945). Aviation psychology in the Army Air Forces. *Psychological Bulletin, 42,* 386–389.

Harrell, T. W. (1949). *Industrial psychology.* New York: Reinhart.

Harrell, T. W., & Churchill, R. D. (1941). Classification of military personnel. *Psychological Bulletin, 38,* 331–353.

Harris, D. H. (Ed.). (1994). *Organizational linkages: Understanding the productivity paradox.* Washington, DC: National Academy Press.

Harris, L. R., Glover, B. J., & Spady, A. A. (1986, July). *Analytic techniques of pilot scanning behavior and their application* (NASA Technical Paper 2525). Moffett Field, CA: NASA-Ames Research Center.

Hart, A. (1985). Knowledge elicitation: Issues and methods. *Computer Aided Design, 17,* 455–462.

Hart, A. (1986). *Knowledge acquisition for expert systems.* London: Kogan Page.

Hart, S. G., & Staveland, L. E. (1988). Development of a NASA-TLX (Task Load Index): Results of empirical and theoretical research. In P. A. Hancock & N. Meshkati (Eds.), *Human mental workload* (pp. 139–183). Amsterdam: Elsevier.

Hartley, R. T. (1981). How expert should an expert system be? In *Proceedings of the seventh international joint conference on artificial intelligence* (pp. 862–867). Vancouver, BC: International Joint Conferences in Artificial Intelligence.

Harvey, N. (1995). Why are judgments less consistent in less predictable task situations? *Organizational Behavior and Human Decision Processes, 63,* 247–263.

Hatala, R., Norman, G. R., & Brooks, L. R. (1999a). Impact of a clinical scenario on accuracy of electrocardiogram interpretation. *Journal of General Internal Medicine, 14,* 126–129.

Hatala, R. M., Norman, G. R., & Brooks, L. R. (1999b). Influence of a single example upon subsequent electrocardiogram interpretation. *Teaching and Learning in Medicine, 11,* 110–117.

Hatala, R. M., Norman, G. R., & Brooks, L. R. (2003). Practice makes perfect: The critical role of deliberate practice in the acquisition of ECG interpretation skills. *Advances in Health Science Education, 8*, 17–26.

Hatano, G., & Inagaki, K. (1983, April). "Two courses of expertise." Paper presented at the Conference on Child Development in Japan and the US. Stanford University, Stanford, CA.

Hatano, G., & Osawa, K. (1983). Digit memory of grand experts in abacus-derived mental calculation. *Cognition, 15*, 95–110.

Hayes, C. C. (1997). A study of solution quality in human expert and knowledge-based system reasoning. In P. J. Feltovich, K. M. Ford, & R. R. Hoffman (Eds.), *Expertise in context: Human and machine* (pp. 339–362). Cambridge, MA: MIT Press/AAAI Books.

Hayes, J. R. (1965). Problem typology and the solution process. *Journal of Verbal Learning and Verbal Behavior, 4*, 371–379.

Hayes, J. R. (1989). *The complete problem solver.* Hillsdale, NJ: Erlbaum.

Hayes, N. A., & Broadbent, D. E. (1988). Two modes of learning interactive tasks. *Cognition, 28*, 249–276.

Hayes, P. J., Ford, K. M., & Agnew, N. (1994, Fall). On babies and bath water: A cautionary tale. *AI Magazine, 15*–26.

Hayes-Roth, F., Waterman, D. A., & Lenat, D. B. (1983). *Building expert systems.* Reading, MA: Addison-Wesley.

Hebb, D. O. (1963). The semi-autonomous process: Its nature and nurture. *American Psychologist, 18*, 16–27.

Hedlund, J., Ilgen, D. R., & Hollenbeck, J. R. (1998). Decision accuracy in computer-mediated versus face-to-face decision making. *Organizational Behavior and Human Decision Processes, 76*, 30–47.

Heimreich, R., & Schaefer, H. (1994). Team performance in the operating room. In M. S. Bogner (Ed.), *Human error in medicine* (pp. 225–253). Hillsdale, NJ: Erlbaum.

Helander, M., & Nagamachi, M. (Eds.). (1992). *Design for manufacturability: A systems approach to concurrent engineering and ergonomics.* London: Taylor & Francis.

Helmholtz, H. (1856–1866). *Handbuch der physiologischen Optik (Handbook of physiological optics)* (J. P. C. Southall, Trans.). Hamburg, Germany: Verlag von Leopold Voss.

Hemple, K. G. (1970). *Aspects of scientific explanation.* New York: Free Press.

Hick, W. E. (1945). *Friction in manual controls with special reference to its effect on accuracy of corrective movements in conditions simulating jolting.* Report No. 18, Applied Psychology Unit, Cambridge University, Cambridge, England.

Hick, W. E. (1951). Information theory and intelligence tests. *British Journal of Psychology, 4*, 157–164.

Hick, W. E. (1952). On the rate of gain of information. *Quarterly Journal of Experimental Psychology, 4*, 11–26.

Hilgard, E. R. (1987). *Psychology in America: An historical survey.* New York: Harcourt Brace Jovanovich.

Hilgard, E. R., Campbell, R. K., & Sears, W. N. (1938). Conditioned discrimination: The effect of knowledge of stimulus-response relationships. *American Journal of Psychology, 51*, 498–506.

Hill, L. B., Rejall, A. E., & Thorndike, E. L. (1913). Practice in the case of typewriting. *Pedagogical Seminary, 20*, 516–529.

Hinsz, V. B., Tindale, R. S., & Volrath, D. A. (1977). The emerging conceptualization of groups as information processes. *Psychological Bulletin, 121*, 43–64,

Hirokawa, R. Y., & Poole, M. S. (Eds.). (1996). *Communication and group decision making.* Thousand Oaks, CA: Sage.

Hmelo-Silver, C. E. (2006). Design principles for scaffolding technology-based inquiry. In A. M. O'Donnell, C. E. Hmelo-Silver, & G. Erkens (Eds.), *Collaborative learning, reasoning, and technology* (pp. 147–170). Mahwah, NJ: Erlbaum.

Hmelo-Silver, C. E., & Pfeffer, M. G. (in press). Comparing expert and novice understanding of a complex system from the perspective of structures, behaviors, and functions. *Cognitive Science.*

Hoc, J.- M., Cacciabue, P. C., & Hollnagel, E. (Eds.). (1995). *Expertise and technology: Cognition and human-computer cooperation.* Mahwah, NJ: Erlbaum.

Hoffman, B. (1962). *The tyranny of testing.* New York: Corwell-Collier.

Hoffman, P. J. (1960). The paramorphic representation of clinical judgment. *Psychological Bulletin, 57,* 116–131.

Hoffman, R. R. (1979). On metaphors, myths, and mind. *Psychological Record, 29,* 175–178.

Hoffman, R. R. (1986). *Procedures for efficiently extracting the knowledge of experts.* Report to the Office of the Deputy for Development Plans, the Strategic Planning Directorate of the Electronic Systems Division, Hanscom AFB, MA. Air Force Office of Scientific Research, Contract No. F49260-85-C-0013.

Hoffman, R. R. (1987a). *A human factors approach to the process of designing the advanced meteorological processing system.* Research conducted at the USAF Geophysics Laboratory, with the support of the U.S. Air Force Office of Scientific Research, Contract No. F49620-85-0013.

Hoffman, R. R. (1987b, Summer). The problem of extracting the knowledge of experts from the perspective of experimental psychology. *AI Magazine, 8,* 53–67.

Hoffman, R. R. (1989a, October). *The design of advanced meteorological information processing workstations.* Paper presented at Electronic Imaging Expo '89, Boston.

Hoffman, R. R. (1989b, May). *Human factors psychology in the support of forecasting: The design of advanced meteorological workstations.* Paper presented at the Artificial Intelligence Research in Environmental Science Conference, Baltimore.

Hoffman, R. R. (1990). Remote perceiving: A step toward a unified science of remote sensing. *Geocarto International, 5,* 3–13.

Hoffman, R. R. (1991a). Human factors psychology in the support of forecasting: The design of advanced meteorological workstations. *Weather and Forecasting, 6,* 98–110.

Hoffman, R. R. (1991b, October). *Novice and expert interpretation of meteorological satellite images.* Paper presented at the session on "Severe Weather Effects and Reporting" held at the 21st Conference on Broadcast Meteorology, sponsored by the American Meteorological Society, held in Washington, DC.

Hoffman, R. R. (1992a, January). *The perceptual skills of expert meteorologists.* Paper presented at the Sixth Conference on Satellite Meteorology, held in conjunction with the 72nd annual meeting of the American Meteorological Society, held in Atlanta, GA.

Hoffman, R. R. (Ed.). (1992b). *The psychology of expertise: Cognitive research and empirical AI.* Mahwah, NJ: Erlbaum.

Hoffman, R. R. (1993, May). *Expertise in context: Perceptual expertise in the interpretation of satellite images.* Paper presented at the Third International Workshop on Human and Machine Cognition, sponsored by the American Association for Artificial Intelligence and the Institute for Human and Machine Cognition of the University of West Florida.

Hoffman, R. R. (1994). Constructivism versus realism or constructivism and realism? *Journal of Experimental and Theoretical Artificial Intelligence, 6,* 431–435.

Hoffman, R. R. (1995a, Fall). *Forecasting operations at the Meteorological Office of the United Kingdom.* Paper presented to the New York City/Long Island Chapter, American Meteorological Society.

Hoffman, R. R. (1995b). Monster analogies. *AI Magazine, 16,* 11–35.

Hoffman, R. R. (1995c). *A review of naturalistic decision making on the critical decision method of knowledge elicitation and the recognition-priming model of decision-making, with a focus on implications for military proficiency.* Report to Epistemics, Ltd., under a contract from the Defense Research Agency, Ministry of Defense, United Kingdom.

Hoffman, R. R. (1997a). How to doom yourself to repeat the past: Some reflections on the history of cognitive technology. *Cognitive Technology, 2,* 4–15.

Hoffman, R. R. (1997b, February). *Human factors in meteorology.* Paper presented at the 77th annual meeting of the American Meteorological Society, held in Los Angeles, CA.

Hoffman, R. R. (1997c, September). *Human factors in radar meteorology.* Paper presented at the 28th Conference on Radar Meteorology, American Meteorological Society, held in Austin, TX.

Hoffman, R. R. (1997d). *A proposed paradigm for the experimental comparison of software tools that are intended to support the process of knowledge acquisition.* Unpublished manuscript.

Hoffman, R. R. (1998a). How can expertise be defined? Implications of research from cognitive psychology. In R. Williams, W. Faulkner, & J. Fleck (Eds.), *Exploring expertise: Issues and perspectives.* London: Macmillan.

Hoffman, R. R. (1998b, May). *Revealing the reasoning and knowledge of expert weather forecasters.* Paper presented at the Fourth International Conference on Naturalistic Decision Making, Warrenton, VA.

Hoffman, R. R. (Ed.) (2007). *Expertise out of context: Proceedings of the Sixth International Conference on Naturalistic Decision Making.* Boca Raton, FL: Taylor & Francis.

Hoffman, R. R., Bradshaw, J. M., Hayes, P. J., & Ford, K. M. (September/October 2003). The Borg hypothesis. *IEEE: Intelligent Systems,* pp. 73–75.

Hoffman, R. R., Cochran, E. L., & Nead, J. M. (1990). Cognitive metaphors in the history of experimental psychology. In D. Leary (Ed.), *Metaphors in the history of psychology* (pp. 173–209). Cambridge: Cambridge University Press.

Hoffman, R. R., Coffey, J. W., & Carnot, M. J. (2000, November). *Is there a "fast track" into the black box? The Cognitive Modeling Procedure.* Paper presented at the 41st Annual Meeting of the Psychonomics Society, New Orleans, LA.

Hoffman, R. R., Coffey, J. W., Carnot, M. J., & Novak, J. D. (2002, September). An empirical comparison of methods for eliciting and modeling expert knowledge. In *Proceedings of the 46th Meeting of the Human Factors and Ergonomics Society* (pp. 482–486). Santa Monica, CA: Human Factors and Ergonomics Society.

Hoffman, R. R., Coffey, J. W., & Ford, K. M. (2000). *A case study in the research paradigm of human-centered computing: Local expertise in weather forecasting.* Report on the Contract, "Human-Centered System Prototype," National Technology Alliance.

Hoffman, R. R., Coffey, J. W., Ford, K. M., & Novak, J. D. (2006). A method for eliciting, preserving, and sharing the knowledge of forecasters. *Weather and Forecasting, 21,* 416–428.

Hoffman, R. R., Coffey, J. W., Novak, J. D., & Cañas, A. J. (2005). Applications of concept maps to Web design and Web work. In R. W. Proctor & K.- P. L. Vu (Eds.), *Handbook of human factors in Web design* (pp. 157–175). Mahwah, NJ: Erlbaum.

Hoffman, R. R., & Conway, J. (1990). Psychological factors in remote sensing: A review of recent research. *Geocarto International, 4,* 3–22.

Hoffman, R. R., Crandall, B., & Shadbolt, N. R. (1998). A case study in cognitive task analysis methodology: The Critical Decision Method for the elicitation of expert knowledge. *Human Factors, 40,* 254–276.

Hoffman, R. R., & Deffenbacher, K. A. (1992). A brief history of applied cognitive psychology. *Applied Cognitive Psychology, 6,* 1–48.

Hoffman, R. R., & Deffenbacher, K. A. (1993). An analysis of the relations of basic and applied science. *Ecological Psychology, 5,* 315–352.

Hoffman, R. R., & Deffenbacher, K. A. (1994). To each his own: Reply to Vicente. *Ecological Psychology, 6,* 125–130.

Hoffman, R. R., Detweiler, M. A., Lipton, K., & Conway, J. A. (1993). Considerations in the use of color in meteorological displays. *Weather and Forecasting, 8,* 505–518.

Hoffman, R. R., & Elm, W. C. (2006, January–February). HCC implications for the procurement process. *IEEE: Intelligent Systems,* pp. 74–81.

Hoffman, R. R., Feltovich, P. J., & Ford, K. M. (1997). A general framework for conceiving of expertise and expert systems in context. In P. J. Feltovich, K. M. Ford, & R. R. Hoffman (Eds.), *Expertise in context: Human and machine* (pp. 543–580). Cambridge, MA: MIT Press/AAAI Books.

Hoffman, R. R., Feltovich, P. J., Ford, K. M., Woods, D. D., Klein, G., & Feltovich, A. (2002, July–August). A rose by any other name ... would probably be given an acronym. *IEEE: Intelligent Systems,* 72–80.

Hoffman, R. R., & Fiore, S. M. (2007, May–June). Perceptual (re)learning: A leverage point for human-centered computing. *IEEE Intelligent Systems,* pp. 79–83.

Hoffman, R. R., & Hanes, L. F. (2003, July–August). The boiled frog problem. *IEEE: Intelligent Systems,* pp. 68–71.

Hoffman, R. R., & Hayes, P. J., (2004, January–February). The pleasure principle. *IEEE: Intelligent Systems,* pp. 86–89.

Hoffman, R. R., Hayes, P. J., & Ford, K. M. (2001, September–October). Human-centered computing: Thinking in and outside the box. *IEEE: Intelligent Systems,* pp. 76–78.

Hoffman, R. R., Hayes, P., Ford, K. M., & Hancock, P. A. (2002, May–June). The triples rule. *IEEE: Intelligent Systems,* pp. 62–65.

Hoffman, R. R., Klein, G., & Laughery, K. R. (2002, January–February). The state of cognitive systems engineering. *IEEE: Intelligent Systems,* pp. 73–75.

Hoffman, R. R., Klein, G., & Schraagen, J. M. (2007). The macrocognition framework of naturalistic decision making. In J. M. Schraagen (Ed.), *Macrocognition* (pp. 2–26). London: Ashgate.

Hoffman, R. R., & Lintern, G. (2006). Eliciting and representing the knowledge of experts. In K. A. Ericsson, N. Charness, P. Feltovich, & R. Hoffman (Eds.), *Cambridge handbook on expertise and expert performance* (pp. 203–222). New York: Cambridge University Press.

Hoffman, R. R., Lintern, G., & Eitelman, S. (2004, March–April). The Janus principle. *IEEE: Intelligent Systems,* pp. 78–80.

Hoffman, R. R., & Markman, A. B. (Eds.). (2001). *The interpretation of remote sensing imagery: The human factor.* Boca Raton, FL: Lewis Publishers.

Hoffman, R. R., Marx, M., & Hancock, P. A. (2008/March-April). Metrics, metrics, metrics: Negative hedonicity. *IEEE: Intelligent Systems,* pp. 69–73.

Hoffman, R. R., & Nead, J. M. (1983). General contextualism, ecological science, and cognitive research. *Journal of Mind and Behavior, 4,* 507–560.

Hoffman, R. R., & Palermo, D. S. (Eds.). (1991). *Cognition and the symbolic processes: Applied and ecological perspectives.* Mahwah, NJ: Erlbaum.

Hoffman, R. R., & Pike, R. J. (1995). On the specification of the information available for the perception and description of the natural terrain. In P. Hancock, J. Flach, J. Caird, & K. Vicente (Eds.), *Local applications of the ecological approach to human-machine systems* (pp. 285–323). Mahwah, NJ: Erlbaum.

Hoffman, R. R., Roesler, A., & Moon, B. M. (2004, July–August). What is design in the context of human-centered computing? *IEEE: Intelligent Systems*, pp. 89–95.

Hoffman, R. R., & Shadbolt, N. R. (1996). *Facilitating the acquisition of expertise in domains involving perceptual skill, mental workload, and situation awareness*. Report under Contract No. ASF/2819U. Defense Research Agency, Ministry of Defense, United Kingdom.

Hoffman, R. R., Shadbolt, N. R., Burton, A. M., & Klein, G. (1995). Eliciting knowledge from experts: A methodological analysis. *Organizational Behavior and Human Decision Processes, 62,* 129–158.

Hoffman, R. R., Trafton, G., & Roebber, P. (2008). *Minding the weather: How expert forecasters think*. Cambridge, MA: MIT Press.

Hoffman, R. R., & Woods, D. D. (2000). Studying cognitive systems in context. *Human Factors, 42,* 1–7.

Hoffman, R. R., & Woods, D. D. (2005, January–February). Steps toward a theory of complex and cognitive systems. *IEEE: Intelligent Systems*, pp. 76–79.

Hoffman, R. R., & Yates, J. F. (2005, July–August). Decision-making. *IEEE: Intelligent Systems*, pp. 22–29.

Hofstadter, D. R. (2001). Analogy as the core of cognition. In D. Gentner, K. J. Holyoak, & B. N. Kokinov (Eds.), *The analogical mind: Perspectives from cognitive science* (pp. 499–538). Cambridge, MA: Bradford Books.

Hofstadter, D., & the FARG. (1995). *Fluid concepts and creative analogies*. New York: Basic Books.

Hoke, R. E. (1922). *The improvement of speed and accuracy in typewriting* (Johns Hopkins University Studies in Education, No. 7). Baltimore: Johns Hopkins University Press.

Holden, C. (1992). Study flunks science and math tests. *Science, 26,* 541.

Holding, D. H., & Pfau, H. D. (1985). Thinking ahead in chess. *American Journal of Psychology, 98,* 271–282.

Hollan, J. D., Hutchins, E. L., & Kirsh, D. (in press). Distributed cognition: A new theoretical foundation for human–computer interaction research. *ACM Transactions on Human-Computer Interaction.*

Hollnagel, E. (1982). *Cognitive task analysis*. Draft Report in a memo to David Woods, Institutt for Atomenergi, Halden, Sweden.

Hollnagel, E., & Cacciabue, P. C. (1999). Cognition, technology, and work: An introduction. *Cognition, Technology, and Work, 1,* 1–6.

Hollnagel, E., Hoc, J.- M., & Cacciabue, P. C. (1995). Expertise and technology: "I have a feeling we're not in Kansas anymore." In J.- M. Hoc, P. C. Cacciabue, & E. Hollnagel (Eds.), *Expertise and technology: Cognition and human–computer cooperation* (pp. 279–286). Mahwah, NJ: Erlbaum.

Hollnagel, E., Mancini, G., & Woods, D. D. (Eds.) (1986), *Intelligent decision support in process environments*. New York: Springer-Verlag.

Hollnagel, E., Pedersen, O. M., & Rasmussen, J. (1981). *Notes on human performance analysis* (Report Riso-M-2285). Roskilde, Denmark: Risø National Laboratory.

Hollnagel, E., & Woods, D. D. (1983). Cognitive systems engineering: New wine in new bottles. *International Journal of Man–Machine Studies, 18,* 583–600.

Hollnagel, E., & Woods, D. D. (2006). *Joint cognitive systems: Foundations of cognitive systems engineering*. Boca Raton, FL: Taylor & Francis.

Holsapple, C. W., & Raj, V. S. (1994). An exploratory study of two KA methods. *Expert Systems, 11,* 77–87.

Holtzblatt, K. (2003). Contextual design. In J. A. Jacko & A. Sears (Eds.), *The human–computer interaction handbook* (pp. 941–963). Mahwah, NJ: Erlbaum.

Holtzblatt, K., & Beyer, H. R. (1995). Requirements gathering: The human factor. *Communications of the ACM, 38,* 31–32.

Holyoak, K. J. (1984). Analogical thinking and human intelligence. In R. J. Sternberg (Ed.), *Advances in the psychology of human intelligence* (Vol. 2, pp. 199–230). Hillsdale, NJ: Erlbaum.

Holyoak, K. J., & Koh, K. (1987). Surface and structural similarity in analogical transfer. *Memory and Cognition, 15,* 332–340.

Holyoak, K. J., Novick, L. R., & Melz, E. R. (1994). Component processes in analogical transfer: Mapping, pattern completion, and adaptation. In K. J. Holyoak & J. A. Barnden (Eds.), *Advances in connectionist and neural computation theory: Analogical connections* (Vol. 2, pp. 113–180). Norwood, NJ: Ablex.

Holyoak, K. J., & Thagard, P. (1989). A computational model of analogical problem solving. In S. Vosniadou & A. Ortony (Eds.), *Similarity and analogical reasoning* (pp. 242–266). Cambridge: Cambridge University Press.

Honeck, R. P., & Temple, J. G. (1992). Metaphor, expertise, and a PEST. *Metaphor and Symbolic Activity, 7,* 237–252.

Howard, G. S. (1994). Why do people say nasty things about self-reports? *Journal of Organizational Behavior, 15,* 399–404.

Howell, W. C. (1984). *Task influences in the analytic-intuitive approach to decision making.* Bethesda, MD: Office of Naval Research.

Howell, W. C., & Cooke, N. J. (1989). Training the human information processor: A look at cognitive models. In I. L. Goldstein (Ed.), *Training and development in work organizations: Frontiers of industrial and organizational psychology* (pp. 121–182). San Francisco, CA: Jossey-Bass.

Hughes, J. A., Randall, D., & Shapiro, D. (1993). From ethnographic record to system design: Some experiences from the field. *CSCW, 1,* 123–141.

Hughes, J., & King, V. (1992). *Sociology for large scale system design.* Paper presented at the Conference on Software Systems and Practice: Social Science Perspectives, University of Reading, Reading, UK.

Humphrey, G. (1963). *Thinking: An introduction to experimental psychology.* London: Methuen.

Hunter, W. S. (1946). Psychology and the war. *American Psychologist, 1,* 479–492.

Husband, R. W. (1934). *Applied psychology.* New York: Harper Brothers.

Hutchins, E. (1990). The technology of team navigation. In J. Galegher, R. Kraut, & C. Egido (Eds.), *Intellectual teamwork: Social and technical bases of cooperative work.* Hillsdale, NJ: Erlbaum.

Hutchins, E. L. (1995a). *Cognition in the wild.* Cambridge, MA: MIT Press.

Hutchins, E. L. (1995b). How a cockpit remembers its speeds. *Cognitive Science, 19,* 265–288.

Hutchins, E. L., & Hinton, G. G. (1984). Why the islands move. *Perception, 13,* 629–632.

Hutchins, E. L., Hollan, J. D., Norman, D. A. (1985). Direct manipulation interfaces. *Human-Computer Interaction, 1,* 311–338

Hyman, R. (1953). Stimulus information as a determinant of reaction time. *Journal of Experimental Psychology, 45,* 188–196.

Indurkhya, B. (1991). On the role of interpretive analogy in learning. *New Generation Computing, 8,* 385–402.

Inhelder, B., & Piaget, J. (1958). *The growth of logical thinking from childhood to adolescence.* New York: Basic Books.

Isenberg, D. J. (1984). How senior managers think. *Harvard Business Review, 6,* 80.

Jackson, W. (Ed.). (1953). *Communication theory.* London: Butterworths Scientific.

Jacob, V. S., Gaultney, L. D., & Salvendy, G. (1986). Strategies and biases in human decision making and their implications for expert systems. *Behavior and Information Technology, 5,* 119–140.

Jacobson, R., Fant, C. G. M., & Halle, M. (1952). *Preliminaries to speech analysis* (Tech. Rep. No. 13). Cambridge, MA: MIT.

Jagacinski, R. J., & Flach, J. M. (2003). *Control theory for humans: Quantitative approaches to modeling performance.* Mahwah, NJ: Erlbaum.

James, W. (1890). *Principles of psychology* (2 vols.). New York: Holt.

Janik, A. (1988). Tacit knowledge, working life, and scientific method. In B. Goranzon & I. Josefson (Eds.), *Knowledge, skill, and artificial intelligence* (pp. 53–63). London: Springer Verlag.

Janik, A. (1990). Tacit knowledge, rule-following, and learning. In B. Goranzon & M. Florin (Eds.), *Artificial intelligence, culture, and language: On education and work* (pp. 45–55). London: Springer-Verlag.

Janis, I. L., & Mann, L. (1977). *Decision-making: A psychological analysis of conflict, choice, and commitment.* New York: Free Press.

Jastrzebowski, W. (1857). An outline of ergonomics, or the science of work based on truths drawn from the science of nature. *Przyroda I Przemysal (Nature and Industry),* No. 29. Warsaw, Poland: The Central Institute for Labour Protection.

Jeffries, R. (1997). Position paper. In J. Flanagan, T. Huang, P. Jones, & S. Kasif (Eds.), *Human-centered systems: Information, interactivity and intelligence* (pp. 277–279). Washington, DC: National Science Foundation.

Jeffries, R., Turner, A., Polson, P., & Atwood, M. (1981). The processes involved in designing software. In R. J. Anderson (Ed.), *Cognitive skills and their acquisition* (pp. 255–283). London: Springer-Verlag.

Jenkins, J. J. (1953). Some measured characteristics of Air Force weather forecasters and success in forecasting. *The Journal of Applied Psychology, 37,* 440–444.

Johannesen, L., Cook, R. I., & Woods, D. D. (1994). *Grounding explanations in evolving diagnostic situations.* Institute for Ergonomics/Cognitive Systems Engineering Laboratory Report, ERGO- CSEL 94-TR-03.

Johnson, B. (Ed.). (1982). *My inventions: The autobiography of Nikola Tesla.* Austin, TX: Hart Brothers.

Johnson, D., Maruyama, G., Johnson, R., Nelson, D., & Skon, L. (1981). The effects of cooperative, competitive and individualistic goal structure on achievement: A meta-analysis. *Psychological Bulletin, 89,* 47–62.

Johnson, L., & Johnson, N. (1987). Knowledge elicitation involving teachback interviewing. In A. L. Kidd (Ed.), *Knowledge elicitation for expert systems: A practical handbook* (pp. 91–108). New York: Plenum Press.

Johnson, N. E. (1985). Varieties of representation in eliciting and representing knowledge in IKBS. *International Journal of Systems Research and Information Science, 1,* 69–90.

Johnson, P. E. (1983). What kind of expert should a system be? *Journal of Medicine and Philosophy, 8,* 77–97.

Johnson, P. E., Duran, A. S., Hassebrock, F., Moller, J. H., Prietula, M. J., Feltovich, P., et al. (1981). Expertise and error in diagnostic reasoning. *Cognitive Science, 5,* 235–283.

Johnson, P. E., Hassebrock, F., Duran, A. S., & Moller, J. H. (1982). Multimethod study of clinical judgment. *Organizational Behavior and Human Performance, 30,* 201–230.

Johnson, P. E., Zualkerman, I. A., & Garber, S. (1987). Specification of expertise. *International Journal of Man–Machine Studies, 26,* 161–181.

Johnson, P. E., Zualkerman, I. A., & Tukey, D. (1993). Types of expertise: An invariant of problem solving. *International Journal of Man–Machine Studies, 39,* 641–665.

Jonassen, D., Ambruso, D., & Olesen, J. (1992). Designing hypertext on transfusion medicine using cognitive flexibility theory. *Journal of Educational Multimedia and Hypermedia, 1,* 309–322.

Jordan, B. (1989). Cosmopolitical obstetrics: Some insights from the training of traditional midwives. *Social Science and Medicine, 28,* 925–944.

Jordan, B., & Henderson, A. (1995). Interaction analysis: Foundations and practice. *Journal of the Learning Sciences, 4,* 39–103.

Josefson, I. (1988). The nurse as engineer: The theory of knowledge in research in the care sector. In B. Goranzon & I. Josefson (Eds.), *Knowledge, skill, and artificial intelligence* (pp. 19–30). London: Springer-Verlag.

Kaempf, G. L., Klein, G., Thordsen, M. L., & Wolf, S. (1996). Decision making in complex command-and-control environments [Special issue]. *Human Factors, 38,* 220–231.

Kaempf, G. L., Thordsen, M. L., & Klein, G. (1991). *Application of an expertise-centered taxonomy to training decisions* (Report No. MDA903-91-C-0050). Alexandria, VA: U.S. Army Research Institute.

Kaempf, G. L., Wolf, S. P., Thordsen, M. L., & Klein, G. (1992). *Decision making in the AEGIS combat information center* (Contract N66001-90-C-6023 for the Naval Command, Control and Ocean Surveillance Center). Fairborn, OH: Klein Associates.

Kahneman, D., Slovic, P., & Tversky, A. (Eds.). (1982). *Judgment under uncertainty: Heuristics and biases.* Cambridge: Cambridge University Press.

Kahneman, D., & Tversky, A. (Eds.). (2000). *Choices, values, and frames.* Cambridge: Cambridge University Press.

Kassirer, J. P., Kuipers, B. J., & Gorry, G. A. (1982). Toward a theory of clinical expertise. *American Journal of Medicine, 73,* 251–259.

Katz, S., Lesgold, A. M., Eggan, G., & Gordin, M. (1993). Modeling the student in Sherlock II. *Journal of Artificial Intelligence in Education* (Special issue on student modeling, G. McCalla & J. Greer, eds.), *3,* 495–518.

Katz, S., Lesgold, A. M., Hughes, E., Peters, D., Eggan, G., Gordin, M., & Greenberg, L. (1998). Sherlock 2: An intelligent tutoring system built on the LRDC framework. In C. P. Bloom & R. B. Loftin (Eds.), *Facilitating the development and use of interactive learning environments* (pp. 227–258). Mahwah, NJ: Erlbaum.

Keane, M., & Brayshaw, M. (1988). The incremental analogy machine: A computational model of analogy. In D. Sleeman (Ed.), *Proceedings of the Third European Working Session on Learning* (pp. 53–62). London: Pitman.

Keane, M., Ledgeway, T., & Duff, S. (1994). Constraints on analogical mapping: A comparison of three models. *Cognitive Science, 18,* 387–438.

Kenny, A. (1980). *Acquinas.* Oxford, England: Oxford University Press.

Kent, R. T. (1911). Introduction. In F. B. Gilbreth (Ed.), *Motion study.* New York: Van Nostrand.

Kidd, A. L. (Ed.). (1987). *Knowledge acquisition for expert systems: A practical handbook.* New York: Plenum Press.

Kidd, A. L., & Cooper, M. B. (1985). Man–machine interface issues in the construction and use of an expert system. *International Journal of Man–Machine Studies, 22,* 91–102.

Kidd, A. L., & Welbank, M. (1984). Knowledge acquisition. In J. Fox (Ed.), *Infotech state of the art report on expert systems.* London: Pergamon.

Kidd, J. S. (1965). Human tasks and equipment design. In R. M. Gagné (Ed.), *Psychological principles in system development* (pp. 159–184). New York: Holt, Rinehart and Winston.

Kiekel, P. A., Cooke, N. J., Foltz, P.W., Gorman, J. C., & Martin, M. J. (2002). Some promising results of communication-based automatic measures of team cognition. In *Proceedings of the Human Factors and Ergonomics Society 46th Annual Meeting* (pp. 298–302). Santa Monica, CA: Human Factors and Ergonomics Society.

Kieras, D. (1988). Towards a practical GOMS model methodology for user interface design. In M. Helander (Ed.), *Handbook of human–computer interaction.* New York: North-Holland.

Kim, J., & Courtney, J. F. (1988). A survey of knowledge acquisition techniques and their relevance to managerial problem domains. *Decision Support Systems, 4,* 269–284.

Kim, Y.- G., & March, S. T. (1995). Comparing data modeling formalisms. *Communications of the ACM, 38,* 103–115.

Kirsch, D. (2001). The contexts of work. *Human–Computer Interaction, 16,* 305–322.

Kirwan, B., & Ainsworth, L. K. (Eds.). (1992). *A guide to task analysis.* London: Taylor & Francis.

Klahr, D. (Ed.). (1976). *Cognition and instruction.* Hillsdale, NJ: Erlbaum.

Klahr, D., & Kotovsky, K. (Eds.). (1989). *Complex information processing: The impact of Herbert A. Simon.* Mahwah, NJ: Erlbaum.

Klein, G. (1987). Applications of analogical reasoning. *Metaphor and Symbolic Activity, 2,* 201–218.

Klein, G. (1989a). Recognition-primed decisions. In W. B. Rouse (Ed.), *Advances in man–machine research* (Vol. 5) (pp. 47–92). Greenwich, CT: JAI.

Klein, G. (1989b). *Utility of the critical decision method for eliciting knowledge from expert C debuggers* (Report on Purchase Order No. 339404, AT&T Bell Laboratories). Yellow Springs, OH: Klein Associates.

Klein, G. (1992). Using knowledge engineering to preserve corporate memory. In R. R. Hoffman (Ed.), *The psychology of expertise: Cognitive research and empirical AI* (pp. 170–190). Mahwah, NJ: Erlbaum.

Klein, G. (1993a). *Naturalistic decision making—Implications for design.* Fairborn, OH: Klein Associates.

Klein, G. (1993b). A recognition-primed decision (RPD) model of rapid decision making. In G. Klein, J. Orasanu, R. Calderwood, & C. E. Zsambok (Eds.), *Decision making in action: Models and methods* (pp. 138–147). Norwood, NJ: Ablex.

Klein, G. (1995). The value added by cognitive task analysis. In *Proceedings of the 39th Annual Human Factors and Ergonomics Society Meeting* (pp. 530–533). Santa Monica, CA: Human Factors and Ergonomics Society.

Klein, G. (1997). The recognition-primed decision (RPD) model: Looking back, looking forward. In C. E. Zsambok & G. Klein (Eds.), *Naturalistic decision making* (pp. 285–292). Mahwah, NJ: Erlbaum.

Klein, G. (1998). *Sources of power.* Cambridge, MA: MIT Press.

Klein, G. (2003). *Intuition at work.* New York: Doubleday.

Klein, G., & Brezovic, C. P. (1986). Design engineers and the design process: Decision strategies and human factors literature. In *Proceedings of the 30th Annual Meeting of the Human Factors Society* (pp. 771–775). Santa Monica, CA: Human Factors Society.

Klein, G., Calderwood, R., & Clinton-Cirocco, A. (1986). Rapid decision making on the fire ground. In *Proceedings of the 30th Annual Meeting of the Human Factors Society* (pp. 576–580). Santa Monica, CA: Human Factors Society.

Klein, G., Calderwood, R., & MacGregor, D. (1989). Critical decision method for eliciting knowledge. *IEEE Transactions on Systems, Man, and Cybernetics, 19,* 462–472.

Klein, G., Feltovich, P. J., Bradshaw, J. M., & Woods, D. D. (2006). Common ground and coordination in joint activity. In W. R. Rouse & K. B. Boff (Eds.), *Organizational simulation* (pp. 139–184). New York: Wiley.

Klein, G., & Hoffman R. R. (1993). Seeing the invisible: Perceptual-cognitive aspects of expertise. In M. Rabinowitz (Ed.). *Cognitive science foundations of instruction* (pp. 203–226). Mahwah, NJ: Erlbaum.

Klein, G., & Hoffman, R. R. (2008). The use of cognitive task analysis methods to capture mental models. In J. M Schraagen (Ed.), Naturalistic decision making and macrocognition: *Proceedings of the Seventh International Conference on Naturalistic Decision Making* (pp. 56–80) London: Ashgate.

Klein, G., Kaempf, G., Wolf, S. P., Thordsen, M., & Miller, T. E. (1997). Applying decision requirements to user-centered design. *International Journal of Human–Computer Studies, 46,* 1–15.

Klein, G., & Militello, L. G., (2001). Some guidelines for conducting cognitive task analysis. In E. Salas (Ed.), *Advances in human performance and cognitive engineering research* (Vol. 1, pp. 163–199). New York: JAI.

Klein, G., & Militello, L. G., (2004). The Knowledge Audit as a method for cognitive task analysis. In H. Montgomery, R. Lipshitz, & B. Brehmer (Eds.), *How professionals make decisions* (pp. 335–342). Mahwah, NJ: Erlbaum.

Klein, G., Moon, B., & Hoffman, R. R. (2006, July–August). Making sense of sensemaking: 1. Alternative perspectives. *IEEE Intelligent Systems,* pp. 22–25.

Klein, G., Orasanu, J., Calderwood, R., & Zsambok, C. E. (Eds.). (1993). *Decision making in action: Models and methods.* Norwood, NJ: Ablex.

Klein, G., Ross, K. G., Moon, B. M., Klein, D. E., Hoffman, R. R., & Hollnagel, E. (2003, May–June). Macrocognition. *IEEE Intelligent Systems,* pp. 81–85.

Klein, G., Schmitt, J., McCloskey, M., Heaton, J., Klinger, D., & Wolf, S. P. (1996). *A decision-centered study of the regimental command post* (Final Contract USC P.O. 681584 for the Naval Command, Control and Ocean Surveillance Center, San Diego, CA). Fairborn, OH: Klein Associates.

Klein, G. A., & Thordsen, M. L. (1989). Recognitional decision making in C2 organizations. In *Proceedings of the 1989 Symposium on Command-and-Control Research* (pp. 239–244). McLean, VA: Science Applications International Corporation.

Klein, G. A., & Thordsen, M. L. (1991). Representing cockpit crew decision making. In R. S. Jensen (Ed.), *Proceedings of the Sixth International Symposium on Aviation Psychology* (pp. 1026–1031). Columbus, OH: Ohio State University.

Klein, G., & Weitzenfeld, J. S. (1982). The use of analogues in comparability analysis. *Applied Ergonomics, 13,* 99–104.

Klein, G. A., & Woods, D. D. (1993). Conclusions: Decision making in action. In G. Klein, J. Orasanu, R. Calderwood, & C. Zsambok (Eds.), *Decision making in action: Models and methods* (pp. 404–411). Norwood, NJ: Ablex.

Klein, G., Woods, D. D., Bradshaw, J. M., Hoffman, R. R., & Feltovich, P. J. (2004, November–December). Ten challenges for making automation a "team player" in joint human-agent activity. *IEEE: Intelligent Systems,* pp. 91–95.

Klein, G., & Zsambok, C. (Eds.) (1995). *Naturalistic decision making.* Hillsdale, NJ: Erlbaum.

Klein, L. (1994). Sociotechnical/organizational design. In W. Karwowski & G. Salvendy (Eds.), *Organization and management of advanced manufacturing* (pp. 197–222). New York: Wiley.

Kleinman, D. L., & Serfaty, D. (1989). Team performance assessment in distributed decision making. In R. Gibson, J. P. Kincaid, & B. Godiez (Eds.), *Proceedings: Interactive networked simulation for training conference* (pp. 22–27). Orlando, FL: Institute for Simulation and Training.

Kleinmuntz, B. (Ed.) (1968). The processing of clinical information by man and machine. In B. Kleinmuntz (Ed.), *Formal representations of human judgment* (pp. 149–186). New York: Wiley.

Klemm, O. (1918). Untersuchungen über die Lokalisation von Schallreizen. *Archiv fur Psychologie, 38,* 71–114.

Klemp, G. O., & McClelland, D. G. (1986). What characterizes intelligent functioning among senior managers? In R. J. Sternberg & R. K. Wagner (Eds.), *Practical intelligence: Nature and origins of competence in the everyday world* (pp. 31–50). Cambridge: Cambridge University Press.

Kline, D. A. (2005). Intuitive team decision making. In H. Montgomery, R. Lipshitz, & B. Brehmer (Eds.), *How professionals make decisions* (pp. 171–182). Mahwah, NJ: Erlbaum.

Kling, R. (1997). Organizational and social informatics. In J. Flanagan, T. Huang, P. Jones, & S. Kasif (Eds.), *Human-centered systems: Information, interactivity and intelligence* (p. 310). Washington, DC: National Science Foundation.

Kling, R., & Iacono, S. (1984). The control of information systems development after implementation. *Communications of the ACM, 27, 1218–1226.*

Klinger, D. W. (1994). A decision-centered design approach to case-based reasoning: Helping engineers prepare bids and solve problems. In P. T. Kidd & W. Karwowski (Eds.), *Advances in agile manufacturing* (pp. 393–396). Manchester, England: IOS Press.

Klinger, D. W., Andriole, S. J., Militello, L. G., Adelman, L., Klein, G., & Gomes, M. E. (1993). *Designing for performance: A cognitive systems engineering approach to modifying an AWACS human–computer interface.* Fairborn, OH: Klein Associates.

Klinger, D. W., & Gomes, M. G. (1993). A cognitive systems engineering application for interface design. In *Proceedings of the 37th Annual Meeting of the Human Factors and Ergonomics Society* (pp. 16–20). Santa Monica, CA: Human Factors and Ergonomics Society.

Knorr-Cetina, K. D. (1981). *The manufacture of knowledge.* Oxford: Pergamon.

Knorr-Cetina, K. D. (1983). The ethnographic study of scientific work: Towards a constructivist interpretation of science. In K. D. Knorr-Cetina & M. Mulkay (Eds.), *Science observed: Perspectives on the social study of science* (pp. 115–140). London: Sage.

Knorr-Cetina, K. (1995). Metaphors in the scientific laboratory: Why are they there and what do they do? In Z. Radman (Ed.), *From a metaphorical point of view: A multidisciplinary approach to the cognitive content of metaphor* (pp. 329–349). Berlin, Germany: Walter de Gruyter.

Knorr-Cetina, K. D., & Mulkay, M. (1983). *Science observed: Perspectives on the social study of science.* Beverly Hills, CA: Sage.

Kolodner, J. L. (1983). Towards an understanding of the role of experience in the evolution from novice to expert. *International Journal of Man–Machine Studies, 19,* 497–518.

Kolodner, J. L. (1991, Summer). Improving decision making through case-based decision aiding. *AI Magazine, 12,* 52–68.

Kommers, P. A., Grabinger, S., & Dunlap, J. C. (Eds.). (1996). *Hypermedia learning environments.* Mahwah, NJ: Erlbaum.

Koonce, J. M. (1984). A brief history of aviation psychology. *Human Factors, 26,* 499–508.

Koopman, P., & Hoffman, R. R. (2003, November–December). Work-arounds, make-work, and kludges. *IEEE: Intelligent Systems,* pp. 70–75.

Kraut, R. E., Egido, C., & Galegher, J. (1990). Patterns of contact and communication in scientific research collaboration. In J. Galegher, R. E. Kraut, & C. Egido (Eds.), *Intellectual teamwork: Social and technological foundations of cooperative work* (pp. 149–171). Mahwah, NJ: Erlbaum.

Krogstad, J. L., Ettenson, R. T., & Shanteau, J. (1984). Context and experience in auditors' materiality judgments. *Auditing, 4,* 54–73.

Kruger, C., & Cross, N. (2006). Solution driven versus problem driven design: Strategies and outcomes. *Design Studies, 27,* 527–548.

Kugler, P. N., & Lintern, G. (1995). Risk management and the evolution of instability in large-scale, industrial systems. In P. Hancock, J. Flach, K. Caird, & K. Vicente (Eds.), *Local applications of the ecological approach to human–machine systems* (pp. 416–450). Hillsdale, NJ: Erlbaum.

Kuhn, T. S. (1962). *The structure of scientific revolutions.* Chicago: Chicago University Press.

Kuhn, T. S. (1977). *The essential tension: Selected studies in scientific tradition and change.* Chicago: Chicago University Press.

Kuipers, B. (1987). New reasoning methods for artificial intelligence in medicine. *International Journal of Man–Machine Studies, 26,* 707–718.

Kuipers, B., & Kassirer, J. P. (1983). How to discover a knowledge representation for causal reasoning by studying an expert physician. In *Proceedings of the 8th International Conference on Artificial Intelligence* (pp. 49–56). Los Altos, CA: Morgan Kaufman.

Kuipers, B., & Kassirer, J. P. (1984). Causal reasoning in medicine: Analysis of a protocol. *Cognitive Science, 8,* 363–385.

Kuipers, B., & Kassirer, J. P. (1987). Knowledge acquisition by analysis of verbatim protocols. In A. L. Kidd (Ed.), *Knowledge acquisition for expert systems: A practical handbook* (pp. 45–71). New York: Plenum Press.

Kuipers, B., Moskowitz, A. J., & Kassirer, J. P. (1988). Critical decisions under uncertainty. *Cognitive Science, 12,* 177–210.

Kulkanni, D., & Simon, H. A. (1988). The process of scientific discovery: The strategy of experimentation. *Cognitive Science, 12,* 139–175.

Kulatanga-Moruzi, C., Brooks, L. R., & Norman, G. R. (2001). Coordination of analytical and similarity based processing strategies and expertise in dermatological diagnosis. *Teaching and Learning in Medicine, 13,* 110–116.

Kulatunga-Moruzi, C., Brooks, L. R., & Norman, G. R. (2004). The diagnostic disadvantage of having all the facts: Using comprehensive feature lists to bias medical diagnosis. *Journal of Experimental Psychology: Learning, Memory and Cognition, 30,* 563–572.

Kundel, H. L., & LaFolette, P. S. (1972). Visual search patterns and experience with radiological images. *Radiology, 103,* 523–528.

Kundel, H. L., & Nodine, C. F. (1978). Studies of eye movements and visual search in radiology. In J. W. Senders, D. F. Fisher, & R. A. Monty (Eds.), *Eye movements and the higher psychological functions* (pp. 317–228). Hillsdale, NJ: Erlbaum.

Kundel, H. L., & Wright, D. J. (1969). The influence of prior knowledge on visual search strategies during the viewing of chest radiographs. *Radiology, 93,* 315–320.

Kurtz, A. K. (1944). *The prediction of code learning ability* (Report OSRD 4059). Washington, DC: Applied Psychology Panel, National Defense Research Council.

Kurz-Milcke, E., & Gigerenzer, G. (Eds.). (2004). *Experts in science and society*. New York: Kluwer Academic.

Kurzweil, R. (1985). What is artificial intelligence anyway? *American Scientist, 73*, 258–264.

Kusterer, K. C. (1978). *Know-how on the job: The important working knowledge of "unskilled" workers*. Boulder, CO: Westview.

LaFrance, M. (1989, April). The quality of expertise: Implications of expert-novice differences for knowledge acquisition. In C. R. Westphal & K. L. McGraw (Eds.), Special Issue on Knowledge Acquisition, *SIGART Newsletter*, No. 108, pp. 6–14. Special Interest Group on Artificial Intelligence: Association for Computing Machinery, New York.

LaFrance, M. (1992). Excavation, capture, collection, and creation: Computer scientists' metaphors for eliciting human expertise. *Metaphor and Symbolic Activity, 7*, 135–156.

Lahy, J.- M. (1923). *Taylorsystem und Physiologie der berufflichen Arbeit*. [The Taylor system and the physiology of professional work] Berlin: Verlag von Julius Springer.

Lahy, J.-M. (1933). *Le premier laboratoire psychotechnique Ferroviaire Français aux Chemins de Fer du Nord* [The first transportation psychotechnics laboratory for the northern railroad]. *Le Travail Humain* [Human Work], *1*, 409–431.

Lajoie, S. P., & Lesgold, A. M. (1989). Apprenticeship training in the workplace: Computer-coached practice environment as a new form of apprenticeship. *Machine-Mediated Learning, 3*, 7–28.

Landauer, T. K. (1995). *The trouble with computers*. Cambridge, MA: MIT Press.

Larkin, J. H. (1981). Enriching formal knowledge: A model for learning to solve textbook physics problems. In J. R. Anderson (Ed.), *Cognitive skills and their acquisition* (pp. 311–334). Mahwah, NJ: Erlbaum.

Larkin, J. H. (1983). The role of problem representation in physics. In D. Gentner & A. Stevens (Eds.), *Mental models*. Hillsdale, NJ: Erlbaum.

Larkin, J. H., McDermott, J., Simon, D. P., & Simon, H. A. (1980). Expert and novice performance in solving physics problems. *Science, 208*, 1335–1342.

Lashley, K. S. (1930). Basic neural mechanisms in behavior. *Psychological Review, 37*, 1–24.

Lashley, K. (1951). The problem of serial order in behavior. In L. A. Jeffress (Ed.), *Cerebral mechanisms in behavior* (pp. 112–136). New York: Wiley.

Laskey, K. B., Cohen, M. S., & Martin, A. W. (1989). Representing and eliciting knowledge about uncertain evidence and its implications. *IEEE Transactions on Systems, Man, and Cybernetics, 19*, 536–545.

Latour, B. (1983). Give me a laboratory and I will raise the world. In K. D. Knorr-Cetina & M. Mulkay (Eds.), *Science observed: Perspectives on the social study of science* (pp. 141–170). London: Sage.

Latour, B. (1992). The sociology of a few mundane artifacts. In W. Bijker & J. Law (Eds.), *Shaping technology/building society* (pp. 225–259). Cambridge, MA: MIT Press.

Latour, B., & Woolgar, S. (1979). *Laboratory life: The social construction of scientific facts*. Beverly Hills, CA: Sage.

Laugier, H., & Weinberg, D. (1936). Le Laboratorie du Travail des Chemins de fer de L'etat Français. [Laboratory of raildroad work for the nation of France]. *Le Travail Humain* [Human Work], *4*, 257–268.

Lave, J. (1988). *Cognition in practice: Mind, mathematics, and culture in everyday life*. Cambridge: Cambridge University Press.

Lave, J. (1993). Situating learning in communities of practice. In L. B. Resnick, J. M. Levine, & S. D. Teasley (Eds.), *Perspectives on socially shared cognition* (pp. 63–82). Washington, DC: American Psychological Association.

Lave, J. (1997). What's special about experiments as contexts for thinking. In M. Cole, Y. Engeström, & O. Vasquez (Eds.), *Mind, culture, and activity* (pp. 57–69). Cambridge: Cambridge University Press.

Lave, J., & Wenger, E. (1991). *Situated learning: Legitimate peripheral participation*. New York: Cambridge University Press.

Lawrence, J. A. (1988). Expertise on the bench: Modeling magistrates' judicial decisions. In M. T. H. Chi, R. Glaser, & J. M. Farr (Eds.) *The nature of expertise* (pp. 229–259). Mahwah, NJ: Erlbaum.

Lawsche, C. H., & Tiffin, J. (1945). The accuracy of precision instrument measurements in industrial inspection. *Journal of Applied Psychology, 29*, 413–491.

Layton, C., Smith, P. J., & McCoy, E. (1994). Design of a cooperative problem-solving system for en-route flight planning: an empirical eveluation. *Human Factors, 36*, 94–119.

Leahy, T. (1987). *A history of modern psychology*. Englewood Cliffs: Prentice Hall.

Lederberg, J., & Feigenbaum, E. A. (1968). Mechanization of inductive inference in organic chemistry. In B. Kleinmuntz (Ed.), *Formal representation of human judgment* (pp. 187–267). New York: Wiley.

Leedom, D. K. (2001). "Sensemaking Symposium." Final Report to the Command and Control Research Program, Office of the Assistant Secretary of Defense for Command, Control, Communications and Intelligence. Washington DC: Department of Defense. [Downloaded 14 April 2006 from http://www.au.af.mil/au/awc/awcgate/ccrp/sensemaking_final_report.pdf].

Legros, L. A., & Weston, H. C. (1926). *On the design of machinery in relation to the operator*. London: His Majesty's Stationery Office.

Leigh, S. (1992). The skin, the skull, and the self: Toward a sociology of the brain. In A. Harrington (Ed.), *So human a brain: Knowledge and values in the neurosciences* (pp. 204–228). Boston: Birkhäuser.

Leishman, T. R., & Cook, D. A. (2002). Requirements risks can drown software projects. *Crosstalk, 15*(4), 4–8.

Lenat, D. B., & Feigenbaum, E. A. (1987, August). On the thresholds of knowledge. In *Procedings of the International Joint Conference on Artificial Intelligence* (pp. 1173–1182). Milano, Italy: International Joint Conferences on Artificial Intelligence.

Leplat, J. (1993). Psychological work analysis: Some historical milestones. *Le Travail Humain, 56*, 115–131.

Leplat, J. (1994). Collective activity in work: Some ways of research. *Le Travail Humain, 57*, 209–226.

Leplat, J., and Pailhous, J. (1981). L'acquisition des habiletés mentales: la place des techniques. [The acquisition of mental habits: The role of skill]. *Le Travail Humain [Human Work], 44*, 275–282.

Lesgold, A. M. (1984). Acquiring expertise. In J. R. Anderson & S. M. Kosslyn (Eds.), *Tutorials in learning and memory: Essays in honor of Gordon Bower* (pp. 31–60). San Francisco, CA: W. H. Freeman.

Lesgold, A. M. (1985). *Cognitive and instructional theories of impasses in learning*. Pittsburgh, PA: University of Pittsburgh.

Lesgold, A. M. (1986). *Toward a theory of curriculum for use in designing intelligent tutoring systems*. Pittsburgh, PA: University of Pittsburgh.

Lesgold, A. M., Katz, S., Greenberg, L., Hughes, E., & Eggan, G. (1992). Extensions of intelligent tutoring paradigms to support collaborative learning. In S. Dijkstra, H. P. M. Krammer, & J. J. G. van Merrienboer (Eds.), *Instructional models in computer-based learning environments* (pp. 291–311). Berlin: Springer-Verlag.

Lesgold, A. M., Lajoie, S., Eastmen, R., Eggan, G., Gitomer, D., Glaser, R., et al. (1986). *Cognitive task analysis to enhance technical skills training and assessment*. Pittsburgh, PA: Learning Research and Development Center.

Lesgold, A. M., Rubinson, H., Feltovich, P., Glaser, R., Klopfer, D., & Wang, Y. (1988). Expertise in a complex skill: Diagnosing X-ray pictures. In M. Chi, R. Glaser, & M. Farr (Eds.), *The nature of expertise* (pp. 311–342). Hillsdale, NJ: Erlbaum.

Lewicki, P. (1986). Processing information about covariance that cannot be articulated. *Journal of Experimental Psychology: Learning, Memory and Cognition, 12*, 135–146.

Lewis, M. W., & Anderson, J. R. (1985). Discrimination of operator schemata in problems solving: Learning from examples. *Cognitive Psychology, 17*, 26–65.

Libby, R., & Lewis, B. L. (1977). Human information processing research in accounting: The state of the art. *Accounting, Organizations, and Society, 21*, 245–268.

Liberman, A. M., Delattre, P. C., & Cooper, F. S. (1952). The role of selected stimulus variables in the perception of unvoiced stop consonants. *American Journal of Psychology, 65*, 497–516.

Lichtenstein, S., Fischhoff, B., & Phillips, L. D. (1982). Calibration of probabilities: The state of the art in 1980. In D. Kahneman, P. Slovic, & A. Tversky (Eds.), *Judgment under uncertainty: Heuristics and biases*. New York: Cambridge University Press.

Lieberman, D. M. (1979). Behaviorism and the mind: A (limited) call for a return to introspection. *American Psychologist, 34*, 319–333.

Lind, M. (1999). Making sense of the abstraction hierarchy. In *Proceedings of the Seventh European Conference on Cognitive Science Approaches to Process Control* (pp. 195–200). Villeneuve d'Asc, France: Presses Universitaires de Valenciennes.

Lindley, E. H. (1895). A preliminary study of some of the motor phenomena of mental effort. *American Journal of Psychology, 7*, 491–517.

Lindsley, D. B. (1945). *Final report in summary of work on the selection and training of radar operators* (Report OSRD 5766). Washington, DC: Applied Psychology Panel, National Defense Research Council.

Lipshitz, R. (1987). "Decision making in the real world: Developing descriptions and prescriptions from decision maker's retrospective accounts." Report, Center for Applied Science, Boston University, Boston MA.

Lipshitz, R. (1989). *Decision making as argument-driven action*. Boston: Boston University Center for Applied Social Science.

Lipshitz, R. (1993). Converging themes in the study of decision making in realistic settings. In G. Klein, J. Orasanu, R. Calderwood, & C. E. Zsambok (Eds.), *Decision making in action: Models and methods* (pp. 103–137). Norwood, NJ: Ablex.

Lipshitz, R., & Ben Shaul, O. (1997). Schemata and mental models in recognition-primed decision making. In C. E. Zsambok & G. Klein (Eds.), *Naturalistic decision making* (pp. 293–304). Mahwah, NJ: Erlbaum.

Lipshitz, R., Klein, G., Orasanu, J., & Salas, E. (2001). Rejoinder: A welcome dialogue—and the need to continue. *Journal of Behavioral Decision Making, 14*, 385–389.

Loftus, E. F., & Suppes, P. (1972). Structural variables that determine problem solving difficulty in computer-assisted instruction. *Journal of Educational Psychology, 63*, 531–542.

Luff, P., Heath, C., & Greatbach, D. (1992). Tasks in interaction: Paper- and screen-based activity in cooperative work. In *Proceedings of the Conference on Computer-Supported Cooperative Work* (pp. 163–170). New York: Association for Computing Machinery.

Lusted, L. B. (1960). Logical analysis and Roentgen diagnosis. *Radiology, 74*, 178–1.

Luton, A. (1926). A correlational analysis of proficiency in typewriting. *Archives of Psychology, 13*, Whole No. 82.

Lynch, M. (1991). Laboratory space and the technological complex: An investigation of topical contextures. *Science in Context, 4,* 51–78.

Lynch, M. (1993). *Scientific practice and ordinary action.* Cambridge: Cambridge University Press.

Lynch, M., & Edgerton, S. Y. (1988). Aesthetics and digital image processing: Representational craft in contemporary astronomy. In G. Fyfe & J. Law (Eds.), *Picturing power: Visual depictions and social relations* (pp. 184–220). London: Routledge.

Lynch, M., Livingston, E., & Garfield, H. (1983). Temporal order in laboratory work. In K. D. Knorr-Cetina & M. Mulkay (Eds.), *Science observed: Perspectives on the social study of science* (pp. 205–238). London: Sage.

Lysinki, E. (1923). *Psychologie des Betriebes.* Berlin: Industrieverlag Spätze and Linde.

MacKay, D. M. (1951). Mindlike behaviour in artefacts. *British Journal of the Philosophy of Science, 2,* 105–121.

MacKay, D. M. (1956a). The epistemological problem for automata. In C. E. Shannon & J. McCarthy (Eds.), *Automata studies* (pp. 235–251). Princeton, NJ: Princeton University Press.

MacKay, D. M. (1956b). Towards an information-flow model of human behaviour. *British Journal of Psychology, 47,* 30–43.

MacKay, D. M. (1969). *Information, mechanism, and meaning.* Cambridge, MA: MIT Press.

Mackay, W. (1990). Patterns of sharing customizable software. In *Proceedings of the Conference on Computer-Supported Cooperative Work* (pp. 209–221). New York: Association for Computing Machinery.

Mackay, W. E. (2000). Is paper safer? The role of paper flight strips in air traffic control. *ACM/ Transactions on computer-human interactions, 6,* 311–340.

Mackenzie, C. F., Hu, P. F., & Horst, R. L. (1995). An audio-video acquisition system for automated remote monitoring in the clinical environment. *Journal of Clinical Monitoring, 11,* 335–341.

Mackworth, N. H. (1950). *Researches on the measurement of human performance.* London: Her Majesty's Stationery Office.

Madni, A. M. (1988). The role of human factors in expert systems design and acceptance. *Human Factors, 30,* 395–414.

Mahew, D. J. (2003). Requirements specifications within the usability engineering life cycle. In J. A. Jacko & A. Sears (Eds.), *The human–computer interaction handbook* (pp. 914–921). Mahwah, NJ: Erlbaum.

Maier, N. R. F. (1946). *Psychology in industry: A psychological approach to industrial problems.* New York: Houghton Mifflin.

Mallory, L. A., & Temple, W. J. (1945). *Final report in summary of work on the selection and training of telephone talkers* (OSRD Report 5497). Washington, DC: Applied Psychology Panel, National Defense Research Council.

Mamede, S., & Schmidt, H. G. (2004). The structure of reflective practice in medicine. *Medical Education, 38,* 1302–1306.

Mandin, H., Harasym, P., Eagle, C., & Watanabe, M. (1995). Developing a "clinical presentation" curriculum at the University of Calgary. *Academic Medicine, 70,* 186–193.

Mandin, H., Jones, A., Woloschuk, W., & Harasym, P. (1997). Helping students learn to think like experts when solving clinical problems. *Journal of the Academy of Medicine, 72,* 173–179.

Mandler, G. (1967). Organization and memory. In K. W. Spence & J. T. Spence (Eds.), *The psychology of learning and motivation, Vol. 1* (pp. 327–372). New York: Academic Press.

Mandler, J. M., & Mandler, G. (1964). *Thinking: From association to Gestalt.* New York: Wiley.

Manes, S. (1997, March 11). Technology in 2047: How smart? *New York Times,* p. C-8.

Mantovani, G. (1996). *New communication environments from everyday to virtual.* Bristol, PA: Taylor & Francis.

Marketplace. (1997). *Marketplace Morning Report for January 31st, 1997.* National Public Radio.

Marti, P., & Scrivani, P. (2003). The representation of context in the simulation of complex systems. *Cognitive Technology, 8,* 34–44.

Matsumoto, E. D., Hamstra, S. J., Radomski, S. B., & Cusimano, M. D. (2002) The effect of bench model fidelity on endourologic skills: A randomized controlled study. *Journal of Urology, 167,* 1243–1247.

Mayer, R. E. (1977). The sequencing of instruction and the concept of assimilation-to-schema. *Instructional Science, 6,* 369–388.

Mayer, R. E. (1997). Multimedia learning: Are we asking the right questions? *Educational Psychology, 32,* 1–19.

Maynard, H. B., Stegemerten, G. J., & Schwab, J. L. (1948). *Methods: Time measurement.* New York: McGraw-Hill.

McCabe, V., & Balzano, G. J. (Eds.). (1986). *Event cognition: An ecological perspective.* Mahwah, NJ: Erlbaum.

McConkie, G. W. (1997). Getting to know you: A requirement of intelligent systems. In J. Flanagan, T. Huang, P. Jones, & S. Kasif (Eds.), *Human-centered systems: Information, interactivity and intelligence* (pp. 280–282). Washington, DC: National Science Foundation.

McCormick, E. J. (1976). Job and task analysis. In M. D. Dunnette (Ed.), *Handbook of industrial and organizational psychology* (pp. 651–696). Chicago: Rand McNally.

McCulloch, W. S. (1949). The brain as a computing machine. *Electrical Engineering, 68,* 492–497.

McDermott, J., & Larkin, J. H. (1978). Representing textbook physics problems. In *Proceedings of the 2nd National Conference of the Canadian Society for Computational Studies of Intelligence* (pp. 156–164). Toronto, Ontario: University of Toronto Press.

McDonald, B. A., & Witten, I. H. (1989). A framework for knowledge acquisition through techniques of concept learning. *IEEE Transactions on Systems, Man, and Cybernetics, 19,* 499–512.

McGeoch, J. A. (1931). The acquisition of skill. *Psychological Bulletin, 28,* 414–415.

McGraw, K. L. (1992). Managing and documenting the knowledge acquisition process. In R. R. Hoffman (Ed.), *The psychology of expertise: Cognitive research and empirical AI* (pp. 149–169). Mahwah, NJ: Erlbaum.

McGraw, K., & Harbison, K. (1997). *User-centered requirements: The scenario-based engineering process.* Mahwah, NJ: Erlbaum.

McGraw, K. L., & Harbison-Briggs, K. (1989). *Knowledge acquisition: Principles and guidelines.* Englewood Cliffs, NJ: Prentice Hall.

McGraw, K., & Riner, A. (1987). Task analysis: Structuring the knowledge acquisition process. *Texas Instruments Technical Journal, 4,* 16–21.

McGraw, K. L., & Seale, M. R. (1988). Knowledge elicitation with multiple experts: Considerations and techniques. *Artificial Intelligence Review, 2,* 31–44.

McGuire, C. H. (1985). Medical problem-solving: A critique of the literature. *Journal of Medical Education, 60,* 587–595.

McKeithen, K. B., Reitman, J. S., Reuter, H. H., & Hirtle, S. C. (1981). Knowledge organization and skill differences in computer programmers. *Cognitive Psychology, 13,* 307–325.

McKenney, J. L., Duncan, C., Copeland, R., & Mason, O. (1995). *Waves of change: Business evolution through information technology*. Boston: Harvard Business School Press.

McKeown, D. M. (1983). *Concept-maps*. Pittsburgh, PA: Carnegie Mellon University.

McMillan, B. (1953). Mathematical aspects of information theory. In B. McMillan, D. A. Grant, P. M. Fitts, F. C. Frick, W. S. McCulloch, G. A. Miller, et al. (Eds.), *Current trends in information theory* (pp. 1–17). Pittsburgh, PA: University of Pittsburgh Press.

McMillan, B., Grant, D. A., Fitts, P. M., Frick, F. C., McCulloch, W. S., Miller, G. A., et al. (1953). *Current trends in information theory*. Pittsburgh, PA: University of Pittsburgh Press.

Means, B., & Gott, S. P. (1988). Cognitive task analysis as a basis for tutor development: Articulating abstract knowledge representations. In J. Psotka, L. D. Massey, & S. A. Mutter (Eds.), *Intelligent tutoring systems: Lessons learned* (pp. 35–57). Mahwah, NJ: Erlbaum.

Medin, D. L., Altom, M. W., & Murphy, T. D. (1984). Given versus induced category representations: Use of prototype and exemplar information in classification. *Journal of Experimental Psychology: Learning, Memory and Cognition, 10*, 333–352.

Medsker, G. J., & Campion, M. A. (1997). Job and team design. In G. Salvendy (Ed.), *Handbook of human factors and ergonomics* (pp. 450–489). New York: Wiley.

Meister, D. (1985). *Behavioral analysis and measurement methods*. New York: Wiley.

Meister, D. (1999). *The history of human factors and ergonomics*. Mahwah, NJ: Erlbaum.

Melcher, J. M., & Schooler, J. W. (1996). The misremembrance of wines past: Verbal and perceptual expertise differentially mediate overshadowing of taste memory. *Journal of Memory and Language, 35*, 231–245.

Merkelbach, E. J. H. M., & Schraagen, J. M. C. (1994). *A framework for the analysis of cognitive tasks* (Report No. TNO-TM-1994-B-13). Soesterberg, Germany: TNO Institute for Human Factors, TNO Defense Research.

Merton, R. K., Fiske, M., & Kendall, P. L. (1956). *The focused interview*. Glencoe, IL: Free Press.

Merton, R. K., & Kendall, P. L. (1946). The focused interview. *American Journal of Sociology, 51*, 541–557.

Merton, T. (1977). *The sociology of science*. Chicago: Chicago University Press.

Meyer, M. A., & Payton, R. C. (1992). Towards an analysis and classification of approaches to knowledge acquisition from examination of textual metaphor. *Knowledge Acquisition, 4*, 347–369.

Meyerheim, W. (1927). *Psychotechnik der Buchführung*. Berlin: Verlag von Julius Springer.

Micciche, P. F., & Lancaster, J. S. (1989, April). Application of neurolinguistic techniques to knowledge acquisition. In C. R. Westphal & K. L. McGraw (Eds.), Special Issue on Knowledge Acquisition, *SIGART Newsletter*, No. 108, pp. 28–33. Special Interest Group on Artificial Intelligence, Association for Computing Machinery, New York.

Michalski, R. S., & Chilausky, R. L. (1980). Knowledge acquisition by encoding expert rules versus computer induction from examples: A case study involving soybean pathology. *International Journal of Man-Machine Studies, 12*, 63–87.

Mieg, H. A. (2001). *The social psychology of expertise*. Mahwah, NJ: Erlbaum.

Mieg, H. A. (2006). Social and sociological factors in the development of expertise. In K. A. Ericsson, N. Charness, P. Feltovich, & R. Hoffman (Eds.), *Cambridge handbook on expertise and expert performance* (pp. 743–760). New York: Cambridge University Press.

Militello, L. G., & Hutton, R. J. B. (1998). Applied Cognitive Task Analysis (ACTA): A practitioner's toolkit for understanding cognitive task demands [Special issue]. *Ergonomics, 41*, 1618–1641.

Militello, L. G., & Lim, L. (1995). Patient assessment skills: Assessing early cues of necrotizing enterocolitis. *Journal of Perinatal and Neonatal Nursing, 9,* 42–52.

Militello, L. G., Patterson, E. S., Bowman, L., & Wears, R. (2007). Information flow during crisis management: Challenges to coordination in the emergency operations Center. *Cognition, Technology, and Work Special Issue on Large-Scale Coordination, 9,* 25–31.

Militello, L. G., Patterson, E. S., Wears, R., & Snead, A. (2005). Emergency operations center design to support rapid response and recovery. In *Proceedings of the Working Together: R&D Partnerships in Homeland Security Conference* (CD-ROM Paper # 1-9). Washington, DC: Department of Homeland Security.

Militello, L. G., Quill, L., Patterson, E. S., Wears, R., & Ritter, J. A. (2005). Large-scale coordination in emergency response. In *Proceedings of the 49th Annual Human Factors and Ergonomics Society Meeting* (pp. 534–538). Santa Monica, CA: Human Factors and Ergonomics Society.

Miller, A. I. (1984). *Imagery in scientific thought.* Boston: Birkhäuser.

Miller, C. A., & Vicente, K. J. (1999). Task "versus" work domain analysis techniques: A comparative analysis. In *Proceedings of the Human Factors and Ergonomics Society 43rd Annual Meeting* (pp. 328–332). Santa Monica, CA: Human Factors and Ergonomics Society.

Miller, G. A. (1979). "A very personal history." Occasional Paper of the MIT Center for Cognitive Science. Massachusetts Institute of Technology, Cambridge, MA.

Miller, G. A. (1953). Information theory and the study of speech. In B. McMillan, D. A. Grant, P. M. Fitts, F. C. Frick, W. S. McCulloch, G. A. Miller, et al. (Eds.), *Current trends in information theory* (pp. 119–139). Pittsburgh, PA: University of Pittsburgh Press.

Miller, G. A., Galanter, E., & Pribram, K. H. (1960). *Plans and the structure of behavior.* New York: Holt.

Miller, G. A., Heise, G. A., & Lichten, W. (1951). The intelligibility of speech as a function of the context of the test materials. *Journal of Experimental Psychology, 41,* 329–355.

Miller, R. B. (1953). *A method for man-machine task analysis* (Report WADC-TR-53-137). Wright Air Development Center, Wright Patterson Air Force Base, Ohio.

Miller, T. E., Wolf, S. P., Thordsen, M. L., & Klein, G. (1992). *A decision-centered approach to storyboarding anti-air warfare interfaces.* Fairborn, OH: Klein Associates.

Miller, T. E., & Woods, D. D. (1997). Key issues for naturalistic decision making researchers in system design. In C. E. Zsambok & G. Klein (Eds.), *Naturalistic decision making* (pp. 141–150). Mahwah, NJ: Erlbaum.

Minsky, M. (1961). Steps toward artificial intelligence. *Proceedings of the Institute of Radio Engineers, 49,* 8–30.

Minsky, M., & Papert, S. (1974). *Artificial intelligence.* Eugene, OR: Oregon State System of Higher Education.

Mintzes, J., Wandersee, J., & Novak, J. (1998). *Teaching science for understanding.* San Diego: Academic Press.

Mintzes, J., Wandersee, J., & Novak, J. (2000). *Assessing science understanding.* San Diego: Academic Press.

Mitchell, C. M., & Sundstrom, G. A. (1997). Human interaction with complex systems: Design issues and research approaches. *IEEE Transactions on Systems, Man, and Cybernetics. Part A: Systems and Humans, 27,* 265–273.

Mitchell, M. (1993). *Analogy-making as perception: A computer model.* Cambridge, MA: MIT Press.

Mitchell, M. J. H. (1948). *Direction of movement of machine controls.* Cambridge, England: Medical Research Council.

Mitchell, M. J. H., & Vince, M. A. (1951). The direction of movement of machine controls. *Quarterly Journal of Experimental Psychology, 3,* 24–35.

Mittal, S., & Dym, C. L. (1985, Summer). Knowledge acquisition from multiple experts. *AI Magazine, 6,* 32–36.

Miyake, N., & Norman, D. A. (1979). To ask a question, one must know enough to know what is not known. *Journal of Verbal Learning and Verbal Behavior, 18,* 357–364.

Moede, W. (1926). Kraftfahrer-Eignungsprüfen beim deutschen heer 1915–1981. *Industrielle Psychotechnik, 3,* 23–28.

Moede, W. (1930). *Lehrbuch der Psychotechnik* (2 vols.). Berlin: Verlag Julius Springer.

Mogensen, A. H. (1932). *Common sense applied to motion and time study.* New York: McGraw-Hill.

Monarch, A., Konda, S. L., Levy, S. N., Reich, Y., Subrahmanian, E., & Ulrich, C. (1997). Mapping sociotechnical networks in the making. In G. C. Bowker, S. L. Star, W. Turner, & L. Gasser (Eds.), *Social science, technology, and cooperative work: Beyond the great divide* (pp. 331–354). Mahwah, NJ: Erlbaum.

Monk, A. (1985). How and when to collect behavioral data. In A. Monk (Ed.), *Fundamentals of human-computer interaction* (pp. 69–79). New York: Academic Press.

Montgomery, H., Lipshitz, R., & Brehmer, B. (Eds.). (2005). *How professional make decisions.* Mahwah, NJ: Erlbaum.

Moon, B. (2002, May). *Naturalistic decision making: Establishing a naturalistic perspective in judgment and decision-making research.* Paper presented at the 19th Qualitative Analysis Conference, McMaster University, Hamilton, Ontario, Canada.

Moore, H. (1942). *Psychology for business and industry.* New York: McGraw-Hill.

Moore, T. V. (1939). *Cognitive psychology.* New York: Lippincott.

Moray, N. (Ed.). (2005). *Ergonomics: Major writings, Volume 1: The history and scope of human factors.* New York: Taylor & Francis.

Moray, N., Sanderson, P. M., & Vicente, K. J. (1992). Cognitive task analysis of a complex work domain: A case study. *Reliability Engineering and System Safety, 36,* 207–216.

Morris, P. E. (1988). Expertise and everyday memory. In M. M. Gruneberg, P. E. Morris, & R. N. Sykes (Eds.), *Practical aspects of memory: Current research and issues, Vol. 1* (pp. 459–465). Chichester, England: John Wiley.

Mosier, K. L. (1997). Myths of expert decision making and automated decision aids. In C. E. Zsambok & G. Klein (Eds.), *Naturalistic decision making* (pp. 319–330). Mahwah, NJ: Erlbaum.

Motta, E., Rajan, T., & Eisenstadt, M. (1989). A methodological tool for knowledge acquisition in KEATS-2. In J. Boose & B. Gaines (Eds.), *Proceedings of the Third Knowledge Acquisition for Knowledge-Based Systems Workshop* (pp. 21.1–21.20). Alberta, Canada: Department of Computer Science, University of Alberta.

Mueller, M. J. (2003). Participatory design: The third space in human–computer interaction. In J. A. Jacko & A. Sears (Eds.), *The human–computer interaction handbook* (pp. 1051–1068). Mahwah, NJ: Erlbaum.

Mullen, C. (2006). All in a day's work. *Reader's Digest Laughlines.* [Downloaded 21 March 2008 at http://www.rd.com/newsletter-archive-parent/laugh-lines].

Mullin, T. M. (1989). Experts' estimation of uncertain quantities and its implications for knowledge acquisition. *IEEE Transactions on Systems, Man, and Cybernetics, 19,* 616–625.

Mumaw, R. J., Roth, E. M., Vicente, K. J., & Burns, C. M. (2000). There is more to monitoring a nuclear power plant than meets the eye. *Human Factors, 42,* 36–55.

Mundel, M. E. (1947). *Systematic motion and time study.* New York: Prentice Hall.

Mundel, M. E. (1948). Motion study techniques which could be brought to bear on desirable size of aircraft crews. In D. Morrison (Ed.), *Scientific methods for use in the investigation of flight crew requirements* (pp. 55–68). Woods Hole, MA: Flight Safety Foundation.

Mundel, M. E. (1978). *Motion and time study: Principles and practice* (5th ed.). Englewood Cliffs, NJ: Prentice Hall.

Münsterberg, H. (1912). *Psychologie und Wirtschaftsleben.* [Psychology and business life.] Leipzig: Barth.

Münsterberg, H. (1913). *Psychology and industrial efficiency.* Boston: Houghton Mifflin.

Münsterberg, H. (1914). *Grundzüge der Psychotechnik.* [Foundations of Psychotechnics.] Lepizig: Barth.

Murphy, G. L., & Wright, J. C. (1984). Changes in conceptual structure with expertise: Differences between real-world experts and novices. *Journal of Experimental Psychology: Learning, Memory, and Cognition, 10,* 144–155.

Murray, P. (1989). Poetic genius and its classical origins. I. P. Murray (ed.), *Genius: the history of an idea* (pp. 9–31). Oxford, England: Basil Blackwell.

Muzzin, L. J., Norman, G. R., Feightner, J. W., & Tugwell, P. (1983). Expertise in recall of clinical protocols in two specialty areas. In *Proceedings of the 22nd Annual Conference of Research on Medical Education* (pp. 122–127). Washington, DC: Association of American Medical Colleges.

Myers, C. S. (1925/1977). *Industrial psychology.* New York: Arno Press.

Myles-Worsley, M., Johnston, W. A., & Simons, M. A. (1988). The influence of expertise on X-ray image processing. *Journal of Experimental Psychology: Learning, Memory and Cognition, 14,* 553–557.

Naikar, N. (2005a). A methodology for work domain analysis: The first phase of cognitive work analysis. In *Proceedings of the Human Factors and Ergonomics Society 49th Annual Meeting* (pp. 312–316). Santa Monica, CA: Human Factors and Ergonomics Society.

Naikar, N. (2005b). Theoretical concepts for work domain analysis, the first phase of cognitive work analysis. In *Proceedings of the Human Factors and Ergonomics Society 49th Annual Meeting* (pp. 249–253). Santa Monica, CA: Human Factors and Ergonomics Society.

Naikar, N. (2006). Beyond interface design: Further applications of cognitive work analysis. *International Journal of Industrial Ergonomics, 36,* 423–438.

Naikar, N., Hopcroft, R., & Moylan, A. (2005). *Work domain analysis: Theoretical concepts and methodology.* Victoria, Australia: Defence Science and Technology Organization.

Naikar, N., Sanderson, P. M., & Lintern, G. (1999). Work domain analysis for identification of training needs and training-system design. In *Proceedings of the Human Factors and Ergonomics Society 43rd Annual Meeting* (pp. 1128–1132). Santa Monica, CA: Human Factors and Ergonomics Society.

Nardi, B. A. (Ed.). (1996). *Context and consciousness: Activity theory and human–computer interaction.* Cambridge, MA: MIT Press.

Nardi, B. A. (1997). The use of ethnographic methods in design evaluation. In M. Helander, T. Landauer, & P. Prabhu (Eds.), *Handbook of human–computer interaction* (2nd ed., pp. 361–366). Amsterdam: North-Holland.

NASA Mars Climate Orbiter Mishap Investigation Board. (2000, March 13). *Report on project management at NASA.* Washington DC: NASA HQ.

National Science and Technology Council. (1999). *Human-centered transportation systems: A federal research and development initiative.* Washington, DC: Author.

Naval Air Training Command (1993). "Flight Training Instruction TH-57, Helicopter Advanced Phase, CNATRA P-457 New (08-93) PAT." U. S. Naval Air Station, Corpus Christi, TX.

Neale, I. M. (1988). First generation expert systems: A review of knowledge acquisition methodologies. *Knowledge Engineering Review, 3,* 105–146.

Nehme, C. E., Scott, S. D., Cummings, M. L., & Furusho, C. Y. (2006). Generating requirements for futuristic heterogeneous unmanned systems. In *Proceedings of the Human Factors and Ergonomics Society 50th Annual Meeting* (pp. 235–239). Santa Monica, CA: Human Factors and Ergonomics Society.

Neisser, U. (1967). *Cognitive psychology.* New York: Appleton Century Crofts.

Neisser, U. (1976). *Cognition and reality: Principles and implications of cognitive psychology.* San Francisco: W. H. Freeman.

Neisser, U. (Ed.). (1982). *Memory observed: Remembering in natural contexts.* San Francisco: W. H. Freeman.

Neisser, U. (1991). A case of misplaced nostalgia. *American Psychologist, 46,* 34–36.

Neisser, U. (1993). Toward a skillful psychology. In D. Rogers & J. A. Sloboda (Eds.), *The acquisition of symbolic skills* (pp. 1–17). New York: Plenum.

Nemeth, C. P. (2004). *Human factors methods for design: Making systems human-centered.* Boca Raton, FL: CRC Press.

Nendaz, M. R., & Bordage, G. (2002). Promoting diagnostic problem representation. *Medical Education, 36,* 760–766.

Nestor, J.- M. (1933). Vocational tests on the European railways, I, II. *Human Factor, 7,* 11–23, 51–58.

Neufeld, V. R., Norman, G. R., Barrows, H. S., & Feightner, J. W. (1981). Clinical problem-solving by medical students: A longitudinal and cross-sectional analysis. *Medical Education, 15,* 315–322.

Newbold, E. M. (1926). *A contribution to the study of the human factor in the causation of accidents.* London: His Majesty's Stationery Office.

Newell, A. F. (1968). On the analysis of human problem solving protocols. In J. C. Gardin & B. Jaulin (Eds.), *Calcul et formalization dans les sciences de l'homme* (pp. 145–185). Paris: Editions du Centre National de la Recherche Scienfitique.

Newell, A. F. (1981). The knowledge level. *Artificial Intelligence, 18,* 87–127.

Newell, A. F. (1985). Duncker on thinking: An inquiry into progress on cognition. In S. Koch & D. E. Leary (Eds.), *A century of psychology as a science* (pp. 392–419). Oxford: Oxford University Press.

Newell, A. F. (1990). *Unified theories of cognition.* Cambridge, MA: Harvard University Press.

Newell, A. F., & Simon, H. A. (1956). The logic theory machine: A complex information processing system. *Institute of Radio Engineers Transactions on Information Theory. IT-2,* 61–79.

Newell, A. F., & Simon, H. A. (1972). *Human problem solving.* Englewood Cliffs, NJ: Prentice Hall.

Nicely, P. E., & Miller, G. A. (1957). Some effects of unequal spatial distribution on the detectability of radar targets. *Journal of Experimental Psychology, 53,* 195–198.

Nickerson, R. S. (1997). Cognitive technology: Reflections on a long history and a promising future. *Cognitive Technology, 2,* 6–20.

Nisbett, R. E. (2003). *The geography of thought: How Asians and Westerners think differently … and why.* New York: Free Press.

Nisbett, R. E., & Wilson, T. D. (1977). Telling more than we can know: Verbal reports on mental processes. *Psychological Review, 84,* 231–259.

Noble, D. F. (1989). Schema-based knowledge elicitation for planning and situation assessment. *IEEE Transactions on Systems, Man, and Cybernetics, 19,* 473–482.

Norman, D. A. (1987). Cognitive engineering-cognitive science. In J. M. Carroll (Ed.), *Interfacing thought: Cognitive aspects of human-computer interaction* (pp. 323–336). Cambridge, MA: The MIT Press.

Norman, D. A. (1988). *The psychology of everyday things.* New York: Basic Books.

Norman, D. A. (1990). The "problem" with automation: Inappropriate feedback and interaction, not "over-automation." *Philosophical Transactions of the Royal Society of London, 327,* 585–593.

Norman, D. A. (1992). *Turn signals are the facial expressions of automobiles.* Reading, MA: Addison-Wesley.

Norman, D. A. (1993). *Things that make us smart.* Reading, MA: Addison-Wesley.

Norman, D. A. (1998). *The invisible computer.* Cambridge, MA: MIT Press.

Norman, G. R. (1992). Expertise in visual diagnosis: A review of the literature. *Academic Medicine, 67,* S78–S84.

Norman, G. R., Brooks, L. R., & Allen, S. W. (1989). Recall by experts and novices as a record of processing attention. *Journal of Experimental Psychology: Learning, Memory and Cognition, 15,* 1166–1174.

Norman, G. R., Brooks, L. R., Colle, C. L., & Hatala, R. M. (2000). The benefit of diagnostic hypotheses in clinical reasoning: Experimental study of an instructional intervention for forward and backward reasoning. *Cognition and Instruction, 17,* 433–448.

Norman, G. R., Eva, K., Brooks, L., & Hamstra, S. (2006). Expertise in medicine and surgery. In K. A. Ericsson, N. Charness, P. Feltovich, & R. R. Hoffman (Eds.), *Cambridge handbook of expertise and expert performance* (pp. 339–353). New York: Cambridge University Press.

Norman, G. R., Trott, A. L., Brooks, L. R., & Smith, E. K. M. (1994). Cognitive differences in clinical reasoning related to postgraduate training. *Teaching and Learning in Medicine, 6,* 114–120.

Novak, J. D. (1977). *A theory of education.* Ithaca, NY: Cornell University Press.

Novak, J. D. (1990). Concept-maps and Vee diagrams: Two metacognitive tools for science and mathematics education. *Instructional Science, 19,* 29–52.

Novak, J. D. (1991). Clarify with concept-maps. *Science Teacher, 58,* 45–49.

Novak, J. D. (1998). *Learning, creating, and using knowledge.* Mahwah, NJ: Erlbaum.

Novak, J. D., & Gowin, D. B. (1984). *Learning how to learn.* Cambridge: Cambridge University Press.

Novak, J. D., & Musonda, D. (1991). A twelve-year longitudinal study of science concept learning. *American Educational Research Journal, 28,* 117–153.

Novak, J. D., & Wandersee, J. (1991). *Special Issue on Concept-mapping of Journal of Research in Science Teaching, 28,* 10.

Ntuen, C. (1997). A model of system science for human-centered design. In J. Flanagan, T. Huang, P. Jones, & S. Kasif (Eds.), *Human-centered systems: Information, interactivity and intelligence* (p. 312). Washington, DC: National Science Foundation.

Nyce, J. M., & Lowgren, J. (1995). Towards foundational analysis in human–computer interaction. In P. J. Thomas (Ed.), *Social and interactional dimensions of human–computer interfaces* (pp. 37–47). Cambridge: Cambridge University Press.

Nyssen, A. S. (2000). Analysis of human errors in anaesthesia: Our methodological approach: From general observations to targeted studies in laboratory. In C. Vincent & B. A. De Mol (Eds.), *Safety in medicine* (pp. 49–63). London: Pergamon.

Nyssen, A. S., & De Keyser, V. (1998). Improving training in problem solving skills: Analysis of anesthetists' performance in simulated problem situations. *Le Travail Humain, 61,* 387–402.

Nyssen, A. S., & De Keyser, V. (2000). *On task and activity analysis in complex work domains.* Paper presented at the Fifth International Conference on Naturalistic Decision Making, Tammsvik, Sweden.

Obradovich, J. H., & Woods, D. D. (1996). Users as designers: How people cope with poor HCI design in computer-based medical devices. *Human Factors, 38,* 574–592.

Ochanine, D. A. (1964). *L'acte et l'*image, probleme d'ergonomie.* Presentation at the 17th International Congress of Applied Psychology, Ljubljana Yogoslavia.

Ocker, W. C., & Crane, C. J. (1932). *Blind flight in theory and practice.* San Antonio, TX: The Naylor Company.

O'Dell, C., & Grayson, C. J. (1998). *If we only knew what we know: The transfer of internal knowledge and best practice.* New York: Free Press.

O'Donnell, A. M., Hmelo-Silver, C. E., & Erkens, G. (Eds.). (2006). *Collaborative learning, reasoning, and technology.* Mahwah, NJ: Erlbaum.

Office of Scientific Research and Development. (1946). *Transmission and reception of sounds under combat conditions* (Summary Technical Report of Division 17, Vol. 3). Washington, DC: National Defense Research Council.

Olson, G. (1994). Collaborative problem solving as distributed cognition. In A. Ram & K. Eiselt (Eds.), *Proceedings of the Sixteenth Annual Conference of the Cognitive Science Society* (p. 991). Hillsdale, NJ: Erlbaum.

Olson, J. R., & Biolsi, K. J. (1991). Techniques for representing expert knowledge. In K. A. Ericsson & J. Smith (Eds.), *Toward a general theory of expertise: Prospects and limits* (pp. 240–285). Cambridge: Cambridge University Press.

Olson, J. R., & Reuter, H. (1987). Extracting expertise from experts: Methods for knowledge acquisition. *Expert Systems, 4,* 152–168.

Olson, G. M., Malone, T. W., & and Smith, J. B. (Eds.) (2001). *Coordination theory and collaboration technology.* Mahwah, NJ: Erlbaum.

Omodei, M. M., McLennan, J., Eliott, G. C., Wearing, A., & Clancy, J. M. (2005). "More is better?": A bias toward overuse of resources on naturalistic decision making settings. In H.Montgomery, R. Lipshitz, & B. Brehgmer (Eds.), How professionals make decisions (pp. 43–56). Mahwah, NJ: Erlbaum.

Orasanu, J. (1990). *Shared mental models and crew decision making* (Report No. 46). Princeton, NJ: Princeton University.

Orasanu, J., & Connolly, T. (1993). The reinvention of decision making. In G. Klein, G. J. Orasanu, R. Calderwood, & C. Zsambok (Eds.), *Decision making in action: Models and methods* (pp. 3–20). Norwood, NJ: Ablex.

Orasanu, J., & Fischer, U. (1997). Finding decisions in natural environments. In C. E. Zsambok & G. Klein (Eds.), *Naturalistic decision making* (pp. 434–458). Hillsdale, NJ: Erlbaum.

Orasanu, J., & Salas, E. (1993). Team decision making in complex environments. In G. A. Klein & J. Orasanu (Eds.), *Decision making in action: models and methods* (pp. 327–345). Westport, CT: Ablex.

Ormerod, T. C. (2000). Using task analysis as a primary design method. In J. M. Schraagen & S. F. Chipman (Eds.), *Cognitive task analysis* (pp. 181–200). Mahwah, NJ: Erlbaum.

Ormerod, T.C. & Shepherd, A. (2004). Using task analysis for information requirements specification: The SGT method. In D. Diaper & N. Stanton (Eds.): *The handbook of task analysis for human-computer interaction* (pp. 347–366). London: Lawrence Erlbaum Associates.

Orr, J. (1985). *Social aspects of expertise.* Palo Alto, CA: Xerox PARC.

Orr, J. (1996). *Talking about machines: An ethnography of a modern job.* Ithaca, NY: Cornell University Press.

Osgood, C. E., & Sebeok, T. A. (Eds.) (1954). *Psycholinguistics: A survey of theory and research problems.* Bloomington, IN: University of Indiana Press.

Osier, D. V., & Wozniak, R. H. (1984). *A century of serial publications in psychology, 1850–1950.* New York: Kraus.

Painvin, C., Norman, G. R., Neufeld, V. R., Walker, I., & Whelan, G. (1979). The triple-jump exercise: A structured measure of problem-solving and self-directed learning. In *Proceedings of the 18th Annual Conference on Research on Medical Education* (pp. 73–77). Washington, DC: Association of American Medical Colleges.

Papa, F. J., Shores, J. H., & Meyer, S. (1990). Effects of pattern matching, pattern discrimination, and experience in the development of diagnostic expertise. *Academic Medicine, 65,* S21–S22.

Patel, V. L., & Arocha, J. F. (2001). The nature of constraints on collaborative decision making in health care settings. In E. Salas & G. Klein (Eds.), *Linking expertise and naturalistic decision making* (pp. 383–405). Mahwah, NJ: Erlbaum.

Patel, V. L., Evans, D. A., & Groen, G. J. (1988). Biomedical knowledge and clinical reasoning. In D. A. Evans & V. L. Patel (Eds.), *Cognitive science in medicine* (pp. 53–112). Cambridge, MA: MIT Press.

Patel, V. L., & Groen, G. J. (1986). Knowledge based solution strategies in medical reasoning. *Cognitive Science, 10,* 91–116.

Patel, V. L., Groen, G. J., & Norman, G. R. (1991). Effects of conventional and problem based medical curricula on problem solving. *Academic Medicine, 66,* 380–389.

Patel, V. L., Kaufman, D. R., & Magder, S. (1991). Causal explanation of complex physiological concepts by medical students. *International Journal of Science Education, 13,* 171–185.

Paterson, D. G. (1940). Applied psychology comes of age. *Journal of Consulting Psychology, 4,* 1–9.

Patterson, E. S., Roth, E. M., & Woods, D. D. (2001). Predicting vulnerabilities in computer-supported inferential analysis under data overload. *Cognition, Technology, and Work, 3,* 224–237.

Patterson, E. S., Watts-Perotti, J. C., & Woods, D. D. (1999). Voice loops as coordination aids in space shuttle mission control. *Computer Supported Cooperative Work, 8,* 353–371.

Patterson, E. S., & Woods, D. D. (2001). Shift changes, updates, and the on-call model in space shuttle mission control. *Computer Supported Cooperative Work, 10,* 317–346.

Patterson, E. S., Woods, D. D., Sarter, N. B., & Watts-Perotti, J. C. (1998, May). Patterns in cooperative cognition. In F. Darses & P. Zarate (Eds.), *Third International Conference on the Design of Cooperative Systems* (pp. 13–23). Rocquencourt, France: INRIA Press.

Payne, J. W. (1994). Thinking aloud: Insights into information processing. *Psychological Science, 5,* 241–248.

Payne, J. W., Bettman, J. R., & Johnson, E. J. (1988). Adaptive strategy selection in decision making. *Journal of Experimental Psychology: Learning, Memory, and Cognition, 14,* 534–552.

Pearce, C. L., & Ensley, M. D. (2004). A reciprocal and longitudinal investigation of the innovation process: The central role of shared vision in product and process innovation teams. *Journal of Organizational Behavior, 25,* 259–278.

Pejtersen, A. M., & Rasmussen, J. (1997). Ecological information systems and support of learning: Coupling work domain information and user characteristics. In M. Helander, T. Landauer, & P. Prabhu (Eds.), *Handbook of human–computer interaction* (2nd ed., pp. 315–346). Amsterdam: North-Holland.

Penner, L. A., & Craiger, J. P. (1992). The weakest link: The performance of individual team members. In R. W. Swezey & E. Salas (Eds.), *Teams: Their training and performance* (pp. 57–73). Norwood, NJ: Ablex.

Pennington, N. (1981). *Causal reasoning and decision making: Two illustrative analyses.* Paper presented at the Second Annual Meeting of the Cognitive Science Society, New Haven, CT.

Pennington, N. (1987). Stimulus structures and mental representations in explicit comprehension of computer programs. *Cognitive Psychology, 19,* 295–341.

Pennington, N., & Hastie, R. (1981). Juror decision making models: The generalization gap. *Psychological Bulletin, 89,* 246–287.

Pennington, N., & Hastie, R. (1988). Explanation-based decision making: Effects of memory structure on judgment. *Journal of Experimental Psychology: Learning, Memory, and Cognition, 14,* 521–533.

Pennington, N., & Hastie, R. (1993). A theory of explanation-based decision-making. In G. Klein, J. Orasanu, R. Calderwood, & C. Zsambok (Eds.), *Decision making in action: Models and methods* (pp. 188–204). Norwood, NJ: Ablex.

Pepper, S. C. (1918). What is introspection? *American Journal of Psychology, 29,* 208–213.

Perby, M.- L. (1989). Computerization and skill in local weather forecasting. In B. Göranzon & I. Josefson (Eds.), *Knowledge, skill, and artificial intelligence* (pp. 39–52). Berlin: Springer-Verlag.

Pillsbury, W. B. (1926). *Education as the psychologist sees it.* New York: Macmillan.

Pillsbury, W. B. (1929). *The history of psychology.* New York: W. W. Norton.

Pinch, T. J. (1985). Towards an analysis of scientific observation: The externality and evidential significance of observational reports in physics. *Social Studies of Science, 15,* 3–36.

Pitz, G. F., & Sachs, N. J. (1984). Judgment and decision: theory and application. *Annual Review of Psychology, 35,* 139–163.

Pliske, R., Crandall, B., & Klein, G. (2004). Competence in weather forecasting. In K. Smith, J. Shanteau, and P. Johnson (Eds.), *Psychological investigations of competent decision making* (pp. 40–70). Cambridge: Cambridge University Press.

Poffenberger, A. T. (1942). *Principles of applied psychology.* New York: Appleton-Century.

Pollack, I. (1952). The information of elementary auditory displays. *Journal of the Acoustical Society of America, 24,* 745–749.

Pollard, P., & Crozier, R. (1989). The validity of verbal reports: Unconscious processes and biases in judgment. In C. Ellis (Ed.), *Expert knowledge and explanation* (pp. 13–37). Chichester, England: Ellis Horwood Ltd.

Polson, P. G. (1987). A quantitative model of human-computer interaction. In J. M. Carroll (Ed.), Interfacing thought: cognitive aspects of human-computer interaction (pp. 184–235). Cambridge, MA: Bradford Book/MIT Press.

Polya, G. (1957). *How to solve it: An aspect of mathematical method.* Princeton, NJ: Princeton University Press.

Popovic, V. (2003). General strategic knowledge models: Connections and expertise development in product design. In Creativity and Cognition Studios (Ed.), *Expertise in design*. Sydney, Australia: Creativity and Cognition Studios, University of Technology. Retrieved September 29, 2006, from http://research.it.uts.edu.au/creative/design/

Popper, K. (1972). *Objective knowledge: An evolutionary approach*. Oxford: Clarendon Press.

Porter, D. B. (1987). Classroom teaching, implicit learning, and the deleterious effects of inappropriate explanation. In *Proceedings of the Human Factors Society 31st annual meeting* (pp. 289–292). Santa Monica, CA: Human Factors Society.

Posner, M. I. (1988). Introduction: What is it to be an expert? In M. T. H. Chi, R. Glaser, & M. J. Farr (Eds.), *The nature of expertise* (pp. xxix–xxxvi). Hillsdale, NJ: Erlbaum.

Potter, S. S., Roth, E. M., Woods, D. D., & Elm, W. C. (2000). Bootstrapping multiple converging cognitive task analysis techniques for system design. In J. M. Schraagen & S. F. Chipman (Eds.), *Cognitive task analysis* (pp. 317–340). Mahwah, NJ: Erlbaum.

Poulton, E. C. (1964). The Medical Research Council's Applied Psychology Unit. *Murmur: The Cambridge University Medical Society Magazine, 36*(10), 3–7.

Pratt, C. C. (Ed.). (1941). Military psychology. *Psychological Bulletin, 38(6),* 311–312.

Prerau, D. (1989). *Developing and managing expert systems: Proven techniques for business and industry*. Reading, MA: Addison-Wesley.

Prereau, D. S., Adler, M. R., & Gunderson, A. S. (1992). Eliciting and using experiential knowledge and general expertise. In R. R. Hoffman (Ed.), *The psychology of expertise: Cognitive research and empirical AI* (pp. 137–148). Mahwah, NJ: Erlbaum.

Pressley, M., & Afflerbach, P. (1995). *Verbal protocols of reading: The nature of constructively responsive reading*. Hillsdale, NJ: Erlbaum.

Prietula, M. J., Feltovich, P. J., & Marchak, F. (2000). Factors influencing analysis of complex cognitive tasks: A framework and example from industrial process control. *Human Factors, 42,* 56–74.

Quastler, H. (Ed.). (1955). *Information theory in psychology: Problems and methods*. Glencoe, IL: Free Press.

Radford, J. (1974). Reflections on introspection. *American Psychologist, 29,* 245–250.

Raiffa, H. (1968). *Decision analysis: Introductory lectures on choices under uncertainty*. Reading, MA: Addison-Wesley.

Rasmussen, J. (1979). *On the structure of knowledge: A morphology of mental models in a man–machine context*. (Report No. Risø-M-219). Roskilde, Denmark: Risø National Laboratory.

Rasmussen, J. (1981). Models of mental strategies in process plant diagnosis. In J. Rasmussen & W. B. Rouse (Eds.), *Human detection and diagnosis of system failures* (pp. 241–258). New York: Plenum Press.

Rasmussen, J. (1983). Skills, rules, and knowledge: Signals, signs, and symbols, and other distinctions in human performance models. *IEEE Transactions on Systems, Man, and Cybernetics, 13,* 257–266.

Rasmussen, J. (1985). The role of hierarchical knowledge representation in decision making and system management. *IEEE Transactions on Systems, Man and Cybernetics, SMC-15,* 234–243.

Rasmussen, J. (1986a). A framework for cognitive task analysis. In E. Hollnagel, G. Mancini, & D. D. Woods (Eds.), *Intelligent decision support* (pp. 175–196). New York: Springer-Verlag.

Rasmussen, J. (1986b). *Information processing and human–machine interaction: An approach to cognitive engineering*. New York: North-Holland.

Rasmussen, J. (1988). Information technology: A challenge to the Human Factors Society? *Human Factors Society Bulletin, 31,* 1–3.

Rasmussen, J. (1992). The use of field studies for design workstations for integrated manu-facturing systems. In M. G. Helander & N. Nagamachi (Eds.), *Design for manufactur-ability: A systems approach to concurrent engineering and ergonomics* (pp. 317–338). London: Taylor & Francis.

Rasmussen, J. (1993). Deciding and doing: Decision making in natural contexts. In G. Klein, J. Orasanu, R. Calderwood, & C.E. Zsambok, (Eds.) (1993). *Decision making in action: Models and methods* (pp. 158–171). Norwood, NJ: Ablex.

Rasmussen, J. (2000). Human factors in a dynamic information society: Where are we heading? *Ergonomics, 43,* 869–879.

Rasmussen, J., & Jensen, A. (1973). *A study of mental procedures in electronic trouble shooting.* Denmark: Danish Atomic Energy Commision, Research Establishment Risø.

Rasmussen, J., & Jensen, A. (1974). Mental procedures in real life tasks: A case study of electronic trouble shooting. *Ergonomics, 17,* 293–307.

Rasmussen, J., & Lind, M. (1981). Coping with complexity. In H. G. Stassen (Ed.), *First European annual conference on human decision making and manual control* (pp. 69–91). New York: Plenum.

Rasmussen, J., & Pejtersen, A. M. (1995). Virtual ecology of work. In J. M. Flach, P. A. Hancock, J. Caird, & K. J. Vicente (Eds.), *Global perspectives on the ecology of human–machine systems* (Vol. 1, pp. 121–156). Hillsdale, NJ: Erlbaum.

Rasmussen, J., Pejtersen, A. M., & Goodstein, L. P. (Eds.). (1994). *Cognitive systems engineering.* New York: Wiley.

Rasmussen, J., Pejtersen, A. M., & Schmidt, K. (1990). *Taxonomy for cognitive work analysis.* Roskilde, Denmark: Risø National Laboratory.

Rasmussen, J., & Rouse, W. B. (Eds.). (1981). *Human detection and diagnosis of system failures.* New York: Plenum Press.

Ravetz, J. R. (1971). *Scientific knowledge and its social problems.* Oxford, UK: Oxford University Press.

Reason, J. (1990). *Human error.* Cambridge: Cambridge University Press.

Reason, J. (1997). *Managing the risks of organizational accidents.* Aldershot, England: Ashgate.

Reber, A. S. (1976). Implicit learning of synthetic languages: The role of instructional set. *Journal of Experimental Psychology: Human Learning and Memory, 2,* 88–94.

Reber, A. S., Allen, R., & Regan, S. (1985). Syntactical learning and judgment: Still uncon-scious and still abstract. *Journal of Experimental Psychology: General, 114,* 17–24.

Reber, A. S., & Lewis, S. (1977). Implicit learning: An analysis of the form and structure of a body of tacit knowledge. *Cognition, 5,* 333–361.

Redding, R. E. (1989). Perspectives on cognitive task analysis: The state of the art. In *Proceed-ings of the Human Factors Society 33rd Annual Meeting* (pp. 1348–1352). Santa Monica, CA: Human Factors Society.

Reder, L. M. (1987). Beyond associations: Strategic components in memory retrieval. In D. S. Gorfein & R. R. Hoffman (Eds.), *Memory and learning: The Ebbinghaus centennial conference* (pp. 203–220). Hillsdale, NJ: Erlbaum.

Reder, L. M., & Anderson, J. R. (1980). A partial resolution of the paradox of interference: The role of integrating knowledge. *Cognitive Psychology, 12,* 447–472.

Redish, J., & Wixon, D. (2003). Task analysis. In J. A. Jacko & A. Sears (Eds.), *The human–computer interaction handbook* (pp. 922–940). Mahwah, NJ: Erlbaum.

Regehr, G., Cline, J., Norman, G. R., & Brooks, L. R. (1994). Effect of processing strategy on diagnostic skill in dermatology. *Academic Medicine, 69,* S34–S36.

Regoczei, S. B., & Hirst, G. (1992). Knowledge and knowledge acquisition in the computational context. In R. R. Hoffman (Ed.), *The psychology of expertise: Cognitive research and empirical AI* (pp. 12–28). Mahwah, NJ: Erlbaum.

Rehak, L. A., Lamoureaux, T. B., & Bos, J. C. (2006). Communication, coordination, and integration of cognitive work analysis outputs. In *Proceedings of the Human Factors and Ergonomics Society 50th Annual Meeting* (pp. 515–519). Santa Monica, CA: Human Factors and Ergonomics Society.

Reichherzer, T., Cañas, A. J., Ford, K. M., & Hayes, P. (1998a, May). *The giant: An agent-based approach to knowledge construction and sharing.* Paper presented at the Eleventh Florida Artificial Intelligence Research Symposium, Sanibel Island, FL.

Reichherzer, T. R., Cañas, A. J., Ford, K. M., & Hayes, P. J. (1998b, August). *The giant: A classroom collaborator.* Paper presented at the Workshop on Pedagogical Agents, San Antonio, TX.

Resnick, L. B. (1976). Task analysis in instructional design: Some cases from mathematics. In D. Klahr (Ed.), *Cognition and instruction* (pp. 51–80). Hillsdale, NJ: Erlbaum.

Resnick, L. B., Levine, J. M., & Teasley, S. D. (Eds.). (1996). *Perspectives on socially shared cognition.* Washington, DC: American Psychological Association.

Resnick, M. (1996). Beyond the centralized mindset. *Journal of the Learning Sciences, 5,* 1–22.

Restle, F., & Davis, J. H. (1962). Success and speed of problem solving by individuals and groups. *Psychological Review, 69,* 520–536.

Ribot, T. (1873). *English psychology* (Anonymous, Trans.). London: Henry King.

Ribot, T. (1879). *German psychology of to-day.* (J. M. Baldwin, Trans.). New York: Scribner.

Ribot, T. (1890). *Psychology of attention.* Chicago: Open Court.

Rice, D., Ryan, J., & Samson, S. (1998). Using concept-maps to assess student learning in the science classroom: Must different methods compete? *Journal of Research in Science Teaching, 35,* 1103–1127.

Rice, R. E., & Shook, D. E. (1990). Voice messaging, coordination, and communication. In J. Galegher, R. E. Kraut, & C. Egido (Eds.), *Intellectual teamwork: Social and technological foundations of cooperative work* (pp. 327–350). Mahwah, NJ: Erlbaum.

Rodi, L. L., Pierce, J. A., & Dalton, R. E. (1989, April). Putting the expert in charge: Graphical knowledge acquisition for fault diagnosis and repair. *SIGART Newsletter,* pp. 56–62.

Rogoff, B., & Lave, J. (Eds.). (1984). *Everyday cognition: Its development in social context.* Cambridge, MA: Harvard University Press.

Rogoff, B., & Mistry, J. J. (1985). Memory development in cultural context. In M. P. C. Brainerd (Ed.), *Cognitive learning and memory in children* (pp. 117–142). New York: Springer-Verlag.

Rommetveit, R. (1987). Meaning, context, and control. *Inquiry, 30,* 77–99.

Rönnberg, J. (1986). Cognitive psychology in Scandinavia: Attention, memory, learning and memory dysfunctions. *Scandinavian Journal of Psychology, 27,* 95–149.

Rook, F. W., & Croghan, J. W. (1989). The knowledge acquisition activity matrix: A systems engineering conceptual framework. *IEEE Transactions on Systems, Man, and Cybernetics, 19,* 586–597.

Ross, B. H., & Kennedy, P. T. (1990). Generalizing from the use of earlier examples in problem solving. *Journal of Experimental Psychology: Learning, Memory and Cognition, 16,* 42–55.

Ross, G. (1995). *Flight strip survey report.* Australia Advanced Air Traffic Control System, Airservices Australia, Canberra, Australia.

Ross, K., & Shafer, J. (2006). Naturalistic decision making and the study of expertise. In A. Ericsson, N. Charness, P. Feltovich, & R. Hoffman (Eds.), *Cambridge handbook of expertise and expert performance*. Cambridge: Cambridge University Press.

Rosson, M. B., & Carroll, J. M. (2003). Scenario-based design. In J. A. Jacko & A. Sears (Eds.), *The human–computer interaction handbook* (pp. 1032–1050). Mahwah, NJ: Erlbaum.

Roth, E. M. (1997a). Analysis of decision making in nuclear power plant emergencies: An investigation of aided decision making. In C. E. Zsambok & G. Klein (Eds.), *Naturalistic decision making* (pp. 175–182). Mahwah, NJ: Erlbaum.

Roth, E. (1997b). Position paper. In J. Flanagan, T. Huang, P. Jones, & S. Kasif (Eds.), *Human-centered systems: Information, interactivity and intelligence* (pp. 247–251). Washington, DC: National Science Foundation.

Roth, E. M., Malin, J. T., & Schreckenghost, D. L. (1997). Paradigms for intelligent interface design. In M. Helander, T. Landauer, & P. Prabhu (Eds.), *Handbook of human–computer interaction* (2nd ed., pp. 1177–1201). Amsterdam: North-Holland.

Roth, E. M., Patterson, E.S. and Mumaw, R. J. (2002). Cognitive engineering: Issues in user-centered system design. In J. J. Marciniak (Ed.), *Encyclopedia of software engineering* (2nd ed.) (pp 163–179). New York: Wiley-Interscience, John Wiley and Sons.

Roth, E. M., Scott, R., Deutsch, S., Kuper, S., Schmidt, V., Stilson, M. And Wampler, J. (2006). Evolvable work-centered support systems for command and control: Creating systems users can adapt to meet changing demands. *Ergonomics, 49,* 688–705.

Roth, E. M., & Woods, D. D. (1989). Cognitive Task Analysis: An approach to knowledge acquisition for intelligent system design. In G. Guida & C. Tasso (Eds.), *Topics in expert system design* (pp. 233–264). New York: North-Holland.

Roth, E. M., Woods, D. D., & Pople, H. E. (1992). Cognitive simulation as a tool for cognitive task analysis. *Ergonomics, 35,* 1163–1198.

Rothkopf, E. Z. (1986). Cognitive science applications to human resources problems. *Advances in Reading/Language Research, 4,* 283–289.

Rouse, W. B., & Morris, N. M. (1986). On looking into the black box: Prospects and limits in the search for mental models. *Psychological Bulletin, 100,* 349–363.

Rowe, A. L., & Cooke, N. J. (1995). Measuring mental models: Choosing the right tools for the job. *Human Resource Development Quarterly, 6,* 243–255.

Rowe, A. L., Cooke, N. J., Hall, E. P., & Halgren, T. L. (1996). Toward an on-line knowledge assessment methodology: Building on the relationship between knowing and doing. *Journal of Experimental Psychology: Applied, 2,* 31–47.

Ruch, T. C. (1951). Motor systems. In S. S. Stevens (Ed.), *Handbook of experimental psychology* (pp. 154–208). New York: Wiley.

Ruger, H. (1910). *The psychology of efficiency: An experimental study of the processes involved in the solution of mechanical puzzles and in the acquisition of skill in their manipulation.* New York: Science Press.

Ruiz-Primo, M., & Shavelson, R. (1996). Problems and issues in the use of concept maps in science. *Journal of Research in Science Teaching, 33,* 569–600.

Rumelhart, D. & Norman, D. (1978). Accretion, tuning and restructuring: Three modes of learning. In. J. W. Cotton & R. Klatzky (Eds.), *Semantic factors in cognition*. Hillsdale, NJ: Erlbaum.

Russo, J. E., Johnson, E. J., & Stephens, D. L. (1989). The validity of verbal reports. *Memory and Cognition, 17,* 759–769.

Ryan, T. A. (1970). *Intentional behavior: An approach to human motivation.* New York: Ronald Press.

Ryan, T. A., & Smith, P. C. (1954). *Principles of industrial psychology.* New York: Ronald Press.

Salas, E., Bowers, C. A., & Edens, E. (Eds.). (2001). *Improving teamwork in organizations.* Mahwah, NJ: Erlbaum.

Salas, E., Burke, C. S., & Stagl, K. C. (2004). Developing teams and team leaders: Strategies and principles. In D. Day, S. J. Zaccaro, & S. M. Halpin (Eds.), *Leader development for transforming organizations: Growing leaders for tomorrow* (pp. 325–355). Mahwah, NJ: Erlbaum.

Salas, E., Cannon-Bowers, J. A., & Blickensderfer, E. L. (1993). Team performance and training research: Emerging principles. *Journal of the Washington Academy of Sciences, 83,* 81–106.

Salas, E., Cannon-Bowers, J. A., & Johnson, J. H. (1997). How can you turn a team of experts into an expert team? Emergency training strategies. In C. E. Zsambok & G. Klein (Eds.), *Naturalistic decision making* (pp. 359–370). Mahwah, NJ; Erlbaum.

Salas, E., & Fiore, S. (2004). *Team cognition.* Washington, DC: APA Books.

Salas, E., & Klein, G. (2001). *Linking expertise and naturalistic decision making.* Mahwah, NJ: Erlbaum.

Salas, E., Rosen, M., Burke, C. S., Goodwin, G. F., & Fiore, S. M. (2006). The making of a dream team: When expert teams do best. In K. A. Ericsson, N. Charness, P. Feltovich, & R. Hoffman, (Eds.), *Cambridge handbook of expertise and expert performance* (pp. 439–453). New York: Cambridge University Press.

Salas, E., Stagl, K. C., & Burke, C. S. (2004). 25 years of team effectiveness in organizations: Research themes and emerging needs. *International Review of Industrial and Organizational Psychology, 19,* 47–91.

Salas, E., Stagl, K. C., Burke, C. S., & Goodwin, G. F. (2007). Fostering team effectiveness in organizations: Toward an integrative theoretical framework of team performance. In W. Spaulding & J. Flowers (Eds.), *Modeling complex systems: Motivation, cognition and social processes* (pp. 185–244). Lincoln: University of Nebraska Press.

Salomon, G. (1991, August–September). Transcending the qualitative–quantitative debate: The analytic and systemic approaches to educational research. *Educational Researcher,* pp. 10–18.

Salomon, G. (Ed.). (1993). *Distributed cognition.* Cambridge: Cambridge University Press.

Salter, W. J. (1988). Human factors in knowledge acquisition. In M. Helander (Ed.), *Handbook of human–computer interaction* (pp. 957–968). Amsterdam: North-Holland.

Salthouse, T. A. (1984). Effects of age and skill in typing. *Journal of Experimental Psychology: General, 113,* 345–371.

Salvendy, G. (Ed.). (1987). *Handbook of human factors.* New York: Wiley.

Sampaio, E., Maris, S., & Bach-y-Rita, P. (2001). Brain plasticity: Visual acuity of blind persons via the tongue. *Brain Research, 908,* 204–207.

Sanders, M. S., & McCormick, E. J. (1992). *Human factors in engineering and design.* New York: McGraw-Hill.

Sanderson, P. M. (1989). Verbalizable knowledge and skilled task performance: Association, dissociation, and mental models. *Journal of Experimental Psychology: Learning, Memory and Cognition, 15,* 729–747.

Sanderson, P. M. (2002). Cognitive work analysis. In J. M. Carroll (Ed.), *HCI models, theories, and frameworks: Toward an interdisciplinary science* (pp. 225–264). New York: Morgan-Kaufmann.

Sanderson, P. M., Eggleston, R., Skilton, W., & Cameron, S. (1999). Work domain analysis workbench: Supporting cognitive work analysis as a systematic practice. In *Proceedings of the Human Factors and Ergonomics Society 43rd Annual Meeting* (pp. 323–327). Santa Monica, CA: Human Factors and Ergonomics Society.

Sanderson, P. M., Haskell, I., & Flach, J. M. (1992). The complex role of perceptual organization in visual display design theory. *Ergonomics, 35,* 1199–1219.

Sanderson, P. M., Naikar, N., Lintern, G., & Goss, S. (1999). Use of cognitive work analysis across the system life cycle: From requirements to decommissioning. In *Proceedings of the Human Factors and Ergonomics Society 43rd Annual Meeting* (pp. 318–322). Santa Monica, CA: Human Factors and Ergonomics Society.

Sanderson, P. M., Verhapge, A. G., & Fuld, R. B. (1989). State-space and verbal protocol methods for studying the human operator in process control. *Ergonomics, 32,* 1343–1372.

Sanjek, R. (Ed.). (1990). *Fieldnotes: The making of anthropology.* Ithaca, NY: Cornell University Press.

Sarter, N. B., & Woods, D. D. (1992). Pilot interaction with cockpit automation: I. Operational experiences with flight management system. *International Journal of Aviation Psychology, 2,* 303–321.

Sarter, N. B, & Woods, D. D. (1994). Pilot interaction with cockpit automation II: An experimental study of pilot's model and awareness of the flight management system. *International Journal of Aviation Psychology, 4,* 1–28.

Sarter, N. B., & Woods, D. D. (1995). "How in the world did we get into that mode?" Mode error and awareness in supervisory control. *Human Factors, 37,* 5–19.

Sarter, N. B., & Woods, D. D. (1997). Teamplay with a powerful and independent agent: A corpus of operational experiences and automation surprises on an airbus A-320. *Human Factors, 42,* 390–402.

Sarter, N., & Woods, D. D. (2000). Team play with a powerful and independent agent: A full mission simulation. *Human Factors, 42,* 390–402.

Sarter, N., Woods, D. D., & Billings, C. E. (1997). Automation surprises. In G. Salvendy (Ed.), *Handbook of human factors/ergonomics* (2nd ed., pp. 1926–1943). New York: Wiley.

Scandura, J. M. (1982). Structural cognitive task analysis: A method for analyzing content: I. Background and empirical research. *Journal of Structural Learning, 7,* 101–114.

Scandura, J. M. (1984a). Structural cognitive task analysis: A method for analyzing content: II. Toward precision, objectivity and systematization. *Journal of Structural Learning, 8,* 1–27.

Scandura, J. M. (1984b). Structural cognitive task analysis: A method for analyzing content: III. Validity and reliability. *Journal of Structural Learning, 8,* 173–193.

Scandura, J. M. (2006). *Structural learning theory: Current status and new perspectives.* Retrieved April 18, 2006, from http://www.scandura.com/Articles/SLT%20Status-Perspectives.PDF

Schaafstal, A., Schraagen, J. M., & van Berlo, M. (2000). Cognitive task analysis and innovation of training: The case of structured trouble shooting. *Human Factors, 42,* 75–86.

Schach, S. R. (1996). *Classical and object-oriented software engineering.* Chicago: Irwin.

Schmidt, H. G., & Boshuizen, H. P. A. (1993a). On the origin of intermediate effects in clinical case recall. *Memory and Cognition, 21,* 338–351.

Schmidt, H. G., & Boshuizen, H. P. A. (1993b). Transitory stages in the development of medical expertise: The "intermediate effect" in clinical case presentations. In *Proceedings of the Annual Meeting of the Cognitive Science Society* (pp. 139–145). Hillsdale, NJ: Erlbaum.

Schmidt, H. G., Norman, G. R., & Boshuizen, H. P. A. (1990). A cognitive perspective on medical expertise: Theory and implications. *Academic Medicine, 65,* 611–621.

Schneiderman, B. (1977). "Measuring computer program quality and comprehension." Report No. 16, Department of Information Systems Management, University of Maryland, College Park, MD.

Schön, D. A. (1982). *The reflective practitioner: How professionals think in action.* New York: Basic Books.

Schön, D. A. (1987). *Educating the reflective practitioner.* San Francisco: Jossey-Bass.

Schooler, J. W. (2002). Verbalization produces a transfer inappropriate processing shift. *Applied Cognitive Psychology, 16,* 989–997.

Schooler, J. W., Ohlsson, S., & Brooks, K. (1993). Thoughts beyond words: When language overshadows insight. *Journal of Experimental Psychology, General, 122,* 166–183.

Schraagen, J. M. C. (2006). Task analysis. In K. A. Ericsson, N. Charness, P. J. Feltovich, & R. R. Hoffman (Eds.), *Cambridge handbook of expertise and expert performance* (pp. 185–202). New York: Cambridge University Press.

Schraagen, J. M. (Ed.). (2008). *Macrocognition.* London: Ashgate.

Schraagen, J. M. C., Chipman, S. F., & Shalin, V. L. (Eds.). (2000). *Cognitive task analysis.* Hillsdale, NJ: Erlbaum.

Schraagen, J. M. C., Militello, L. G., Ormerod, T., & Lipshitz, R. (Eds.). (2007). *Naturalistic decision making and macrocognition.* Aldershot, UK: Ashgate Publishing Limited.

Schumacher, R. M., & Czerwinski, M. P. (1992). Mental models and the acquisition of expert knowledge. In R. R. Hoffman (Ed.), *The psychology of expertise: Cognitive research and empirical AI* (pp. 61–79). Mahwah, NJ: Erlbaum.

Schunn, C. D., & Dunbar, K. (1996). Priming, analogy, and awareness in complex reasoning. *Memory and Cognition, 24,* 271–284.

Schvaneveldt, R. (Ed.). (1990). *Pathfinder associative networks: Studies in knowledge organization.* Norwood, NJ: Ablex.

Schvaneveldt, R. W., Durso, F. T., Goldsmith, T. E., Breen, T. J., Cooke, N. J., Tucker, R. G., & DeMaio, J. C. (1985). Measuring the structure of expertise. *International Journal of Man–Machine Studies, 23,* 699–728.

Schwager, J. D. (1989). *Market wizards: Interviews with top traders.* New York: New York Institute of Finance.

Schweikert, R., Burton, A. M., Taylor, N. K., Corlett, E. N., Shadbolt, N. R., & Hedgecock, A. P. (1987). Comparing knowledge elicitation techniques: A case study. *Artificial Intelligence Review, 1,* 245–253.

Scott, P. C. (1988). Requirements analysis assisted by logic modeling. *Decision Support Systems, 4,* 17–25.

Scott, R., Roth, E., Deutsch, S., Kuper, S., Schmidt, V., Stilson, M., and Wampler, J. (2005). Envisioning evolvable work-centered support systems: Empowering users to adapt their systems to changing world demands. *Proceedings of the Human Factors and Ergonomics Society 49th Annual Meeting* (pp. 244–248). Santa Monica, CA: Human Factors and Ergonomics Society.

Scott, R., Roth, E., Deutsch, S., Kuper, S., Schmidt, V., Stilson, M., & Wampler, J. (2006). Evolvable work-centered support systems: Creating systems users can adapt to changing demands. *Ergonomics, 49,* 688–705.

Scott, R., Roth, E., Deutsch, S., Malchiodi, E., Kazmierczak, T., Eggleston, R. G., et al. (2005, March–April). Work-centered support systems: A human-centered approach to system design. *IEEE Intelligent Systems,* pp. 73–81.

Scott, W. D. (1921). *Increasing human efficiency in business.* New York: Macmillan.

Scribner, S. (1984). Studying working intelligence. In B. Rogoff & S. Lave (Eds.), *Everyday cognition: Its development in social context* (pp. 9–40). Cambridge, MA: Harvard University Press.

Scribner, S. (1986). Thinking in action: Some characteristics of practical thought. In R. J. Sternberg & R. K. Wagner (Eds.), *Practical intelligence: Nature and origins of competence in the everyday world* (pp. 14–30). Cambridge: Cambridge University Press.

Sell, P. S. (1985). *Expert systems: A practical introduction.* New York: Wiley.

Selz, O. (1922). *Zur Psychologie der produktiven Denkens und des Irrtums.* Bonn: F. Cohen.

Senjen, R. (1988). Knowledge acquisition by experiment: Developing test cases for an expert system. *AI Applications in Natural Resource Management, 2,* 52–55.

Serfaty, D., MacMillan, J., Entin, E. B., & Entin, E. E. (1997). The decision making expertise of battle commanders. In G. A. Klein & C. E. Zsambok (Eds.), *Naturalistic decision making* (pp. 243–246). Hillsdale, NJ: Erlbaum.

Seubert, R. (1920). *Aus der Praxis des Taylor-Systems.* Berlin: Verlag von Julius Springer.

Sewell, D. R., Geddes, D., & Rouse, W. B. (1987). Initial evaluation of an intelligent interface for operators of complex systems. In G. Salvendy (Ed.), *Cognitive engineering in the design of human–computer interaction and expert systems* (pp. 551–558). New York: Elsevier.

Seymour, W. D. (1954). *Industrial training for manual operations.* London: Pitman.

Seymour, W. D. (1968). *Skills analysis training.* London: Pittman.

Shadbolt, N. R., & Burton, A. M. (1990a). Knowledge elicitation techniques: Some experimental results. In C. R Westphal & K. L. McGraw (Eds.), *Special Issue on Knowledge Acquisition, SIGART Newsletter,* No. 108, 21–33.

Shadbolt, N. R., & Burton, A. M. (1990b). Knowledge elicitation. In E. N. Wilson & J. R. Corlett (Eds.), *Evaluation of human work: Practical ergonomics methodology* (pp. 321–345). London: Taylor & Francis.

Shannon, C. E. (1948). A mathematical theory of communication. *Bell Systems Technical Journal, 27,* 379–423, 623–656.

Shannon, C. E. (1951). Prediction and entropy of printed English. *Bell System Technical Journal, 30,* 50–64.

Shannon, C. E., & Weaver, W. (1949). *The mathematical theory of communication.* Urbana: University of Illinois Press.

Shanteau, J. (1984). Some unasked questions about the psychology of expert decision makers. In M. E. El Hawary (Ed.), *Proceedings of the 1984 IEEE Conference on Systems, Man, and Cybernetics* (pp. 23–45). New York: IEEE.

Shanteau, J. (1988). Psychological characteristics and strategies of expert decision makers. *Acta Psychologica, 68,* 203–215.

Shanteau, J. (1989). Cognitive heuristics and biases in behavioral auditing: Review, comments and observations. *Accounting, Organizations and Society, 14,* 165–177.

Shanteau, J. (1992). Competence in experts: The role of task characteristics. *Organizational Behavior and Human Decision Processes, 53,* 252–266.

Shanteau, J., & Stewart, T. R. (1992). Why study expert decision making? Some historical perspectives and comments. *Organizational Behavior and Human Decision Processes, 53,* 95–106.

Shapiro, J. P. (2000, July). Taking the mistakes out of medicine. *U.S. News and World Report,* pp. 50–66.

Shartle, C. L. (1950). Job analysis. In D. H. Fryer & E. R. Henry (Eds.), *Handbook of applied psychology* (pp. 135–142). New York: Rinehart.

Shattuck, L., & Woods, D. D. (1994). The critical incident technique 40 years later. In *Proceedings of the 38th Annual Meeting of the Human Factors and Ergonomics Society* (pp. 1080–1084). Santa Monica, CA: Human Factors and Ergonomics Society.

Shavelson, R. J. (1972). Some aspects of the correspondence between content structure and cognitive structure in physics instruction. *Journal of Educational Psychology, 63,* 225–234.

Shaw, A. G. (1952). *The purpose and practice of motion study.* New York: Harlequin Press.

Shaw, R., & Wilson, B. E. (1976). Abstract conceptual knowledge: How we know what we know. In D. Klahr (Ed.) *Cognition and instruction* (pp. 197–221). Hillsdale, NJ: Erlbaum.

Shen, W., Chao, K.-M., Lin, Z., Barthès, J.-P. A., & James, A. (Eds.). (2006). *Computer supported cooperative work in design: The 10th international conference.* New York: Springer.

Shepherd, A. (1976). An improved tabular format for task analysis. *Journal of Occupational Psychology, 49,* 93–104.

Shepherd, A. (2001). *Hierarchical task analysis.* London: Taylor & Francis.

Sheridan, T. B. (1997). Task analysis, task allocation, and supervisory control. In M. G. Helander, T. K. Landauer, & P. Prabhu (Eds.), *Handbook of human–computer interaction* (2nd ed., pp. 87–105). Amsterdam: Elsevier Science.

Sheridan, T. B., Jenkins, J., & Kisner, R. (Eds.). (1982). *Proceedings of Workshop on Cognitive Modeling of Nuclear Plant Control Room Operators* (Nuclear Regulatory Commission Report NUREG/CR-3114). Washington, DC: Nuclear Regulatory Commission.

Sierhuis, M. (2001). *Modeling and simulating work practice. BRAHMS: A multiagent modeling and simulation language for work system analysis and design.* Unpublished doctoral dissertation, University of Amsterdam, the Netherlands.

Simon, D. P. (1979). A tale of two protocols. In J. Lockhead & J. Clement (Eds.), *Cognitive processes in instruction* (pp. 119–132). Philadelphia: Franklin Institute.

Simon, D. P., & Simon, H. A. (1978). Individual differences in solving physics problems. In R. Siegler (Ed.), *Children's thinking: What develops?* (pp. 325–348). Hillsdale, NJ: Erlbaum.

Simon, H. A. (1955). A behavioral model of rational choice. *Quarterly Journal of Economics, 69,* 99–118.

Simon, H. A. (1972). *The sciences of the artificial.* Cambridge, MA: MIT Press.

Simon, H. A. (1973a). Does scientific discovery have a logic? *Philosophy of Science, 40,* 471–480.

Simon, H. A. (1973b). The structure of ill-structured problems. *Artificial Intelligence, 4,* 181–201.

Simon, H. A. (1981). *The sciences of the artificial* (2nd ed.). Cambridge, MA: MIT Press.

Simon, H. A. (1991). Cognitive architectures in a rational analysis: Comment. In K. VanLehn (Ed.), *Architectures for intelligence* (pp. 25–39). Mahwah, NJ: Erlbaum.

Simon, H. A., & Gilmartin, K. (1973). A simulation of memory for chess positions. *Cognitive Psychology, 5,* 29–46.

Simon, H. A., & Hayes, J. R. (1976). Understanding complex task instructions. In D. Klahr (Ed.), *Cognition and instruction* (pp. 269–186). Hillsdale, NJ: Erlbaum.

Simon, H., Langley, P., Bradshaw, G., & Zytkow, J. (1987). *Scientific discovery: Computational explorations of the creative processes.* Cambridge, MA: MIT Press.

Simoneau, G. G., Leibowitz, H. W., Ulbrecht, J. S., Tyrrell, R. A., & Cavanagh, P. R. (1992). The effects of visual factors and head orientation on postural steadiness in women 55 to 70 years of age. *Journal of Gerontology, 47,* M151–M158.

Sinaiko, H. W., & Buckley, E. P. (1957). *Human factors in the design of systems* (Report No. 4996, Naval Research Laboratory). Washington, DC: Naval Research Laboratory.

Singleton, W. T. (1974), *Man-machine systems.* London: Penguin.

Slade, S. (1991, Spring). Case-based reasoning: A research paradigm. *AI Magazine,* 42–55.

Sleeman, D., & Shadbolt, N. R. (1996). *Report of the ESPRC Workshop on Software Assisted Knowledge Acquisition.* Computing Science Department, University of Aberdeen, Aberdeen, Scotland.

Slovic, P. (1966). Cue consistency and cue utilization in judgment. *American Journal of Psychology, 79,* 427–434.

Slovic, P. (1982). Toward understanding and improving decisions. In W. C. Howell & E. A. Fleishman (Eds.), *Human Performance and productivity, Volume 1* (pp. 157–183). Hillsdale, NJ: Erlbaum.

Smith, C. C. (1922). *The expert typist.* New York: Macmillan.

Smith, E. E., Adams. N., & Schor, D. (1978). Fact retrieval and the paradox of interference. *Cognitive Psychology, 10,* 438–464.

Smith, E. M., Ford, J. K., & Kozlowski, S. W. (1997). Building adaptive expertise: Implications for training design strategies. In M. A. Quinones & A. Ehrenstein (Eds.), *Training for a rapidly changing workplace: Applications of psychological research* (pp. 89–118). Washington, DC: American Psychological Association.

Smith, H. H., & Wiese, E. G. (1921). *Seven speed secrets of expert typing.* New York: Gregg.

Smith, P. J., & Geddes, N. D. (2003). A cognitive systems engineering approach to the design of decision support systems. In J. A. Jacko & A. Sears (Eds.), *The human–computer interaction handbook* (pp. 656–676). Mahwah, NJ: Erlbaum.

Smith, P. J., Geddes, N., & Beatty, R. (in press). Human-centered design of decision support systems. In A. Sears & J. Jacko (Eds.), *Handbook of human–computer interaction* (2nd ed.). Mahwah, NJ: Erlbaum.

Smith, P. J., Woods, D. D., McCoy, E., Billings, C., Sarter, N. B., Denning, R., et al. (1998). Using forecasts of future incidents to evaluate future ATM system designs. *Air Traffic Control Quarterly, 6,* 71–85.

Société d'Ergonomie de Langue Française (2008). [Downloaded 21 March 2008 at http://www.ergonomie-self.org/self/desnoyers.html].

Soloway, E., Adelson, B., & Ehrlich, K. (1988). Knowledge and process in the comprehension of computer programs. In M. T. H. Chi, R. Glaser, & M. J. Farr (Eds.), *The nature of expertise* (pp. 129–152). Hillsdale, NJ: Erlbaum.

Solvberg, I., Nordbo, I., Vestli, M., Aakvik, G., Amble, T., Eggen, J., et al. (1988). *METAKREK: Methodology and toolkit for knowledge acquisition.* Trondheim, Norway: Univeristy of Trondheim.

Sonnentag, S., Niessen, C., & Volmer, J. (2006). Expertise in software design. In K. A. Ericsson, N. Charness, P. Feltovich, & R. Hoffman (Eds.), *Cambridge handbook on expertise and expert performance.* New York: Cambridge University Press.

Sowa, J. F. (1984). *Conceptual structures: Information processing in mind and machine.* Reading, MA: Addison-Wesley.

Spector, P. E. (1994). Using self-report questionnaires in OB research: A comment on the use of a controversial method. *Journal of Organizational Behavior, 15,* 385–392.

Spellman, B. A., Holyoak, K. J., & Morrison, R. G. (2001). Analogical priming via semantic relations. *Memory and Cognition, 29,* 383–393.

Spilich, G. J., Vesonder, G. T., Chiesi, H. L., & Voss, J. F. (1979). Text-processing of domain-related information for individuals with high and low domain knowledge. *Journal of Verbal Learning and Verbal Behavior, 18,* 275–290.

Spiro, R. J., Coulson, R. L., Feltovich, P. J., & Anderson, D. K. (1988). Cognitive flexibility theory: Advanced knowledge acquisition in ill-structured domains. In *Proceedings of the 10th Annual Conference of the Cognitive Science Society* (pp. 375–383). Hillsdale, NJ: Erlbaum.

Spiro, R. J., Feltovich, P. J., Coulson, R. L., & Anderson, D. K. (1989). Multiple analogies for complex concepts: Antidotes for analogy-induced misconception in advanced knowledge acquisition. In S. Vosniadou & A. Ortony (Eds.), *Similarity and analogical reasoning* (pp. 498–531). Cambridge: Cambridge University Press.

Spiro, R. J., Feltovich, P. J., Jacobson, M. J., & Coulson, R. L. (1991). Knowledge representation, content specification, and the development of skill in situation-specific knowledge assembly: Some constructivist issues as they relate to cognitive flexibility theory and hypertext. *Educational Technology, 31,* 22–25.

Spiro, R. J., Feltovich, P. J., Jacobson, M. J., & Coulson, R. L. (1992). Cognitive flexibility, constructivism, and hypertext: Random access instruction for advanced knowledge acquisition in ill-structured domains. In T. M. Duffy & D. H. Jonassen (Eds.), *Constructivism and the technology of instruction: A conversation* (pp. 57–76). Hillsdale, NJ: Erlbaum.

Spiro, R. J., & Jehng, J. (1990). Cognitive flexibility and hypertext: Theory and technology for the non-linear and multidimensional traversal of complex subject matter. In D. Nix & R. Spiro (Eds.), *Cognition, education, and multimedia* (pp. 163–205). Hillsdale, NJ: Erlbaum.

Spradley, J. P. (1979). *The ethnographic interview.* New York: Holt, Rinehart and Winston.

Staff of the Personnel Research Section to the Adjutant General's Office. (1943). Personnel research in the Army IV: The selection of radiotelegraph operators. *Psychological Bulletin, 40,* 357–371.

Stahl, G. (2006). *Group cognition: Computer support for building collaborative knowledge.* Cambridge, MA: MIT Press.

Stanard, R., Uehara, M., & Hutton, R. J. (2003). *Year One Final Report: Decision-Centered Design: Principles and Processes.* Report to the Advanced Decision Architectures Collaborative Alliance, Army Research Laboratory, Aberdeen, MD.

Stanton, N. A. (2004). The psychology of task analysis today. In D. Diaper & N. Stanton (Eds.), *The handbook of task analysis for human-computer interaction* (pp. 569–584). Mahwah, NJ: Erlbaum.

Stanton, N. A., Salmon, P. M., Walker, G. H., Baber, C., & Jenkins, D. P. (2005). *Human factors methods: A practical guide for engineering and design.* London: Ashgate.

St-Cyr, O., & Burns, C. M. (2001). Mental models and the abstraction hierarchy: Assessing ecological compatibility. In *Proceedings of the Human Factors and Ergonomics Society 45th Annual Meeting* (pp. 297–301). Santa Monica, CA: Human Factors and Ergonomics Society.

Steels, L. (1990, Fall). Components of expertise. *AI Magazine, 11,* p. 2.

Stein, E. (1992). A method to identify candidates for knowledge acquisition. *Journal of Management and Information Systems, 9,* 161–178.

Stein, E. (1997). A look at expertise from a social perspective. In P. J. Feltovich, K. M. Ford, & R. R. Hoffman (Eds.), *Expertise in context: Human and machine* (pp. 181–194). Cambridge, MA: MIT Press/AAAI Books.

Stein, G. (1989). Cultivated motor automatism. *Psychological Review, 5,* 295–306.

Stern, W. (1927). William Stern. In R. Schmidt (Ed.), *Philosophie der Gegenwart in Selbstdarstellungen, Vol. 6 (Philosophy of the present in autobiography).* Reprinted in C, Murchison (Ed.) (1961). *A history of psychology in autobiography, volume 1* (pp. 335–338). (S. Langer, Trans). New York: Russell & Russell.

Stern, W. (1961). William Stern. In C. Murchinson (Ed.), *A history of psychology in autobiography* (Vol. 1, pp. 355–388). Worcester, MA: Clark University Press.

Sternberg, R. J. (1977). *Intelligence, information processing, and analogical reasoning: The componential analysis of human abilities.* Hillsdale, NJ: Erlbaum.

Sternberg, R. J., & Frensch, P. A. (Eds.). (1991). *Complex problem solving: Principles and mechanisms*. Mahwah, NJ: Erlbaum.

Sternberg, R. J., & Frensch, P. A. (1992). On being an expert: A cost-benefit analysis. In R. R. Hoffman (Ed.), *The psychology of expertise: Cognitive research and empirical AI* (pp. 191–203). New York: Springer-Verlag.

Stevens, A. L., & Collins, A. (1978). *Multiple conceptual models for a complex system* (Report 3923). Cambridge, MA: Bolt, Beranek, and Newman.

Stevens, S. S. (Ed.). (1951). *Handbook of experimental psychology*. New York: John Wiley and Sons.

Stewart, T. R. (2001). Improving reliability of judgmental forecasts. In J. S. Armstrong (Ed.), *Principles of forecasting: A handbook for researchers and practitioners* (pp. 81–106): Kluwer Academic Publishers.

Stewart, T. R., Roebber, P. J., & Bosart, L. F. (1997). The importance of the task in analyzing expert judgment. *Organizational Behavior and Human Decision Processes, 69*, 205–219.

Still, D. L., & Temme, L. A. (2006). Configuring desktop helicopter simulation for research. *Aviation Space and Environmental Medicine, 77*, 323.

Stout, R., Cannon-Bowers, J. A., & Salas, E. (1996). The role of shared mental models in developing team situation awareness: Implications for training. *Training Research Journal, 2*, 85–116.

Stout, R. J., Cannon-Bowers, J. A., Salas, E., & Milanovich, D. M. (1999). Planning, shared mental models, and coordinated performance: An empirical link is established. *Human Factors, 41*, 61–71.

Stratton, G. H. (1896). Über die Wharnehmung von Druckänderungen bei verscheidenen Geschwindigkeiten. *Philosophische Studien, 12*, 525–586.

Stratton, G. M. (1909). Some experiments on the perception of the movement, color, and direction of lights, with special references to railway signaling. *Psychological Review Monograph Supplements, 10*(1) (Whole No. 40), 85–104.

Stratton, G. M. (1919). Psycho-physical tests of aviators. *Scientific Monthly, 8*, 421–426.

Suchman, L. A. (1987). *Plans and situated actions: The problem of human–machine communication*. Cambridge: Cambridge University Press.

Suchman, L. A. (1988). Representing practice in cognitive science. *Human Studies, 11*, 305–325.

Summers, W. C. (1996, March). 50 years of human engineering. *Human Factors and Ergonomics Society Bulletin, 39*, 1–3.

Sundali, J. A., & Atkins, J. B. (1994). Expertise in investment analysis: Fact or fiction. *Organizational Behavior and Human Decision Processes, 59*, 223–241.

Sundstrom, G. A. (1989). Information search and decision making: The effects of information displays. *Acta Psychologica, 65*, 165–179.

Sutcliffe, A. G. (1985). Use of conceptual maps as human–computer interfaces. In P. Johnson & S. Cook (Eds.), *People and computers: Designing the interface* (pp. 117–127). Cambridge: Cambridge University Press.

Svenson, O. (1979). Process descriptions of decision making. *Organizational Behavior and Human Performance, 23*, 86–112.

Swets, J. A., Dawes, R. M., & Monahan, J. (2000). Psychological science and improve diagnostic decisions. *Psychological Science in the Public Interest, 1*, 1–26.

Swift, E. J. (1904). The acquisition of skill in typewriting. *Psychological Bulletin, 1*, 295–305.

Swift, E. J. (1910). Learning to telegraph. *Psychological Bulletin, 6*, 149–153.

Tambe, M., Shen, W., Mataric, M., Pynadath, D. V., Goldberg, D., Modi, P. J., et al. (1999). Teamwork in cyberspace: Using TEAMCORE to make agents team-ready. In *Proceedings of the AAAI Spring Symposium on Agents in Cyberspace* (pp. 136–141). Menlo Park, CA: AAAI Press.

Taylor, F. W. (1911). *Principles of scientific management.* New York: Harper and Row.

Taynor, J., Crandall, B., & Wiggins, S. (1987). *The reliability of the critical decision method* (Technical Report on Contract No. MDA903-86-C-0170). Alexandria, VA: U.S. Army Research Institute; Yellow Springs, OH: Klein Associates.

Taynor, J., Klein, G., & Thordsen, M. (1987). Distributed decision making in wetland firefighting. Report, Contract MDA-903-85-C-0327, U. S. Army Research Institute, Alexandria, VA.

Temme, L. A., Woodall, J., & Still, D. L. (1998). *Calculating a helicopter pilot's instrument scan patters from discrete 60 Hz measures of the line-of-sight: The evaluation of an algorithm. NAMRL-1403.* Pensacola, FL: Naval Aerospace Medical Research Laboratory, Naval Air Station.

Terkel, S. (1972). *Working.* New York: New Press.

Thibos, L. N., Still, D. L., & Bradley, A. (1996). Characterization of spatial aliasing and contrast sensitivity in peripheral vision. *Vision Research, 36,* 249–258.

Thomas, J. L. (1974). An analysis of behavior in the hobbits-orcs problem. *Cognitive Psychology, 6,* 257–269.

Thordsen, M. L., McCloskey, M. J., & Heaton, J. K. (1996). *Decision-centered development of a mission rehearsal system* (Final Technical Report on Contract No. N61339-95-C-0101, SPONSOR). Fairborn, OH: Klein Associates.

Thordsen, M. L., Militello, L. G., & Klein, G. A. (1992). *Cognitive task analysis of critical team decision making during multiship engagements* (Technical Report on Contract No. F33615-90-C-0005, U.S. Air Force Armstrong Laboratory). Fairborn, OH: Klein Associates.

Thordsen, M. L., Wolf, S. P., & Crandall, B. (1990). *User defined requirements for the JSTARS self defense suite* (Report on Subcontract No. A62497L, UNISYS Corporation). Fairborn, OH: Klein Associates.

Thorndike, E. L. (1920). The selection of military aviators. *U.S. Air Service, 1–2,* 14–17, 28–32, 29–31.

Thorsrud, E. (1972). Policy making as a learning process. In A. B. Cherns, R. Sinclair, & W. I. Jenkins (Eds.), *Social science and government: Policies and problems* (pp. 39–81). London: Tavistock Institute.

Thumb, A., & Marbe, K. (1901). *Experimentelle Untersuchungen über die psychologischen Grundlagen der sprachlichen Analogiebildung.* Leipzig, Germany: Verlag von Wilhelm Engelmann.

Titchener, E. B. (1912). The schema of introspection. *American Journal of Psychology, 23,* 485–508.

Titchener, E. B. (1929). *Systematic psychology: Prolegomena.* New York: Macmillan.

Todd, P., & Benbasat, I. (1987, December). Process tracing methods in decision support systems research: Exploring the black box. *MIS Quarterly,* pp. 493–514.

Tolcott, M. A., Marvin, F. F., & Lehner, P. E. (1989). Expert decision making in evolving situations. *IEEE Transactions on Systems, Man, and Cybernetics, 19,* 606–615.

Towne, B. M. (1922). An individual curve of learning: A study in typewriting. *Journal of Experimental Psychology, 5,* 79–92.

Tramm, K. A. (1921). *Psychotechnik und Taylor-System.* Berlin: Verlag von Julius Springer.

Trist, E. L., & Bamforth, K. W. (1951). Some social and psychological consequences of the longwall method of coal-getting. *Human Relations, 4,* 3–38.

Tulving, E. (1983). *Elements of episodic memory.* Oxford: Clarendon Press.

Turano, K., Herdman, S. J., & Dagnelie, G. (1993). Visual stabilization of posture in retinitis pigmentosa and in artificially restricted visual fields. *Investigative Ophthalmology and Vision Science, 34,* 3004–3010.

Turner, P., & McEwan, T. (2004). Activity theory: another perspective on task analysis. In D. Diaper & N. Stanton (Eds.), *The handbook of task analysis for human–computer interaction* (pp. 423–444). Mahwah, NJ: Erlbaum.

Tyzska, T. (1985). Simple decision strategies versus multi-attribute utility theory approach to complex decision problems. *Praxiology Yearbook, 2,* 159–172.

Umbers, I. G., & King, P. J. (1981). An analysis of human decision-making in cement kiln control and the implications for automation. In E. H. Mamdani & B. R. Gaines (Eds.), *Fuzzy reasoning and its applications* (pp. 369–381). London: Academic Press.

U.S. Department of Transportation. (2000). *Federal Aviation Regulations and Aeronautical Information Manual.* Newcastle, WA: Author.

van Berlo, M. P. W., Lowyck, J., & Schaafstal, A. (2007). SDupporting the instcuctional design process for tream training. *Comptuers in Human Behavior, 23,* 1145–1161,

van Charante, E. M., Cook, R. I., Woods, D. D., Yue, L., & Howie, M. B. (1993). Human-computer interaction in context: Physician interaction with automated intravenous controllers in the heart room. In H. G. Stassen (Ed.), *Analysis, design, and evaluation of man–machine systems* (pp. 263–274). New York: Pergamon Press.

van Someren, M. W., Barnard, Y. F., & Sandberg, J. A. C. (1994). *The think aloud method: A practical guide to modeling cognitive processes.* London: Academic Press.

van Strien, P. J. (1998). Early applied psychology between essentialism and pragmatism: The dynamics of theory, tools, and clients. *History of Psychology, 1,* 205–234.

Vekirl, I. (2002). What is the value of graphical displays in learning? *Educational Psychology Review, 14,* 261–298.

Verkoeijen, P. P. J. L., Rikers, R. M. J. P., Schmidt, H. G., van der Weil, M. W. J., & Koomna, J. P. (2004). Case presentation by medical experts, intermediates and novices for laboratory data presented with or without a clinical context. *Medical Education, 38,* 617–627.

Vernon, H. M. (1918). *Industrial fatigue and efficiency.* London: His Majesty's Stationery Office.

Vessey, I. (1985). Expertise in debugging computer programs: A process analysis. *International Journal of Man-Machine Studies, 23,* 459–494.

Vicente, K. J. (1997). Heeding the legacy of Meister, Brunswik, and Gibson: Toward a broader view of human factors research. *Human Factors, 39,* 323–328.

Vicente, K. J. (1999). *Cognitive work analysis: Toward safe, productive, and healthy computer-based work.* Mahwah, NJ: Erlbaum.

Vicente, K. J. (2000). Work domain analysis and task analysis: A difference that matters. In J. M. Schraagen, S. F. Chipman, & V. L. Shalin (Eds.), *Cognitive task analysis* (pp. 101–118). Mahwah, NJ: Erlbaum.

Vicente, K. J. (2001, November). Cognitive work analysis: An ecological approach to the design of computer-based work. CTA Resource Online Seminar Series. Boston, MA: Aptima.

Vicente, K. J. (2002). Ecological interface design: Progress and challenges. *Human Factors, 44,* 62–78.

Vicente, K. J., Burns, C. M., & Pawlak, W. S. (1997, January). Muddling through wicked design problems. *Ergonomics in Design,* pp. 25–30.

Vicente, K. J., Christoffersen, K., & Pereklita, A. (1995). Supporting operator problem solving through ecological interface design. *IEEE Transactions on Systems, Man, and Cybernetics, 25,* 529–545.

Vicente, K. J., & Rasmussen, J. (1992). Ecological interface design: Theoretical foundations. *IEEE Transactions on Systems, Man, and Cybernetics, 22,* 589–606.

Vidulich, M. A. (1989). The use of judgment matrices in subjective workload assessment: The Subjective Workload dominance (SWORD) technique. In *Proceedings of the Human Factors and Ergonomics Society 33rd Annual Meeting* (pp. 406–1410). Santa Monica, CA: Human Factors and Ergonomics Society.

Viteles, M. S. (1922). Job specification and diagnostic tests of job competency for auditing division of a street railway company. *Psychological Clinic, 14,* 83–105.

Viteles, M. S. (1932). *Industrial psychology.* New York: Norton.

Viteles, M. S. (1945). The aircraft pilot: 5 years of research; A summary of outcomes. *Psychological Bulletin, 42,* 489–526.

von Drunen, P. (1997). Psychotechnics. In W. G. Bringmann, H. E. Lück, R. Miller, & C. E. Early (Eds.), *A pictorial history of psychology* (pp. 480–484). Chicago: Quintessence.

von Helmholtz, H. (1866/1962). *Treatise on physiological optics.* New York: Dover.

von Neumann, J. (1958). *The computer and the brain.* New Haven, CT: Yale University Press.

Voss, J. F., Greene, J. R., Post, T. A., & Penner, B. C. (1983). Problem solving skill in the social sciences. In G. H. Bower (Ed.), *The psychology of learning and motivation: Advances in research and theory, Volume 17* (pp. 165–213). New York: Academic Press.

Voss, J. F., & Post, T. A. (1988). On the solving of ill-structured problems. In M. T. H. Chi, R. Glaser, & M. J. Farr (Eds.), *The nature of expertise* (pp. 261–285). Hillsdale, NJ: Erlbaum.

Voss, J. M., Tyler, S., & Yengo, L. (1983). Individual differences in social science problem solving. In R. F. Dillon & R. R. Schmeck (Eds.), *Individual differences in cognitive processes* (Vol. 1, pp. 205–232). New York: Academic Press.

Vygotsky, L. S. (1962). *Thought and language.* Cambridge, MA: Harvard University Press.

Wagner, R. K., & Sternberg, R. J. (1986). Tacit knowledge and intelligence in the everyday world. In R. J. Sternberg & R. K. Wagner (Eds.), *Practical intelligence: Nature and origins of competence in the everyday world* (pp. 51–83). Cambridge: Cambridge University Press.

Waldron, V. (1985). Process tracing as a means of collecting knowledge for expert systems. *TI Engineering Journal, 2,* 90–94.

Waldrop, M. (1992). *Complexity: The emerging science at the edge of order and chaos.* New York: Simon & Schuster.

Walls, M. (2006, Winter). Review of TaskArchitect. *Ergonomics in Design,* pp. 27–29.

Wampler, J., Roth, E., Whitaker, R. D., Conrad, K., Stilson, M. T., Thomas-Meyers, G., et al. (2006). Using work-centered specifications to integrate cognitive requirements into software development. In *Proceedings of the Human Factors and Ergonomics Society 50th Annual Meeting* (pp. 420–244). Santa Monica, CA: Human Factors and Ergonomics Society.

War Manpower Commission Bureau of Training. (1945). *Training within industry.* Washington, DC: War Manpower Commission Bureau.

Warwick, W., & Hutton, R. (2007). Computational and theoretical perspectives on recognition primed decision making. In R. R. Hoffman (Ed.), *Expertise out of context: Proceedings of the Sixth International Conference on Naturalistic Decision Making* (pp. 429–451). Boca Raton, FL: CRC Press.

Waterman, D. A. (1986). *A guide to expert systems.* Reading, MA: Addison-Wesley.

Watson, J. (1913). Psychology as the behaviorist views it. *Psychological Review, 20,* 158–177.

Watts-Perotti, J. C., & Woods, D. D. (1999). How experienced users avoid getting lost in large display networks. *International Journal of Human–Computer Interaction, 11,* 269–299.

Waugh, N. C., & Norman, D. A. (1965). Primary memory. *Psychological Review, 72,* 89–104.

Way, D. S. (1978). *Terrain analysis.* Stroudsburg, PA: Dowden, Hutchinson, & Ross.

Weaver, W. (1949). The mathematics of communication. *Scientific American, 181,* 11–15.

Wei, J., & Salvendy, G. (2004). The cognitive task analysis method for job and task design: Review and reappraisal. *Behavior and Information Technology, 23,* 273–299.

Weitzel, J. R., & Kerschberg, L. (1989). A system development methodology for knowledge-based systems. *IEEE Transactions on Systems, Man, and Cybernetics, 19,* 598–605.

Weitzenfeld, J. S., & Klein, G. (1979). *Analogical reasoning as a discovery logic* (Technical Report on Contract No. F49620-79-C-0179, Air Force Office of Scientific Research, Bolling AFB, DC). Yellow Springs, OH: Klein Associates.

Weitzenfeld, J. S., Riedl, T. R., Freeman, J. T., Klein, G., & Musa, J. (1991). Knowledge elicitation for software engineering expertise. In J. E. Tomayko (Ed.), *Proceedings of the 1991 Software Engineering Education (SEI) Conference* (pp. 283–296). New York: Springer-Verlag.

Weldon, M. S. (2001). Remembering as a social process. *Psychology of Learning and Motivation, 40,* 67–120.

Wells, F. L. (1916). On the psychomotor mechanisms of typewriting. *American Journal of Psychology, 27,* 47–70.

Wenger, E. (1998). *Communities of practice: Learning, meaning, and identity.* New York: Cambridge University Press.

Wertheimer, M. (1912). Experimentelle Studien über das Sehen von Bewegung. [Experimental studies of motion perception]. *Zeitschrift für Psychologie [Journal for Psychology], 61,* 161–265.

Wertheimer, M. (1945). *Productive thinking.* NY: Harper and Row.

West, M. A. (1996). *Handbook of work group psychology.* Chichester, England: Wiley.

Weston, H. C. (1923). A note on machine design in relation to the operative. In *Third Annual Report of the Industrial Fatigue Research Board to 31 December, 1922* (pp. 71–75). London: His Majesty's Stationery Office.

Wexley, K. N., & Yukl, G. A. (1984). *Organizational behavior and personnel psychology.* Homewood, IL: Irwin.

Whitaker, R. D., Scott, R., Roth, E., Militello, L. G., Quill, L. L., Stilson, M. T., et al. (2005). *Work-centered Technology Development (WTD).* Report No. AFRL-HE-WP-TR-2005-0149. Human Effectiveness Directorate, USAF, Wright-Patterson AFB, Ohio.

Wickens, C. D., Merwin, D. H., & Lin, E. L. (1994). Implications of graphics enhancements for the visualization of scientific data: Dimensional integrity, stereopsis, motion, and mesh. *Human Factors, 36,* 44–61.

Wielinga, B. J., & Breuker, J. A. (1984). Interpretation of verbal data for knowledge acquisition. In T. O'Shea (Ed.), *Advances in artificial intelligence* (pp. 3–12). Amsterdam: North-Holland.

Wiendieck, G. (1997). Industrial psychology. In W. G. Bringmann, H. E. Lück, R. Miller, & C. E. Early (Eds.), *A pictorial history of psychology* (pp. 514–517). Chicago: Quintessence.

Wiener, N. (1948). *Cybernetics.* Cambridge, MA: MIT Press.

Williams, R., Faulkner, W. & Fleck, J. (Eds.), (1998). *Exploring expertise: Issues and perspectives.* London: Macmillan.

Willis, P. (1977). *Learning to labour: How working class lads get working class jobs.* New York: Columbia University Press.

Wilson, P. (1991). *Computer supported cooperative work: An introduction.* London, England: Kluwer Academic Publisher.

Wilson, T. D. (1994). The proper protocol: Validity and completeness of verbal reports. *Psychological Science, 5,* 249–252.

Wilson, T. D., & Schooler, J. W. (1991). Thinking too much: Introspection can reduce the quality of preferences and decisions. *Journal of Personality and Social Psychology, 60,* 181–192.

Winograd, T. (1997). Position paper. In J. Flanagan, T. Huang, P. Jones, & S. Kasif (Eds.), *Human-centered systems: Information, interactivity and intelligence* (pp. 285–287). Washington, DC: National Science Foundation.

Winograd, T., & Flores, F. (1986). *Understanding computers and cognition.* Norwood, NJ: Ablex.

Winograd, T., & Woods, D. D. (1997). *The challenge of human-centered design.* National Science Foundation Workshop on Human-Centered Systems. In J. Flanagan, T. Huang, P. Jones, S. Kasif (Eds.) Human-Centered Systems: Information, Interactivity, and Intelligence final report (pp. 61–90). Urbana, IL: Beckman Institute for Advanced Science and Technology.

Wolf, S. P., Hutton, R., Miller, T., & Klein, G. (1995). *Identification of the decision requirements for Air Defense planning* (Report prepared for Litton Data Systems, OSI, Los Angeles, CA). Fairborn, OH: Klein Associates.

Wong, B. L. W. (2004). Critical Decision Method data analysis. In D. Diaper & N. Stanton (Eds.), *Handbook of task analysis for human-computer interaction* (pp. 327–346). Mahwah, NJ: Erlbaum.

Wood, L. E., Davis, T. C., Clay, S. L., Ford, J. M., & Lammersen, S. (1995). Evaluation of interviewing methods and mediating representations for knowledge acquisition. *International Journal of Expert Systems, 8,* 1–23.

Wood, L. E., & Ford, K. M. (1993). Structuring interviews with experts during knowledge elicitation. In K. M. Ford & J. M. Bradshaw (Eds.), *Knowledge acquisition as modeling* (pp. 71–90). New York: Wiley.

Woods, D. D. (1982a). *Cognitive Task Analysis* (Report No. 82-1C57-CONMR-R5). Pittsburgh, PA: Westinghouse Research and Development Center.

Woods, D. D. (1982b). Visual momentum: An example of cognitive models applied to interface design. In T. Sheridan, J. Jenkins, & R. Kisner (Eds.), *Proceedings of Workshop on Cognitive Modeling of Nuclear Plant Control Room Operators* (pp. 63–72) (Nuclear Regulatory Commission Report NUREG/CR-3114). Washington, DC: Nuclear Regulatory Commission.

Woods, D. D. (1986). Paradigms for intelligent decision support. In E. Hollnagel, G. Mancini, & D. D. Woods (Eds.), *Intelligent decision support in process environments* (pp. 154–173). New York: Springer-Verlag.

Woods, D. D. (1988). Coping with complexity: The psychology of human behaviour in complex systems. In L. P. Goodstein, H. B. Andersen, & S. E. Olsen (Eds.), *Tasks, errors and mental models: A Festschrift to celebrate the 60th birthday of Professor Jens Rasmussen* (pp. 128–148). London: Taylor & Francis.

Woods, D. D. (1993). Process tracing methods for the study of cognition outside of the experimental psychology laboratory. In G. A. Klein, J. Orasanu, R. Calderwood, & C. E. Zsambok (Eds.), *Decision making in action: Models and methods* (pp. 228–251). Norwood, NJ: Ablex.

Woods, D. D. (1994a, April). Automation: Apparent simplicity, real complexity. In R. Parasuraman & M. Mouloula (Eds.), *Proceedings of the First Automation Technology and Human Performance Conference* (pp. 7–8). Hillsdale, NJ: Erlbaum.

Woods, D. D. (1994b, August). Keynote address: Observations from studying cognitive systems in context. In *Proceedings of the 16th Annual Conference of the Cognitive Science Society* (pp. 3–4). Mahwah, NJ: Erlbaum.

Woods, D. D. (1995). Towards a theoretical base for representation design in the computer medium: Ecological perception and aiding human cognition. In J. Flach, K. Vincente, P. Hancock, & J. Caird (Eds.), *Global perspectives on the ecology of human–machine systems* (pp. 157–188). Hillsdale, NJ: Erlbaum.

Woods, D. D. (1996). Designs are hypotheses about how artifacts shape cognition and collaboration. *Ergonomics, 41,* 168–173.

Woods, D. D. (1997). Human-centered software agents: Lessons from clumsy automation. In J. Flanagan, T. Huang, P. Jones, & S. Kasif (Eds.), *Human-centered systems: Information, interactivity, and intelligence* (pp. 288–293). Washington, DC: National Science Foundation.

Woods, D. D. (1998a). Designs are hypotheses about how artifacts shape cognition and collaboration. *Ergonomics, 41,* 168–173.

Woods, D. D. (1998b). *Multiple threads in the rise of cognitive task analysis.* Online paper from Ohio State University Cognitive Systems Engineering Laboratory. Retrieved April 20, 2006, from csel.eng.ohio-state.edu/woodscta/

Woods, D. D. (2000, October 8–10). *Lessons from beyond human error: Designing for resilience in the face of change and surprise.* NASA Design for Safety Workshop, NASA-Ames Research Center, Moffett Field, CA.

Woods, D. D. (2002). Steering the reverberations of technology change on fields of practice: Laws that govern cognitive work. In W. Gray & C. Schunn (Eds.), *Proceedings of the 24th Annual Meeting of the Cognitive Science Society* (pp. 14–17). Mahwah, NJ: Erlbaum.

Woods, D. D., & Cook, R. I. (1991). Nosocomial automation: Technology-induced complexity and human performance. In *Proceedings of the 1991 IEEE International Conference on Systems, Man, and Cybernetics: Decision Aiding for Complex Systems* (Vol. 2, pp. 1279–1282). New York: Institute for Electrical and Electronics Engineers.

Woods, D. D., & Cook, R. I. (1999). Perspectives on human error: Hindsight biases and local rationality. In F. T. Durso, R. S. Nickerson, R. W. Schvaneveldt, S. T. Dumais, D. S. Lindsay, & M. T. H. Chi (Eds.), *Handbook of applied cognition* (pp. 141–171). New York: Wiley.

Woods, D. D., & Dekker, S. W. A. (2000). Anticipating the effects of technological change: A new era of dynamics for human factors. *Theoretical Issues in Ergonomic Science, 1,* 272–282.

Woods, D. D., & Hollnagel, E. (1987). Mapping cognitive demands in complex problem-solving worlds. *International Journal of Man–Machine Studies, 26,* 257–275.

Woods, D. D., & Hollnagel, E. (2006). *Joint cognitive systems: Patterns in cognitive systems engineering.* Boca Raton, FL: CRC Press.

Woods, D. D., Johannsen, L., Cook, R. I., & Sarter, N. B. (1994). *Behind human error: Cognitive systems, computers and hindsight.* Report to the Crew Systems Ergonomic Information and Analysis Center, Wright Patterson Air Force Base, Ohio.

Woods, D. D., & Patterson, E. S. (2000). How unexpected events produce an escalation of cognitive and coordinative demands. In P. A. Hancock & P. A. Desmond (Eds.), *Stress, workload, and fatigue* (pp. 290–304). Hillsdale, NJ: Erlbaum.

Woods, D. D., Patterson, E. S., & Roth, E. M. (1998). Can we ever escape from data overload? A cognitive systems diagnosis. *Cognition, Technology, and Work, 4,* 22–36.

Woods, D. D., & Roesler, A. (2007). Connecting design and cognition. In H. N. J. Schifferstein & P. Hekkert (Eds.), *Product experience: A multidisciplinary approach* (pp. 199–213). Amsterdam: Elsevier.

Woods, D. D., & Roth, E. M. (1988a). Cognitive engineering: Human problem solving with tools. *Human Factors, 30,* 415–430.

Woods, D. D., & Roth, E. M. (1988b). Cognitive systems engineering. In M. Helander (Ed.), *Handbook of human–computer interaction* (pp. 1–43). Amsterdam, Netherlands: Elsevier Science.

Woods, D. D., Roth, E. M., and Bennett, K. B. (1990). Explorations in joint human-machine cognitive systems. In S. Robertson, W. Zachary, and J. Black (Eds.), *Cognition, computing and cooperation* (pp. 123–158). Norwood, NJ: Ablex.

Woods, D. D., & Sarter, N. B. (2000). Learning from automation surprises and "going sour" accidents. In N. B. Sarter & R. Amalberti (Eds.), *Cognitive engineering in the aviation domain* (pp. 327–353). Hillsdale, NJ: Erlbaum.

Woods, D. D., & Shattuck, L. G. (2000). Distant supervision: Local action given the potential for surprise. *Cognition, Technology, and Work, 2,* 242–245.

Woods, D. D., & Tinapple, D. (1999, September). *W3: Watching human factors watch people at work.* Presidential address, 43rd Annual Meeting of the Human Factors and Ergonomics Society. Retrieved April 20, 2006, from http://csel.eng.ohio-state.edu/hf99/

Woods, D. D., & Watts, J. C. (1997). How not to have to navigate through too many displays. In M. G. Helander, T. K. Landauer, & P. Prabhu (Eds.), *Handbook of human–computer interaction* (2nd ed., pp. 617–650). Amsterdam: Elsevier Science.

Woods, N. N., Brooks, L. R., & Norman, G. R. (2005). The value of basic science in clinical diagnosis: Creating coherence among signs and symptoms. *Medical Education, 39,* 107–112.

Woodson, W. E., Tilman, B., & Tilman, P. (1992). *Human factors design handbook* (2nd ed.). New York: McGraw-Hill.

Woodworth, R. S. (1899). The accuracy of voluntary movement. *Psychological Review Monographs,* Whole No. 3.

Woodworth, R. S. (1903). *Le Mouvement.* Paris: O. Doin.

Woodworth, R. S. (1938). *Experimental psychology.* New York: Holt.

Woolgar, S. (1987). Reconstructing man and machine: A note on sociological critiques of cognitivism. In W. E. Bijker, T. P. Hughes, & T. J. Pinch (Eds.), *The social construction of technological systems: New directions in the sociology and history of technology* (pp. 311–328). Cambridge, MA: MIT Press.

Wortham, S. (2001). Interactionally situated cognition: A classroom example. *Cognitive Science, 25,* 37–66.

Wright, G., & Ayton, P. (1987). Eliciting and modeling expert knowledge. *Decision Support Systems, 3,* 13–26.

Wulfleck, J. W., & Zeitlin, L. R. (1965). Human capabilities and limitations. In R. M. Gagné (Ed.), *Psychological principles in system development* (pp. 115–156). New York: Holt, Rinehart and Winston.

Wundt, W. (1874). *Grundzuge der physiologischen Psychologie* [Foundations of physiological psychology] (2nd ed.). Leipzig: Englemann.

Wyatt, S., Fraser, J. A., & Stock, F. G. L. (1929). *The effects of monotony in work* (Report No. 56, Industrial Fatigue Research Board). London: His Majesty's Stationery Office.

Wynn, E. (1991). Taking practice seriously. In J. Greenbaum & M. Kyng (Eds.), *Design at work: Cooperative design of computer systems* (pp. 45–64). Hillsdale, NJ: Erlbaum.

Xiao, Y., Plasters, C., Seagull, F. J., Mackenzie, C., Kobayashi, M., Fussell, S., & Kiesler, S. (2005). Negotiation and coordination: A preliminary field study of conflict management in large scale collaboration. In *Proceedings of the Human Factors and Ergonomics Society 49th Annual Meeting* (pp. 539–543). Santa Monica, CA: Human Factors and Ergonomics Society.

Xiao, Y., & Vicente, K. J. (2000). A framework for epistemological analysis in empirical (laboratory and field) studies. *Human Factors, 42,* 87–101.

Yerkes, R. M. (1919). Report of the Psychology Committee of the National Research Council, 3: The Committee on Psychological Problems of Aviation, including examination of aviation recruits. *Psychological Review, 26,* 83–149.

Yerkes, R. M. (1945). Plan for a history of psychological services in the war. *Psychological Bulletin, 42,* 87–90.

Young, A. T. (1985, May). What color is the solar system? *Sky and Telescope,* p. 399.

Young, R. M., & Gammack, J. (1987). The role of psychological techniques and intermediate representations in knowledge elicitation. In *Proceedings of the First European Workshop on Knowledge Acquisition for Knowledge-Based Systems.* Reading, England: Reading University.

Zakay, D., & Wooler, S. (1984). Time pressure, training, and decision effectiveness. *Ergonomics, 27,* 273–284.

Zhang, J., & Norman, D. A. (1994). Representations in distributed cognitive tasks. *Cognitive Science, 18,* 87–122.

Zmuidzinas, M., Kling, R., & George, J. (1990). Desktop computerization as a continuing process. In *Proceedings of the 11th International Conference on Information Systems.* Copenhagen, Denmark.

Zsambok, C. E. (1997). Naturalistic decision making research and improving team decision making. In C. E. Zsambok & G. Klein (Eds.), *Naturalistic decision making* (pp. 111–120). Mahwah, NJ: Erlbaum.

Zsambok, C. E., Beach, L. R., & Klein, G. (1992). *A literature review of analytical and naturalistic decision making.* Fairborn, OH: Klein Associates.

Zsambok, C. E., Kaempf, G. L., Crandall, B., & Kyne, M. (1996). *A cognitive model of a prototype training program for OJT providers.* (Technical Report Contract No. MDA903-93-C-0092, U.S. Army Research Institute, Alexandria, VA). Fairborn, OH: Klein Associates.

Zsambok, C. E., & Klein, G. (1997). *Naturalistic decision making.* Mahwah, NJ: Erlbaum.

Subject Index

N

O

X

Author Index

A

Aakvik, G., 64, 470
Abbott, A., 283, 403
Abelson, R., 71, 403
Acquisti, A., 365, 410
Adams, N., 150, 470
Adams-Webber, J. R., 129, 428
Adelman, L., 155, 404, 445
Adelson, B., 148, 149, 470
Adler, M. H., 22, 403
Adler, M. R., 129, 461
Afflerbach, P., 461
Agnew, N. M., 274, 275, 403, 435
Agre, P., 95, 403
Ainger, A., 266, 403
Ainsworth, L. K., 4, 36, 44, 443
Akerstrom-Hoffman, R. A., 403
Albright, C. A., 254, 403
Alexander, H., 136, 433
Allee, V., 403
Allen, G., 139, 403
Allen, J. F., 363, 365, 403, 410
Allen, R., 153, 462
Allen, R. B., 348, 403
Allen, S. W., 137, 148, 404, 411, 457
Alluisi, E. A., 4, 404
Altom, M. W., 452
Alvarado, G., 127, 404
Amble, T., 64, 470
Ambruso, D., 147, 442
Amirault, R. J., 128, 404
Anastasi, A., 4, 31, 404
Andersen, H. B., 223, 431
Anderson, A., 429
Anderson, D. K., 130, 143, 470, 471
Anderson, J. R., 79, 138, 139, 150, 151, 152, 154, 161, 404, 449, 462
Anderson, R. J., 80, 121, 260, 261, 291, 292, 296, 404
Andre, A. D., 64, 404
Andreas, B. G., 46, 404
Andrews, E. J., 428
Andriole, S. J., 404, 445
Annett, J., 4, 37, 44, 73, 75, 184
Anonymous, 36, 42, 404
Ansbacher, H. L., 36, 48, 49, 404, 405

Applebaum, S. H., 265, 405
Aquinas, T., 16, 405
Ark, T. K., 405
Arkes, H. R., 150, 405
Arocha, J. F., 367, 459
Aston, B., 153, 154, 410
Atkins, J. B., 283, 472
Atkinson, M. L., 119, 405
Atkinson, R. C., 71, 405
Attewell, P., 303, 305, 307, 308, 405
Atwood, M. E., 59, 122, 132, 139, 148, 159, 432, 441
Ausubel, D. P., 55, 146, 405
Avrahami, J., 405
Axtell, C. M., 265, 416
Ayton, P., 479

B

Baars, B. J., 71, 405
Babcock, C. J., 137, 405
Baber, C., 8, 116, 471
Bach-y-Rita, P., 313, 405, 465
Badham, R. J., 265, 405
Baecker, R. M., 362, 405
Bailey, A. A., 17, 405
Bailey, W. A., 6, 17, 62, 131, 132, 163, 405
Bain, A., 5, 405
Bainbridge, L., 6, 74, 97, 102, 103, 104, 159, 163, 364, 405, 406
Bakan, D., 17, 406
Baker, D. P., 366, 408, 429
Balick, M. J., 419
Ball, L. J., 80, 81, 289, 406
Ballas, J. A., 352, 385, 406
Balzano, G. J., 79, 451
Bamforth, K. W., 262, 263, 474
Banaji, M. R., 79, 406
Bandura, A., 406
Bannon, L., 387, 406
Barber, P., 79, 406
Barclay, J. R., 151, 410
Barile, A. B., 254, 403
Barley, S., 80, 406
Barloon, T. J., 407

501